Country Studies in International Accounting – Americas and the Far East

The Library of International Accounting

Series Editor: Christopher W. Nobes
Coopers & Lybrand Professor of Accounting
Department of Economics, University of Reading, UK

1. International Accounting – General Issues and Classification
   Christopher W. Nobes

2. Country Studies in International Accounting – Europe
   Peter J. Walton

3. Country Studies in International Accounting – Americas and the Far East
   Gary K. Meek

4. International Harmonization of Accounting
   Christopher W. Nobes

5. Financial Reporting by Multinationals
   Carol A. Adams and Clare B. Roberts

Country Studies in International Accounting – Americas and the Far East

Edited by

Gary K. Meek

Oscar S. Gellein/Deloitte & Touche Professor of Accounting
Oklahoma State University, US

THE LIBRARY OF INTERNATIONAL ACCOUNTING

An Elgar Reference Collection
Cheltenham, UK • Brookfield, US

Published by
Edward Elgar Publishing Limited
8 Lansdown Place
Cheltenham
Glos GL50 2HU
UK

Edward Elgar Publishing Company
Old Post Road
Brookfield
Vermont 05036
US

British Library Cataloguing in Publication Data
Country studies in international accounting
  Americas and the Far East. – (The library of international
  accounting ; v. 3)
  1. Accounting – America 2. Accounting – East Asia
  I. Meek, Gary K.
  657'.095

Library of Congress Cataloguing in Publication Data
Country studies in international accounting. Americas and the Far
  East / edited by Gary K. Meek.
      p. cm. — (The library of international accounting : v.3)
  (An Elgar reference collection)
  Includes bibliographical references and index.
    1. Accounting—North America. 2. Accounting—Latin America.
  3. Accounting—East Asia. 4. Financial statements—North America.
  5. Financial statements—Latin America. 6. Financial statements—East Asia.
  7. Accounting—Standards—North America. 8. Accounting—Standards—
  Latin America. 9. Accounting—Standards—East Asia. 10. Comparative accounting.
  I. Meek, Gary. II. Series. III. Series: An Elgar reference collection.
  HF5616.N7C68 1996
  657.095—dc20   96-2504
                                                                            CIP

ISBN 1 85898 225 1

Printed in Great Britain by Galliard (Printers) Ltd, Great Yarmouth

Contents

Acknowledgements

The editor and publishers wish to thank the authors and the following publishers who have kindly given permission for the use of copyright material.

American Accounting Association for articles: Lawrence Revsine (1984), 'The Rationale Underlying the Functional Currency Choice', *Accounting Review*, **LIX** (3), July, 505–14; Chee W. Chow and Adrian Wong-Boren (1987), 'Voluntary Financial Disclosure by Mexican Corporations', *Accounting Review*, **LXII** (3), July, 533–41.

Basil Blackwell Ltd for articles: Paul A. Griffin (1983), 'Management's Preferences for FASB Statement No. 52: Predictive Ability Results', *Abacus*, **19** (2), December, 130–38; Bimal K. Prodhan and Malcolm C. Harris (1989), 'Systematic Risk and the Discretionary Disclosure of Geographical Segments: An Empirical Investigation of US Multinationals', *Journal of Business Finance & Accounting*, **16** (4), Autumn, 467–92; Charles Hall, Yasushi Hamao and Trevor S. Harris (1994), 'A Comparison of Relations Between Security Market Prices, Returns and Accounting Measures in Japan and the United States', *Journal of International Financial Management and Accounting*, **5** (1), February, 47–73; Frances L. Ayres and Jacci L. Rodgers (1994), 'Further Evidence on the Impact of SFAS 52 on Analysts' Earnings Forecasts', *Journal of International Financial Management and Accounting*, **5** (2), June, 120–41.

Canadian Academic Accounting Association for articles: Daniel W. Collins and William K. Salatka (1993), 'Noisy Accounting Earnings Signals and Earnings Response Coefficients: The Case of Foreign Currency Accounting', *Contemporary Accounting Research*, **10** (1), Fall, 119–59; Jennifer L. Kao (1993), 'Discussion of "Noisy Accounting Earnings Signals and Earnings Response Coefficients: The Case of Foreign Currency Accounting"', *Contemporary Accounting Research*, **10** (1), Fall, 161–6; Paul A. Griffin (1993), 'Discussion of "Noisy Accounting Earnings Signals and Earnings Response Coefficients: The Case of Foreign Currency Accounting"', *Contemporary Accounting Research*, **10** (1), Fall, 167–78.

T.E. Cooke and Accountancy Magazines for article: T.E. Cooke (1992), 'The Impact of Size, Stock Market Listing and Industry Type on Disclosure in the Annual Reports of Japanese Listed Corporations', *Accounting and Business Research*, **22** (87), Summer, 229–37.

R.G. Walker and Accountancy Magazines for article: R.G. Walker (1987), 'Australia's ASRB. A Case Study of Political Activity and Regulatory "Capture"', *Accounting and Business Research*, **17** (67), Summer, 269–86.

Every effort has been made to trace all the copyright holders but if any have been inadvertently overlooked the publishers will be pleased to make the necessary arrangement at the first opportunity.

In addition the publishers wish to thank the Library of the London School of Economics and Political Science and the Marshall Library, Cambridge University, for their assistance in obtaining these articles.

Introduction
Gary K. Meek

The articles in this volume, concerning international accounting issues related to countries of the Americas and Far East, are representative of the kinds of research currently being conducted. The bulk of this research has a US focus. This is because data on US companies are widely available and because a large number of accounting researchers are American. While the amount of international accounting research on issues of interest to Asia is growing, it is still rather slight overall. In addition, there is almost no international accounting research in English dealing with Latin America. Therefore, the emphasis here on the United States reflects the nature of the existing literature. In the future, this balance may change.

The articles in this volume have counterparts in three of the other four volumes in this series. Similar articles to those in Part I 'Aspects of Standard Setting in Certain Countries' are contained in Volume II (Walton, *Country Studies in International Accounting – Europe*). Part III 'Comparisons with US GAAP' is related to the papers in the section entitled 'The Measurement and Effects of Diversity' in Volume I (Nobes, *International Accounting – General Issues and Classification*). The articles in Part IV 'Foreign Currency Translation by US Multinationals' can be read in conjunction with the more general papers in the section 'Foreign Currency Translation' in Volume V (Roberts and Adams, *Financial Reporting by Multinationals*). Finally, Volume V in this series also has chapters corresponding to those in Part V 'Geographic Segment Reporting by US Multinationals'.

This volume is arranged in five parts. The following provides background discussion and a brief introduction to each article.

Aspects of Standard Setting in Certain Countries

Accounting standards are the regulations or rules (including, in many countries, laws and statutes) followed in preparing financial statements. Standard setting is the regulatory framework – the process – by which accounting standards are formulated. Thus, accounting standards are the outcomes of accounting standard setting. Understanding how accounting standards are established and the influences on the process is important for appreciating why, for example, a country requires that accounting be done one way and not another. Further, differences in standard setting across countries help explain why accounting standards vary around the world.

Chapter 1 by Puxty, Willmott, Cooper and Lowe provides a theoretical framework for examining how accounting is regulated in advanced capitalist countries. According to this framework, accounting can variously be regulated through forces of the market, the state or the 'community' of accounting professionals and others. In most countries, all three forces exert some influence, though in varying amounts. The authors apply their model to the US and three European countries, though it is also relevant elsewhere. Their framework is useful for understanding both differences in standard setting across countries and the shape of the standards that emerge from the process.

The remaining five chapters in Part I examine standard setting in specific countries of the Americas and Far East. All go beyond merely describing the procedures followed and the parties involved. In one way or another, they look at the influences on the process and/or where the real authority for standard setting lies.

McKinnon and Harrison begin by using the implementation of consolidation accounting in Japan to show how Japanese culture influences the involvement of both the corporate and government sectors in standard setting. It vividly demonstrates how the standard setting process impacts on the accounting standards that finally emerge, and shows why it is important to go beyond merely describing the mechanism of a nation's standard setting and instead to illuminate the actual dynamics of the process.

Chapter 3 by Walker focuses on Australia. It documents the evolution of a standard setting authority in the first two years after the government-sponsored Accounting Standards Review Board (ASRB) was formed in 1984. The author argues that the accounting profession initially lost, but later regained, authority over standard setting. Thus, the ASRB was effectively 'captured' by the Australian accounting profession which it was designed to regulate.

In Chapter 4 Young looks at the behaviour of the Financial Accounting Standards Board (FASB) in the US in enacting changes to accounting regulations. Three issues that were targeted for inclusion on the FASB's technical agenda are analysed. How the FASB came to define whether these were problems worthy of its attention and the resolution of each issue differed. The article demonstrates the complexity of the accounting regulatory space in the United States. Similar analyses on other countries would no doubt show comparable complexities.

Chapter 5 by McKinnon analyses how political and economic factors have influenced the accounting regulatory framework in Australia. McKinnon extends her analysis to cultural values by contrasting the accounting regulatory framework in Australia with that in Japan. She shows how the ambiguous balance of power between the Australian government and the accounting profession is consistent with underlying cultural norms in Australia. At the same time, government domination of accounting regulation in Japan is consistent with Japanese cultural norms. This article complements Chapters 2 and 3, discussed above.

The final article in Part I, by Ge and Lin, is about a developing, socialist country – the People's Republic of China. It thus provides an interesting contrast to the previous articles which have considered the regulation of accounting in advanced, capitalist states. The authors show how new, market-oriented accounting standards have been evolving as a result of outside, international influences in line with China's implementation of recent economic and market reforms.

(Volume II of this series contains similar articles on standard setting in Europe. For example, Standish examines France, Schroer focuses on Germany, Nobes and Turley are both about the UK, Achleitner looks at Switzerland, and Schoonderbeck describes the Netherlands. For details, see listing at the end of this Introduction.)

Disclosure Choices

The disclosure of accounting information is necessary to gain access to capital market funds. Stock exchanges and standard setters require certain information disclosures from companies whose securities are publicly traded. However, disclosure requirements vary widely around the world. Companies also disclose voluntary information in excess of requirements. Companies disclose accounting information in a number of ways, for example through annual reports, filings with regulators, through press releases and in meetings with financial analysts.

The three papers in Part II assess why companies disclose accounting information. However, they differ in terms of the nationalities of the companies investigated, whether voluntary or required disclosures are at issue, as well as the type and means of disclosure. The papers also examine a range of different factors as explanatory variables for disclosure. The issue of why companies disclose accounting information is relevant for the users of such information (e.g., investors), standard setters, and preparers of accounting information (i.e., other companies).

The Cooke paper (Chapter 7) examines the effects of size, stock market listing and industry type on the amount of voluntary and required disclosure contained in Japanese company annual reports. The study is similar to others focusing on US and European companies and, indeed, reaches similar conclusions. It would appear that disclosure decisions by Japanese companies are not significantly different from those of comparable Western firms, at least insofar as these three variables are concerned.

Chapter 8 by Chow and Wong-Boren indicates the extent of voluntary annual report disclosures by Mexican companies and relates this to three factors suggested by the agency theory literature. One implication of their findings is that agency theory may not be very relevant to corporate voluntary disclosure by Mexican companies. Alternatively, it may be that agency conflicts are controlled in Mexico by some means other than annual report disclosure.

The article by Cheung, Li and Wu looks at Taiwanese firms' voluntary earnings forecast disclosures contained in press releases. Seven factors derived from the positive accounting theory literature are chosen to explain these disclosures, and the results then compared to the behaviour of a set of US companies. The findings suggest that positive accounting theory better explains the motivations for voluntary earnings forecast disclosures by US than by Taiwanese firms. When transferring a theory from one nation to another, it is important to examine the assumptions and institutional frameworks that underlie it.

Comparisons with US GAAP

Accounting information plays an important role in the valuation of equity securities traded in stock markets around the world. Investors, financial analysts and others use accounting information in order to assess the amounts, timing and uncertainty of future cash flows from firms' securities. Thus, accounting information is used to price securities and, hence, determine their rates of return. However, the analysis of accounting information for such purposes is complicated by differences in financial reporting standards and practices. The significant, and still growing, amount of global trading in equity securities has highlighted international differences in accounting and reporting. Is this lack of international comparability important economically, or is it merely a nuisance which investors should be able to overcome? The issue is controversial.

The US Securities and Exchange Commission (SEC) allows non-US companies to use the generally accepted accounting principles (GAAP) of their home country in financial statement filings with the SEC. However, the companies must also reconcile net income and stockholders' equity based on home-country GAAP to corresponding amounts based on US GAAP. Implicit in the SEC requirement is a presumption that US GAAP accounting information has relevance to US investors over and above accounting information based on the company's home-country GAAP.

The first two papers in Part III address the 'value relevance' of reconciliations to US GAAP. (Value relevance means that the information has an impact on share prices and returns.) Bandyopadhyay, Hanna and Richardson find no evidence that Canadian firms' reconciliations to US GAAP are value relevant, despite the fact that US-Canadian GAAP differences are sometimes quite material. This finding has implications for SEC policy regarding Canadian companies. Until 1993, the SEC had been moving towards a policy of reciprocity (or mutual recognition) with respect to financial statement filings by Canadian companies: financial statements by Canadian companies based on Canadian GAAP would be accepted for US securities trading. However, in 1993, the SEC decided to continue the reconciliation requirement for Canadian companies. The findings of this study support reciprocity.

In Chapter 11, Amir, Harris and Venuti find that the reconciliations for their sample of firms (a cross-section of companies from 20 countries, excluding Canada) are, on average, value relevant. Thus, these findings support the SEC's reconciliation requirement. In discussing the paper by Amir, Harris and Venuti, Pope notes that their evidence seems to be time specific, which could affect the general applicability of their results. Pope also notes that the evidence seems to be specific to systems of financial accounting. This point, along with the results of Bandyopadhyay, Hanna and Richardson in Chapter 10, suggest that the significance of the reconciliation information for capital market participants may differ depending on the company's home country.

The remaining three papers in Part III are broadly concerned with differences between US and Japanese GAAP. That there are worldwide variations in price-earnings (PE) ratios is a well documented phenomenon. In particular, the significantly higher PE ratios of Japanese compared to US companies have puzzled accountants, financial analysts and others for some time. A commonly cited explanation is that the more conservative way that Japanese companies calculate earnings (i.e., the denominator in the PE ratio) explains some or all of the difference.

Bildersee, Cheh and Lee adjust earnings for a variety of differences between Japanese and US accounting principles and business practices in Chapter 12. They conclude that their adjustments to earnings eliminate nearly all of the difference between Japanese and US PE ratios. However, it is unclear how to interpret their restated ratios, since some of the adjustments to earnings that they make might also affect a company's share price.

The study by Brown, Soybel and Stickney represents another approach to explaining differences between Japanese and US PE ratios. Unlike Bildersee, Cheh and Lee, they focus strictly on differences in accounting principles that are cosmetic in nature. Their approach to restating earnings is also unique in the literature in that they do not attempt to adjust from Japanese to US GAAP, or vice versa. Instead, they adjust both Japanese and US GAAP earnings to a common basis, depending on available information. Their results indicate that adjusting for GAAP differences explains very little of variation in PE ratios. Therefore, differences in Japanese and US PE ratios are due to other, more substantive divergences between Japanese and American firms and their operating environments.

Whether or not the PE ratios should converge by adjusting for GAAP difference presupposes that securities are priced the same way in both Japanese and US capital markets. In particular, it presupposes that Japanese investors consider accounting numbers in their pricing decisions in a similar manner as US investors. This issue is examined in Chapter 14 by Hall, Hamao and Harris who are concerned with the relative role of accounting information in determining share prices and returns in Japan and the United States. They find that Japanese investors use accounting numbers, particularly earnings, less than US investors in their pricing of companies' equity securities. The implication of their finding is that fundamental structural differences between the two capital markets account for variations in PE ratios. Controlling for GAAP differences to account for such variations is highly questionable. This is consistent with the results presented in the previous chapter by Brown, Soybel and Stickney.

(Several papers in Volume I of this series relate to those in this section. Choi, Hino, Sang, Sang, Ujiie and Stonehill – one of the first empirical studies to examine the effect of international diversity on financial statement analysis – concerns Japanese and Korean GAAP. Weetman and Gray compare UK, Swedish and Dutch GAAP to that in the United States. Choi and Lee and Lee and Choi investigate the effects of international differences in accounting for goodwill on premia paid in international mergers. For details, see listing at the end of this Introduction.)

Foreign Currency Translation by US Multinationals

Foreign currency translation is the process of restating financial statement data from one currency to another. It typically arises in the context of preparing consolidated (or group) financial statements. Foreign currency translation has proved to be one of the most vexing issues faced by accountants and accounting standard setters. In the United States, *Statement of Financial Accounting Standards (SFAS) No. 8* governed foreign currency translaion from the mid-1970s to early 1980s. This required a temporal method of translation, with the translation gain or loss included in current period income. During the years that *SFAS No. 8* was in effect, exchange rates were highly volatile, as were reported income amounts. Understandably, *SFAS No. 8* proved to be controversial and unpopular. In 1981, it was replaced by *SFAS No. 52*.

The new standard requires US multinationals to classify foreign subsidiaries as either autonomous of or integral to the operations of the US parent. This classification, in turn, determines the foreign subsidiary's so-called functional currency. For autonomous subsidiaries, the current rate method of translation is used, with the translation gain or loss included in stockholders' equity instead of income. The functional currency is said to be the subsidiary's local currency. However, for integral subsidiaries, the temporal provisions of *SFAS No. 8* continue to apply. The parent's currency (i.e., the US dollar) is said to be the foreign subsidiary's functional currency. US multinationals have tended to report less volatile (quarterly and annual) income amounts under *SFAS No. 52* than they previously did under *SFAS No. 8*. (These two US accounting standards for foreign currency translation have been extensively monitored over the last 20 years, the article by Houston in Volume V of this series providing an overview of this research.)

Chapter 15 by Revsine clarifies the rationale underlying the functional currency choice in *SFAS No. 52*. Using three numerical examples, he explains the objectives behind the functional currency notions and shows how the translation methods required in *SFAS No. 52* are consistent with the intended translation objectives.

The remaining papers in Part IV are empirical studies relating to the implementation or the effects of *SFAS No. 52*. Chapters 16 and 17 by Griffin and Ayres are based on positive accounting theory, specifically as it relates to the self-interested behaviour of managers regarding preferences for accounting methods and their impacts on reported income. In general, positive accounting theory seeks to explain or predict choices about accounting practice. Griffin develops a model using factors derived from positive accounting theory to distinguish and predict which managers lobbied the Financial Accounting Standards Board regarding the exposure draft that eventually became *SFAS No. 52*. Such behaviour was essentially a choice to engage in a political process that US standard setting represents. Overall, Griffin's model adequately describes manager behaviour in this case, but has only slight predictive ability.

The paper by Ayres concerns management's choice of adoption date for *SFAS No. 52*. US companies could choose one of three years for implementing the new standard, with managers aware of the income implications in the choice of adoption date. If this choice could be identified by positive accounting theory, then factors consistent with the theory should be able to distinguish early versus late adopters. It would also suggest that managers chose an adoption date with a view to managing income. Her evidence, which supports positive accounting theory, indicates that a strategy of earnings manipulation was involved in the choice of adoption date for *SFAS No. 52*.

Chapter 18 by Ayres and Rodgers examines the impact of *SFAS No. 52* on the accuracy of analysts' forecasts of earnings. One criticism of *SFAS No. 8* was that the impact of currency fluctuations on earnings made it difficult to assess reported earnings amounts. Therefore, if analysts' forecasts of earnings became less biased after *SFAS No. 52*, then one of the criticisms of *SFAS No. 8* would be resolved. In general, the authors find that forecast accuracy improved: there tended to be an overstatement bias in forecasts under *SFAS No. 8*, whereas forecasts became relatively unbiased under *SFAS No. 52*.

The Collins and Salatka paper uses a research approach that is relatively new to capital markets studies. So-called earnings response coefficients are used to assess the quality of accounting earnings signals. Collins and Salatka examine whether the quality of earnings signals improved with the implementation of *SFAS No. 52*. They conclude that capital markets participants perceived earnings signals to be of higher quality under *SFAS No. 52* than under *SFAS No. 8*. Discussions of the Collins and Salatka paper by Kao and by Griffin end this section. They raise several theoretical and research design issues that should temper conclusions about their colleagues' results. For example, Collins and Salatka omit the effects of exchange rate variability and inflation rates in their analysis. Both factors potentially affected the market's response to accounting earnings signals produced under both of the foreign currency translation standards.

Geographic Segment Reporting by US Multinationals

Risk and return opportunties vary by country and by region. The purpose of disaggregated geographic segment reporting is to make risk and return relationships of multinational operations more transparent than consolidated information alone. In the absence of costs, the fineness theorem argues that disaggregated disclosures – in addition to consolidated information – are preferred to consolidated information only. However, when costs are introduced, the fineness theorem is not sufficient to justify the relevance of geographic segment disclosures. For example, if geographic disclosures are reported with error, users face costs of interpreting imperfect information in their analyses. Additionally, the discretion available to companies in presenting this information may make it difficult to interpret. Thus, the pertinence of geographic segment reporting is not a foregone conclusion. The three papers in Part V are concerned with the relevance of geographic segment information as reported by US multinational corporations. *SFAS No. 14* has required this information since 1977.

Balakrishnan, Harris and Sen examine whether *SFAS No. 14* disclosures improve the ability to forecast annual sales and income. If predictive ability is not improved, then an important motivation for the requirements of *SFAS No. 14* is lost. The overall findings are that geographic segment information, in compliance with *SFAS No. 14*, does enhance predictive ability for annual sales and income.

In Chapter 21, Doupnik and Rolfe construct hypothetical data and test it on actual financial analysts to see whether increasingly disaggregated geographic segment information changes their assessments of risk. This study is not about the actual impact of geographic information, but its potential impact. The results show that the level of disaggregation of geographic information can influence risk assessments of financial analysts. However, their results also suggest that disaggregration itself does not automatically provide useful information: risk assessment is clouded when countries or regions with different risks are combined.

The Prodhan and Harris study is concerned with whether the introduction of *SFAS No. 14* changed the capital market's assessment of the systematic risk of affected US multinational corporations. 'Beta' measures systematic risk; it is the volatility of a share's return compared to the return of the capital market as a whole. Given that investor perceptions and expectations about a company's risks and returns are embedded in share prices (and returns), anything changing these perceptions and expectations (for example, new information) potentially affects beta. Thus, Prodhan and Harris look for changes in beta after *SFAS No. 14* was introduced. The decreases in beta they document after companies began disclosing the required *SFAS No. 14* geographic segment information indicates that stock market investors found the disclosures useful in assessing risk.

(Volume V of this series has a section entitled 'Segmental Reporting'. Papers by Rennie and Emmanuel, Roberts, Boatsman, Behn and Patz, and Hussain and Skerratt complement those in this section. For details, see listing at the end of this Introduction.)

References

Volume I International Accounting – General Issues and Classification
Choi, Frederick D.S., Hisaaki Hino, Sang Kee Min, Sang Oh Nam, Junichi Ujiie and Arthur I. Stonehill (1983), 'Analyzing Foreign Financial Statements: The Use and Misuse of International Ratio Analysis', *Journal of International Business Studies*, Spring/Summer, 113–31.
Choi, Frederick D.S. and Changwoo Lee (1991), 'Merger Premia and National Differences in Accounting for Goodwill', *Journal of International Financial Management & Accounting*, **3** (3), Autumn, 219–40.

Part I
Aspects of Standard Setting
in Certain Countries

Accounting, Organizations and Society, Vol. 12, No. 3, pp. 273–291, 1987.
Printed in Great Britain

0361–3682/87 $3.00+.00
Pergamon Journals Ltd.

MODES OF REGULATION IN ADVANCED CAPITALISM: LOCATING ACCOUNTANCY IN FOUR COUNTRIES*

A. G. PUXTY
University of Sheffield

HUGH. C. WILLMOTT
University of Aston

and

DAVID J. COOPER and TONY LOWE
University of Manchester Institute of Science and Technology

Abstract

The paper presents a framework for examining how accounting practices are regulated within advanced capitalist societies. Through the critical use of Streeck & Schmitter's (*Private Interest Government and Public Policy*, Sage, London, 1985) exploration of models of social order, regulation is theorised as an expression of the combination of the organising principles of Market, State and Community. The analytical framework is then applied to compare modes of accounting regulation in the Federal Republic of Germany, the United Kingdom, Sweden and the United States of America. The paper highlights the significance of contradictions within and between the organising principles of advanced capitalism and seeks to display the regulation of accounting as a medium and outcome of the articulation of these contradictions.

The social context of accountancy, has not been given the emphasis we believe it warrants. A concern with the social context is important if accountants are to understand their position and roles in society and if the significance of accountancy is to be assessed. Accountancy practices may be significant in relation to their social and economic consequences which include not only the more obvious and direct effects on resource allocation in society (Zeff, 1978) but also the extensiveness and legitimacy of economic calculative discourses and practices, the reinforcement of organisational boundaries (what is to count as internal and what is not to count because it is external to the enterprise) and the reproduction of the relations of production and distribution more generally.

This paper focusses on the roles of accountancy in regulating economic and social activities in society and the manner in which the institutions of accountancy are themselves regulated. These aspects are intertwined. The study of the regulatory institutions of accountancy involves an examination of the interpolation of accounting technologies and ideologies in regulating the relations and practices of social repro-

* We gratefully acknowledge the financial assistance of the Economic and Social Research Council, who are funding the project "Accounting Regulation as Corporatist Control" as part of their initiative on Corporatism and Accountability. This paper is a product of initial theorising on this project and an earlier version of this paper was presented at the Accounting and Culture Conference in Amsterdam, the EGOS Colloquium in Stockholm, and the Interdisciplinary Perspectives on Accounting Conference in Manchester. We appreciate the comments made by contributors at each of these Conferences, and notably Simon Archer, Sten Jonsson, Keith Robson, Tony Tinker and Grahame Thompson. Any errors or misunderstandings are our own responsibility.

duction. The mode of regulating accountancy is likely to affect the content and consequences of accounting policy and practices. Conversely, the form of accounting rules will have implications for the mode of their regulation.

The paper analyses the roles of accountancy in regulating social and economic activities in society by developing a framework for understanding a variety of principles of regulation.[1] It then explores the scope and variation in modes of accounting regulation in a number of late capitalist societies (using the U.K., U.S.A., Sweden and West Germany as examples). It presents a relatively elaborate framework for understanding principles of regulation in order to contribute to a comparative analysis of accountancy in which different modes of its regulation are associated with the distinctive histories and institutional specificities of different nations. However, in highlighting different modes of regulation, a fundamental commonality amongst the four countries studied is also recognised. All are advanced capitalist economies in which systematic and persistent patterns of inequalities in power and resources exist between (fractions of) capital and labour. To talk of advanced or organised capitalism is to acknowledge that the contradictions of capitalism are reflected and sustained not only through increasingly internationalised and monopolised markets but also through various forms of state and neo-corporatist modes of socio-economic regulation (Mandel, 1975; O'Connor, 1973; Offe, 1984; Streeck & Schmitter, 1985).

More substantively, the paper provides a framework for exploring and evaluating contemporary challenges to the authority of the regulatory institutions of accountancy, a challenge which is perhaps most visible in the United States, but is also emerging in Western Europe. This challenge comes from at least two sources. Emerging from the political Left in the 1970s, there has been a critical appraisal of the monopolisation of the market for accounting

services and challenges to the lack of accountability of professional bodies (Tinker, 1985). At the same time, the radical Right has re-asserted the value of unfettered market forces and thereby challenged the efficacy of professional self regulation (Benston, 1978–80). Concurrently, the relationship between the modern state, large multinational corporations and multi-national accountancy companies has brought into question the most appropriate mode of regulation of accountancy institutions and the roles of accountants in modern society.

The paper is structured into four main sections. The first offers a framework, developed by Streeck & Schmitter (1985), for exploring the varying approaches to regulation in advanced capitalism and the roles of accounting therein. Three organising principles — the market, the state and the community — are identified as providing modes of regulation. In the second section we advance a critique of the limitations of the Streeck & Schmitter framework in which it is argued that their framework is deficient in maintaining a focus on the nation state, thereby ignoring the increasingly significant international and transnational institutions of regulation. Further, the framework is shown to be flawed by its somewhat ahistoric and asocial character. In consequence, it provides neither an explanation for the origins, reproduction or transformation of the modes of regulation, nor an indication of the role of human agency in such dynamic processes. Despite these failings, their framework is valuable in highlighting the contradictory nature of regulatory modes. More specifically, it provides considerable insight into the comparative analysis of accounting regulation which is offered in the third section of the paper. Finally we offer a commentary on the comparative analysis of accountancy regulation, showing how the organising principles of State, Community and Market apply to the regulation of accountancy institutions and how these principles exist in relation to one another.

---

[1] This paper is intended to contribute to the growing concern to locate and analyse accountancy in its social context (see for example, Scott, 1931; Lowe & Tinker, 1977; Burchell *et al.*, 1980, 1985; Benston, 1979/80; Tinker, 1984, 1985; Cooper & Sherer, 1984).

TOWARDS A CONCEPTUAL FRAMEWORK

The institutions and processes of accounting regulation in different nation-states cannot be understood independently of the historical and politico-economic contexts of their emergence and development. For this reason, we view the particular institutional forms and social processes of regulation as an outcome of distinctive constellations of material and ideological forces that are present within different nations. To take the example of the U.K., we would highlight the hardiness of laissez-faire ideology and the significance of the City as a world financial centre. The conjuncture of these associated elements has created conditions favourable for accountants to occupy a key position as "the watchdogs of Financial Capital" (Armstrong, forthcoming).

However, while requiring sensitivity with respect to the existence of significant differences between economies and societies, it is also relevant to recognise their similarities. This consideration has already been alluded to in characterising them as "advanced capitalist". This label is intended to signify a number of common features of our four nation-states. First, it implies that they are part and parcel of a monopolistic stage of capitalism in which the political economy of nation-states is increasingly conditioned by transnational forces, particularly multinational corporations and military and economic alliances (e.g. NATO, EEC). Second, the label implies that, as capitalism "advances", institutions of the state have tended to become increasingly intertwined with the operation of market forces. Third, it allows that, despite the historical tendency towards rationalisation and disenchantment, modern nation-states harbour and depend upon the existence of the values and ideals of community. Albeit in distorted form, these values may still exert a powerful, if anachronistic, influence in the regulation of everyday economic and political life. However, as with the other principles, this influence will differ according to the contrasting histories, cultures and paths of development of different nation states.[2]

We have suggested that an analysis of accounting regulation as a social and organisational phenomenon requires critical appreciation of its construction within a nexus of "market forces", "bureaucratic controls" and "communitarian ideals". In stressing the importance of appreciating the importance of the nexus or fusion of these organising principles, we seek to avoid forms of analysis in which the contradictory policies and practices emanating from both capitalist enterprises and state institutions disappear from view (Frankel, 1983, pp. 11–12). To this end, we draw initially upon the work of Streeck & Schmitter (1985) who have identified three ideal-typical principles of coordination and allocation "dispersed competition" (Market), "hierarchical control" (State) and "spontaneous solidarity" (Community). Figure 1 illustrates their model.

The differences between these principles can best be appreciated by comparing and contrasting them in terms of their respective sources of motivation and authority, on the one hand, and sources of tension and cleavage, on the other. For example the operation of the principle of dispersed competition is seen to generate both economic entrepreneurs who maximise profits and consumers who are satisfied with the material benefits derived from competition. But tensions are understood to arise from the basic conflict of interest between sellers and buyers of products as well as factors of production. In contrast, the authority of hierarchical control, as operationalised by career civil servants for example, is vested in agreed rules and procedures backed up by the state's monopoly of legitimate coercion. This principle of coordination and allocation is characterised by its successful protection of actors from external threats and its

---

[2] As Frankel (1983, p. 14) notes, "While it is perfectly reasonable to speak of the French state, or the Turkish state, or any such shorthand term which implies a set of historically specific social institutions and relations, it is quite another matter to involve concepts of 'the State' and 'the capitalist State' as if they were self-evident or empirically visible and similar in all societies and over long periods of time".

Fig 1. Three principles of social order.

	Market	State	Community
1. Guiding principle of coordination and allocation	Dispersed competition	Hierarchical control	Spontaneous solidarity
2. Predominant collective actor	Firms	Bureaucratic agencies	Families
3. Principal medium of exchange	Contracts	Authoritative regulation	Compacts
4. Predominant resources	Economic entrepreneurship, calculative rationality	Legitimate control over means of coercion	Respect, trust, inherited status
5. Principal motives of superordinate actors	Profit	Career advancement; bureaucratic stability	Esteem of followers
6. Principal motives of subordinate actors	Material benefit	Fear of punishment	Belonging to group; desire to share in common values
7. Common motive of all actors	Maximising advantage	Maximising predictability; minimising risk	Satisfying identity
8. Principal line of cleavage	Sellers vs buyers	Rulers vs ruled	Natives vs foreigners
9. Principal pay-offs	Material prosperity	External security; equitable and predictable treatment	Mutual affection; collective identity

Adapted from Streeck & Schmitter (1985).

securing of equitable and predictable treatment for all its citizens. Tensions arise, nonetheless, in relation to privileges that rulers provide for themselves and obligations they impose on others. Finally, with spontaneous solidarity, leaders are described as enjoying the esteem of followers who themselves benefit from a sense of belonging. As members of a community both groups are able to "satisfy their mutual needs for a shared affective existence and a distinctive collective identity" (Streeck & Schmitter, 1985, p. 7), but tensions are generated by the appearance of outsiders who fail to respect the sanctity of dominant norms and values.

Although Streeck & Schmitter stress the presence of internal tension and cleavage, they also emphasise that the main threat to the persistence and legitimacy of these organising principles is external — that is, it is posed by the co-existence of other, competing principles of order. For, as they see it, under the conditions of "modernity", each of these principles of order is in competition for "the allegiance of specific groups, for the control of scarce resources, for the incorporation of new issues, for the definition of rules regulating exchanges between them, and so forth" (1985, p. 9). And yet, paradoxically, each order is also acknowledged to feed off the fruits of its "competitors". Capitalist market relations, for example, are recognised to be dependent upon the authority of the state for ensuring "the policing of contracts" no less than it is upon the presence of "trust, deference, esteem and consent rooted in communitarian practices" (p. 9). Likewise, the state's authority is seen to be reliant upon "the socialised identification of its subjects who associate it with a particular nation, ethnic group, religion or 'community of fate'" (p. 9).[3]

To sum up, Streeck & Schmitter attend to

_____

[3] Our conceptual framework focusses on the social and organisational shaping of accounting practice by nation-state specific forces of regulation that have a degree of national specificity. But, equally it has been necessary for this framework to be sensitive to accounting practices as *condition and medium* of these forces as well as a product of them. Accounting itself plays a formative role in advancing, mediating and legitimising the principles and mechanisms that underpin and condition its own

"modernity" as a composite order in which a delicate balance is maintained between three formally incompatible, yet substantively interdependent, guiding principles of coordination and allocation.[4] In our view, the value of Streeck & Schmitter's discussion resides in its sensitivity to the complexity and multi-dimensionality of "modernity" and its provision of a detailed framework of analysis. It recognises how the institutions and practices of modernity are conditioned by the presence of ordering principles that are simultaneously interdependent and contradictory. However, we have reservations about the analytical commitment and points of departure of their framework.

These reservations can be summarily stated by highlighting a number of absences within their discussion of how social order is accomplished. First, it lacks an historical dimension. There is little appreciation of how the presence and interpretation of the three organising principles is historically specific. Second, their analysis tends to be couched in terms of the examination of social order within nation states. There is little space, or signs of invitation, to appreciate the limited political and economic autonomy of states within a world system. Third, and most crucially, Streeck & Schmitter's framework offers no attempt to discern *which* contradictions within "modernity" are *central* in generating change both generally and also in the relative presence and influence of the three organising principles within contemporary social practices. Before advancing a critique of their position, though, we explore more fully its contribution to sensitising us to the principles that may inform accounting as a social practice.

Accounting as a social practice

Our argument so far is that an adequate study of accountancy regulation must attend to its institutions and its practices as emergent within,

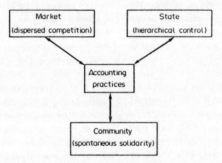

Fig. 2. Accounting and the intersection of ordering principles.

practices. Double entry book-keeping, for example, is widely recognised as a critical technique for the establishment and universalisation of capitalist relations of production. More particularly, where states have supported and/or licenced the operation of professional bodies, these associations have selectively sought the preservation of ideals of community (i.e. service to the public interest) as a means of vouchsafing their authority (Willmott, 1985b). In doing so, they may be seen to offer themselves and their clients a degree of protection from the "twin evils" of the anarchic irrationality of the market and the bureaucratic surveillance of the state.

[4] Here it is relevant to note that Streeck & Schmitter go on to identify what they regard as a fourth principle, an inter- and intra-organisational consertation, which is attributed to the associative model of social order. As will become clear, we accept that this fourth principle has assumed greater significance in modern capitalist societies, and is of relevance to our study in so far as accounting regulation is accomplished through inter- and intraorganisational concertation (e.g. the role of professional associations in the U.K.). However, we believe that the properties of the Associative model of social order are better understood as an outcome of the intersection of "Market", "State" and "Community" than as properties that can be analysed independently (see Willmott, 1985a).

and reproductive of, the intersections between ordering principles (see Fig. 2). We now explore the relevance of each of these principles, with reference to accounting in the U.K.

Dispersed competition. Accountancy practice is regulated by market principles in a variety of ways. First, with respect to internal "management" accounting private firms are the major providers or generators of accounting information. Accounting practices pervade the modern organisation and take on increasing significance as they are used to control and improve, as well as monitor, employee and organisational performance. Indeed, the expansion of accounting practices into virtually every area of corporate life is promoted and supported as the pressures to maintain or improve the extraction of surplus value mount in the face of competition (Hopper *et al.*, 1986). Second, within the U.K., capital market pressures have stimulated the development of accounting disclosures. Indeed it has been suggested that company accounts, produced to facilitate the smooth operation of capital markets, would be, or have been, constructed and audited without the goad of regulation. (Watts, 1977; Benston, 1973).

Hierarchical control. The principle of hierarchical control is also significant in the formation and reproduction of accountancy practice. For example, of considerable importance is the passing of legislation (e.g. Company Acts, commercial codes, market regulations) that make the preparation and publication of company accounts a legal requirement. In this way, the state, or associated agencies, seeks to hold companies accountable for their activities and ensures that costly information is made available for both market and non-market actors — something that the market mechanism could not be relied upon to provide. The principle of hierarchical control intervenes, therefore, to ensure that basic accounting practices are undertaken as a means of reducing the turbulence and uncertainties associated with the erratic discipline of the market. However, in the U.K., the state does not exercise this control directly by passing detailed

statutes. Instead, the legislation governing accounting practice merely indicates in very general terms the minimum requirements in respect, for example, of the preparation and auditing of company accounts. The detail of how accounts are to be drawn up is left to the "discretion" of the accountancy profession. It is the members of the profession, in consultation with advisors from a plurality of interest groups, who formally specify the precise content of the standards which determine how accounts are prepared. And it is members of the profession, not the state, who are responsible for verifying (i.e. auditing) the position presented in published accounts.

Spontaneous solidarity. A recognition of the role of the profession brings us to a consideration of "community" in shaping accounting practice. Clearly, it would be a mistake to equate the organisation or the profession with the operation of the principle of spontaneous solidarity. For, in essence, the formal organisation of an occupation into professional associations in the U.K. was promoted, historically, by the unreliability of an unregulated, "free" market for accounting expertise (Willimott, 1986). In this market, sellers of accounting labour who possessed a measure of expertise and honesty were being brought into disrepute by those who possessed little save the ability to make a fast buck in an unregulated market in which many buyers were unable to assess the quality and reliability of the product. To justify their monopolistic efforts to restrict the supply of accounting labour the emergent, "industrial" professions drew heavily upon the ideals of community — of gentlemanly conduct and public service. To attain and legitimise social closure, emphasis has been placed upon "good breeding", upon being well-connected and upon the "personal" qualities associated with such characteristics as reliability, trustworthiness and fellowship. Even as training and qualifications have been introduced to provide impersonal validations of technical competence, the trappings of Establishment virtues have been retained, not least because these have an instrumental value in legitimising market practices and, thereby, securing the market value of accounting labour (Macdonald, 1984). But equally, it is important to acknowledge that accounting activities may also be defended and reproduced by practitioners because they offer a valued source of personal satisfaction, collective identity and social esteem, and not solely because they are of instrumental, material value.

The principles of dispersed competition, hierarchical control and spontaneous solidarity all play a role in the regulation of accountancy practice. Accountancy regulation is something that cannot be analysed by reference to only one or even two of these principles since it is clearly a mix of all three of them. Recent debates over inflation accounting in the U.K. indicate the problematic and potentially volatile nature of this mix. The U.K. state may have produced a blueprint in the form of the Sandilands Report (Cmnd 6225, 1975) but the Accounting Standards Committee, having earlier tried to produce a blueprint themselves, were expected to implement the State blueprint. Market resistance has resulted in the withdrawal of a standard, with calls for either the State or the Stock Market to provide mandatory backing for any future standard (Cooper *et al.,* forthcoming).

The above observations beg the question of which of the principles is dominant in the conditioning of the institutions and practices that constitute accountancy regulation. If the carriers of these institutions and practices (e.g. accountants) are analysed in isolation from the economic and political contexts in which they are shaped, the answer might well be "spontaneous solidarity" or, at least, the selective borrowing and embellishment of communitarian principles by professional associations. If the activities of accountants are abstracted from the wider context, accountants alone appear to be responsible for determining the specific contents of accounting policy, standards and practice. It is only when the formation and development of the institutions and practices of accounting regulation are theorised as an outcome as well as a medium of advanced capitalist structures of economic and political relationships that it becomes evident that the very presence of an or-

ganised "profession" depends upon the presence of other organising principles. It is to a consideration of the significance of these principles that we now turn.

BEYOND THE EQUILIBRIUM MODEL

It has been suggested that Streeck & Schmitter's framework is analytically useful in disclosing the presence, absence, characteristics and inter-relations of the three principles of order. However, the potential value of Streeck & Schmitter's framework is constrained by its fragmented focus upon the constituent elements of the ideal-typical orders, to the neglect of the *totality* that is constituted through their intersection. Absent from their discussion is any general theory of society that offers an analysis of the principle or principles that are more, or less, *dominant* in the constitution and reproduction of modernity. Even when disclosing the existence of cleavage and contradiction, their examination of models of order only emphasises the presence of checks and balances within and between principles. It offers little or no indication of the force of each principle either in relation to the others or, more importantly, in relation to their intersection.

Of course, there is no easy or definitive answer to the question of which forces or principles are dominant or determinant in the constitution of accounting in modern society. As Tinker (1984) stresses, in exploring the conjuncture between advanced capitalism and accounting regulation, it is also necessary to be sensitive to the ways in which structured social inequality and conflict is "mediated, modified and transformed" and that other conflicts are also present. Amongst these, Tinker numbers racial, sexual and psychological conflict. Of equal relevance to the present argument, perhaps, are the conflicts over professional identity (which may well include strong sexual and racial strains) that cannot be reduced to structural (class) conflict. Yet, while recognising the (muted) presence of what we refer to as the Community principle of organisation, we concur with Tinker that there is a considerable danger in the analysis of regulation becoming preoccupied with the manifest tension and conflicts within and between interest groups. Analysis should not overlook the deeper, defining structural relations of advanced capitalism which both enable and constrain the expression and resolution of such conflicts. Or, as Tinker, in emphasising the importance of the historical context, puts it:

> it is important not to lose a sense of proportion by letting the "moderators" and "intervening factors" take on greater significance than that which is being moderated — structural conflict itself.

But, equally, we believe that it is a mistake to stress the explanatory-power of "structural conflict" *if* the effect is to deny or neglect the critical role of agents in the reproduction of social systems. For although agents are positioned in a structure of class relations, they are still obliged to respond inventively to the manifestation of contradictions that are continuously "thrown up" by this structure. Although clearly conditioned by the location of their positions within the class structure, these responses are not programmed by this location. Indeed, what is crucial to realise is that there are ideological (as well as material) conditions for the reproduction of class relations and, more specifically, the positions/subjects within these relations (Coward & Ellis, 1977; Therborn, 1980; Pecheux, 1982).

With the reservation that the continuation of advanced capitalism is conditioned by the ideological production of compliant subjects, we are persuaded that an appreciation of the structural contradictions endemic to advanced capitalist modes of production is an important key to understanding the fundamental dynamics of regulating accounting policy and practice. For example, the free operation of the Market principle of "dispersed competition" tends to frustrate its own reproduction since, by definition, each participant in a competitive market — labour as well as capital — has a vested interest in excluding, or wiping out, the competition — by buying it up, by pricing it out and/or by erecting massive barriers to entry. Indeed the very operation of

the market stimulates a cyclical crisis of overproduction during periods of "boom" which are then drastically terminated by "slump". During this cycle, there is a continuous crisis of underinvestment as demand falls and the competitive response of substituting capital for labour has the effect of reducing future opportunities for realising a surplus. Finally, by commodifying labour and by socialising and rationalising the process of production, there is a tendency for labour to become homogenised, deskilled and generally "proletarianised". This process can lead to a situation where labour is more likely to discern a collective interest in withdrawing consent from, if not actively resisting, the oppressive demands of capital for relations of production and consumption whose primary concern is sustaining a political economy of private appropriation.

And yet, in each case, the flexibility and adaptability of the capitalist mode of production, the capacity for its contradictions to be contained and displaced but not removed, also needs to be recognised. For example, with the development of the market, a limited number of very large, often multinational competitors can become sufficiently big to be unconcerned by the continuous emergence of numerous small firms that compete for very localised and specialist segments of their market. Frequently, it is these small firms that smooth the periods of "boom" and "slump" as their entrance is stimulated by a rise in demand (just as their exit is promoted by its fall), whereas the bigger firms draw upon their reserves to weather the storm. The existence of reserves also offers the latter the possibility of strategic restructuring through diversification, for example by investing in new technologies as a means of "outpacing" the tendency for the rate of profit to fall. Similarly, potential crises of over production and under-investment are averted or buffered by the realisation that demand can be created through the stimulation of mass needs. Thus, in advanced capitalist nation states at least, it is the affluent worker with money to invest as well as spend, not the impoverished worker, who has become the boon of capitalist development — development which, of course, requires continuous expansion into new markets in order to ensure accumulation. In this process, the division between the "political" and "economic" spheres has encouraged trade unionists and employers alike to formulate and interpret employee demands in narrow, economic terms. The basic, exploitative structure of capitalist society is then largely taken for granted as the focus of debate turns upon notions of "fair wages" and "ability to pay" within the cash nexus. Effectively excluded from the economic sphere are issues, for example, relating to the control and accountability of capital in relation to those who produce the wealth (cf. Haworth & Ramsie, 1985).

In the context of advanced capitalism, however, it is insufficient to limit analysis to those contradictions which are essentially economic in nature. This is because during the development of the capitalist mode of production, the state has played an increasingly important and quasi-autonomous role in mediating and organising the contradictory tendencies of capitalism. For example, in its limited responsiveness to the demands of labour and its concern with formally democratic decision making, the state has both facilitated and frustrated the operation of the Market principle as the dominant means of regulating social and economic relations (Poulantzas, 1975; Offe, 1984). In recognising the influence of State principles in the regulation of capitalist development, including accounting, it is necessary to reject the crude Marxian formulation of the state as an instrument or "executive committee" of a unified capitalist clans as well as the idea that its power is always tightly coupled to class interests (Lenin, 1971; Miliband, 1973). Instead, the state is seen to make often poorly coordinated and pragmatic responses to the constraining influence and re-

sistance of organised labour as well as the power exerted by fractions of capital. In this light, the state is theorised as a complex and loosely coupled set of institutions that enjoy a degree of "relative autonomy" from economic class interests. In responding to class pressures to pursue policies and develop institutions of mediation (e.g. corporatist forms of economic regulation), regulation through the state secures and extends its power base as it simultaneously facilitates accumulation for capital and employment for labour.

In large part, the development of the apparatus of the state as a third force has arisen from organised labour's formally successful pursuit of the demand for political representation through universal suffrage. Although this achievement has not resulted in the transformation of the state, it has produced support for policies that may run counter to the liberal principles of the Market. Amongst such policies are those that expand demand, promote regional development, subsidise declining industries, and exclude capital from participation in potentially profitable markets (e.g. by nationalisation) or regulate the pricing of commodities, including labour. Of course, many of these policies have also been indirectly advantageous to capital, especially when the cost of expanding demand, improving competitiveness or attracting investment has been socialised through selective changes in taxation and public expenditure. However, universal suffrage (and proportional representation) has also had the largely unintended consequence of stabilising and legitimising the *status quo* of welfare capitalism since political parties are obliged to appeal to the "middle ground" of political opinion in order to secure a working majority.[5]

Yet, in order to secure political legitimacy

---

[5] Although we have noted the (unintendedly) "functional" role of the state in preserving the *status quo*, we would wish to reassert our emphasis upon the presence and critical importance of contradictions within the capitalist mode of production that are displaced into, and not resolved by, the political sphere following interventions by the state (Offe, 1984). Late capitalism enters a political crisis as the shortfall between the demands of the electorate on the one hand, and the suppliers of goods and tax revenue, on the other, is widely perceived as *its* failure, and not attributed either to a lack of realism on the part of the electorate, to profligate state expenditure and/or economic mismanagement by the party in power. Needless to say, the task of avoiding and discrediting such a perception is undertaken by the leaders and spokesmen of those parties and interest groups most committed to the "free enterprise", Market principles of capitalism.

through the ballot box, the managers of the state are under pressure to intervene in the economy at all levels to counter the deficiencies and irrationalities of the operation of Market principles. And, in doing so, they create an army of unproductive bureaucrats whose allegiance is neither directly to "capital" nor "labour" but rather, to the security (i.e. preservation) of the modern state, to its elected representatives and, not least, to themselves. Moreover, the managers of the state (i.e. politicians and senior civil servants) have come to depend upon various agencies of interest representation (e.g. professional associations) to whom state power is "licensed", and over whom control is exercised only indirectly — through the threat of withdrawal of the licence. The tendential effect of state managers' positioning in relation to the demands of diverse capitals, organised labour, the electorate and its licensees is towards the uneasy, restless reproduction of the *status quo.*.

COMPARATIVE ACCOUNTANCY REGULATION

Theorising accountancy regulation

It should now be clear that our understanding of the relationship between "Market", "State" and "Community" principles of societal regulation is that they are both essential and problematical for the "ordering" of advanced capitalism.

In examining accountancy regulation, we theorise its institutions and practices as an outcome of interactions between parties (e.g. diverse state managers, agents of fractions of capital and representatives of organised interest groups) who are positioned within a structure of politico-economic relations that is simultaneously united and divided by internal contradictions, tensions and struggles. Accordingly, the actions and accounts of these parties will be

theorised as an expression of the fusing of the principles of Market, State and Community. In this light, the reproduction/reform of the prevailing structure of politico-economic relations is seen as an (often unintended) consequence of these parties' efforts to mobilise their stock of material and ideological resources (including institutions) to negotiate policies and practices of regulation that are perceived, within the terms of their own frames of reference, to safeguard or advance their own individualistic career interests as well as the class interests of those on whose behalf they act.[6]

Reflecting historical and cultural differences between nation-states, variations in the combination of principles that regulate institutions and practices of regulation are to be expected. Facilitated by the in-built flexibility and adaptability of the capitalist mode of production, the structures of advanced capitalism invite and accommodate a number of nation-state specific strategies dealing with emergent problems (cf. Strinati, 1982). Once applied, and embodied in modes of regulation, these strategies shape and constrain the conditions and directions of future development.

By returning to our earlier discussion and critique of models of social order, we can identify a number of theoretically possible modes of regulation (see Fig. 3). Mirroring our argument that, in this context, the organising principles of Community are subordinated to those of Market and State, these modes are seen to rely most heavily upon some mix of the latter elements. So, at one extreme, there is the ideal-typical mode of Liberalism whereby regulation is provided exclusively by the discipline of Market principles. That is to say, activity occurs, and information is provided, only if it is found to be commercially demanded. At another extreme is the conceptual possibility of Legalism, which relies upon the unreserved application of State principles. In

---

[6] When saying this, it is not assumed that these perceptions are "accurate", or that they are devoid of undesirable unintended consequences, or indeed that there is a well defined link between interests, actions and outcome (Foucault, 1977). On the contrary, there is every expectation that actions and accounts will be informed by unexamined and indelible prejudices, assumptions and rationalisations about the purpose and process of accountancy regulation. But, as researchers, our role is not to mirror and thereby legitimise these actions and accounts as the reality of regulation but, rather, to illuminate this "reality" from an intellectually coherent perspective.

Fig. 3. Strategies of regulation situated in relation to dominant models of social order.

this case, behaviour is sanctioned only if it follows the letter of the law — law that is enforced not by commercial failure, but by the state's monopoly of the means of coercion. Because neither Market nor State principles exist in a pure form actual modes of regulation can only approximate to the ideal-types of Liberalism and Legalism. More useful for empirical analysis, then, is the notion that, within different nation-states, the regulation of accounting, for example, can be compared along the Liberalism–Legalism axis. Between these poles, different diluted *combinations* of Market and State principles, with remnants of Community principles, are to be expected (discussed below).

Clearly, an adequate analysis of accountancy regulation requires a grounded study of policy makers and their social context. In the absence of such studies, we may make a preliminary assessment of the dominant, but ever shifting, combinations of mode of regulation in the four nation states, using evidence about their formal institutions of regulation. This will provide an indication of the utility of the framework adopted and a theoretically grounded appreciation of the different patterns which currently exist in late capitalist nation-states.

Modes of accounting regulation in four nation-states

An example of predominantly Legalist modes would appear to be the Federal Republic of Germany. Regulation there is predominantly the outcome of statute law, both the *Aktiengesetz*, 1965, and tax legislation. "The regulations of German tax law for the determination of taxable income are (almost) as important as regulations of commercial law" (Wysocki, 1983, p. 59). These laws, though created by lawyers and administrators in the Ministry of Justice, are also influenced by representations, and relevant bodies including Wirtschaftsprufer, accountants in industry, and accounting academics (Busse von Colbe, 1984) now concentrate on attempting to influence the process of developing new laws by lobbying. Additional regulatory institutions which indicate the significance of State principles in developing a Legalistic mode include the Commercial Code (*Handelsgesetzbuch*) of 1897 "finally amended 4 July 1980" (Wysocki, 1983, p. 58) and decisions by the courts. As with all codified legal systems, the latter involves an interpretation by the judicature of the intention of statute and the commercial code; the principle of the precedent does not apply.

These legalist influences have been modified, however, by the introduction of other principles of regulation. Market principles may be evidenced in the charts of accounts of individual industries that tend to be followed by the firms in that industry. Combinations of Market and Communitarian principles seem to apply in two further elements.

The *"Grundsatze Ordnungsmassiger Buchfuhrung"* (variously translated as "Generally Accepted Accounting Principles" and as "the principles of proper book-keeping") influences accountancy regulations. For, according to Wysocki (1983): "Even given the above legal regulations concerning accounting standards in the Federal Republic of Germany there is considerable scope for some form of accounting standards for external accounting. This scope, according to the will of the German Legislature, is to be filled by the *Grundsatze Ordnungsmassiger Buchfuhrung* i.e. by generally accepted accounting principles".

Finally, Wysocki refers to another body not alluded to by other authors:

An organization which is quite active in the interpretation of GAAP is the *"Institut der Wirschaftsprufer…"* and its professional committee, the *"Hauptfachauschuss"* … the *Hauptfachauschuss* has since the thirties published many pronouncements, comments and releases about accounting principles under German legal provisions. Although these pronouncements, comments and releases are formally private opinions, they are taken to be equivalent to GAAP in many cases. There are only a few of these pronouncements which have not been accepted by the public in Germany … (p. 62).

Although other sources suggest that the Institute does not formally issue accountancy regulations, this body seems, to some extent at least, to have a parallel authority not through issuing specific regulations but by adjudicating or advising on fundamental principles.

While West Germany appears to quite closely approximate legalism, other nation states seem to adopt a combination of modes. As a first approximation, two mixed modes can be identified. In the first of these, regulation is accomplished through the development of organisations that are formed to represent and advance the interests of their members. In relation to accountancy, the presence and influence of professional bodies is the most obvious example of the strategy of Associationism. In this mode, there is some dependence upon principles of Community. However, such principles are routinely subordinated to those of the Market. Membership is founded principally upon calculative rationality rather than a desire to share in common values.

The other "mixed" mode along the Liberalism–Legalism axis involves a greater reliance upon State principles of "hierarchical control". Here the State does not simply license the existence of organised interest groups but incorporates them into its own centralised, hierarchical system of regulation. In doing so, the state simultaneously recognises its dependence upon these associations and seeks to use them as an instrument in the pursuit and legitimation of its policies. This mode of regulation, which we describe as Corporatism, has received most attention in relation to the macro level where governments conduct tri-partite negotiations with representatives of industrial capital and labour (e.g. in the U.K. context, the Confederation of British Industry and the Trades Union Congress). However, more generally, Corporatism describes any "attempt to assign to interest associations a distinct role between the State and 'civil society' (market and community) *so as to put to public purposes* the type of social order that associations can generate and embody" (Streeck & Schmitter, 1985, pp. 20–21, emphasis added). Thus, although the strategies of Associationism and Corporatism can be seen to shade into each other, the basic difference between them lies in the extent to which the State "leans" on interest groupings to achieve "public" (i.e. State), as contrasted with "private" (i.e. Market) purposes.

In the light of this model, the U.K. is seen to be principally Associationist in organisation. U.K. professional bodies have not been set up by the State [although the State may have been influential in their development (Loft, 1986)] and the professional bodies are nominally, at least, independent of it (Willmott, 1986). In this context, accounting standards are set by a body, the Accounting Standards Committee (ASC) whose membership still overwhelmingly consists of representatives of the six major professional bodies and which is indeed a subcommittee of the coordinating committee (i.e. the Consultative Committee of Accounting Bodies) of these six bodies (Willmott, 1985a). Its rulings do not have the force of law and are not infrequently ignored by reporting companies. In principle it has the power to discipline members of the accounting bodies for failure to comply with the standards for financial statements. However, this power has not been widely used in the fifteen years the system has existed. The standards produced by the ASC are supported, but not enforced, by the Stock Exchange and generally attract favourable comment from the government. Members of the ASC are part-time (as with the ASB in Sweden, but in contrast to the FASB in the United States — see below), and may tend to act as representatives of the institutions they represent (although that may not be the intention).

To the extent that the rhetoric (that the ASC acts in the public interest through trust and respect) actually informs its practices, so it may be regarded as embodying communitarian principles. However several analyses of the U.K. accounting profession (Johnson, 1980; Puxty, 1984; Cooper, 1984; Willmott, 1985b, 1986) and standard setting (Hope & Gray, 1982) suggest that the Market principle of dispersed competition through economic entrepreneurship and calculative rationality is predominant.

However, the principles of hierarchical control are gradually becoming felt in the U.K., largely through its membership of the European Community. This is most noticeable in changes to the law. The Companies Acts of 1949, 1967, 1976, 1980 and 1981, consolidated into one large Act, in 1985, were orientated to increased disclosure and the discretion of the accounting profession in defining "true and fair". Although embodied into the latest Acts, the undefined principle of true and fair is somewhat problematic in relation to both professional discretion and authoritative regulation. Within the U.K., the overt relationship of the state to the accountancy profession is one in which there is little in the formal structure (only recognition for audit purposes of members of certain bodies) but more considerable informal pressure (for instance the state is represented at the meetings of the ASC and the professional institutes keep in touch with their "sponsoring" Ministry, the Department of Trade and Industry). Further in the U.K. system the courts and judiciary attempt to understand the letter of the law rather than the intention behind it. There is a system of precedence whereby previous legal decisions are to some extent binding for subsequent court decisions.

The relatively direct involvement of the Swedish state in the regulation of accountancy in that nation state leads us to suggest that Corporatism is the best description of how accountancy regulation appears to operate there. The State has passed various pieces of legislation governing financial reporting, of which the most important are the Bookkeeping Act 1976, the Companies Act 1975 and the Municipal Tax Act 1926. The requirements are quite detailed. The courts, as in other countries with codified legal systems, interpret the law. Accountancy regulations appear to be particular to broad sectors of the economy (there are separate regulations for the public sector, local government and private sectors, for example). For quoted companies, the Stock Exchange has issued guidelines on both the disclosure of information and the form of financial statements.

The auditors in Sweden have attempted to emulate the influence of the accounting professions in Anglo-American practice and thereby to introduce Market and Communitarian principles of regulation. The *Foreningen Aukterisade Revisover* (hereafter FAR) has issued a number of recommendations (using special committees) on auditing, and a few on accounting. However, these are not binding and indeed government legislation set up the Accounting Standards Board (hereafter ASB). This is a product of the Bookkeeping Act (SFS) of 1976 and reflected in part governmental feeling that the FAR was itself an interested party that was not unbiased in issuing accounting standards. The ASB consists of experts from various interested parties such as auditors, business, academia, small firms, tax authorities and unions. The 1976 Act required it to "further the development of good accounting practices in company books and their published reports" (SFS 1976, p. 377 quoted by Jonsson, forthcoming) intending that it "should with participation from different interested parties in industry . . . work for the improvement of published accounts" (p. 112). The statements of the ASB do not have the force of law "unless the content of the directive is covered by a court ruling or by administrative decisions" (Jonsson, forthcoming).

The Swedish state is also directly involved in the authorisation of candidate members of the accountancy profession. After obtaining the appropriate academic qualifications and practical experience, the candidate applies for registration with the Royal Board of Trade. Following this, he may (but need not) apply to join the professional body (FAR). The FAR is not a State body.

The duality of the FAR and the ASB appears to make Sweden unique. It is of note that the FAR issues exposure drafts for comment before deciding on a recommendation. The ASB does not, and its decisions have, until 1986, been unanimous. After an initial period in which the FAR was unhappy with the establishment of an alternative source of rules, the two boards have now, according to Jonsson, developed a coordinated way of working. However, the FAR is strongly represented on the ASB.

The fourth country with which we are concerned, the U.S.A., cannot be typified quite so easily. As a federation of states, much of the hierarchical control takes place at individual state level. Corporate legislation is a matter for the individual states, as is the recognition of the qualified accountant. There is hence a relationship between the state and the profession in that each aspiring Certified Public Accountant (CPA) must obtain recognition from his or her state licensing authority before being allowed to practice. However the American Institute of Certified Public Accountants (AICPA) is a national body; and its examinations are common to all states and recognised by them. Membership of the AICPA is not compulsory for those who wish to practice as CPAs.

Accountancy regulation in the U.S.A. as it relates to the corporate reporting of larger companies, is governed principally by a state agency, the Securities and Exchange Commission. Financial statements in the U.S.A. are heavily influenced by the Federal Securities Acts of 1933 and 1934. These incorporated disclosure provisions for companies with assets over $1m. The latter Act set up the Securities and Exchange Commission (SEC) which undertakes the detailed regulation of corporate disclosure and has considerable powers (which it uses).

Whilst these arrangements appear to vest considerable authority in State and (capital) Market principles of regulation, the SEC has generally taken the view that detailed accounting regulation should be undertaken by a more "independent" body organised by the U.S. accounting profession. The latest of such bodies is the Financial Accounting Standards Board (FASB), set up in 1974. If the SEC does not like the regulations set by the FASB, however, it is willing to take action to change them. The U.S. Congress, in addition to its influence through the Securities Acts, is willing to overrule the SEC on accounting regulations when it feels it is necessary. As a result, it can be the subject of (sometimes intense) lobbying by affected companies.

The FASB is appointed by the Financial Accounting Foundation which itself is funded half by business firms and half by public accounting firms. The FASB consists of seven full-time members who are backed up by a large and extensive organization. Its members are *not* intended to be delegates of other bodies. They are specifically required to sever links with existing employers when appointed, which contrasts with Swedish and U.K. practice. The standards produced are mandatory on the companies concerned (as a result of SEC backing). In sum, there is a close relationship between the SEC and the FASB and the accounting profession has some influence both as a lobbying body and, as suppliers of expertise to the Financial Accounting Standards Board. U.S. accounting regulations thus contain elements of Legalism and Associationism, with the latter subordinated to the former.

Above, we have identified the formal modes of accountancy regulation in the U.K., U.S.A., Sweden and Germany. Whilst this may contribute to comparative accounting theory, it is clear that much remains to be done. The dynamic of accountancy regulation could be made more explicit by an historical analysis of advanced capitalism and accounting change. The apparent convergence of modes of accountancy regulation between the four nations states suggests that more attention needs to be paid to international and trans-national pressures. And greater emphasis could be placed on the roles of accountancy rules (which would include standard setting and law making) in regulating advanced capitalism in order that the interaction between the regulatory rules and the regulatory bodies could be more thoroughly appreciated.

Finally, we have said little of the effect of these differing modes of regulating accountancy. Leaving aside the problematic nature of concepts such as effectiveness, democracy, utility and sophistication, we can nonetheless share the recognition of Muis that different regulations and principles of regulation are likely to have profoundly different material and ideological effects:

> We can broadly categorise countries into "sophisticated" (U.S., U.K., Netherlands), "legalistic/formalistic" (Germany and France) and the so-called "primitives" (Switzerland, Japan, Italy)... I would like to point out ... that this classification says little or nothing about the social-economic utility of public accounting as such: a country may well be classified as "sophisticated", as an index of the thoroughness of its accounting and reporting doctrine, but in an economic sense far worse than the so-called "primitives". We should remember that no one has so far been able to prove a causal relationship between a well-developed public accounting system with an informal but effective communication system among the happy few wielding economic power, take, for example, Switzerland, France and, until recently, Belgium ... I believe in it (i.e. the sophisticated model) not for the sake of rational (or rather quasi-rational) economic decision-making but rather because a sound framework of accounting enhances the decision-making process in our democratic society — of which our economic financial fabric is no more, but also no less, than one of the cornerstones. Transparency in our financial reporting enhances the transparency of our society and thus *democracy* (Muis, 1984, p. 264).

COMMENTARY

It will be clear from our cursory examination of these four nation-states that accounting is regulated differently within Germany, the U.K., Sweden and the U.S.A. In reviewing these cases, a starting point is to examine their respective features in terms of *commonality* and *contrast*. In doing so, it is worth recalling our view that the principles of Market, State and to a lesser extent Community, in the form of "Associationism", are present in all four countries. The presence and extensiveness of these principles is however problematic.

It is fundamental to countries with codified legal systems that the legal codes attempt to regulate all conduct. It is to be expected therefore that Market principles will have a limited influence in accountancy regulation in countries with legal systems of this kind. Germany is the clearest example of the four considered here. At first sight, it would appear that the state is fundamental in understanding the regulation of accountancy information. However, as with so many systems, this is a *minimum* and the market doubtless operates to increase or modify this minimum. One further feature of the German system must be mentioned, however; the preponderance of power inherent in the banks which own and/or control a substantial portion of the equity of industry, have substantial representation on the supervisory boards (*Aufsichstrate*) of major industrial enterprises and often have a substantial ownership interest in firms of auditors. Given the resulting knowledge of affairs by the banks, there has been a lack of interest in the F.R.G. (and, to a lesser extent, in Sweden) in disclosure for investment purposes (as opposed to disclosure for the needs of creditors). This power relationship has therefore had a marked influence on the market for information in the F.R.G. The influence of the capital market has been more important to the U.K. and U.S.A. though even here, there has been considerable state involvement.

Second, it can be seen that in each case there is some provision for the accountancy profession to share with the state in the control mechanism over financial reports. This may be through representations and argument over the substance of statute law (Germany), promulgating its own standards and being presented on the government's own standards board (Sweden), administering a standards board itself (U.K.) or partly funding and partly having its members staff the quasi-independent (of the state, that is) standard-setting authority (U.S.A.). Although the form of the institutions varies between countries, the parties involved do not; and though the overt structures vary, the extent to which different interests have influence over the actual regulations that take place cannot be deduced from the formal structures.

Third, there is in all cases some state control over the entrance to the accountancy profession. This is weakest in the U.K.: in the other three countries the state must either register a candidate directly before s/he is permitted to practise as an accountant (Germany, Sweden and the U.S.A.) or there is a state-designed organization to supervise accountancy (as in the German *Kammer*). In the U.K. the government sanction is indirect: the professional bodies admit candidates to membership on the same terms as the state registering bodies in other countries (with requirements to be satisfied concerning education, practical training and integrity) and it does so in the knowledge that State approval for the self-governance of the profession will continue only so long as they exercise the privilege in a way acceptable to the State.

Fourth, the different forms of regulation present different potentials and problems. In each country there are likely variations in the roles of accounting and auditing in the accountability of third parties. These variations may reflect the histories and specific features of the State, Market and Community principles of regulation in individual nation-states. These variations may themselves reflect to whom, by what means and for what aspects of behaviour, accountability is present. Accounting and auditing appears to be more extensive as a regulator in the market orientated countries of the U.S. and U.K., yet the institutions of accountancy and auditing may themselves be less subject to pressures for accountability in these nation-states, pressures which may exist in countries more familiar with problems of the accountability of state bodies.

These four matters however constitute only the statics of the structural and procedural commonalities and differences among the four countries. Located as they are in different spatial configurations within Fig. 3, the four countries inevitably face different dynamics as a result of the different ways the contradictions of the ad-

vanced capitalist system are worked out. It is the recognition of this process which distinguishes the argument of this paper from the social order suppositions of Streeck & Schmitter.

In essence, the argument of Streeck & Schmitter is one of social order. That is to say, the three organising principles associated with Market, State and Community provide the means whereby society is integrated. The argument of this paper is that any such "integrated" order is illusory, and that the characteristics of advanced capitalist countries are essentially ones in which the contradictions of the system lead to continual ruptures and crises which are enacted and managed, often with unanticipated effects, through the (conditioned) medium of human agency. For example, a particular accountancy standard may have been particularly influenced by the community ideals of an accountancy profession. But the resulting draft standard may then become unacceptable more generally. Under these conditions either market forces (in the shape of objections to the draft by industry, the securities industry, or some other body) may move to change the standard, or the government may step in to oblige some change. *For this standard alone*, therefore, the mix will have shifted to one with a greater preponderance of influence from Market or the State principles and only in the new form will the issue be "acceptable". This is not to claim that it will remain acceptable: social change may make the new mix likewise subject to challenge. Since contradiction is immanent to the system, no permanent location within the Market–State–Community configuration can finally resolve the tensions and processes that result from them.

CONCLUSION

It has been stressed that there will be no single matrix of Market, State and Community principles of organisation which will apply to all arenas of regulation. Rather, the extent to which each of these regulatory forms is prominent in its influence upon the arena under investigation (such as, for example, the treatment of research and development in accounts, or the method of currency translation deemed appropriate) will vary from one issue to another. In this sense, the location of the nation-state in the conceptual space of Fig. 3 may be taken to be an arena within which such differences vary, rather than a specifiable point. For any such issue, each of the three organising principles are likely to be implicated in the definition and (temporary) resolution of the issue. Further, the saliency of each is likely to vary over the period of the issue's visibility.

The dynamics within each such issue will revolve around the tensions resulting from the systemic contradictions as these are expressed and encountered by agents of the organising principles. For any such issue solutions will be suggested that favour and combine one or more of the regulatory modes: Legalism, Liberalism, Association and Corporatism. The exploration of such process, provides an illuminating insight into the way in which the three organising principles of advanced capitalism intersect, collide and shift.

We are conscious that the framework elaborated in this paper is neither simple nor complete. Our concern is to point out that the different modes of regulating accountancy in specific nation states (and indeed the differing means by which accountancy regulations may be implicated in the regulation of economies and societies) cannot be read off from a description of advanced capitalism, with its alleged characteristics, needs and interests. But, conversely, it would seem fallacious to ignore the location of accountancy regulations and regulatory institutions in their social context of advanced capitalism, with its tendencies to fissure and crisis. The actions of policy makers are based on their frame of reference, including their enactment of opportunities and constraints, and thereby reproduce their own social context; but policy makers are not autonomous in their actions. An adequate analysis of accountancy regulation can no more ignore the systemic contradictions of advanced capitalism than it can disregard the everyday practices of the agents who embody, confront and reproduce them.

To conclude, the value of the Streeck &

Schmitter framework, elaborated and extended, is that it offers a concrete analysis of the specific principles of regulation that can be accommodated within advanced capitalism. Our concern in this paper has been limited to developing and applying the framework for identifying differences in the organisation of accountancy regulations in a number of advanced capitalist nation states. We appreciate that a more complete account would identify the historical conditions that are associated with the changing nature of accountancy regulation and its specific features in each nation state. Such an account, we believe, would need to address both the structural location of policy makers as part of the process by which the contradictions of advanced capitalism are managed and displaced and the opportunities for those policy makers to enact their own frame of reference in the ways in which they deal with these contradictions. For this reason an adequate examination of the alternative modes of problem-dealing (for example, with respect to the regulation of accountancy) must attend to the following.

First, it must explore how the status of the activities of policy-makers is a condition and consequence of contradictions and struggles within the political economy of different nation-states. That is, accountancy regulation is recognised to be implicated in the contradictions of capitalist societies, as a means through which struggles are conducted. Clearly then, we do not share a vision of accountancy regulation as being the outcome of rational administration or being achieved through the interplay of great leaders — visions that are commonplace in official histories of the accountancy profession. Second, we suggest that an adequate account of accountancy regulation should acknowledge the frames of reference within which policy makers identify and integrate the issues or puzzles which they face. The culture, history and experience of policy makers in different nation states means that they may take specific views of what is an acceptable, tolerable, sensible or even efficient response to the dilemmas and contradictions they face. And finally, it must be appreciated how these frames of reference fundamentally inform the responses of policy makers. For example, to the extent to which Market principles of regulation have been perceived to offer an acceptable resolution to contradictions within specific nation states, so policy makers will formulate responses to their problems in terms of these principles. However, since, as we have argued, all principles of regulation have contradictions within them, it is unlikely that any nation-state will display an entirely consistent set of institutions and practices of accountancy regulation at any point in time.

BIBLIOGRAPHY

Armstrong, P., The Rise of Accounting Controls in British Capitalist Enterprises, *Accounting, Organizations and Society* (forthcoming).

Benston, G., Required Disclosure and the Stock Markets: An Evaluation of the Securities and Exchange Act of 1934, *American Economic Review* (March 1973) pp. 132–155.

Benston, G., The Market for Public Accounting Services: Demand, Supply and Regulation, *The Accounting Journal* (Winter 1979–1980) pp. 2–47.

Bornstein, S., Held, D. & Krieger, J. (eds) *The State in Capitalist Europe* (London: George Allen & Unwin, 1984).

Burchell, S., Clubb, C. & Hopwood, A., Accounting in its Social Context: Towards a History of Value Added in the U.K., *Accounting, Organizations and Society* (1985) pp. 381–413.

Burchell, S., Clubb, C., Hopwood, A., Hughes, J. & Nahapiet, J., The Roles of Accounting in Organisations and Society, *Accounting, Organisations and Society* (1980) pp. 5–28.

Busse von Colbe, W., Financial Accounting Research in Germany. Some Socio-economic Determinants, in Hopwood, A. G., and Schrueder, H., (eds) *European Contributions to Accounting Research* (Amsterdam: The Free University Press, 1984).

Cooper, D. J., A Political Economy of the U.K. Accounting Profession, unpublished paper, UMIST (1984).

Cooper, D. J., Lowe, E. A. & Puxty, A. G., The Accounting Profession, Corporation and the State, in Chua, W. F., Lowe, E. A. and Puxty, A. G. (eds) *Critical Perspectives in Management Control* (London: Macmillan, forthcoming).

Cooper, D. J. & Sherer, M. J., The Value of Corporate Accounting Reports: Arguments for a Political Economy of Accounting, *Accounting Organisations and Society* (1984) pp. 207–232.

Coward, R. & Ellis, J., *Language and Materialism* (London: Routledge & Kegan Paul, 1977).

Fielding, A. G. & Portwood, D., Professions and the State — Towards a Typology of Bureaucratic Professions, *Sociological Review* (1980) pp. 23–53.

Foucault, M., *Discipline and Punish* (Harmondsworth: Penguin, 1977).

Frankel, B., *Beyond the State?* (London: Macmillan, 1983).

Habermas, J., *Legitimation Crisis* (London, Heinemann, 1976).

Haworth, N. & Ramsie, R., Workers of the World Untied, unpublished paper, University of Strathclyde, 1985.

Holloway, J. & Picciotto, S., *State and Capital* (London: Edward Arnold, 1978).

Hope, A. & Gray, R., Power and Policy Making, *Journal of Business Finance and Accounting* (1982).

Hopper, T. M., Cooper, D. J., Capps, T., Lowe, E. A. & Mouritsen, J., Financial Control and the Labour Process in the National Coal Board, in Knights, D. R. and Willmott, H. (eds) *Management and the Labour Process* (Aldershot: Gower, 1986).

Hopwood, A. G., Accounting Research and Accounting Practice. The Ambiguous Relationship between the Two, unpublished paper, London Business School (1984).

Hopwood, A. G., Burchell, S. & Clubb, C., The Development of Accounting in its International Context: Past Concerns and Emergent Issues, in Roberts, A., (ed.), *An Historical and Contemporary Review of the Development of International Accounting* (Atlanta, GA: Georgia State University, 1979).

Jessop, B., *The Capitalist State* (Oxford: Martin Robertson, 1982).

Johnson, T., *Professions and Power* (London: Macmillan, 1972).

Johnson, T., 1980 Work and Power, in Esland, G. & Salaman, G. (eds) *The Politics of Work and Occupations* (Milton Keynes: Open University Press, 1980).

Jonsson, S., *The Elite and the Norms: Driving Forces in the Development of Accounting Policy* (Chichester: John Wiley, forthcoming).

Lenin, V. I., *State and Revolution* (New York: International Publishers, 1971).

Loft, A. Towards a Critical Understanding of Accounting: The Case of Cost Accounting in the U.K., 1914–1925, *Accounting, Organizations and Society* (1986) pp. 137–169.

Lowe, E. A. & Tinker, A., Sighting the Accounting Problematic, *Journal of Business Finance and Accounting* (1977).

Macdonald, K., Professional Formation: The Case of Scottish Accountants, *British Journal of Sociology* (1984) pp. 174–189.

Mandel, E., Late Capitalism (London: New Left Books, 1975).

Marx, K., *Capital* (Harmondsworth: Penguin Books, 1976).

Middlemas, K., *Politics in Industrial Society* (London: Andre Deutsch, 1979).

Milibrand, R., Poulantzas and the Capitalist State, *New Left Review* (1973).

Muis, J., The Interface of Financial Accounting Research and Practice, in Hopwood, A. and Schrueder, H., (eds), *European Contributions to Accounting Research* (Amsterdam: Free University Press, 1984).

O'Connor, J., *The Fiscal Crisis of the State* (New York: St Martin's Press, 1973).

Offe, C., *Contradiction of the Welfare State* (London, Hutchinson, 1984).

Oldham, K. M., *Accounting Systems and Practice in Europe* (Aldershot, Hants: Gower, 1981).

Pecheux, M., *Language, Semantics and Ideology*, Nagpal, H. (trans) (London: Macmillan 1982).

Poulantzas, N., *Classes in Contemporary Capitalism* (London: New Left Books, 1975).

Puxty, A. G., Decision Usefulness in Accounting: A Contribution to the Critical Theory of the Professions, unpublished PhD, University of Sheffield (1984).

Scase, R. (ed.) *The State in Western Europe* (London: Croom Helm, 1980).

Scott, D. R., *The Cultural Significance of Accounts* (New York: H. Holt, 1931; reprinted, Houston, TX: Scholars Book Co. 1973).

Securities and Exchange Commission, *Staff Report on Corporate Accounting* (U.S.A., 1980).

Stamp, E. & Marley, C., *Accounting Principles and the City Code — The Case for Reform* (London: Butterworths, 1970).

Streeck, W. & Schmitter, P. C., Community Market, State — and Associations? in Streeck, W. and Schmitter, P. C., (eds) *Private Interest Government and Public Policy* (London: Sage, 1985).

Strinati, D., *Capitalism, the State and Industrial Relations* (London: Croom Helm, 1982).

Therborn, G., *The Ideology of Power and the Power of Ideology* (London: Verso, 1980).

Tinker, A. M., Theories of the State and the State of Accounting: Economic Reductionism and Political Voluntarism in Accounting Regulation Theory, *Journal of Accounting and Public Policy* (1984).

Tinker, A. M., *Paper Prophets* (London: Holt, Rinehart & Winston, 1985).

Tinker, A. M., Merino, B. D. & M. Niemark, The Normative Origins of Positive Theories: Ideology and Accounting Thought, *Accounting Organizations and Society* (1982) pp. 167–200.

Tweedie, D. & Whittington, G., *The Debate on Inflation Accounting* (Cambridge: Cambridge University Press, 1984).

Watts, R., Corporate Financial Statements: A Product of the Market and Political Processes, *Australian Journal of Management* (April 1977) pp. 53–75.

Westergaard, J., Inequality and Corporatism, in Hunt, A. (ed.), *Class and Class Structure* (London: Lawrence & Wishart, 1977).

Willmott, H., Setting Accounting Standards in the UK: The Emergence of Private Accounting Bodies and their Role in the Regulation of Public Accounting Practice, in Streeck, W. & Schmitter, P. C. (eds) *Private Interest Government and Public Policy* (London: Sage, 1985a).

Willmott, H., Serving the Public Interest: A Critical Examination of a Professional Claim, unpublished paper, University of Aston (1985b).

Willmott, H., Organising the Profession: A Theoretical and Historical Examination of the Development of the Major Accountancy Bodies in the UK, *Accounting Organizations and Society* (1986) pp. 555–580.

Wysocki, K. von, Research into the Processes of Accounting Standard Setting in the Federal Republic of Germany, in Bromwich, M., and Hopwood, A. G., (eds), *Accounting Standard Setting in an International Context* (London: Pitmans, 1983).

Zeff, S., The Rise of Economic Consequences, *Journal of Accountancy* (December 1978) pp. 56–63.

[2]

Cultural Influence on Corporate and Governmental Involvement in Accounting Policy Determination in Japan

Jill L. McKinnon and Graeme L. Harrison

This study examines the impact of culture on the motivation for, and mode of involvement of, the corporations and the government in accounting policy determination in Japan. Three propositions are developed and evaluated against the events that occurred in the formulation and implementation of the 1976 ordinances on consolidation. Data are derived from source documentation and personal interviewing. Cultural determinants are seen to position the corporations and bureaucracy as influential and conflicting interest groups in accounting standard-setting in Japan and to predetermine a mode of conflict resolution in policy determination that maintains the "balance of forces" between those parties.

Introduction

Accounting policy determination has been seen as the outcome of complex interactions among parties interested in or affected by accounting standards (Kelly-Newton 1980, p. 5); Watts and Zimmerman 1978, p. 112); Zeff 1978, p. 56). Research into the sociopolitical and socioeconomic dimensions of such policy determination has emanated largely from Anglo-American nations, and in particular, the U.S.

By contrast, very little research has been directed toward the process of accounting policy determination in non-Anglo-American nations. The need to understand the process of accounting-principles development and standard-setting in different nations is widely recognized (Schoenfeld 1981, p. 96; Choi and Mueller 1978, p. 22). So too is the need to consider the influence of the nation-specific cultural environment on that process (Benston 1976, p. 3); Zeff

Address reprint requests to: Dr. Jill McKinnon, School of Economic and Financial Studies, Macquarie University, North Ryde, N.S.W. 2113 Australia.

The authors wish to acknowledge the Australia-Japan Foundation as sponsor of the research for this paper and the two anonymous reviewers who assisted preparation of the final manuscript.

1972, p. 306; Zeff and Defliese 1974, pp. 42–43; Schoenfeld 1981, pp. 84–85; Previts 1975, p. 4; Nair and Frank 1980, p. 449).

Research into accounting standard-setting in the U.S. has treated the environmental setting *implicitly*. This research has proceeded on the researchers' (and their audiences') familiarity with a cultural environment, a behavioral philosophy, and a set of commercial and political institutions seen as pertaining to that nation. Underlying these studies are implied assumptions about the behavior and motivation of corporate managers, bureaucrats, bondholders, and shareholders, and the premise of "arms-length" relationships among individuals and specific groups.

The results of this research provide insights into the standard-setting process in the U.S. and in Anglo-American nations generally. However, the premises and hypotheses of these studies may not be transferred to analyses of accounting policy determination in non-Anglo-American nations without prior investigation of: 1) the environmental setting in different nations; and 2) the influence of cultural environment on the motivation and behavior of parties involved in the process of accounting policy determination in those nations.

This paper is an exploratory study of the impact of cultural environment on the process of accounting policy determination in Japan. Three propositions are formulated. The first two propositions relate to the *motivation* for bureaucratic and corporate involvement in accounting standard-setting in Japan and the third to the *mode* of such involvement. Japan was chosen as the nation for study because, despite its emergence over the past two decades as a leading power in international trade and finance, little attention in the English language literature has been directed toward its process of accounting policy formulation. The bureaucracy and corporate management were chosen as the initial interest groups for study because they are generally recognized as the two most influential parties in public and economic policy determination in Japan (Fukui 1981, pp. 297–298; Reischauer 1977, p. 191).

The three propositions are developed from the literature on Japanese society and culture and from previous studies conducted by the authors on corporate reporting regulation in Japan. Preliminary evaluation of the propositions is provided by an analysis of and interpretation of the events that occurred in the process of formulation and implementation of the 1976 ordinances on consolidation. The ordinances constitute a significant instance of standard-setting in Japan (Aida 1982; Someya 1982), and reflect the approach to and process of accounting policy formulation in that nation generally (Ballon 1982). They are therefore used in this paper as an "insight-stimulating" example (Selltiz et al. 1976, p. 970) of corporate and governmental involvement in accounting policy determination in Japan.[1] Data on this instance of policy

---

[1] Selltiz et al. (1976, p. 98) noted the appropriateness of the use of insight-stimulating examples in allowing the researcher to seek rather than test and to be receptive to a broad range of factors or attributes of the phenomenon being studied. The approach allows (and relies on) the integrative powers of the researcher "to draw together many diverse bits of information into a unified interpretation" (Selltiz et al. 1976, p. 98).

determination are drawn from source documentation and personal interviews conducted in Japan with selected respondents. The use of selected respondents in this way is termed an "experience survey" by Selltiz et al. (1976, p. 94) and "inductive argument from authority" by Salmon (1963, p. 63). To maintain the validity of the approach, careful selection of the interview respondents is required in terms of the respondents' experience and authority.

The interview respondents were selected on two sets of criteria. The first set classified respondents as: 1) participants in the formulation and implementation of the consolidation requirements (specifically, senior representatives of the Ministry of Finance, the Business Accounting Deliberation Council,[2] and the Japanese Institute of Certified Public Accountants); and 2) objective observers. Objective observers were drawn from senior partners in Japanese accounting firms and the Tokyo offices of international accounting firms and from accounting academics of professorial status and with long-standing experience and expertise in the subject area.

Fifteen respondents were interviewed over a four-week period in interviews ranging from three to six hours.[3] Participant respondents comprised: two representatives from the Corporation Finance Division (Securities Bureau) of the Ministry of Finance; one from the Civil Affairs Bureau of the Ministry of Justice; two of the 21 permanent members of the Business Accounting Deliberation Council; and two from the Japanese Institute of Certified Public Accountants. The objective observers were six certified public accountants and two accounting professors.[4]

The second set of criteria for respondent selection was based on Selltiz et al.'s (1976, pp. 99-100) classification of types for the analysis of insight-stimulating examples. The categories used were: 1) respondents in different positions (representatives of different policy-determination authorities); 2) respondents in marginal or dual capacities (respondents who were representatives of more than one authority); and 3) "strangers and newcomers" (nonindigenous participants in and objective observers of the policy-determination process).

Respondents in different policy-formulation authorities were selected to allow the analysis to include and balance the potentially diverse perceptions of individual respondents. Respondents in marginal or dual categories were selected because these individuals are exposed to the conflicting processes of more than one element or group, and frequently reveal the major influences operating in each group. "Strangers and newcomers" were selected as respondents because of their greater sensitivity to social customs and practices that may be taken for granted by indigenous individuals.

---

[2] The Business Accounting Deliberation Council is a deliberative body attached to the Ministry of Finance. It comprises representatives of parties involved in or affected by accounting policy determination in Japan. Details of the composition of the Council and its activities are given later in the paper.

[3] Interview transcripts are available from the authors.

[4] Four accounting professors were interviewed; however two were members of the Business Accounting Deliberation Council and were interviewed in that capacity.

J. L. McKinnon and G. L. Harrison

Of the 15 respondents, eight occupied positions in different policy-formulation authorities, four occupied dual membership within policy bodies or across participant/observer categories, and three were nonindigenous to Japan. The latter three were selected on the basis of differing lengths of exposure to the Japanese standard-setting process: 20, ten, and two years, respectively.

The analysis in this paper proceeds as follows. First, the three propositions are formulated. Second, the events that marked the formulation and implementation of the consolidation ordinances are documented. Third, the motivation for corporate and government involvement in the consolidation issue is evaluated in terms of Propositions 1 and 2. The mode of involvement of these parties in the formulation of the consolidation ordinances is then evaluated in terms of Proposition 3. Finally, conclusions about the influence of cultural environment on the process of accounting policy determination in Japan are presented.

Propositions

In this section, two propositions are formulated about the motivation for bureaucratic and corporate-management involvement in accounting policy determination in Japan. A third proposition relates to the mode of involvement of these parties.

Motivation for Bureaucratic Involvement

The involvement of the bureaucracy in accounting-policy determination in Japan must be considered in the light of governmental influence in all areas of public and economic policy determination in that nation.

The source of that influence resides formally in the constitutional and legislative stature of parliament (Diet), and sociologically in the cultural acceptance in Japan of the moral basis of government (Reischauer 1977, p. 139). This cultural attribute of Japanese society derives from the confucianist precept of the natural existence of "the ruler" (Diet and bureaucracy) and "the ruled" (the people) (Reischauer 1977, p. 139). The role of government in policy determination operates through heavy reliance on the bureaucracy, which, relative to Diet, typically assumes the dominant position in drafting, supporting, and implementing legislation (Fukui 1981, pp. 186–188).

The Japanese bureaucracy is seen as possessing a "legal consciousness," premised on implicit assumptions about the duty of the bureaucrats to fulfill the central role in the formulation and administration of Japanese law and on their superior ability to do so (Henderson 1973, p. 195; Tanaka and Takeuchi 1976, p. 347).[5] Such a legal consciousness does not encourage a social perception of

---

[5] The most accomplished and successful law graduates in Japan have typically joined the higher echelons of the ministries rather than the judicial system. Consequently, people in the ministries tend to view the judiciary as being of lesser ability and feel more qualified to interpret laws, which they themselves, in many cases, have previously drafted. Furthermore, an unfavorable precedent established by judicial review may be overruled by petitioning Diet to revise the law (Rex Coleman, cited in Hashimoto 1963, p. 273; Henderson 1973, pp. 208–210).

the law as the joint responsibility of the bureaucracy, the judiciary, and the people. Instead, it reinforces traditional Japanese beliefs in the moral basis of government and supports the active role of the bureaucracy in public policy determination and administration.

Bureaucratic involvement in accounting policy formulation may be viewed, therefore, as a natural extension of the government's role in public policy formulation and administration. We propose that the behavior exhibited by the Japanese bureaucracy in accounting-policy determination is motivated broadly in the manner suggested by Watts (1977, p. 67); i.e., that such behavior is designed to avoid an imputation of blame on the government that may arise from future "crises" of inadequate policy.

Such motivation is intensified in Japan, however, because the Japanese Diet and bureaucracy may be seen as more directly associated with "crises" in corporate disclosure than are their counterparts in Anglo-American nations. Several factors contribute to this intensification. First, the administration of corporate financial disclosure under the Securities Exchange Law is the direct responsibility of the Ministry of Finance. Second, accounting standards in Japan are formulated by the Business Accounting Deliberation Council (BADC) but are issued and enforced as Ministry of Finance ordinances (McKinnon 1984a, p. 318). And third, the Ministry of Finance, through its administration of the Certified Public Accountants Law, controls the registration and deregistration of certified public accountants in Japan and oversees the activities of the Japanese Institute of Certified Public Accountants (JICPA).[6]

Consequently, "blame" for perceived "crises" of inadequate financial disclosure at both national and international levels in Japan is channelled directly to the Ministry of Finance and Diet. In most Anglo-American nations, by contrast, this "blame" is typically spread more broadly over the accounting profession and independent or quasi-governmental regulatory authorities. In these nations, accounting standards and principles frequently lack legislative status and responsibility for their enforcement is shared by the accounting profession and other regulatory authorities.

> PROPOSITION 1. *The involvement of Diet and bureaucracy in accounting policy determination stems from its central involvement in public policy generally. Specifically, Diet and the Ministry of Finance will support an accounting policy that results in increased corporate financial disclosure, because that lessens the potential for "blame" associated with inadequate corporate disclosure.*

Motivation for Corporate Involvement

The source of corporate influence in public and economic policy determination in Japan lies in: 1) the concentration of economic power in the large financial

---

[6] For a detailed discussion of the relationship between the Ministry of Finance, the JICPA, and certified public accountants in Japan, see McKinnon (1983, pp. 406–408, 410).

and industrial groupings; and 2) their politically powerful representative body, Keizai Dantai Rengo-Kai (Federation of Economic Organizations, hereafter referred to as Keidanren). Keidanren represents the views of the largest 798 corporations in Japan (Dodwell Marketing Consultants 1980/81, p. 34).

Keidanren operates at two levels. First, it undertakes research and detailed discussion in a process of consensus-building among the corporations it represents. Second, it provides a powerful link between the corporations and the government ministries by communicating the consensus of its members to the ministries (Vogel 1978, pp. 164–166). Corporate lobbying in Japan, therefore, takes the form of a unified voice in Keidanren, supported by detailed research and the backing of the economically powerful corporations.

The specific motivation for corporate involvement in the process of accounting policy determination lies in the strong resistance of Japanese corporations and corporate groups to financial disclosure *per se*. This resistance has been documented throughout the historical development of corporate reporting in Japan during the twentieth century (Fujita 1968, p. 137; McKinnon 1984a, pp. 321–322). It is reflected in contemporary attitudes of "keeping everything within the group" (Sawa and Takeyama 1982) and in "an abhorrence of the insides of the company coming out" (Ministry of Finance 1982). The strength and persistence of corporate resistance to financial disclosure in Japan derive from fundamental cultural characteristics of *group consciousness* and *interdependence*.

Cultural Determinants of Corporate Resistance to Financial Dislcosure

Japanese social relationships are generally accepted as based on group consciousness (*dantai ishiki*) and interdependence (Nakane 1970, pp. 1–3; Robinson et al. 1981, pp. 371–374). Group consciousness is manifested in the tendency of an individual in Japanese society to perceive him/herself in terms of a group location and, therefore, to accept and emphasize the interdependence among group members. A major focus of group consciousness is the corporation and the corporate group (Horie 1966, p. 15; Nakane 1970, pp. 3, 8).

In Anglo-American nations, by contrast, individuals view themselves as separate from each other and separate from the groups to which they belong. The result is that gaps exist between both individuals and groups and human made "links" or "bonds" are used to bridge relational gaps (Rix 1975, p. 5; Robinson et al. 1981, pp. 371–372; McKinnon 1984b, p. 26). These gaps, however, allow the types of "arms-length" relationships that support professional and contractual arrangements among individuals and groups in Anglo-American societies.

Hence, the cultural characteristics of group consciousness and interdependence in personal and corporate relations in Japan contrast with the independent or "arms-length" relationships among individuals and groups in Anglo-

American nations. This contrast produces different perceptions of corporate disclosure in Anglo-American societies than in Japan. In Anglo-American nations, one of the "links" supporting relationships between corporations and associated or interested individuals is external financial reporting, typically involving the verification of the report by an independent third party (auditor). This link, however, is not as intrinsically appropriate in Japan, where interdependent relationships embody implicit and mutual trust in personal and corporate interactions (Pascale and Athos 1981, p. 27). In respect of the corporations, cultural characteristics of group consciousness and interdependence result in the propensity for corporate managers to retain responsibility for and knowledge of corporate activity within the corporation itself or within the corporate group.[7]

> PROPOSITION 2. *The involvement of corporate management in accounting policy determination in Japan is driven by the strong resistance of Japanese corporations and corporate groups toward public financial disclosure. On behalf of the corporations, Keidanren will oppose accounting policy that results in increased corporate financial disclosure.*

Mode of Bureaucratic and Corporate Involvement

It is proposed here that the mode of bureaucratic and corporate involvement in accounting policy determination in Japan is circumscribed by: 1) the long-term collaborative relationship between these parties in public and economic policy determination generally; and 2) the culturally prescribed mode of maintaining that long-term relationship.

The special relationship of collaboration between the corporations and Diet and the bureaucracy has been identified as a critical contributory factor in Japan's post–World War II prosperity (Curtis 1975, pp. 33–34; Reischauer 1977, p. 191). It is supported by the mutual perception of common objectives in many areas of economic policy (Tanaka and Smith 1976, p. 359; Reischauer 1977, pp. 191–192). Objectives are not shared, however, in *all* areas of policy; for example, the choice of accounting policy concerned with increased corporate disclosure. In such instances, the government and corporations may be seen as influential, competing interest groups. However, the resolution of conflict between the corporations and Diet and the bureaucracy in these instances is constrained by the economic and political importance of maintaining the long-term cooperative relationship between the parties.

The relationships between the corporations and the government in Japan are viewed as continuous, long-term, and interdependent (Ballon 1982; Vogel 1978, pp. 164–165). The mode of behavior in such relationships is directed by specific

---

[7] This propensity reflects the codes of conduct and standards of behavior associated with interdependent relationships in Japan; e.g., *nai nai ni sumaseru* (the internal settlement of disputation) and *tasuke ai* (mutual help and the protection of mutual interests) (Ballon et al. 1976, p. 159; McKinnon, 1984b, p. 26).

cultural determinants that emphasize the maintenance of harmony across interacting groups (Pascale and Athos 1981, p. 110).[8] The concept of harmony itself stems from the duality of *yang* and *yin*; that is, from the confucianist idea of complementary forces (lightness and darkness) that alternate with and balance each other. Confucianism allows no strict "good-bad" or "right-wrong" dichotomies, but rather asserts a sense of harmony and a "balance of forces" (Reischauer 1977, p. 139).

These cultural attributes carry two significant implications for the process of conflict resolution in policy determination and decision making generally. First, the preservation of harmony in intergroup decision making in Japan emphasizes: 1) the avoidance of open confrontation both within and across groups (Reischauer 1977, p. 139); and 2) participation, consultation, and a readiness to extend the deliberation process to incorporate a reconciliation of competing interests (Pascale and Athos 1981, pp. 110-113).

Second, a consequence of the perceptions of continuity, interdependence, and the preservation of harmony in intergroup relationships is that the ability to abstract any one instance of conflict out of the long-term relationships among parties is reduced. This contrasts with group relationships in many Western societies, in which the consequences of differential benefits perceived by interest groups as arising from the resolution of an instance of conflict are less prejudicial to the long-term relationships among these parties. The orientation to the individual in Western societies, which produces discontinuities among groups and individuals, also allows an ability to abstract and isolate the short-term from the long-term relationships.

PROPOSITION 3. *The modes of involvement of bureaucratic and corporate representation in accounting policy determination in Japan are directed toward the resolution of conflict between those parties. As such, the process of policy determination accommodates the maintenance of the long-term collaborative relationship and the "balance of forces" between the Japanese bureaucracy and the corporations.*

Chronology of Events in Formulation of Consolidation Ordinances

The 1976 ordinances on consolidation introduced the requirement of consolidated financial statement reporting for all corporations subject to the Securities Exchange Law of Japan and provided for the concurrent introduction of a "cost-plus" equity method of accounting for investments in related companies (Ministry of Finance Ordinances Nos. 27, 28, 29, 30).

The major events in the process of formulation and implementation of the ordinances are detailed in Table 1. These events provide the reference points for our analysis of corporate and governmental involvement in that process. The

---

[8] This characteristic of Japanese society is traceable to the entry of confucianist ideas between the sixth and ninth centuries AD with the first "great wave" of Chinese influence (Reischauer 1977, p. 214).

Table 1.   Chronology of Events in Formulation of Consolidation Ordinances

Event Number	Date	Event
1	1965	Diet requests the Ministry of Finance to improve corporate disclosure under the Securities Exchange Law (Ballon 1982)
2	1965	The Ministry of Finance requests the Business Accounting Deliberation Council (BADC) to prepare an interim report on consolidated financial statements, with the idea of improving corporate disclosure (Ayukawa 1982; Ballon 1982; BADC 1975, p. 4)
3	1966	The BADC reports to the Ministry of Finance and the ministry releases an Exposure Draft on Consolidation for public review (BADC 1975, p. 4)
4	1966	Keidanren reports that it supports the exposure draft in principle, but that it strongly opposes the implementation of consolidation in the near future (Ballon 1982)
5	1967	The Ministry of Finance releases its "Opinion on Consolidated Statements," which supports the introduction of consolidation (Ballon 1982; BADC 1975, p. 4)
6	1971	Diet revises the Securities Exchange Law to require that the financial statements of important subsidiaries be attached to the parent-only statements and calls on the Ministry of Finance to draft the necessary new provisions and revision clauses for the introduction of consolidation (Ministry of Finance 1982; Aida 1982)
7	1971	The BADC resumes discussion on consolidation (Ministry of Finance 1982)
8	1975	The BADC releases financial accounting standards for consolidated financial statements (BADC 1975, p. 5)
9	1976	The Ministry of Finance issues Ordinances Nos. 27, 28, 29, and 30, operational from the fiscal periods commencing on or after April 1, 1977 (Ministry of Finance 1982)
10	1980	Ministry of Finance statistics for 1978/1979 and 1979/1980 reveal that approximately 50% of the corporations subject to Securities Exchange Law did not submit consolidated statements. Those corporations preparing consolidated statements excluded approximately 67% of their total subsidiaries from the consolidation (Ministry of Finance 1981, Chapter 8)
11	1981	The Ministry of Finance revises the consolidation ordinances to make equity accounting mandatory from April 1, 1983 (Sawa and Takeyama 1982; Yamauchi 1982)

events demonstrate the state of conflict that developed between the two parties in both the formulation and implementation of the consolidation requirements. Conflict in the process of formulation was demonstrated in the lobbying stances adopted by each party. Events 1, 2, 3, 5, and 6 evidence the support of Diet and the bureaucracy for the introduction of consolidation, whereas Event 4 illustrates the strong opposition of Keidanren of behalf of the corporations.

Conflict was also present in the implementation of the ordinances. Event 10 reveals that, in 1978/1979 and 1979/1980, many corporations did not submit consolidated statements and those that did excluded a large number of subsidiaries from the consolidated statements. In 1981, the Ministry of Finance acted to strengthen the consolidation requirements and to make equity accounting mandatory. That process itself took 12 years from the initial Diet request until the implementation of consolidation, and a further six until the mandatory application of equity accounting.

Motivation for Corporate and Governmental Involvement in the Consolidation Ordinances

The involvement of Diet and the bureaucracy in these instances of accounting policy determination provides support for Proposition 1; that is, that the Japanese government favors an accounting policy that increases corporate financial disclosure because such policy lessens the potential "blame" for "crises" of inadequate disclosure. Evidence to support this motivation was provided in the interviews that identified the sociopolitical stimuli giving rise to the introduction of the consolidation ordinances. Those stimuli were three separate but reinforcing events occurring during the 1960s and early 1970s in Japan.

Sociopolitical Stimuli for the Consolidation Ordinances

The first event motivating the Japanese government toward the introduction of consolidation was the declared insolvency of a major steel manufacturer in early 1965. This event was identified in the interviews as the incident that focused public and governmental attention in Japan on the need to improve corporate disclosure under the Securities Exchange Law (Ministry of Finance 1982; Aida 1982; Someya 1982). Investigations of that steel company and more than ten medium-sized companies that declared bankruptcy at approximately the same time revealed that almost all had manipulated their financial statements. A good deal of the manipulation was done through fictitious (intercompany) sales at overly high prices between the parent companies and their subsidiaries and related companies. These companies were not subject to the Securities Exchange Law, and the fictitious sales, designed to disguise parent company losses or to inflate profits, were disclosed only by investigations into the parent companys' bankruptcies (McKinnon 1984b, pp. 19–20).

The characteristics of the steel company case, however, were neither exceptional nor uncommon in Japan at the time. For several years previously, professional accountants and academics had been aware of numerous unreported instances of fraudulent activity and financial statement manipulation that had ultimately ended in corporate bankruptcies (Nakajima 1973, p. 35). By contrast, the steel company was the first such case to receive widespread publicity in Japan. The strength of the public outcry, based on the social and political ramifications of corporate bankruptcies and the potential of fraudulent reporting to prejudice the operations of the Japanese securities markets, created intense pressure on Diet and the Ministry of Finance to improve corporate disclosure under the Securities Exchange Law.

The intensity of pressure stemming from the adverse public reaction reflects underlying cultural values of Japanese society. In a society in which group relationships are based on interdependence and in which implicit and mutual trust are valued and assumed to underlie those relationships, violations of trust assume great and far-reaching social significance. Additionally, when seen in conjunction with the Japanese emphasis on viewing corporations as the *people* constituting them rather than as legal or separate entities (Ballon et al. 1976, p. 158), such violations cannot be lessened or depersonalized by recourse to the veil of incorporation.

Concurrent with this domestic pressure for improved disclosure was international pressure on Japan to introduce consolidation practices. This pressure occurred in two forms, both related to the international listing of corporate securities. In the early to mid-1960s, a number of Japanese corporations sought listing on the New York Stock Exchange (Ministry of Finance 1982). Entry to the U.S. financial market was initially barred, however, because the parent-only financial statements of the Japanese corporations did not meet the consolidated statement disclosure requirements of the NYSE (Ballon 1982).

This pressure intensified in the early 1970s when overseas (primarily U.S.) corporations sought listing on the Tokyo Stock Exchange on the basis of the information disclosed in the overseas corporations' consolidated financial statements. As a consequence of these events, the Ministry of Finance came to perceive that Japan's parent-only financial statements carried relatively low international status (Ministry of Finance 1982).

Bureaucratic motivation in the formulation of the 1976 consolidation ordinances may, therefore, be attributed to perceived crises of inadequate corporate disclosure. Crises were perceived by Diet and the Ministry of Finance at both *national* and *international* levels.

Corporate management involvement in this instance of policy formulation is consistent with Proposition 2. The consolidation (and equity accounting) requirements on the corporations were to substantially increase the number of subsidiary and related companies that would be subject to the disclosure requirements of the Securities Exchange Law and to independent (CPA) audit. Previously, these companies were subject only to the far less stringent disclosure and audit requirements of the Commercial Code (Aida 1982; Someya 1982).[9]

The effect of the consolidation ordinances was to require much greater disclosure by Japanese corporations. Against the cultural and historical

---

[9] Additionally, financial statements prepared under the Commercial Code were subject only to statutory audit. The statutory auditor in Japan need not be a qualified CPA (Nakajima 1982) and, in practice, is typically a retired employee of the company.

background of corporate resistance to disclosure (discussed earlier), the introduction of consolidation (and equity accounting) may therefore be viewed as a particularly sensitive issue. The motivation for corporate opposition to the consolidation ordinances was seen as being driven by this general resistance to increased public disclosure (Aida 1982; Ballon 1982; Someya 1982).

Conflict Resolution in the Process of Accounting Policy Determination

Proposition 3 is evaluated in this instance of policy determination by examining: 1) the mode of involvement of corporate management and Diet and bureaucracy in the formulation of the consolidation ordinances; 2) the implementation of the ordinances by the corporations; and 3) subsequent Ministry of Finance reaction to that implementation.

The formulation of the consolidation ordinances was carried out within the forum of the Business Accounting Deliberation Council (BADC). The BADC is the deliberation council attached to the Ministry of Finance. It is the representative body of the interest groups most affected by policy changes to corporate disclosure under the Securities Exchange Law. Comprising delegates of Keidanren, the Japanese Institute of Certified Public Accountants (JICPA), the Tax Accountants Society, the Japanese Stock Exchanges, and the Ministry of Justice,[10] the council represents a broad range of views and expertise. The technical expertise in the formulation of the consolidation ordinances was provided by the accounting professors and the representatives of the JICPA and the stock exchanges (Aida 1982; Someya 1982).

In contrast to Keidanren, the Ministry of Finance is not directly represented in the formal membership of BADC. However, the ministry maintains a strong, indirect influence over the four JICPA and three stock exchange representatives on the council. This influence derives from the ministry's control over the licensing of CPAs and stock exchange members and its close supervision of the activities of the JICPA (Ministry of Finance 1982; Sawa and Takeyama 1982). In practice, the ministry "uses its experts" to present the theoretical case for its policy proposal to BADC (Ayukawa 1982).

Furthermore, officers of the Securities Bureau of the ministry fulfill the secretarial function for the BADC, and the council meets on premises of the Ministry of Finance (Ministry of Finance 1982). The interviews conducted in this research allow the conclusion that, although the ministry's involvement in the deliberation council appears to be passive, the ministry utilizes the secretarial function to keep informed of the progress of deliberations and to provide feedback on the acceptability of the BADC proposals. The use of the secretarial function in this way, and the indirect influence over JICPA and stock exchange

---

[10] As at January 1982, there were 32 members of BADC, consisting of 16 accounting professors, seven members of Keidanren, four of the JICPA, one of the Tax Accountants Society, three of the Japanese stock exchanges, and one representative of the Ministry of Justice.

representatives, allows and results in active Ministry of Finance representation on the deliberation council.

The process of formulation of the ordinances on consolidation required 12 years (1965–1976) and approximately sixty BADC meetings (Ministry of Finance 1982). However, the majority of discussion was devoted not to the technical issues of consolidation as an accounting procedure, but to accommodating corporate resistance to consolidation and to determining compromise solutions to the conflict between the corporations and the Ministry of Finance (Aida 1982; Someya 1982).

Analysis of that process shows, first, that it was consistent with the general nature of conflict resolution in policy formulation in Japan, relying on the consensus rather than the dominance mode of resolution (Horne 1982, p. 40). The consensus mode emphasizes harmony and compromise in attaining a solution acceptable to affected interest groups (Reischauer 1977, p. 135; Pascale and Athos 1981, pp. 110–113).

The maintenance of harmony in the resolution of conflict in this instance was facilitated by: 1) the ways in which influential competing parties conveyed their initial negotiating positions and their subsequent confirmation or modification of those positions; and 2) the preparedness to promote and accept compromises and concessions in specific instances of conflict in order to maintain the long-term relationships and balance of forces among those parties.

Negotiating Positions

Although Keidanren, and the corporations it represents, were in strong opposition to the introduction of consolidation, their response to the interim report contained an acceptance "in principle" but objection to implementation "in the near future" (Event 4 in Table 1). This seemingly ambiguous response served two purposes. First, it conveyed Keidanren's opposition to increased financial disclosure. Second, and most importantly, it provided Keidanren with the flexibility to negotiate in the deliberation process and to promote and accept compromises in the final form of the consolidation ordinances while still maintaining its original opposition to consolidation.

Similarly, the strength of the Ministry of Finance commitment to consolidation was conveyed at different stages in the deliberation process through means *external* to the BADC. These means included: 1) the release by the Ministry of a report confirming its favorable disposition to the introduction of consolidation in May 1967 (Event 5 in Table 1); 2) the 1971 revision to the Securities Exchange Law, which required that the financial statements of important subsidiaries be attached to and filed with parent company statements (Event 6); and 3) the release of a statement by Diet calling on the Ministry to draft new provisions and revision clauses for the introduction of consolidation (Event 6).

Each of these events served to communicate to Keidanren and the corporations (and, equally importantly, to the BADC) the ministerial response to corporate objections to the introduction of consolidation. Although that communication was definitive and public, it was also indirect. It therefore allowed the ministry's position to be made clear without the prejudice to the BADC's discussions that would have arisen from the direct confrontation of conflicting interests.

Compromise and Concession

Examination of the formulation of the consolidation ordinances also reveals the processes of compromise and concession entered into by the corporations and the bureaucracy. The Ministry of Finance, through the BADC deliberations, eventually obtained a consensus on the introduction of consolidation. This consensus, however, involved the protraction of "seemingly endless discussions" over "some sixty meetings of the BADC" (Ministry of Finance 1982). Additionally, Keidanren agreement was not forthcoming until it received five major concessions in the ordinances (Yonke 1982; Vines et al. 1982; Aida 1982; Someya 1982).

The first concession provided that Japanese corporations that were already preparing consolidated statements to meet the listing requirements of the U.S. Securities Exchange Commission could submit the same statements to the Ministry of Finance and be regarded as meeting the requirements of the consolidation ordinances (Ordinance No. 28, Supplementary Provisions). Although U.S. and Japanese consolidation statements are similar in many respects, there are a number of differences of sufficient significance to reduce their immediate comparability (Sawa and Takeyama 1982; Ayukawa 1982).

The second concession introduced a materiality exclusion clause, which provided that a subsidiary, the assets and sales of which are not material, need not be included in the consolidated financial statements, providing such exclusion does not make the statements misleading in judging the financial position and results of operations of the consolidated group [Ordinance No. 28, Article 5(2)]. The ordinance provides "rule of thumb" criteria for the application of the materiality clause, under which exclusion from disclosure in consolidated financial reports is permissible if the following ratios are equal to or less than 10%:

$$\text{Asset (sales) standard:} \quad \frac{\text{Total assets (sales) of nonconsolidated subsidiary companies}}{\text{Total assets (sales) of parent and total assets (sales) of consolidated subsidiaries}}.$$

Although materiality is a concept employed in Anglo-American nations, there are several reasons for the materiality exclusion clause being interpretable here as a "concession" to corporate representation. First, it was acknowledged as such by the interview respondents (Aida 1982; Someya 1982; Sawa and Takeyama 1982). Corporate resistance to consolidation was perceived by the interviewees to be founded on an objection to parent company subsidiaries becoming subject to the stricter disclosure and audit requirements of the Securities Exchange Law. Hence, a clause that provided for the exclusion of a number of subsidiaries from consolidation (and hence from Securities Exchange Law) may be reasonably termed a concession. The second reason is that it is not generally accepted practice in Anglo-American nations to allow subsidiaries to be excluded from consolidation solely on the grounds of materiality, given that the objective of consolidation is to provide a picture of the entire group as an economic unit. And third, the Exposure Draft for the International Accounting Standard No. 3 on Consolidated Financial Statements, which was drawn on by the BADC in the formulation of the consolidation ordinances (JICPA 1975, Preface), contains no reference to the exclusion of subsidiaries based on materiality.

The third concession was that an income-based criterion, which was proposed in the BADC discussions, was removed from the materiality clause of Ordinance No. 28. This criterion would have placed substantial restriction on the ability of Japanese corporations to exclude subsidiary companies from consolidation. Keidanren claimed that some foreign subsidiaries (for example, those based in Hong Kong) have high income figures because of the lower sales taxes and other taxes in foreign nations in which the subsidiaries are located, and yet those subsidiaries are "insignificant" in terms of sales and assets (Aida 1982). Keidanren's claim was acceded to, although the claim was acknowledged as weak by the interview respondents and the underlying motive was interpreted as a desire by the corporations to shield overseas subsidiaries from consolidation and disclosure (Aida 1982; Sawa and Takeyama 1982).

The fourth concession was the provision allowing the consolidation of foreign subsidiaries' statements without adjustment to meet Japanese disclosure requirements, providing material differences are disclosed in the notes to the accounts (Ordinance No. 28, Article 13).

The final concession involved the postponement of the mandatory application of the equity method of accounting for investments in related companies. Although Article 10 of Ordinance No. 28 required the implementation of the equity method with consolidation, the supplementary provisions to the ordinance allowed that the provisions of Article 10 "need not be applied for the time being."

These five concessions were attained by Keidanren in the face of Ministry of Finance opposition and with relatively low numerical representation on the BADC compared to that of parties that supported the intrinsic merit of consolidation (particularly the JICPA, the accounting professors, and the stock exchange representatives). The ability of Keidanren to achieve a substantial dilution of the consolidation disclosure requirements demonstrates the considerable influence exercised by the corporations in accounting policy determination in Japan.

Correspondingly, however, it must be recognized that the Ministry of Finance succeeded in gaining corporate acceptance of the legal requirement for consolidated financial statement reporting. The compromises embodied in the legal fabric of the ordinances, and the granting of "acceptance time" in the application of equity accounting, allowed the ministry to achieve a consensus on the consolidation issue and forced the eventual agreement of Keidanren to the introduction of consolidation (Aida 1982; Someya 1982). There is little doubt that the corporations and Keidanren retained their opposition to increased financial disclosure associated with the introduction of consolidation but were induced to accept the ordinances with the "compensating favors" allowed as compromise concessions.

The process of conflict resolution evident in the formulation of the consolidation ordinances reflects not only the power of the corporations and the Ministry of Finance in accounting policy determination, but also the importance of not prejudicing the broader long-term and continuous relationship between them. The ministry has the statutory power to legislate the corporate disclosure requirements it desires, regardless of corporate opposition. Its reluctance to do this, and its behavior in granting concessions to the corporations on specific issues, maintains a "balance of forces" in the relationship between these two influential, interacting groups.

Implementation of the Consolidation Ordinances

Analysis of the implementation of the consolidation ordinances since 1977 reinforces: 1) the evidence relating to the strength of corporate resistance to financial disclosure in Japan; and 2) the continuation of compromise between the corporations and the bureaucracy in implementing accounting policy in that nation. These attributes are visible in the extent of corporate implementation of the ordinances following their introduction and in the revisions to the ordinances effected by the Ministry of Finance in 1981.

Corporate Implementation of the Consolidation Ordinances

Statistical data provided by the Ministry of Finance for the years 1978/1979 and 1979/1980 show little acceptance by the corporations of the underlying objective of the consolidation ordinances. That objective may be viewed as the preparation of financial statements showing the financial position and profit performance of the parent company and its subsidiaries. First, 50.3% of corporations subject to the Securities Exchange Law and with subsidiaries as described by the ordinances did not submit consolidated financial statements in 1979/1980 (53.6% for 1978/1979) (Ministry of Finance 1981, Ch. 8). Second, those corporations submitting consolidated statements in each of these years excluded from consolidation 67.7% and 68.4% (in 1979/1980 and 1978/1979, respectively) of their subsidiaries (Ministry of Finance 1981, Ch. 8).

Two practices were widespread among Japanese corporations during this period. The first was the reduction of parent company shareholdings in subsidiaries to below 50% (Ministry of Finance 1981, Ch. 8; Sawa and Takeyama 1982). [11] The second was the extensive use of the materiality clause that allowed the exclusion from consolidation of subsidiaries whose aggregate total sales (assets) amounted to 10% or less of the consolidated total sales (assets) of the parent company and its consolidated subsidiaries (Aida 1982; Someya 1982).

Aggregation of the Ministry of Finance figures for consolidating and nonconsolidating corporations reveals that, of a total of 20,818 companies classified as subsidiaries under the ordinances, only 5,617 (27%) were consolidated in 1979/1980 (26.3% for 1978/1979) (Ministry of Finance 1981, Ch. 8). The vast majority of the remainder were excluded under the materiality clause inserted into the ordinances as a concession to corporate lobbying during the formulation of the ordinances (Ministry of Finance 1981, Ch. 8; Aida 1982). In the opinion of the interview respondents, the corporations paid little attention to the overriding requirement that the exclusion of subsidiaries from the consolidation should not make the statements misleading in judging the financial position or operations of the group (Aida 1982; Someya 1982; Nakajima 1982).

The corporations not only relied extensively on the materiality clause to minimize the number of subsidiary companies included in the consolidated statements, but they also utilized the postponement of the mandatory application of the equity method of accounting for investments in nonconsolidated and related companies. The Ministry of Finance data show that of 2,726 corporations subject to the equity accounting provisions, only 54 (2%) applied these provisions voluntarily (Ministry of Finance 1981, Ch. 8).

1981 Revisions to the Consolidation Ordinances

The Ministry of Finance regarded as excessive the reliance by the corporations on both the materiality exclusion clause of Ordinance No. 28 and the supplementary provisions postponing mandatory equity accounting (Someya 1982; Aida 1982). In response to this, two revisions were promulgated by the ministry in 1981, effective from April 1, 1983. The first revision tightened the provisions of the materiality exclusion clause by returning the income criterion, which had been omitted in the 1976 ordinances as a concession to corporate representation.

However, the selection of a 10% ratio for the income criterion must be seen as a further compromise between Keidanren and the ministry. Keidanren contends that the income criterion should be removed from the clause altogether, whereas officers of the Ministry of Finance believe that the income criterion is necessary

---

[11] Although the potential effect of coincident economic events on disinvestment by Japanese corporations during this period cannot be completely ruled out, it was generally accepted among the interview respondents that disinvestment prior to the introduction of consolidation was directly associated with its introduction.

and that the 10% rule is too liberal (Aida 1982; Ayukawa 1982). The materiality clause remains a contentious issue in corporate reporting in Japan and continues to allow corporations substantial opportunity to exclude many subsidiaries from consolidation.

The second revision repealed the supplementary provision that allowed the nonmandatory application of equity accounting. Theoretically, equity accounting may be seen as very important in improving corporate financial disclosure in Japan, because more of the corporate relationships based on shareholding criteria are of a parent-related rather than parent-subsidiary nature (Ayukawa 1982; Yamauchi 1982; McKinnon 1984b, p. 23). For this reason, those parties concerned with increasing financial disclosure have expressed strong support for the implementation of equity accounting, particularly accounting academics (Aida 1982; Someya 1982; Nakajima 1982), certified public accountants and the JICPA (Ayukawa 1982; Yamauchi 1982), and the Securities Bureau of the Ministry of Finance (Ministry of Finance 1982).

In practice, however, projections for the success of equity accounting, in terms of increasing the number of nonconsolidated subsidiaries and related companies included in consolidated financial statements, must take account of two important characteristics of the corporations in Japan. First, the shareholding relationships among many group corporations are already less than the 20% equity criterion (McKinnon 1984a, p. 288) and will therefore remain excluded from the equity method of accounting (Yamauchi 1982; Aida 1982). Second, the underlying corporate resistance to increased financial disclosure may be presumed to determine corporate reaction to mandatory equity accounting. The interviews revealed that some corporations had already reduced their share ownership in related companies to below the 20% significance criterion. Our respondents considered this action to be a means of avoiding the equity accounting requirement (Yamauchi 1982; Vines et al. 1982) and expected other corporations to take similar action before the mandatory implementation of equity accounting on April 1, 1983.

Additionally, the 1981 revisions to the consolidation ordinances also introduced a materiality clause that restricts the scope of application of equity accounting.[12] It might be expected that corporations will make equally extensive use of this materiality clause to limit the scope of their application of equity accounting as they did to limit the scope of consolidation.

---

[12] The scope of consolidation is considered adequate if the following ratio is 10% or less:

$$\frac{\text{Investor's equity in net income of unconsolidated subsidiaries and affiliated companies to which the equity method is not applied}}{\text{Total net income of the parent and its equity in net income of unconsolidated subsidiaries and affiliated companies to which the equity method is applied}}$$

Conclusions

This study examined the introduction of the 1976 ordinances on consolidation as an "insight-stimulating" example of 1) the nature of corporate and governmental influence on accounting policy determination in Japan, and 2) the underlying cultural determinants of that influence. Preliminary support was provided for three propositions about the motivation for and mode of involvement of these parties in accounting standard-setting.

The motivation for corporate and governmental involvement is driven by cultural environmental characteristics that differ substantially from those in Anglo-American nations. Underlying cultural philosophies of group consciousness and interdependence produce corporate attitudes and behavior opposed *intrinsically* to increased public financial disclosure. Bureaucratic involvement in all areas of public and economic policy determination in Japan is supported by the confucianist-based belief in the "moral basis of government" and is reinforced by the bureaucrats' perceived duty and superior ability to formulate and administer law. The consequence for bureaucratic motivation in accounting standard-setting in Japan is that a *very* direct association exists between the Ministry of Finance and "crises" of inadequate disclosure.

These cultural determinants carry two major implications for the process of accounting policy determination in Japan. First, they position the corporations and the bureaucracy as conflicting and influential interest groups in accounting standard-setting. Second, they predetermine the mode of conflict resolution in that process.

Corporate influence in the formulation and implementation of the consolidation ordinances was evident at three levels: 1) the amount of time and discussion devoted in BADC deliberations to accommodating corporate resistance to the introduction of consolidation; 2) the capability of Keidanren to obtain movements (through concessions) in both the nature of policy and the timing of its implementation in the direction desired by the corporations; and 3) the ability of corporations to affect the implementation of policy through their heavy reliance on the concession clauses.

The Japanese consolidation requirements retain certain features that limit the informational utility of the consolidated statements for shareholder and investor decisions. Retained are: 1) the provision allowing Japanese corporations to file for Japanese reporting purposes consolidated statements based on U.S. Securities Exchange Commission requirements; 2) the provision allowing foreign subsidiary consolidation without adjustment to meet Japanese requirements; and 3) the materiality exclusion clauses that continue to allow corporations to limit the scope of their consolidated statements. Additionally, parent-only financial statements remain the primary report required of corporations in Japan.

It may be argued that the retention of the concession clauses represents effective subversion of the intrinsic accounting objectives of consolidated financial statements. Equally, however, it must be recognized that the Ministry of Finance has succeeded in "attaining" the introduction of the legal requirement for consolidation in Japan in a corporate climate opposed to increased financial disclosure.

The description of "attained," however, must be interpreted against the stimuli that gave rise to the introduction of consolidation. The importance of the ordinances to the Japanese bureaucracy may be seen to lie less in the criterion of intrinsic content of accounting policy than in the use of such policy to further the economic and public policy objectives of the bureaucracy. The events associated with the introduction of consolidation, from the viewpoint of the bureaucracy, are interpretable as more directly related to enhancing the international status of corporate disclosure in Japan and to overcoming specific prior instances of accounting manipulation than to improving the inherent usefulness of corporate reports for investor decisions.

The second implication of cultural influences on the process of accounting policy determination in Japan lies in their predetermination of the mode of conflict resolution between the corporations and bureaucracy. The emphasis on harmony and consensus in Japanese society produces a mode of conflict resolution that avoids overt confrontation between interacting groups and emphasizes pragmatic compromise rather than conceptual or theoretic resolution. Resolution of conflict between the corporations and the bureaucracy in the formulation of the consolidation ordinances was not sought through conceptual analysis to achieve the theoretically "best" solution, which may have required a dominance mode of implementation. Rather, resolution was sought through the search for harmonious compromises that would achieve and maintain the "balance of forces" between those parties.

The influence relationship between the corporations and the government in accounting policy determination in Japan must be viewed not as an isolated and discontinuous relationship, but as part of the continuous and long-term relationship that has characterized corporate and governmental interactions in the areas of economic and public policy generally in that nation. The "balance of forces" between these two complementary interest groups is maintained in and circumscribes the Japanese approach to accounting policy formulation and implementation.

Our study has examined one instance of accounting policy determination in Japan. Its generalizability is restricted accordingly. Given the limited state of knowledge of the process of accounting standard-setting in Japan, and the increasing importance of this nation in international affairs, we would encourge further research into other instances of policy determination. Such research, however, should take account of the cultural determinants of interpersonal and intergroup relationships in Japanese society generally and their impact on the motivation and behavior of parties involved in the standard-setting process.

Additionally, this study has focused on the relationship between culture and the process of accounting policy determination in Japan. Japan, however, is just one of many non-Anglo-American nations for which little is known about the processes of accounting principles development. Further research into the link between culture and accounting principles formulation is required in order that our understanding of that process may be extended beyond the present Anglo-American boundaries.

References

Aida, Yoshio (Professor). Jan. 11 and 16, 1982. Interviews.

Ayukawa, Masaaki (CPA). Jan. 18, 1982. Interview.

BADC, Ministry of Finance. 1975. *Principles of Consolidated Financial Statements and Notes Thereto, and the 1976 Amendment to Financial Statements Regulation. Japan Accounting Series, Vol. IV.* Tokyo: Trade Bulletin Corp.

Ballon, R. J. (Director, International Management Development Seminars, Sophia University, Tokyo), Jan 12, 1982. Interview.

Ballon, R. J., Tomita Iwao, and Usami Hajime. 1976. *Financial Reporting in Japan.* Tokyo: Kodansha International Ltd.

Benston, G. J. 1976. *Corporate Financial Disclosure in the U.K. and the U.S.,* Westmead, Engl.: Saxon House D. C. Heath.

Choi, F. D., and Mueller, G. G. 1978. *An Introduction to Multinational Accounting.* Englewood Cliffs, N.J.: Prentice-Hall.

Curtis, G. L. 1975. Big business and political influences. In *Modern Japanese Organization and Decision-Making* (E. F. Vogel, ed.). Berkeley, CA.: University of California Press, pp. 54–68.

Dodwell Marketing Consultants. 1980/81. *Industrial Groupings in Japan 1980/81.* Tokyo: Dodwell Marketing Consultants.

Fujita, Yukio. 1968. An analysis of the development and nature of accounting principles in Japan. Unpublished doctoral thesis. Department of Accounting, University of Illinois.

Fukui, Haruhiro. 1981. Bureaucratic power in Japan. In *Japan and Australia: Two Societies and Their Interactions* (P. Drysdale and Kitaoji Hironobu, eds.). Canberra: Australian National University Press, pp. 275–303.

Hashimoto, K. (assisted by D. B. Maggs). 1963. The rule of law: Some aspects of judicial review of administrative action. In *Law in Japan—The Legal Order in a Changing Society* (A. T. von Mehren, ed.). Cambridge, Mass.: Harvard University Press, pp. 239–273.

Henderson, D. F. 1973. *Foreign Enterprise in Japan: Law and Politics.* Chapel Hill, N.C.: The University of North Carolina Press.

Horie, Yasuzo. Apr. 1966. The role of the IE in the economic modernization of Japan. *Kyoto University Economic Review* 36(1) 1–16.

Horne, J. Dec. 1982. National, international and sectional interests in policymaking: The evolution of the yen bond market 1970–82. *Australia-Japan Research Centre Paper,* No. 98. Canberra: Research School of Pacific Studies, Australian National University.

JICPA. 1975. *Financial Accounting Standard on Consolidated Financial Statements* (issued by BADC). Tokyo: Japanese Institute of Certified Public Accountants.

Kelly-Newton, L. 1980. *Accounting Policy Formulation: The Role of Corporate Management*. Reading, Mass.: Addison-Wesley.

Marks, B. 1978. *Australian-Japanese Business Transactions: Legal Aspects.* Sydney: CCH Australia Ltd.

McKinnon, J. L. July 1983. The accounting profession in Japan. *The Australian Accountant* July 406–408, 410.

McKinnon, J. L. 1984a. The historical development and operational form of corporate reporting regulation in Japan. Ph.D. thesis. Macquarie University.

McKinnon, J. L. June 1984b. Application of Anglo-American principles of consolidation to corporate financial disclosure in Japan. *Abacus* 16–33.

Ministry of Finance. Oct. 30. 1976. *Ordinance No. 27: Partial Amendment to the Regulations Concerning the Terminology, Form and Methods of Preparation of Financial Statements, etc.* Tokyo: Trade Bulletin Corp.

Ministry of Finance. Oct. 30, 1976. *Ordinance No. 28: Regulations Concerning the Terminology, Form and Methods of Preparation of Consolidated Financial Statements.* Tokyo: Trade Bulletin Corp.

Ministry of Finance. Oct. 30, 1976. *Ordinance No. 29: Partial Amendment to the Ministerial Ordinance Concerning Audit Certification of Financial Statements, etc.* Tokyo: Trade Bulletin Corp.

Ministry of Finance. Oct. 30, 1976. *Ordinance No. 30: Institutionalization of Consolidated Financial Statements under the Securities Exchange Law.* Tokyo: Trade Bulletin Corp.

Ministry of Finance. 1981. *Negotiable Securities Annual.* Tokyo: Ministry of Finance.

Ministry of Finance. Jan. 19, 1982. Interviews with officers of the Corporation Finance Division, Securities Bureau.

Nair, R. D., and Frank, W. G. July 1980. The impact of disclosure and measurement practices on international accounting classifications. *The Accounting Review* 426–450.

Nakajima, Seigo. 1973. Economic growth and corporate financial reporting in Japan. *International Journal of Accounting Education and Research* 9(1):36–41.

Nakajima, Seigo (Professor). Jan. 21, 1982. Interview.

Nakane, Chie. 1970. *Japanese Society*. London: Weidenfeld & Nicolson.

Pascale, R. T., and Athos, A. G. 1981. *The Art of Japanese Management*. Middlesex, Engl.: Penguin Books.

Previts, G. J. Spring 1975. On the subject of methodology and models for international accountancy. *International Journal of Accounting Education and Research* 1–12.

Reischauer, E. O. 1977. *The Japanese.* Tokyo: Charles E. Tuttle.

Rix, A. G. 1975. An analysis of Japanese responses to foreign societies: A critique of Nakane's work on Japanese mentality and social structure. *Research Paper.* Canberra: Australian National University, Australia-Japan Economic Relations Research Project.

Robinson, P., Rix. A., and Newell, W. 1981. Perspectives on cultural and social factors in Australia-Japan relations. In *Japan and Australia: Two Societies and Their Interaction* (P. Drysdale and Kitaoji Hironobu, eds.). Canberra: Australian National University Press, pp. 366–384.

Salmon, W. C. 1963. *Logic.* Englewood Cliffs, N.J.: Prentice-Hall.

Sawa, Etsuo, and Takeyama, Tetsuo (CPAs) Jan 18, 1982. Interview.

Schoenfeld, H-M.W. Fall 1981. International accounting: Development, issues and future directions. *Journal of International Business Studies* 83-100.

Selitiz, C., Wrightsman, L. S., and Cook, S. W. 1976. *Research Methods in Social Relations,* 3rd ed. N.Y.: Holt, Rinehart and Winston.

Someya, Kyojiro (Professor). Jan. 13, 1982. Interview.

Tanaka, Hideo, and Takeuchi, Akio. 1976. The role of private persons in the enforcement of law. In *The Japanese Legal System* (Hideo Tanaka and M. D. H. Smith, eds.). Tokyo: University of Tokyo Press, pp. 331-351.

Vines, G., Tomita, T., and Watanabe, M. (CPAs). Jan 20, 1982. Interview.

Vogel, E. F. May-June 1978. Guided free enterprise in Japan. *Harvard Business Review*

Watts, R. L. Apr. 1977. Corporate financial statements: A product of the market and political process. *Australian Journal of Management* 53-75.

Watts, R. L., and Zimmerman, J. L. 1978. Towards a positive theory of the determination of accounting standards. *The Accounting Review* 52(1):112-134.

Yamauchi, Yoshiaki (CPA). Jan. 14, 1982. Interview.

Yonke, R. (CPA) Jan. 14, 1982. Interview.

Zeff, S. A. 1972. *Forging Accounting Principles in Five Countries: A History and Analysis of Trends.* U.S.A.: Stripes Publishing Co.

Zeff, S. A. 1972. *Forging Accounting Principles in Five Countries: A History and Analysis of Trends.* Champaign, Ill: Stipes Publishing Co.

Zeff, S. A., and Defliese, P. L. 1974. Search for standards: U.S. and abroad. In *Accounting in Transition: Oral Histories of Recent U.S. Experience* (T. J. Burns, ed). Columbus, Ohio: College of Administrative Science, The Ohio State University, pp. 16-46.

[3]

Australia's ASRB. A Case Study of Political Activity and Regulatory 'Capture'

R. G. Walker*

Abstract—The establishment of an Accounting Standards Review Board (ASRB) in Australia followed proposals for greater government and community involvement in the development of accounting rules, and concern about the low level of compliance with the accountancy profession's standards. The profession had opposed proposals for a review board. The Ministerial Council for Companies and Securities overrode these objections, yet avoided giving any formal authority to the ASRB. In this environment the way was left open for renewed opposition to arrangements which had reduced the profession's capacity to control the standard-setting process. The newly-formed ASRB was vulnerable if it was unproductive—and it encountered delays and difficulties in receiving and processing submissions from the profession. The Board lacked the authority (and the will) to enforce its priorities. After two years the Board abandoned earlier efforts to secure wider community participation in its activities, and announced 'fast track' procedures which were to be applied only to those standards which the profession chose to submit for review.

This history suggests that the ASRB had been 'captured' by interest groups that it had been established to regulate. The history also casts doubts on claims that the political processes adopted in Australia for the development of accounting rules are consistent with notions of 'pluralism'; rather, those arrangements seem closer to the form of interest-group politics labelled 'neo-corporatism'.

The establishment of the Accounting Standards Review Board (ASRB) in January 1984 introduced a new set of arrangements for the regulation of corporate financial reporting in Australia. This paper (i) reviews these arrangements; (ii) outlines the ASRB's activities in its first 24 months, and the responses of the accounting profession to those initiatives; and (iii) speculates about the future direction of the ASRB in the light of subsequent changes in its policies. The early history of the ASRB can be interpreted as a case study of regulatory 'capture'. Or it can be seen as illustrating a change in the overall political processes associated with the development of accounting rules.

The profession and its standards

Australian corporate financial reporting has long been regulated by a combination of statutory requirements and profession-sponsored standards (with listed companies also being subject to rules promulgated by the Australian Associated Stock Exchanges).

There are two major accountancy bodies in Australia—the Institute of Chartered Accountants in Australia (ICAA) and the Australian Society of Accountants (ASA). The ICAA first issued 'Recommendations on Accounting Principles' in 1946; these were virtually copies of similarly titled documents produced by the Institute of Chartered Accountants in England and Wales. In 1965 the title of these professional pronouncements was changed to 'Statements on Accounting Principles and Recommendations on Accounting Practice' (later abbreviated to 'Statements on Accounting Practice'). In 1971 the Institute encouraged compliance with its statements by issuing Statement K1, 'Conformity with Institute Technical Statements' and by monitoring the reporting practices 'of a number of public companies'. In 1972 the ICAA was joined by the ASA in a programme of co-operative rule-making—initially through Society endorsement of Institute statements, later through the joint production of those rules. In 1973 the ASA required Society members to comply with ICAA/ASA accounting rules—which were to be described as 'accounting standards'.

The ICAA and ASA jointly fund the Australian Accounting Research Foundation (AARF) which is a rule-drafting body currently operating through three subsidiary 'boards' dealing with 'Accounting Standards', 'Public Sector Accounting Standards' and 'Auditing Standards' respectively. The ICAA and ASA appoint all members of these Boards. Proposed 'standards' must be approved by the councils of both the ICAA and ASA prior to release. Subsequent monitoring of compliance with accounting standards has been minimal, and

*The author was a member of the ASRB from 1984-85. There is a further note on this in an appendix. The views expressed in this paper are the author's, and it is possible that they do not reflect the views of other members of the ASRB, past or present.

though failure to observe Australian Accounting Standards supposedly exposes members to the possibility of disciplinary action, in practice the two bodies have avoided imposing such sanctions.

Proposals for greater government involvement in the development of accounting rules were advanced regularly since the early 1970s:

—In 1970 a Commonwealth and State Company Law Advisory Committee recommended the establishment of a 'Companies Commission' with power to alter or add to the provisions of the Act as to the form and content of a company's accounts (Company Law Advisory Committee, 1970, para. 49).

—In 1974 the Commonwealth Attorney-General (Senator Murphy) introduced a Companies and Securities Industry Bill which embodied proposals for the establishment of a Corporations and Exchange Commission which would have been empowered to make rules 'prescribing accounting principles' (Clause 129(1) and (3)). However this bill was not enacted before a change of government in 1975.

—In 1978 a committee appointed by the NSW Attorney General (Frank Walker) recommended the appointment of 'a national authority' to be 'delegated the task of ensuring that standards proposed for adoption by the professional bodies conform with the requirements of the Companies Act and of other Acts relating to the accounts of companies' (*Company Accounting Standards*, para. 10.18).

During the 1970s monitoring activities by government agencies revealed the high incidence of non-compliance with profession-sponsored accounting rules. The NSW Corporate Affairs Commission reviewed the financial statements of 8,699 companies over the period 1978–82, with the finding that 3,528 (41%) had failed to comply with one or more accounting standards. The profession's main public response was to attribute non-compliance to the difficulty of imposing the profession's standards on company directors. It was argued that the profession's standards should receive automatic 'statutory backing' (Bishop, 1978, p. 3; 'Professional standards review report', 1979; *Australian Financial Review*, 5 October 1982) and suggested that if statutory backing was forthcoming then membership of AARF could be expanded to make it a more representative body ('Government involvement in accounting standards', 1979; 'Joint submission', 1979). The executive director of the ASA later openly stated that the counter-proposals were designed to 'safeguard the profession's control' over accounting standards (Vincent, 1982, p. 19). The outcome of public debate about this proposal was the establishment of the ASRB.

Changed regulatory arrangements

Institutional Background

The ASRB was not established by statute, though the Companies Act and Codes refer to the Board in section 266:

> "Board" means the body, known as the Accounting Standards Review Board, established by the Ministerial Council.

The ASRB was established by a resolution of the Ministerial Council for Companies and Securities, and presumably it exists for as long as the Ministerial Council wishes. Accordingly, one cannot sensibly examine the role of the ASRB without some understanding of the role of the Ministerial Council and the operations of the Co-operative Scheme for Companies and Securities.

In 1978 a 'formal agreement' between state governments and the Commonwealth Government led to the establishment of the Co-operative Scheme, which aims at uniform companies and securities legislation, and establishing uniform administration of those statutes. Before 1961, the various Australian states had framed their own company laws; in 1960–61 the Commonwealth and States developed 'uniform' legislation which was separately enacted in each jurisdiction. In order to secure some degree of uniform administration, three of the states (NSW, Victoria and Queensland) formed the Interstate Corporate Affairs Commission in 1974 (and were joined by Western Australia in 1975). However, experience showed that such arrangements were cumbersome. In the 1978 'formal agreement', the states agreed to automatically adopt the Commonwealth companies and securities legislation as state 'Codes'.

The principal body in the Co-operative Scheme is the Ministerial Council for Companies and Securities, the members of which are the Commonwealth Attorney-General and the Attorneys-General of the six states and (since 1 July 1986) the Northern Territory. The principal administrative agency of the Scheme is the National Companies and Securities Commission (NCSC), created by the National Companies and Securities Commission Act of 1979. The NCSC has responsibility for administering legislation of the Scheme, principally through its delegates, the state Corporate Affairs Commissions (CACs). The NCSC was also given authority to exercise responsibility for policy making and adjudication arising from that legislation, on a national basis. Responsibility for formulating certain law reform proposals was assigned to a further body, the Companies and Securities Law Reform Committee (CSLRC), which was established in 1983. The CSLRC undertakes assignments on reference from the Ministerial Council.

On paper, the Scheme promised to simplify regulatory arrangements by giving the NCSC a central policy-making role in relation to company law and securities matters throughout Australia. However, the Commonwealth and state bureaucracies continue to advise their individual ministers and so play an important role in the framing of policies. As the NCSC has no power to direct resource allocation at state level, the various state CACs maintain considerable autonomy in the administration of the Scheme.

On 23 May 1980 the Ministerial Council formally resolved that the formation of an Accounting Standards Review Board should be considered by the NCSC. In 1981 the NCSC published its views on the role and functions of an ASRB: it recommended the establishment of a Board which was to review accounting standards formulated *by the accountancy bodies* and, if thought fit, to recommend their endorsement by the Commission (NCSC Release 401). At the request of the Ministerial Council, the NCSC invited public submissions on those proposals, and later prepared a revised set of recommendations (NCSC Release 405). The principal change in those recommendations concerned the possibility of 'recognising' accounting standards which had been developed *by organisations other than the Australian accountancy bodies*.

The accounting profession strongly opposed the 'costly and possibly bureaucratic step' of involving government in the preparation of accounting rules. It publicised counter-proposals that existing rules contained in Schedule 7 of the Companies Act and Codes should be scrapped and that legislative backing be extended to the profession's own standards (see, e.g., Australian Financial Review, 5 October 1982).

The files of the Commonwealth Attorney-General's Department relating to the establishment of the ASRB (copies of which were obtained in terms of Commonwealth Freedom of Information legislation) record that NCSC chairman Leigh Masel referred to 'a concerted lobby by the accounting profession' on these matters. Masel telexed members of the Ministerial Council advising that the NCSC had received submissions opposing the profession's proposals.

A particular concern expressed in discussions with some respondents was that, if the accounting profession's proposals are accepted, the status and income of the profession would, effectively, be accorded statutory protection without any corresponding requirement for public reporting and accountability by that profession. For reasons readily apparent, there are many in the profession who would welcome the safe harbour which legislative recognition would provide (Document 4, File CA82/5777).

The profession's counter-proposals for legislative backing for standards stood little chance of success in the face of this opposition. The final decisions of the Ministerial Council regarding the ASRB were based on a further set of recommendations, prepared jointly by the NCSC and the NSW Corporate Affairs Commission.[1] The NCSC/NSW CAC recommendations referred to 'approved' (rather than 'recognised') accounting standards: and they required the ASRB to report directly to the Ministerial Council (rather than through the NCSC). They also provided that standards which had been formally 'approved' by the ASRB through publication in the Commonwealth Government Gazette could be vetoed by the Ministerial Council within 60 days.

The 1983 decisions of the Ministerial Council envisaged a far more activist role for the ASRB than had been canvassed in the NCSC's 1981 proposals. The Ministerial Council endorsed a set of recommendations proposing that the ASRB be empowered to:

(a) determine priorities for the consideration of accounting standards referred to it;
(b) review standards referred to it;
(c) sponsor the development of standards;
(d) seek expert advice as it deems necessary;
(e) conduct public hearings into whether a proposed accounting standard should be approved;
(f) invite public submissions into any aspect of its functions;
(g) approve accounting standards.

Successive proposals significantly widened the ambit of standards that the Board could 'approve'. Initially, the NCSC argued that the ASRB should review standards developed by the Australian accounting bodies; then it argued that the ASRB should review standards developed by the Australian accounting bodies *and* 'other private organisations'; and finally the NCSC-NSW CAC submission proposed that the ASRB should be empowered to determine priorities, review standards referred to it, and sponsor the development of standards (see Peirson and Ramsay, 1983, p. 297).

The 1983 guidelines can be interpreted as authorising the ASRB to *commission* the preparation of 'high priority' standards, which could then be 'reviewed' by the Board. This possibility was supported in the NCSC-NSW CAC report, together with the suggestion that the source of proposed standards should not be restricted to 'private

---

[1]Document 196, File CA82/17743; this report had earlier been made available to the two accounting bodies 'on a confidential, not for publication basis'—Document 69, File E83/10597; it was made public when cited by Peirson and Ramsay, 1983, p. 297.

organisations', but that standards could also be submitted by public bodies or private persons (Peirson and Ramsay, 1983, p. 297).

A further extension of the role originally proposed for the ASRB was the suggestion in the NCSC-NSW CAC recommendations that one of the first tasks of the ASRB should be 'to sponsor or encourage the development of a conceptual framework for accounting standards in Australia'.

These background documents (and in particular the NCSC-NSW CAC report) assume considerable significance since, in the absence of any statutory statement of the Board's powers and duties, they reflect the Ministerial Council's 1983 intentions, and in particular have a bearing on later claims that the ASRB's powers were limited to accepting or rejecting standards submitted to it. They indicate that in 1983 the Ministerial Council saw the ASRB's brief as proactive rather than reactive.

The significance of the Ministerial Council's 1983 decisions is reinforced when viewed in the light of prior lobbying activities of the accountancy profession. The files of the Commonwealth Attorney-General's Department contain letters and records of oral submissions to the Attorney, his staff, and officers of the Department and the NCSC, and indicate that two main proposals were pressed. First, the profession argued that the ASRB should not be empowered to consider standards from sources other than the profession, asserting that 'the recognition and possible use of alternative sources of standards is unnecessary and undesirable', and that such a draft power 'should be deleted entirely'. Second, the profession claimed that the ASRB should not have the authority to establish priorities, but should rely on the priorities 'agreed' with AARF.[2]

In 1983 the Ministerial Council rejected both proposals, perhaps heeding the NCSC's advice that providing the ASRB with the power to set priorities and commission the preparation of draft standards was intended to enable the ASRB to ensure that its priorities for the development of standards could not be frustrated by delay or inaction on part of the AARF.[3] Despite the NCSC's and the Ministerial Council's intentions, the question of whether the Board had these powers became the source of conflict between the Board and representatives of the profession, and the question of whether the 'commissioning' power should be exercised became the subject of some disagreement within the Board itself.

The profession may have had more success with its opposition to the appointment of an academic as chairman of the ASRB. This opposition may have been associated with the NSW Attorney-General's appointment in November 1977 of an 'Accounting Standards Review Committee' chaired by Prof. R. J. Chambers of the University of Sydney. This Committee was to have included representatives of both the ICAA and the ASA but the ICAA failed to nominate a member and the ASA's representative then withdrew (see 'Accounting Standards Review Committee', March 1978). The Committee's report was highly critical of existing standards and of the standard-setting process, and was not well received within the profession. When in 1983 it was rumoured that an academic (probably Chambers) was a favoured candidate for chairmanship of the ASRB, the accountancy bodies argued that 'academic knowledge would not be the appropriate requirement for the post' of chairman; rather, selection criteria 'should properly reflect the important considerations of practicality, acceptability and need in the community.[4] (In contrast, the legal profession apparently had no difficulty with the appointment of an academic as chairman of the ASRB's sister organisation, the CSLRC.)

The accountancy profession also vigorously opposed proposals that the Board should be supported by a 'research director'—arguing that the Board should not have an independent research capacity but should rely on materials presented to it by AARF. Memoranda record that the ICAA and ASA argued that the Board 'should not be a high-powered initiating and research body'.[5] Subsequent advertisements for the initial appointment to the ASRB's staff described the position as administrative.

Rule Development and Rule Administration

Any set of regulatory arrangements reflects choices about:

(a) the processes to be used to develop rules;
(b) the mechanisms to be used to monitor compliance with rules, and to impose sanctions for non-compliance.

An examination of the role and functions of the ASRB in terms of its contribution to rule development and rule administration highlights the significance of the adoption of the concept of 'approved accounting standards'.

(a) Processes

The establishment of the ASRB in 1984, together with decisions later taken by the Board about its proposed procedures, constituted changes in the *political process* used for the prepa-

---

[2]Letter, ASA and ICAA to NCSC, 16 May 1983: Document 64, File E83/10597.
[3]Memorandum, L. Masel, 3 June 1983, Document 68, File E83/10597.

[4]Letter, ICAA to Ministerial Council, 16 September 1983, Document 123, File E83/10597.
[5]Minute, 22 June 1983, File G83/4211; NCSC Staff Paper, Document 66, File E83/5211.

ration of accounting standards in Australia (though, as suggested below, these changes were short-lived).

During the course of debate about proposals for statutory backing of profession-sponsored accounting standards, public servants and politicians suggested that any such step should be conditional on the involvement of a wide range of community interests (see, e.g., 'Government involvement in accounting standards', 1979). The joint accountancy bodies consistently expressed the view that if government required some involvement, this should be achieved 'either through direct external representation in [the] existing AARF structure, or through a profession-sponsored ASRB' (see, e.g., Prosser, 1983, p. 18).

In the event, the Ministerial Council resolved to appoint an ASRB which was 'independent' of the profession. In practice, while ICAA and ASA nominees filled only two of the seven positions on the Board, a majority of ASRB members held (or had held) senior positions in those bodies. The chairman, Geoff Bottrill (68) was a former national president of the ASA. Other members of the foundation Board were selected from panels of names solicited from the Australian Council of Trade Unions, the Company Directors' Association of Australia, the Business Council of Australia, the NCSC, AARF, the Australian Shareholders' Association, and the Accounting Association of Australia and New Zealand (an organisation whose membership was drawn primarily from the academic community). All appointees held accounting qualifications of some kind, leading to suggestions that the profession had 'every reason to be pleased with the composition of the new ... Board' (Business Review Weekly, 21 January 1984).

North American experience has been interpreted as showing that the appointment of a widely-representative standard-setting Board would constitute a more politically viable or stable arrangement than prior arrangements (see Hines, 1983; Bromwich, 1986, p. 118). Indeed, a submission from the ICAA and ASA to the Ministerial Council in August 1981 acknowledged that proposals for the establishment of an ASRB were intended to secure 'the public acceptability of accounting standards' (Document 42, File CA82/7529).

As noted earlier, the accountancy bodies had strongly opposed proposals that other organisations might be able to submit accounting rules to the ASRB. To some who were unaware of the profession's prior lobbying activities, this reaction was surprising: the occasional submission of standards from non-professional sources could only enhance the ASRB's appearance of independence, and it could also protect the profession from criticism, since critics of accounting standards

could be invited to 'put up or shut up'. However the first standard submitted to the ASRB came from the Australian Shareholders' Association, and concerned a subject that AARF had been tardy in addressing: the preparation of consolidated statements. Press reports claimed that a consolidation standard was 'urgently needed' and that the submission was 'a show of frustration at the slowness of the major accounting bodies on this subject' (*Australian Financial Review*, 22 August 1984). Such reports appear to have exacerbated the profession's sensitivities.

The ASRB had been directed to determine priorities for its review of accounting standards, and in Release 200 the Board indicated that it would review all submissions in terms of those priorities before actively considering any draft standard. But the Board had no authority to enforce its priorities on other bodies, and it encountered reluctance on the part of AARF to submit those Australian Accounting Standards which (in the light of public submissions) it regarded as the most pressing candidates for 'approval'. Perhaps this difficulty could have been overcome if the Board had been prepared to follow its brief to 'sponsor the development of standards'. But this was an ambiguous directive and the ASRB—while trying to establish a good working relationship with AARF—found representatives of the profession arguing that the Board could or should not initiate the drafting of standards, but only 'review' standards submitted to it by third parties.

(b) Compliance and sanctions

A feature of the ASRB arrangements is the manner in which legislative amendments established a process enabling government agencies to monitor compliance with approved accounting standards.

The legislation requires directors who fail to comply with an approved standard to justify why compliance would not provide 'a true and fair view' (and to report the quantified financial effects of non-compliance); auditors must comment on those explanations and notify the ASRB of instances of non-compliance. This arrangement would provide the ASRB with both information concerning non-compliance and the arguments of those company directors or auditors who favoured alternative procedures. The ASRB later resolved to maintain a register of instances of non-compliance, and to make that register available to the NCSC and its delegates.

The ASRB's activities in the first two years

During its first two years, the Board followed the guidelines set by the Ministerial Council and published a statement of the criteria it would employ in reviewing accounting standards (Release 100)—which included a partial 'conceptual framework'. However, the first 'approved accounting standards' did not appear until September 1985—20 months after the ASRB's establishment.

This lack of productivity can be partly explained by the difficulties faced by a part-time Board in establishing operating procedures and securing funding for its operations within the labyrinth of the Co-operative Scheme. The Board began with minimal funding ($35,000) for the first five months, and was serviced by staff seconded from the NCSC. Until it was allocated further resources (1984–5, $200,000), the Board was unable to recruit staff or to engage consultants—and even then, given the manner in which the ASRB had been established, the Board had to enter into contracts through public service intermediaries.

A major source of delay in the 'approval' process was the need to establish ground-rules for the ASRB's operations. The Board also become embroiled in efforts by the ICAA and ASA to persuade the Ministerial Council that they should be permitted to retain the copyright in 'approved accounting standards'—and the commercial benefits flowing from the sale of those regulations.

ASRB Procedures

The ASRB had been established in 1984 with no formal terms of reference. Members had been given copies of the 1983 recommendations of the NCSC and NSW CAC (described earlier) concerning the powers and duties of the Board, together with the advice that the Ministerial Council had approved the recommendations and supporting argument 'in principle'. This document had not been made available to the public. A request by one organisation for a copy was initially denied, but later upheld in terms of Commonwealth Freedom of Information legislation.[6] As noted above, copies or drafts of this document had earlier been provided to the accountancy bodies, so that representatives of the profession were well informed about the broad intentions of the Ministerial Council when it established the ASRB.

In this situation (and despite the decisions of the Ministerial Council in 1983) the ICAA and ASA continued to seek changes in the powers and duties of the Board. The Board elected to negotiate with the accountancy bodies in an effort to establish a harmonious working relationship. Indeed, the Board found itself trying to explain its powers, as originally delineated by the Ministerial Council, in the face of what it saw as misconceptions about its role. Some of these 'misconceptions' were that the ASRB, upon receiving a standard from a source other than AARF, was required to give AARF the

⁶Personal communication, chairman, Australian Shareholders' Association.

right to submit a standard of its own on the same topic, and that the ASRB was obliged to either wholly 'approve' or wholly reject a standard submitted to it, without any amendment.

Perhaps the most difficult issue was whether the Board had the capacity to amend the text of standards. In Release 200 the Board outlined an abbreviated statement of the procedures it intended to follow in handling the submission of accounting standards. (The full statement had been 'noted', though not 'endorsed' by the Ministerial Council.) These procedures were based on the assumption that public submissions might suggest the need for some changes to the text of proposed standards. Release 200 indicated that the Board would advise submitting parties of proposed changes (in the expectation that they would be prepared to make minor revisions and resubmit the standard). However, it became evident that the ASRB could not adhere to that process if it was to produce any standards within a reasonable period. The Board could go through the process of inviting public comments on proposed standards, receive and analyse those comments—and then find that the submitting party objected to any amendments, or suggested that amendments should be set forth in an exposure draft reissued to its own constituency.

These difficulties were compounded by uncertainties as to the ownership of copyright in approved accounting standards. During discussions in February 1984, the joint accountancy bodies expressed concern about having to relinquish copyright in standards submitted to the ASRB. In February 1985, the Board (with Ministerial Council approval) published Release 200 which affirmed that parties submitting standards would be required to assign copyright to the Board. Apparently the accountancy bodies refused to accept this requirement (but did not formally communicate this refusal until 27 June 1985). This delayed the formal approval of any standard, since a majority of the Board opposed the publication of any standards until the copyright dispute was settled.

The Board referred the matter to the Ministerial Council which (according to later reports) concluded 'that it was not permissible for a body to have copyright over what would be essentially a public piece of legislation' (*Australian Business*, September 1985). This decision did not settle the matter, and the accountancy bodies refused to assign copyright. A press report suggested that the ASA, ICAA and AARF were 'at war with the ASRB' over the issue (*Australian Business*, 4 September 1985). In the face of the profession's intransigence the ASRB still had several options open to it if it was to get on with its job of 'approving' accounting rules: it could examine standards submitted by other bodies, it could commission the drafting of standards, or it could examine overseas standards which were free of copyright restrictions. The Board elected not to pursue any of these options.

In July 1985 the Ministerial Council directed the newly-appointed chairman of the NCSC, Mr Henry Bosch, to investigate the copyright issue. In due course the copyright problem was said to have been 'smartly resolved': the joint accountancy bodies were to assign copyright provided they obtained a licence for any royalties over standards they submit' (*Australian Business*, 4 September 1985). In effect, the Ministerial Council reversed its earlier decision that private bodies should not hold copyright over public regulations.

Shortly afterwards, the Board was able to approve two standards in terms of an 'interim agreement' about licensing (*Business Review Weekly*, 27 September 1985). Those standards bore a 'copyright warning':

> The copying of this standard is only permitted in certain circumstances. Enquiries should be directed to the offices of the Accounting Standards Review Board.

The same copyright warning was still appearing on ASRB-approved standards late in 1986—indicating that the interim agreement had still not been finalised.

Priorities Established by the Board

In mid-1985 the then president of the ICAA claimed that it had been 'generally expected' that soon after its establishment the ASRB would give 'approval, or at least some form of provisional approval' to all of the Australian Accounting Standards then on issue (Edwards, 1985, p. 6). However the evidence is to the contrary. Soon after its formation in 1984 the ASRB invited public submissions on its priorities and received a clear message from respondents that it would be inappropriate to approve existing standards. The principal reasons advanced were dissatisfaction with the substance of a number of those standards, and a belief that the processes used to develop standards had not taken account of the views of different interest groups. Table 1 summarises those responses.

Nevertheless the Board was attracted by the idea of 'approving' those provisions of existing Australian Accounting Standards which seemed technically sound and to have secured widespread support. It explored the possibility of preparing a re-numbered collation of clauses from existing standards, presented along the lines adopted by the Canadian Institute of Chartered Accountants in its *CICA Handbook*. It was thought that this exercise might lead to the short-run approval of relatively uncontentious rules. However the Board abandoned the idea after concluding that the existing standards needed extensive redrafting if they were to be legally enforceable, and in the face of opposition to the use of a format which differed from that presently adopted by AARF. It was also realised that the legislative requirements for the formal notification of the approval or revocation of standards did not readily accommodate line-by-line amendments.

Many respondents suggested that high priority should be given to some contentious standards: equity accounting, revaluations, leases and 'goodwill'. However the Board was also considering its brief to foster the development of a conceptual framework and it was examining weaknesses in the drafting of existing Australian Accounting Standards. Accordingly, the Board decided to try to resolve drafting issues in the course of examining some less controversial topics.

At its May 1984 meeting the Board discussed priorities with AARF and suggested that it first review existing standards dealing with the presentation of balance sheets and profit and loss statements. AARF explained that it was in the process of re-examining these standards, and would not be able to present revised versions before late 1986. The Board accepted this—and in any event saw no reason to press the issue, given that the NCSC had published a 'green paper' proposing amendments to Schedule 7 of the Com-

Table 1 Responses to ASRB on priorities			
Category of respondent	No priority stated	Immediately approve existing standards	Review or amend existing standards
Academics	4	—	4
Corporations	4	3	19
Practitioners	1	4	9
ASA and ICAA	—	2	—
Other organisations	5	—	7
Govt. bodies or depts.	3	—	4
Others	2	1	2
Total: 74	19	10	45

panies Act and Codes (NCSC, 1983) and that a subsequent draft revision of Schedule 7 covered most of the matters incorporated in the profession's 1973 standard on profit and loss statements.

The Board then nominated other 'general' standards as vehicles for resolving drafting issues: those dealing with 'materiality', 'statement of accounting policies', and 'post-balance date events' (AAS 5, AAS 6 and AAS 8). Several members of the Board expressed the hope that most of the work on these 'low priority' standards could be completed by July 1984. Such optimism proved ill-founded.

Some respondents and members of the Board were of the view that a high priority should be given to the development of standards on consolidated statements. It seemed important to sort out ideas about consolidation accounting before handling standards dealing with equity accounting or the treatment of goodwill on consolidation (or other related topics such as merger accounting, the proposed 'partial consolidation' of joint ventures, and the application of foreign currency translation techniques to overseas subsidiaries). Accordingly, the submission by the Australian Shareholders' Association of a standard on consolidation accounting was welcome. However, shortly after its submission the Shareholders' Association suggested to the ASRB that examination of the standard be delayed pending the Association's consideration of submissions it had received and expected to receive from interested parties. The standard was not 'withdrawn' (as suggested in the *Australian Financial Review*, 8 November 1984, and subsequently reported by a representative of AARF—see McGregor, June 1985, p. 5).

In a letter dated 29 May 1985 the Australian Shareholders' Association proposed that the ASRB could now proceed with its review of that standard. Meantime the ASRB had published Releases 100 and 200 which required bodies submitting standards to provide other material in support of the submission (e.g. particulars of responses to any prior public exposure of the standards submitted to the Board). The Australian Shareholders' Association was asked to submit all of the supporting material specified in Release 200—but it did not immediately comply. The ASRB's 1984–85 Annual Report noted that the consolidation standard submitted by the Australian Shareholders' Association had not been reviewed during 1984–85 because of the lack of supporting material (p. 9). However late in 1985 these requirements were waived for both submissions and promised submissions from AARF, while the consolidation standard remained off the Board's formal agenda.

After prior discussions with AARF representatives the ASRB formally advised AARF in May 1984 that there was a need for existing Australian Accounting Standards to be redrafted before they could be 'approved'. This was accepted, but AARF

took time to make those revisions, and more rigorously drafted versions were not finally submitted until 12 December 1984. The Board invited public submissions on those standards by the following February, and concluded its examination of all three in June 1985 (subject to a final review by a drafting sub-committee, completed in July). But the failure of AARF to provide an assignment of copyright prevented publication of the two standards 'approved' until September 1985. The standard on 'materiality' was rejected, principally because while it purported to establish general principles for financial reporting it was drafted imprecisely or ambiguously.

Meantime the Board had determined that 'in view of the importance it attaches to the preparation and presentation of group accounts', it would next examine 'Revaluation of non-current assets', 'Equity method of accounting' and 'Accounting for goodwill' (Release 300, 'Progress report', December 1984). AARF was advised of these priorities, and the ASRB engaged consultants from three major accountancy firms to report on anomalies which had emerged in the practical application of those standards. Consultants' reports were considered in January 1985.

In May 1985 AARF submitted those three standards, together with six others (equivalent to versions of Australian Standards AAS 10–AAS 18). The Board did not consider that it should invite public submissions on any of these documents, since AARF had failed to provide all of the materials required in terms of ASRB Releases 100 and 200. The Board formally reconsidered its priorities in the light of the six additional submissions, but resolved to maintain its existing plan to review the standards on asset revaluations, equity accounting and goodwill. By late 1985 redrafted versions of these standards had still not appeared, and the Board again reviewed its priorities in the light of a submission from the NCSC concerning foreign currency translation. The Board also discussed the possibility of further NCSC submissions in the new year.

However, close to the expiration of the term of office of four of the seven members of the Board, negotiations between AARF and the ASRB's chairman led to the announcement of a different set of priorities from those which had been formally adopted by the Board. Advertisements appearing in the national press on 23 October 1985—placed the day before a scheduled Board meeting—announced that AARF had 'advised that it will shortly be submitting four further standards for approval by the ASRB': 'Disclosure of revenue', 'Accounting for leases', 'Accounting for interests in joint ventures', and 'Foreign currency translation'.

In effect, the actions by the ASRB's chairman meant that the Board had abandoned its stated policy of setting priorities in the light of 'community needs', after consultation with 'preparers and users' of financial statements (Release 200, para 4.2.2). It had also ignored some of its procedural rules requiring the submission of full documentation before standards could be placed on its agenda (Release 200, para 4.4). But the Board continued to apply those rules to the earlier submission from the Australian Shareholders' Association.

Criteria for Evaluating Standards

In its first months, the first task addressed by the Board was the articulation of criteria it would use to evaluate accounting standards. The Ministerial Council had approved in principle a set of guidelines which the ASRB was to follow in the performance of its tasks. In February 1984 the Board decided to invite interested parties to comment on this material and, in the light of public submissions, restated and combined the 'guidelines' to produce four criteria:

1. Whether the information generated by application of the proposed standard is relevant to informed decision-making and discharges directors' accountability in a manner consistent with community requirements and expectations.
2. Whether the proposed standard is well-formulated and logically derived.
3. Whether the proposed standard is consistent with approved accounting standards.
4. Whether the standard is practicable (for some or all companies) having regard to the commercial and economic consequences which might flow from its implementation.

Baldly stated, these propositions seem trite: after all, who would suggest that accounting standards should be 'poorly formulated' or 'illogically derived'? However, the adoption of these criteria reflected the Ministerial Council's instructions that the Board should examine standards systematically, in terms of a 'decision usefulness' framework. Further, Release 100 indicated that the Board planned to have regard to the so-called 'economic consequences' of standards in a very limited way (e.g. for the purpose of considering whether different reporting rules should apply to different classes of company, or to establish transitional provisions for the adoption of newly-approved standards which might disturb existing commercial arrangements). However, to those familiar with the history of standard setting activities in other countries, possibly the most significant steps taken by the Board were the publication of a set of 'fundamental assumptions' concerning the accounting process, and the announcement that the Board would place weight on the findings of 'decision-usefulness' research.

Key Accounting Assumptions

The ASRB's brief was to foster the development of a 'conceptual framework' of accounting. The Ministerial Council had been advised that without such a framework, it would be difficult for the Board to ensure that approved accounting standards 'were logically well developed and consistent' (Release 100, para. 20).

When the ASRB sought advice about priorities, there were some expressions of concern that the Board should contemplate any involvement with a conceptual framework project—particularly in the light of the FASB's slow progress with such a venture over 12 years. However other respondents urged the ASRB to attempt to outline a conceptual framework so that the 'review' process could be less amenable to pressure from sectional interests.

The Board concluded that it could not assess whether arguments in support of a standard were 'logically derived' (Criterion 2) unless those arguments were fully stated and that it would be unable to ensure that standards were inter-consistent (Criterion 3) unless arguments in support of those standards were founded on consistent assumptions. Accordingly, the Board sought to articulate certain assumptions concerning the accounting process (Release 100, para. 21).

Release 100 was drafted by August 1984, completed in October 1984 and published in February 1985 (after further review within the Co-operative Scheme). It set forth nine 'assumptions':

Purpose of corporate financial reporting
Reporting entity
Concept of 'asset'
Concept of 'liability'
Concept of 'residual equity'
Concept of 'contributions'
Concept of 'distributions'
Concept of 'revenues'
Concept of 'expenses'.

This mini 'conceptual framework' was obviously incomplete; for example, it said nothing about the attributes of assets and liabilities which are to be measured in accounting (though the Board's Release 101 published December 1985 expressed the view that measurement procedures were to be applied to individual items rather than to collections of assets and liabilities). Several of the assumptions in Release 100 were derived from the FASB's Statement of Financial Accounting Concepts 3, 'Elements of financial statements of business enterprises' (December 1980). However, the ASRB's assumptions differed in the specification of a 'holding company' (rather than a 'group') as the reporting entity in consolidated statements, in the definition of 'asset' (which referred to the characteristic of 'legal rights'), in the adoption of simple definitions of 'asset' and 'liability' (rather than the separate specification of definitional and recognition criteria), and in the restriction of changes in residual equity to 'contributions' or 'revenues', 'distributions' or 'expenses' (thus excluding other categorisations of 'gains' and 'losses').

The Board described these assumptions as 'tentative':

> The statements of assumptions reflect pre-liminary views and should be helpful both in focussing the Board's attention on relevant issues, and in assisting those interested in making submissions on proposed standards to address issues of particular concern to the Board (Release 100, para. 24).

Thus in 1984 the Board signalled that standards submitted to it which outlined treatments *consistent* with those assumptions should have an easy passage through the review process. If prospective standards incorporated treatments which were *inconsistent* with those assumptions then the onus was on the submitting party to explain why those rules could be regarded as presenting information relevant to users.

A copy of the draft Release 100 had been forwarded to AARF for comment. AARF responded vigorously, claiming that publication would 'pre-empt' AARF's own 'due process' procedures for the development of a conceptual framework. The ASRB unanimously decided to proceed with publication. However the first members of the Board did not have the opportunity to apply the procedures outlined in Release 100, since the standards on 'goodwill' and 'asset revaluations' (which *prima facie* required treatments which were inconsistent with some of the 'fundamental assumptions' outlined in Release 100) were not submitted during 1984–5.

The Role of Research in Evaluation

The Board also indicated its intention to have regard to the findings of research. Release 100 explained that the evaluative criterion of whether standards were 'well formulated and logically derived' was intended:

> to encompass both the quality of argument expressed in support of a standard, and *evidence* that approval of the standard would lead to the presentation of information of the character indicated by Criterion 1 (i.e. information relevant to 'users').

Further clauses indicated that the Board saw present and potential shareholders and creditors as the principal users—and that it considered that key financial indicators derived from reports to those users could also be relevant to other interested parties.

Only a relatively small proportion of published academic 'research' has had much bearing upon the technical accounting issues which have been examined by regulatory agencies. An even smaller proportion has been concerned with amassing 'evidence' on such questions. So the ASRB faced little risk of being swamped with academic submissions. Nevertheless, it appears that this was the first time that a newly-established standard-setting body had expressed a desire to link its deliberations with the findings of 'decision-usefulness' empirical research.

Drafting of 'Approved Accounting Standards'

After taking advice from the Commonwealth Attorney-General's Department early in 1984, the Board agreed that existing Australian Accounting Standards would need some redrafting before 'approval' to ensure consistency with the Companies Act and Codes, and to ensure that they were enforceable. Strangely, AARF had apparently given little thought to these issues, despite the profession's long-standing requests for 'statutory backing' of its standards.

The Board concluded that existing professionally sponsored standards should be redrafted as imperatives rather than as statements of guidance about what practices 'should' be followed. The Board also wished to discourage a literal approach to interpretation, and sought to foster a concern with the overall *intent* of accounting rules. Accordingly, in Release 100 the Board reported its decision to require a purposive style of drafting. Another aspect that received attention was the fact that existing standards were accompanied by passages explaining the content and rationale for those standards. Some of this material merely paraphrased the rules; some paragraphs canvassed the merits of alternatives to the procedures adopted in the standard; some paragraphs described theoretical justifications for those procedures—justifications which at times were contentious, or which could create difficulties and delays if members of the Board were prepared to 'approve' a standard but disagreed with the stated rationale. The Board concluded that much of the 'explanatory material' accompanying existing standards was superfluous, and reported its decision that 'explanatory material should not form part of an approved accounting standard' (Release 200, para. 8).

Despite earlier explanations of the Board's views, representatives of AARF continued to express concern about the exclusion of educational and other 'explanatory' material. Board members pointed out that statutes were generally devoid of illustrations and explanations, and that nothing prevented the profession from initiating the publication of 'guidance notes' to offer the profession's view of how approved standards were to be interpreted (a policy which was in fact adopted by AARF late in 1985 in respect of its own standards). Representatives of the profession indicated that whatever changes were made, they wanted to be able to adopt a drafting style which minimised the differences between 'approved standards' (which applied only to corporations) and the existing Australian Accounting Standards (which would remain in force for other entities). The ASRB indicated its willingness to discuss the issues and rethink its position. In February–April 1985 the Board committed its views to writing in an effort to foster debate; and then enlisted the co-operation of the NCSC in the establishment of a three-party project team (ASRB, NCSC and AARF) to seek agreement on a drafting style. Subsequently a working party involving staff of AARF, the ASRB, the NCSC and representatives of the Commonwealth Attorney-General's Department endeavoured to apply those drafting principles to several standards. An invitation was extended to AARF's Accounting Standards Board to comment on a draft ASRB Release 202 which proposed guidelines on drafting.

After these meetings and other discussions, the Board considered that it had secured agreement on drafting, and reached a satisfactory compromise about explanatory material. Approved accounting standards were to be prefaced by a 'statement of purpose' which was to indicate the linkage between rules on a given topic, and the objectives of financial reporting. This statement of purpose was to be framed as an overriding requirement. The text of approved standards was to be accompanied by cross-references to other standards on related topics, by examples of items which fell within given definitions or the ambit of certain rules, and by certain other 'explanatory material'. While most of this explanatory material was to be interpolated between substantive clauses (so that it assisted in the interpretation of specific clauses), it was agreed that additional 'explanatory material' could be provided in the form of a supplementary 'commentary'.

Negotiations with AARF during early 1985 focussed on the three standards selected back in March 1984 as suitably uncontroversial vehicles for the sorting out of drafting issues. Yet after these discussions, the preparation of drafting guidelines, and detailed analysis of the three standards, the next batch of standards submitted by AARF in December 1985 failed to conform to the Board's requirements. For example, the 36-page 'Foreign currency translation' standard (Release 406, December 1985) contained no less than 23 pages of 'explanatory material', including clauses which were not commentaries on the standards themselves but 'recommendations' on additional aspects of accounting practice. Another feature of these submissions was the fact that while the mandatory 'shall' had been substituted for the directory 'should', this change was often neutralised by qualifications to the effect that disclosure was required only if the information was 'material'.

AARF's proposed foreign currency standard (published as ASRB Release 406, December 1985) contained no less than 30 references to 'materiality' in 23 substantive clauses.

This lack of conformity with the agreed drafting guidelines was noted in a low-key way when the Board commented that the draft standards were being published 'as submitted', and that the ASRB proposed to review 'all aspects of the proposed standard' including 'the adequacy of the statement of purpose, the appropriateness of the explanatory material and the method of drafting' (Releases 404–6). Plainly after almost two years of debate the ASRB's policies on drafting remained under challenge.

NCSC Intervention

The ASRB's efforts to 'approve' standards had been stalled by the profession's attempts to retain copyright over 'approved' standards. The Board was ready to publish two standards in June 1985 but refrained from doing so to avoid a full-scale confrontation with the leadership of the ICAA and ASA. However the Board had considered consultants' reports on three other topics, and had arranged for the standard on 'goodwill' to be redrafted in accord with its guidelines. A copy had been forwarded to AARF to assist in the review of that standard.

Meantime the ASRB was being criticised for its lack of productivity. A paper delivered at the ASA's Victorian congress in June 1985 by an AARF staff member pointed out that no standards had been approved after 18 months, 'and unless there is a marked change in direction, we will be lucky to see any standards approved before year end' (*Melbourne Herald*, 20 June 1985). Other press reports alluded to 'mud throwing' at the ASRB (*Australian Business*, 4 September 1985). A member of AARF's Accounting Standards Board presented a paper at the annual conference of the Accounting Association of Australia and New Zealand (AAANZ) which was critical of the ASRB for not giving interim approval of all the profession's standards, and suggested that delays were attributable to the ASRB's insistence upon the need for redrafting into literal, 'black letter' rules (Boymal, 1985, pp. 18–9).

As the tensions between the ASRB and the profession became a matter of public knowledge, press reports indicated that the Ministerial Council had directed NCSC chairman, Henry Bosch, to examine the problems (*The Age*, 7 August, 1985). Events moved rapidly in the following weeks. Late in August the NCSC gave the ASRB something to do by submitting a draft standard titled 'Foreign Exchange—Disclosure'. And a few days later Bosch began criticising the elongated nature of the standard-setting process—in an address at the annual conference of the AAANZ, in press releases and interviews with journalists. Bosch's main target was the 'small number of rather loose standards' that had been produced by the profession—and the fact that the ASRB had passed only two standards since its establishment (Bosch, 1985, p. 20).

As noted earlier in this paper, in 1983 the then NCSC chairman, Leigh Masel, had warned that the ASRB risked being frustrated by delay and inaction from AARF. Bosch observed delay and inaction, but apparently was persuaded that this was the product of personality clashes rather than the outcome of a dispute over control of the standard-setting process. He suggested that 'one of the biggest stumbling blocks' preventing a greater output of standards was the relationship between AARF and the ASRB (*Business Review Weekly*, 30 August 1985). Bosch's intervention had some effect: while the ASRB had 'passed' two standards, it had not formally 'approved' them by publication in the Commonwealth of Australia Gazette because of the lingering copyright dispute. The Ministerial Council's decision to permit the accounting profession to earn revenues from these regulations enabled the ASRB to gazette its first two standards on 18 September 1985. The NCSC-submitted standard was gazetted nine days later—demonstrating that the Board could move quickly when given standards to approve, but also re-activating the profession's sensitivity about the submission of standards from organisations other than AARF.

A New Agenda, Procedures and Board

Bosch's criticisms may also have prompted a change in the public position of the ASRB concerning its priorities. As noted earlier, the ASRB's chairman, Geoff Bottrill, authorised press advertisements appearing in late October 1985 which announced that the ASRB 'expected to receive' four standards from AARF, and invited submissions on this material—thus establishing priorities consistent with AARF's wishes. This list of proposed standards was markedly different from the priorities formally established by the Board in response to public submissions early in 1984—and which had subsequently been re-affirmed in the Board's 1984 'progress report' (Release 300, December 1984) and in its 1984 Annual Report.

But by this time the life of the foundation Board was drawing to a close—with the expiration of the two-year term of four of the seven members. All four offered themselves for reappointment, amid rumours of strong lobbying by elements of the accountancy profession to secure changes in ASRB membership and policies. Three members were not reappointed.

In a press release issued by the NCSC in December 1985, Bottrill announced the appointment of new members and the adoption of new 'fast track

procedures' aimed at 'clearing the backlog of standards awaiting approval'.

A year later, details of these new procedures had not been published. But the Board had rapidly 'approved' six of the profession's standards—though apparently without linking its decisions to its prior statement of criteria to be used in the 'approval' process (Release 100, February 1985). The 'approved' standards dealt with disclosure of operating revenue, segment reporting, joint ventures, funds statements, leases and construction contracts. Standards on the topics which the 1984 Board had regarded as warranting urgent attention 'in view of the importance it attaches to the preparation and presentation of group accounts' (Release 300, December 1984) remained off the agenda.

The ASRB's first two years: in retrospect

The ASRB was established without a 'constitution' or a formal statement of objectives—but prior political debate suggested that those objectives were to ensure that accounting rules were to be enforceable, and that they were to have legitimacy in the eyes of preparers of financial statements, auditors, shareholders and other users of accounting reports. This 'legitimacy' was to be attained through the appointment of a Board which was to be representative of a wide range of interests, to follow procedures which ensured widespread discussion and consultation, and to base its deliberations on an articulated set of accounting concepts.

The first steps undertaken by the ASRB were consistent with that brief: the Board established its priorities in the light of public submissions, enunciated criteria to be used in the review process, outlined its views about basic assumptions of accounting, and sought to establish drafting guidelines so that standards could be enforceable. But these policies brought the Board into conflict with AARF and the leadership of the ICAA and ASA. The initial composition of the Board had ensured strong representation from the accountancy bodies. The chairman and the profession's nominees were elected for three-year terms; all three were past national presidents of the ICAA or ASA. The ASA's nominee also became an ex officio member of AARF's Accounting Standards Board during 1985—an appointment which some consider should have contributed to greater harmony between the AARF and the ASRB (though others might intepret that appointment as giving rise to a conflict of interests).

With the benefit of hindsight, it is difficult to avoid the conclusion that representatives of the accountancy bodies and AARF ensured that the ASRB was unproductive. The Board was hampered by the tardiness of those bodies in formally

SUMMER 1987   281

communicating their demands about copyright, by delays in the submission of redrafted versions of two relatively uncontentious standards, and by the failure of AARF to redraft and submit the three standards which the Board considered should have priority.

Back in 1983, NCSC chairman Masel had warned of the possibility that the Board might be 'frustrated by delay and inaction on the part of the AARF'. But Masel had retired, and the Ministerial Council was a new set of ministers. The professional bodies were able to create a climate in which they could press for some review of the powers and duties of the Board (or even, perhaps, for the total abandonment of the ASRB in favour of some form of statutory endorsement of the profession's standards). Indeed, late in 1985 (when changes in the ASRB's powers and policies had been announced) there was open discussion about the profession's past strategies—and the outcome. Press reports indicated that the adoption of new procedures meant that the ASRB would now have 'the co-operation' of the ICAA and ASA (see, e.g., *The Age*, 10 December 1985). Items in the profession's journals reported triumphantly,

> Legal backing for the profession's standards! (McGregor, December 1985, p. 27).

Some Generalisations on the ASRB's Early History

Different observers may interpret the early history of the ASRB in different ways. Possibly those interpretations would be influenced by their circumstances and be coloured by the likely effect of the ASRB's activities upon their interests (see Appendix).

Members of the Ministerial Council had not displayed great interest in the activities of the ASRB; indeed Board representatives had not been invited to meet the Ministerial Council or address its meetings. By the end of 1985 the composition of the Ministerial Council had undergone around 30 changes since its formation in 1978, and in those circumstances its members (as lawyers) may have had little or no understanding of the background debate prior to the establishment of the Board, or the history of similar initiatives in other countries, or of the passions that can be aroused by choices of accounting rules. In these circumstances, the Ministerial Council's decisions about the role and functions of the Board may have owed much to the advice tendered by the public service (including the NCSC). Perhaps the Ministerial Council saw the apparent lack of productivity of the ASRB as politically hazardous, with no vote winning outcomes likely from any well publicised conflict with the accounting profession.

The staff of AARF constituted the interest group with most at stake during these episodes: they had a career commitment to the continuing dominance of the profession as the prime source of accounting rules in Australia. With a responsibility to brief members of AARF and the councils of the two accountancy bodies prior to negotiations with the ASRB, they were well placed to influence the tone and direction of those discussions. There is evidence that members of AARF were hostile to the notion of other bodies submitting standards to the ASRB (see Miles, 1986, p. 51; Boymal, 1986, p. 40). The ASRB's publication of Release 100 had been strongly opposed as 'pre-empting' AARF's own conceptual framework project. AARF promoted the idea that the task of redrafting standards for the ASRB had involved it in significant costs (a claim difficult to reconcile with a textual analysis of the changes actually made in those standards) and prevented it from addressing more pressing issues. An AARF staff member's speech had been the catalyst for press speculation about the lack of productivity of the ASRB (*Melbourne Herald*, 20 June 1985)—at a time when the Board was waiting in vain for the submission of redrafted standards. All things considered, AARF's employees may have been well pleased by the review of the ASRB's power late in 1985.

Other interest groups within the profession may have viewed the ASRB's efforts to secure tighter drafting of accounting standards with considerable concern. Tighter drafting was characterised as excessive legalism. Most criticisms of the 'legalistic' nature of the ASRB's drafting were made informally (though see Boymal, 1986, p. 39), with fears being expressed that accounting standards might become as lengthy and complicated as the 'tax act'—a comment which hardly withstood scrutiny, since the ASRB's drafting style was more parsimonious than AARF's, and the incorporation of an overriding 'statement of purpose' promised to avoid the necessity for detailed, loophole-closing clauses.

Regulatory Capture?

The general literature on 'regulation' is replete with allusions to the tendency for regulatory agencies to be 'captured' by interest groups and thereafter to operate in the interest of those elements of the community that the agencies were established to regulate. Mitnick (1980) offered the following summary:

> 'Capture' is said to occur if the regulated interest *controls* the regulation and the regulated agency; or if the regulated parties succeed in *co-ordinating* the regulatory body's activities with their activities so that their private interest is satisfied; or if the regulated party somehow manages to neutralize or ensure *nonperformance* (or mediocre performance) by the regulating body; or if in a subtle process of interaction with the regulators the regulated party succeeds

(perhaps not even deliberately) in *coopting* the regulators into seeing things from their own perspective and thus giving them the regulation they want; or if, quite independently of the formal or conscious desires of either the regulators or the regulated parties the basic structure of the *reward system* leads neither venal nor incompetent regulators inevitably to a community of interests with the regulated party (pp. 95–6).

The ASRB's early history can be considered a case study in regulatory capture. Consider the evidence:

—Before the Board was established, the accountancy bodies lobbied to ensure that the ASRB was not to have an independent research capability, was not to have an academic as chairman (since 'academic knowledge' was claimed to be of no relevance to its functions) and was to be provided with an administrative officer rather than a 'research director' (for the same reasons); all of these objectives were achieved.

—In 1984 the Board established its priorities on the basis of public submissions; by November 1985 its agenda represented the standards that AARF initimated it was prepared to submit; in December 1985 new ASRB procedures ensured that 'priorities would only be set after consultation with AARF' (*Sydney Morning Herald*, 10 December 1985).

—In 1984 the Board published a set of procedures (Release 200) which treated AARF and other interest groups on a similar footing. Accordingly, the Board refused to place a standard submitted (earlier) by the Australian Shareholders' Association on its agenda, on the ground that the Association had not provided all of the supporting documentation and an assignment of copyright as required by Release 200. Yet in November 1985 an ASRB advertisement announced that the Board would be reviewing a series of standards, yet to be submitted by AARF; the Board, while abandoning the requirements of Release 200 for AARF, continued to impose them on the Australian Shareholders' Association. In December 1985 the ASRB reported that it had adopted 'fast track' procedures for handling standards—but after six months had only applied these to submissions from AARF while it imposed more stringent requirements to submissions from other sources.

—The ASRB's Release 100, 'Criteria for the evaluation of accounting standards', indicated that it would not approve standards unless they were consistent with 'fully stated valid arguments derived from a set of explicit assumptions' and for that purpose tentatively adopted a series of

assumptions about the accounting process, indicating that in the light of experience it might amend those assumptions. Early in 1986 the Board approved several standards which *prima facie* were not consistent with previously-published assumptions (see Wise and Wise, 1986, pp. 26, 28; Currie, 1987, p. 61).

—In 1984 the ASRB indicated that it would issue periodic 'progress reports' about its activities—but issued only one (Release 300, December 1984). No statements were issued by the Board indicating why it had rejected the materiality standard or required changes in other standards submitted to it. But in December 1985 the staff of AARF were explaining the 'minor refinements' allegedly made by the profession to the 'handbook versions' of several standards prior to their 'formal approval by the ASRB' (McGregor, December 1985, p. 27).

—Prior to its establishment, it was suggested that the ASRB would be independent of the accountancy profession, and representative of a wide range of community interests. In 1984 the Board membership included nominees of the Australian Council of Trade Unions, and the Australian Shareholders' Association and (it is understood) the Australian Merchant Bankers Association. The 1986 membership consisted of: two former national presidents of the ASA (including one who was a current member of AARF's Accounting Standards Board); a former national president of the ICAA; a former state president of the ASA; a state councillor of the ASA (and former chairman of AARF), an academic active in committee work for the ASA—and only one other (the executive director of the Australian Associated Stock Exchanges).

During 1984–5 the profession had ensured the non-performance of the ASRB; by the beginning of 1986 the profession had managed to influence the procedures, the priorities and the output of the Board. It was controlling both the regulations and the regulatory agency; it had managed to achieve co-ordination of the ASRB's activities with AARF's activities; and it appears to have influenced new appointments so that virtually all members of the Board might reasonably be expected to have some community of interests with the professional associations. The ASRB had been 'captured' by the profession, within only 24 months.

The Political Process—Pluralism or Corporatism?

This examination of the ASRB's early history may also provide insights into the type of political processes undertaken in Australia in the development of accounting rules. Many (principally

North American) studies of standard setting have examined agency responses to written submissions to assess whether or not those agencies are responsive to that form of lobbying behaviour and whether or not they tend to place greater weight on the responses of particular interest groups. The authors of several of these studies have claimed that this evidence indicates that the standard setting process is 'pluralist'—a conclusion which must be greeted with more than a little scepticism, given the limited scope of such studies (i.e. examining only written submissions on matters which have permitted agenda entrance by bodies which had been established by a particular 'interest group'—the accountancy profession). However, in Australia the 'pluralist' ideal has been invoked in the context of discussions of rule making in accounting: for example, the NCSC had promoted the retention of both government-sponsored and profession-sponsored accounting rules as a means of permitting different interests to pursue their own priorities while limiting the capacity of particular interest groups to dominate the rule-development process—claiming that such an arrangement was 'valued in Australia's pluralistic society' (NCSC, 1983, p. 20).

The ASRB's membership and first published procedures seem to have been consistent with the pluralistic ideal: efforts had been made to ensure that the Board was widely representative, and that various individuals or interest groups were permitted to make submissions about priorities, to submit standards, to have opportunities to examine proposals and to express their views, perhaps through public hearings (see Release 200, paras. 4.2, 4.5, 4.6).

By the end of 1985, the regulation of accounting seems to have become more closely aligned to the form of interest group politics that has been labelled *neo-corporatism* (see Schmitter and Lehmbruch, 1979; Lehmbruch and Schmitter, 1982; Wilson, 1983). In 'neo-corporatist' arrangements, efforts to secure consensus are achieved through government recognition of interest groups and the granting to those groups of privileged access to the policy making process. The 'approval' process had been transformed by 'government' (through the Ministerial Council) effectively abrogating responsibility for the regulation of financial reporting to a private interest group: the accountancy profession. The Companies Act and Codes required conformity with 'approved accounting standards' and the profession had been given control of the 'approval' process. The profession had even been licensed to exploit commercially the sale of these government regulations.

Moreover, early in 1986 plans were announced for the abandonment of the major form of government involvement in accounting regulation. In 1982 the accountancy profession had campaigned

for the repeal of Schedule 7 of the Companies Act and proposed that this material should be included in accounting standards to be produced by a new board administered by the joint accountancy bodies. The Ministerial Council firmly rejected this proposal; the NCSC proceeded with its previously initiated review of Schedule 7—publishing a 'Green Paper' (NCSC, 1983), reviewing public responses, and drafting a revised version. Finally in February 1986 the Commonwealth Attorney-General's Department published a Schedule 7 'exposure draft', re-written by legislative draftsmen. There was widespread criticism of the drafting and the accountancy bodies again campaigned for the repeal of Schedule 7 (see *Australian Financial Review*, 11 March 1986)—advancing much the same arguments as they had put forward in 1982. Shortly afterwards the chairman of the Ministerial Council announced that the introduction of Schedule 7 would be delayed until it could be more plainly drafted (*Business Review Weekly*, 4 April 1986). Subsequently it was reported that the Ministerial Council 'agreed in principle' to the progressive transfer of Schedule 7 to approved accounting standards (*Financial Markets Briefing*, 29 August 1986). Thus, the proposal which had been so firmly rejected by the Ministerial Council in 1982 was accepted in 1986.

If fully implemented, the decision to abandon Schedule 7 in favour of standards to be approved by a professionally dominated ASRB would give a private interest group a monopoly over the regulation of financial reporting—and complete the transfer of responsibility for this area of social control from government to the profession.

ASRB in prospect

The domination of the ASRB by auditors and preparers of accounting reports, and the pursuit of policies which do not treat the submissions of other interest groups in an even-handed manner, seem likely to increase the probability of critical reactions to the activities of the ASRB and the way it frames its agenda. If it has been 'captured', it has also been *seen* to be captured. If the political processes reflected in the recent operations of the ASRB reflect the conscious adoption by government of a 'neo-corporatist' approach in the handling of interest groups, then it might be noted that corporatist arrangements may be unstable—as collaborating interest groups disengage themselves, or as other interest groups which were not recognised in a particular arrangement become more militant (see, e.g., Panitch, 1980, pp. 174–5).

The Board's rapid 'approval' in 1986 of many existing Australian Accounting Standards proceeded without any public explanation of the underlying rationale for those decisions—despite some lack of conformity of those standards with

284

the precepts and assumptions set forth in the ASRB's early Releases (see Wise and Wise, 1986; Currie, 1987). The Board's brief to develop a 'conceptual framework' might have been effective in giving some credibility to its deliberations. But for such a strategy to work, a standard-setting body must 'use the concepts and be seen to use them' (Storey, 1981, p. 651). In 1986, the Board was pursuing the exactly opposite strategy in relation to the basic assumptions: it was not using them, and was seen to be not using them (Wise and Wise, 1986; Currie, 1987). These actions have already led to the ASRB's recent policies being characterised as involving the expensive 'rubber stamping' of AARF standards.[7] The Board may provoke responses from the corporate sector over unpopular standards. So long as the ASRB reviews standards which have been on issue for some time, public submissions may well be 'informed' submissions. But 'fast track' procedures may mean that newly developed standards are approved before preparers, auditors and 'users' are fully aware of their technical features. Further, after a decade or more of relative inactivity, AARF has accelerated the promulgation of new rules: only 10 standards were on issue in January 1983 but the total had risen to 21 within three years. Moreover, AARF has turned to some contentious topics—so that the 'fast track' approval of new rules seems likely to lead to some critical responses from the corporate sector. The tacit acceptance by business interests of the 'corporatist' arrangement between government and the profession may enter a phase of instability.

It will be recalled that the ASRB was established in the wake of criticisms of the low level of compliance with the profession's accounting rules. It seems reasonable to suppose that there could be higher levels of compliance with 'approved' standards, given their greater authority and the Board's tighter drafting practices. But there are signs that some are trying to persuade the ASRB to make its drafting style more permissive. Late in 1985 AARF was submitting standards which were drafted so as to make compliance more discretionary. Early in 1986 representatives of the ASA were openly attacking the ASRB's drafting style.

When the ASRB's first standards were 'approved' in 1985 and the profession was actively negotiating to retain copyright in accounting standards, it was reported by AARF that drafting changes had been made 'by the profession' (McGregor, December 1985). One year later, the national president of the ASA (Bernard Wright) claimed that drafting changes had been made by

the ASRB—which in the process had translated standards 'from English into 'Bureaucratese'':

> As a result, we now have two standards on accounting matters, one authored (sic) by the profession in English, and one mutilated by Bureaucratese—a scenario for chaos (Wright, 1986), p. 13).

Wright also alleged that the ASRB's exposure and consultation practices were a waste of time and money: suggesting perhaps that the ASA nurtured hopes that the ASRB could be made to reduce the scope of its review. Paradoxically, the ICAA's journal in the same month carried an article criticising the ASRB for superficiality and inconsistency in its approval process, and claiming that several recently approved standards were both unpopular and technically deficient (Wise and Wise, 1986).

Whatever the merits of this criticism, the simultaneous publication in the Society and Institute journals of these vastly different commentaries seems to reflect the divergence of views within the Australian accounting community about the ASRB experiment. There appears to have been greater support for the venture from members of the auditing profession (who dominate the ICAA) than from accountants in industry and commerce (who dominate the ASA). The interaction of these interests seems likely to affect the future of the ASRB.

Those familiar with the history of standard setting ventures may doubt whether the ASRB will prove to be viable, unless it can establish intellectual credibility and some wider political legitimacy. Meantime the Ministerial Council's policies in making appointments to the ASRB seem modelled on those adopted for the USA's ill-fated Accounting Principles Board: a majority of members have been chosen on the basis of their 'leadership' roles within the profession rather than for their technical expertise.

But it would be a mistake to look at the ASRB in terms of US or UK institutional arrangements or political structures. In some respects, Australian society is less 'open' than in those countries—particularly with regard to relations between executive government or the public service and the community. The ASRB is a creature of a Cooperative Scheme between the Commonwealth and State governments; its role and functions are shaped by the unpublished decisions of the Ministerial Council, and the Scheme does not require a high level of public accountability by the bodies established and operating in terms of those arrangements.

It would also be a mistake to disregard the influence of key players in the evolution of policies about accounting regulation. Though not explored in detail in this paper, proposals for the establish-

---

[7]Address by A. E. F. Rofe to ICAA seminar, Sydney, 12 November 1986.

ment of the ASRB were largely the product of the influence of a NSW Attorney-General, Frank Walker, who had instigated a state based enquiry into accounting regulation (*Company Accounting Standards*, 1978). Later those proposals were supported by the foundation chairman of the NCSC, Leigh Masel, and an activist Commonwealth Attorney, Gareth Evans; decisions about the powers and duties of the proposed ASRB had been taken with the advice of senior public servants. The reshuffling of portfolios in both State and Commonwealth arenas, the retirement of Masel, and the reassignment of public servants led to a lack of continuity of involvement by leading participants in the government sector, and accordingly some volatility in policies. On the other hand, there was a high level of continuity in the leadership and staffing of the two accountancy bodies. In this environment, the profession found that when lobbying about the ASRB or the future of Schedule 7, it did not need to take 'no' for an answer.

In looking at the ASRB's prospects, it may be that a new set of key players will emerge, taking the ASRB in new directions (or proposing some wholesale review of the Co-operative Scheme). But meanwhile the potential of the ASRB to enhance the quality of information available to the securities market remains somewhat problematic—and of less concern to some parties than the locus of control over the regulation of financial reporting.

Appendix. A personal note

Since the author was a member of the ASRB during 1984–5, some readers may choose to regard the analysis as a jaundiced and biased account, and attribute uncomplimentary motives to the author ('sour grapes'?).

Writing in 1987, the author felt sufficiently detached from the events of 1984–5 to try to provide a balanced account of the early history of the ASRB. The aim was not 'to set the record straight' about the apparent inactivity of the ASRB during those years; nor to offer any assessment of the ASRB's performance during 1986–7 nor to criticise individuals. The main concern was to highlight the way that a set of standard setting arrangements designed to permit widespread consultation and participation were subverted by some likeable, well-meaning individuals who were trying only to promote the interests of their fellow accountants.

Overall, the paper reflects the belief that accounting regulation is too important to be left to the preparers and auditors of financial statements—and that political arrangements which require openness, consultation and widespread participation are both fragile and worth defending.

The author would be very happy if his interpretation of events in 1984–5 were proved wrong.

Indeed, 'regulatory capture' is not necessarily a permanent state, and putting the spotlight on capture relationships may itself encourage change. Recently the ASRB has been given a new chairman and three new members, through a nomination and selection process which remains obscure. The lack of openness about these selection processes is depressing; but the rumoured distress of some interest groups about their failure to secure the nominations of their choice makes one more optimistic about future developments.

A few words about citations in the paper. The author has felt bound to observe the ASRB's guidelines on confidentiality, and so has sought to describe events in terms of publicly available documents. Much more could have been said about personalities and events, but (as mentioned above) there was no wish to criticise individuals.

Selected references

——First Interim Report to the Standing Committee of Attorneys-General on Accounts and Audit, Company Law Advisory Committee, Melbourne, 1970.

——Report of the Accounting Standards Review Committee, *Company Accounting Standards*, NSW Government Printer, May 1978.

——'Accounting Standards Review Committee', *Chartered Accountant in Australia*, March 1978, p. 9.

——'Government Involvement in Accounting Standards', *Chartered Accountant in Australia*, April 1979, p. 5.

Accounting Standards Review Board, *Criteria for the Evaluation of Accounting Standards*, Release 100, February 1985.

Accounting Standards Review Board, *Procedures for the Approval of Accounting Standards*, Release 200, February 1985.

Accounting Standards Review Board, *Progress Report*, Release 300, December 1984.

Bishop, J., 'A Challenging Year', *Chartered Accountant in Australia*, December 1978, p. 3.

Bosch, H., 'Profit is a Measure', address to AAANZ 1985 Conference, Sydney.

Boymal, D., 'The Setting of Accounting Standards—Threats and Opportunities', paper presented at AAANZ 1985 Conference, Sydney.

Boymal, D., 'Accounting Standards: The Profession's Spectator Sport', *Chartered Accountant in Australia*, February 1986, pp. 36–40.

Bromwich, M., *The Economics of Standard Setting*, Prentice-Hall, 1985.

Currie, C., 'Should Cash Statements Replace Funds Statements?', *Chartered Accountant in Australia*, March 1987, pp. 61–4.

Edwards, B., 'Accounting Standards—the Long Hard Road to Approval', *Chartered Accountant in Australia*, June 1985, p. 6.

Hines, R. D., 'Economic Consequences of Accounting Standards: A Good Reason for a Representative ASRB', *Chartered Accountant in Australia*, July 1983, pp. 24–27.

Lehmbruch, G. and P. C. Schmitter (eds.), *Patterns of Corporatist Policy Making*, Sage, London, 1982.

McGregor, W. J., 'Accounting Standards Update', Proceedings of the Australian Society of Accountants Victorian Division 1985 State Congress, June 1985.

McGregor, W. J., 'New ASRB Approved Accounting Standards—Legal Backing for the Profession's Standards!', *Chartered Accountant in Australia*, December 1985, pp. 27–8.

Miles, J., 'Accounting Standards—in Retrospect and Prospect', *Australian Accountant*, March, 1986, pp. 62–71.

Mitnick, B. M., *The Political Economy of Regulation*, Columbia University Press, 1980.

National Companies and Securities Commission, *Financial Reporting Requirements of the Companies Act and Codes*, Australian Government Publishing Service, 1983.

Panitch, L., 'Recent Theorizations of Corporatism: Reflections on a Growth Industry', *British Journal of Sociology*, June 1980, pp. 159–87.

Peirson, G. and A. L. Ramsay, 'A Review of Regulation of Financial Reporting in Australia', *Company and Securities Law Journal*, November 1983, pp. 286–300.

Prosser, V., 'Accounting Standards Review Board', *Chartered Accountant in Australia*, February 1983, p. 10.

Schmitter, P. C. and G. Lehmbruch (eds.), *Trends Towards Corporatist Intermediation*, Sage, London, 1979.

Storey, R. K., 'Conditions Necessary for Developing a Conceptual Framework', *Financial Analysts Journal*, May/June 1981, pp. 51–58.

Vincent, G., 'Do We Need an Accounting Standards Review Board?', *Australian Accountant*, January/February 1982, pp. 18–20.

Wilson, F. L., 'Interest Groups and Politics in Western Europe: the Neo-Corporatist Approach', *Comparative Politics*, October 1983, pp. 105–23.

Wise, T. and V. Wise, 'ASRB Under Pressure', *Chartered Accountant in Australia*, July 1986, pp. 26–9.

Wright, B., 'A View of the Future', *Australian Accountant*, July 1986, pp. 12–14.

[4]

Accounting, Organizations and Society, Vol. 19, No. 1, pp. 83–109, 1994.
Printed in Great Britain

0361–3682/94 $6.00+.00

OUTLINING REGULATORY SPACE: AGENDA ISSUES AND THE FASB*

JONI J. YOUNG

Anderson School of Management, University of New Mexico

Abstract

Research examining the process of accounting change has focussed upon dramatic changes such as the rise of discounted cash flow analysis. However, much of accounting change centers around recognition issues and serves to expand and enhance the domain of accrual accounting. This paper employs three studies (accounting for loan fees, leases and nonprofit organizations) to examine the process of enacting change in accounting recognition practices. The paper follows the construction of accounting issues as accounting problems within a regulatory space, and the subsequent construction of these problems as appropriate for standard-setting action. The study employs a regulatory space metaphor and a "logic of appropriateness" to examine the complex processes through which accounting change occurs.

Several scholars have examined the process of innovation in accounting practice including the rise of discounted cash flow analysis (Miller, 1991), the rise and decline of value added accounting (Burchell *et al*, 1985), the production of product costs (Hopwood, 1987), the production of standard costs and budgets (Miller & O'Leary, 1987), and the emergence of an accounting standard-setting group (Robson, 1991). In contrast to these major changes in accounting practice, much of accounting change may appear less innovative and more mundane. Changes in accounting practices in the financial accounting domain often center around recognition issues — when to recognize assets, liabilities, revenues and expenses. Changes in these practices may require the reporting entity to recognize "liabilities" previously excluded from the balance sheet, to delay the recognition of income or to hasten the recognition of expense. These accounting changes typically expand and enhance the domain of accrual accounting (and often historical cost accounting). The processes underlying these types of accounting changes remain largely unexamined.

In the United States, the Financial Accounting Standards Board (FASB) is perceived as the entity responsible for enacting changes in accounting practices. The FASB maintains a technical agenda of accounting projects that will eventually alter existing recognition practices. The addition of an accounting problem to the technical agenda of the FASB is a necessary condition for the subsequent issuance of accounting standards. Indeed, FASB chairman Dennis Beresford has indicated that "setting the agenda may be the most important single activity of the Board" (Previts, 1991, p. 71). Financial accounting standards have far-reaching economic consequences from their potential redistributive effects (Zeff, 1978) as well as social consequences from the potential use of accounting reports as instruments of social

---
* This paper has benefited greatly from the comments of Ted O'Leary, Orace Johnson, Tony Cebuhar, Ivan Bull, Ruth Hines, Dean Neu, the participants of the Third Interdisciplinary Perspectives in Accounting Conference, the University of New Mexico accounting workshop and two anonymous reviewers as well as from comments at various other workshops. Any errors are mine. I wish to thank the many individuals in accounting practice and at the FASB who gave freely of their time to talk with me. Finally, I wish to acknowledge the dissertation support provided by Deloitte and Touche.

control (Zeff, 1978) and from the subtle reinforcement by accounting standards of which things are "worth" capturing in accounting reports (Burchell *et al.*, 1980; Tinker *et al.*, 1982; Hines, 1988, 1991).

This paper explores the processes through which changes in financial accounting practices occur or fail to occur, by examining three accounting issues (accounting for loan fees, leases and nonprofit organizations) that were considered for inclusion on the FASB technical agenda. This paper emphasizes the construction of accounting issues as accounting problems and the interpretation of actions as appropriate by the accounting standard-setter within the broader space in which accounting regulation occurs.

REGULATORY SPACE

Although the formation of the FASB technical agenda is an important element of accounting standard-setting and the processes of changing financial accounting practices, it would be a serious mistake to study the emergence of issues onto this agenda by focussing solely upon the internal dynamics of the FASB. Such a study would presume that strict organizational boundaries can be drawn between the FASB and its environment. Such a study would presume that it is the decisions of the FASB that are most "important" in studying the issues included on its agenda. Such a study would ignore that FASB decisions are embedded in social and historical contexts, and would assume that accounting "problems" are obvious and uncontested.

Accounting and accounting change are inter-related with events occurring elsewhere (Burchell *et al.*, 1985; Miller, 1991; Robson, 1991). The FASB (often thought of as the primary change agent for U.S. financial accounting) resides within an uneasy institutional nexus located between the accounting profession and the state and operates within a broader social and economic environment. The FASB both responds to this environment and contributes to changes in the environment.

Although events and practices intertwine in the emergence of a project onto the FASB agenda, these events and practices may not have been directed specifically towards this outcome. The initiation of accounting change may emerge from the unanticipated consequences of actions or events and at the intersection of disparate practices that give rise to requests for accounting change. To understand the emergence of issues onto the FASB agenda, one must look beyond the boundaries of this organization and examine the broader space in which the FASB operates and accounting regulation occurs.

This paper adopts the perspective that accounting standards are produced within a regulatory space (Hancher & Moran, 1989). Regulatory space is an analytical construct that is defined "by the range of regulatory issues subject to public decision" (Hancher & Moran, p. 277). The shape of this space and the allocation of power within the space are affected by the political and legal setting, history, organizations and markets (Hancher & Moran, p. 271). Hancher and Moran develop this concept as a means to summarize and integrate a set of studies about economic regulation and suggest that regulation can be best understood through the use of regulatory space.

Regulatory space bears some resemblance to the "accounting constellation" usefully employed to examine the emergence of value added accounting (Burchell *et al.*, 1985), the rise of discounted cash flow in capital expenditure analysis (Miller, 1991) and the formation of a British accounting standard-setting group (Robson, 1991). This accounting constellation is formed by the intertwining of forms of knowledge, institutions, economic and administrative processes, systems of norms and measurements, and classification techniques (Burchell *et al.*, 1985, p. 400).

In this paper, regulatory space is an abstract conceptual space within which changes in the recognition and measurement practices of financial accounting occur. This space is constructed by people, organizations and events that act upon accounting and accounting practices. Regulatory space encompasses the set of accounting problems for which a rationale for standard-setting action can be developed. It is within this space that the process of change in financial accounting practices occurs.

Regulatory space is an arena where the accounting standard-setter issues standards that in the FASB's words "refine" and "improve" the financial reports of the organization. Regulatory space is not a space within which dramatic changes in accounting practices occur. Instead, it is a space for tinkering with existing practices and financial statements. However, this tinkering is significant given the social and economic consequences arising from accounting standards. It is within regulatory space that the fundamental claims made for accounting and accounting reports are defended, maintained and promoted.

Regulatory space is a very particular arena of accounting change in which the accounting standard-setter or FASB is expected to participate and alter the accounting practices of individual companies. This is the space within which the accounting standard-setter requires, permits and proscribes specific accounting measurement methods and recognition practices. Because these accounting standards and practices highlight certain features of an organization and render an organization calculable by transforming it into material traces, regulatory space is a highly contested space. (See for example Latour, 1987; Rose, 1990; and Miller & Rose, 1990, for a discussion of the importance of such traces.) These material traces created in regulatory space are the financial reports of an entity including its balance sheet and income statement. It is within regulatory space that the content of these reports, the timing of the recognition of profits and the amounts of the carrying values of assets and liabilities are decided. Through the production of accounting standards, the participants acting within regulatory space develop and direct the methods of producing material traces for organizations. If accounting reports and profits are score-keeping mechanisms, then regulatory space is the abstract locale in which the rules for keeping score (measuring profitability) are selected.

The use of the regulatory space metaphor recognizes the complexity of the standard-setting and agenda formation processes and serves as a broad theoretical lens to focus upon the issue of agenda formation. Several benefits arise from the choice of this theoretical lens. First, because regulatory space is "a space, it is available for occupation" (Hancher & Moran, 1989, p. 277). This lens forces the researcher to ask: who is involved in the process? The researcher must look beyond the organizational boundaries of the FASB and consider the roles of other actors including the SEC, auditors and preparers of financial statements.

By focussing upon accounting "issues" rather than upon the operations of a regulatory organization such as the FASB, this research recognizes that accounting change and the shaping of demands for accounting change occur both inside and outside the boundaries marked by the FASB. This lens emphasizes the interconnectedness of the FASB with other actors and other organizations as well as the importance of the broader social and economic environment. The FASB is not acting in a vacuum.

Second, using this lens, the researcher does not assume the dominance of interests as explanations for the actions of the FASB and other groups. Instead, no one-to-one correspondence may exist between the "demands" of various groups or entities for accounting change and the issues included on the agenda of the FASB. Demands for accounting change may be unfocussed, lacking in specificity, and ambiguous. Pressures from many institutional and policy arenas impinge on accounting and increase the difficulty of ascribing accounting change to a single interest imperative (Hopwood, 1989, p. 151; Burchell *et al.*, 1985). Interests are themselves constructed and interpreted in particular situations (Hindess, 1986). Interests do not unambiguously define the actions of actors involved in the regulatory process nor do interests inhere to actors as a result of their membership in a particular category (Hindess, 1982, 1986). Instead, these actors interpret, construct and reconstruct their interests while constructing and linking problems, actions and solutions.

Finally, this lens permits the researcher to "lighten the weight of causality" (Foucault, 1981) and to provide explanations in terms of conditions of possibility rather than employing causal explanations that omit the political, cultural and technical conditions that create a "space" in which change becomes possible (Miller, 1991). The U.S. mainstream accounting models that employ a supply and demand metaphor (Watts & Zimmerman, 1979; Johnson & Messier, 1982) implicitly stress the importance of disruptive events in upsetting a regulatory equilibrium. However, the implicit assignment of causality in these models to specific event types is overly simplistic. These models cannot help us understand why events that exhibit surface similarities are "disruptive" in some circumstances but not others, nor can these models help us to understand why some accounting issues emerge onto agendas in the apparent absence of disruptive events. Several researchers have questioned the usefulness of simple deterministic models to understand complex processes as they omit much of the institutional structure through which politics (March & Olsen, 1984, 1989), accounting (Burchell *et al.*, 1980, 1985; Hopwood, 1987; Lowe *et al.*, 1983; March, 1987), and organizations (Meyer & Scott, 1983) operate and occur. The metaphor of regulatory space demands that one pay closer attention to the actors and institutions that contribute to the processes of accounting change.

In this paper, the process of accounting change is seen to consist of several stages (that may occur simultaneously or sequentially). Accounting conditions must be constructed as accounting problems. Accounting problems must be constructed as appropriate for standard-setting action. Solutions must be constructed as appropriate resolutions to particular accounting problems. While this construction and linkage occurs in regulatory space, the actions of the standard-setter and others are constrained by expectations that exist about their role and purpose. These expectations are drawn upon by the standard-setter to construct an "appropriate" response to constructed accounting problems. This paper argues that the standard-setter employs a "logic of appropriateness" (March & Olsen, 1989) in constructing responses to accounting problems. It is to the logic of appropriateness that we now turn.

THE CONSTRUCTION OF APPROPRIATE PROBLEMS

The issues that emerge onto the agenda of the FASB are those classified as "problems". However, within this perspective accounting problems are not seen to be simply "there", rather they must be constructed as problems by participants in regulatory space. The changes in accounting practices enacted through FASB accounting standards are typically justified by references to getting the accounting "right". These changes are depicted as facilitating accounting progress and allowing accounting to become what it should be (Hopwood, 1987), as well as eliminating what accounting should not be.

Central to getting accounting "right" and eliminating what is "wrong" is the issue of diversity in practice. In accounting standard after accounting standard, and in statement after statement, the FASB explains and thereby justifies its decisions to undertake a particular accounting project by reference to diversity in accounting practice. For example, because of "the diversity in practice among the different types of financial institutions making loans" (Agenda Decisions, 1984), the FASB justified adding a loan fees project to its agenda. Because "inconsistencies exist in practice and in the authoritative specialized industry literature" (FASB, 1987), the FASB justified adding to its agenda a project on accounting for nonprofit organizations. Despite such explanations and justifications, however, I argue that diversity in practice is a condition not a problem and the FASB's explanation of the agenda decision is at best incomplete. Diversity in practice becomes constructed as a problem within a particular intersection of events, conditions and demands placed upon accounting and accounting reports.

This process of constructing diversity in practice as a problem may be evidenced by the fact that the FASB does not interpret diversity in accounting practice as a problem in all situations nor advocate the elimination of all such diversity.[1] Instead, the FASB emphasizes that only certain variations in accounting practice should be eliminated to ensure that "like" things will look alike and "unlike" things will look different (FASB submission in U.S. House, 1985a, p. 214). I suggest that diversity in practice becomes a "problem" only when it is judged to clash with such accounting claims as relevance, reliability and representational faithfulness. Despite the problematic nature of these claims, they nevertheless play an important role in constructing accounting conditions as accounting problems within regulatory space. These claims about accounting and accounting reports are reiterated in the conceptual framework of the FASB. Thus, "good" accounting information is claimed to balance the characteristics of relevance, information useful in making economic decisions (FASB, 1980, para. 47), and reliability, information relatively free from error that represents what it purports to represent and possesses the quality of representational faithfulness (FASB, 1980, para. 59).

Actors in regulatory space draw upon these accounting claims and, particularly, the accounting claim of representational faithfulness to justify the construction of accounting conditions such as diversity in practice as problems. This construction occurs within highly visible arenas amid historically specific contexts and situations. Thus, diversity in practice is used to justify the inclusion of projects on the FASB agenda and representational faithfulness is used to justify the designation of diversity in practice as a problem.

The emergence of projects on accounting for loan fees and accounting for depreciation and contributions by nonprofit organizations onto the FASB agenda provides examples of the importance of attending to the process and circumstances by which an accounting condition such as diversity in practice becomes constructed as an accounting problem that requires the attention of the FASB. Similarly, the case of leases illustrates how a former "solution" may become constructed as an accounting problem.

However, constructing an accounting issue as an accounting problem is not sufficient to ensure the emergence of a project onto the FASB agenda; not all accounting problems result in FASB standard-setting projects. Accounting problems must also be constructed and interpreted as appropriate for FASB standard-setting action.

The studies contained in this paper suggest the relevance of a "logic of appropriateness" (March & Olsen, 1989) in understanding the emergence of issues onto the FASB standard-setting agenda. This logic involves "fulfilling the obligations of a role in a situation, and so of trying to determine the imperatives of holding a position" (p. 161). The emphasis is upon upholding duties and obligations rather than selecting outcomes to promote self-interested behavior. Behavior is driven by rules, and actions are matchings of situations to the demands of a position (p. 23). Ambiguity is resolved by "trying to clarify the rules, make distinctions, determine what the situation is and what definition 'fits'" (p. 161). Thus, rules provide "good" reasons for actions. For March and Olsen, rules include "the routines, procedures, conventions, role, strategies, organizational form, and technologies around which political activity is constructed" (p. 22).

Within this framework, one understands the FASB response to constructed accounting problems as a process of interpreting the situation and matching an appropriate action to the demands of this situation. In this way, the

---

[1] See Merino & Coe (1978) for a historical perspective on uniformity in accounting practice.

actions of the FASB are seen to arise from "duties and obligations rather than anticipatory, consequential decision-making" (March & Olsen, 1989, p. 23). The process of agenda formation and constructing standard-setting actions as appropriate within regulatory space is heavily mediated by language and the ways in which the participants discuss an accounting issue and compare it to other issues.

Because the FASB is not the only actor in regulatory space and is neither of the profession nor of the state, it may experience considerable "difficulties in establishing a mandate for action that is accepted as legitimate by significant groups" (Hopwood, 1983a, p. 13). Because the standard-setting group cannot appeal to the traditions of the profession or to the prerogatives of the state, a different rationale for action may be needed (Hopwood, 1983b, p. 172). Thus, the logic of appropriateness may be especially important for understanding the actions of an organization such as the FASB that resides in an uneasy authority position.

I believe that deploying the logic of appropriateness as an analytical lens provides several benefits. First, the actions of the FASB must be perceived as consistent with the constructed contemporary role and purpose of an accounting standard-setting organization. Institutionalized expectations attach to particular roles such as the standard-setter and these expectations create obligations that bind the actor. The actions of the FASB must be interpreted as consistent with the expectations held by the other actors in regulatory space about the role and purpose of the FASB. In other words, the FASB must be seen as exercising a logic of appropriateness. By upholding norms and signalling one's willingness to play by the rules, social action can proceed even in changeable settings such as political organizations and regulatory space (Biggart & Hamilton, 1984, p. 548).

The procedures followed by the FASB in promulgating accounting standards may reflect the expectations of participants in regulatory space. (See for example Johnson & Solomons, 1984; Dyckman, 1988.) These expectations limit the role of the FASB to promulgate accounting standards that are interpreted by participants as somehow "improving" financial accounting and reporting in a fashion consistent with accounting claims. For example, the Wheat Committee (AICPA, 1972, p. 20) stated that the most important aspect of accounting standards is "whether they contribute to progress in achieving the objectives of financial accounting and reporting" and, by inference, sustaining the accounting claims contained in the conceptual framework. (Also see Financial Accounting Foundation, 1977; Beresford, 1989, p. 24; Chandler, 1990.)

Second, this "logic" suggests the importance of expectations and the ways that these expectations may be interpreted to limit the types of actions that are seen as appropriate for a standard-setter to undertake. The studies in the following sections suggest that the emergence of agenda projects is based on an interpretation of which projects are appropriate for the FASB to undertake and an interpretation of when expectations exist about the need for FASB action. The studies show that agenda formation includes the interpretation of expectations about the role and purpose of standard-setters and is not a simple response to "pressures" from various interested actors. Agenda formation is more than a FASB effort to promote organizational survival by reacting to constituent demands.

Finally, the necessity for standard-setter interpretations suggests that a variety of responses by the standard-setting organization is possible and may be interpreted as appropriate. The following studies suggest that agenda formation is more than a yes/no action and illustrate various responses to expectations about the role of the standard-setter. While these studies do not exhaustively detail the set of responses available to the standard-setter and other actors, they demonstrate that agenda formation is a complex process.

As illustrated by the leases study, agenda formation was seen to be used by the FASB to argue that no feasible solutions exist and to develop a rationale for inaction. As illustrated by the nonprofit organizations study, agenda formation was seen to be used to increase the scope of FASB operations while enacting expectations that the FASB be the standard-setter for all organizations. As illustrated by each of these studies and accounting for loan fees, agenda formation was seen to be used to develop arguments by the FASB and other members of regulatory space to suggest the necessity of altering accounting practices in specific situations.

However, a logic of appropriateness does not preclude self-interested actions. Rather, it does limit the circumstances and situations within which self-interested actions may be construed as consistent with the expectations of other actors in regulatory space. Further, this logic does not deny the possibility that actors such as the FASB may (over time) alter the expectations of other actors and expand or diminish the set of "appropriate" actions.

The three studies contained in the following sections examine the emergence of issues onto the technical agenda of the FASB. These studies illustrate the operation of regulatory space in constructing existing accounting conditions as accounting problems and constructing accounting standard-setting action as appropriate for these problems. These studies suggest that accounting claims and expectations about the role and purpose of the standard-setter are important elements in the operation of regulatory space. Accounting claims play an important role in constructing accounting conditions as accounting problems. Expectations about the standard-setter are critical in con-

structing accounting problems as appropriate for standard-setting action. The studies of agenda formation draw upon regulatory space as an organizing framework and begin to develop its theoretical contours.[2]

ACCOUNTING FOR LOAN FEES

Background

With the advent of the Reagan era and increased deregulation, the financial industry underwent significant changes. Deregulation blurred the sharp distinctions that had existed between the banking, savings and loan and securities industries (AICPA, 1981, 1982; U.S. Senate, 1983b; McQuade, 1984) and increased the competition for capital and deposits among these institutions. These changes also heightened interest in the comparability of accounting practices between the various financial institutions (McQuade, 1984; AICPA, 1981) and occurred in a hostile economic climate. In the early 1980s, interest rates reached record high levels and threatened the viability of many financial institutions particularly the savings and loan industry. In 1981, the Federal Home Loan Bank Board (FHLBB) Chairman reported that 25% of savings and loan institutions were not viable in an economic environment with high interest rates (Washington Post, 15 July 1981). In 1982, the FHLBB Chairman reported that 80% of savings and loans were unprofitable and stated that these entities were "experiencing their worst period since the Depression" (U.S. House, 1982a, pp.

[2] These studies were developed using a variety of data sources including confidential interviews. The author conducted these interviews with participants in the standard-setting process during the summer and fall of 1990. These participants included members of the FASB, the FASB staff, and the Securities Exchange Commission staff as well as the members of other organizations that interact more frequently with the FASB (e.g. the Accounting Standards Executive Committee of the American Institute of Certified Public Accountants, the Committee on Corporate Reporting of the Financial Executives Institute, and the Management Accounting Practices Committee of the National Association of Accountants). These interviews were taped and transcribed by the author. The following studies include quotes from the interviews. These quotes have been edited (as indicated by [] or ...) to conform the oral English of the interview to written standards of English. References to FASB members include both FASB members and FASB staff. Documentary and secondary data sources were also employed. The documentary data consisted of FASB documents such as meeting summaries (minutes), exposure drafts, discussion memoranda, concepts statements, standards and invitations to comment; Financial Accounting Standards Advisory Committee documents and U.S. Congressional hearing transcripts and documents. The secondary data sources included newspaper and business periodical articles on the FASB and the accounting issues included in this study.

201–213). Based upon concerns about the economic health of the banking and savings and loan industries, Congress held several hearings to examine the competitive and economic conditions of these industries (e.g. U.S. House, 1981b, 1982b; U.S. Senate, 1981a, b) and to discuss ways to assist these entities (e.g. U.S. House, 1981a).

In this climate of economic distress and deregulation, Congress lessened restrictions on the activities and asset powers of financial institutions. Even so, financial regulators continued to employ solvency and capital requirements to monitor the "health" of these institutions and to provide a basis for regulatory intervention. Financial accounting was a significant input in assessing whether an entity met these capital and solvency requirements. In response to the difficult economic environment, federal regulators such as the FHLBB altered the accounting measurements used to assess compliance with regulatory capital and solvency requirements. To minimize the number of "sick" classifications, the FHLBB began to permit savings and loan institutions to accelerate income recognition and to delay loss recognition (Baker, 1981; Auerbach & McCall, 1985; U.S. Senate, 1990; White, 1991). Savings and loans also increased recorded income and "improved" the appearance of their income statements by originating risky loans and recognizing immediately as income the fees received for originating these loans (Berton, 1985; Rudnitzky & Sloan, 1984).

Participants in regulatory space

The American Institute of Certified Public Accountants (AICPA) and the FASB viewed the actions of the FHLBB and savings and loan organizations as accounting gimmickry designed to conceal the "true" financial condition of these organizations (Deloitte, Haskins & Sells, 1981; Kirk, 1982, 1987). For example, FASB chairman, Donald Kirk condemned FHLBB actions that permitted the deferral of losses on the sale of low-yield mortgages:

> I also recognize that bookkeeping entries do not make an S&L any more solvent or any less solvent than it otherwise would be. It should be the overriding purpose of a statement of financial position to measure and report real world phenomena *as faithfully and as factually* as possible. If the FHLBB believes its net worth requirements or other solvency tests may no longer be valid, it should consider revising those tests. ... But revising the financial statements so that the tests are not violated, in my opinion, does little for the credibility of the S&Ls or financial reporting in general (in Deloitte, Haskins & Sells, 1981, p. 2, emphasis added).

The AICPA and FASB began acting to eliminate these perceived abuses. In 1981, the AICPA issued a notice to practitioners directing auditors not to apply new FHLBB guidelines on loan fee recognition in external financial statements. In May 1982, the FASB staff began to monitor the accounting implications of Congressional proposals to aid the savings and loan industry and the Board directed the staff to prepare a discussion paper analyzing issues affecting savings institutions (FASB minutes, 5 May 1982). The AICPA's Accounting Standards Executive Committee worked to prepare an issues paper relating to accounting for loan fees and urged the FASB to undertake an agenda project on this topic. A FASB member later noted:

> We had a meeting ... with a cross-section of representatives for the AICPA banking committee, S&L committee and all the rest of the financial institution area ... We said look we can't put a project like accounting for all financial institutions on the agenda. But, if there was anything we could do that would improve financial reporting in the area, what would it be? And [they] absolutely overwhelmingly said you got to clean up the loan fee mess. You've got to clean up the guys that are out there just front-ending income and the only way they are remaining solvent is doing that ... [e2,1].

Others also expressed particular concerns about loan fee accounting. Federal bank regulators indicated that neither GAAP nor regulatory accounting principles specifically addressed the recognition of fee income by banks and substantial discretion had resulted in diversity in practice (U.S. Senate, 1983a, p. 257). The U.S. General Accounting Office also voiced concerns:

Banks can appear more profitable *than they actually are* when loans are rescheduled and large rescheduling fees are posted to current income. This result is especially anomalous when loan portfolios have typically become riskier and less profitable (U.S. Senate 1983a, p. 22, emphasis added).

In 1983, Congress directed the Federal Financial Institution Examination Council in Title IX of Public Law 98–181 to develop income recognition rules to be used in recording fees from restructuring international loans in regulatory reports.[3] When asked about the relevance of congressional attention to the emergence of a project on loan fees on the FASB agenda, a FASB member commented:

... that was a factor at the time. And it was one of those things that gives a topic a high profile which is one of the things that gets them on our agenda, if they begin to stir interest broadly and particularly Congressional concerns [b3a].

Auditors (as represented by the AICPA), financial regulators, the General Accounting Office, Congress and the FASB all expressed concerns about the interest in the accounting for loan fees and all occupied regulatory space. Although the AICPA, Congress and the FASB indicated that diversity in practice was a problem, their primary concerns appeared to center on whether some of the accounting practices for loan fees "misrepresented" the financial condition of the organization. These concerns about misrepresentation were especially acute in light of the precarious financial health of many savings and loan and other financial institutions. Thus, practices that increased recorded income and maintained required solvency and capital requirements became labelled as "abusive" (Deloitte, Haskins & Sells, 1981; Kirk, 1982, 1987; General Accounting Office in U.S. Senate, 1983a; Baker, 1981; Auerbach & McCall, 1985; Berton, 1985;

Rudnitzky & Sloan, 1984). In recalling the reasons underlying the decision to examine loan fee accounting, a FASB member discussed the accounting practices used in the savings and loan industry:

I've forgotten the dates now but the crisis [in S&Ls] has been going on for quite a long time and one of the factors that was of concern was the fact that they had been taking the points, mortgage points, up front and taking them into income immediately. And we didn't agree that that was proper. ... There was a lot of concern at that time about bad accounting in the S&L industry and this one seemed to be getting more flagrant as time went on and involved a lot of money. ... But it was really the S&L crisis and the concern that they were taking in a lot more income than *they had really earned* [b3, emphasis added].

The accounting practices in a highly visible and closely monitored segment of the economy were considered to conceal the "true" picture and therefore contradict a central claim contained in the conceptual framework. Congress, AICPA, the General Accounting Office and others called into question the validity of the claim of representational faithfulness for the accounting reports of financial institutions. Some of the accounting practices used to construct these reports were labelled as abusive and misleading and considered unreliable and perhaps not relevant for economic and financial decision-making.[4] These accounting practices were judged to fall short of the claims made for accounting. If one accepts these claims, then financially unstable entities should be depicted as unprofitable and accounting practices should emphasize and highlight this instability. Instead, some accounting practices for loan fees increased the recorded profits of some financially unstable institutions. One financial article described these practices: "Taking points into income as they are paid has helped many a thrift ... report healthy profits even as it was going

---

[3] These bills also addressed nonaccounting issues and the accounting for loan loss reserves, a topic that did not emerge onto the FASB agenda.

[4] The business press also questioned the accounting practices of financial institutions (e.g. S&L's Various Strategies, 1984; Baker, 1981).

down the tubes" (Hayes, 1986, p. 97). Within this perspective, the accounting practices for loan fees failed to emphasize sufficiently the "badness" of these entities. In this way, diversity in practice for loan fees was constructed as abusive accounting that required the attention of the standard-setter. Diversity in practice here may be seen to represent a shorthand to describe an intersection of events, conditions, and demands upon accounting that suggest the "need" to eliminate accounting alternatives. As another FASB member commented:

> ... you have to think about that one [loan fees addition] in the context of S&L problems in general and I think a recognition on the Board's part that it was an industry that was full of abuses and gimmicks and the regulators were fostering it. So we would have been very sensitive to ... issues that were in the S&L area [o7a].

An "appropriate" action

In February 1984, the FASB members voted to add to the FASB technical agenda a project to address the accounting for loan fees because "of concerns expressed to it that current guidance provides for different accounting for similar transactions by the various kinds of entities in the financial services industry" (FASB, 1984a, p. i). This diversity in practice was constructed as a problem within a set of concerns about whether some of the accounting practices for loan fees "misrepresented" the financial viability of financial institutions. Questions about misrepresentation provided the FASB with a rationale for action to eliminate the diversity in practice among various types of financial institutions. No single event "triggered" the emergence of an agenda project. Instead, general concerns about the financial viability of financial organizations coupled with concerns that management and regulators were employing accounting to conceal the "ill-health" of these organizations were combined to construct diversity in practice as an accounting "problem". A FASB

member interpreted the decision to undertake the loan fee project as follows:

> This was an area where we knew the criticism would be severe because the practices were questionable. In some instances, they were far from reality. The whole notion that it really wasn't a yield adjustment that it was something different. [That it] was really compensation for doing something else was always very suspect. We, I think, knew well here that the S&L thing was just going to get worse and then there would be finger pointing. We knew that to at least demonstrate we were on top of things this was an issue we had to deal with [o8a].

The savings and loan industry and its then powerful lobbying arm, the League of Savings Institutions, opposed the FASB decision to examine accounting for loan fees. The association periodical *Savings Institutions* closely followed the progress of the AICPA issues paper on accounting for loan fees and the subsequent FASB agenda project. These articles predicted dire consequences to arise from any action by the FASB to change accounting for loan fees (AICPA Issues Paper, 1984; FASB Loan Fee Stance, 1986). Financial organizations (particularly the savings and loan industry) undertook a lobbying campaign to mitigate the extent of changes arising from the FASB project. A FASB member later commented:

> ... but we put it [the agenda] on because we thought there was something abusive going on and we knew the response would be very strong because some of them [savings and loan institutions] really needed that income to maintain their capital standards [b5].

These entities responded to the subsequent invitation to comment and exposure draft in large numbers. In their comment letters, many organizations claimed that changes in accounting practices for loan fees would harm their operations. Other respondents predicted that financial institutions would simply change their operations to avoid the impact of changes in accounting rules.[5] The executives in savings

---

[5] In order to maintain reported profitability levels after the FASB issued its standard on accounting for loan fees, portfolio lenders and mortgage bankers engaged in transactions more influenced by favorable short-term accounting results than long-term economic considerations (Parks, 1988).

and loan organizations attempted to occupy regulatory space and challenged, in a variety of ways, the appropriateness of FASB actions.

Despite this vocal opposition, the FASB presented itself as working to improve financial accounting and reporting even if that meant changing predominant accounting practices of financial institutions and ignoring their intensive lobbying efforts.[6] They could, however, do this because of the support of other influential occupants of regulatory space. Business periodicals published FASB staff comments that presented the staff as antagonistic to the savings and loan industry and striving to end the "bad" accounting practices in this industry. The staff evinced little sympathy for the predicted economic consequences of the proposed accounting changes and stressed the importance of getting the accounting "right":

> Those arguments are completely irrelevant. The Board is here for the purpose of improving financial reporting, and if it tells you your baby's ugly, then your baby's ugly (FASB project manager quoted in Hayes, 1986, p. 98).

Thus, standard-setting action was constructed as an appropriate response to eliminate the "bad" accounting practices of the financial industry. The FASB observed the practices of these entities and shared the concerns voiced by others about these practices. In the case of accounting for loan fees, the actions of the Board can be interpreted as acting upon its mission statement — to consider promptly significant areas of deficiency in financial reporting that might be improved through standard-setting (FASB, 1990). The Board acted upon these expectations to end accounting "abuse" in a highly visible and financially troubled industry.

The efforts of the savings and loan industry to stop the FASB failed. The industry was unable to gain a foothold in regulatory space. The FASB ignored the savings and loan industry complaints as it pursued a course of action to alter loan fee accounting practices. FASB efforts were buttressed by the support of powerful allies within regulatory space including Congress. Within this context, the FASB could more easily act out its mission statement and further enhance its own legitimacy as the organization acting to eliminate "bad" accounting, in a highly visible arena.

ACCOUNTING FOR LEASES

Background

The FASB inherited accounting for leases from the Accounting Principles Board and included this matter on its initial technical agenda. The FASB "solved" accounting for leases in 1976 with the issuance of Financial Accounting Standard (FAS) 13 (FASB, 1976). This standard established criteria to classify leases as either capital or operating leases and required lessees to record an asset and associated liability for those leases classified as capital leases. The solution required substantial subsequent clarification and interpretation. Almost immediately upon issuing FAS 13, the FASB began to amend and interpret the standard. Between 1977 and 1979, the FASB issued seven amending standards and six interpretations and, in 1979, released nine technical bulletins.[7] Thus, the "solution" to the problem of accounting for leases created its own difficulties.

---

[6] The FASB recounted its efforts to eliminate "bad" accounting from the financial institution arena in two appearances before the Dingell committee investigations into the auditing and accounting practices in the financial services industry. On both occasions, the FASB cited its efforts to reduce the diversity in practice for loan fees (US. House, 1985b, pp. 333–335, 1986, p. 456).

[7] See FAS 17 (FASB, 1977a), FAS 22, (FASB, 1987a), FAS 23 (FASB, 1978b), FAS 26, (FASB, 1979a); FAS 27, (FASB, 1979b); FAS 28 (FASB, 1979c); FAS 29 (FASB, 1979d); Financial Interpretation (FIN) 19 (FASB, 1977b); FIN 21 (FASB, 1978c); FIN 23 (FASB, 1978d); FIN 24 (FASB, 1978e); FIN 26 (FASB, 1978f); FIN 27 (FASB, 1978g); Technical Bulletin (TB) 79-10 (FASB, 1979e); TB 79-11 (FASB, 1979f); TB 79-12 (FASB, 1979g); TB 79-13 (FASB, 1979h); TB 79-14 (FASB, 1979i); TB 79-15 (FASB, 1979j); TB 79-26 (FASB, 1979k); TB 79-17 (FASB, 1979l); TB 79-18 (FASB, 1979m).

A crowded regulatory space

In issuing FAS 13, the FASB had attempted to implement the perspective that "a lease that transfers substantially all of the benefits and risks incident to the ownership of property should be accounted for as the acquisition of an asset and the incurrence of an obligation by the lessee and a sale or financing by the lessor" (FASB, 1976, para. 60). Despite this intent, the FASB standard was later criticized for failing to capture and record the "true" economic substance of many leasing transactions. Accounting theorists and practitioners were concerned that the application of FAS 13 resulted in too little capitalization of leases (Phalen, 1978; Dieter, 1979; FASB's Rule 13, 1979; Abdel-Khalik, 1981). Many individuals also believed that companies structured new lease contracts and renegotiated existing lease contracts to avoid the FAS 13 capitalization requirements (Abdel-Khalik, 1981). It was believed by many that the arbitrary criteria outlined in FAS 13 to classify leases as either capital or operating leases had contributed to this "game playing" by corporate entities. In doing so, it may be interpreted as increasing diversity in practice and of contradicting the accounting claim of representational faithfulness. A FASB member recalled:

> [There was] theoretical dissatisfaction among some Board members who might not have been among the original ones [to issue FAS 13] and some outsiders like [a Big 6 firm] that we had [drawn] an arbitrary line ... people were structuring deals to avoid it. What kind of standard was that? [o2,1b].

And another individual noted:

> ... one of the problems of Statement 13 [is] it is a form not a substance standard and people will continue to structure leases to get around that form standard [p 2– 3b].

In light of this "game playing", several accounting theorists and practitioners believed that the application of FAS 13 failed to represent faithfully the perceived purpose of many leasing transactions, an "in substance" purchase of assets.

A separate set of concerns also arose around FAS 13. The amendments, interpretations and technical bulletins issued to clarify and interpret FAS 13 accented the "cookbookish" nature of lease accounting and increased the complexity of implementing FAS 13 into accounting practice. While the FASB and its staff worked to issue these documents, special committees of the AICPA discussed the burden that numerous accounting standards placed on small, closely held and medium-sized firms (AICPA, 1976, 1983). The Financial Executives Research Foundation and the FASB also studied these issues. In study after study, FAS 13 was criticized for its complexity (AICPA, 1983; Arthur D. Little, Inc., 1983; FASB, 1983a; Abdel-Khalik, 1983) and several studies recommended its revision (AICPA, 1983; Arthur D. Little, Inc., 1983).

Regulatory space was crowded with theoreticians, small audit practitioners, preparers of financial statements, and the FASB and its staff. While regulatory space was crowded with individuals and groups who agreed that FAS 13 *was* a problem, these occupants disagreed about not only a solution but also importantly on an appropriate construction of the problem. Was it too much complexity or too little capitalization?

Further crowding of regulatory space

In 1983, the FASB began to explore publicly alternatives to the existing standard. The FASB staff readily acknowledged the complexity of FAS 13 and claimed an inability to suggest a solution to reduce its complexity. Instead of recommending the immediate addition of a technical agenda project, the staff suggested studying the feasibility of developing a "better" answer to replace FAS 13 (FASB Minutes, 18 May 1983). The Board later indicated that a simplification of lease accounting could not result from minor changes to FAS 13. Instead, a fundamental change in lessee accounting was needed to simplify this accounting. The Board specifically discussed two alternatives: no capitalization of leases[8] and capitalization of all leases (FASB Minutes, 8 June 1983).

The FASB presented these alternatives to its Financial Accounting Standards Advisory Committee (FASAC)[9] for consideration and advice in July 1983. Many FASAC members identified the no capitalization "solution" as the alternative more likely to satisfy small business concerns and to reduce accounting complexity (FASAC, 1983, p. 10). However, the members questioned the theoretical support for this alternative and whether foregoing the capitalization of all leases would "improve" financial reporting. Several FASAC members characterized this alternative as a "step backwards" in accounting practice and expressed their beliefs that bankers and analysts would not accept this "solution". These members indicated that this alternative would exacerbate existing criticisms about too little lease capitalization. The FASB staff also raised the bogey of SEC intervention if the no capitalization alternative was selected:

> Before Statement 13 was issued, the Securities and Exchange Commission had taken a strong stand against lessees' accounting for leases at that time. Virtually no leases were being capitalized then. An FASB decision to eliminate capitalization of leases could result in a confrontation between the FASB and SEC (FASB, 1983b, p. 5).

The FASB also explored another alternative — capitalization of all leases. This alternative had been considered during the FASB deliberations leading to the issuance of FAS 13 (FASB, 1976, para. 63) but had been dismissed as too radical a departure from then existing practice to gain acceptance in the business community. A FASB member indicated:

> ... you say capitalize all [leases] but you don't really mean capitalize all [leases] because you're not going to capitalize car rentals. So you say that's easy just capitalize those [leases] with [terms of] 1 or 2 or 3 years or whatever, pick your time. But that immediately begins to get you into the sort of drawing of lines that are easy to get around. ... which is one of the problems with [FAS] 13. So you can't totally escape the problems ... [b,89].

Further, there was no assurance that this alternative would simplify lease accounting (e.g. Baker, 1980). A FASB member later discussed whether capitalizing all leases would simplify lease accounting:

> You'd be introducing more and more present value notions into what people have always thought [were] rental agreements. And you'd be creating more timing differences for tax purposes and as a result adding to what was another complex statement, deferred tax accounting [o,89].

Many FASAC members also expressed the opinion that this alternative would not address complexity concerns, achieve broad support among the FASB's constituency, or "improve" financial reporting (FASAC, 1983).

The FASB and its staff gathered information, discussed lease accounting issues at several Board meetings, used staff time to develop project proposals, and discussed lease accounting issues with FASAC. The Board employed the agenda process to highlight the conflicting problem constructions for lease accounting arising from the complexity and theoretical concerns. Those solutions likely to address complexity concerns were theoretically unacceptable. Those solutions likely to address theoretical concerns were unlikely to alleviate complexity concerns. A FASB member recalled the conflicting perspectives of the complexity and theoretical concerns about lease accounting:

---

[8] The no capitalization alternative required only disclosure of information about lease commitments.

[9] FASAC has responsibility for consulting with the FASB about major policy questions, technical issues, project priorities and other matters (FASB, 1990). The Council consists of members selected by the Financial Accounting Foundation. These members are broadly representative of preparers, auditors, and users of financial information (FASB, 1990).

... then the Institute standards overload complexity concerns came in and you had a combining of overload and theoreticians pushing for reconsideration whose motives were entirely different and expectations were entirely different ... so there was sort of a convergence of entirely different perspectives that put pressure on the Board [o,1b].

The FASB had accepted the alternative problem constructions of the other participants in regulatory space as "given" and explored these alternatives. This exploration brought other actors such as FASAC into the regulatory space. In calling on FASAC, the FASB further crowded regulatory space as FASAC members speak as unofficial representatives for the banking, analyst, preparer and auditor communities. The FASB also called on the SEC to cast its shadow onto the regulatory space and to buttress the inappropriateness of foregoing the capitalization of leases. This further crowded regulatory space with multiple opinions and responses and assisted the FASB in classifying accounting for leases as an intractable accounting problem.

Constructing inaction as appropriate

In February 1984, the FASB staff recommended the Board add a project to its agenda to reconsider leases. Paul LePage, FASB project manager, indicated: "... it's a very controversial item and there's a question as to whether the Board needs more controversy" (quoted in Berton, 1984). The Board declined to add the project to its agenda but requested that the staff outline the full range of conceptual and implementation issues to be addressed in a reconsideration of FAS 13 (FASB, 1984d).

In September 1984, the Board again discussed whether to undertake a project to reconsider lessee accounting. At this meeting, the FASB staff reviewed the problems associated with lessee accounting including complexity concerns and lessee avoidance of the arbitrary rules contained

in FAS 13. The Board voted again not to undertake the project and later indicated that the agenda criterion, general acceptance of a solution, was not met (FASB, 1984b).

Through these meetings, the FASB accomplished much more than a simple refusal to add a project to its technical agenda. The Board also communicated that an "improvement" in lease accounting would be defined as capitalizing more leases. (The no capitalization alternative was not discussed at the September 1984 Board meeting.) A member described the Board's action as follows:

we frequently are urged to reconsider a standard and people have an answer that they want in mind. When we put it on the agenda and come to a different answer, then they're horrified. In effect, that was all we were trying to do in that case ... [b,10–11].

Through this extended discussion, the FASB previewed the likely answer that would emerge from a reconsideration of FAS 13. Despite its theoretical "purity", this answer was not preferred by many of the FASB's constituents.[10] As one individual commented:

... we've learned to live with [FAS 13] and we're not sure that if they [the FASB] undertook to relook at the whole thing that they would come out with anything better short of capitalizing all leases which at least gets away from the arbitrary threshold ideas. Capitalize all leasehold rights no matter what the nature of the lease. Nobody, preparers at least, are very happy with that [d,6–7].

Although the FASB indicated that "improvement" meant capitalize more leases, the extended process also raised questions about how much improvement to financial accounting and reporting could be expected to arise from this change in accounting practices.

Through these meetings and discussions with participants, the FASB formally acknowledged that the previous solution to the problem of

---

[10] Survey respondents (including preparers, loan officers and auditors) had previously revealed strong negative attitudes toward capitalizing all leases (Abdel-Khalik, 1981, p. 109).

accounting for leases, FAS 13, could itself be constructed as an accounting problem. Thus, the FASB demonstrated responsiveness to the various criticisms of FAS 13 that had been documented in studies, reports, articles and discussions. The FASB exhibited its awareness of the concerns of the actors in regulatory space. The FASB also worked to establish that the imaginable alternatives to FAS 13 were unlikely to improve accounting substantially from the perspective of many participants in regulatory space or to gain the general acceptance of these participants. Some Board members, including FASB chairman Donald Kirk (Schildneck & Berton, 1983), were skeptical whether the FASB could develop an answer that would improve upon the answer in FAS 13. A FASB member recalled:

> ... the [members who were on the Board when FAS 13 was issued] were vehemently against 13 being reconsidered. Because they didn't believe that in the final analysis you would do anything but rehash a lot of the old issues that were essentially unresolvable the first time [e2,5].

The Board highlighted the incompatibility of the overload and too little capitalization concerns and constructed accounting for leases as an intractable problem. In establishing the problem as intractable, the FASB could refuse to "waste" its time by undertaking a project on lease accounting. The following comments underscore this point:

> ... We have a line and some leases are capitalized and some are not and [we] probably [will] never go to capitalize every single lease ... It's a question of maybe capitalizing some more. And it just doesn't seem to be the best use of our resources [bf16].

> ... the reaction against putting it [accounting for leases] on [the agenda] is that you, first going into saying yes to it, have to accept that you will either capitalize essentially all leases or no leases. If you're not willing to admit that then you must be only talking about moving the line a little bit. And a lot of us thought that moving the line is not cost-beneficial. There is nothing really dramatically going to improve the reporting by changing an arbitrary line from one point to another and the Board will incur incredible costs [e2,5].

In accounting for leases, participants crowded the regulatory space and spurred the FASB to act in developing a rationale for inaction. At the outset, the space was crowded by participants with conflicting perspectives about the description of the problem and conflicting expectations about an acceptable solution to the problem. The FASB called upon still other actors to enter the space and to heighten further the intractability of the problem in terms of finding an acceptable solution. Neither of the solutions discussed was likely to reconcile the conflicting perspectives. Thus, these conflicting perspectives were employed to construct inaction as appropriate.

DEPRECIATION AND CONTRIBUTION ACCOUNTING FOR NONPROFIT ORGANIZATIONS

Constructing nonprofit accounting as a problem

The Committee on Accounting Practices and the Accounting Principles Board, predecessors of the FASB, directed none of their standard-setting efforts toward establishing accounting guidance for the nonprofit sector. Instead, various associations and agencies such as the Municipal Finance Officers Association and American Hospital Association independently established accounting guidance for their specific types of organizations (American Accounting Association, 1971, p. 84).

In 1975, the Commission on Private Philanthropy and Public Needs (Filer Commission), a committee formed by a group of private citizens, issued a study of philanthropic giving in the U.S. Two accounting proposals were included among the recommended ways to strengthen the nonprofit sector and the practice of private giving. First, the Commission recommended increased accountability for NPOs through the distribution of detailed annual reports that would document finances, programs and priorities. Second, the commission urged the adoption of uniform accounting measures by comparable NPOs to improve accountability (Commission on Private Philanthropy, 1975, p. 165):

One obstacle in the path of accountability is the tangle of accounting definitions and principles that are in effect among nonprofit organizations which makes examination of any particular organization's basic finances often difficult if not impossible, especially for nonexperts, and compounds the problems of comparing one organization with another. . . . greater uniformity, at least among comparable types of organizations, is clearly possible and desirable.

Diversity in accounting definitions and principles was viewed as an obstacle to understanding the accounting reports of NPOs. The committee's position suggested that NPOs should work to eliminate this diversity. However, several committee members objected to the view that NPOs could accomplish this task and called for outside initiative to improve NPO accounting: "Further progress [in accounting] is dependent on the readiness of the AICPA and the FASB to move ahead — not alone on the agencies which have heretofore taken the initiative" (Commission on Private Philanthropy, p. 213).

While the Filer Commission questioned the accounting practices of NPOs, major U.S. cities such as New York City, Cleveland, and Chicago faced fiscal crises. The financial crises of these cities and particularly New York City raised questions about the adequacy of the accounting practices and accounting reports of municipalities (Klapper, 1978a). Congressmen, accountants, and regulators discussed the inadequacies of municipal accounting practices and the need for change. For example, a 1978 Coopers and Lybrand study concluded that municipal accounting practices failed to meet the needs of taxpayers and investors (Klapper, 1978b). These concerns about the accounting practices of municipalities led several actors to suggest that an authoritative entity be established to provide accounting guidance to state and municipal organizations.

In linking uniform accounting measures for comparable organizations with improved financial accountability of NPOs, the Filer Commission established a link between accounting standard-setting and more general concerns about the financial viability of the nonprofit sector. This linkage, coupled with the concerns about the accounting practices of New York City and other municipalities, constructed accounting in the nonprofit area as a problem and once again centered the problem around the issue of diversity in practice. However, this was a process of problem construction in which the FASB was apparently not a participant. The Filer Commission report and the discussions about municipal accounting suggest the sense that the accounting and reporting practices of municipalities and nonprofit organizations had failed to provide sufficient information to assist in the allocation of resources to these organizations. The concerns of participants in regulatory space were vague and general but suggested that efforts were needed to get the accounting "right".

While the AICPA, FASB and other organizations had ignored accounting by NPOs, these organizations began to attend to the area after the reports of the Filer commission and the wide publicity arising from the near bankruptcy of New York City. The AICPA ended its traditional disinterest in nonprofit accounting by appointing a committee to establish accounting guidance — a statement of position covering the accounting practices of nonprofit organizations such as churches and museums. In addition, U.S. Congressional members considered nonprofit solicitation activities and proposed at least two bills to govern these activities. Each bill would have likely resulted in a government agency to establish accounting rules for nonprofit organizations (Gross, 1977). Other members of Congress proposed forming a committee to establish disclosure and accounting rules for municipalities issuing bonds. Sen. Harrison Williams circulated several bills in Congress designed to grant the SEC the authority to establish accounting practices for municipalities that issued bonds or to create a private institution to establish accounting standards for state and local governments. The regulatory space was thus becoming crowded with groups and organizations proposing alternative ways to provide accounting guidance for nonprofit entities.

Is FASB action appropriate? Regulatory space shrinks

While the AICPA had begun to act and certain Congressional members were also trying to act upon NPO accounting practices, the FASB, the organization designated by the AICPA, Financial Analysts Federation, Financial Executives Institute, National Association of Accountants and American Accounting Association and the SEC as the entity responsible for improving financial accounting and reporting, had failed to act. However, participants in regulatory space were working to construct NPO accounting practices as appropriate for FASB action. In this respect, the FASB was being drawn into the space and FASB action was being constructed as appropriate by those who had already entered the regulatory space. Although a number of reasons might explain the FASB's inaction on NPOs, for example the intractable nature of the "problem" or a lack of interest in nonprofit accounting, the FASB was nevertheless drawn into the regulatory space. This reinforces the necessity for analyzing the agenda process within a wider context as other participants may construct appropriateness and thereby define the role of the FASB within a particular regulatory space.

Yet other conditions must be considered to penetrate the complexity of the FASB's position on NPOs. For example, in 1977 the Financial Accounting Foundation Structure Committee published its evaluation of the operations of the FASB and recommended several structural changes.[11] Among its many recommendations, the Structure Committee included its belief that "the Board must deal with municipal accounting" (Financial Accounting Foundation,

1977, p. 27). The Structure Committee accepted as a fact that municipal accounting was an accounting problem and encouraged the FASB to address this problem. The Structure Committee urged the FASB to leverage its work in this and other areas to avoid delays in undertaking and completing projects as "abstinence invites other standard-setting bodies into the act" (p. 26). Similarly, the Study on Establishment of Accounting Principles (AICPA, 1972, p. 72) had recommended "financial accounting standards be in only one set of hands ..." These committees asserted that only one standard-setting group was required and that the FASB should be the standard-setter.

Others also urged the FASB to establish accounting standards for municipalities. In noting that municipal accounting practices failed to meet user needs, Coopers and Lybrand called for FASB action (Klapper, 1978b). A former New York City deputy mayor for finance also urged the FASB to act (Axelson, 1977). Thus, more and more participants encouraged the FASB to define NPO accounting as an appropriate arena for action. However, in the above cases, the rationales were not couched only in terms of getting the accounting "right", but rather were apparently concerned with occupying regulatory space. It was a concern not so much with defining NPO accounting as a problem but with defining regulatory space itself. As such, the Structure Committee's call for action was tinged with concerns that the newly organized FASB would be supplanted by other organizations in establishing guidance for NPOs.

In 1977, the FASB responded to these expectations and announced its intention to study the entire area of nonprofit accounting. The Board commissioned Robert Anthony of Harvard University to study the objectives and

---

[11] The structure committee was composed of six Financial Accounting Foundation trustees. The Foundation is responsible for selecting the members of the FASB, funding their activities and exercising general oversight (except with regard to the FASB's resolution of technical issues) (FASB, 1990). The committee report was prepared in part due to the interest of two congressional committees in the work of the FASB and their concern about whether the FASB was the appropriate entity to establish accounting rules.

basic concepts underlying financial accounting and reporting for NPOs. Chairman Donald Kirk later explained the FASB decision to address accounting for NPOs:

> There is growing concern regarding the relevance and reliability of financial reports of nonbusiness organizations and this concern has been expressed in legislation proposed in both houses of Congress. Against this backdrop, persons representing a wide range of interests have called upon the FASB to become involved in the nonbusiness sector (Different Rules, 1978).

It should be noted that, rather than elevating NPO accounting to the status of an agenda item immediately, the Anthony study delayed the FASB's decision on this matter while allowing it to be seen as active.

The FASB's entry into regulatory space was still tentative. Although the FASB began to enter regulatory space, not all entities accepted its authority as the accounting standard-setter nor shared expectations that the FASB should be *the* standard-setter for all reporting entities. Regulatory space was contested. This jurisdictional matter was open to debate as those urging the FASB to establish accounting rules were acting upon an absence of an "official" mandate. Because there were no restrictions to prevent the FASB from establishing accounting standards for NPOs, those calling for action had assumed the existence of an implicit mandate (see for example Anthony, 1978). Those calling for action by the FASB in the nonprofit area assumed or at least intended that the FASB should be the entity to establish accounting rules for both for-profit and nonprofit organizations. However, state and local government officials resisted the efforts of the FASB and denied the authority of the Board to establish accounting standards for governmental entities (Mautz, 1981). These officials vigorously opposed FASB standard-setting efforts (Klapper, 1978a; Accounting Panel, 1978; FASAC minutes, April 1979; FASB Head, 1978) and began to

conduct lengthy discussions with the Financial Accounting Foundation about an "appropriate" entity to establish accounting rules for government entities. In part, this resistance arose from the conflicting views of FASB members and state and local officials. The FASB members believed that NPOs differed little from for-profit organizations and that many of the accounting differences between NPOs and for-profits should be eliminated. State and local officials argued that their entities pursued fundamentally different objectives and that the accounting for government entities should reflect these differences. The members of other nonprofit entities such as hospitals, museums and churches offered no resistance to the role of the FASB as standard-setter and remained out of regulatory space during the jurisdiction discussions.[12] In light of this ongoing jurisdictional dispute, the FASB members agreed unanimously in May 1978 to defer any decisions about undertaking projects to develop specific accounting standards for NPOs and in doing so withdrew itself from the contested domain. The decision to withdraw was described as an "apparent bid to avoid controversy, particularly in the government sector" (Accounting Panel, 1978). Rather than being seen to completely capitulate, the Board added to its agenda a project to address selected conceptual issues.

The negotiations between the Financial Accounting Foundation and state and local government officials ended in 1981. The Financial Accounting Foundation approved a proposal to establish a second standard-setting body, the Governmental Accounting Standards Board (GASB), to promulgate accounting standards for state and local government officials (FAF Position, 1981). FASB members opposed this decision. The FASB chairman charged: "multiple accounting standard-setting bodies will be costly, inefficient, conflicting, confusing and therefore unfair to external users" (Chairman Presents, 1981). Ignoring this

---

[12] Whether the lack of resistance arose from passive acceptance of FASB jurisdiction, lack of awareness of FASB intentions, or other reasons is unknown.

opposition, the Financial Accounting Foundation action in effect established a separate regulatory space for state and local government accounting practices. By establishing the GASB, the Financial Accounting Foundation removed the accounting practices of governmental entities from the jurisdiction of the FASB and the regulatory space in which it operated. Ironically, this action also removed those actors who had forcefully challenged the FASB's authority in the domain of the NPO and as we shall see cleared the way for the FASB to act in providing guidance for other NPOs.

Action in the absence of controversy

During and after the jurisdiction controversies, the FASB continued to examine conceptual issues relating to accounting and reporting for NPOs and to delay undertaking projects to establish specific accounting standards (FASB, 1981). Although the Board agreed that specific standards should focus on pervasive accounting issues affecting all NPOs, the Board also decided it would develop standards only in situations where an immediate need for a project was demonstrated (FASB Minutes, 23 September 1981). A FASB member later commented:

> We did concepts statement 4 and then there was quite a bit of pressure for us to go into standard-setting at that point. But we decided instead to incorporate the nonprofits into concepts statement 3. And the board felt that until you get the concepts laid out you have difficulty with standards. We decided that it was more important to establish that an asset is an asset whether it's a nonprofit or so on ... [b18].

The role of the concepts statements and other strategies such as commissions are interesting in that they permitted the FASB to remain active on the fringes of regulatory space without fully committing itself to a project on accounting for NPOs. As we shall see, this presence allowed the FASB to reactivate itself when the conditions within the regulatory space turned in its favor.

The FASB finally issued Concepts Statement No. 6 in December 1985. After its completion, the FASB added to its agenda in March 1986 a project to develop specific accounting standards on depreciation and contributions for NPOs. In selecting projects for accounting standards, the Board returned to those areas of accounting practice that its staff had identified in 1981 as requiring standards work. Very little external "pressure" was placed on the FASB to undertake these standards projects in 1986, nor was there much opposition to these projects at the outset.[13] The earlier concerns expressed by members of Congress and others had subsided and eased and few individuals or entities outside the Board were interested in the project. In the annual FASAC questionnaire on projects and priorities, FASAC members consistently assigned a lower priority to the development of NPO financial reporting concepts than to other major projects. A FASB member commented:

> CPAs were the only ones pressing the Board to address the issues. Nonprofit organizations provided no impetus for change. They were content with the way things were and perceived no problems with differences [g,3]

Another individual stated:

> There is a wide divergence of practice with respect to nonprofits [but] I don't know where the hue and cry [for these projects] came from [r,7].

Despite the relative lack of interest in the project, the FASB continued its work and followed along the course the Board had charted initially in the late 1970s and early 1980s. In discussing the Board's decision to continue working in the nonprofit area, an individual painted a picture of inertia:

---

[13] Later, regulatory space became highly contested again. The depreciation project reopened the jurisdiction issue for those "industries" (such as colleges and universities) which have both private and governmental organizations. The contributions project generated significant controversy over the "appropriate" accounting for museum collections and other items.

Until [the New York City bankruptcy], the FASB had very little to do with nonprofits. And then there was a lot of pressure on them to get involved in the governmental side. The government sector successfully avoided the FASB jurisdiction and got their own board set up. Meanwhile, the nonprofit thing had started. They had done concepts statement 4 and that just carried forward. ... So I think it was just that momentum of getting involved initially [1,4].

In contrast to other projects, FASB members did not discuss an urgent need to address these issues. Instead, members discussed the decision in terms of responsibility, commitment and embarrassment at the slow progress in establishing standards:[14]

But the Board has always felt a responsibility for it because it was a real problem and a real need. So despite the kind of FASAC attitude, [the Board] just kept plowing along and figured they had a responsibility and has continued to pursue it [b,21].

We knew that GASB might start dealing with it but we were really underway with it before that became an issue. I think in part it was frustration that we had decided to do this issue well before [in 1977]. We decided that we needed to deal with this issue which had been stepchild within the institute [AICPA] in a way. We needed to deal with it. ... So we were committed. After all those years, it was an embarrassment that we hadn't done anything yet. So I think that probably was the biggest issue. We weren't going to drop it from the agenda [o,1c].

Note the emphasis on commitment, a commitment to be *the* standard setter for all organizations within the jurisdiction of the FASB.

Initially, the FASB began work within regulatory space amid an environment of concern about the accounting practices of NPOs including government units. The FASB had been urged to be the standard-setter (AICPA, 1972; FAF, 1977, 1979) and acted as the "official" standard-setter as it began to study how to "improve" the accounting practices of NPOs. Thus, the FASB listened to and acted upon the expectations voiced by those in regulatory space. However, it was discovered that these were not the only actors in regulatory space as state and local government officials began to contest whether the FASB actions were "appropriate" and whether the FASB had jurisdication over the accounting for governmental entities. While the arguments about the jurisdiction of the regulatory space in which the FASB operated continued, the FASB focussed its attention upon developing accounting concepts. Because accounting concepts have little immediate impact upon accounting practices, these efforts delayed standard-setting while permitting the FASB to establish its presence in the area and to incorporate accounting issues for nongovernment NPOs within the regulatory space in which the FASB operates. By focussing on items with little immediate impact, the FASB could avoid further provoking state and local officials with action and avoid annoying the other interested parties by FASB inaction.

These jurisdictional debates ended by establishing that the FASB was not the standard setter for government entities. This action removed the contentious state and local government officials from the regulatory space in which the FASB operates. By default, these debates and the concepts work completed by the FASB constructed FASB actions on the accounting practices of other nonprofit entities as "appropriate". The FASB eventually acted upon this construction of "appropriate" behavior and began standard-setting projects on depreciation and contribution accounting. It was no longer an issue as to whether the FASB should act but became a responsibility of the FASB to act and a source of "embarrassment" that action had not occurred earlier. This study illustrates the construction of action as appropriate and suggests that FASB actions are bounded by the expectations of participants in regulatory space who also may work to establish the boundaries of regulatory space.

---

[14] Several members indicated that this "slowness" resulted in part from the difficulty of finding qualified individuals to staff the project.

CONCLUDING COMMENTS

The studies on loan fees, leases and nonprofit accounting suggest that accounting problems are not simply there. Instead, these problems are constructed by the occupants of regulatory space. In this process, the FASB does not act alone in constructing accounting issues as problems. Instead, many other actors such as the AICPA, the SEC and Congress are also involved. AICPA committees prepare issues papers, statements of position and other documents to highlight those issues that these committees perceive as accounting "problems". Congress holds hearings and discusses accounting matters. Many actors work to construct an issue as a "problem".

Accounting change is not an "anything goes" process. Instead, accounting claims and concepts of what accounting should be and what accounting should do may be seen to establish bounds for accounting change. Accounting claims such as relevance, reliability and representational faithfulness, are among the elements that construct the regulatory space and limit the issues that can be included on the FASB technical agenda.[15] In this paper, the rationale presented for agenda formation is seen to depend heavily upon the perceived divergences between accounting claims and accounting practices. Constituent demands for accounting change arise from this perceived divergence.

In each of the three case studies, the process of constructing accounting problems depended upon the presence and interpretations of various participants in regulatory space. Congress, the AICPA, FASB, financial regulators and the General Accounting Office were each important in the process of constructing accounting for loan fees as an accounting problem. Savings and loan organizations were effectively excluded from regulatory space. The powerful allies of the FASB reduced the ability of these organizations to lobby effectively and precluded them from an active role in regulatory space. In this case, the FASB was seen to act decisively.

AICPA committees representing small audit practitioners, preparers, bankers, analysts, FASAC, SEC, and the FASB were all involved in the case of accounting for leases. Regulatory space was crowded with conflicting perspectives on the description of the accounting problem and with views about the constitution of "appropriate" solutions. The FASB further increased the crowding in regulatory space with its solicitation of FASAC and its invocation of the preferences of the SEC. In this case, the FASB was seen to use delaying tactics to avoid including accounting for leases as an agenda item and thereby being forced to take action which would inevitably be unpopular with some participants. Instead, it created inaction as appropriate.

In the case of accounting for nonprofit entities, the occupants of regulatory space changed over time. The Filer Commission, Congress, AICPA, FAF and auditors acted to construct accounting for nonprofit entities as a problem for the FASB. The FASB began reluctantly to address these problems at the urging of these entities. State and local government officials later entered regulatory space to protest vigorously FASB involvement in establishing accounting guidance for their organizations. Again, faced with a contested regulatory space, the FASB withdrew. However, the FASB remained along the sidelines until the space calmed and then returned to establish accounting standards for NPOs. Congress lost interest in these matters and exited regulatory space before the FASB made any noticeable progress in their resolution.

With each accounting issue, the occupants of regulatory space may vary. Actors enter and exit regulatory space. Some actors participate in the

---

[15] Although these claims are historically contingent concepts that may and probably do change over time, tracing changes in these claims is a subject for future research efforts. For the current project, the important observation lies in noting the interactions among claims, practices and the social and economic environment.

construction of some problems but not others. Some actors participate in the construction of problems but lose interest in their resolution. Although participation in the process is fluid and changing, some actors do consistently participate in the process of constructing accounting problems and resolving these problems. However, consistent involvement is highly institutionalized. Frequent participants tend to be those individuals serving on committees (such as the AICPA Accounting Standards Executive Committee and FASAC) or fullfilling their employee roles (i.e. members of large accounting firms). Participation occurs primarily by individuals associated with the largest public accounting firms, large manufacturing or service companies, Congress or other public organizations.[16] Academics and the assumed users of financial statements such as investors and creditors seldom occupy regulatory space.

The members of the FASB and its staff occupy a prominent position within regulatory space. The FASB does not simply respond to pressures from the participants in regulatory space. Sometimes the FASB reacts to such pressures (i.e. loan fees). Sometimes, it does not (i.e. leases). Sometimes, the FASB acts in the absence of such pressures (i.e. NPOs). The common thread in these cases is the development of a need for standard-setting action on an accounting problem and an evaluation that such action is appropriate.

The cases in the preceding sections suggest that the FASB employs a logic of appropriateness in conducting its activities in regulatory space. Instead of evaluating the benefits and assessing the consequences of alternative actions in reaching a decision, the FASB appears both to evaluate and to construct actively what a standard-setter should do in a specific situation. In assessing the situation, the standard-setter

interprets its obligation and selects an action construed as appropriate (March & Olsen, 1989, p. 160).

This logic contrasts with a logic of consequences. The application of this latter logic and its sole reliance upon assessments of consequences in selecting actions tends to imply that the actor is separate from the environment. Models of organizational behavior that employ this logic understate the extent to which organizations are internally constituted by a wider environment that contains prescriptions regarding the types and structure of organizational actors (Meyer *et al.*, 1987, p. 19). Thus, these models understate the importance of societal expectations about the role and purpose of the standard-setter to all facets of the standard-setting process, including agenda formation.

The cases in the preceding sections suggest that the process of agenda formation includes interpretation by the standard-setter about the expectations held by participants in regulatory space on the role and purpose of the standard-setter. This process is more than a simple response to "pressures" from various interested actors or an effort by the FASB to promote its organizational survival. A variety of responses by the standard-setting organization is possible and may be interpreted as appropriate.

The appropriateness of standard-setting action is inextricably linked to the development of accounting problems. There is little need for standard-setter action to address issues that have not been constructed as accounting problems. However, this does not exclude the FASB from a role in constructing these problems. In the case of loan fees, the FASB assisted in labelling some accounting practices of financial institutions as abusive and then proceeded to act upon its mission statement to eliminate these abuses. The powerful allies of the FASB assisted it in

---

[16] Whether this limited involvement results from the cost of attention (March & Olsen, 1976) or from limited opportunities for early participation remains a subject for future research. However limited involvement implies that the few people primarily involved in constructing accounting issues as problems are those individuals that tend to be successful within the existing accounting system.

overcoming the objections of S&L organizations and supported the FASB efforts as appropriate and "right". In the case of leases, the FASB accepted the descriptions of leases as an accounting problem and employed these conflicting perspectives (again with the assistance of others in regulatory space such as FASAC and the SEC) to establish the intractability of the problem and the appropriateness of inaction. In accounting for nonprofit organizations, the FASB and others attempted to establish the domain of regulatory space to include state and local governments and the "appropriateness" of the FASB in acting to develop accounting standards for all entities. However, state and local government officials opposed this interpretation of appropriateness and successfully gained the creation of a separate regulatory space for their accounting problems. After FASB action was established as inappropriate for state and local government accounting, the FASB began to develop accounting standards for other nonprofit entities and established standard-setting action as appropriate for these entities.

A duality exists. Although the FASB appears to employ a logic of appropriateness, FASB actions (if uncontested) also tend to solidify and perpetuate those actions that will be considered appropriate in the future. The necessity for standard-setter interpretations does not preclude a role for the standard-setter in developing and perpetuating the expectations of regulatory space occupants about its "proper" role and assisting these other occupants in establishing what constitutes "appropriate" actions.

An analysis of events or actions alone is insufficient to understand the emergence of issues onto the FASB agenda. Conditions problematize divergences between accounting practices and accounting claims and are interpreted as requiring standard-setting action. General conditions interact with expectations about accounting to construct accounting problems. These expectations about accounting also interact with expectations about the role and purpose of the accounting standard-setter to construct an agenda project. The agenda process may not be dominated by assessments of consequences so much as by an interpretation of expectations by the groups and individuals that participate in standard-setting and occupy regulatory space.

Baier *et al.* (1988, p. 157) argue that "understanding administrative implementation cannot be separated from understanding the ways in which policies are made and the implications of the policy-making process for administrative action". The studies in this paper illustrate that an understanding of accounting standard-setting cannot be separated from an understanding of the role of accounting claims and expectations about standard-setters that construct a regulatory space for accounting change.

BIBLIOGRAPHY

Abdel-Khalik, A. R., *The Economic Effects on Lessees of FASB Statement No. 13, Accounting for Leases* (Stamford: FASB, 1981).

Abdel-Khalik, A. R., *Financial Reporting by Private Companies: Analysis and Diagnosis* (Stamford, CT: FASB, 1983).

Accounting Panel Sets Study of Government, Institution Practices, *Wall Street Journal* (12 May 1978) p. 48.

Agenda Decisions, *FASB Status Report* (12 March 1984) p. 1.

AICPA Issues Paper Sparks Anger, Dread Among Institutions, *Savings Institutions* (April 1984) pp. 168–170.

American Accounting Association, Report of the Committee on Accounting for Not-for-profit Organizations, *Accounting Review* (Supplement 1971) pp. 81–163.

American Institute of Certified Public Accountants, Study on Establishment of Accounting Principles, *Establishing Financial Accounting Standards* (New York: AICPA, 1972).

American Institute of Certified Public Accountants, *Report of the Committee on Generally Accepted Accounting Principles for Smaller and/or Closely Held Businesses* (New York: AICPA, August 1976).

American Institute of Certified Public Accountants, *Accounting for Installment Lending Activities of Financial Companies*, issues paper draft (6 April 1981).

American Institute of Certified Public Accountants, *Accounting for Nonrefundable Fees and Loan Acquisition Costs*, issues paper draft (17 September 1982).

American Institute of Certified Public Accountants, *Report of the Special Committee on Accounting Standards Overload* (New York: AICPA, February 1983).

Anthony, R. N., *Financial Accounting in Nonbusiness Organizations: An Exploratory Study of Conceptual Issues* (Stamford, CT: Financial Accounting Standards Board, 1978).

Arthur D. Little, Inc., *Financial Reporting Requirements of Small Publicly Owned Companies* (New York: FERF, 1983).

Auerbach, R. P. & McCall, A. S., Permissive Accounting Practices Inflate Savings and Loan Industry Earnings and Net Worth, *Issues in Bank Regulation* (Summer 1985) pp. 17–21.

Axelson, K. S., Crisis in New York City: The Case for Municipal Accounting Reform, *Journal of Contemporary Business* (Winter 1977) pp. 1–17.

Baier, V. E., March, J. G. & Saetren, H., Implementation and Ambiguity, *Scandinavian Journal of Management Studies* (May 1986), reprinted in March J. G. (ed.), *Decisions and Organizations*, pp. 150–164 (Oxford: Basil Blackwell, 1988).

Baker, C. R., Leasing and the Setting of Accounting Standards: Mapping the Labyrinth, *Journal of Accounting Auditing and Finance* (Winter 1980) pp. 197–206.

Baker, T., Bad Will, *Forbes* (11 May 1981) pp. 90, 93.

Beresford, D. R., How Well Does the FASB Consider the Consequences of Its Work? *Financial Executive* (March/April 1989) pp. 24–28.

Berton, L., FASB to Begin Study on Changing 76 Rule for Lease Accounting, *Wall Street Journal* (8 February 1984) p. 8.

Berton, L., Accounting at Thrifts Provokes Controversy as Gimmickry Mounts, *Wall Street Journal* (21 March 1985) p. 1.

Biggart, N. W. & Hamilton, G. G., The Power of Obedience, *Administrative Science Quarterly* (1984) pp. 540–549.

Burchell, S., Clubb, C., Hopwood, A., Hughes, J. & Nahapiet, J., Roles of Accounting Organizations and Society, *Accounting Organizations and Society* (1980) pp. 5–27.

Burchell, S., Clubb, C. & Hopwood, A., Accounting in Its Social Context: Towards a History of Value Added in the United Kingdom, *Accounting, Organizations and Society* (1985) pp. 381–413.

Chairman Presents FASB's Views on Proposed Structure to Set Standards for Governments, *Status Report* (8 May 1981) pp. 1–2.

Chandler, C. H., A Businessman's View of the Standard-setting Process, *Financial Executive* (March/April 1990) pp. 46–50.

Commission on Private Philanthropy and Public Needs, *Giving in America: Toward a Stronger Voluntary Sector*, Report of the Commission on Private Philanthropy and Public Needs (1975).

Deloitte, Haskins & Sells, FASB Chairman on Self-Regulation in a Deregulatory Environment, *The Week In Review* (30 October 1981) pp. 1–2.

Different Rules for the Nonbusiness Sector?, *CA Magazine* (August 1978) p. 26.

Dieter, R., Is Lessee Accounting Working? *CPA Journal* (August 1979) pp. 13–19.

Dyckman, T., Credibility and the Formulation of Accounting Standards Under the Financial Accounting Standards Board, *Journal of Accounting Literature* (1988) pp. 1–30.

The FAF Position on a Governmental Accounting Standards Board, *Status Report* (24 September 1981) pp. 3–4.

FASB Head Criticizes Government Auditing, Says Rules Are Needed, *Wall Street Journal* (18 May 1978) p. 22.

FASB Loan Fee Stance Has Dire Implications, *Savings Institutions* (April 1986) pp. S21–S23.

FASB's Rule 13: Enough Loopholes for Everybody, *Dun's Review* (November 1979) p. 87.

Financial Accounting Foundation, *Report of the Structure Committee* (Stamford, CT, April 1977).

Financial Accounting Foundation, *Report of the Structure Committee: Interim Review of the FASB and FASAC* (Mimeo, May 1979).

Financial Accounting Standards Advisory Committee, *Summary of Responses of Council Members to the July 1983 Post-meeting Questionnaire on Statement No. 13, Accounting for Leases* (Mimeo, 1983).

OUTLINING REGULATORY SPACE 107

Financial Accounting Standards Board, *Financial Accounting Standard No. 13*, Accounting for Leases (November 1976).

Financial Accounting Standards Board, *Statement of Financial Accounting Standard No. 17*, Accounting for Leases — Initial Direct Costs (Stamford, CT: FASB, 1977a).

Financial Accounting Standards Board, *FASB Interpretation No. 19*, Lessee Guarantee of the Residual Value of Leased Property, (Stamford, CT: FASB, 1977b).

Financial Accounting Standards Board, *Statement of Financial Accounting Standard No. 22*, Changes in the Provisions of Lease Agreements Resulting from Refundings of Tax-Exempt Debt (Stamford, CT: FASB, 1978a).

Financial Accounting Standards Board, *Statement of Financial Accounting Standard No. 23*, Inception of the Lease (Stamford, CT: FASB, 1978b).

Financial Accounting Standards Board, *FASB Interpretation No. 21*, Accounting for Leases in a Business Combination (Stamford, CT: FASB, 1978c).

Financial Accounting Standards Board, *FASB Interpretation No. 23*, Leases of Certain Property Owned by a Governmental Unit or Authority (Stamford, CT: FASB, 1978d).

Financial Accounting Standards Board, *FASB Interpretation No. 24*, Leases Involving Only Part of a Building (Stamford, CT: FASB, 1978e).

Financial Accounting Standards Board, *FASB Interpretation No. 26*, Accounting for Purchase of Leased Asset by the Lessee during the Term of the Lease (Stamford, CT: FASB, 1978f).

Financial Accounting Standards Board, *FASB Interpretation No. 27*, Accounting for a Loss on a Sublease (Stamford, CT: FASB, 1978g).

Financial Accounting Standards Board, *Statement of Financial Accounting Standard No. 26*, Profit Recognition on Sales-type Leases of Real Estate (Stamford, CT: FASB, 1979a).

Financial Accounting Standards Board, *Statement of Financial Accounting Standard No. 27*, Classification of Renewals or Extensions of Existing Sales-types or Direct Financing Leases (Stamford, CT: FASB, 1979b).

Financial Accounting Standards Board, *Statement of Financial Accounting Standard No. 28*, Accounting for Sales with Leasebacks (Stamford, CT: FASB, 1979c).

Financial Accounting Standards Board, Statement of Financial Accounting Standard No. 29, Determining Contingent Rentals (Stamford, CT: FASB, 1979d).

Financial Accounting Standards Board, *FASB Technical Bulletin No. 79–10*, Fiscal Funding Clauses in Lease Agreements (Stamford, CT: FASB, 1979e).

Financial Accounting Standards Board, *FASB Technical Bulletin No. 79–11*, Effect of a Penalty on the Term of a Lease (Stamford, CT: FASB, 1979f).

Financial Accounting Standards Board, *FASB Technical Bulletin No. 79–12*, Interest Rate Used in Calculating the Present Value of Minimum Lease Payments (Stamford, CT: 1979g).

Financial Accounting Standards Board, *FASB Technical Bulletin No. 79–13*, Applicability of FASB Statement No. 13 to Current Value Financial Statements (Stamford, CT: 1979h).

Financial Accounting Standards Board, *FASB Technical Bulletin No. 79–14*, Upward Adjustment of Guaranteed Residual Values (Stamford, CT: 1979i).

Financial Acounting Standards Board, *FASB Technical Bulletin No. 79–15*, Accounting for Loss on a Sublease Not Involving the Disposal of a Segment (Stamford, CT: 1979j).

Financial Accounting Standards Board, *FASB Technical Bulletin No. 79–16*, Effect of a Change in Income Tax Rate on the Accounting for Leveraged Leases (Stamford, CT: 1979k).

Financial Accounting Standards Board, *FASB Technical Bulletin No. 79–17*, Reporting Cumulative Effect Adjustment from Retroactive Application of FASB Statement No. 13 (Stamford, CT: 1979l).

Financial Accounting Standards Board, *FASB Technical Bulletin No. 79–18*, Transition Requirement of Certain FASB Amendments and Interpretations of FASB Statement No. 13 (Stamford, CT: 1979m).

Financial Accounting Standards Board, *Statement of Financial Accounting Concepts No. 2*, Qualitative Characteristics of Accounting Information (Stamford, CT: FASB, December 1980).

Financial Accounting Standards Board, *Action Alert* No. 81–39 (1981).

Financial Accounting Standards Board, *Financial Reporting by Privately Owned Companies: Summary of Responses to FASB Invitation to Comment* (Stamford, CT: FASB, 1983a).

Financial Accounting Standards Board, *Staff Briefing Paper for FASAC — Accounting for Leases* (Mimeo, 1983b).

Financial Accounting Standards Board, *Invitation to Comment, Accounting for Nonrefundable Fees and Costs Associated with Originating and Acquiring Loans* (Stamford, CT: FASB, 1984a).

Financial Accounting Standards Board, Board Decides Not to Reconsider Lessee's Accounting for Leases, *Status Report* (25 October 1984b) pp. 1–2.

Financial Accounting Standards Board, Agenda Decisions, *Status Report* (12 March 1984c) p. 1.

Financial Accounting Standards Board, Agenda Decisions Made, *Status Report* (6 April 1984d) p. 1.

Financial Accounting Standards Board, *Statement of Financial Accounting Standards*, Recognition of Depreciation by Not-for-profit Organizations (Stamford, CT: FASB, 1987).

Financial Accounting Standards Board, *FACTS about FASB* (Stamford, CT: FASB, 1990).

Foucault, M., Questions of Method, *I&C* (Spring 1981) pp. 3–14.

Gross, M. J., Recent Accounting and Legislative Developments Affecting Nonprofit Organizations, *Journal of Contemporary Business* (Winter 1977) pp. 19–30.

Hancher, L. & Moran, M., Organizing Regulatory Space, in Hancher, L. & Moran, M. (eds), *Capitalism, Culture and Regulation* (Oxford: Clarendon Press, 1989).

Hayes, J. R., Party Pooping, *Forbes* (20 October 1986) pp. 97–98.

Hindess, B., Power, Interests and the Outcomes of Struggles, *Sociology* (November 1982) pp. 498–511.

Hindess, B., 'Interests' in Political Analysis, in Law, J. (ed.), *Power, Action and Belief*, pp. 112–131 (London: Routledge & Kegan Paul, 1986).

Hines, R. D., Financial Accounting: In Communicating Reality, We Construct Reality, *Accounting Organizations and Society* (988) pp. 251–261.

Hines, R. D., The FASB's Conceptual Framework, Financial Accounting and the Maintenance of the Social World, *Accounting, Organizations and Society* (1991) pp. 313–331.

Hopwood, A. G., Accounting Research and Accounting Practice: The Ambiguous Relationship Between the Two, The Deloitte, Haskins and Sells Accounting Lecture (University College of Wales, Aberystwyth, 1983a), in Hopwood, A. (ed.) *Accounting from the Outside*, pp. 549–578.

Hopwood, A. G., On Trying to Account for Accounting, in Bromwich, M. & Hopwood, A. G. (eds), *Accounting Standards Setting: An International Perspective*, pp. 168–173 (Pitman, 1983b).

Hopwood, A. G., The Archaeology of Accounting Systems, *Accounting, Organizations and Society* (1987) pp. 207–234.

Hopwood, A. G., Accounting and the Pursuit of Social Interests, in Chua, W. F., Lowe, T. & Puxty, T. (eds), *Critical Perspectives in Management Control*, pp. 141–157 (London: MacMillan, 1989).

Johnson, S. & Messier, W., The Nature of Accounting Standards Setting: An Alternative Explanation, *Journal of Accounting Auditing and Finance* (Spring 1982) pp. 195–213.

Johnson, S. & Solomons, D., Institutional Legitimacy and the FASB, *Journal of Accounting and Public Policy* (Fall 1984) pp. 165–183.

Kirk, D. J., The FASB and Industry, *Journal of Accountancy* (October 1982) pp. 82–92.

Kirk, D. J., The Costs of Accounting Legerdemain, *New York Times* (6 September 1987), Section III, p. 2.

Klapper, B., FASB Will Face Opposition in Its Move to Set Accounting Rules for Nonbusiness, *Wall Street Journal* (21 June 1978a) p. 18.

Klapper, B., Accounting Study Could Set Off Sparks at Municipal Finance Officers' Meeting, *Wall Street Journal* (15 May 1978b) p. 35.

Latour, B., *Science in Action* (Cambridge: Harvard University Press, 1987).

Lowe, E. A., Puxty, A. G. & Laughlin, R. C., Simple Theories for Complex Processes: Accounting Policy and the Market for Myopia, *Journal of Accounting and Public Policy* (1983) pp. 19–42.

March, J. G., Ambiguity and Accounting: The Elusive Link between Information and Decison-making, *Accounting, Organizations and Society* (1987) pp. 153–168.

March, J. G. & Olsen, J. P., Ambiguity and Choice in Organizations (Bergen: Universitetsforlaget, 1976).

March, J. G. & Olsen, J. P., The New Institutionalism: Organizational Factors in Political Life, *American Political Science Review* (1984) pp. 734–749.

March, J. G. & Olsen, J. P., *Rediscovering Institutions* (New York: The Free Press, 1989).

Mautz, R. K., A Government Accounting Standards Board? Pro GASB, *CPA Journal* (August 1981) pp. 14–18.

McQuade, E. M., Loan Fee Accounting: The Controversy Heads Toward Resolution, *Magazine of Bank Administration* (October 1984) pp. 48–50.

Merino, B. D. & Coe, T., Uniformity in Accounting: A Historical Perspective, *Journal of Accountancy* (August 1978) pp. 62–69.

Meyer, J. W. & Scott, W. R. (eds), *Organizational Environments* (Beverly Hills: Sage, 1983).

Meyer, J. W., Boli, J. & Thomas, G. M., Ontology and Rationalization in the Western Cultural Account, in Thomas, G. M., Meyer, J. W., Ramirez, F. O. & Boli, J. (eds), *Institutional Structure: Constituting State, Society, and the Individual* (Beverly Hills: Sage, 1987).

Miller, P., Accounting Innovation Beyond the Enterprise: Problematizing Investment Decisions and Programming Economic Growth in the U.K. in the 1960s, *Accounting, Organizations and Society* (1991) pp. 733–762.

Miller, P. & O'Leary, T., Accounting and the Construction of the Governable Person, *Accounting, Organizations and Society* (1987) pp. 235–265.

Miller, P. & Rose, N., Governing Economic Life, *Economy and Society* (February 1990) pp. 1–31.

Parks, J. T., How Accounting Standards Are Changing the Home Finance Industry, *Journal of Accountancy* (November 1988) pp. 59–62.

Phalen, F., The Impact of SFAS 13 on the Retail Industry, *Financial Executive* (November 1978) pp. 52–56.

Previts, G. (ed.), *Financial Reporting and Standard Setting*, Symposium Proceedings sponsored by the American Institute of Certified Public Accountants (New York: AICPA, 1991, forthcoming).

Robson, K., On the Arenas of Accounting Change: The Process of Translation, *Accounting, Organizations and Society* (1991) pp 547–570.

Rose, N., *Governing the Soul* (London: Routledge, 1990).

Rudnitzky, H. & Sloan, A., Full Speed Ahead, Damn the Torpedos, *Forbes* (30 July 1984) pp. 34–37.

S&L's Various Strategies, Accounting Methods are Leading Investors to Focus on Core Earnings, *Wall Street Journal* (16 April 1984) p. 61.

Schildneck, B. J. & Berton, L., The FASB's Second Decade: A Focus on Twelve Issues [interviews with D. J. Kirk, J. J. Leisenring and P. Pacter], *Journal of Accountancy* (December 1983) pp. 94–102.

Tinker, A. M., Merino, B. D. & Neimark, M. D., The Normative Origins of Positive Theories: Ideology and Accounting Thought, *Accounting, Organizations and Society* (1982), pp. 167–200.

U.S. House of Representatives Committee on Banking, Finance and Urban Affairs, *Financial Institutions in a Revolutionary Era* (1981a).

U.S. House of Representatives Subcommittee on Financial Institutions, Supervision, Regulation and Insurance, *Deposit Insurance Flexibility Act* (1981b).

U.S. House of Representatives Committee on the Budget, *Budget Issues for Fiscal Year 1983* (1982a) Vol. 5.

U.S. House of Representatives Subcommittee on Housing and Community Development, *Housing and Urban-Rural Recovery Act of 1982* (1982b) Part 2.

U.S. House Subcommittee on Oversight and Investigations, *SEC and Corporate Audits Part 1* (Washington, DC: Government Printing Office, 1985a).

U.S. House Subcommittee on Oversight and Investigations, *SEC and Corporate Audits Part 4* (Washington, DC: Government Printing Office, 1985b).

U.S. House Subcommittee on Oversight and Investigations, *SEC and Corporate Audits Part 5* (Washington, DC: Government Printing Office, 1986).

U.S. Senate Committee on Banking, Housing and Urban Affairs, *Financial Institutions Restructuring and Services Act of 1981* (1981a) Parts 1 and 2.

U.S. Senate Committee on Banking, Housing and Urban Affairs, *Competition and Conditions in the Financial System* (1981b) Parts 1 and 2.

U.S. Senate Subcommittee on Financial Institutions Supervision, Regulation and Insurance, *International Bank Lending* (1983a).

U.S. Senate Committee on Banking, Housing and Urban Affairs, *Moratorium Legislation and Financial Institutions Deregulation* (1983b).

U.S. Senate, *Banking Regulators' Report on Capital Standards*, Hearing before the Committee on Banking, Housing, and Urban Affairs (1990).

Watts, R. & Zimmerman, J., The Demand for and Supply of Accounting Theories: The Market for Excuses, *Accounting Review* (April 1979) pp. 273–305.

White, L., *The S&L Debacle* (New York: Oxford University Press, 1991).

Zeff, S., The Rise of Economic Consequences, *Journal of Accountancy* (December 1978) pp. 56–63.

[5]

Corporate Disclosure Regulation in Australia

Jill McKinnon

This article discusses the system of regulating corporate financial disclosure in Australia. The first part describes the framework of the system in structural and operational form and explains how the system's development has been influenced by political and economic factors. The second part explores the notion that the system of regulation in a nation is likely to take a form, and operate in a manner, consistent with that nation's cultural values. This is explored by comparing the Australian system with that of Japan and noting how differences between the systems are consistent with differences in the cultural values of each nation.

While the regulation of corporate financial disclosure is a feature of most developed nations, the way in which corporate regulation is conducted varies between and across nations. Variations stem from a number of factors including historical events, political and economic links with other countries, and the underlying social and cultural values of the nations concerned.

This article examines the system of regulating corporate financial disclosure in Australia. The article has two objectives. The first is to describe the framework of the system, in terms of its contemporary structure and operational form, giving attention to the economic and political events which have influenced the system's development. The second objective is to explore the notion that the system of corporate disclosure regulation in a nation is likely to take a form and operate in a manner that is consistent with the cultural values of that nation. This notion is explored by comparing features of the Australian regulation system with features of the Japanese system and noting how differences between the two systems are consistent with differences in the cultural values of each nation. The article is organized into two parts consistent with the two objectives.

Journal of International Accounting Auditing & Taxation, 2(1):1-21   ISSN: 1061-9518

Jill McKinnon ● School of Economic and Financial Studies, Macquarie University, Sydney, NSW, 2109, Australia.

2   INTERNATIONAL ACCOUNTING AUDITING & TAXATION, 2(1)   1993

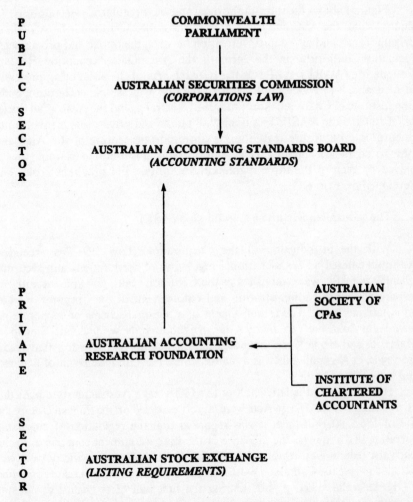

Figure 1.   *The Framework of Corporate Disclosure Regulation in Australia*

THE FRAMEWORK OF REGULATION IN AUSTRALIA

The responsibility for corporate disclosure regulation in Australia vests in three main authorities: the Australian Securities Commission, the Australian Stock Exchange, and the Australian Accounting Standards Board. Each authority employs a different mechanism of regulation. The Securities Commission (ASC) regulates disclosure through the Corporations Law. The Stock Exchange (ASX) influences disclosure through its Listing Requirements, and the Accounting Standards Board (AASB) uses accounting standards as its regulatory mechanism.

Figure 1 shows the three authorities and their regulatory mechanisms. The figure locates the ASC and the AASB in the public sector and the ASX in the private sector, and also depicts a relation between the public and private sector regulation authorities in the form of the Australian Accounting Research Foundation (AARF). AARF is the research arm of the accounting profession in Australia; it provides a link between the two professional accounting bodies (the Institute of Chartered Accountants in Australia, and the Australian Society of CPAs) and the AASB. This duality of public and private sector involvement in corporate disclosure regulation is an important feature of the Australian system. To understand how the system operates, it is useful to examine the role played by each of the three regulation authorities and how these roles have developed over time.

The Australian Securities Commission (ASC)

With the introduction of the Corporations Law 1991 (as amended), Australia entered an era of national regulation of corporations and securities, whereby the ASC was established as the Commonwealth government authority responsible for the administration and enforcement of the Corporations Law on a national basis.[1] The establishment of a national scheme of corporate law may seem "old hat" to many—our neighbours: New Zealand, Singapore, Malaysia, and Hong Kong, have had national companies laws for many years. However, in Australia this was a major achievement and the result of a lengthy and hard-fought battle.

Historically, in the latter half of the 1800s, each Australian state passed its own Companies Act. These Acts were largely modeled on the English Companies Act of 1862. At that time, it was regarded that the regulation of companies operating in a state was the province of the state Parliament concerned, so that when the federal Constitution was drawn up in 1900, no specific powers were included to give the Commonwealth Parliament direct power to create companies (CCH Australia, 1991, p. 14). During the first half of the century, the state governments jealously guarded their powers to formulate and administer corporate regulations, with each state developing its requirements along different lines. However, with the widespread growth of companies operating on a nationwide basis, the inconvenience of registering corporations in each state, and the potential for fraudulent practices by less scrupulous company directors and security brokers operating across state borders became apparent (Miller, 1991, p. 31). The problems associated with the state-based corporate legislation received prolonged and intense press criticism, particularly in the 1960s and 1970s, and a number of government-sponsored enquiries into corporations and securities were conducted during this period (Baxt, 1974, pp. 80-90). A common theme in their recommendations was the need for uniformity in the legislation and for a central "watchdog" to administer the corporate legislation.

4   INTERNATIONAL ACCOUNTING AUDITING & TAXATION, 2(1)   1993

Major steps toward uniformity in the corporate law were achieved in 1961 when the states cooperated and passed amendments to eliminate major differences between the individual legislations. Over the next 20 years, however, amendments were adopted by some states but not others and hence differences reappeared (Lipton and Herzberg, 1988, p. 4). The first steps toward a national scheme of regulating companies and securities occurred in 1976 when the Commonwealth and state governments agreed to a general framework for a cooperative scheme which was formalized in December 1978. After considerable dispute and compromise, our first efforts at national corporate regulation commenced in 1981. Complete uniformity was achieved in the legislations of the individual states and a national administrator of corporate law was established in 1981 in the form of the National Companies and Securities Commission (NCSC). This scheme, which operated until 1991, was quite fragile. At any time, any state could withdraw from the agreement and go its own way and, as administrator of the scheme, the NCSC was hampered by a paltry budget and political interference at the state level. In addition, the Commonwealth government was never happy with the fact that the effective power to amend the uniform corporate legislation adopted by the states lay with the states in consultation, and not with the Commonwealth itself.

In 1988, the Commonwealth government sought to introduce Commonwealth legislation for corporate regulation. Encouraged by a court case which implied a wider interpretation of federal powers,[2] the Commonwealth Parliament enacted The Corporations Bill in May 1989. The constitutional validity of this action was immediately challenged in the High Court by three Australian states, and six of the seven High Court justices held that the Commonwealth had no power to make laws for the incorporation of companies (CCH Australia, 1991, p. 17). However, while the states won the day, the move toward Commonwealth domination of corporate regulation was inexorable. Soon after the states' public victory, a compromise was reached to shift power for the legislation and administration of corporate law to the Commonwealth government. This compromise was sweetened by the generous compensation paid by the Commonwealth to the states for the loss of revenues from their day-to-day administration of the legislation.

Hence, while we still do not have a national corporations law in the sense of a law being based upon Commonwealth constitutional power and applying as a Commonwealth Statute throughout Australia, we have achieved an "effectively" national scheme of corporate legislation operated by the Commonwealth government (CCH Australia, 1991, p. 2). It is a regime of applied law whereby all Australian states and the Northern Territory passed application laws adopting the Corporations Act 1989 and the Australian Securities Commission Act 1989, and recognize the ASC (replacing the NCSC) as the sole administrator of the laws and the Commonwealth Parliament as having the dominant influence on matters of reform and amendment. The adopted laws are referred to collectively as the Corporations Law.

As administrator of the Corporations Law, the ASC is responsible for legislation dealing with companies, takeovers, securities, and futures. The ASC is an independent statutory commission accountable to the Commonwealth Attorney General and, ultimately, Parliament. In comparison with its predecessor (the NCSC), the ASC has a much healthier funding base, strengthened inspection and investigation powers, and, at least in structure, less potential for political interference. The ASC is supported by state Business Centers and Regional Offices to facilitate its administrative activities nationwide.

Regulation of corporate disclosure under the Corporations Law is orientated toward accountability and shareholder and investor protection. Corporate directors are required to disclose an audited profit-and-loss statement, balance sheet, and accompanying notes, together with a directors' statement and audit report. The financial statements must comply with prescribed regulations contained in Schedule 5 of the Corporations Law, and with accounting standards issued by the Australian Accounting Standards Board (AASB). The statements are required to give a "true and fair" view of the company's state of affairs.

The "true and fair" view requirement (and the predecessor term of "true and correct") is Australia's oldest specific disclosure requirement and, indeed, was the only requirement in early Companies Acts. Prescriptions for disclosure of certain items which enter into the determination of profit and the composition of financial position have steadily been introduced to the law in the form of Schedule 5 (and its predecessors, Schedules 7 and 9). With the introduction of the legal requirement for compliance with accounting standards in the mid 1980s, the need for the overriding "true and fair" view (a term which remains undefined in the legislation) has been increasingly questioned. An amendment to the Corporations Law in June 1991 has perhaps signalled the beginning of the end for "true and fair." The amendment reversed the rankings of giving a "true and fair view" and compliance with accounting standards, with the latter now taking precedence. Directors may provide additional information if they consider such compliance with accounting standards fails to give a "true and fair" view.[3]

The Australian Stock Exchange (ASX)

The second regulation authority discussed is the Australian Stock Exchange. Official records of stockbroking in Australia date back to 1828, when Matthew Gregson was granted permission by the Bank of New South Wales to trade in its shares. Stock exchanges were formally established in the capital cities of each of the six Australian states from 1871 to 1889 (Bruce, McKern,

Pollard, and Skully, 1991, p. 79). From 1972 to 1987, the exchanges operated under the umbrella of the Australian Associated Stock Exchanges and, in 1987, they amalgamated to form a national organization, the present-day Australian Stock Exchange (ASX). The ASX is a nonprofit, private sector body comprising, in 1991, 98 stockbroker corporations and partnerships (Bruce et al., 1991, p. 81). The conduct of the exchanges and their members is governed by securities legislation which dates back to the mid 1970s and currently forms part of the Corporations Law, 1991. Within this legislative framework, the ASX operates effectively as a self-regulatory body with its own strict and comprehensive Listing Requirements.[4]

As an authority of corporate disclosure regulation, the ASX is oriented toward the protection of shareholders and investors, and the promotion of share market efficiency. This orientation is reflected in the ASX's concern with timely disclosure as seen in its requirement for half-yearly and preliminary final reports in addition to the statutorily required annual report.

The ASX affects corporate financial disclosure through its Listing Requirements. These requirements, like those of the Corporations Law, have traditionally been concerned with disclosure rather than with technical accounting issues. In its concern with corporate disclosure, the ASX has to a large extent relied on compliance with accounting standards and corporate legislation. However, where it has considered that these regulatory mechanisms have lagged behind, it has been quick to insert additional disclosure items into the Listing Requirements. For example, turnover and funds statements (since replaced by cash flow statements) were included in the Listing Requirements many years before they were required disclosure in accordance with accounting standards. The Listing Requirements have been revised on a fairly regular basis, reflecting the Exchange's concern with promoting a "fair and efficient" market. The most recent of these revisions was in June 1991, when the ASX again required additional disclosure, including particularly onerous requirements in respect of related party transactions (Whittred and Zimmer, 1992, p. 7). Noncompliance with Listing Requirements may result in delisting of the offending corporation. This is a potent and immediate sanction which is used occasionally.

The Australian Accounting Standards Board (AASB)

The Australian Accounting Standards Board (AASB) is the third main authority of regulation in Australia. Standard setting in Australia has been in a state of flux for much of the past two decades. During this time, a battle has been waged between the professional accounting bodies and the government for domination of the standard-setting process. To say that we have reached a stable state in this process would be more a case of wishful thinking than supportable fact. In order to gain an appreciation of this conflict, and to place perspective on the current state of standard setting in Australia, the background is provided.

The development of standard setting in Australia may be divided into four phases. The first, termed a pre-standard-setting phase, can be viewed as running from the 1920s to the late 1960s. While various organizations were formed from 1886 onward to represent the interests of accountants in Australia, it was during this phase that the two present-day professional accounting bodies were established; the Institute of Chartered Accountants in Australia (ICAA) by Royal Charter in 1928 as representing the interests of accountants in public practice, and the Australian Society of Accountants (ASA) in 1953 as the representative body of accountants employed in commerce and industry (Allen, 1991, p. 54). From time to time during this period, both professional bodies issued pronouncements offering relatively brief technical guidance to their members. These pronouncements were issued on an ad hoc basis and were not substantive in nature. This first phase in the development of accounting standard setting in Australia was one of little activity; however, it does provide evidence that the professional accounting bodies regarded the regulation of technical accounting issues as their domain.

The second phase of standard setting covered the period from the late 1960s to 1983 and may be described as the introduction of formal accounting standards in Australia. During this period, accounting standard setting was the domain of the accounting profession. In 1965, the Australian Accounting Research Foundation (AARF) was established as a cooperative venture by the two professional accounting bodies. After a relatively slow start, by 1972 the AARF was clearly operating as the research arm and accounting standard-drafting body of the accounting profession. Accounting standards formulated by the AARF were issued jointly by the ICAA and the ASA and have become known as the AAS (Australian Accounting Standards) series of standards. Thirteen such standards were issued during this period.

In contrast to the relative calm and inactivity that characterized the previous phase, the second phase of standard setting was lively and conflictual. In the mid to late 1970s, the accounting profession came under intense and sustained press and government criticism on two main counts. The first criticism related to the poor level of corporate compliance with the standards. A review of the financial statements of 8,699 companies over the period 1978 to 1982 by the NSW Corporate Affairs Commission showed that 41% had not complied with one or more accounting standards (Walker, 1987, p. 270). The standards were only binding on members of the accounting profession and, as far as it is possible to ascertain, no disciplinary action was taken during this period against members of the profession for instances of noncompliance with the standards (Whittred and Zimmer, 1992, p. 2). The second criticism related to the lack of "due process" in the standard-setting process, and the lack of outside representation in that process (Henderson and Peirson, 1992, p. 90).

As a consequence of these criticisms, several government-sponsored committees were set up to enquire into the adequacy of existing mechanisms of regulating corporate disclosure in Australia. The first of these, the Chambers Committee (1978), recommended that accounting standards be given statutory recognition, but that the existing standards were not suitable for such recognition (Peirson, 1988, p. 1). The second, the Campbell Committee (1981), recommended that the accounting profession should continue to be responsible for the development of accounting standards, but that a "higher" body representing users, the government, and the accounting profession should review and approve standards.

In a joint response to these recommendations, the two professional accounting bodies proposed that, preferably, Australia should follow the Canadian precedent and give legislative backing to accounting standards designed and approved by the accounting profession, but that if the "more costly and possibly bureaucratic" step of establishing a "higher" review body were to be adopted, this should be sponsored by the profession or should at least be independent rather than government sponsored (Peirson, 1988, p. 2).

The government, on the other hand, was clearly displeased with how the profession was formulating and implementing accounting standards. Inadequate or fraudulent corporate disclosure attracted lively press criticism and was attributed in large part to the failure of accounting standards and accounting standard setters. The press criticism was directed not only toward the accounting profession but also toward the government. In order to deflect the criticism, the government needed to be seen to take action in this crisis, and such action was certainly not going to be to "reward" the accounting profession by giving it legislative backing for its existing standards. The government argued that the profession had had plenty of time to "get its house in order" and had failed to do so.

The action taken by the government in response to the criticisms of corporate disclosure ushered in the third phase in the development of standard setting in Australia. This phase, which covered the period from 1983 to 1988, was a time of government domination (at least in structural form) of standard setting. The government-sponsored Accounting Standards Review Board (ASRB) was established in January 1984 by a formal resolution of the Ministerial Council.[5] The ASRB was initially comprised of seven, primarily part-time, members appointed by the Ministerial Council, with nominations for appointment being called from a wide range of interest groups including the two professional accounting bodies, the stock exchanges, the Institute of Directors, the Shareholders Association, and the Business Council of Australia. The ASRB was empowered to review accounting standards referred to it and to approve those it considered appropriate. Accounting standards could be submitted to the ASRB by any group, not just the accounting profession, although the majority of submissions came from the AARF, the research arm of the accounting profession. In fulfilling its review function, the ASRB followed "due process," issuing standards submitted to it as exposure drafts, requesting and reviewing submissions from interested parties, seeking expert advice, and, where deemed necessary, holding public hearings into the appropriateness of proposed standards. Accounting standards approved by the ASRB were given backing in corporate legislation.

In operational form, this phase was again conflictual. Understandably, the accounting profession resented the imposition of the ASRB. The first two years of the ASRB's life saw great arguments over trivial issues such as who held copyright on accounting standards submitted by the AARF to the ASRB, the legal wording and arrangement of material in the standards, and the priority of accounting issues in terms of the need for standards dealing with these issues (Walker, 1987, pp. 274-275). The tensions between the ASRB and the accounting profession received considerable press coverage and drew strong public criticism of both parties from the (then) Chairman of the NCSC (Bosch, 1985).

Hence, in the first two years of the life of the ASRB, little progress was made in terms of approving accounting standards. While the next six years saw a much greater rate of progress in issuing accounting standards, substantial frustration with the system remained. The ASRB, with an annual budget of about $A 200,000, was never in a position financially either to sponsor the development of accounting standards or to obtain expert advice from sources other than the AARF. It was the AARF, funded by the profession, which had both the financial resources and the accounting expertise. However, the ASRB was sensitive about being seen as just "rubber stamping" accounting standards proposed by the AARF. It was able to show in a number of small ways that this was not the case, but in 1986 it "flexed its muscles" and forced the AARF to change its mandated method of accounting for unrealized exchange gains on foreign currency transactions. This enforced change was very public and embarrassing for the AARF, which had spent considerable time and resources formulating and taking submissions on this standard.[6]

The public conflict between the AARF and the ASRB probably brought to the boil frustrations simmering in other areas. With the AARF submitting its AAS series of standards, which had already been through exposure drafts and public submissions, and the ASRB then re-exposing the proposed standards and taking further submissions, it was claimed that standards were being subjected to a dual "due process" and that this was wasting time and limited standard-setting resources (Peirson, 1988, p. 4). In addition, corporations were technically subject to both the AAS and the ASRB series of standards and many preparers and others complained that the situation was confusing (McGregor, 1989, pp. 48-49). Henderson and Peirson noted that the AARF and the professional accounting bodies believed at this stage that "while the objective of statutory backing for accounting standards was desirable, the current arrangements were unworkable." The profession believed that a merger of the standard-setting activities was essential, and instigated negotiations for such a merger with the NCSC (Henderson and Peirson, 1992, p. 95).

The fourth and current phase in the development of our standard-setting process may be termed dual government/profession regulation. This phase commenced in 1989, when the AARF and the ASRB entered what they described as a "joint venture" in standing setting. While the structure of the new regime is somewhat fuzzy, it primarily has the following features. The AARF and the ASRB remain as separate bodies, but their standard-setting functions have been merged. As part of the merger, the ICAA and the Australian Society of CPAs (formally the Australian Society of Accountants), representing the accounting profession, have been given two more positions on the ASRB, bringing the profession's representation to four of the nine positions. The dual "due process" has been removed and the two bodies work together in the formulation of accounting standards. The AARF is the research arm of the merged process, providing administrative and technical services. Proposed standards are issued as exposure drafts and submissions are invited by the ASRB, which, with the introduction of the Corporations Law and the new centralized system of corporate regulation in 1991, was reconstituted as the Australian Accounting Standards Board (AASB).

The AASB is a federal statutory board accountable to the Commonwealth Parliament rather than to the Ministerial Council, which had been the case with the ASRB. Additionally, the functions and powers of the AASB are embodied in the law rather than being issued as a resolution of the Ministerial Council. These changes have had the effect of formally moving the government's involvement in the standard-setting process from the state to the Commonwealth level and generally "cleaning up" the structure. The functions of the AASB, which are broadly similar to those of the old ASRB, are formally stated in the Australian Securities Commission Act (1989, section 226) as follows.

The Standards Board has such functions as are conferred on it by or under a national scheme law, and also the following functions:

- (a)   to develop a conceptual framework, not having the force of an accounting standard, for the purpose of evaluating proposed accounting standards;
- (b)   to review proposed accounting standards;
- (c)   to sponsor or undertake the development of possible accounting standards;
- (d)   to engage in such public consultation as may be necessary to decide whether or not it should make a proposed accounting standard;
- (e)   to make such changes to the form and content of a proposed accounting standard as it considers necessary.

The Standards Board has power to do whatever is necessary for or in connection with, or reasonably incidental to, the performance of its functions.

Under the current standard-setting arrangements, accounting standards are formulated jointly by the AARF and the AASB and are then issued separately as the AASB series and the professional AAS series. The AASB series applies only to corporations, their application stemming from the Corporations Law, while the AAS series is now restricted in application to noncorporate entities, including the large number of public sector organizations in Australia. The status of AAS standards remains as it was in the 1970s, that is, binding on members of the two professional bodies but with no legal backing.

The current standard-setting process in Australia may be described as dual government and accounting profession regulation. It represents a compromise between the two parties and, as such, the relationship may continue to be an evolving one, with each party making moves from time to time to improve its position. Such a move was made by the accounting profession in late 1990 when the Peirson report, commissioned by the AARF to review existing arrangements for standard setting in Australia and to recommend changes, was released (Peirson, 1990, p. 2). The Peirson report proposed the establishment of a body that would be largely independent of the accounting profession, business, and government, and whose funding would be broadly based (Miller, 1991, p. 35). The government's reply to this proposal came in February 1992, when the federal Attorney General announced that the government would not be implementing the proposals contained in the Peirson report. In addition, the Attorney General announced that from 1 April 1992, the membership of the AASB would be increased from nine to eleven by increasing the representation of the user/preparer group from two to four (Soh, 1992, p. 1).

THE INFLUENCE OF CULTURAL VALUES ON REGULATION

The first part of the article has described the structure and operational form of the system of regulating corporate financial disclosure in Australia and noted how the system and its development have been influenced by a number of different political and economic factors. The second part explores how the cultural values underlying Australian society have also influenced the structure and form of the system and, in doing so, draws on Hofstede's (1980, 1983) concept of national culture and on Gray's (1988) hypotheses about the link between national culture and corporate reporting regulation systems. The potential influence of culture on the Australian regulation system is explored in two ways; first, by examining the consistency of the Australian system with Australian cultural characteristics, and second, by comparing Australia with Japan, a nation which exhibits substantial contrasts with Australia both in terms of cultural characteristics and corporate reporting regulation.

Hofstede defined culture as "the collective programming of the mind which distinguishes the members of one human group from another" (1980, p. 25).

He described the content of mental programs as values, where a value is "a broad tendency to prefer certain states of affairs over others" (1980, p. 19). From a survey of the attitudes and values of nearly 90,000 employees of a multinational company across more than 60 countries, Hofstede identified four norm values which he termed "dimensions" of culture. These were: power distance (low to high), individualism (versus collectivism), uncertainty avoidance (low to high), and masculinity (versus femininity). Hofstede ranked some 50 of the nations studied on each of these four dimensions (Hofstede, 1984, 1980). Although there are many different ways of conceptualizing and operationalizing national culture, Hofstede's approach has received considerable subsequent support and is being used increasingly by accounting and organizational researchers (see, for example, Gray, 1988; Soeters and Schreuder, 1988; Chow, Shields, and Chan, 1991; Harrison, 1992, 1993; Pratt and Beaulieu, 1992).

Gray developed four hypotheses linking Hofstede's cultural dimensions to differences in accounting practices and systems in different nations (Gray, 1988). The first of those hypotheses related to a difference in the nature of corporate reporting regulation across nations; specifically, whether the regulation system was based on professionalism or statutory control. Gray described professionalism as "a preference for the exercise of individual professional judgment and the maintenance of professional self-regulation as opposed to compliance with prescriptive legal requirements and statutory control" (1988, p. 8). Gray theorized that three of Hofstede's cultural dimensions would be relevant in influencing whether a nation's approach to corporate reporting regulation relied on professionalism or statutory control. The dimensions were individualism, uncertainty avoidance, and power distance.

The cultural dimension of individualism is based on the relationship between an individual and his/her fellow individuals in society. A high individualism culture is characterized by people focusing on themselves rather than on the group(s) to which they belong. Under this perspective, an individual is seen as unique and whole, that is, having a self-identity which is separable from and independent of a group affiliation (Hofstede, 1980, p. 235). By contrast, in a low individualism society (also referred to as a collectivist society), a person is seen as whole only when considered in terms of an in-group affiliation. It is the group, not the individual, that is seen as the basic unit of society (Hui, 1984, p. 28). Gray (1988, p. 9) hypothesized that, in a high individualism culture, there will be a preference for independent professional judgment because this is consistent with the emphasis on independence and the belief in individual decisions inherent in the value systems of such a culture.

Uncertainty avoidance is:

> the degree to which the members of a society feel uncomfortable with uncertainty and ambiguity. This feeling leads them to beliefs promising certainty and to maintaining institutions protecting conformity. Strong Uncertainty Avoidance societies maintain rigid

codes of belief and behaviour and are intolerant towards deviant persons and ideas. Weak Uncertainty Avoidance societies maintain a more relaxed atmosphere in which practice counts more than principles and deviance is more easily tolerated (Hofstede, 1984, pp. 83-84).

Gray (1988, p. 9) theorized that a weak uncertainty-avoidance culture will manifest professionalism in regulation because of its belief in "as few rules as possible, and where a variety of professional judgments will tend to be more easily tolerated." By contrast, a high uncertainty-avoidance culture will prefer codification and statutory control to promote conformity and uniformity.

The cultural dimension of power distance refers to the way societies handle the problem of human inequality. Low power distance societies are characterized by a norm value that inequalities between people should be minimized; and, to the extent that hierarchies exist within the society and its organizations, they exist only for administrative convenience (Hofstede, 1980, p. 122). High power distance societies are characterized by the acceptance of inequality and its institutionalization in hierarchies, which locate people in their "rightful" places. Here, the hierarchy reflects and reinforces inequality. In a high power distance culture, the right of the powerful to create rules and direct behavior is accepted and expected, regardless of whether the power is exercized legitimately or not. In a low power distance culture, the stress is on expert power, and the exercise of power is subject to evaluation of its legitimacy (Hofstede, 1980, p. 122). Gray (1988, p. 9) hypothesized that professionalism in regulation is likely to be associated with low power distance cultures because it is consistent with low power distance characteristics of a concern with equal rights and a belief in the need to justify any imposition of laws and codes. The acceptance and expectation of rules directing behavior in a high power distance culture allows the expectation of an association with statutory forms of regulation.

Gray did not operationalize or test his hypotheses. However, his hypothesis regarding the cultural conditions associated with professionalism and statutory forms of regulation allows a lens through which the regulation system in Australia may be viewed and compared with the Japanese system. That hypothesis was stated by Gray (1988, p. 9) as:

> The higher a country ranks in terms of individualism and the lower it ranks in terms of uncertainty avoidance and power distance then the more likely it is to rank highly in terms of professionalism.

Cultural Characteristics of Australia and Japan

Based on his (1980) measurement, Hofstede classified Australia as a high individualism, low power distance nation with a low to moderate level of

14   **INTERNATIONAL ACCOUNTING AUDITING & TAXATION, 2(1)   1993**

uncertainty avoidance. In terms of individualism, Australia ranked second highest among 40 nations classified by Hofstede (1980, p. 158). Only the United States ranked higher. For each of the other dimensions, Australia clustered with a number of nations, including the United States, Great Britain, Canada, and New Zealand, all of which have Anglo-American origins.

Australia's modern-day origin lay in its settlement in 1788 as a penal colony to take the overflow from Britain's cramped jails. Along with the convicts, Australia's free settlers and earliest immigrants came predominantly from Britain and Ireland. Since the Second World War, our immigration policy has been more broadly based, and we have to some extent become a multicultural nation. Nonetheless, the cultural characteristics attributed to Australia by Hofstede are supported by contemporary social commentators and sociologists. For example, Australia's high individualism ranking is consistent with the observations of social commentators who note our emphasis on individuality, individual achievements and self-reliance (Horne, 1985; Younger, 1970). The norms and values attributed to low power distance nations, such as an emphasis on democratic processes, less emphasis on class and status, the presence of two major political parties (rather than one dominant one), and a central role played by the courts of law in monitoring the relationship between government and society, are all clearly present in Australia (Aitken and Castles, 1989). Withers (1989) described Australia as a fairly affluent, easy-going, and egalitarian society, further supporting a low power distance classification. Australia's low to moderate uncertainty avoidance ranking is also fairly consistent with the nation's reasonable tolerance for differences, dissent, and eccentrics, accompanied by an acceptance of a moderate level of rules and regulations as a necessary means of ordering economic and social activity.

By contrast with Australia, Hofstede (1980, p. 159) classified Japan as a low individualism nation with moderate to high levels of power distance and high uncertainty avoidance. On this latter dimension, Japan ranked fourth highest of the 40 countries classified by Hofstede (p. 122). Again, sociological literature supports Hofstede's classifications. For example, Japan's ranking as low individualism is consistent with the widely recognized "group consciousness" of Japanese society (Nakane, 1970; Reischauer, 1977). Its moderate to high power distance is consistent with the importance of relative rank in fixing social position in Japan (Nakane, 1970) and with the Japanese belief in the moral basis of government, which draws from the Confucian precept of the natural existence of the "ruler" and the "ruled" (Reischauer, 1977, p. 139). These norms and values are realized in the greater level of active involvement of the Diet (the Japanese Parliament) and bureaucracy in all areas of social and economic policy formulation and administration in Japan than in Anglo-American nations (Harrison and McKinnon, 1986, p. 243). The high uncertainty avoidance ranking is also broadly consistent with the pattern of interpersonal relations in Japan. Social order is clearly established and defined through group membership and rank. The emphasis is on particularistic relations, rather than universal ethics, producing a very detailed set of situational codes of conduct, which are meticulously observed (McKinnon, 1986, p. 88). Bloom and Naciri (1989, p. 88), in their multination study, also pointed out the low threshold for uncertainty in Japanese society.

Using Gray's (1988, p. 8) description of professionalism in regulation as a preference for the exercise of individual professional judgement and the maintenance of professional self-regulation as opposed to compliance with prescriptive legal requirements and statutory control, the regulation systems in Australia and Japan exhibit clear consistencies with the contrasting cultural characteristics of the societies in which they operate in terms of responsibility for corporate reporting regulation and the process of standard setting. The Japanese situation is discussed first to provide a contrast and perspective on the subsequent discussion of regulation and culture in Australia.

Regulation and Culture in Japan—Contrast with Australia

Government and bureaucratic dominance, and statutory control, are primary features of corporate disclosure regulation in Japan. The responsibility for regulation vests in two government departments: the Ministry of Justice and the Ministry of Finance. The Ministry of Justice regulates disclosure by all Japanese corporations through the Commercial Code 1899 (as amended), while the Ministry of Finance regulates disclosure through the Securities Exchange Law (SE Law) 1947 (as amended), which applies to all listed corporations. The Commercial Code and SE Law are accompanied by Ministerial Ordinances which specify disclosure requirements in detail. The Ministry of Finance, through the SE Law, also closely controls the operations of the Japanese stock exchanges and licenced securities companies.

Standard setting in Japan is also government dominated. Accounting standards are formulated by the Business Accounting Deliberation Council (BADC), which is a deliberative council attached to the Ministry of Finance. Appointments to the BADC are made by the Ministry, which also provides the secretariat (Nakajima, 1980, p. 60). Representation on the BADC is broad, comprising representatives from academia, the Japanese Institute of Certified Public Accountants (JICPA), the Japanese Stock Exchange, and *Keidanren* (the representative body of the large corporations). However, despite this representation, McKinnon and Harrison (1985) and Bloom and Naciri (1989, p. 87) provide evidence that it is undoubtedly the Ministry of Finance that exercises control over standard setting in Japan. Reinforcing this is the fact that accounting and auditing standards are issued as Ministry of Finance Ordinances.

Government domination of Japan's regulation system extends into the role and operation of the accounting profession. The profession is relatively small (approximately 11,000 CPAs for a population of 124 million) and primarily engaged in audit and taxation. The CPA Law accords the Ministry of Finance jurisdiction over the examination, registration, deregistration, and suspension of CPAs (Japanese Institute of Certified Public Accountants, 1987).

Bureaucratic dominance and statutory control in Japan's regulation system are not the result of historical accident or the nonexposure to alternative forms of regulation. Harrison and McKinnon (1986, pp. 242-243) discussed the attempt by the United States during the allied occupation of Japan from 1946 to 1952 to democratize the monolithic Japanese corporate system and to provide fair protection for Japanese investors by establishing a sound and democratic securities system. Specifically, the allies established the Securities Exchange Commission (SEC), the JICPA, and the Investigation Committee on Business Accounting Systems (ICBAS) as independent and autonomous regulatory authorities. All were modeled on U.S. exemplars, as, too, were the SE Law and the Certified Public Accountants Law (CPA Law) and the accounting and auditing principles and standards. A revision to Japan's Commercial Code was also enforced in 1950, with the objective of "promoting democracy and the rights of the individual in law by strengthening the status of the shareholder" (Harrison and McKinnon, 1986, pp. 242-243).

Within two years of the end of the occupation, however, the Diet abolished the Japanese SEC and ascribed its functions to the Ministry of Finance and converted ICBAS (renamed the Business Accounting Deliberation Council) from an independent advisory body to the Diet to a deliberative council to the Ministry of Finance. Additionally, the Diet revised the Commercial Code to restrict the rights of shareholders accorded to them under the occupation reforms. While these actions did not remove the bodies and laws put in place by the allies to "improve corporate reporting," they diminished substantially the democratization and decentralization of autonomy of the regulatory authorities. Bringing all aspects of corporate disclosure regulation back under bureaucratic control was a deliberate choice and reflected the reemergence of Japanese cultural influences, which had been suppressed during the allied occupation. The actions taken to restore bureaucratic dominance and statutory control to the regulation system were entirely consistent with and illustrative of both high power distance and high uncertainty avoidance cultural characteristics in that those actions restored the natural existence of the ruler and the ruled, and were designed to remove ambiguity and uncertainty from the regulation process.

Regulation and Culture in Australia

In contrast to Japan's public sector dominance, corporate disclosure regulation in Australia has both private and public sector influences. As outlined in the first section of the article, the Australian Securities Commission (ASC) and the Australian Accounting Standards Board (AASB) are located in the public sector, while the Australian Stock Exchange (ASX), the Australian Accounting Research Foundation (AARF), and the two professional accounting bodies (the ICAA and the Australian Society of CPAs) are all well-established private sector bodies.

The accounting profession in Australia is large, with approximately 22,000 Chartered Accountants (CAs) and 63,000 Certified Practising Accountants (CPAs) for a population of 17 million. The profession is self-regulating in all respects. Educational study programs and examinations for CA and CPA qualifications are controlled by the professional bodies, as are codes of professional conduct and disciplinary action. Professional accountants in Australia are engaged in a wide range of commercial activities including audit, tax, accounting services, insolvency and liquidation, management consulting, and executive placement.

Australia's regulation system has traditionally exhibited a clear preference for professionalism. Indeed, it is only in the last two decades and as a direct result of the press criticism of corporate disclosure practices that reflected adversely on the government as well as the accounting profession, that the profession's role has come under attack by the government. This itself was sufficiently unusual that it, also, received widespread media coverage. Never before had the government threatened to invade the territory of the accounting profession. Impinging on the territory of professions is not something governments in Australia have tended to do, with other professions such as medical and legal being left largely alone. This traditional and typical approach of relying on professional self-regulation is consistent with Gray's hypothesis about professionalism in regulation in a high individualism, low power distance, and low uncertainty avoidance culture.

The events and conflicts that surrounded the government's intervention in the regulation process are also consistent with a basic philosophy of professionalism in Australian regulation. On the surface, the government may be seen to have made greater inroads into the corporate reporting and standard-setting process in Australia than in other Western nations with similar cultural values (the United States, Great Britain, and Canada, for example).[7] However, the strength with which government intervention has been openly and publicly resisted by the accounting profession indicates the extent to which the profession has, and does, regard itself as the primary authority on accounting issues. The resistance and conflict between the profession and the government discussed in the first part of this article in respect of the third and fourth phases of development of standard setting in Australia is clear evidence of this. So, too, is the fact that it was the profession which instigated discussions on the merger of the standard-setting roles of the then ASRB (subsequently the AASB) and the AARF. In no way was this action motivated by an acceptance or recognition of an intrinsic right of the government to be involved in the standard-setting

18   INTERNATIONAL ACCOUNTING AUDITING & TAXATION, 2(1)   1993

area. Rather, it was a move away from the hierarchical structure imposed by the government originally and toward a structure reflecting equality.

In addition, the question as to which party (the profession or the government) has the most influence in the standard-setting process does not have an obvious answer. The situation is probably best described as a balance of power between government and profession which shows evidence of a continuing tendency to lurch from time to time in favor of one of the two parties as each seeks to advance its regulatory authority. The attempt by the profession to use the Peirson Report to improve its position relative to the government is an example of such a move.

An important weapon in the accounting profession's armoury in this power play is the conceptual framework of accounting that the AARF has been actively developing since the mid 1980s. Considerable time and resources have been expended on this project and substantial progress has been made. Since the merger of the standard-setting functions of the AARF and the AASB and the passing of the Corporations Law, the responsibility for the development of a conceptual framework has been stated in the Law as being that of the AASB. However, there can be no doubt about the profession's claim to the accounting knowledge that constitutes the conceptual framework. In addition, the funding, research, and project management for the conceptual framework have all been provided by the AARF. The conceptual framework has been given a central role in the standard-setting arena, being the body of knowledge from which future accounting standards will be developed and against which existing accounting standards will be evaluated. Hence, consistent with a number of other Anglo-American nations and in contrast to Japan, the accounting profession in Australia has placed great importance on the conceptual framework as an illustration of its claim to professional accounting expertise.

The ambiguous nature of the balance between the profession and government in terms of regulation influence is well demonstrated by the various views of academic observers and commentators, particularly Professors Walker and Miller. Walker (1987, pp. 274-275), the first academic representative on the ASRB, claimed that although the government seemed to have gained control of standard setting in Australia through the ASRB/AASB, in reality this was a "reverse takeover" and the ASRB/AASB had in fact been "captured" by the profession. Miller (1991, p. 35), the third and current academic representative on the board, commented, however, that "if that was so, the ASRB was a very troublesome captive."

The ability of the regulation system in Australia to continue to operate with this ambiguous balance of power is evidence of the consistency of the Australian system with the cultural characteristic of low power distance. Specifically, there is an acceptance of relative equality of influence among the participating parties, and strong belief and practice in the need to question and justify government intervention. Open conflict, where both parties survive the battle and continue to vie for an increasing share of power in an economically important arena, is a feature of low power distance societies. In a high power distance society, such conflict is likely to be much less public and, indeed, is less likely to occur, as the accepted hierarchical structure will have established the permanently dominant position of one of the parties. The Australian system is also consistent with the cultural characteristic of low uncertainty avoidance in that it continues to function in uncertain balance rather than with closure, as well as in tolerance of the duality of the public/private sector influences and the multiple judgments and opinions that such an approach embodies.

NOTES

1. A Westminster bicameral system of government operates in Australia at both state and federal levels. The state governments are the oldest, as from 1788 Australia was progressively settled as a number of separate colonies which later became states. Federal government commenced in 1900 with the passing of the Commonwealth of Australia Constitution, whereby the states unified to form a federal Commonwealth.
2. *Commonwealth & Anor v The State of Tasmania & Ors*, 57 A.L.J.R., 1983, p. 450.
3. Prior to this, directors were not required to comply with accounting standards if they considered such compliance did not give a "true and fair" view, and providing they also explained why.
4. At 30 June 1991, 1151 companies were listed on the Main Board of the ASX. There are approximately 788,000 operating corporations in Australia.
5. The Ministerial Council, comprised of the attorney general for each state and a federal government minister, was itself established by an agreement between the state and federal governments.
6. The defer and amortize method advocated by the AARF on this controversial issue was also favored by the majority of submissions received by both the AARF and the ASRB on the three separate occasions that public submissions were invited on the proposed standard.
7. Social commentators such as Aitken and Castles (1989) and Withers (1989) suggest that Australia probably suffers a little more government intervention than comparable Anglo-American nations.

REFERENCES

Aitken, D., and F. Castles. 1989. "Democracy Untrammelled: The Australian Political Experience Since Federation," in *Australian Society*, edited by K. Hancock. Cambridge: Cambridge University Press. 1989, pp. 208-227.

Allen, K. 1991. "In Pursuit of Professional Dominance: Australian Accounting 1953-1985," *Accounting, Auditing & Accountability Journal*, 4 (1): 51-67.

Baxt, R. 1974. *The Rae Report–Quo Vadis?* Melbourne: Butterworths.

Bloom, R., and M.A. Naciri. 1989. "Accounting Standard Setting and Culture: A Comparative Analysis of the United States, Canada, England, West Germany, Australia, New Zealand, Sweden, Japan and Switzerland," *The International Journal of Accounting*, 24 (1): 70-97.

Bosch, H. 1985. "Profit is a Measure." Address to Conference of Accounting Association of Australia and New Zealand, Sydney, August.

Bruce, R., B. McKern, I. Pollard, and M. Skully. 1991. *Handbook of Australian Corporate Finance*, 4th ed. Sydney: Butterworths.

CCH Australia. 1991. *Guidebook to Australian Company Law*. Sydney: CCH Australia Limited.

Chow, C.W., M.D. Shields, and Y.K. Chan. 1991. "The Effects of Management Controls and National Culture on Manufacturing Performance: An Experimental Investigation," *Accounting, Organizations and Society*, 16 (3): 209-226.

Gray, S.J. 1988. "Towards a Theory of Cultural Influence on the Development of Accounting Systems Internationally," *Abacus*, 24 (1): 1-15.

Harrison, G.L. 1992. "The Cross-Cultural Generalizability of the Relation between Participation, Budget Emphasis and Job Related Attitudes," *Accounting, Organizations and Society*, 17 (1): 1-15.

Harrison, G.L. 1993. "Reliance on Accounting Performance Measures in Superior Evaluative Style: The Influence of National Culture and Personality," *Accounting, Organizations and Society*, 18 (4): 319-339.

Harrison, G.L., and J.L. McKinnon. 1986. "Culture and Accounting Change: A New Perspective on Corporate Reporting Regulation and Accounting Policy Formulation," *Accounting, Organizations and Society*, 11 (3): 233-252.

Henderson, S., and G. Peirson. 1992. *Issues in Financial Accounting*, 5th ed. Melbourne: Longman Cheshire.

Hofstede, G.H. 1980. *Culture's Consequences: International Differences in Work-Related Values*. Beverly Hills, CA: Sage.

Hofstede, G.H. 1983. "The Cultural Relativity of Organizational Practices and Theories," *Journal of International Business Studies*, (Fall): 75-89.

Hofstede, G.H. 1984. "The Cultural Relativity of the Quality of Life Concept," *Academy of Management Review*, pp. 389-398.

Horne, D. 1985 *The Story of the Australian People*. Sydney: Readers' Digest.

Hui, C.H. 1984. "Development and Validation of an Individualism-Collectivism Scale." ONR Technical Report No. 31, Department of Psychology, University of Illinois, Champaign.

Japanese Institute of Certified Public Accountants. 1987. *CPA Profession in Japan*, 5th ed. Japanese Institute of Certified Public Accountants, Tokyo.

Lipton, P., and A. Herzberg. 1988. *Understanding Company Law*, 3rd ed. Sydney: The Law Book Company.

McGregor, W. 1989. "The New Standard Bearer," *Chartered Accountant*, (September): 48-49.

McKinnon, J.L. 1986. *The Historical Development and Operational Form of Corporate Reporting Regulation in Japan*. New York: Garland Publishing.

McKinnon, J.L., and G.L. Harrison. 1985. "Cultural Influence on Corporate and Governmental Involvement in Accounting Policy Determination in Japan," *Journal of Accounting and Public Policy*, 4 (3, Fall): 201-233.

Miller, M. 1991. "Shifts in the Regulatory Framework for Corporate Financial Reporting," *Australian Accounting Review*, 1 (2, November): 30-39.

Nakajima, S. 1980. "Corporate Accounting," in *Lectures on Japanese Securities Regulation*. Tokyo: Japan Securities Research Institute, pp. 53-63.

Nakane, C. 1970. *Japanese Society*. London: Weidenfeld and Nicolson.

Peirson, G. 1988. "The Role of the ASRB in the Standard-Setting Process," *Accounting Communique No. 6*, Australian Society of Accountants, Melbourne

Peirson, G. 1990. "A Report on Institutional Arrangements for Accounting Standard Setting in Australia." Report prepared for the Board of Management of the Australian Accounting Research Foundation, Melbourne.

Pratt, J., and P. Beaulieu. 1992. "Organizational Culture in Public Accounting: Size, Technology, Rank and Functional Area," *Accounting, Organizations and Society*, 17 (7): 667-684.

Reischauer, E.O. 1977. *The Japanese.* Tokyo: Charles E. Tuttle Company.

Soeters, J., and H. Schreuder. 1988. "The Interaction between National and Organizational Cultures in Accounting Firms," *Accounting, Organizations and Society*, 13 (1): 74-85.

Soh, D. 1992. "AG Decides Against Pierson Plan," *New Accountant*, 5 (4, February 20): 1.

Walker, R.G. 1987. "Australia's ASRB. A Case Study of Political Activity and Regulatory Capture," *Accounting and Business Research*, 17 (67): 269-286.

Whittred, G., and I. Zimmer. 1992. *Financial Accounting: Incentive Effects and Economic Consequences*, 3rd ed. Sydney: Holt, Rinehart and Winston.

Withers, G. 1989. "Living and Working in Australia." In *Australian Society*, edited by K. Hancock. Cambridge: Cambridge University Press, pp. 1-22.

Younger, R.M. 1970. *Australia and the Australians–A New Concise History.* Adelaide: Rigby Ltd.

[6]

Economic Reforms and Accounting Internationalization in The People's Republic of China

Jiashu Ge
Z. Jun Lin

This research article surveys accounting internationalization in the People's Republic of China, an underdeveloped socialist country. The internationalization movement stems from the significant changes in the social and economic environment, as a result of China's ambitious economic reforms in the last decade. The gap between Chinese accounting and common practices in industrial countries has been reduced remarkably. The research commences with the motives of the internationalization contextual to the specific environmental changes in China. The developments of accounting internationalization in the areas of accounting principles and standards, accounting regulations for foreign-capital-affiliated business, public accounting practice, and international accounting research and education are examined respectively.

With expansion of international trade and capital flow, business activities in various countries have increasingly infiltrated each other. This development has brought about an internationalization of accounting at the global level, because accounting (a business language) is an important instrument in facilitating capital flow and economic exchanges across borders (Choi, 1981; Enthoven, 1981; Doyle and Spencer, 1986; Irvine, 1988; and Rivera, 1989).

Generally speaking, internationalization of accounting could refer to the developments of: (1) a unique accounting system in the world; (2) a descriptive and informative approach covering all accounting practices in various countries; and (3) an operational accounting system for multinational corporations

Journal of International Accounting Auditing & Taxation, 2(2):129-143   ISSN: 1061-9518
Copyright © 1993 by JAI Press, Inc.   All rights of reproduction in any form reserved.

Jiashu Ge ● Professor of Accounting, College of Economics, Xiamen University, People's Republic of China, and Vice President of the Accounting Society of China. **Z. Jun Lin** ● Assistant Professor of Accounting, Faculty of Management, University of Lethbridge, Lethbridge, Alberta, Canada T1K 3M4.

130   INTERNATIONAL ACCOUNTING AUDITING & TAXATION, 2(2)   1993

(Weirich, Clarence, and Anderson, 1971). Clearly, the first dimension, although quite desirable, is difficult to achieve at present. Thus, the major developments in accounting internationalization today are aimed at promoting the understanding of all accounting methods and procedures applied in varied countries, and harmonizing the diverse accounting and financial reporting practices on a worldwide scale (Choi and Mueller, 1992). Harmonization of accounting will help to produce more comparable and understandable accounting information that could help international investors and creditors to make correct and efficient economic decisions about global concerns (Turner, 1983; IASC, 1989; Wyatt, 1989; Beresford, 1990).

Accounting has a common heritage in human civilizations. Although accounting evolved in varied forms in individual countries owing to the unbalanced developments of a specific economy, culture and technology, it is possible for accounting to grow beyond the specific borderlines (AAA, 1978; Needles, 1985; Gray and Roberts, 1991). The internationalization of accounting has gained a remarkable momentum in the world, although its progress has varied in different social and economic environments. Even in socialist countries, internationalization of accounting has progressed steadily resulting from significant social and economic changes (Ash, 1985; Lin, 1988; Cheney, 1990; Aurichio, 1991; Fang and Tang, 1991).

DETERMINANTS OF ACCOUNTING INTERNATIONALIZATION IN CHINA

Accounting operates in specific social, cultural, and economic settings. None of its significant developments can be separated from the conditions of a given environment. This is particularly true for the internationalization progress of Chinese accounting.

After the founding of the People's Republic of China (PRC) in 1949, an early Soviet-style economic system was installed, that is, China adopted a highly centralized planning economy: the state controlled the ownership, the right to use, and the distribution of all production means and carried out rigid economic planning and control from the highest level to the grass roots. The state-owned enterprises were designed only as the basic production units; their operations, sales, and product pricing were all stipulated by the state's planning authorities, and their financing, spending (product costing), and profits allocation were subject to the strict administration or control of the state's public finance departments.

Under such a centralized economic and administrative system, the basic objective of accounting was to serve the needs of the state for economic planning and control. Enterprise accounting must: (1) provide data for the preparation of state economic plans and facilitate the implementation or statistical analysis of the plans; and (2) check and record all receipts and disbursements in individual enterprises in order to ensure their compliance with the state's public finance policies or regulations. In other words, performing a duty of "stewardship" for the state was the major obligation of Chinese accountants. Bookkeeping was the main task. All accounting procedures, the type of information, and the format of financial statements, had to follow the nationwide accounting regulations, called "The Uniform Accounting System" (UAS), promulgated by the central authority. In addition, as restrained by ideological influences, accounting was labelled with a distinct attribute of "class." Western accounting theories and practices were rejected entirely. In such an environment, Chinese accounting practices were quite different from the rest of the world.

Significant changes, however, have taken place in Chinese economic and business administrations since the late 1970s, resulting from China's ambitious economic reforms. A new economic system with the following characteristics has been gradually developed:

Increasing market mechanism. There was a strategic change to replace the highly centralized planning economy, first with a "Planned Commodity Economy," and more recently with the "Socialist Market Economy."[1] The state reduced its administrative controls over economic and business activities; many reform measures such as decentralization of decision-making, relaxation of price control, "tax instead of profit remittance," contract responsibility, and a share-capital (stock company) system were introduced, step by step, to develop a market-oriented economy. Enterprises were increasingly exposed to the pressure of market mechanics;

Expanding enterprise autonomy. The state has adjusted and readjusted its economic relations and financial responsibilities with enterprises by granting them a status of independent commodity producers with self-existing and self-developing capacity (i.e., economic entities). With a relative separation of ownership and operations, managements now possess greater power to make operating and financing decisions;

Introducing a multi-ownership economy. Many new business patterns such as associated-operation, business contracting or leasing, stock companies, and private business (called "individualized economy"), were all encouraged and experienced, aimed at promoting a diversification of the economy and enhancing business productivity. Corporate bond and stock transactions were initiated on an experimental basis. These changes broadened sources of financing for enterprises and enlarged the outside interest parties or user groups of accounting;

Developing foreign-affiliated business. Economic exchanges between China and other countries (Western countries in particular) were expanded, and the volume of foreign trade and other economic cooperations rose dramatically. Many "Special Economic Zones" and "Opening Coastal Cities" have been

132   INTERNATIONAL ACCOUNTING AUDITING & TAXATION, 2(2)   1993

established across the country since 1979 to attract and facilitate foreign investments.[2] Joint ventures using Chinese and foreign investments, and businesses with exclusive foreign ownerships, have increased steadily in the last decade.

All of those changes in economic and business environments have generated a need for accounting internationalization in China. With enlarged user groups of accounting information, diversified business patterns, and a decentralized decision-making process, accounting now must also serve the information needs of managements and other outside investors and creditors, in addition to the requirements of state economic planning and administration. Many new accounting issues rooted in market economy have surfaced. The original accounting framework of a simple "stewardship for the state" came to appear unfit. It became necessary to reconstruct Chinese accounting to meet challenges from the emerging market-oriented economy. In addition, the development of foreign-capital-affiliated business and other economic exchanges with the world market has demanded the introduction and adoption of internationally accepted business and accounting practices in China.

Thus, accounting internationalization in China, aimed at understanding and harmonizing international practices, became inevitable. It has brought about significant changes in Chinese accounting in the past decade. Particularly, developments in the areas of accounting principles and standards setting, accounting regulations for foreign-capital-affiliated businesses, public accounting practice, and international accounting research and education have evidenced the most remarkable progress toward internationalization of Chinese accounting.

IMPROVEMENT OF ACCOUNTING PRINCIPLES AND STANDARDS

Accounting practice is subject to the guidance of certain accounting principles or standards, although those principles or standards may have varied formats and applications in different social environments. In China, accounting has long been restrictively regulated by central authorities to ensure accounting data could meet the state's information needs for economic planning and control. The national accounting regulations, *The Uniform Accounting Systems for Industrial Enterprises* (UAS), formulated by the Ministry of Finance of the PRC, are the mandatory and all-inclusive accounting rules for state-owned enterprises across the country.[3]

Unfortunately, many inconsistencies existed in the detailed rules or procedures laid out in the UAS due to a lack of basic accounting principles and sound conceptual framework in standard setting in the past. The uniformity and authoritativeness of the UAS have long been overstressed under the highly centralized economic system. Accounting research and education were reduced to simply interpreting the UAS instead of examining its rationale. Furthermore, the contents of the UAS, serving as a tool of business administration, have been altered frequently to reflect changes in state economic and financial policies. Such fluctuations in accounting regulations have generated a negative impact on the comparability and understandability of accounting practices.

The deficiencies of the UAS had been voiced by accounting academicians and practitioners since the beginning of the 1980s. Following the introduction and analysis of the *Generally Accepted Accounting Principles* (GAAP) in the West, Chinese accountants began to pay attention to the studies of accounting principles. Many argued that the UAS, as the guidance for accounting practices, should embody the basic accounting principles derived from accounting work. Hence, those internationally accepted accounting principles (e.g., Entity, Measurement Unit, Period, Going-concern, Accrual-base, Actual/Historical Cost, Realization, Matching, Consistency, Comparability, Truthfulness (Reliability), Timeliness, etc.), as well as some specific principles unique to socialist accounting (e.g., Economic-planning-orientation, Regulation-compliance, Politicization, etc.), were examined and generalized theoretically, as an initial attempt to justify the formulation of the UAS (Li, 1982).

In pace with the progress of economic and accounting reforms, more discussions appeared to probe the rationale of the UAS. Some academics contended that the UAS gave too much weight to the state's needs for economic planning and control but insufficient consideration to the information needs of the enterprise's management and other external users. They advocated a reform of existing accounting regulations in China by drawing a line of demarcation between accounting guidelines and specific economic and finance policies, and replacing the UAS with a set of less rigorous "accounting standards," like the common practice in most other industrialized countries (Xue and Shi, 1982; Yang and Yian, 1985). This proposal earned the recognition of the government authority in charge of accounting affairs, and it has been identified as a key issue on the agenda of accounting reform since the late 1980s.

Therefore, the state would only establish some "directive" accounting standards concerning the general quality of accounting information instead of mandatory and all-inclusive accounting rules or procedures for businesses. In December of 1992, a new set of national accounting standards, "The Accounting Standards for Business Enterprises," was issued by the Ministry of Finance after several rounds of public discussion and revision.[4] In addition, 13 new industrial accounting regulations were formulated in accordance with "Accounting Standards for Business Enterprises." The new accounting standards and regulations, officially implemented on July 1, 1993, attempt to establish a better balance between information needs of the state, management, and external investors or other users. Industries or enterprises, conditional on compliance with the guidelines in the Accounting Standards and industrial accounting

134   INTERNATIONAL ACCOUNTING AUDITING & TAXATION, 2(2)   1993

regulations, are allowed to make certain modifications in terms of their own operating conditions to better serve management and external users.

Accounting academics have further proposed that the existing standard-setting process should also be reformed to involve the accounting profession. In February 1989, the Study Group on Accounting Principles and Standards of the Accounting Society of China (the national academic association consisting of accounting administrators, practitioners, and educators) adopted a motion at the Society's annual conference that it would study and periodically issue *Recommendations of Financial Accounting Standards for Business Enterprises*. It was decided that the six recommendations below would be examined and issued in 1990-1995:

1. *The Qualitative Requirements of Accounting Information;*
2. *The Truthfulness of Accounting Information;*
3. *Depreciation Accounting for Fixed Assets;*
4. *Accounting for Foreign Currency Translation;*
5. *Off-Financial-Statements Disclosure of Supplementary Information on Price Changes;* and
6. *Accounting Issues under the Share Capital System.*

These studies represent an attempt to build a new theoretical foundation for accounting standards setting in China, which can be regarded as a Chinese version of accounting conceptual framework studies with an assimilation of the same efforts in many Western countries. Although much has to be done in this area, the implementation of such a new standard-setting process will improve understandableness of Chinese accounting and enhance its comparability with prevailing practices in the world.

DEVELOPMENT OF ACCOUNTING REGULATIONS FOR FOREIGN-CAPITAL-AFFILIATED BUSINESSES

During the last decade, China has expanded its economic ties with other countries. The volume of its international trade and foreign capital inflow increased dramatically. By the end of 1991, according to official statistics, there were more than 28,000 foreign-capital-associated enterprises operating in China with U.S.$30.7 billion of foreign investments (including joint ventures, associated operations, and exclusive foreign ownership). The growth of foreign-capital-affiliated businesses has contributed to the progress of internationalization of Chinese accounting.

To improve the investment environment and protect the interests of foreign investors and other capital providers, the Chinese government has made considerable efforts, since 1980, to enact a series of legislation for foreign-capital-affiliated businesses. Related to accounting, the Ministry of Finance of the PRC stipulated a draft of "The Accounting Regulations of the People's Republic of China for Joint Ventures Using Chinese and Foreign Investments" (the "Accounting Regulations For Joint Ventures," or ARFJV) in 1983, which was formally approved and implemented on July 1, 1985. The essential purpose of the ARFJV is to incorporate internationally accepted accounting standards and practices into accounting regulations for the joint ventures and other business patterns associated with foreign capital.

The formulation and implementation of the ARFJV is a successful attempt to enhance understanding of, and harmonization with, international accounting standards by the Chinese accounting profession. For example, the ARFJV contains explicit provisions for accounting that deal with capital transactions, fund/cash flows, inventory, investments, fixed assets, intangible and other assets, liabilities, costs and expenses, currency exchanges and translation, sales and profits, auditing, business dissolution and liquidation, as well as the categorization of accounts (i.e., chart of accounts) and format of financial statements, in terms of internationally accepted practices. Many of these were completely new accounting procedures for state-owned enterprises. In particular, the ARFJV departed significantly from the existing UAS, and it is fairly similar to common practices around the world.

Technically, the ARFJV has adopted accounting practices prevailing in the West (in particular, the International Accounting). A major exception is the exclusion of the "Conservatism" convention (prudence principle). With an emphasis on the state's economic planning and the historical cost accounting principle, no provisions are allowed for bad debts or inventory write-downs. These losses can only be recognized as an operating expense or nonoperating loss when they actually occur.

However, the legitimacy of this procedure was challenged by accounting practitioners and academicians in recent years, and some alternatives appeared in practice. Support for certain conservative (prudent) accounting treatments, such as allowance for bad debts or contingent losses, mounted (Ge, Lin. and Wei, 1988; Hu, 1992). The government authority in charge of accounting regulations therefore reexamined the issue. A conditional application of the conservative treatment is now allowed according to the new version of the accounting regulation for foreign-capital-affiliated businesses.[5]

The ARFJV is not only applicable to joint ventures but also suitable for other forms of business with foreign investments or exclusively foreign-funded enterprises. Actually, it was revised and renamed the "Accounting Regulation for Business Enterprises with Foreign Capitals"(ARFFCB) in 1992. In addition, after the successful implementation of the ARFJV, more and more Chinese accountants came to believe that the ARFJV might have a wider application in a new economic environment with increasing market mechanics. Suggestions calling for revision of the current UAS by modeling it on the ARFJV emerged.

This view became a central theme in the "Symposium on Accounting Reform in China" held by the Administrative Bureau of Accounting Affairs of the Ministry of Finance in 1989 and has gained much support since then. In particular, the ARFJV (now the ARFFCB) has served as a model for the formulation of a new Accounting Regulation for Enterprises Experimenting the Share-capital System (AREESC) in 1992, applicable to the state-owned enterprises converting to stock companies. Doubtless, a greater comparability between Chinese accounting and common practices in the world will be achieved, following an expansion of the capitalist-style experimentation in the current wave of economic reforms.

RESTORATION OF PUBLIC ACCOUNTING PRACTICE

Generally speaking, the growth of the accounting profession is associated with the development of a public accounting practice, which refers to auditing and accounting services (including consulting) rendered by independent public accountants. Although public accounting practice existed in China as early as the 1920s, its growth was fairly slow. In fact, when the former Soviet-style economic and business administrative pattern was adopted after 1949, public accounting practice and the state audit system were all suspended.

Chinese authorities recognized the need to enhance economic supervision (inspection) in the early 1980s as economic reforms resulted in a decentralization of decision making and a much diversified economy. The Standing Committee of the People's Congress legalized the restoration of the state audit system in 1982. The State Auditing Administration (SAAC) was created and empowered to conduct audits for all government departments and state-owned enterprises across the country.

In addition, with a rapid increase in international economic exchanges and capital inflows, foreign investors, creditors, and other interested groups required more independent (or nongovernmental) auditors to attest to the creditability of accounting information relating to their businesses. Responding to such a demand, the Chinese government decided to resume the public accounting practice, along with the resumption of the state audit system, as an effort to improve the investment environment. Since then, Chinese Certified Public Accountants (CPAs) have resurfaced and they have played an important role in promoting the development of economic reforms and foreign-capital-affiliated business.

Public accounting practice in China is modeled after that of Western countries (U.S. practices in particular) and has progressed smoothly. Some major characteristics are listed below:

1.   According to "The Regulation of The People's Republic of China on Certified Public Accountants" promulgated by the State Council on July 3,

1986, a Chinese CPA must have a Bachelor's degree (or equivalent training or experience) and at least two to three years working experience in accounting or auditing. A candidate must pass uniform professional examinations and receive the approval of the Ministry of Finance or a provincial Bureau of Finance before receiving the CPA certificate;[6]

2. Public accountants can pursue their business only by organizing a CPA firm as a partnership (consisting of three or more CPAs approved by the Chinese authority). CPA firms (about 600 at present) must file registration with the Ministry of Finance (or provincial bureaus of finance) and apply for business licenses to the local branch of the Administration of Industry and Commerce. CPA firms are independent (nongovernmental), self-financed professional organizations (legal and economic entities), not subject to the jurisdiction of the State Auditing Administration (SAAC). They operate on a client-engagement basis but must accept the professional supervision of the Administrative Bureau of Accounting Affairs in the Ministry of Finance.

3. The primary business areas of CPA firms, according to the provisions of the "Law of The People's Republic of China on Joint Ventures Using Chinese and Foreign Investments" as well as related tax laws and accounting regulations, are validation of paid-in capital and annual audit of financial statements for business entities associated with foreign investments. It is a legal obligation that all foreign-capital-affiliated businesses within Chinese territory must hire CPA(s) registered with the Chinese government to issue validation certificates on paid-in capital and audit reports on annual financial statements. More recently, according to the newly issued regulations on securities issuance and trading, all publicly listed companies in China are required to engage CPA firms to provide accounting and auditing services.

4. CPA firms can render a wide range of other professional services, such as management consulting, business feasibility studies, tax services, design of accounting system, settlement of claims and debts, corporate registration, business dissolution and liquidation, and training of accounting personnel. They may also accept engagements from the state administrations of auditing, public finance, and taxation, or other authorities, to perform asset appraisal and annual financial statement audits for state-owned enterprises, as well as to participate in preparation of business contracts and investigation or testimony of economic lawsuits.

5. Chinese CPAs have developed various professional associations on the national and provincial levels. Bilateral exchanges with professional organizations in other countries have been established. For example, the Chinese Institute of Certified Public Accountants (CICPA) has developed various exchange programs with "Big Six" accounting firms since the beginning of the 1980s, by inviting foreign CPAs to lecture on training classes in China and selecting Chinese auditing personnel to be trained by foreign CPA firms. Foreign CPA firms are allowed to practice in China in cooperation, or as joint

138   **INTERNATIONAL ACCOUNTING AUDITING & TAXATION, 2(2)**   **1993**

ventures, with Chinese CPAs. Currently, the CICPA is actively preparing to join the International Federation of Accountants (IFAC).

Obviously, the restoration and expansion of public accounting practice in China has progressed rather rapidly in recent years. Since the early 1990s, the Chinese accounting profession has been in existence, and the CICPA has made considerable efforts to develop a series of auditing standards and guidelines, such as the Generally Accepted Auditing Standards (GAAS) in developed countries. An ethical code of professional conduct and guidelines for continuous education of public accountants have also been issued. Internationally accepted professional ethics and auditing standards, such as independence, personal competence, objectivity, materiality, due care, client confidentiality, audit planning, and supervision, have all been introduced into Chinese CPA regulations and the practicing standards and guidelines issued by the CICPA. Efforts have also been devoted to studying and standardizing audit procedures and the format of auditor reports nationwide.

ENHANCEMENT OF INTERNATIONAL ACCOUNTING RESEARCH AND EDUCATION

As part of internationalization of Chinese accounting, international accounting research and education in China have been stimulated with two objectives: (1) to study the accounting experience of other countries in order to assimilate or incorporate advanced accounting theories and practices into Chinese accounting; and (2) to train a large number of accounting personnel to be able to understand and apply knowledge of international accounting (Western accounting, in particular) to meet the business demands of the new economic environment. International accounting research and education boomed in the past decade and have become an important motivation for the promotion of accounting internationalization in China.

Stimulation of International Accounting Research

Research on international accounting has flourished in China since the end of the 1970s. Initially, the major effort was concentrated on introducing Western accounting. A great deal of Western literature and textbooks on financial accounting, managerial accounting, GAAP, analysis of financial statements, and auditing was introduced systematically.

Later, research focus switched to comparative studies of accounting systems in various countries to analyze the commonality and differences of varied accounting systems in different social, economic, and cultural contexts. For example, the Accounting Society of China sponsored a joint research project on comparative study of Sino-U.S. accounting systems in the mid-1980s. Accounting scholars from both countries have conducted a systematic comparison of accounting objectives, accounting functions, basic accounting assumptions and principles, structure of the profession, and accounting education programs in the two countries. Such studies were not limited to accounting practices in the industrialized Western world but also embraced accounting developments in Eastern Europe and other less developed countries.

In addition, some worldwide accounting issues were closely examined in light of Chinese circumstances. In pace with the advance of economic reforms, for example, many common accounting issues such as accounting for price changes, foreign currency translation, and business combinations surfaced in China. This forced Chinese accountants to study international practices and relevant accounting procedures in other countries, and to develop solutions suitable to Chinese situations.

Redesign of the Accounting Curriculum

Accounting curriculum is a key factor in promoting the development of accounting education and practices in a given country. Hence, redesign of accounting curriculum has been an essential task of accounting reform in China since the early 1980s. Accounting curriculum has been reexamined in most educational institutions across the country. Some accounting educators have advocated revamping the existing accounting curriculum and developing a new pattern similar to the knowledge and pedagogical requirements in other developed countries. Many Western accounting courses have been incorporated into the Chinese accounting curriculum. In particular, China's State Education Commission organized a Joint Symposium on Curriculum Development for Business Education in 1987, attended by prominent Chinese and Western business educators. A series of core courses and other innovative teaching methods for accounting programs were recommended by participants, and at present these recommendations have been adopted and implemented in most Chinese universities.

Initiation of the International Accounting Major

The demand for accounting personnel with broad knowledge and skills in international accounting has kept growing in the past decade, owing to increased international economic exchanges and foreign-capital inflows in China. Since graduates from accounting programs were unable to meet such a demand, a more specialized accounting program was initiated. A new accounting major—International Accounting—was formally established in leading universities, with the approval of the State Education Commission, in the late 1980s. This new accounting major aims at fostering accounting personnel who will be competent to work in joint ventures or associated operations using Chinese and foreign investments, as well as Chinese enterprises or other economic entities operating abroad.

The new program focuses on intensive training of foreign-investment-oriented business knowledge and skill. Its curriculum is comprised of core accounting courses in the West, including international economics, international finance, international taxation, international marketing, foreign trade, and foreign languages, in addition to general education. Although the new program remains an experiment, it has bright prospects as the demand for it is high.

CONCLUSION

Chinese accounting has made remarkable advances toward internationalization in the past decade. This movement stems from changing social and economic conditions in China. Economic reforms have resulted in a partial market economy with much closer ties to world markets. The demands for accounting information to aid business decisions other than the information needs of the state have been emphasized. This development has stimulated the Chinese accounting profession to enhance its understanding and adoption of international practices. Progress in internationalization of Chinese accounting is now evident.

Accounting internationalization in China has now progressed from introducing or importing Western accounting practices to a new stage of analyzing, comparing, and integrating effective accounting theories and practices in China and other countries, with an aim of narrowing the differences between Chinese accounting and those of the rest of the world. Meanwhile, most internationally accepted accounting practices are in place in China, with certain modifications in light of specific Chinese circumstances. Although considerable differences between Chinese accounting and international practices remain at present, the internationalization drive has narrowed the gap remarkably. In addition, significant progress has been made in Chinese accounting research and education in the last decade to facilitate progress toward the internationalization. The process was temporarily interrupted after the "Tiananmen Event" in 1989, but the momentum of accounting internationalization in China never faded. In fact, the movement rebounded in full swing with the new round of economic reform that began in early 1992.

Internationalization of accounting, for the time being, does not mean a uniformity of accounting in all countries. Since accounting is a product of a given social, culture, and economic environment, accounting practices may vary in certain aspects in different countries. The goal of international accounting harmonization is to enhance understanding of accounting developments in different countries and to narrow the differences between, or improve gradually the comparability of, varied accounting practices. Doubtless, recent developments in Chinese accounting have made a significant contribution to the progress of accounting internationalization.

Acknowledgment: The authors are grateful to two anonymous reviewers for their comments on a previous draft.

NOTES

1. There have significant changes in economic policy in China over the past decade. In the mid 1980s, the Chinese government intended to pursue an economic pattern of "Planned Commodity Economy," which refers to a planned economy with incorporation of market mechanics to an extent, or a partial market economy. In 1992, a new economic strategy of the "Socialist Market Economy" was officially adopted by the 14th National Congress of the Chinese Communistic Party. Although it is difficult to interpret the restrictive attribute of "Socialist," the new policy emphasizes a market economy rather than a partial pattern as the ultimate goal of economic reforms.

2. At present, there are five "Special Economic Zones" in China—Shenzheng, Xiamen, Zhuhai, Shantou, and Hainan; and 14 "Opening Coastal Cities"—Shanghai, Tianjin, Guangzhou, Ninbo, Wenzhou, Fuzhou, Dalian, Qingdao, Yantai, Qinhua Dao, Zhangjian, Beihai, Lianyun Gan, and Nantong. A set of flexible economic policies, such as discretionary investment, low taxation or tax holiday, preferential tariff, and flexible labor policy, are adopted in those areas, in order to attract foreign investors. The preferential economic policies have also been extended to other coastal areas and border regions in the new round of economic reforms that began in early 1992.

3. Under the original system of accounting administration, the state's Ministry of Finance is responsible for setting the leading accounting regulations (UAS) for state-owned enterprises in manufacturing industry, whereas other ministerial authorities are allowed to set more specific accounting regulations for particular industries such as commerce, railway, chemistry, and capital construction. However, all of these industry-specified accounting regulations must be, in the main, consistent with the UAS.

4. Simultaneously, the Ministry of Finance has issued "General Standards for Business Financing," which lay down general guidelines and rules for corporate financial management and expenditure control and are expected tp have an impact on an enterprise's accounting activities.

5. According to the new accounting regulation for foreign-capital-affiliated businesses, a company may establish allowances for bad debts or possible losses, but it should obtain the consent of government financial departments in advance.

6. Meanwhile, Chinese CPAs, in a very small number, are mainly people who earned their CPA certificate and experience before 1949, as well as those who were granted the certificate through a process of evaluation based on requirements of schooling, experience, and professional competence established by the Ministry of Finance or provincial bureaus of finance. The first nationwide CPA examination was scheduled to be held in 1990 but was postponed to December 1991. Four subjects—Accounting, Auditing, Taxation, and Economic Laws—were covered in the examinations. The pass rate of the first CPA examination was about 4%. The second examination was scheduled for late 1993. However, according to current regulation, some accounting experts, such as accountants with senior professional ranks or senior professors of accounting in universities, may apply for exemption from the examinations.

142   INTERNATIONAL ACCOUNTING AUDITING & TAXATION, 2(2)   1993

REFERENCES

American Accounting Association (AAA). 1978. *Accounting Education and the Third World: A Report by Committee on International Operation and Education.* Sarasota, FL: AAA.

Ash, E. 1985. "Social Style of Teaching Accounting." *The Journal of Accounting Education,* (Spring).

Aurichio, K. 1991. "Western Accounting Principles Head East." *Management Accounting,* 73(2, August): 54-56.

Beresford, D. 1990. "Internationalization of Accounting Standards." *Accounting Horizons,* (March): 99-107.

Cheney, G.A. 1990. "Western Accounting Arrives in Eastern Europe." *Journal of Accountancy,* (September): 40-43.

Choi, F.D.S. 1981), A Cluster Approach to Accounting Harmonization, *Management Accounting,* (August): 17-31.

Choi, F.D.C., and G.G. Mueller. 1992. *International Accounting* (2nd edn.). Englewood Cliffs, NJ: Prentice-Hall.

Doyle, B.R., and S.D. Spencer. 1986. "International Accounting Standards: Why They Merit Support?" *Management Accounting,* (October): 28-29.

Enthoven, A.J. 1981. *Accounting Education in Economic Development.* Amsterdam: North Holland Publishing.

Fang, Z.L., and Y.W. Tang. 1991. "Recent Accounting Development in China: An Increased Internationalization." *International Journal of Accounting,* 26(2): 88-103.

Fitzgerald, R.D. 1981. "International Harmonization of Accounting and Reporting." *International Journal of Accounting Education and Research,* (Fall): 21-32.

Ge, Jiashu, Z.J. Lin, and M.H. Wei. 1988. "Conservatism Principle and the Accounting Regulations for Foreign-capital-affiliated Business." *Accounting Research* (Beijing, PRC, in Chinese), 2: 15-22.

Gray, S.J., and C.B. Roberts. 1991. "East-West Accounting Issues: A New Agenda." *Accounting Horizons,* (March): 42-50.

Hu, C.Y. 1992. "Problems and Solutions to Accounting Practices for the Joint Ventures with Chinese and Foreign Investments." *Fujian Accounting* (Fuzhou, PRC, in Chinese), (June): 41-43.

International Accounting Standards Committee (IASC). 1989. *Exposure Draft 32- Comparability of Financial Statements.* London: IASC.

Irvine, V.B. 1988. "Setting Accounting Standards for the World." *CMA Magazine,* (April): 13-17.

Li, Baozheng. 1982. "The Accounting Principles in the Socialist Countries." *Accounting Research* (Beijing, in Chinese), 3: 10-15.

Lin, Zhijun, 1988. "A Survey of Current Accounting Development in the People's Republic of China." Pp. 99-110 in *Advances in International Accounting,* Vol. 2, edited by K. Most. Greenwich, CT: JAI Press.

Needles, B.E. 1985. *Comparative International Auditing Standards.* Sarasota, FL: AAA.

Rivera, J.M. 1989. "The Internationalization of Accounting Standards: Past Problems and Current Prospects." *The International Journal of Accounting,* (Autumn): 120-141.

Turner, J.N. 1983. "International Harmonization: A Professional Goal." *Journal of Accountancy,* (January): 58-66.

Weirich, T.R., G.A. Clarence, and H.R. Anderson. 1971. "International Accounting: Varying Definitions." *International Journal of Accounting,* (Fall): 80-81.

Wyatt, A. 1989. "International Accounting Standards: A New Perspectives." *Accounting Horizons,* (September): 105-108.

Xue, Zhendan, and Chengyu Shi. 1982. "Enterprise Accounting Standards in China." *Shanghai Accounting* (Shanghai, in Chinese), 5: 2-8.
Yang, Jiwan, and Yian Dawu. 1985. "On Accounting Management." *Sciences on Economics and Management* (Beijing, in Chinese), 4: 32-41.

Part II
Disclosure Choices

[7]

Accounting and Business Research, Vol. 22, No. 87, pp. 229-237, 1992

The Impact of Size, Stock Market Listing and Industry Type on Disclosure in the Annual Reports of Japanese Listed Corporations

T. E. Cooke*

Abstract—This paper represents a contribution to rigorous testing of Japanese financial reporting and specifically reports on the impact of size, stock market listing and industry type on disclosure, both voluntary and mandatory, in the annual reports of Japanese listed corporations. The topic is of interest because findings in one country may not be applicable to Japan because of its so-called unique business environment and unique culture. It is found that size and listing status are important explanatory variables. In addition, manufacturing corporations were found to disclose significantly more information than other types of Japanese corporations. The interaction between industry type and quotation status was also found to be significant.

Japan has become a major world economic power and yet knowledge of Japanese '... accounting and reporting practices remains in its infancy. This knowledge gap poses a major obstacle to more effective [international] business communications' (Choi and Hiramatsu, 1987, p. xv) with Japan. This observation is still true in 1992, particularly with respect to empirical work on Japanese corporate annual reports. This paper investigates, by way of a pilot study, the influence of size, stock market listing and industry type on the extent of disclosure in the annual reports of 35 listed Japanese corporations.

Size has been found to be a significant factor in explaining differences in the extent of disclosure in a number of different countries (see, for example, Cerf, 1961; Singhvi, 1967; Singhvi and Desai, 1971; Stanga, 1976; Belkaoui and Kahl, 1978; Firth, 1979; Firth, 1980; and Cooke, 1989a). There are two reasons for including it in this study. First, if size is an important explanatory variable then stock market listing and industry type may be important interacting variables. Secondly, whilst size has been found to be significant in Anglo-Saxon countries this need not be the case for Japan which is sometimes considered to have a unique

*The author would like to acknowledge the assistance of M. Kikuya, and the comments received from B. Pearson, R. S. O. Wallace and the anonymous referees. He would also like to thank the Institute of Chartered Accountants in England and Wales (ICAEW) for their financial support. The author is reader in accountancy at the University of Exeter and holder of an academic fellowship of the Institute of Chartered Accountants in England and Wales.

business environment and culture. Indeed, there is a substantial Japanese literature that is often referred to as the *nihonjinron* (literally, discussions of the Japanese). The *nihonjinron* emphasises differences between Japan and the Occident that encompass climate, race, productive base, social base, socio-cultural mode and intellectual style (Dale, 1986, pp. 42–6). Whilst the environment may affect the level of disclosure in a particular country, size may be important in determining the extent of compliance with mandatory disclosures. It may be that large companies are more likely to comply with mandatory disclosures because they receive more public attention than smaller sized companies (Cooke, 1989b). Cooke (1989a) found that in the case of Swedish companies size was significant in explaining differences in corporate disclosure levels. However, if size is not found to be significant for Japanese companies this may be the result of differences in environment between Sweden and Japan.

Japan is also a country of interest because it is a major economic power, has many multinational organisations, some with overseas quotations, and has a domestic stock exchange in its capital city that has the second largest market capitalisation in the world.

Differences in culture may help explain why Japanese corporate organisations are unlike those in the West. For example, Kagono *et al.* (1985) argue that cultural differences between Japan and the US affect their strategic and structural orientations. Their research suggests that Japanese corporations face less rivalry than their US counterparts but are continually subject to demands for new products and have low mobility of capital and labour. In contrast, US corporations face intense rivalry, discontinuous jumps in technology and high labour and capital mobility. As a consequence, US firms are characterised by 'bureaucratic dynamics' with emphasis on products while Japanese corporations are epitomised by 'group dynamics' and are operations orientated.

Another important characteristic of Japan is that interdependence rather than independence is a cultural attribute. For example, 73% (in 1990) of the shares of Japanese listed corporations are held by financial institutions (43.5%) and other business corporations (29.5%). These shareholdings are maintained, in part, to consolidate business relationships and have the effect of making it extremely difficult for a hostile takeover to succeed. Reciprocal shareholdings and interlocking directorships are characteristics of the so-called *keiretsu* (corporate groups).

These characteristics of the Japanese environment make an investigation into the relationship between a number of independent variables and the extent of disclosure worthwhile. Unique cultural and environmental factors may lead to conclusions that are fundamentally different from those established for other countries.

Before discussing the research methodology and hypothesis development a brief resumé of the regulatory system is provided in the following section. A detailed analysis can be found in McKinnon (1986), Choi and Hiramatsu (1987) and Cooke and Kikuya (1992).

Japan's dual regulatory financial reporting system

An unusual feature of the post-war accounting regulatory framework in Japan is its dual nature (Oguri and Hara, 1990) in which listed companies produce one set of accounts based on the requirements of the Commercial Code (CC) and a second set based on the requirements of the Securities and Exchange Law (SEL).

Before the Second World War the Ministry of Justice had been the major influence on financial reporting in Japan since it administered financial reporting based on the CC 1899 and as subsequently amended. The underlying objective of financial statements prepared in accordance with the CC is to protect creditors and current investors. Consequently, disclosure of information on the availability of earnings for dividend distributions, creditworthiness and earning power is considered to be important (JICPA, 1984, pp. 4–5).

The role of the Ministry of Justice remains the same, although, particularly for listed corporations, its importance diminished considerably as a result of the post-war democratisation programme

imposed by the US which gave the Ministry of Finance considerable power. As part of this programme an independent Securities and Exchange Commission (SEC) was formed and the SEL was introduced under the auspices of the Ministry of Finance. Both changes were based on the position in the US. However, within a few months of the departure of the Allied Forces the SEC had been abolished and its role transferred to the Finance Bureau of the Ministry of Finance, thereby conferring additional authority on this Ministry.

The introduction of the SEL was a major change in the orientation of corporate financial reporting since disclosure required by the SEL is oriented to general investors (JICPA, 1984, p. 32). The requirements of the SEL apply to all companies that have issued securities to the public (i.e., in the main those corporations with a listing on a Japanese stock exchange). They affect about 3,000 corporations out of a total of about one million joint stock corporations. However, corporations subject to the requirements of the SEL represent a significant proportion of economic activity. The Ministry of Finance must be kept informed, not only through disclosures at the time of issuing securities by a registration statement, for which Ministry approval must be obtained by the issuing corporation, but also by continuous disclosure.

The dual nature of the regulatory system inevitably affects disclosure in corporate annual reports. All corporations produce one set of accounts prepared in accordance with the CC and these are distributed to shareholders and may be available to others if a request is made to head office. In addition all listed entities must prepare a second set of accounts that comply with the SEL. These accounts are rarely distributed to shareholders but must be filed with the Ministry of Finance and the appropriate stock exchange. Copies of the SEL accounts may also be purchased through designated bookshops or scrutinised at the appropriate stock exchange. The information in both sets of accounts may thus be considered to be in the public domain.

Purpose of the study and theoretical background

The purpose of this research is to examine the extent of financial disclosure in Japanese corporate annual reports and to assess whether a number of independent variables (viz. size, stock market listing and industry type) affect levels of disclosure. This research differs in a number of ways from those that have included Japanese corporations as part of their samples. First, this study covers 35 Japanese corporations compared with much smaller samples included in works by Choi (1973), Barrett (1977), Cairns, Lafferty and Mantle (1984), Stilling, Norton and Hopkins (1984) and Tonkin

(1989). Secondly, this study differs from Campbell's (1985) research in that it is not solely based on accounts prepared in accordance with the SEL but extends to annual reports prepared in accordance with the CC.

The disclosure of information in annual reports involves a company in costs. These costs involve information gathering, management supervision, audit and legal fees and the dissemination of the information. Whilst firms are obliged to disclose certain items of information because of statutory regulations—although, of course, they may not comply—it is often the case that corporations voluntarily disclose more information than is required by statute. When voluntary disclosures are made it can reasonably be assumed that the benefits of disclosure are perceived to exceed the costs.

Disclosure is defined here as consisting of both voluntary and mandatory items of information provided in the financial statements, notes to the accounts, management's analysis of operations for the current and forthcoming year and any supplementary information. Such a definition corresponds closely with that proposed by Wolk *et al.* (1989, p. 246). The definition of disclosure is operationalised as those items of information included in both the annual reports prepared in accordance with the requirements of the CC and the SEL. If an item of information is required to be disclosed in either the CC or SEL accounts then this constitutes a mandatory disclosure and all other items are considered to be voluntary. Thus, the definition of mandatory items is quite restrictive and consequently voluntary disclosure is wide-ranging. The distinction between voluntary and mandatory disclosures is provided for information purposes and serves to get 'behind' the aggregate data. However, in formulating the disclosure model the distinction was not considered important for a number of reasons. First, not all companies comply with mandated disclosures even though Japanese society is considered to be conformist. Secondly, the distinction between mandatory and voluntary disclosures is often blurred in Japan since companies must comply with GAAP (generally accepted accounting principles) even though the principles are not well specified (Cooke and Kikuya, 1992). Consequently the distinction is subjective. This is emphasised in the definitions of mandatory and voluntary disclosures used in this paper in which the narrow definition for mandatory items leads to the disclosure model being dominated by voluntary items.

Corporations with their headquarters in Japan are classified as those listed solely on the Tokyo Stock Exchange (25 in the TSE group) or those with a listing on the TSE plus at least one overseas quotation (10 companies in the multiple group). This distinction may be important since it is possible that corporations with multiple listings may disclose more information in their domestic accounts than corporations with a listing only on a home stock exchange. Indeed, Cooke (1989a), in an analysis of Swedish corporations, found that disclosure in the corporate annual reports of domestically listed corporations was significantly lower than that reported by multiple listed corporations. However, the Swedish situation is different from that in Japan because Swedish corporations with overseas quotations usually produce one corporate report in Swedish and this is translated into a number of foreign languages. In contrast, Japanese listed corporations not only produce two sets of annual reports for the domestic market but some produce a third set designed to meet the needs of the international reader, where the latter is normally perceived to be a US investor.

The independent variables

Choi (1973) suggested that corporations are motivated by the need to obtain scarce money capital as cheaply as possible. The demand for information from investors is likely to be greater in an international setting than in a domestic one (Choi, 1973, p. 159). Thus, public disclosures in corporate annual reports published in Japan may reflect the demands placed upon managers by sophisticated suppliers of capital, both nationally and internationally, or their advisors (Bevis, 1965, p. 9).

Size

Size can be measured in a number of different ways. In this paper, eight size variables are considered, viz. capital stock, turnover, number of shareholders, total assets, current assets, fixed assets, shareholders' funds and bank borrowings. Many of these variables have been used individually in previous research studies; for example, Cooke (1989a) used turnover, number of shareholders and total assets separately as measures of size.

Each of the variables used in this study is a measure of size in some respect and virtually all are used as size measures in ratio analysis. Perhaps the one unusual measure of size is bank borrowings. This is included because of the relationship in Japan between the banks and the corporate sector. The banks, under the direction of the bureaucracy, have been instrumental in the rapid post-war growth of corporations. As van Wolferen (1989, p. 121) notes: 'Another of the major functions of the Ministry of Finance is to regulate the flow of funds from banks into the business sector. Since the war Japanese corporations have had little choice but to rely for capital on bank borrowings rather than on equity raised in the public markets.' Therefore, it is possible that in the case of Japanese corporations, bank borrowings may be a measure of size in some sense. Indeed, the correlation between bank borrowings and the other size variables suggests that this is the case.

There is no overwhelming theoretical reason to prefer one size variable to another. However, each variable may contain an interesting and possibly unique aspect of size, despite any multicollinearity between the size variables. Consequently it was decided to use factor analysis to identify the internal structure of the set of variables. In the light of information on size, appropriately measured using factor analysis, the paper examines the effect of listing status and industry type on the extent of disclosure by Japanese corporations.

Reasons why large corporations might disclose more information than other corporations can be found in Buzby (1972), Choi (1973), Firth (1979), Schipper (1981) and Cooke (1989b). One aspect that is worth emphasising is that the potential for agency costs may be greater in Japan than in the UK or US because there are fewer bonding activities in Japan that create symmetry between the objectives of management and those of shareholders (Pettway *et al.*, 1990). Furthermore, because of the interrelationship between businesses and the existence of the *keiretsu* there are few monitoring activities in Japan.

Listing Status

Given the importance of size, listing status can also be a factor in explaining variability in the extent of disclosure. This is because multiple listed corporations may well incorporate certain aspects of foreign regulation into their domestic accounts. Again, this can be linked to the capital-need hypothesis since those corporations that wish to raise money at the lowest cost of capital through a stock exchange are likely voluntarily to increase disclosure. Consequently, multiple listed corporations, raising capital on the international markets, will have a higher level of disclosure than purely domestically listed enterprises if the requirements of overseas stock markets are greater than those of their domestic exchanges. Indeed, Cooke (1989a) found that this was the case and Singhvi and Desai (1971) and Choi (1973) also found that listing status was an important explanatory variable. Spero (1979) found support for the capital-need hypothesis and Firth (1979) found that UK listed corporations disclosed significantly more information than unlisted corporations.

Industry Type

Levels of disclosure in corporate annual reports are not likely to be identical throughout all sectors of the economy. This may occur for a number of reasons. For example, 'Japan's unparalleled econ-omic growth and the extraordinary efficiency and productivity of Japanese manufacturing' (Lincoln and Kalleberg, 1990, p. 3) together with the international exposure of the manufacturing sector may have an effect on the extent of disclosure in corporate annual reports that differs from other sectors.

In addition, there may be historical reasons for differences in levels of disclosure. For example, during the war years accounting in certain businesses was heavily regulated (Choi and Hiramatsu, 1987, p. 34). Such regulations included the issuance of Working Rules for the Calculation of Manufacturing Costs in 1937, cost accounting regulations for industries supplying war materials in 1939 and 1940, and in 1941 the Planning Board's Tentative Standards for Financial Statements of Manufacturing Companies. While all these regulations were abolished after the Second World War it is possible that they have had a lasting effect on disclosure in the manufacturing sector. Similarly, Cooke (1989c, p. 33) suggested that historical factors may have been important in the development in financial reporting in different sectors in the Swedish economy. He found that when Swedish corporations were classified into manufacturing, trading, services or conglomerate industry types, aggregate disclosure and voluntary disclosure was lower in those corporations classified as 'trading'. Stanga (1976) also found industry type to be a significant explanatory variable.

In the case of Japan, post-war economic success has been founded on manufacturing industry in which the '. . . economy prospers because areas of industry that show promise are stimulated by fiscal policies favouring investment' (van Wolferen, 1989, p. 7). Since manufacturing is of fundamental importance to Japan it is possible that levels of disclosure in their corporate annual reports may differ from those in other business sectors. Consequently, corporations included in this research are categorised as either manufacturing (21 firms) or non-manufacturing (14 companies).

Based upon the preceding arguments, the hypothesis to be tested is:

There is an association between size, listing status and industry type and the extent of disclosure by Japanese corporations.

Research method

The Annual Report Sample

In order to obtain a satisfactory sample, 100 Japanese corporations were contacted by letter (in English and Japanese) and requests were made for the 1988 annual reports. The corporations were selected by simple random sampling without replacement from the entire population of listed companies which are published in the *Japan*

Company Handbook.[1] The overall response rate was 35 per cent.

A major task is the selection of items of information that might be expected to be reported in corporate reports. Since the focus of this paper is disclosure of information to a wide range of users, an extensive (165) list of items, including both voluntary and mandatory disclosures, is included in the scoring sheet.[2] The selection of items for inclusion is influenced by previous research studies, recommended disclosures by the IASC, accounting standards issued by the Business Accounting Deliberation Council (BADC), Ordinances of The Ministry of Finance, statements and opinions issued by the JICPA, and the law. Thus, the list of disclosures is not directed at specific user groups, and is not constrained by the exclusion of statutorily required items (Firth, 1980) or by the exclusion of items likely to be irrelevant to a user group (Barrett, 1977).

The disclosure scoring sheet was pre-tested on three Japanese corporate annual reports and after consultation with Japanese accounting professionals the research instrument was modified. A similar wide-ranging approach to the measurement of the extent of disclosure was adopted by Spero (1979), Wallace (1987) and Cooke (1989a). The split between mandatory and voluntary disclosure items was as follows:

	Commercial Code accounts	Securities and Exchange Law accounts
Voluntary	107 (65%)	76 (46%)
Mandatory	58 (35%)	89 (54%)
	165 (100%)	165 (100%)

Scoring the Disclosure Items

The approach to scoring items is essentially dichotomous in that an item scores one if disclosed and zero if it is not disclosed in either the CC or SEL accounts. However, where an item of disclosure is clearly not relevant to a particular company, the entity is not penalised for non-disclosure. Whilst this introduces a judgemental element into

the scoring procedure, this was considered to provide a more realistic assessment of corporate disclosure than a strict dichotomous approach. Judgement in the dichotomous procedure was made after reading the entire contents of both the CC and SEL annual reports. Failure to adopt such a procedure would have meant that larger more diversified enterprises would be able and likely to disclose more information. A modified dichotomous approach was adopted also by Buzby (1972), Wallace (1987) and Cooke (1989a).

The disclosure index I_j for a set of accounts is defined as:

$$I_j = \frac{\sum_{i=1}^{n_j} x_{ij}}{n_j}$$

where

n_j = number of relevant items for jth firm, $n_j \leqslant 165$.

x_{ij} = 1 if ith (relevant) item disclosed,

= 0 if ith (relevant) item not disclosed,

so that $0 \leqslant I_j \leqslant 1$.

In determining the weights, if an item of information in either set of accounts is disclosed then the item is part of the information set, whereas if an item is not disclosed in either corporate report the item is classified as not being part of the information set.

The implied assumption when an item is relevant is that each item of disclosure is equally important. Clearly one class of user will attach different weights to an item of disclosure than another class of user. However, the focus of this research is not on one particular user group but rather on all users of corporate annual reports. An approach which tried to encapsulate the subjective weights of a multitude of user groups would be unwieldy, and probably futile. Thus, the approach here is in effect to assume that the subjective weights will average each other out. Support for not attaching weights can be found in Spero (1979, p. 57) and Robins and Austin (1986).

Descriptive Statistics

Table 1 provides some descriptive statistics categorised by type of disclosure. Whilst disclosure is split into voluntary and mandatory items, the regression analysis is based on aggregate disclosure, i.e. voluntary and mandatory disclosure together. It is noticeable that the mean scores for mandatory items are very high, reflecting a high level of compliance. However, the mean scores for voluntary disclosures are low and have a higher standard deviation compared to mandatory disclosures. Whilst the range of mandatory disclosure was from 88% to 100% the range of voluntary disclosure was from 7% to 41%.

One of the conditions necessary for regression analysis is that the sample must be random and

---

[1] Thus, there was considerable non-response to requests for corporate annual reports despite two follow-up letters in Japanese and English to non-responders. The low response rate may yield a non-response bias to the results given here, inasmuch as it may be considered that corporations which did not respond may be reluctant to disclose information generally. Thus, responding corporations are likely to disclose more information in their annual reports and hence the indices of disclosure calculated are likely to be biased upwards. However, there is no reason to believe that the bias varies between corporations in the different groups or has any effect on the interrelationship between the dependent variable and the independent variables. Thus, the sample is considered to be soundly based.

[2] A copy of the research instrument may be obtained from the author.

Table 1

Descriptive Statistics of the Disclosure Indexes by Type of Disclosure

	Voluntary	Mandatory	Aggregate
Mean	0.200	0.950	0.558
Standard deviation	0.095	0.027	0.060
Minimum	0.070	0.880	0.460
Maximum	0.410	1.000	0.680

drawn from a normal distribution. Standard tests (Stuart and Ord, 1983, p. 144) of the data set on the skewness and kurtosis for the values 0 and 3 respectively indicate the acceptance of the hypothesis that the data is normally distributed.

Model

A linear regression model is used to test the hypothesis. The problem of multicollinearity between the size variables was resolved by factoring and the principal factors were used as regressors. Standard factor analysis statistics established that the technique is appropriate in this case.[3,4] The full specification of the regression is:

$$Y_i = \beta_1 + \beta_2 X_{2i} + \beta_{31} X_{31i} + \beta_{32} X_{32i}$$
$$+ \beta_{41} X_{41i} + \beta_{42} X_{42i} + \beta_{51} X_{51i}$$
$$+ \beta_{52} X_{52i} + \beta_{53} X_{53i} + \beta_{54} X_{54i} + \epsilon_i$$

where

Y = disclosure index scores,

X_2 = factvar = (0.12736 capital stock + 0.13563 turnover + 0.13160 number of shareholders + 0.14327 total assets + 0.13715 current assets + 0.13863 fixed assets + 0.13913 shareholders' funds + 0.11949 bank borrowings).

Listing status

X_{31} = the company is multiple listed,
X_{32} = the company is listed on the TSE.

Industry sector

X_{41} = the company is a manufacturing enterprise,
X_{42} = the company is not a manufacturing enterprise.

---

[3] Bartlett test statistic, $p = 0.00001$; Kaiser–Meyer–Olkin, 0.81098.

[4] Estimates of the factors were obtained using principal components analysis from the correlation matrix. Since factor one dominates with 86.73% of the total variation and the second factor only contributes 8.41%, it is considered appropriate to incorporate one factor in the linear regression. The unobservable construct is referred to as 'factvar' and the observable variables are the eight size variables (capital stock, turnover, number of shareholders, total assets, current assets, fixed assets, shareholders' funds and bank borrowings). As the structure is fairly simple no rotation was adopted. It is a property of factor analysis that the (unrotated) factors are uncorrelated.

Interactive terms

X_{51} = a manufacturing company and listed on the TSE,

X_{52} = a non-manufacturing company and listed on the TSE,

X_{53} = a manufacturing company and multiple listed,

X_{54} = a non-manufacturing company and multiple listed,

ϵ = error term,

$i = 1, \ldots, 35$,

β = parameters (where the constant β_1 adjusts for any excluded dummy variables)

and where at least one of X_{31} and X_{32}, one of X_{41} and X_{42}, one of X_{51}, X_{52}, X_{53} and X_{54} is zero.

The regression analysis was undertaken with the interactive variables, X_{51}, X_{52}, X_{53}, X_{54}, set at zero; then this assumption was relaxed permitting some of β_{51}, β_{52}, β_{53}, β_{54} to be non-zero. Furthermore, since listing status and industry type are categorical variables, dummy variables were used for each of these variables, omitting one from each category to avoid perfect collinearity. Given the characteristics of the data, a first approximation of the relationship between the independent and dependent variables is a linear response function. Since this is a pilot study with no prior information as to the distribution of the residuals a reasonable assumption is that the errors have a homoscedastic independent structure which enables t-statistics to be derived. An analysis of the standardised residuals against the predicted values of the index for the models reported in the tables suggests that the assumption is reasonable.

Results

Multiple. Linear Regression

A summary of the first regression is provided in Table 2. Independent variables in the equation consist of the manufacturing group, the composite variable (factvar) and the type of company classified as multiple listed. The TSE group is left out of the equation since it acts as a dummy variable for the quotation status category.

Manufacturing corporations were found to disclose significantly more information than non-manufacturing companies and this was true

Table 2

Regression with no Interactive Coefficients

	Constant	Factvar X_2	Multiple X_{31}	Manufacturing X_{41}
β	0.510322	0.022747	0.044018	0.046659
T	38.278	3.013	2.173	3.074
Sig T	0.0000	0.0051	0.01080	0.0044

$\bar{R}^2 = 0.60417$, standard error $= 0.03744$, F $= 18.29823$.

regardless of quotation status. However, there was no significant difference in levels of mandatory disclosure between manufacturing and non-manufacturing corporations. The difference in levels of disclosure between manufacturing and non-manufacturing corporations resulted, therefore, from voluntary disclosure. The motivational force appears not to be government driven since there are no additional requirements for disclosure which apply to the manufacturing sector. The motivation seems rather to be capital markets based, although it would be a simplification in the case of Japan to conclude that corporations seek capital at the lowest cost and therefore obtain overseas quotations since rates of interest in Japan's domestic market have been traditionally low. There is no doubt that deregulation in the capital markets which led to easier issuing terms was important and as a consequence the proportion of total funds raised abroad by Japanese corporations increased substantially during the 1980s. However, part of the motivation is to match foreign exchange risk with foreign trade and earnings. Another reason for obtaining an overseas quotation has been to increase Japanese corporate presence and public awareness of their operations in the markets in which they serve and rely upon. Indeed, post-war economic growth has been founded on development in the manufacturing sector in which corporations have sought to expand, often by obtaining foreign market share.

Another feature of the regression equation is that the β of the multiple listed group is positive, providing evidence that multiple listed corpor-

ations disclose more information in their Japanese accounts than those companies with a domestic listing only. The Japanese regulatory environment is the same for both groups so it is possible that multiple listed corporations internalise some aspects of foreign regulation. To be categorical on this point would require a separate investigation which analysed levels of disclosure by each Japanese corporation with an overseas listing with the disclosure requirements of each foreign stock exchange. This would require a larger sample of Japanese listed corporations with overseas listings and is beyond the scope of this paper.

The second regression relaxes the assumption that the interactive coefficients are zero and the results are summarised in Table 3. Independent variables in the equation consist of the composite variable (factvar), X_{52} (non-manufacturing × TSE) and X_{53} (manufacturing × multiple listed group). The listing status categories, manufacturing companies, X_{51} (manufacturing × TSE) and X_{54} (non-manufacturing × multiple listed) were all excluded from the regression equation. X_{51} and X_{54} were excluded because they served as the dummies with which X_{52} and X_{53} were compared. For example, the β for X_{52} is negative, demonstrating that the impact on disclosure of this interaction term is inferior to the X_{51} category. Furthermore, the β for X_{53} is positive, demonstrating that the impact on disclosure of this interaction term is superior to the X_{54} category. This is consistent with the regression reported in Table 2, i.e. manufacturing companies in the TSE group disclose more information than non-manufacturing corporations in that group and

Table 3

Regression with Interactive Coefficients

	Constant	Factvar (X_2)	X_{52}	X_{53}
β	0.554493	0.022049	−0.042061	0.049311
T	61.683	2.882	−2.626	2.813
Sig T	0.0000	0.0071	0.0133	0.0084

$\bar{R}^2 = 0.60498$, standard error $= 0.03740$, F $= 18.35727$.

secondly, manufacturing companies in the multiple listed group disclose more information than non-manufacturing companies in the same group.[5] The inclusion of any one of the omitted variables reduces $\bar{R}^2$.[6]

Concluding comments, limitations and further research

The research set out to examine whether the extent of disclosure by Japanese corporations in their annual reports that are published domestically is associated with the size of the corporation, stock-market listing and industry type. It has been found that multiple listed corporations disclose more information in their Japanese annual reports than corporations listed only on the Tokyo Stock Exchange. Multiple listed corporations are much more in the public eye than other corporations and pressures for adequate levels of disclosure are placed upon them by investors, their agents, and other users. These pressures are not as great on corporations with a domestic listing only. Whilst this result is to be expected it is interesting to note that an overseas quotation has an effect on the extent of information disclosed in the domestic annual reports of Japanese corporations rather than on reports prepared for the international reader or for a foreign stock exchange. Corporations are willing to behave in this way, not only because of the differences in needs to raise external capital, but to match foreign exchange risks and to increase international awareness of their existence.

Size was found to be an important influence. The composite size variable (factvar), derived by factor analysis, was included in the multiple linear re-

gression equation. Total assets, shareholders' funds and fixed assets were most highly correlated with this factor. It appears that sheer size in terms of controlling assets is more influential on this factor than the number of shareholders.

It also appears that Japanese manufacturing corporations disclose significantly more information than other types of corporations, a finding consistent with the economic significance of manufacturing in that economy. In addition, interaction effects between industry type and quotation status were also found to be significant.

There are a number of limitations of this type of research. First, the focus of disclosure discussed in this paper has been on corporate annual reports which are only a part of the information set. In the context of Japan, external finance has often been raised from banks and these institutions have the power to demand inside information. However, in the second half of the 1980s Japanese companies raised considerable sums of money from international capital markets. Casual empiricism suggests that this, had the effect of increasing disclosure over time, with the added managerial bonus of increasing autonomy to the detriment of the banks. Such an assertion could be tested rigorously.

Other weaknesses include the lack of concentration on any single user group. This could be remedied by ascertaining a specific user group's information values and reflecting these in weightings of the items of disclosure in the model.

Another area for future research is to assess both qualitative and quantitative disclosure differences between Japan and other countries.

---

[5] If each of the size variables is used separately in place of factvar there are only small variations in $\bar{R}^2$ compared with the results reported in this section. The only exception to this is if bank borrowings are used as the size variable. In this case the R^2 with interactive effects increases from 0.60498 to 0.6410. This is of some interest since traditionally Japanese companies have been supported greatly by banks, as is the case in Germany, and is one reason why Zysman (1983) has described their financial systems as being credit based rather than capital market based as in the UK and the US. In the case of some Far Eastern countries such as Japan and Korea the level of bank borrowings is probably a good measure of size.

[6] Alternatively the sectoral effect may be modelled by introducing the interaction between X_{41} (manufacturing) and the size measure (X_2). The difference in the index between the two sectors is explained through the responsiveness to size rather than to a shift in the intercept in the regression. The regression result:

$$\hat{Y} = 0.567 - 0.076X_{41}X_2 + 0.109X_2 \quad R^2 = 0.4795$$

$$(68.928) \quad (-2.418) \quad (3.618)$$

$$0.0000 \quad 0.0215 \quad 0.0010$$

suggests this may be an appropriate model but it has inferior measures of fit and significance to the result reported in Table 3.

References

Barrett, M. E. (1977), 'The Extent of Disclosure in Annual Reports of Large Companies in Seven Countries', *International Journal of Accounting*, Spring.

Belkaoui, A. and Kahl, A. (1978), *Corporate Financial Disclosure in Canada*, Research Monograph No. 1 of the Canadian Certified General Accountants Association (Vancouver: Canadian Certified General Accountants Association).

Bevis, B. (1965), *Corporate Financial Reporting in a Competitive Economy* (New York: Macmillan).

Buzby, S. L. (1972), *An Empirical Investigation of the Relationship between the Extent of Disclosure in Corporate Annual Reports and Two Company Characteristics*. Unpublished doctoral dissertation, Pennsylvania State University.

Cairns, D., Lafferty, M. and Mantle, P. (1984), *Survey of Accounts and Accountants 1983–84* (London: Lafferty Publications).

Campbell, L. G. (1985), *Accounting and Financial Reporting in Japan* (London: Lafferty Publications).

Cerf, A. R. (1961), *Corporate Reporting and Investment Decisions* (California: University of California).

Choi, F. D. S. (1973), 'Financial Disclosure and Entry to the European Capital Market', *Journal of Accounting Research*, Autumn.

Choi, F. D. S. and Hiramatsu, K. (1987), *Accounting and Financial Reporting in Japan* (Wokingham: Van Nostrand Reinhold, UK).

Cooke, T. E. (1989a), 'Disclosure in the Corporate Annual Reports of Swedish Companies', *Accounting and Business Research*, Spring.

Cooke, T. E. (1989b), *An Empirical Study of Financial Disclosures by Swedish Companies* (New York: Garland Publishing).

Cooke, T. E. (1989c), 'Voluntary Corporate Disclosure by Swedish Companies', *Journal of International Financial Management and Accounting*, Summer.

Cooke, T. E. and Kikuya, M. (1992), *Financial Reporting in Japan: Regulation, Practice and Environment* (Oxford: Blackwell Publishing, and London: ICAEW).

Dale, P. N. (1988), *The Myth of Japanese Uniqueness* (London: Routledge).

Firth, M. (1979), 'The Impact of Size, Stock Market Listing and Auditors on Voluntary Disclosure in Corporate Annual Reports', *Accounting and Business Research*, Autumn.

Firth, M. (1980), 'Raising Finance and Firms' Corporate Reporting Policies', *Abacus*, December.

Japanese Institute of Certified Public Accountants (1984), *Corporate Disclosure in Japan: Reporting* (Tokyo: JICPA).

Kagono, T., Nonaka, I., Sakakibara, K. and Okamura, A. (1985), *Strategic vs Evolutionary Man: A U.S.-Japan Comparison of Strategy and Organization* (New York: North-Holland).

Lincoln, J. R. and Kalleberg, A. L. (1990), *Culture, Control and Commitment* (Cambridge: Cambridge University Press).

McKinnon, J. L. (1986), *The Historical Development and Operational Form of Corporate Reporting Regulation in Japan* (New York: Garland Publishing).

Oguri, T. and Hara, Y. (1990), 'A Critical Examination of Accounting Regulation in Japan', *Accounting, Auditing and Accountability*, Vol. 3.

Pettway, R. H., Sicherman, N. W. and Yamada, T. (1990), 'The Market for Corporate Control, the Level of Agency Costs, and Corporate Collectivism in Japanese Mergers', in E. J. Elton and M. J. Gruber, *Japanese Capital Markets* (London: Harper and Row).

Robins, W. A. and Austin, K. R. (1986), 'Disclosure Quality in Governmental Financial Reports', *Journal of Accounting Research*, Autumn.

Schipper, K. (1981), 'Discussion of Voluntary Corporate Disclosure. The Case of Interim Reporting', *Journal of Accounting Research*, Supplement.

Singhvi, S. S. (1967), *Corporate Disclosure through Annual Reports in the USA and India*. Unpublished doctoral dissertation, Columbia University.

Singhvi, S. S. and Desai, H. (1971), 'An Empirical Analysis of the Quality of Corporate Financial Disclosure', *Accounting Review*, January.

Spero, L. L. (1979), *The Extent and Causes of Voluntary Disclosure of Financial Information in Three European Capital Markets: An Explanatory Study*. Unpublished doctoral dissertation, Harvard University.

Stanga, K. (1976), 'Disclosure in Published Annual Reports', *Financial Management*, Winter.

Stilling, P., Norton, R. and Hopkins, L. (1984), *World Accounting Survey* (London: Financial Times).

Stuart, A. and Ord, J. K. (1983), *Kendall's Advanced Theory of Statistics* (London: Financial Times).

Tonkin, D. J. (1989), *World Survey of Published Accounts: An Analysis of 200 Annual Reports from the World's Leading Companies* (London: Lafferty Publications).

van Wolferen, K. (1989), *The Enigma of Japanese Power* (London: Macmillan).

Wallace, R. S. O. (1987), *Disclosure of Accounting Information in Developing Countries: A Case Study of Nigeria*. Unpublished doctoral thesis, Exeter University.

Wolk, H. I., Francis, J. R. and Tearney, M. G. (1989), *Accounting Theory: A Conceptual and Institutional Approach* (PWS-Kent Publishing).

Zysman, J. (1983), *Government, Markets and Growth: Financial Systems and the Politics of Industrial Change* (Ithaca: Cornell University Press).

[8]

THE ACCOUNTING REVIEW
Vol. LXII, No. 3
July 1987

Notes

Voluntary Financial Disclosure by Mexican Corporations

Chee W. Chow and Adrian Wong-Boren

ABSTRACT: This paper reports on voluntary financial disclosure practices of Mexican corporations and relates the extent of disclosure to firm size, financial leverage, and proportion of assets in place. Studying the voluntary disclosure of Mexican firms yields additional insights into factors behind voluntary disclosure choices, and enhances our understanding of the accounting institutions and practices of non-Anglo-American nations. Voluntary disclosure varies widely within a sample of 52 Mexican Stock Exchange-listed firms, and the extent of disclosure is significantly and positively related to firm size but not to financial leverage and assets in place.

THIS paper reports on the extent of voluntary financial disclosure by a set of Mexican corporations and tests the effects of three firm characteristics on disclosure. There are two objectives of this study. The first is to advance our understanding of accounting institutions and practices in non-Anglo-American nations. The second objective is to provide additional evidence on the factors behind voluntary financial disclosure. Many recent studies have hypothesized that firms' voluntary accounting and disclosure choices are aimed at controlling the interest conflicts among shareholders, debtholders, and management (see Holthausen and Leftwich [1983], Kelly [1983], and Watts and Zimmerman [1986] for reviews). It is held that the extent of these interest conflicts—hence the incentives behind voluntary accounting/disclosure choices—varies with certain firm characteristics. Since Mexico has a relatively unregulated accounting environment, it provides a suitable setting for testing the effects of these variables.

This Note is organized as follows. The first section provides an overview of the Mexican accounting environment. The next section describes the data collection procedures and reports descriptive statistics for the sample of Mexican firms. Results of cross-sectional regressions are then presented, followed by concluding remarks.

The authors are indebted to Mike Shields, the Editor, and two anonymous reviewers for many helpful suggestions.

Chee W. Chow is Vern Odmark Professor of Accountancy, and Adrian Wong-Boren is Assistant Professor of Accountancy, both at San Diego State University.

Manuscript received August 1985.
Revisions received May 1986 and November 1986.
Accepted January 1987.

ACCOUNTING REGULATIONS AND PRACTICE IN MEXICO[1]

Operations of business firms in Mexico are regulated by a number of federal agencies. The Ministry of Finance and Public Credit is by far the most important. This ministry includes the National Securities Commission (NSC), which administers Mexico's Securities Market Law and regulates the securities market.

The current version of the Mexican Securities Market Law was enacted in 1975. This Law regulates public offering and trading of securities, the Mexican Stock Exchange (a private corporation), and the activities of securities brokers and traders. Listing on the Mexican Stock Exchange requires approval by the NSC. Firms seeking such approval are required to submit a prescribed set of financial and non-financial information. Annual financial statements of listed firms must be certified by a Mexican certified public accountant, filed with the NSC, and published in a nationally-circulated medium.[2]

The NSC is the primary source of Mexican disclosure regulations. To date, the Commission's pronouncements in this area are contained in three "circulars" (similar to the U.S. Securities and Exchange Commission's Accounting Series Releases). While these regulations cover a large number of topics, their scope is still quite limited compared to what most larger U.S. firms are required to disclose. Further, they are mostly silent on issues of accounting procedures. There are also no federal or state laws that specify accounting practices. The primary source of accounting standards is the quasi-public Mexican Institute of Certified Public Accountants (IMCP). To date, the Institute's Accounting Principles Commission has issued 20 statements on generally accepted accounting principles. While these statements cover a broad range of accounting issues, they still appear to be far less comprehensive than their U.S. counterparts.[3]

The preceding summary of Mexican accounting and disclosure regulations suggests a much more *laissez-faire* environment than that in the U.S. An extensive search of the published accounting and business literature did not reveal any systematic study on how accounting/disclosure practices have responded to this environment in the period since the 1975 Securities Market Law.[4] Unstructured interviews with seven Mexican CPA firms' managing partners suggested that law enforcement is generally lax, and fraudulent accounting practices are common. Thus, firms in Mexico seem to have much more flexibility in accounting and disclosure practices than those in the U.S. Consequently, their accounting and disclosure choices are also more likely to reflect voluntary responses to market forces.

EMPIRICAL TESTS

This section addresses three topics. First, sample selection is explained. Then descriptive statistics on the extent of voluntary disclosure are presented and dis-

[1] More detailed discussions of the Mexican accounting environment are available in AICPA [1975], Ernst & Whinney [1983], and Price Waterhouse [1981].

[2] The specific reporting requirements are contained in the Securities Market Law (Diario Oficial de la Federación [1975]).

[3] Overviews of U.S. accounting practices and regulations are provided by Benston [1976] and Nobes and Parker [1981]. A detailed comparison of U.S. and Mexican accounting regulations is beyond the scope of this study. However, an examination of the sources cited in footnote 1 suggests that this general observation is valid.

[4] Our primary focus was the *Business Periodicals Index* from 1978 to 1985. We also searched selected Mexican business periodicals and accounting texts. Mexican accounting practices in an earlier period are discussed in Zeff [1972].

cussed. Finally, results of cross-sectional regressions are reported.

Sample Selection

The sample firms were chosen from the Mexican federal government's 1982 *Official Gazette*. This daily (except Saturdays and Sundays) publication is the primary outlet for exchange-listed firms' required annual reports to external users. For the year 1982, the *Gazette* contained annual reports of 73 listed firms. The 13 banks within this set were dropped because they are subject to additional reporting regulations. We also eliminated eight firms from the service industry. The final sample of 52 firms all belonged to the manufacturing sector.[5] As such, their operations, and thus the types of information available for voluntary disclosure, should be relatively homogeneous in nature.

Extent of Voluntary Disclosure

A firm's extent of voluntary financial disclosure was operationalized with two alternate disclosure scores. These scores were obtained using a three-step process:

1. *Identifying Voluntary Disclosure Items.* By referring to the pronouncements of the Mexican authorities, Mexican accounting texts, and prior studies [Choi, 1973; Buzby, 1975; Barrett, 1976; Firth, 1979; and McNally, Eng, and Hasseldine, 1982], we generated a preliminary list of financial items that Mexican firms may disclose. This list was reviewed by the credit department heads of eight Mexican banks. Their feedback was used to compile a final list of 89 items.

Next, the managing partners of four large Mexican CPA firms were asked to indicate which items from the list were required to be disclosed by exchange-listed firms. Fifty-three items were unan-

imously classified as being required, and the remaining 36 were identified as being optional. These classifications were validated by examining the NSC and IMCP pronouncements.[6] Of the 36 voluntary disclosure items, 12 did not apply equally to all sample firms because they required an antecedent event (e.g., disclosure of lawsuits or auditor changes would require that such events had occurred). Hence, only the remaining 24 items were used to construct the disclosure scores.

2. *Rating the Importance of Each Disclosure Item.* Cooperation was obtained from the credit department heads of 16 Mexican banks, who distributed 106 survey instruments to loan officers in their departments. These officers were asked to indicate, on a seven-point scale, the importance they placed on each of the 89 items in evaluating an average loan application. The end-points were: (1) "Of no importance at all," and (7) "Of utmost importance." Respondents were asked to take into account the cost of information production in rating the importance of each item (in the manner of Choi [1973]). To control for order effects, eight random sequences of presenting the items were used.

A total of 67 completed responses were received, yielding a 63 percent response rate. The respondents had a mean of 4.6 years' experience as a loan officer ($s=3.6$ years). The mean number of loans each respondent processed per year was 102 ($s=144$), and the mean

---

[5] These manufacturing firms came from a variety of industries. However, since there were only a few firms from each industry, it was not feasible to test for industry effects.

[6] All of the items classified as required were traced to NSC and IMCP pronouncements. We also verified that the items classified as not required were not part of these pronouncements. However, since it was not feasible to check all industry-specific regulations, there is still the potential for some items to be misclassified.

The Accounting Review, July 1987

loan size processed was 43,122,000 pesos ($s = 76,130,000$ pesos).[7] Since the survey was anonymous and all responses were received in a two-week period, data were not available for an effective test for non-response bias. However, given the high response rate and the profile of the respondents, the responses should be reasonably indicative of the judgments of experienced Mexican loan officers.[8]

Table 1 presents the means, medians, and standard deviations of the voluntary disclosure items' importance ratings. These are rather widely dispersed. The highest-rated item—breakdown of borrowings—has a mean (median) rating of 6.194 (7.0), while the lowest-rated item—amount of past pension fund liability—is rated at 3.194 (3.0). Consensus among the respondent ratings was tested using an approach common in accounting research (see Libby [1981] and Ashton [1982] for reviews). For all possible pairs ($N = 2,211$) among the respondents, the Pearson correlation was computed between the two respondents' 89 ratings. The mean (median) of these correlations was 0.24 (0.27) ($s = 0.24$). These values are comparable to prior studies of judgment consensus (e.g., Wright [1977], Schultz and Gustavson [1978]; also see Ashton [1982]). Both the t-test and the nonparametric Wilcoxon rank-sum test indicated that the mean (median) of these pairwise correlations was significantly greater than zero ($t = 46.60$, $p < 0.0001$; $Z = 33.43$, $p < 0.0001$). Thus, on the whole, there is evidence of weak to moderate consensus among the respondents' ratings.

3. *Computing Disclosure Scores.* The reports in the *Gazette* were used to generate two disclosure scores for each sample firm. One was a weighted score (WTDSCORE); this was the sum of all the items (out of 24) that the firm had voluntarily disclosed, with each item

being weighted by its mean importance rating. The other was an unweighted score (UNWTSCORE), which was the number of items voluntarily disclosed. The unweighted score was introduced to compensate for two potential limitations of the importance ratings. First, since these ratings were obtained through a survey and without real economic consequences to the respondents, they may not fully reflect loan officers' actual use of each item. Second, bank loan officers are only a subset (though an important one) of financial report users in Mexico. Using an unweighted score permits an analysis independent of the perceptions of a particular user group.

To control for subjectivity in interpreting the annual reports, two independent raters were used to determine which items were disclosed. Both raters were Mexican CPAs, and their ratings were in substantial agreement. For both WTDSCORE and UNWTSCORE, the Pearson correlation between their ratings was 0.98 ($p < 0.0001$). In the statistical analyses, almost identical results were obtained by using either rater's ratings or their equally-weighted composite. Thus, only the results based on the composite measure will be reported here.[9]

---

[7] Using an exchange rate of 300 pesos to one U.S. dollar, the average loan size processed would be U.S. $143,740.

[8] Since we emphasize disclosure incentives due to external financing, another important user group would have been financial analysts. Unfortunately, efforts to obtain such a sample were unsuccessful. Zeff [1972] suggests that Mexican firms are generally reluctant to reveal much about their financial affairs to the public, and that banks are often used as sources of outside capital to avoid public disclosure of sensitive financial information. Hence, our respondents should still represent a key user group.

[9] The composite WTDSCORE and UNWTSCORE measures were obtained by adding the scores assigned by the two raters and dividing the sum by two. Since the two raters did not agree perfectly, fractional values for UNWTSCORE (number of items disclosed) were possible. These were rounded up to the next whole number.

TABLE 1
VOLUNTARY DISCLOSURE ITEMS:
DESCRIPTIVE STATISTICS AND FREQUENCY OF DISCLOSURE

	Importance Rating			Number (%) of Firms Disclosing This Item
	Mean	Median	Std. Dev.	
1. Breakdown of borrowings (e.g., lending institution, date of maturity, security)	6.194	7	1.28	39 (75%)
2. Description of major products produced	5.821	6	1.35	15 (29%)
3. Forecast of next year's profits	5.701	6	1.56	6 (12%)
4. Cash projections for the next one to five years	5.636	6	1.60	0 (0%)
5. Description of major plants, warehouses, and properties, including location, function, and size	5.582	6	1.45	23 (44%)
6. Discussion of the company's operating results for the past year	5.567	6	1.50	5 (10%)
7. Overall financing cost	5.254	5	1.42	38 (73%)
8. Names of company directors	5.224	5	1.71	46 (88%)
9. Information relating to capital expenditures (e.g., expenditure in the past year, planned expenditures)	5.209	5	1.46	20 (38%)
10. Disclosure of the responsibilities, experience, and background of corporate executives, and other key personnel such as research scientists and production managers	5.200	5	1.75	0 (0%)
11. Statement of company objectives	5.119	5	1.63	18 (35%)
12. Capitalized interests during the period	4.925	5	1.39	18 (35%)
13. Description of marketing network for finished goods/services	4.894	5	1.56	1 (2%)
14. Method used to determine cost of inventories	4.848	5	1.72	40 (77%)
15. Current resale value of the firm's assets	4.791	5	1.45	26 (50%)
16. The principal business or professional affiliation of each outside director	4.463	5	1.55	0 (0%)
17. Index of sales prices	4.246	4	1.81	14 (27%)
18. Breakdown of earnings by major product lines, customer classes, and geographical location	4.194	4	1.81	0 (0%)
19. Information relating to research and development (e.g., progress with new product development, planned expenditures)	4.167	4	1.53	5 (10%)
20. Number and type of ordinary shareholders (e.g., institutions, individuals)	4.136	4	1.86	5 (10%)
21. Specification of the method used to compute depreciation	3.877	4	1.68	39 (75%)
22. Information on corporate social responsibility (e.g., attitude of company, expenditures)	3.851	4	1.62	3 (6%)
23. Historical summary of price range of ordinary shares in past few years	3.288	4	1.51	4 (8%)
24. Amount of past pension fund liability	3.194	3	1.62	40 (77%)

TABLE 2

DESCRIPTIVE STATISTICS FOR THE INDEPENDENT AND DEPENDENT VARIABLES
($N=52$)

Variable	Mean	Median	Std. Dev.	Range
Firm Size (SIZE) (10^3 pesos)	10,608,851	4,492,290	14,087,692	293,764–54,796,299
Financial Leverage (LEVG)	.79	.88	.21	.04–1.00
Proportion of Assets in Place (ASSETPLC)	.510	.542	.220	.002–.873
Unweighted Disclosure Score (UNWTSCORE)	7.86	9.0	3.90	0.0–17.00
Weighted Disclosure Score (WTDSCORE)	38.25	40.28	18.96	0.0–79.37

The last column of Table 1 presents the number of sample firms disclosing each item. In Table 1, the number of firms disclosing each item ranges from zero to 46, with a mean of 16.87. Five items are disclosed by at least 75 percent of the firms: (1) the names of company directors ($N=46$), (2) inventory costing method ($N=40$), (3) amount of past pension fund liability ($N=40$), (4) depreciation method ($N=39$), and (5) breakdown of borrowings ($N=39$). At the other extreme, no firm disclosed these four items: (1) cash projections for the next one to five years; (2) responsibilities and experiences of key executives and personnel; (3) principal business or professional affiliations of outside directors; and (4) breakdown of earnings by major product lines, customer classes, and geographical location. The number of firms disclosing an item is not significantly related to the item's rated importance. The Pearson and Spearman correlations between these variables were 0.086 ($p=0.34$) and 0.122 ($p=0.28$).

In addition to variation in the items' rated importance and disclosure frequencies, considerable divergence also exists among the sample firms' extent of voluntary disclosure. Table 2 shows that UNWTSCORE has a range of zero to 17, with a mean (median) of 7.86 (9.0). The range for WTDSCORE is zero to 79.37, and the mean (median) is 38.25 (40.28). The correlation between UNWTSCORE and WTDSCORE is positive and significant ($r=0.99$, $p<0.0001$).

Agency theory suggests several variables for explaining cross-sectional variation in voluntary accounting and disclosure choices. Firm size, financial leverage, and proportion of assets in place have been hypothesized to affect voluntary financial disclosure by influencing the magnitude of agency costs and/or the costs of manager-external owner contracting [Leftwich, Watts, and Zimmerman, 1981; Holthausen and Leftwich, 1983; Kelly, 1983]. Regressions using these three variables are reported below.

Cross-Sectional Regressions

The independent variables used are firm size, financial leverage, and proportion of assets in place:

1. *Firm size* (SIZE) is measured as the market value of equity plus the book value of debt. Jensen and Meckling

TABLE 3
RESULTS OF CROSS-SECTIONAL REGRESSIONS
(*N*=52)

Coefficient
(*t*-statistics in parentheses)

Dependent Variable Predicted Sign	Intercept N/A	SIZE (10⁷ PESOS) +	LEVG +	ASSETPLC −	Adj. R^2	F- (sig.)	Kolomogorov-Smirnov Z (sig.) for the residuals
WTDSCORE	26.26 (2.70)	5.16* (2.76)	13.35 (1.01)	−7.90 (−0.64)	.14	3.77 (0.02)	.73 (.66)
UNWTSCORE	5.41 (2.72)	1.11* (2.92)	2.54 (0.94)	−1.46 (−0.58)	.15	4.05 (0.01)	.82 (.52)

* $P<0.01$

[1976] have shown analytically that agency costs increase with the amount of outside capital, while Leftwich, Watts, and Zimmerman [1981] have suggested that the proportion of outside capital tends to be higher for larger firms. Accordingly, the potential benefits from shareholder-debtholder-manager contracting—including the extent of financial disclosure—would also increase with firm size.

2. *Financial Leverage* (LEVG) is measured by the book value of debt divided by SIZE. Fama and Miller [1972], Jensen and Meckling [1976], and Smith and Warner [1979], among others, have observed that agency costs are higher for firms with proportionally more debt in their capital structures, suggesting a positive relationship between the extent of voluntary financial disclosure and LEVG.

3. *Proportion of assets in place* (ASSETPLC) is computed by dividing the book value of fixed assets, net of depreciation, by total assets. Myers [1977] has suggested that wealth transfers are more difficult (hence agency costs are lower) with assets that are already owned than assets as yet to be acquired, implying

that the extent of voluntary financial disclosure would be inversely related to a firm's proportion of assets in place.

The descriptive statistics in Table 2 indicate considerable cross-sectional variation in the three independent variables. Of the bivariate correlations among these variables, only that between SIZE and LEVG is statistically significant ($r=0.34$, $p=0.013$). The magnitude of this correlation does not suggest a serious collinearity problem. Both WTDSCORE and UNWTSCORE are significantly correlated with SIZE (respectively, $r=0.41$, $p=0.002$; and $r=0.43$, $p=0.001$), and both correlations with LEVG are marginally significant (respectively, $r=0.24$, $p=0.08$, and $r=0.24$, $p=0.08$). Neither disclosure score's correlation with ASSETPLC approaches statistical significance.

Table 3 reports the regression results using WTDSCORE and UNWTSCORE alternately as the dependent variable.[10]

---

[10] Regressions were also run by replacing the market value of equity with its book value. The conclusions were unchanged. To allow for a nonlinear effect due to SIZE, the regressions were also repeated using this variable's natural logarithm instead of raw value. Again the conclusions were unaffected.

540   The Accounting Review, July 1987

Both models are statistically significant, and the Kolmogorov-Smirnov test indicates that neither set of residuals deviates significantly from normality. However, of the three independent variables, only SIZE has statistically significant coefficients. The positive signs of these coefficients are consistent with the prediction of more extensive voluntary disclosure by larger firms. The predicted effects of leverage and assets in place are not supported.

CONCLUDING REMARKS

An overview of Mexican accounting and disclosure regulations suggests a more *laissez-faire* environment than that in the U.S. Using a sample of 52 Mexican Stock Exchange-listed firms, it is found that the extent of voluntary disclosure varies widely within this environment. Three variables suggested by agency theory—firm size, financial leverage, and proportion of assets in place—are used to explain this cross-sectional variation. The extent of voluntary disclosure is found to increase with firm size. No significant effects due to financial leverage or assets in place are observed.

This study has contributed evidence on disclosure practices in a non-Anglo-American country that has not been extensively examined. However, much effort is needed to refine and expand this investigation. First, the variables used should be refined and expanded. As Leftwich, Watts, and Zimmerman [1981] have observed, voluntary public disclosure is only one mechanism for containing shareholder-debtholder-manager interest conflicts. Alternative mechanisms include the use of outside directors, executive compensation schemes, restrictions on certain resource allocation activities (e.g., mergers, dividends, new financing, and disposal of assets), private disclosure, and indirect monitoring through exchange-listing requirements. To the extent these other mechanisms complement or substitute for corporate financial disclosure, their inclusion can shed further light on both the accounting environment and firm practices. Second, the effects of other factors (e.g., political costs) and motivations (e.g., signaling) on accounting/disclosure choices should also be explored [Watts and Zimmerman, 1986]. Finally, besides studying accounting/disclosure choices, the scope of analysis can be expanded to include the effects of such choices (e.g., wage negotiations and security prices).

Chow and Wong-Boren   **541**

REFERENCES

American Institute of Certified Public Accountants—International Practice Executive Committee, *Professional Accounting in 30 Countries* (New York: AICPA, 1975), pp. 367–387.

Ashton, R., *Human Information Processing in Accounting: Studies in Accounting Research #17* (American Accounting Association, 1982).

Barrett, E., "Financial Reporting Practices: Disclosure and Comprehensiveness in an International Setting," *Journal of Accounting Research* (Spring 1976), pp. 10–26.

Benston, G., *Corporate Financial Disclosure in the UK and the USA* (Westmead, UK: Saxon House, 1976).

Buzby, S., "Company Size, Listed versus Unlisted Stocks, and the Extent of Financial Disclosure," *Journal of Accounting Research* (Spring 1975), pp. 16–37.

Choi, F., "Financial Disclosure and Entry to the European Capital Market," *Journal of Accounting Research* (Autumn 1973), pp. 159–175.

Diario Oficial de la Federación, *Ley del Mercado de Valores* (Securities Market Law) (Mexico City, January 2, 1975).

Ernst & Whinney, *International Series—Mexico* (E & W, July 1983).

Fama, E., and M. Miller, *The Theory of Finance* (Hinsdale, IL: Dryden Press, 1972).

Firth, M., "The Impact of Size, Stock Market Listing, and Auditors on Voluntary Disclosure in Corporate Annual Reports," *Accounting and Business Research* (Autumn 1979), pp. 273–280.

Holthausen, R., and R. Leftwich, "The Economic Consequences of Accounting Choice: Implications of Costly Contracting and Monitoring," *Journal of Accounting and Economics* (August 1983), pp. 77–117.

Instituto Mexicano de Contadores Públicos, *Campo de Actuación Profesional del Contador Público en México* (Editorial, Instituto Mexicano de Contadores Públicos, 1985).

Jensen, M., and W. Meckling, "Theory of the Firm: Managerial Behavior, Agency Costs and Ownership Structure," *Journal of Financial Economics* (October 1976), pp. 305–360.

Kelly, L., "The Development of A Positive Theory of Corporate Management's Role in External Financial Reporting," *Journal of Accounting Literature* (Spring 1983), pp. 111–150.

Leftwich, R., R. Watts, and J. Zimmerman, "Voluntary Corporate Disclosure: The Case of Interim Reporting," *Journal of Accounting Research* (Supplement 1981), pp. 50–77.

Libby, R., *Accounting and Human Information Processing: Theory and Applications* (Englewood Cliffs, NJ: Prentice-Hall, 1981).

McNally, G., L. Eng, and C. Hasseldine, "Corporate Financial Reporting in New Zealand: An Analysis of User Preferences, Corporate Characteristics and Disclosure Practices for Discretionary Information," *Accounting and Business Research* (Winter 1982), pp. 11–20.

Myers, S., "Determinants of Corporate Borrowing," *Journal of Financial Economics* (November 1977), pp. 147–175.

Nobes, C., and R. Parker (Eds.), *Comparative International Accounting* (Homewood, IL: Irwin, 1981).

Price Waterhouse & Co., "Doing Business in Mexico," in *Information Guide* (PW & Co., November 1984).

Schipper, K., "Discussion of Voluntary Corporate Disclosure: The Case of Interim Reporting," *Journal of Accounting Research* (Supplement 1981), pp. 85–88.

Schultz, J., and S. Gustavson, "Actuaries' Perceptions of Variables Affecting the Independent Auditors' Legal Liability," THE ACCOUNTING REVIEW (July 1978), pp. 626–641.

Smith, C., and J. Warner, "On Financial Contracting: An Analysis of Bond Covenants," *Journal of Financial Economics* (June 1979), pp. 117–161.

Watts, R., and J. Zimmerman, *Positive Accounting Theory* (Englewood Cliffs, NJ: Prentice-Hall, 1986).

Wright, W., "Financial Information Processing Models: An Empirical Study," THE ACCOUNTING REVIEW (July 1977), pp. 676–689.

Zeff, S., *Forging Accounting Principles in Five Countries: A History and Analysis of Trends* (Champaign, IL: Stipes Publishing Company, 1972).

[9]

Int J Acctg (1991) 26:264–276
© 1991 The University of Illinois

The International
Journal of
Accounting

A Comparative Analysis of US and Taiwanese Firms' Decisions to Issue Earnings Forecasts

Joseph K. Cheung,[a] Mandy Li[b] and Anne Wu[c]

[a]Department of Accounting and Business Legal Studies, George Mason University, Fairfax, Virginia 22030–4444, USA
[b]University of Maryland, College Park, Maryland 20742, USA
[c]National Chengchi University, Wenshan, Taipei, Taiwan, ROP

Key words: Positive accounting theory; Management earnings forecasts

Abstract: This study evaluates whether hypotheses of US management's earnings forecast decisions can explain similar decisions in Taiwan. It considers the applicability of positive accounting theories across national boundaries. A match-pair design is used to test the explanatory power of the hypotheses, on two forecast-release samples, one US and one Taiwanese. Both a univariate test and a multivariate test indicate that the hypotheses are more descriptive of management's behavior in the United States than in Taiwan. This leads to the conclusion that positive accounting theories have limited validity internationally because they are heavily dependent on the background institutions.

Research Question

This study investigates whether positive accounting theories developed in one socio-economic environment have comparable explanatory power in another socioeconomic environment. Positive accounting theories are hypotheses of managerial decisions regarding financial reporting choices.[1] The financial reporting choice of interest here is management's decision to release earnings forecasts voluntarily. In this context, the paper addresses whether hypotheses developed of managerial behavior in the United States are equally applicable in a different socioeconomic environment such as Taiwan.

The basic thesis is that positive accounting theories are products of economic, legal, and cultural forces. As these forces vary from one country to another, the explanatory power of the theories may be altered. Rather than painting a bleak

Accepted for publication: August 2, 1991

picture of positive accounting theories, this study shows how such theories can be enriched and checked for external validity when the assumptions of the background institutions are varied. Thus, an intended contribution of this study is to highlight the importance of institutional backgrounds when applying positive accounting theories in different environments. The specific focus of this study is management's behavior in regard to earnings forecast releases. Numerous analytical and empirical studies have investigated why some US firms issue such releases and others do not. The same question can be asked of Taiwanese firms, since some of them do release such forecasts and others shy away from doing so. What this paper attempts to determine is whether the same theories for explaining the behavior of US firms have comparable explanatory power when applied to Taiwanese firms.

One reason for choosing these two countries for a comparative analysis is that there are sharp contrasts between the two environments, in terms of securities laws, institutions of security trading, ownership structure of firms, etc. Moreover, earnings forecasts by Taiwanese firms has been a subject of much attention in recent years. Since the 1986 stock market boom in Taiwan, the Taiwanese Security Administration Commission has been concerned with the level of speculation in the market. One of the measures considered by the Commission to deal with the speculation was to regulate earnings forecasts by management. Eventually, in December 1989, the Financial Accounting Standards Committee, a delegated organization of the Commission, issued guidelines for such management forecasts. To be implemented in 1991, these guidelines would leave management the discretion whether or not to release earnings forecasts.[2] Thus, why some Taiwanese firms decide to issue earnings forecasts voluntarily while others decide otherwise is an interesting research question in its own right. Therefore, an additional purpose of this research is to determine the extent to which existing theories of US managers can explain similar behavior in Taiwan.

The results basically confirm our expectation that positive accounting theories are not readily applicable across national boundaries. The methodology is a match-pair design tested via both a univariate analysis, where the prediction of each existing theory is evaluated, and a logit analysis, where the joint explanatory power of the theories is evaluated.

The next section reviews the various positive theories that attempt to explain why some US firms choose to release earnings forecasts voluntarily. The third section discusses the paper's hypotheses based on the differences between the US and the Taiwanese environments. The fourth section describes the methodology and data. The fifth section presents the test results, and the last section concludes.

Theories Explaining Firms' Decisions to Issue Earnings Forecasts

Why do some firms issue earnings forecasts voluntarily and others do not? This section summarizes seven theories that have been put forth in the literature.

1. *Agency cost theory.* When a business is run by managers who are not owners, the managers do not always act in the best interest of the firm. This is the essence of the agency cost theory.[3] One of the components of agency cost is the cost to monitor the manager. It has been argued that earnings forecasts are a relatively cost-effective monitoring device.[4] Thus, by voluntarily issuing such forecasts, managers can help reduce the firm's agency cost to the benefit of all parties who have an interest in the firm. By this theory, one would predict that firms burdened with large agency costs are more likely to issue earnings forecasts. Since firm size is usually viewed as positively correlated with agency cost,[5] the agency cost theory would predict *that large firms are more likely to issue earnings forecasts*. This prediction statement will be referred to as P_1 below.

2. *External capital theory.* Previous research finds that large firms with greater reliance on external capital are more likely to release insider information voluntarily.[6] Earnings forecasts by management is one form of insider information. Thus, firms seeking external capital are more likely to issue earnings forecasts. voluntarily, which is in keeping with the finding of a survey by Francis Lees.[7] Based on these findings, one would predict *that the firm's likelihood to issue earnings forecasts in a particular period is positively correlated with the amount of new external capital raised during the period* (P_2).

3. *Signaling theory.* A buyer possesses less information on a product than the seller. Hence, the seller has an incentive to offer the buyer more information in order to induce the buyer to buy. Since management has insider information on the firm, issuing earnings forecasts can be said to serve a similar purpose of reducing the information asymmetry between the firm and the buyers of the firm's securities.[8] However, the most that can be achieved by issuing bad news is to confirm the market's negative expectations about the firm. Thus, firms tend to issue good news more frequently and more speedily than bad news. This hypothesis has found to be consistent with existing empirical findings.[9] Therefore, the signaling theory would predict that *firms with good news to report are more likely to issue earnings forecasts* (P_3).

4. *Disclosure cost theory.* One of the skills investors prefer managers to have is the ability to anticipate changes in the firm's economic environment and to make adjustments accordingly. Brett Trueman maintains that this ability is factored into the market value of the firm.[10] This suggests that managers have every incentive to issue forecasts and to update them continuously because this would demonstrate their ability to collect and process future-oriented information. On the other hand, however, such releases can hurt the firm's competitive position if competitive information is revealed to rival firms. So a prudent manager would balance the market-value gain from disclosing and the competitive loss from doing so. All else being the same, therefore, firms with lower competitive costs are more likely to issue forecasts. Since competitive cost is negatively correlated with market power, this theory would predict *that firms with a large market share are more likely to issue earnings forecasts* (P_4).

5. *Expectation adjustment theory.* Expectations as to the firm's performance are formed in the market, as represented by earnings forecasts prepared by security

analysts. Existing evidence shows that management is motivated to issue earnings forecasts in order to correct the market's expectations if such expectations are either overly optimistic or overly pessimistic.[11] Thus, the expectation adjustment theory would predict *that the likelihood for firms to issue earnings forecasts is positively correlated with the magnitude of forecasting errors committed by security analysts* (P_5).

6. *Managerial influence theory.* Existing evidence shows that security analysts often revise their previously issued forecasts of a firm after the firm's own forecast is released.[12] One can therefore argue that management has more incentive to issue forecasts if such forecasts are more influential in the market's expectation formation. By this theory, one would predict *that a firm's tendency to issue earnings forecasts is correlated with analysts' revision of their previous earnings predictions* (P_6).

7. *Earnings variability theory.* According to empirical evidence, firms that release earnings forecasts voluntarily usually have lower variability in their earnings.[13] An obvious reason is that future earnings can be predicted more accurately if the earnings process is more stable. Conversely, firms with unstable earnings are less likely to issue earnings forecasts for fear that inaccuracies of such forecasts at hindsight could bring about adverse legal consequences. Therefore, this theory would predict *that firms with low earnings variability are more likely to issue earnings forecasts* (P_7).

In summary, the seven predictions, referred to concisely as P_1 to P_7 result in the following function mapping seven explanatory variables to the probability that a firm will issue earnings forecasts:

$$Y = f(X_1, X_2, X_3, X_4, X_5, X_6, X_7) \hspace{3cm} \text{Eq. (1)}$$

where Y is the probability to issue earnings forecasts, $f(\cdot)$ is the mapping function, and X_i is the independent variable in prediction statement P_i.

Testable Hypotheses Due to US–Taiwan Environmental Differences

Table 1 lists a number of differences between the environments of the two countries. In spite of a continuous stock market boom since 1986, Taiwan's security market institutions are still at a developing stage. This lack of maturity is particularly evident when such institutions are contrasted with their US counterparts. The following sets forth a number of testable implications from these contrasts.

First, Taiwanese corporations tend to be more family owned as opposed to publicly owned. This implies that managers and owners are less likely to be different parties pursuing conflicting goals. Consequently, agency cost is lower for the average firm in Taiwan. All else being equal, therefore, one would expect firm size, a surrogate for the level of agency cost, to be less predictive of management's tendency to issue earnings forecasts. Thus, we hypothesize *that prediction statement P_1 is less descriptive in the Taiwanese environment than in the US environment.*

Table 1. Key environmental differences between US and Taiwanese firms

Characteristics	United States	Taiwan
Corporate ownership profile	Public	Family
Investor profile	Institutional	Individual
Security analysis industry	Mature	Developing
Legal liability due to incorrect management-issued information	Limited but exists	None

This difference in corporate ownership structure has yet another empirical implication. The external capital theory predicts that management is more likely to issue earnings forecasts when they want to raise capital through the capital market. While publicly placed securities are a crucial source of long-term financing for publicly owned firms, family owned firms are more likely to place securities privately. Since the average source of financing is different in the two environments, one would expect the external capital theory to be less applicable in the Taiwanese environment. Therefore, we hypothesize *that prediction statement P_2 is less applicable to Taiwanese firms than to US firms.*

Second, investor profile also differs in the two countries. Institutional investors play a significant role in making security investment decisions in the United States. This would imply that security investment decisions in the United States are, to a large extent, shaped by professional managers. To deal with questions about accountability and fiduciary duties, professional managers are more likely to follow a methodical investment process, including the use of future-oriented information, such as earnings forecasts, in making the investment decision. But this is not equally the case in Taiwan, where individual investors dominate investment decision making. This difference would imply that earnings forecasts are not perceived to be equally useful in the two countries. If earnings forecasts are perceived to be less useful, as it is in Taiwan, one would expect their supply to fall, including the supply by management. Thus, all else being equal, the signaling theory about management release of earnings forecasts has reduced explanatory power in the Taiwanese environment. In short, we expect *prediction statement P_3 to be less descriptive in the Taiwanese environment than in the US environment.*

Additionally, the difference in investor profile has critical implications for the disclosure cost theory. Management's ability to make forecasts and to adjust the firm's operations accordingly critically hinges on investors' having the capacity to process this information. With resources at their disposal, professional managers can be expected to perform such a task. Lacking similar economies of scale, however, individual investors are expected to be less successful in doing so. We therefore hypothesize *that prediction statements P_4 is less descriptive in the Taiwanese environment than in the US environment.*

Third, the security analysis industry is much less well developed in Taiwan than it is in the US.[14] In the US, on the other hand, security analysis was a highly mature industry. This difference suggests that professionally prepared security analysis in Taiwan lacks the same degree of depth and breadth possessed by its US counterpart. This implies that management forecasts in Taiwan have more influence on the market's expectation formation and adjustment. Accordingly, we expect *prediction statements*

P_5 and P_6 *to be valid descriptions of management forecast behavior in the Taiwanese environment.*

Finally, the difference in potential legal liabilities regarding management forecasts also has a bearing on management's tendency to issue such forecasts. Because of a safe harbor rule, US firms are protected to a degree from potential litigations when forecasts made in good faith later prove incorrect. Yet, such legal liabilities do not vanish completely. This contrasts the Taiwanese environment where such legal liabilities are absent. The earnings variability theory hinges on the assumption that such legal liabilities do exist. When such liabilities are absent, there is no basis to suggest that firms with lower earnings variabilities are more likely to issue forecasts. Therefore, we hypothesize that *prediction statement P_7 is less powerful an explanation of the behavior of Taiwanese firms.*

In summary, this section argues that, although the prediction function as given in Equation 1 may be descriptive of US firms' behavior, it is not expected to have comparable explanatory power when applied to Taiwanese firms, X_4 and X_5 being the only exceptions. These hypotheses of the study are evaluated empirically below.

Methodology and Data

In accordance with the overall hypothesis, the empirical analysis evaluates how well model (1) discriminates forecast-release firms from non-release firms in both the US and the Taiwanese environments.

Test Designs

For each environment, two samples of firms are selected. Release firms are the treatment sample and non-release firms the control sample. If P_1 to P_7 explain the managerial behavior in question, then one would expect X_1 through X_7 to be good descriptors of the release firms *and* poor descriptors of the non-release firms. Both a univariate and a multivariate test are used.

Univariate Test: A release firm will be assigned a value of 1, and a non-release firm a value of 0. That is, the dependent variable Y in Equation 1 will be a dichotomous variable. The univariate analysis correlates each X_i, $i = 1,...,7$, with Y. The point biserial correlation is used, which is calculated as:[15]

$$r_{X_i Y} = [(X_i^R - X_i^N)/S_{X_i}] \sqrt{pq} \qquad\qquad \text{Eq. (2)}$$

where $r_{X_i Y}$ = correlation between X_i and Y

X_i^R = average of X_i for the release firms

X_i^N = average of X_i for the non-release firms

S_{X_i} = standard deviation of X_i

p, q = proportion of release and non-release firms, respectively.[16]

A statistically significant $r_{X_i Y}$ indicates that X_i is a good descriptor of the decision to issue forecasts. That is, the univariate test indicates how valid the prediction statements are when taken one at a time.

Multivariate Test. The joint explanatory power of all seven independent variables is tested via logit analysis. Two logit models are estimated, one for the US firms and the other for the Taiwanese firms, and their explanatory powers are compared.[17]

Sample Selection

The sample period for the US firms runs from 1984 through 1987. The data source is the Dow Jones News Retrieval Service. A sample of 151 observations resulted from the following set of criteria:[18]

a. The firm must have made a point, interval, or percentage forecast of earnings per share or of profits.
b. The forecast must have been made by an official of the firm.
c. The firm's fiscal year end must be December 31. This was needed to ensure comparability in cross-sectional comparisons.
d. The firm's common stock must be traded on either the American or the New York Stock Exchanges. This criterion ensures that the sample firms are of sufficient size and stability.

The sample period for the Taiwanese firms runs from 1985 through 1989. The data were extracted from articles published in 19 large newspapers in Taiwan. Criteria a, b and c above were also applied. Instead of criterion d, the Taiwanese firms must have their common stocks listed on the Taiwan Stock Exchange. These procedures resulted in 189 observations in the Taiwanese sample.[19]

To apply a match-pair design to each sample, a control group of firms was randomly selected from the non-release firms with the same industry classifications as the treatment firms. A four-digit SIC code was used for the US sample, and a two-digit code was used for the Taiwanese sample.

Measuring the Dependent and Independent Variables

The dependent variable in Equation 1 is coded as a zero-one variable, with 0 indicating a non-release firm and 1 indicating a release firm. The independent variables are measured as follows:

1. X_1 represents firm size and is measured as a natural logarithmic transformation of the total book value of the firm's assets. This will be referred to as the *SIZE* variable.
2. X_2 represents the amount of new external capital raised immediately after management's earnings forecast. It is defined as (New debt + New equity)/Total assets, where the numerator variables are measured within three months of the forecast date (the *CAPITAL* variable).
3. X_3 represents the level of good news and is measured as the firm's average accounting rate of return for the most recent three years *minus* the industry's average accounting rate of return for the same period (the *NEWS* variable).[20]
4. X_4 represents the firm's market share and is measured as the firm's total sales divided by total sales of the industry (the *MSHARE* variable).

5. X_5 represents the magnitude of forecast errors made by financial analysts. Following usual practice,[21] it is measured as $|(b - a)/a|$ where a is analyst earnings forecast and b is actual earnings (the *ERROR* variable).

6. X_6 represents the influence of management forecast on security analysts' expectation formation. It is measured by $(c - b)/(b - a)$, where a and b are defined above and c is analyst earnings forecast subsequent to the release of management's earnings forecast (the *INFLUENCE* variable).

7. X_7 represents the variability of the firm's earnings over time. A ten-year period is used to estimate the variability.[22] It is measured by the variance of the series $(E_t - E_{t-1})/E_{t-1}$, $t = 1, 2, 3, ..., 10$, where E_t is the firm's earnings per share in year t (the *EVAR* variable).

Results

Sample Characteristics

Table 2 summarizes the mean and variance of each independent variable for the release firms (treatment group) and the non-release firms (control group). US firms are presented in Panel A and Taiwanese firms in Panel B. It should be noted that some data are not available for some of the independent variables. This missing observation problem is particularly noticeable in the cases of *ERROR* and *INFLUENCE*, and this is true for both Panels A and B.

Table 2 gives several impressions of the two samples. First, the release firms taken as a whole are slightly larger than the non-release firms in the US sample, but

Table 2. Descriptive statistics of explanatory variables

Panel A, US sample: 150 release firms and 150 non-release firms; 1984–1987

Variable	Hypothesis tested	Sample size	Release firms		Non-release firms	
			Mean	S.D.	Mean	S.D.
X_1 (SIZE)	Agency cost	150	7.56	1.90	6.96	2.00
X_2 (CAPITAL)	External financing	150	0.06	0.12	0.11	0.28
X_3 (NEWS)	Signaling	150	0.02	0.05	−0.01	0.06
X_4 (MSHARE)	Disclosure cost	140	0.16	0.23	0.11	0.18
X_5 (ERROR)	Expectation adjustment	55	0.75	2.53	0.59	1.66
X_6 (INFLUENCE)	Managerial influence	55	0.81	0.39	1.02	0.69
X_7 (EVAR)	Earnings variability	147	104.00	619.00	96.00	428.00

Panel B, Taiwan sample: 188 release firms and 188 non-release firms; 1985–1989

Variable	Hypothesis tested	Sample size	Release firms		Non-release firms	
			Mean	S.D.	Mean	S.D.
X_1 (SIZE)	Agency cost	188	22.08	1.21	22.03	1.27
X_2 (CAPITAL)	External financing	188	0.01	0.03	0.11	0.03
X_3 (NEWS)	Signaling	171	−0.01	0.07	0.01	0.08
X_4 (MSHARE)	Disclosure cost	187	0.11	0.14	0.11	0.14
X_5 (ERROR)	Expectation adjustment	103	1.08	2.09	0.55	0.69
X_6 (INFLUENCE)	Managerial influence	97	0.85	1.28	2.91	13.68
X_7 (EVAR)	Earnings variability	169	37.00	207.00	28.67	136.00

the same is not true in the Taiwanese sample.[23] Second, in both samples the release firms tend to raise *less* external capital than the non-release firms, which is inconsistent with the prediction of the external capital theory. Third, US release firms tend to report more good news, as the signaling theory would predict. But this phenomenon is reversed in the Taiwanese sample. Fourth, as indicated by the *MSHARE* variable, US release firms are in a more competitive position to issue forecasts than US control firms. Yet, in the Taiwanese sample, the treatment and control groups are nearly the same in this regard.

Interestingly, in both samples the *ERROR* variable indicates some correspondence between the firm's tendency to issue forecasts and the level of inaccuracy in analyst forecasts. Moreover, the *INFLUENCE* variable also indicates that management forecasts have an impact on security analysts' revision of their previously issued forecasts. This impact is particularly significant in the Taiwanese sample. Finally, contrary to the prediction of the earnings variability theory, both samples suggest that the treatment firms on average have higher, rather than lower, earnings variability.

Univariate Tests

Results from the univariate test are presented in Table 3. Panel A indicates that *SIZE, NEWS, MSHARE*, and *INFLUENCE* are all significantly correlated with the firm's choice to issue earnings forecasts in the United States. The signs of their correlations are also as expected. These results support the agency cost, the signaling, the competitive disclosure cost, and the managerial influence theories as useful

Table 3. Univariate test results

Panel A, US sample: 150 release firms and 150 non-release firms; 1984–1987

Independent Variable	Hypothesis tested	Expected sign	Correlation[a]
X_1 (SIZE)	Agency cost	+	0.16*
X_2 (CAPITAL)	External financing	+	0.03
X_3 (NEWS)	Signaling	+	0.20*
X_4 (MSHARE)	Disclosure cost	+	0.13*
X_5 (ERROR)	Expectation adjustment	+	0.04
X_6 (INFLUENCE)	Managerial influence	–	-0.18*
X_7 (EVAR)	Earnings variability	–	0.02

Panel B, Taiwan sample: 188 release firms and 188 non-release firms; 1984–1987

Independent Variable	Hypothesis tested	Expected sign	Correlation[a]
X_1 (SIZE)	Agency cost	+	0.01
X_2 (CAPITAL)	External financing	+	0.02
X_3 (NEWS)	Signaling	+	-0.02
X_4 (MSHARE)	Disclosure cost	+	0.01
X_5 (ERROR)	Expectation adjustment	+	0.17*
X_6 (INFLUENCE)	Managerial influence	–	-0.10
X_7 (EVAR)	Earnings variability	–	0.02

* Significant at the 0.05 level.
[a] Point biserial correlation as defined in eq. (2). The Y variable in the correlation is a zero-one variable with one indicating a treatment firm and zero indiating a control firm.

Management's Earnings Forecast Decisions   273

Table 4. Cross-correlations between independent variables

Panel A, US sample: 150 release firms and 150 non-release firms; 1984–1987

	X_1	X_2	X_3	X_4	X_5	X_6	X_7
SIZE	–	–0.13	0.03	0.16	0.03	–0.07	0.04
CAPITAL		–	–0.08	0.10	0.11	0.04	0.00
NEWS			–	0.16	–0.26	–0.10	–0.09
MSHARE				–	0.00	–0.16	–0.04
ERROR					–	–0.01	0.31
INFLUENCE						–	0.04
EVAR							–

Panel B, Taiwan sample: 188 release firms and 188 non-release firms; 1985–1989

	X_1	X_2	X_3	X_4	X_5	X_6	X_7
SIZE	–	–0.02	0.09	0.41*	–0.08	–0.02	–0.14
CAPITAL		–	–0.04	–0.06	–0.01	–0.05	–0.02
NEWS			–	0.14	–0.16	–0.06	–0.08
MSHARE				–	–0.13	–0.03	–0.04
ERROR					–	–0.07	0.03
INFLUENCE						–	–0.02
EVAR							–

* Significant at the 0.05 level.

explanations of management forecasts in the United States. On the whole, the data lend substantial support to the theories set forth in the literature.

However, the same cannot be said about the Taiwanese data. Our overall hypothesis is that most of the theories are less useful explanations when applied to Taiwanese firms, the exceptions being the expectation adjustment and the managerial influence theories (*ERROR* and *INFLUENCE*). Panel B in Table 2 clearly bears out this contention. The only variable with the traditional level of significance is *ERROR*. Contrary to the findings for US firms, this result suggests that the primary objective for Taiwanese managements to issue earnings forecasts is to correct biased forecasts issued by financial analysts. To conclude, the univariate test unambiguously supports the overall hypothesis of this study.

Multivariate Tests

Pearson cross-correlations are first computed for the independent variables in each sample. Table 4 presents these correlations, which indicate that multicollinearity does not seem to be a concern.

Table 5 presents two logit models, the US model in Panel A and the Taiwanese model in Panel B. The overall goodness-of-fit of each model is indicated by the model χ^2. Based on this, the US model is statistically significant at the 0.01 level. Unlike the univariate test results, however, only two of the independent variables are significant at the 0.05 level. The results consistently support two of the four theories found to be valid based on the univariate tests. These are the signaling and the managerial influence theories. The agency cost and the disclosure cost theories are not supported by the logic analysis although they were supported by the univariate analysis. Finally, in keeping with the univariate test results, neither the external capital nor the earnings variability theories are supported by the data.

Table 5. Multivariate test results via logit analysis

Panel A. Logit model for US firms: 67 release firms and 67 non-release firms
(Model χ^2 = 18.1; Prob > χ^2 = 0.01)

Independent variable	Hypothesis tested	χ^2	Prob > χ^2
X_1 (SIZE)	Agency cost	0.27	0.61
X_2 (CAPITAL)	External financing	0.75	0.39
X_3 (NEWS)	Signaling	5.09	0.02*
X_4 (MSHARE)	Disclosure cost	0.45	0.50
X_5 (ERROR)	Expectation adjustment	1.10	0.29
X_6 (INFLUENCE)	Managerial influence	4.39	0.04*
X_7 (EVAR)	Earnings variability	0.00	0.99

*Panel B. Logit model for Taiwanese firms: 90 release firms and 90 non-release
firms* (Model χ^2 = 14.83; Prob > χ^2 = 0.04)

Independent variable	Hypothesis tested	χ^2	Prob > χ^2
X_1 (SIZE)	Agency cost	0.21	0.65
X_2 (CAPITAL)	External financing	2.91	0.09
X_3 (NEWS)	Signaling	0.11	0.75
X_4 (MSHARE)	Disclosure cost	0.12	0.73
X_5 (ERROR)	Expectation adjustment	3.47	0.06
X_6 (INFLUENCE)	Managerial influence	0.86	0.35
X_7 (EVAR)	Earnings variability	0.70	0.40

* Significant at the 0.05 level.

In the case of the Taiwanese firms, the univariate and the multivariate results are more in agreement with one another. In the univariate test, the *ERROR* variable is correlated with the decision to release forecasts, with the traditional 0.05 level of significance. This is approximately the impression given by the logit analysis as presented in Panel B, Table 1, which indicates that the *ERROR* variable is significant at the 0.06 level.

Taken as a whole, both the univariate and the multivariate tests lend support to the overall hypothesis of this study. That is, positive theories as to management's decision to release earnings forecasts better explain US firms' behavior than Taiwanese firms' behavior.

Conclusion

Two research questions motivated this study. First, do positive accounting theories have universal validity, or are their explanatory powers dependent on institutional and cultural preconditions? Second, given the recent interests in management earnings forecasts in Taiwan, can one apply existing positive theories developed in the US to analyze Taiwanese managers' behavior in this regard?

These two questions led us to evaluate the validity of a number of such theories to a sample of Taiwanese firms. For comparison purposes, these theories were also applied to a sample of US firms. A univariate analysis was used to evaluate the validity of theories taken one at a time. In addition, a multivariate analysis was used to evaluate their validity jointly. The results allow us to draw an unambiguous conclusion. The theories are largely valid when applied to US firms, but such validity is drastically reduced when applied to Taiwanese firms. So the answer to the two research questions is no. Since we are able to predict this difference in explanatory power based on differences in institutional backgrounds, this evidence supports our contention that institutional backgrounds are crucial to the validity of positive accounting theories. When applying such theories across national boundaries, therefore, one has to be careful in checking whether the underlying assumptions of the theories remain valid, as they often are not.

It should be emphasized that, in spite of the negative tone, the implication of this finding is constructive because it not only strengthens our understanding of the positive theories, but also leaves further questions for future research. For example, it seems that positive economic theories are more universal than positive accounting theories. Is it because external financial reporting is much more institutionally dependent? Additionally, accounting inevitably relates to the information process. Is it because information processing is culturally dependent such that positive accounting theories lose their validity when cultural boundaries are crossed? Furthermore, one of the preconditions for positive accounting theories developed in the US seems to be the existence of efficient markets for securities, managerial labor, information, etc. To what extent will such theories break down when these market efficiencies are in doubt? In short we believe that cross-country development and testing of positive accounting theories can further enhance our understanding of the underlying phenomena.

Notes

1   See Ross Watts and Jerald Zimmerman, *Positive Accounting Theory* (Englewood Cliffs, New Jersey: Prentice-Hall, 1986), ch.1.
2   But if they choose to do so, such forecasts need to be first reviewed by a certified public accountant.
3   Michael Jensen and William Meckling, "Theory of the Firm: Managerial Behavior, Agency Costs and Ownership Structure." *Journal of Financial Economics* (October 1976), 305–360.
4   Richard Morris, "Signalling, Agency Theory, and Accounting Policy Choice." *Accounting and Business Research* (Winter 1987), 47–56.
5   Ross Watts and Jerald Zimmerman, *Positive Accounting Theory* (Englewood Cliffs, New Jersey: Prentice-Hall, 1986), p. 235.
6   Gerald Salamon and Dan Dhaliwal, "Company Size and Financial Disclosure Requirements with Evidence from the Segmental Reporting Issue." *Journal of Business Finance & Accounting* (Winter 1980), 555–568.
7   Francis Lees, *Public Disclosure of Corporate Earnings Forecasts* (New York: The Conference Board, 1981).
8   Stephen Ross, "Disclosure Regulation in Financial Markets: Implications of Modern Finance Theory and Signaling Theory." In *Issues in Financial Regulation: Regulation of American Business and Industry*, edited by F.R. Edwards (New York: McGraw-Hill, 1979), 177–216.
9   Victor Pastena and Joshua Ronen, "Some Hypotheses on the Pattern of Management's Informal Disclosures." *Journal of Accounting Research* (Autumn 1979), 550–564; and Eugene Imhoff and Paul Pare, "Analysis and Comparison of Earnings Forecast Agents." *Journal of Accounting Research* (Autumn 1982), 429–439.
10 Brett Trueman, "Why Do Managers Voluntarily Release Earnings Forecasts?" *Journal of Accounting and Economics* (March 1986), 53–71.
11 Bipin Ajinkya and Michael Gift, "Corporate Managers' Earnings Forecasts and Symmetrical Adjustments of Market Expectations." *Journal of Accounting Research* (Autumn 1984), 425–444.
12 John Hassell and Robert Jennings, "Relative Forecast Accuracy and the Timing of Earnings Forecast Announcements." *The Accounting Review* (January 1986), 58–75; and Robert Jennings, "Unsystematic Security Price Movements, Management Earnings Forecasts, and Revisions in Consensus Analyst Earnings Forecasts." *Journal of Accounting Research* (Spring 1987), 90–110.

276   J.K. Cheung et al.

13 Eugene Imhoff, "The Representativeness of Management Earnings Forecasts." *The Accounting Review* (October 1978), 836–850; and Gregory Waymire, "Earnings Volatility and Voluntary Management Forecast Disclosure." *Journal of Accounting Research* (Spring 1985), 268–295.
14 In fact, during the sample period of this study, there were only two security analysis firms in Taiwan.
15 This statistic is designed to discriminate between two groups based on the characteristic of a continuous explanatory variable. See G. Ferguson, *Statistical Analysis in Psychology and Education*, 5th edn. (New York: McGraw-Hill, 1981) p. 428.
16 Because of the match-pair design, they are both equal to 0.5.
17 An alternative approach to the multivariate analysis would be to pool the two countries' data and use a dummy variable technique. This alternative was not pursued because the financial statements of the two countries were denominated in different currencies.
18 Since some of the firms had more than one forecast releases during the sample period, there are 122 different firms in the treatment sample.
19 Because of multiple releases by the same firm, there are 104 different release firms in the treatment group.
20 Accounting rate of return is defined as net income over book value of net assets.
21 Eugene Imhoff and Paul Pare, "Analysis and Comparison of Earnings Forecast Agents." *Journal of Accounting Research* (Autumn 1982), 429–439.
22 We follow Gregory Waymire, "Earnings Volatility and Voluntary Management Forecast Disclosure." *Journal of Accounting Research* (Spring 1985), 268–295.
23 Additionally, the two samples differ in average size because the two currencies are of vastly different values.

Correspondence and offprint requests to: Professor J.K. Cheung, Department of Accounting and Business Legal Studies, George Mason University, 4400 University Drive, Fairfax, Virginia 22030–4444, USA.

Part III
Comparisons with US GAAP

[10]

Journal of Accounting Research
Vol. 32 No. 2 Autumn1994
Printed in U.S.A.

Capsules and Comments

Capital Market Effects of U.S.–Canada *GAAP* Differences

SATI P. BANDYOPADHYAY,* J. DOUGLAS HANNA,†
AND GORDON RICHARDSON*

1. Introduction

Canadian firms that list securities on U.S. stock exchanges are generally required to provide a reconciliation of reported income measured using Canadian generally accepted accounting principles (*GAAP*) to reported earnings measured using U.S. *GAAP*. This paper examines both the magnitudes and the information content of the reported reconciliations between Canadian-*GAAP* income and U.S.-*GAAP* income.

Two recent studies of cross-country *GAAP* differences do not address U.S.–Canada differences because of perceived similarities between *GAAP* in the two countries (Amir, Harris, and Venuti [1993] and McQueen [1993]). If U.S.–Canada *GAAP* differences are in fact unimportant, then no further examination is warranted. Professional bodies, however, are

*University of Waterloo; †University of Chicago. We acknowledge and appreciate valuable comments from workshop participants at the University of Alberta, SUNY Buffalo, and the University of Waterloo, and from participants at the 1993 American Accounting Association and Canadian Academic Accounting Association meetings. Specific comments from A. Ahmed, Lawrence Brown, Lane Daly, Jennifer Francis, Carol Frost, Jerry Han, David Jobson, P. O'Malley, Vic Pastena, Grace Pownall, Mike Rozeff, Kevin Strain, and an anonymous reviewer were also appreciated. This study received financial support from the Social Sciences and Humanities Research Council of Canada. Finally, we are grateful for the research assistance of Doug Dover and Carol Leaman.

concerned about the nature and magnitude of U.S.–Canada *GAAP* differences. Largely in response to the North American Free Trade Agreement, the Financial Accounting Standards Board, the Canadian Institute of Chartered Accountants, and the Institute Mexicano de Contadores Publicos Ac in Mexico initiated a project to document the degree of consistency and comparability among the *GAAP* of the three countries.

We find that the magnitude of reported U.S.–Canada *GAAP* differences can be very large. Although one-third of the sample reconciliations have no material *GAAP* differences, the reported U.S.–Canada income differences for the remainder exceed 2% of the market value of equity, on average.[1]

In June 1991, the United States Securities and Exchange Commission (*SEC*) adopted forms F-10 and 40-F as part of a multijurisdictional disclosure system for Canadian issuers. If the *SEC* took no action by July 1, 1993, the requirement that Canadian issuers provide reconciliations of their Canadian-*GAAP* financial statements to U.S. *GAAP* would be dropped (a reciprocal privilege was offered to U.S. issuers by the Ontario Securities Commission (*OSC*)). In fact, the *SEC* took further action and decided to continue the reconciliation requirement (*International Series Release No. 556;* SEC [1993]). Finding that the reconciliations contain value-relevant information would support the *SEC*'s position, although there may be other valid political or strategic reasons for their retention.

Two concurrent studies examine the issue of the information content of U.S.–Canada *GAAP* differences. Barth and Clinch [1993] compared U.S. *GAAP* to that of Canada, the United Kingdom, and Australia. They found that U.K. and Australian firms' reconciliations contained information useful for explaining stock returns, but that the reconciliations of Canadian issuers did not. Using a sample of 25 Canadian issuer firms (one observation per firm), Frost and Kinney [1993] found a significant association between security prices and these firms' reconciliations. Our results, based on a sample of 96 Canadian firms (299 firm-year observations) and knowledge of the *SEC* and *OSC* filing dates, do not indicate a significant association between the reconciliation from Canadian to U.S. *GAAP* and the returns on the reporting firm's stock.

We conclude that the reconciliations do not appear to be value-relevant, even though the magnitude of the *GAAP* differences is sometimes large relative to a firm's earnings or its market value of equity. It may be the case that the reconciling items are not the result of events that have a continuing effect on a firm's future cash flows. One-time shocks to income should not be impounded in price the same way that earnings changes of a continuing nature are impounded. Alternatively,

---

[1] On average, the U.S.–Canada income differences are 25.9 times U.S. *GAAP* earnings and 2.7 times Canadian *GAAP* earnings. These large numbers are less a result of large differences and more a result of small earnings numbers. The use of market value of equity as a deflator throughout the paper mitigates this problem.

264   JOURNAL OF ACCOUNTING RESEARCH, AUTUMN, 1994

if financial markets can predict the reconciliation numbers sufficiently early, prices might impound any value-relevant information prior to the 12- and 24-month return windows used in this study.

Section 2 describes the sample and documents the nature and magnitude of the differences between income measured using Canadian *GAAP* and U.S. *GAAP.* In section 3, we provide evidence on the association between firms' stock returns and U.S.–Canada *GAAP* income differences using long-window tests. Section 4 presents the results of short-window tests of the market reaction to the 10K or 20F report filings. Section 5 summarizes the results and concludes the paper.

2. Sample Selection and Description of GAAP Differences

Our sample consists of Canadian firms listed on the Toronto Stock Exchange (*TSE*) which are also traded on the New York Stock Exchange (*NYSE*), the American Stock Exchange (*ASE*), or the National Association of Security Dealers and Quotation (*NASDAQ*) system during 1983–89. Each firm-year observation satisfies three data-availability criteria: (*i*) an annual report available at either Wilfred Laurier University or the University of Waterloo; (*ii*) stock returns available on the *CRSP* tapes or in Standard and Poor's *Daily Stock Price Record*; and (*iii*) a nonzero reported difference between income measured using Canadian *GAAP* and U.S. *GAAP.*

The initial sample consisted of 772 firm-year observations. Constraint (*i*) eliminated 74 firm years; constraint (*ii*) eliminated 243 firm years, leaving 455 reconciliation schedules with available data. Of these, 156 firm years have no material differences between Canadian *GAAP* and U.S. *GAAP* income. Constraint (*iii*) reduced the sample to 299 firm-year observations representing 96 firms. Of the 299 firm-year observations, 204 (52 firms) are cross-listed on either the *NYSE* or the *ASE* and 95 (44 firms) are traded on the *NASDAQ.* Of these 95 *NASDAQ* firm-year observations, 60 (28 firms) were required to file 10Ks and 35 (16 firms) were required to file 20Fs.[2]

The 299 nonzero reconciliations had 567 reconciling items, representing 49 types of *GAAP* differences. We combined the 49 types into six homogeneous categories (with at least 20 observations each) based on a review of several "Big Six" public accounting firms' publications describing U.S.–Canada *GAAP* differences.[3] As indicated in table 1, we

---

[2] Listed firms and *NASDAQ* firms filing under the 1933 Act are required to file form 10K within 90 days of their fiscal year-ends. *NASDAQ* firms filing under the 1934 Act may file form 20F (the Foreign Private Issuer form) instead of form 10K. Form 20F must be filed within six months after the fiscal year-end. For further details, see Bloomenthal [1989].

[3] Publications from four of the "Big Six" firms were reviewed in determining these six categories of *GAAP* differences. The publications include Price Waterhouse [1987] and internal documents from three other firms who asked us not to reference the firms or their publications.

TABLE 1

Description of the Six Major Categories of Differences between
U.S. GAAP Income and Canadian GAAP Income[a]

GAAP Difference	Nature of Difference
FOREXCH (N = 154)	Canadian *GAAP* (*CICA Handbook*, section 1650) requires the deferral and amortization of unrealized foreign exchange gains or losses on foreign long-term debt. U.S. *GAAP* (*SFAS No. 52*) requires the immediate recognition of such items.
OILGAS (N = 67)	Canadian *GAAP* allows the use of worldwide cost centers. U.S. *GAAP* stipulates that cost centers must not extend beyond the geographic boundaries of a country. Canadian *GAAP* allows the use of a zero discount rate in calculations regarding the ceiling test. U.S. *GAAP* stipulates a 10% rate.
INTCAP (N = 45)	The Canadian *Handbook* is silent on the issue of interest capitalization. U.S. *GAAP* (*SFAS No. 34*) requires interest capitalization on certain qualifying fixed assets under construction.
XINOTUS[b] (N = 65)	Canadian *GAAP* (prior to January 1, 1990) was more liberal regarding extraordinary items. Gains or losses on the disposal of fixed assets or losses on asset writedowns were frequent Canadian extraordinary items that did not qualify as extraordinary items according to U.S. *GAAP* (*APB Opinion No. 30*).
DEFTAX (N = 30)	Canadian *GAAP* (*CICA Handbook*, section 1580) allows the carryforward of the deferred tax balances of an acquired company when using the purchase method of accounting for business combinations. U.S. *GAAP* (*APB Opinion No. 16*) assigns these amounts to specific assets and liabilities.
XINOTCDN[b] (N = 32)	Similar to *XINOTUS*, U.S. *GAAP* allows extraordinary items that would not be accorded extraordinary item treatment in Canada. Gains and Losses on the extinguishment of debt, for which *SFAS No. 4* requires extraordinary item treatment in the United States, would be shown "above the line" in Canada.
OTHER (N = 174)	Any other items.

[a] These six categories of *GAAP* differences were identified based on a review of "Big Six" public accounting firms' publications describing U.S.–Canada *GAAP* differences.

[b] The *XINOTUS* and *XINOTCDN* categories represent disclosure differences and not income differences. We emphasize income before extraordinary items in this study. Therefore, different definitions of extraordinary items in the United States and Canada are differences in reconciling income before extraordinary items measured using U.S. *GAAP* to that determined using Canadian *GAAP*.

were able to classify 393 of the 567 sample reconciling items into the six categories; the remaining 174 items were classified as "other."

Table 2 reports descriptive statistics on Canadian *GAAP* earnings and U.S.–Canada earnings differences deflated by the market value of equity (the sample mean market value of equity is U.S. $764.2 million and the median is U.S. $235.4 million). All of the announced earnings numbers in our sample were measured in accordance with Canadian *GAAP*.

TABLE 2

Descriptive Statistics on Canadian Earnings and the Magnitude of GAAP Differences (U.S. minus Canadian) Deflated by Market Value of Equity at the Beginning of the Fiscal Period[a]

	E_{CA}	Aggregate Net Difference	FOREXCH	OILGAS	INTCAP	XINOTUS	DEFTAX	XINOTCDN	OTHER
N^b	299	299	154	67	45	65	30	32	174
Mean	−0.018	−0.022	−0.004	−0.018	−0.001	0.030	0.000	−0.004	−0.007
5th Percentile	−0.271	−0.239	−0.043	−0.190	−0.033	−0.093	−0.011	−0.041	−0.053
25th Percentile	−0.016	−0.019	−0.003	−0.032	−0.000	−0.022	−0.003	−0.008	−0.007
Median	0.029	−0.000	−0.000	−0.002	0.001	−0.002	0.000	−0.001	−0.002
75th Percentile	0.081	0.005	0.005	0.003	0.003	0.041	0.002	0.004	0.004
95th Percentile	0.178	0.055	0.023	0.018	0.015	0.339	0.017	0.018	0.041
Mean Absolute Value	0.118	0.046	0.017	0.041	0.007	0.070	0.005	0.011	0.023
Median Absolute Value	0.063	0.010	0.004	0.009	0.002	0.028	0.002	0.007	0.006

Variable definitions:

E_{CA} is Canadian GAAP earnings before extraordinary items measured in U.S. dollars; Aggregate Net Difference is the difference between income measured using Canadian GAAP and income measured using U.S. GAAP; FOREXCH, OILGAS, INTCAP, XINOTUS, DEFTAX, XINOTCDN, and OTHER are types of reconciling differences and are described in table 1.

[a] The sample mean market value of equity is U.S. $764.2 million and the median is U.S. $235.4 million.

[b] The 299 nonzero reconciliations consist of 567 items. The reconciliations are from a sample of 96 Canadian firms traded on American equity markets and required to file periodic financial reports with the SEC during 1983–89.

Preliminary earnings are almost always measured in Canadian dollars; only 3 of 96 sample firms reported Canadian *GAAP* earnings in U.S. dollars. We converted the reported earnings numbers into U.S. dollars using the exchange rate at the end of the return accumulation period.[4]

As reported in the second column of table 2, the mean absolute value of the aggregate net differences between U.S. and Canadian *GAAP* income is 4.6% of the market value of common equity measured at the beginning of the fiscal year. In addition, half of the aggregate net differences lie outside the range negative 1.9% (U.S. *GAAP* earnings less than Canadian) to positive 0.5% (U.S. *GAAP* earnings greater than Canadian) of market capitalization. The aggregate *GAAP* differences are about one-quarter to one-third the magnitude of unexpected Canadian earnings (calculated using an annual random-walk model—results not reported).[5]

The second column of table 2 also shows that, on average, U.S. *GAAP* earnings are lower than Canadian *GAAP* earnings by about 2.2% of the market value of equity. There are 170 aggregate net differences that decrease income and 129 differences that increase income. The median decrease is −1.2% of market value, while the median increase is 0.6%. A Wilcoxon rank-sum test rejects the null hypothesis that the distributions of the absolute values of decreases and increases are equal at the 0.042 level. These results are consistent with relatively greater conservatism of U.S. *GAAP* (Irwin and Mason [1989]).

Table 2 also reports descriptive statistics for the six categories of *GAAP* difference described in table 1. The most frequent category of reconciling items is differences related to foreign currency (*FOREXCH*, 154 differences). Although the median foreign currency difference is zero, the median absolute value of the *FOREXCH* differences is 0.4% of market value, indicating both income-increasing and income-decreasing differences in this category. The largest reconciling-item category in terms of median absolute value is Canadian *GAAP* extraordinary items not treated as extraordinary items in the United States (*XINOTUS*, 65 differences, 2.8% of market value). The remaining categories all have median absolute values less than 0.01 of market value.[6]

---

[4] The conversion to U.S. dollars is arbitrary and is done solely to ensure the comparability of the earnings numbers. Results based on Canadian returns and prices are qualitatively similar and are not reported. The return accumulation period is the 12 months ending in the month that a firm files its financial information with Canadian or U.S. regulatory authorities (assumed to be the latest date that reconciliations become publicly available).

[5] The mean and median absolute values and the interquartile range of the aggregate U.S.–Canada *GAAP* differences are all one-quarter to one-third the magnitude of these statistics calculated for unexpected Canadian earnings.

[6] In 1984, Page Petroleum Ltd. reported the largest income-decreasing difference. This firm, with a market value of equity of U.S. $5.675 million and a Canadian *GAAP* net loss before extraordinary items of U.S. $17.09 million, reported a U.S. $5.038 million foreign currency loss in its reconciliation to U.S. *GAAP* income. In 1983, Dome Petroleum Ltd.

3. Long Return-Window Tests

We use contemporaneous return–earnings models to examine the association between U.S.–Canada *GAAP* reconciliations and share returns. We measure the return (R) over the 12 months ending in the month a firm first files a reconciliation with either the *SEC* or *OSC*.[7] The reconciliation schedule is contained in an audited footnote to the financial statements. There are at least four dates on which U.S. investors might first receive the information contained in the reconciliations: (*i*) the receipt date of the annual report at the *OSC* in Toronto; (*ii*) the receipt date of the 10K or 20F filing at the *OSC* (a voluntary filing); (*iii*) the receipt date of the 10K or 20F filing at the *SEC*; and (*iv*) the receipt date of the annual report at the *SEC* (a voluntary filing). For (*i*) and (*ii*), the *OSC* filing date was collected. For *SEC* filings, (*iii*) and (*iv*), the date filings are processed by Disclosure Inc. is used as a proxy for the *SEC* receipt date.[8] The earliest of these four dates is used to identify the twelfth month of the return window. Monthly returns are used to calculate the annual return in this window.

Following Easton and Harris [1991], we cross-sectionally regress stock return on both the level of earnings (E_{US}) and the annual change in earnings (ΔE_{US}):[9]

$$R_{ij} = \varphi_0 + \varphi_1 (E_{US})_{ij} + \varphi_2 (\Delta E_{US})_{ij} + (\varepsilon_1)_{ij} \qquad (1)$$

where:

R_{ij} is the raw annual return for firm *i* in year *j*;
E_{US} is the firm's earnings measured using U.S. *GAAP* and deflated by beginning-of-period market value of equity;

---

reported the largest income-increasing difference. This firm, which had a market value of equity of U.S. \$772.2 million and a Canadian *GAAP* net loss before extraordinary items of U.S. \$1,105 million, reported a U.S. \$341 million increase to income related to accounting for oil and gas reserves.

[7] Alternatively, returns were cumulated over the 24 months ending in the same month as the 12-month period (Kothari and Sloan [1992]). Including returns prior to the period for which earnings are measured can improve the fit of the return–earnings model. The results using the longer holding period are similar to those reported, except that the adjusted R^2 statistics are slightly larger.

[8] Hanna [1991] shows that the Disclosure Inc. processing date is a reliable proxy for the date 10K and annual reports are filed with the *SEC*. The lag between the receipt of documents at the *SEC* and at Disclosure Inc. is generally one or two days. Processing dates were unavailable for 20F filings (35 firm years). If the *OSC*'s annual report filing deadline of 140 days is compared to the *SEC*'s 20F filing deadline of 6 months, the earlier of the two dates is likely to be the *OSC* annual report filing date. This date is used for the 20F firms.

[9] Results are not sensitive to alternative specifications using levels-only and changes-only, or to different deflators for the accounting variables (total assets, market value of equity, and previous year's Canadian *GAAP* income).

ΔE_{US} is the annual change in deflated U.S. *GAAP* earnings; and φ_0, φ_1, φ_2, and ε_1 are *OLS* regression parameters and a normally distributed residual term.

The independent variables in the aggregate models are accounting earnings before extraordinary items calculated in accordance with either Canadian *GAAP* (E_{CAN}) or U.S. *GAAP* (E_{US}). The aggregate net *GAAP* difference is the difference between these two income measures (E_{US} – E_{CAN}). All right-hand-side variables in the regressions are measured in U.S. dollars and are deflated by beginning-of-period market value of equity. We examine both the aggregate difference between Canadian and U.S. *GAAP* income, and the components of this difference described in table 1.

Substituting the identity, $E_{US} = E_{CAN} + (E_{US} - E_{CAN})$, into equation (1), and allowing for different slope coefficients yields:

$$R_{ij} = \beta_0 + \beta_1 (E_{CAN})_{ij} + \beta_2 (\Delta E_{CAN})_{ij} + \beta_3 (E_{US} - E_{CAN})_{ij} +$$

$$\beta_4 (\Delta E_{US} - \Delta E_{CAN})_{ij} + (\varepsilon_2)_{ij} \qquad (2)$$

where:

R_{ij} is the raw annual return for firm i in year j;
E_{US} and E_{CAN} are the firm's earnings measured using U.S. *GAAP* and Canadian *GAAP*, respectively, and deflated by beginning-of-period market value of equity;
Δ represents the annual change in a variable; and
β_0, β_1, β_2, β_3, β_4, and ε_2 are *OLS* regression parameters and a normally distributed residual term.

We test the hypotheses that $\beta_3 = 0$ and $\beta_4 = 0$. Rejection of these hypotheses is consistent with the aggregate U.S.–Canada *GAAP* difference containing value-relevant information, beyond the information in Canadian *GAAP* earnings.

Table 3 reports the results of estimating equation (2) on both a pooled and a year-by-year basis. Results for the pooled estimation confirm that Canadian-*GAAP* earnings are an informative signal to the market ($\beta_1 = 0.440$; $t = 3.974$). Neither β_3, the coefficient on the difference between U.S. and Canadian earnings, nor β_4, the coefficient on the year-to-year change in this difference, is significantly different from zero at any conventional level.[10] An *F*-test of the restriction that $\beta_3 = \beta_4 = 0$ fails to reject the null hypothesis ($\alpha = 0.79$). Moreover, the year-by-year results yield a mean estimate of β_3 of 0.661 ($t = 0.592$); the mean

---

[10] In the pooled time-series cross-sectional regression, the White *t*-statistics for β_3 and β_4 are –0.613 and 0.165, respectively. The White [1980] chi-square test does not reject the null hypothesis of homoscedastic error structures for either the pooled time-series cross-sectional regression or the year-by-year regressions, with the exception of the 1983 regression. In that year, only β_3 is significantly positive ($\alpha = 0.05$).

270   S. P. BANDYOPADHYAY, J. D. HANNA, AND G. RICHARDSON

TABLE 3
Regressions of Returns on the Levels and the Changes of Canadian GAAP Earnings and the Aggregate
Difference between Canadian and U.S. GAAP Earnings (1983–89)[a]

	N	α	β_1	β_2	β_3	β_4	Adj. R^2
All Years	299	0.057	0.440	−0.118	−0.267	0.049	0.044
		(2.003)	(3.974)	(−1.063)	(−0.595)	(0.151)	
1983	29	0.173	0.968	0.954	6.868	−2.949	0.232
		(1.723)	(1.550)	(1.868)	(1.833)	(−0.708)	
1984	31	−0.076	0.893	0.553	−2.193	1.410	0.082
		(−1.042)	(1.787)	(1.556)	(−1.155)	(1.086)	
1985	37	−0.068	2.122	−1.448	−0.534	0.889	0.190
		(−1.054)	(2.378)	(−1.578)	(−0.429)	(0.866)	
1986	47	0.535	1.192	−0.878	−0.656	0.973	−0.016
		(4.478)	(1.369)	(−1.153)	(−0.443)	(0.677)	
1987	40	−0.175	0.760	0.678	0.462	1.087	0.040
		(−2.831)	(0.700)	(0.581)	(0.360)	(1.554)	
1988	59	−0.022	0.535	0.490	1.415	−0.831	0.243
		(−0.518)	(2.866)	(1.614)	(1.299)	(−1.089)	
1989	56	−0.052	0.837	−0.321	−0.736	−0.408	0.125
		(−1.312)	(3.099)	(−1.594)	(−0.693)	(−0.933)	
Mean over seven years			1.044	0.004	0.661	0.024	
Standard error of mean			0.195	0.341	1.117	0.587	
t-test of H_0: $\beta = 0$			5.356	0.012	0.592	0.042	

[a] For a sample of 96 Canadian firms traded on American equity markets and required to file periodic financial reports with the *SEC*. All accounting variables are deflated by the beginning-of-period market value of equity. We report the coefficient estimates (t-statistics) for the following regression:

$$R_{i,j} = \alpha + \beta_1 (E_{CAN})_{i,j} + \beta_2 (\Delta E_{CAN})_{i,j} + \beta_3 (E_{US} - E_{CAN})_{i,j} + \beta_4 (\Delta E_{US} - \Delta E_{CAN})_{i,j} + \varepsilon_{i,j}$$

where:

$R_{i,j}$ is the raw return for firm i in year j measured over the 12-month period ending with the month the firm releases a *GAAP* reconciliation;
E_{CAN} is the Canadian *GAAP* annual earnings deflated by market value of equity;
E_{US} is the U.S. *GAAP* annual earnings deflated by market value of equity; and
Δ represents the year-to-year change in a variable.

estimate of β_4 is 0.024 ($t = 0.042$). These results suggest that the null hypothesis of no value-relevant information cannot be rejected.

Equation (2) constrains all reconciling items to have equal effects on market prices. It is possible, however, that some items have a greater effect on security prices than others.[11] To investigate this issue, we expand the *GAAP* difference component of equation (2), $(E_{US} - E_{CAN})$,

---

[11] Of course, individual income statement components will have higher standard errors than aggregate earnings (which enjoy a portfolio effect). Also, the methodology employs an "as if" approach that uses the firm as its own control, so there is no need to control for cross-sectional variation in the determinants of earnings response coefficients (see Pincus [1991]). However, for the disaggregated models, the "as if" approach is less than ideal because different firms are members of different partitions. Coefficients on disaggregated components may vary from component to component because the determinants of earnings response coefficients (such as size, risk, growth, and persistence) are not controlled. To control for this complication, separate regressions were estimated that considered only one type of reconciling item at a time. These results (not reported) are similar to those of the pooled disaggregated model.

into the six components described in table 1. The "*OTHER*" component is assumed to be a part of the error term. Substituting the six components into equation (2) yields the following disaggregated model:

$$R_{ij} = \beta_0 + \beta_1 (E_{CAN})_{ij} + \beta_2 (\Delta E_{CAN})_{ij} + \beta_3 (FOREXCH)_{ij} +$$

$$\beta_4 (OILGAS)_{ij} + \beta_5 (INTCAP)_{ij} + \beta_6 (XINOTUS)_{ij} +$$

$$\beta_7 (DEFTAX)_{ij} + \beta_8 (XINOTCDN)_{ij} + \beta_9 (\Delta FOREXCH)_{ij} +$$

$$\beta_{10} (\Delta OILGAS)_{ij} + \beta_{11} (\Delta INTCAP)_{ij} + \beta_{12} (\Delta XINOTUS)_{ij} +$$

$$\beta_{13} (\Delta DEFTAX)_{ij} + \beta_{14} (\Delta XINOTCDN)_{ij} + (\varepsilon_3)_{ij} \qquad (3)$$

where:

R_{ij} is the raw annual return for firm i in year j;

E_{CAN} is the firm's earnings measured using Canadian *GAAP* and deflated by beginning-of-period market value of equity;

FOREXCH, OILGAS, INTCAP, XINOTUS, DEFTAX, and *XINOTCDN* are the six categories of *GAAP* differences used to reconcile Canadian *GAAP* earnings to U.S. *GAAP* earnings (described in table 1);

Δ represents the annual change in a variable; and

β_0, β_1, β_2, β_3, β_4, and ε_3 are *OLS* regression parameters and a normally distributed residual term.

We investigate whether the variables associated with coefficients β_3 through β_{14} in equation (3) add explanatory power beyond Canadian *GAAP* earnings. Coefficient estimates, t-statistics, and an F-test of H_0: $\beta_3 = \beta_4 = \ldots = \beta_{14} = 0$ are reported in table 4. The individual coefficients, β_3 through β_{14}, are insignificantly different from zero and the F-statistic is insignificant ($F = 0.744$). These results suggest that none of the reconciling items has value relevance.[12]

It is possible that our tests lack the power necessary to detect value relevance for small U.S.–Canada *GAAP* differences. To provide evidence on this issue, we partitioned the sample based on the magnitude of the aggregate difference between U.S. *GAAP* earnings and Canadian *GAAP* earnings. Observations in the second and third quartiles were discarded and the remaining 149 observations were used to reestimate equations (2) and (3). Although the explanatory power of the models is slightly larger, the inferences are essentially unchanged.

4. Short Return-Window Tests

For the subset of firm-year observations with available announcement dates, short-window tests of abnormal returns are performed for the four potential financial statement filing dates and two preliminary

---

[12] Similar results (not reported) were obtained after deleting observations where any of the independent variables exceeded unity (Collins and Kothari [1989]; recall that all accounting variables are deflated by the market value of equity).

272   S. P. BANDYOPADHYAY, J. D. HANNA, AND G. RICHARDSON

TABLE 4

Regression of Returns on the Level and Change in Canadian GAAP Earnings and the Level and Change in the Components Reconciling Canadian GAAP Earnings to U.S. GAAP Earnings (1983–89) [a]

	Coefficient	Estimate	t-Statistic
Intercept	α	0.052	1.808
E_{CAN}	β_1	0.520	3.685
ΔE_{CAN}	β_2	−0.066	−0.452
FOREXCH	β_3	−1.969	−1.098
OILGAS	β_4	−0.567	−0.478
INTCAP	β_5	0.087	0.095
XINOTUS	β_6	0.088	0.015
DEFTAX	β_7	−13.201	−1.615
XINOTCDN	β_8	−3.372	−0.213
ΔFOREXCH	β_9	2.182	1.148
ΔOILGAS	β_{10}	−0.165	−0.178
ΔINTCAP	β_{11}	−0.073	−0.105
ΔXINOTUS	β_{12}	−13.078	−1.229
ΔDEFTAX	β_{13}	3.564	0.631
ΔXINOTCDN	β_{14}	2.024	0.180

Adjusted R^2 = 0.039

299 firm-year observations

F-test of restriction that β_3 through β_{14} = 0: F = 0.744, α < 0.71

[a] For a sample of 96 Canadian firms traded on American equity markets and required to file periodic financial reports with the *SEC*. All accounting variables are deflated by the beginning-of-period market value of equity. We report the coefficient estimates (t-statistics) for the following regression:

$$R_{i,j} = \alpha + \beta_1 (E_{CAN})_{i,j} + \beta_2 (\Delta E_{CAN})_{i,j} + \beta_3 (FOREXCH)_{i,j} + \beta_4 (OILGAS)_{i,j} + \beta_5 (INTCAP)_{i,j} +$$
$$\beta_6 (XINOTUS)_{i,j} + \beta_7 (DEFTAX)_{i,j} + \beta_8 (XINOTCDN)_{i,j} + \beta_9 (\Delta FOREXCH)_{i,j} +$$
$$\beta_{10} (\Delta OILGAS)_{i,j} + \beta_{11} (\Delta INTCAP)_{i,j} + \beta_{12} (\Delta XINOTUS)_{i,j} + \beta_{13} (\Delta DEFTAX)_{i,j} +$$
$$\beta_{14} (\Delta XINOTCDN)_{i,j} + \varepsilon_{i,j}$$

where:

$R_{i,j}$ is the raw return for firm i in year j measured over the 12-month period ending with the month the firm releases a *GAAP* reconciliation;

E_{CAN} is the Canadian *GAAP* earnings;

FOREXCH (foreign exchange), OILGAS (oil and gas), INTCAP (interest capitalization), XINOTUS (extraordinary items in Canada but not in the U.S.), DEFTAX (deferred taxes), and XINODTCDN (extraordinary items in the U.S. but not in Canada) are the reconciling *GAAP* differences described further in table 1; and

Δ represents the year-to-year change in a variable.

earnings announcement dates: (*i*) the date a firm files its annual report at the *OSC*; (*ii*) the date a firm files its 10K or 20F report with the *OSC* (a voluntary filing); (*iii*) the date a firm files its 10K or 20F report with the *SEC*; (*iv*) the date a firm files its annual report to shareholders with the *SEC* (a voluntary filing); (*v*) the preliminary earnings announcement in the Canadian media; and (*vi*) the preliminary earnings announcement of Canadian *GAAP* earnings in the *Wall Street Journal*. An examination of the price reactions to the earnings announcements offers a standard of comparison for the price reactions to the financial statement filings.

The information in the reconciliations should have a "surprise" component only if this information has not been previously available. An examination of the preliminary earnings announcements contained in the press releases issued by the sample firms (available for 190 of the 299 firm-years) indicates that reconciliations of Canadian to U.S. *GAAP* earnings are not typically available at the date of the preliminary earnings announcement.

Our examination of preliminary earnings announcements suggests that both Canadian and U.S. investors received preliminary earnings information at the same time (recall that all sample firms report preliminary earnings figures using Canadian *GAAP*). Moreover, a comparison of the *Wall Street Journal Index* and Canadian news releases indicates that the *Wall Street Journal* (*WSJ*) reports the same Canadian *GAAP* earnings numbers reported in the Canadian news releases; the *WSJ* does not provide information about U.S.–Canada *GAAP* reconciliations for the firm years used in this study.[13]

There is no pattern regarding which of the four financial statement dates is the earliest. For 34% of the sample of 10K filers (264 total firm-years), the earliest of the four dates was the date the annual report was received at the *OSC.* The 10K filing date at the *OSC* was the earliest date for 29%; the 10K filing date at the *SEC* was the earliest date for 25%; and the annual report filing date at the *SEC* was the earliest date for 12%.[14]

The lack of a distinct pattern of disclosure dates indicates there may be considerable measurement error in identifying the date when investors first become aware of U.S.–Canada *GAAP* reconciliations. The date that investors receive annual reports or fourth-quarter reports in the mail is also unknown. Given this event-date uncertainty, as well as the difficulty inherent in modeling investor expectations for the various reconciling items found in the U.S.–Canada *GAAP* reconciliations, we do not regress abnormal returns on the unexpected component of the accounting variables. Instead, we perform short-window tests similar to those described in Easton and Zmijewski [1993]. Easton and Zmijewski compute squared market-model prediction errors for each day in a five-day window around each event-date and determine the rank of each day's squared prediction error in a vector of estimation-period squared

---

[13] For 60% of the 190 firm years for which press releases were available, the preliminary earnings announcement was disclosed through Canada NewsWire Ltd. (*CNW*). CNW has information terminals in major media outlets in Canada, such as newspaper offices and stock exchanges. In the U.S. *CNW*'s press releases are disseminated through PR Newswire Inc., its U.S. affiliate. For 90% of the sample firm years, the earnings report is published in the *WSJ* within four days of the earnings release date in Canada.

[14] Only the 10K must be filed at year-end at the *SEC.* The *OSC* in Canada requires that annual reports be filed within 140 days of the fiscal year-end, but some firms file 10Ks or 20Fs (which typically include the information in the annual report filing) in addition to annual reports in advance of the required annual report filing. Thus, the 10K or 20F filings at the *OSC* and the annual report filings at the *SEC* are voluntary and not always available. Specifically, 10K or 20F reports are available at the *OSC* for 175 of the 299 sample firm years. Filing dates for annual reports were available at the *SEC* for 217 of the 299 firm years.

274   S. P. BANDYOPADHYAY, J. D. HANNA, AND G. RICHARDSON

TABLE 5

Squared Market Model Prediction Errors for Days −2 to +2 around Two Earnings Announcement Dates and around Four Financial Statement Filing Dates (1983–89)[a]

	Day −2	Day −1	Day 0	Day +1	Day +2
Earnings Announcement Dates:					
Canadian NewsWire Earnings					
Announcement Date	0.261	0.094	4.111**	2.016*	0.855
Wall Street Journal Earnings					
Announcement Date	1.466	3.235**	1.481	2.380**	0.580
Financial Statement Filing Dates:					
Date Annual Report Filed with the *SEC*	−0.157	−0.535	0.050	−0.514	2.069*
Date 10K Filed with the *SEC*	−0.454	−2.830**	0.042	0.358	−1.050
Date Annual Report Filed with the *OSC*	0.086	−1.580	0.542	−0.596	−1.497
Date 10K Filed with the *OSC*	0.075	−2.336**	−1.520	1.535	0.731

[a] For a sample of 42 Canadian firms (99 firm-year observations) traded on American equity markets and required to file periodic financial reports with the *SEC* and with all of the above six dates available for a given year, we report the Easton and Zmijewski [1993] z-statistics for the mean squared prediction errors; *(**) indicates statistical significance at the 5% (1%) level. Positive (negative) z-scores indicate abnormally large (small) squared prediction errors.

prediction errors. A standard normal z-score is then derived from this rank for each day examined. The z-scores are aligned in event-time and are aggregated across the observations. These tests document any abnormal price movements in the days surrounding an information release, regardless of the direction.

The short return-window tests are conducted on the 99 firm-year observations with all six event dates and available Center for Research in Security Prices (*CRSP*) return data for a five-day window surrounding each of the six event dates and for at least 100 days in a 300-day estimation period that ends with the last day of the fiscal period related to the filings. The results for the short-window tests on these 99 observations are reported in table 5 and are consistent with the long-window association test results presented earlier. Specifically, significant z-scores are found for earnings announcement dates but not for the financial statement filing dates. The z-score on the day of the preliminary earnings announcement in the Canadian media is 4.11 ($p < 0.01$). The mean z-score for day −1 relative to the *WSJ* preliminary earnings announcement (frequently the Canada NewsWire date) is 3.24 ($p < 0.01$). With few exceptions, the z-scores are not significantly different from zero on any of the five days surrounding the financial statement receipt dates at the *SEC* and the *OSC*. The one day with a significantly large squared prediction error at the 5% level is day +2 relative to the *SEC* annual report filing date.[15] A significant z-score for the preliminary earnings announcement date and insignificant z-scores for each of the

---

[15] The Z-score for day −1 relative to the *SEC* 10K filing date is −2.83 and the Z-score for day −1 relative to the *OSC* 10K filing date is −2.34. The negative sign indicates an unusually small (in magnitude) prediction error.

four reconciliation filing dates (with the *OSC* and the *SEC*) is consistent with no incremental information content of reconciliations beyond that of Canadian *GAAP* earnings.[16]

To address the concern that the information in the reconciliations is known before the reconciliations are filed with the *OSC* or the *SEC*, two additional tests were performed. First, to test whether the reconciliation information was impounded in stock prices at the time of the preliminary earnings announcement, we reestimated equation (2) using market-adjusted stock returns measured for days –1 and 0 relative to the preliminary earnings announcement date (284 firm years). Second, to test whether the reconciliation information was impounded in stock prices between the earnings announcement and the filing of the reconciliation with the *OSC* or *SEC*, we reestimated equation (2) using market-adjusted stock returns measured from day +1 relative to the *WSJ* earnings announcement to day +3 relative to the earliest reconciliation filing date (76 firm years).[17] Results of these tests (not reported) show no evidence of any important association between returns and *GAAP* differences in the time periods examined.

5. Conclusions

This study examines the capital market effects of differences in reported earnings caused by the application of both U.S. and Canadian *GAAP* for a sample of 96 Canadian firms listed on the Toronto Stock Exchange and either cross-listed on the *NYSE/ASE* or traded on the *NASDAQ* system during 1983–89. The reconciliations of Canadian *GAAP* earnings to U.S. *GAAP* earnings provided in the 10K or 20F filings of the sample firms contained as many as 49 types of differences between the two numbers. These differences were grouped into six categories for the purpose of empirical analysis: foreign exchange, oil and gas, deferred taxes, interest capitalization, and two types of extraordinary items.

Our analysis indicates that *GAAP* differences can have a large impact on reported earnings. For example, half the sample firms experienced an aggregate U.S.–Canada *GAAP* difference in earnings that lies outside a range of positive 0.5% of market capitalization (U.S. *GAAP* earnings

---

[16] An alternative explanation for these results is that the short return-windows do not capture the time period when information contained in the reconciliations is impounded in share prices. Also, information allowing investors to forecast reconciling differences could become available during the firm's fiscal year (i.e., investors could track exchange rates and forecast likely foreign exchange differences). The lack of expectations models for the various reconciling items complicates the identification of the portion of the reconciling information that is new to investors at the time these reconciliations become public information.

[17] Because this period could be different for each firm year in the sample, the compounded market-adjusted return was calculated and then the average return per day was used as a dependent variable in the regression.

276   S. P. BANDYOPADHYAY, J. D. HANNA, AND G. RICHARDSON

greater than Canadian *GAAP* earnings) to negative 1.9% of market capitalization (U.S. *GAAP* earnings less than Canadian). However, our empirical tests indicate that investors do not act as if these differences are material. This lack of value relevance is observed for both the aggregate difference between U.S. and Canadian *GAAP* earnings and the individual reconciling items comprising the difference.

Although the results suggest that, on average, investors act as if U.S.–Canada *GAAP* differences do not affect pricing decisions, the tests cannot and do not speak to the costs incurred by investors as a result of such differences. These costs include preparation costs, attestation costs, and the costs of "coping mechanisms" adopted by investors when faced with an unfamiliar foreign *GAAP* and a multitude of sources of *GAAP* differences (see Choi and Levich [1990]). Nor do the tests speak to the other information contained in the *SEC*'s 10K or 20F documents.

With these caveats in mind, we believe our results have at least two policy implications. First, our findings have implications for the North American Free Trade Agreement and the recent creation of a tripartite study group charged with examining *GAAP* differences in the United States, Canada, and Mexico. For the U.S.–Canada issue, our results support reciprocity rather than harmonization. Second, the *SEC* has adopted amendments to their multijurisdictional disclosure system to continue the requirement that Canadian firms provide, at some cost, reconciliations from Canada *GAAP* earnings to U.S. *GAAP* earnings. Results consistent with U.S.–Canada *GAAP* differences containing price-relevant information would have provided an economic justification for retaining the reconciliations. Our evidence that such differences are irrelevant for valuation purposes does not, however, imply that the reconciliations have no value. To determine whether to continue the policy of requiring the reconciliations, the *SEC* would need to consider alternative uses of this information and the costs of providing it. These issues are beyond the scope of this study.

REFERENCES

AMIR, E.; T. HARRIS; AND E. VENUTI. "A Comparison of the Value Relevance of U.S. versus Non-U.S. *GAAP* Accounting Measures Using Form 20F Reconciliations." *Journal of Accounting Research* (Supplement 1993): 230–64.

BARTH, M., AND G. CLINCH. "International Accounting Differences and Their Relation to Share Prices: Evidence from U.K., Australian, and Canadian Firms." Working paper, Harvard Business School and Australian Graduate School of Management, March 1993.

BLOOMENTHAL, H., ed. *International Capital Markets and Securities Regulation.* 1st ed. Revised 1989; Volume 10A, Release No. 7, October 1989. New York: Clark Boardman, 1989.

CHOI, F., AND R. LEVICH. *The Capital Market Effects of International Accounting Diversity.* New York: New York University, 1990.

COLLINS, D., AND S. P. KOTHARI. "An Analysis of Intertemporal and Cross-Sectional Determinants of Earnings Response Coefficients." *Journal of Accounting and Economics* 11 (1989): 143–81.

EASTON, P., AND T. HARRIS. "Earnings as an Explanatory Variable for Returns." *Journal of Accounting Research* 29 (1991): 19–36.

EFFECTS OF U.S.–CANADA *GAAP* DIFFERENCES   277

EASTON, P., AND M. ZMIJEWSKI. "*SEC* Form 10K/10-Q Reports and Annual Reports to Share-holders: Reporting Lags and Squared Market Model Prediction Errors." *Journal of Accounting Research* 31 (1993): 185–209.

FROST, C., AND W. KINNEY. "Regulation S-X and Comparability of Disclosure for Foreign Registrants in the U.S." Working paper, Washington University and University of Texas at Austin, June 1993.

HANNA, D. "A Further Examination of the Incremental Information Content of Cash-Flow Announcements." Ph.D. dissertation, Cornell University, 1991.

IRWIN, D., AND A. MASON. "Closing the GAAP." *CA Magazine* (December 1989): 54–57.

KOTHARI, S. P., AND R. SLOAN. "Information in Prices about Future Earnings." *Journal of Accounting and Economics* 15 (1992): 143–71.

McQUEEN, P. "The Information Content of Foreign and U.S. GAAP Earnings in SEC Form 20F." Working paper, New York University, January 1993.

PINCUS, M. "Accounting Methods and Differential Stock Market Response to the Announcement of Earnings." Working paper, Washington University, May 1991.

PRICE WATERHOUSE. *Accounting Principles and Practices in Canada and the United States of America 1987: A Survey of Significant Differences.* Ottawa, July 1987.

SECURITIES AND EXCHANGE COMMISSION. *International Series Release No. 556: Amendments to the Multijurisdictional Disclosure System for Canadian Issuers.* New York: SEC, July 1, 1993.

WHITE, H. "A Heteroskedasticity-Consistent Matrix Estimator and a Direct Test for Heteroskedasticity." *Econometrica* (May 1980): 817–38.

[11]

Journal of Accounting Research
Vol. 31 Supplement 1993
Printed in U.S.A.

A Comparison of the Value-Relevance of U.S. versus Non-U.S. GAAP Accounting Measures Using Form 20-F Reconciliations

ELI AMIR, TREVOR S. HARRIS, AND
ELIZABETH K. VENUTI*

1. Introduction

Firms registered outside the United States and listed on a primary U.S. exchange may provide their U.S. shareholders with financial statements prepared under their domestic (non-U.S.) generally accepted accounting principles (*GAAP*). The Securities and Exchange Commission requires such firms to reconcile their reported earnings and shareholders' equity to U.S. *GAAP* as part of a Form 20-F filing. These reconciliations provide a set of precise measures of the differences created by alternative accounting practices.

We use the reconciliations to address two questions. First, are the differences in U.S. and non-U.S. *GAAP* as summarized in the aggregate reconciliations of earnings and shareholders' equity value-relevant? That is, do the reconciliations of accounting data to U.S. *GAAP* increase the associations between accounting measures and price (or return)?

*Columbia University. We thank Tom Sandford of the Bank of New York for helpful discussions. We also benefited from the comments of Mary Barth, Vic Bernard, Peter Pope, an anonymous reviewer, and participants at the *Journal of Accounting Research* Conference. We are grateful to the Faculty Research Fund of Columbia Business School for their financial support of this project. Eli Amir is grateful to the KPMG Peat Marwick Foundation for financial support; Trevor Harris's research was partially funded by the Rudolph Schoenheimer Fellowship.

Second, which differences in accounting practices summarized in the components of the reconciliation are value-relevant? Addressing this second question provides insights about the value-relevance of alternative measurement practices. In this study, we evaluate the questions by considering the associations between accounting earnings and security returns, and whether the accounting measures partially explain the ratio of market price to book value of shareholders' equity. Our results suggest that the reconciliations of earnings and shareholders' equity to U.S. *GAAP* are value-relevant. This result holds both in aggregate and for some specific components, in particular property revaluations and capitalized goodwill.

There has been extensive coverage in the popular press questioning the necessity for non-U.S. companies to reconcile their financial statements to U.S. *GAAP* in order to be listed on a U.S. securities exchange (for example, Fuerbringer [1992], Jarrell [1992], and Siconolfi and Salwen [1992]). If the reconciliation data cannot be shown to be value-relevant, then it is harder to argue that such data are necessary.[1] Hence, our results can contribute to the policy debate, even though we do not attempt to ascertain whether any information in the reconciliations can be gleaned from the published non-U.S. *GAAP* financial statements.

We describe some institutional background in the next section. We then describe the sample selection process, related research, and the basic research design in sections 3 and 4. The results of the tests using aggregate reconciliations are presented in section 5 followed by analysis of the components in section 6 and various specification checks in section 7.

2. Background and Research Design

The shares of non-U.S. companies may be traded in several different ways within U.S. markets. The basis of trade is frequently an American Depositary Receipt (*ADR*), a negotiable certificate created when some of the company's shares (or debentures) are deposited with a U.S. depositary bank. The bank holds these American Depositary Shares (*ADSs*) and issues *ADRs* representing some multiple of one issued share, known as the *ADR* ratio.[2] The *ADRs* are priced, and dividends paid, in U.S. dollars although the underlying security and dividend payments are in the company's local currency.

An *ADR* facility created without the company's involvement is an "unsponsored" *ADR*; trading occurs in the over-the-counter (*OTC*)

---

[1] Based on a survey of senior money managers at 70 of the largest non-U.S. institutional investment firms, Harris and Yurko [1993] find a preference for U.S. *GAAP* among survey respondents.

[2] For example, British Airways has an *ADR* ratio of 10 and British Petroleum had an *ADR* ratio of 4, changed to 12 in 1986.

market. These *ADRs* are not subject to the SEC registration and reporting requirements discussed below. When the company participates in the sale of its securities in the United States the facility is in the form of sponsored *ADRs*, at one of three levels.[3]

With a "sponsored level-I" *ADR* there cannot be a listing or public issuance of securities and the shares are traded in the *OTC* "Pink Sheet" market. The company usually obtains section 12g3-2(b) exemption from 1934 Exchange Act registration and reporting requirements, and is therefore not required to present reconciliations to U.S. *GAAP*. This is an increasingly popular form of foreign listing (Bank of New York [henceforth BNY] [1992]) but since reconciliations are rarely disclosed by these firms and U.S. prices are difficult to obtain we do not consider these companies in our analysis.[4]

An *ADR* is described as "sponsored level-II" when a company lists its shares on NASDAQ or a U.S. stock exchange but does not make a public offering in the United States.[5] An *ADR* is classified as "sponsored level-III" when a firm's listing on NASDAQ or a U.S. stock exchange is accompanied by a public offering in the United States.[6] In both cases, the firms are required to file a Form 20-F (or a Form 10-K) annually, within six months of the fiscal year-end. The 20-F is analogous to a 10-K filing for a U.S.-domiciled public company but allows the non-U.S. company to retain its domestic (non-U.S. *GAAP*) reporting for the primary financial statements provided to U.S. shareholders.[7]

If the domestic statements are presented as the primary statements in a 20-F filing, then the company has two options for explaining the differences between domestic and U.S. *GAAP*.[8] First, the firm can present a reconciliation of earnings and shareholders' equity under Item 17 of Form 20-F. The earnings reconciliation must be in a tabular format beginning with earnings as reported under its domestic *GAAP* with material income-increasing and income-decreasing items separately disclosed and ending with earnings based on U.S. *GAAP*. Share-

---

[3] The description of *ADR* levels is a convention with no legal standing.

[4] Companies which have sponsored level-I *ADR* facilities include Allied Lyons, Clarins, Foster's Brewing Group, Roche Holdings, Jardine Matheson, Nintendo, and Ponderosa Industrial. German and Swiss companies appear to be reluctant to perform reconciliations; we find that companies from these countries have no "higher level" *ADRs* and so are not in our sample.

[5] Examples of sponsored level-II *ADRs* are: Gambro, Glaxo, Montedison, and Western Mining.

[6] Examples of sponsored level-III *ADRs* are: Bass, Repsol, and Rhone-Poulenc.

[7] There are several other differences between a 10-K and 20-F. In general, the 10-K requires more detail.

[8] While it is rare, a company may file a 20-F and reconciliation even if it has no securities listed on a U.S. exchange, so that reconciliations are available but U.S. prices are not. For example, Wellcome P.L.C. has issued 20-Fs since 1986 as it had many U.S. investors (registered in the United Kingdom) but its first listing as a sponsored *ADR* on the NYSE originated in 1992.

holders' equity must also be reconciled but there is no required format. A firm utilizing Item 17 need not provide any additional disclosures required under U.S. *GAAP* and Regulation S-X but not required under the firm's domestic *GAAP* (unless the 20-F is being used for a public offering in the United States).

Alternatively, a firm may utilize Form 20-F Item 18 to present its reconciliation. In addition to the Item 17 reconciliations, a firm must supply all information necessary to comply with U.S. *GAAP*, for example, comprehensive segment data. For our purposes the distinction between Item 17 and 18 disclosures is not important since the reconciliation aspects are the same and we do not consider the impact of disclosure choices. Three groups of non-U.S. companies are excluded from our analysis because they are not required to perform the 20-F reconciliations. One group is the firms trading in the OTC market prior to 1983, which were given a "grandfather" exemption. A second group of non-U.S. firms, including most of the Israeli and Japanese companies listed in the United States, use U.S. *GAAP* for their primary financial statements.[9] The third group we exclude is Canadian companies.[10] The SEC has long recognized that Canadian accounting practices are similar to U.S. *GAAP*; and we believe the differences between U.S. and Canadian *GAAP* are unlikely to be sufficiently large to have value-relevance.[11]

3. Sample Description

To identify potential sample firms we searched the *Nexis/Lexis*, *Compustat*, and *Disclosure* data bases and scanned the *Standard & Poors' Stock Guide* to identify firms with a suffix of *ADR*, *ADS*, or certain abbreviations indicating foreign corporations (for example, PLC, NV, or SA); used a 1990 listing of *ADRs* from the Bank of New York; and obtained a listing of foreign registrants from the SEC.

Excluding the Canadian firms, this search yielded 431 firms. Since most of the reconciliation data must be hand-collected, we limited our search for 20-F information to 1981–91. Many of the data are not available until 1987, probably because of coverage of the *Nexis/Lexis* and

---

[9] Most Japanese companies listed on a U.S. exchange use U.S. *GAAP* because at the time they originally listed in the United States Japan did not require consolidated financial statements. Since the companies had no domestic equivalent they chose U.S. *GAAP* and were allowed to retain this for Japanese reporting purposes once Japan adopted full consolidation. The Israeli companies do not fully comply with U.S. *GAAP* because they do not use historical cost accounting. However, Items 17 and 18 of Form 20-F allow companies operating in a hyperinflationary environment to retain their domestic practice which deals with the inflationary effect. Since all other practices conform to U.S. *GAAP* for Israeli companies no reconciliation is necessary.

[10] The SEC rules refer to foreign registrants "other than Canadian." Also, recently the SEC has adopted a "mutual recognition" policy for Canadian companies.

[11] Barth and Clinch [1993] perform price and return association tests on reconciliation items for Canadian firms and find no statistically significant results.

234   E. AMIR, T. S. HARRIS, AND E. K. VENUTI

Disclosure data bases and the increase in *ADR* activity in the last five years (BNY [1992]). We wrote to each firm requesting copies of 20-F forms for 1981–91, and to brokerage firms which specialize in investments in non-U.S. firms to request copies of 20-F forms.

Firms were eliminated for the following reasons: use of U.S. *GAAP* (95); not a listed depositary share (154); exempt from filing Form 20-F (58); and type of depositary receipt unknown and 20-F not traceable (23). The final sample contains 101 firms.[12]

The latest date for filing the 20-F is six months after the fiscal year-end (*FYE*). As indicated in table 1, on average 20-Fs are filed between five and six months after the *FYE*. The *FYE* plus six months period, therefore, is chosen to ensure that the reconciliations are available, but this period also means that the potential for confounding effects increases.[13]

Our resources for the data on prices, dividends and returns were: (*i*) *Center for Research in Security Prices* (*CRSP*) and *Datastream* for the U.S. prices (and returns) in dollars; (*ii*) *Standard & Poors' Daily Stock Price Record* for U.S. prices which were unavailable from other sources;[14] (*iii*) *Datastream* and *Moody's International Manuals* for domestic prices and dividends.

We have a maximum of 467 observations representing 101 firms in 20 countries for which we have a stock price and the accounting data from a 20-F. We have both a U.S. price and the domestic (non-U.S.) price for 374 (359) observations for *FYE* plus six months (*FYE*) price. We extracted the relevant exchange rates from the International Financial Statistics and compared the two prices. The Pearson (Spearman) correlations are 0.998 (0.999) for the *FYE* prices, 0.988 (0.992) for the *FYE* plus six months prices. We run all tests using prices in the domestic market.[15] In the small number of cases where there is no local securities market, we use the U.S. dollar price.[16]

---

[12] Of the 101 firms, 77 file 20-Fs under Item 18 and 24 file 20-Fs under Item 17.

[13] Since some companies submit their reports within three months (which reduces the potential for confounding information) and since more prices were available to us for three months after the *FYE* at the time of original data collection, we also considered this date. We report only results for the six-month prices since the results were qualitatively equivalent for the other prices.

[14] While some shares and *ADRs* are thinly traded, for the sample we use there is a traded price at or within five days of the relevant date for all hand-collected prices. Thus we should avoid the problems described for a different sample in Frost and Pownall [1992].

[15] Simple arbitrage conditions suggest that the domestic and U.S. prices are equal. If they are not, then it is likely to be a result of lack of trading in one market, exchange rate concerns, or some other form of transaction cost. Frost and Pownall [1992] find results which suggest a weaker correlation between U.S. and non-U.S. prices but they have a very different sample including many firms with little trading volume.

[16] These companies are domiciled in countries such as the Bahamas, Bermuda, and Liberia. Since the accounting measures are reported in U.S. dollars we do not have any translation problem for these firms.

U.S. VS. NON-U.S. GAAP ACCOUNTING MEASURES   **235**

TABLE 1
Summary of Filing Dates for Sample Firms:[1] *1981–91*

Annual report filed after 20-F or not filed	421
Annual report received prior to 20-F	
—with U.S. *GAAP* reconciliation	31
—with no reconciliation	<u>15</u>
Total observations	<u>**467**</u>

Average number of days between fiscal year-end and filing of Form 20-F = 154.4

[1]Sample firms are non-U.S. firms listed on a U.S. stock exchange or NASDAQ and filing Form 20-F.

As many firms enter the U.S. market for the first time during the sample period, we have a maximum of 355 observations with both annual returns based on domestic prices and dividends and change in fiscal year earnings. For the annual returns obtained from *CRSP* the maximum sample size is 149. For these observations the Pearson (Spearman) correlation for the two return measures is 0.92 (0.88). We lose additional observations because we could not obtain earnings announcement or 20-F filing dates so that the maximum number of observations for the shorter window returns is 306.[17]

The *ADR* ratios were initially collected from 1990 and 1992 lists from the Bank of New York and checked against each year's financial statements, where possible. We also checked the ratio against the *Standard & Poors' Stock Guide*. The check of U.S. and non-U.S. prices also serves as a test of the *ADR* ratio.

The sample contains varying numbers of firms and observations within 20 countries. Table 2 summarizes the country distribution of the price and annual return samples. Approximately 40% of the sample consists of firms registered in the United Kingdom. Australia, the Netherlands, and Sweden have the next largest numbers of firms and observations, with the rest distributed across the other 16 countries.

4. Research Design

4.1 INFORMATION CONTENT AROUND AN EVENT WINDOW

One approach to evaluating the value-relevance of the 20-F reconciliations is to consider the price reaction to new information in the data. One possibility within this general approach is to consider the reaction to the announcement of U.S. *GAAP* earnings relative to non-U.S. *GAAP* earnings in the spirit of Beaver [1968] and Wilson [1986].

Identification of information releases in each domestic market is not practicable. In addition, U.S. regulations require price-sensitive information released in a domestic market to be released simultaneously in

---

[17] For 37 of the 306 observations for which we could not obtain dividend information we assumed a zero dividend. The results are unaffected if we eliminate these observations.

236   E. AMIR, T. S. HARRIS, AND E. K. VENUTI

TABLE 2
Summary of Country Distribution of Sample Firms:[1] 1981–91

Country	Observations	Firms
Australia	49	10
Bahamas	2	1
Bermuda	7	2
Cayman Islands	4	1
Denmark	7	1
Finland	9	1
France	4	2
Hong Kong	4	1
Ireland	13	4
Italy	16	4
Liberia	4	1
Mexico	5	3
Netherlands	51	8
New Zealand	3	1
Norway	3	1
Philippines	12	2
South Africa	4	1
Spain	26	6
Sweden	48	7
United Kingdom	196	44
Total	467	101

[1]Sample firms are non-U.S. firms listed on a U.S. stock exchange or NASDAQ and filing Form 20-F.

the United States. Hence, to identify dates on which U.S. *GAAP* and non-U.S. *GAAP* earnings are first announced we used the *Wall Street Journal Index* (*WSJI*) to establish U.S. announcement dates and the *Financial Times Index* (*FTI*) to compare the announcement dates reported in the U.K. press. Table 3 reports the results of these tests.

We find that more than 96% of the earnings announcements in the *WSJI* are non-U.S. *GAAP* earnings only. Furthermore, for the 297 announcements in the *FTI*, 81% are announced on the same day in the United States and the United Kingdom. Thus, it appears that for most firms the U.S. *GAAP* earnings, shareholders' equity, and reconciliation items are first made public with the 20-F or annual report.[18]

We also documented the dates on which sample firms' 20-Fs and annual reports were filed with the SEC. The pattern of filing dates is re-

---

[18] If accounting systems reflect a market equilibrium within an institutional environment, then it should not be surprising that the first earnings announced are those based on the measurement system of the domestic market, that is, using non-U.S. *GAAP*.

TABLE 3
Summary of First Earnings Announcement Dates for Sample Firms:[1] 1981–91

Announcements in the *Wall Street Journal* only	45
Announcements in *Financial Times* only	63
Announcements in both papers	302
Announcements in neither paper	57
Total observations	467
Of which:	
—U.S. *GAAP* earnings	16
—Non-U.S. *GAAP* earnings	451

[1]Sample firms are non-U.S. firms listed on a U.S. stock exchange or NASDAQ and filing Form 20-F.

ported in table 1. As in the United States (Easton and Zmijewski [1993]), for most observations (90%) either no annual report was filed with the SEC or the annual report was filed later than the 20-F. For 31 of the 46 cases in which the annual report filing date precedes the 20-F filing date, the reconciliation was provided in the annual report. For these cases we use the earlier annual report filing as the information release date. For the remaining cases, since annual reports do not have to be filed, we cannot be certain that the 20-F filing date is the earliest information release date. Hence, use of this date as the information release date is expected to introduce error.

Identifying the news in the information release presents several problems. First, we know that the non-U.S. *GAAP* earnings are released prior to the U.S. *GAAP* earnings which suggests one measure of unexpected earnings is the reconciliation itself.[19] However, some reconciliation items can be anticipated. For example, as we discuss in section 6, one of the major reconciliations to U.S. *GAAP* is the treatment of purchased goodwill. The reconciliation often requires a large (initial) adjustment to shareholders' equity at the first reconciliation, with the impact on the earnings reconciliation being a function of the amortization period chosen. If the amortization period is known, then the annual reconciliation will be anticipated unless additional acquisitions occur. But even in the first year, the goodwill reconciliation might be anticipated if the size of the acquisition premium is estimable at an earlier acquisition date.

Because there are numerous cases in which we need not expect a significant price reaction to one or more components of earnings reconciliation, we use the change in the aggregate reconciliation and the level and change in each component as possible measures of news in

---

[19] The correlation between the two earnings measures is high. The Spearman (Pearson) correlations are 0.95 (0.99) for reported earnings and 0.84 (0.83) for earnings deflated by price. The yearly cross-sectional correlations display a similar pattern.

238   E. AMIR, T. S. HARRIS, AND E. K. VENUTI

the reconciliation. These proxies for new information are used in the general model:

$$R_{jt} = \omega_0 + \omega_{1k}NI_{kjt} + \pi_{jt} \tag{1}$$

where:

R_{jt} is the return of firm j for period $t - \tau$ through t, that is, $(P_{jt}^F + d_{jt}^F - P_{jt-\tau}^F)/P_{jt-\tau}^F$;

P_{jt}^F is the market price of firm j in domestic currency at time t;

d_{jt}^F is the dividend of firm j in domestic currency for period $t - \tau$ through t;

NI_{kjt} is new information of type k for firm j at time t; and

π_{jt} is a random error term assumed i.i.d.

The initial proxies for NI_{kjt} are (*i*) the aggregate earnings reconciliation and (*ii*) the change in the annual aggregate earnings reconciliation, defined as:

$$\frac{DE_{jt}}{P_{jt-\tau}} \equiv \frac{E_{jt}^{US} - E_{jt}^F}{P_{jt-\tau}} \; ; \; \frac{\Delta DE_{jt}}{P_{jt-\tau}} \equiv \frac{DE_{jt} - DE_{jt-1}}{P_{jt-\tau}}$$

where:

E_{jt}^F is the fiscal year earnings of firm j in domestic currency at time t, reported in non-U.S. *GAAP*, and

E_{jt}^{US} is the fiscal year earnings of firm j in domestic currency at time t, reported in U.S. *GAAP*.

Additional proxies based on the components of the reconciliation will be considered in section 6.

We consider the associations between the information proxies and returns over a five-day window around the 20-F or annual report filing date and returns calculated from two days after the earliest earnings announcement to two days after the earlier of the 20-F or annual report (with reconciliation) filing date. In both cases we assume that investors have efficiently impounded the non-U.S. *GAAP* earnings in prices at the start of the return period.

One problem in estimating equation (1), and return models that follow, is the definition of the return measure R_{jt}. The standard valuation model assumes that price equals the discounted value of expected dividends. Returns for non-U.S. firms, however, should reflect the effects of ex post deviations from interest parity (or shifts in tax aspects) relative to expectations at time $t - 1$. That is, U.S. dollar returns presumably contain the effect of unexpected exchange rate and tax changes beyond those incorporated in the domestic currency returns. In addition, dividends incorporated in the U.S. dollar return calculation will be proportionately different from those incorporated in the domestic currency return, again because of tax and exchange rate effects. Assuming the information in SEC-mandated reconciliations will be reflected in *all* prices, we use domestic currency prices and dividends to calculate returns, although we perform checks using dollar returns.[20]

A further question arises about whether an adjustment should be made for the market return. Use of a standard market model with a single-country's market return seems problematic given a sample of firms listed in at least two national markets.[21] Consequently, we adjust each return using the Morgan Stanley Capital International Index as a proxy for a broad international market return. The market adjustment yields a second form of (1):[22]

$$R_{jt} - R_{mt} = \rho_0 + \rho_{1k} NI_{kjt} + \psi_{jt} \qquad (2)$$

where R_{mt} is the return based on the Morgan Stanley Capital International Index over the period τ through t.

It is conceivable that parts of the reconciliation information could be gleaned from the non-U.S. *GAAP* annual report. Because we are concerned with the value-relevance of the measurement differences reflected in the 20-F reconciliations and not with their timeliness, we view a comprehensive analysis of the new information issue beyond the scope of this research.[23] Hence, we do not consider more complicated filters of the data to test the sensitivity of our proxies for new information.

4.2 LONGER WINDOW RETURN–EARNINGS ASSOCIATIONS

A second approach to evaluating the value-relevance of the reconciliation items is to consider associations between stock market returns and accounting earnings. We adopt the approach initiated in Easton and Harris [1991] which follows from the more formal valuation models in Ohlson [1989]. Easton and Harris [1991] show that both earnings levels and changes deflated by beginning price are associated with annual returns. Hence, we assess the value-relevance of the reconciliations by considering whether they help to explain annual returns. We begin with a model:

$$R_{jt} = \alpha_0 + \alpha_1 \frac{E_{jt}^F}{P_{jt-1}^F} + \alpha_2 \frac{\Delta E_{jt}^F}{P_{jt-1}^F} + \alpha_3 V_{jt} + \varepsilon_{jt} \qquad (3)$$

where:

---

[20] If the reconciliation to U.S. *GAAP* contained value-relevant information impounded in one market but not another, then an arbitrage opportunity would be present. We assume these do not exist.

[21] Adler and Dumas [1983] summarize the issues surrounding international asset-pricing models.

[22] We do not estimate residuals from a market model since we are uncomfortable making the assumptions necessary for the estimation of market betas.

[23] McQueen [1993] finds mixed results in tests for security market reactions around 20-F filing dates for a sample of 153 firm-year observations.

240   E. AMIR, T. S. HARRIS, AND E. K. VENUTI

ΔE_{jt}^F is the change in fiscal year earnings of firm j at time t, reported in non-U.S. *GAAP*, that is, $E_{jt}^F - E_{jt-1}^F$;

V_{jt} is nonrandom "other information" which explains returns for firm j at time t; and

ε_{jt} is a random error term, assumed to be i.i.d.

In (3), if the domestic *GAAP* earnings measures are valuation sufficient, then V_{jt} can be omitted. However, if the earnings reconciliations to U.S. *GAAP* reflect other information associated with returns, then we can rewrite equation (3) as:

$$R_{jt} = \alpha_0 + \alpha_1 \frac{E_{jt}^F}{P_{jt-1}^F} + \alpha_2 \frac{\Delta E_{jt}^F}{P_{jt-1}^F} + \alpha_{31} \frac{DE_{jt}}{P_{jt-1}^F} + \alpha_{32} \frac{\Delta DE_{jt}}{P_{jt-1}^F} + \varepsilon_{jt}. \quad (4)$$

The model in equation (4) assumes that all other information affecting R_{jt} is incorporated in the error term. If the reconciliation to U.S. *GAAP* contains incremental value-relevant information, we expect α_{31} and/or α_{32} to be nonzero.

Equation (4) can be used to obtain an equivalent return–earnings specification based on U.S. *GAAP* and non-U.S. *GAAP* earnings separately. We view our model definition as being closer to the logic adopted by the SEC in requiring non-U.S. firms to reconcile to U.S. *GAAP*. It also helps to focus on whether the reconciliation *to* U.S. *GAAP* is value-relevant.

Two other studies evaluate return–earnings associations for samples of firms presenting 20-F reconciliations. Pope and Rees [1993] consider a model similar to equation (4) with market-adjusted returns for 85 firm-year observations for U.K. companies in 1987–90. Their evaluation of the relative information content of U.K. and U.S. *GAAP* measures suggests a difference for the earnings levels and changes variables. Barth and Clinch [1993] consider a model with the level of U.S. earnings and non-U.S. earnings for a sample of Australian, U.K., and Canadian firms with 24, 115, and 261 firm-year observations respectively. They find negative coefficients on the non-U.S. earnings variable for the U.K. and Australian samples with varying degrees of statistical significance.

The returns–earnings association analysis has the problem that the reconciliation items can sometimes be anticipated. Another problem with return–earnings associations is that they do not explicitly consider the shareholders' equity reconciliations. These concerns are mitigated in the third approach we consider.

4.3 MARKET-TO-BOOK RATIO ANALYSIS

Another approach for evaluating the value-relevance of reconciliation items is to consider whether they explain the difference between market value (P) and book value of shareholders' equity (BV). The difference between P and BV is unrecorded goodwill, which will be related to the market's perception of expected earnings and especially any "excess" or "abnormal" earnings. This concept has been formalized in Edwards and Bell [1961], Ohlson [1989; 1991], and Ou and Penman [1992].

P and BV may also differ because of accounting differences; for example, the ratio of P to BV (the market-to-book ratio) will be higher when conservative practices are used. Hence, if reconciliations to U.S. *GAAP* reflect value-relevant measurement practices, we should expect them to help explain the market-to-book ratio when BV is measured in non-U.S. *GAAP*. This idea is discussed also in Bernard, Merton, and Palepu [1992], Easton, Eddey, and Harris [1993], Feltham and Ohlson [1993], and Ou and Penman [1992].[24] More formally, assume:

$$\frac{P_{jt}^{F}}{BV_{jt}^{F}} = \beta_0 + \beta_1 \frac{E_{jt}^{F}}{BV_{jt}^{F}} + \beta_2 W_{jt}^{F} + \eta_{jt} \qquad (5)$$

where:

BV_{jt}^{F} is the book value of shareholders' equity of firm j, in domestic currency, at time t reported in domestic *GAAP*;

W_{jt}^{F} is nonrandom "other information" explaining the market-to-book ratio of firm j at time t; and

η_{jt} is a random variable, assumed to be i.i.d.

If we assume that the shareholders' equity and earnings reconciliations are the only components of W_{jt}^{F}, we can rewrite (5) as:

$$\frac{P_{jt}^{F}}{BV_{jt}^{F}} = \beta_0 + \beta_1 \frac{E_{jt}^{F}}{BV_{jt}^{F}} + \beta_{21} \frac{DBV_{jt}}{BV_{jt}^{F}} + \beta_{22} \frac{DE_{jt}}{BV_{jt}^{F}} + \eta_{jt} \qquad (6)$$

where DBV_{jt} is the difference between shareholders' equity measured under U.S. *GAAP* and shareholders' equity measured under non-U.S. *GAAP*, that is, $BV_{jt}^{US} - BV_{jt}^{F}$, and all other variables are as defined.[25]

The coefficient β_1 reflects the extent to which current return on equity (*ROE*), measured under non-U.S. *GAAP* practices, reflects expected future profitability and hence explains the (domestic *GAAP*) market-to-book premium or discount. The variable DBV_{jt}/BV_{jt}^{F} is equal to the ratio of BV_{jt} measured under U.S. *GAAP* (BV_{jt}^{US}) to the BV_{jt} measured under non-U.S. *GAAP* (BV_{jt}^{F}) minus one. Hence, if the U.S. *GAAP*

---

[24] The market-to-book ratio has also been the focus of recent research in Rosenberg, Reid, and Landstein [1985], Fairfield and Harris [1991], Amir [1993], and Fama and French [1992].

[25] Barth and Clinch [1993] consider a model with price as a function of shareholders' equity measures, analogous to our model with only the second explanatory variable on the right-hand side.

242   E. AMIR, T. S. HARRIS, AND E. K. VENUTI

measure of shareholders' equity is more closely aligned with price, then we should expect the coefficient β_{21} to be positive. Similarly, DE_{jt}/BV^F_{jt} reports the extent to which adjusting the *ROE* measure to incorporate U.S. *GAAP* practices in earnings (but not shareholders' equity) explains the market-to-book ratio based on non-U.S. *GAAP* shareholders' equity. If a reconciliation to U.S. *GAAP* earnings (deflated by non-U.S. *GAAP BV*) reflects a measure of *ROE* closer to the one used by the market, then the coefficient, β_{22}, should be positive. As in the returns–earnings model we use non-U.S. *GAAP* earnings as the measure of *ROE* and the reconciliation to U.S. *GAAP* because this is the process followed by the companies.

The market-to-book model presented in (5) and (6) is a function of the measurement practices implicit in the non-U.S. *GAAP* book value of shareholders' equity. The right-hand-side variables in (6) reflect both future profitability and adjustments of measurement differences implicit in the non-U.S. *GAAP* measures of shareholders' equity and earnings. To differentiate the two effects, we also consider the market-to-book ratio defined in terms of U.S. *GAAP*. We rewrite equations (5) and (6) as:[26]

$$\frac{P^F_{jt}}{BV^{US}_{jt}} = \theta_0 + \theta_1 \frac{E^F_{jt}}{BV^{US}_{jt}} + \theta_2 W^{US}_{jt} + v_{jt} \qquad (7)$$

and:

$$\frac{P^F_{jt}}{BV^{US}_{jt}} = \theta_0 + \theta_1 \frac{E^F_{jt}}{BV^{US}_{jt}} + \theta_{21} \frac{DBV_{jt}}{BV^{US}_{jt}} + \theta_{22} \frac{DE_{jt}}{BV^{US}_{jt}} + v_{jt} \qquad (8)$$

where W^{US}_{jt} represents nonrandom "other information" affecting the market-to-book ratio as measured under U.S. *GAAP*, and all other variables are as previously defined.

As before, we assume that the only components of W^{US}_{jt} are DBV_{jt} and

DE_{jt}. The market-to-book ratio in (8) can be rewritten as $\dfrac{P^F_{jt}}{BV^F_{jt} + DBV_{jt}}$;

this measure differs from the market-to-book measure in (6) because of differences in measurement practices for *BV*. If the difference between U.S. *GAAP* and non-U.S. *GAAP* shareholders' equity is value-irrelevant noise, then the market-to-book value measure in (8) should be noisier than the measure in (6). On the other hand, if the adjustment is value-relevant, then we expect the market-to-book ratio based

---

[26] BV^{US}_{jt} and E^{US}_{jt} are reported in local currency so no translation is necessary to ensure consistency in the units of account.

on the U.S. *GAAP* measure to be closer to one and to have a lower variance than the non-U.S. *GAAP* measure.[27]

The inclusion of BV_{jt}^{US} as a denominator in (8) is not a simple linear transformation of (6) except under restrictive assumptions.[28] While (6) will demonstrate the potential value-relevance of the reconciliations of earnings and shareholders' equity, it does not reflect the relative impact of the two measures nor does it facilitate differentiation between the profitability and measurement error explanations. Equation (8) facilitates some separation. We expect the coefficient on the *ROE* measure in (8), θ_1, to be positive if the non-U.S. *GAAP* earnings reflect firms' profitability. However, if the U.S. *GAAP* shareholders' equity reduces the measurement error component of the market-to-book ratio, we expect θ_1 to be smaller than the equivalent coefficient, β_1, in (6). Similarly, a nonzero coefficient, β_{22}, in (6) might result from the earnings reconciliation or the measurement error inherent in the non-U.S. *GAAP* shareholders' equity. If the adjustment of the equity to U.S. *GAAP* reduces this error, we can evaluate whether the earnings reconciliation is still value-relevant. That is, if the adjustment to U.S. *GAAP* shareholders' equity is value-relevant, then a nonzero coefficient, θ_{22}, will indicate the value-relevance of the earnings reconciliation beyond that contained in the reconciliation of shareholders' equity.

Similarly, if the reconciliation to U.S. *GAAP BV* is value-relevant and non-U.S. *GAAP BV* has no incremental information, then the reconciliation measure DBV_{jt} divided by U.S. *GAAP BV* should not contribute to explaining the market-to-book ratio based on U.S. *GAAP*. Hence, we would expect the coefficient, θ_{21}, to be zero.

The models in (2), (4), (6), and (8) form the basis of our primary tests. But, as indicated, the reconciliations also include information about material-specific components. Some of these components are specific to countries for which the sample sizes are too small to perform a robust analysis. However, there are several components which are sufficiently systematic to allow us to test their value-relevance using these models. These will be discussed after we describe the results of tests based on aggregate reconciliations.

5. Basic Test Results

Table 4 contains descriptive statistics for the primary variables used in our aggregate analyses. For the market-to-book value tests we exclude 18 observations where *BV* is negative since this distorts all statistics

---

[27] This argument is also used in Bernard, Merton, and Palepu [1992] and Easton, Eddey, and Harris [1993].

[28] A formal model in the spirit of Feltham and Ohlson [1993], with biased measures in earnings and shareholders' equity without complementary clean surplus, would demonstrate this point. We view this demonstration as beyond the scope of this research. We are grateful to Vic Bernard for helpful discussions on this issue.

244   E. AMIR, T. S. HARRIS, AND E. K. VENUTI

TABLE 4
Summary Statistics for Primary (Annual) Variables for All Sample Firms:[1] 1981–91

	Median	Mean	Standard Deviation	First Quartile	Third Quartile	Number of Observations
R_{jt}	0.10	0.15	0.44	−0.09	0.32	355
$\dfrac{E_{jt}^{F}}{P_{jt-1}^{F}}$	0.08	0.09	0.16	0.06	0.12	355
$\dfrac{\Delta E_{jt}^{F}}{P_{jt-1}^{F}}$	0.007	−0.001	0.14	−0.019	0.027	355
$\dfrac{DE_{jt}}{P_{jt-1}^{F}}$	−0.005	−0.006	0.12	−0.016	0.005	355
$\dfrac{\Delta DE_{jt}}{P_{jt-1}^{F}}$	−0.002	0.017	0.53	−0.013	0.008	355
$\dfrac{P_{jt}^{F}}{BV_{jt}^{F}}$	1.74	2.91	4.38	0.90	3.21	449
$\dfrac{P_{jt}^{F}}{BV_{jt}^{US}}$	1.51	2.38	3.01	0.93	2.63	449
$\dfrac{E_{jt}^{F}}{BV_{jt}^{F}}$	0.15	0.15	0.23	0.09	0.22	449
$\dfrac{DEPS_{jt}}{BV_{jt}^{F}}$	−0.01	−0.01	0.11	−0.03	0.01	449
$\dfrac{DBV_{jt}}{BV_{jt}^{F}}$	0.01	0.25	1.03	−0.10	0.35	449

[1]Sample firms are non-U.S. firms listed on a U.S. stock exchange or NASDAQ and filing Form 20-F.

R_{jt} is the annual (domestic) return of firm j for the period ending six months after the fiscal year-end;

P_{jt}^{F} is the domestic price of firm j at time t (fiscal year-end plus six months);

BV_{jt}^{F} is the fiscal year-end book value of shareholders' equity of firm j as reported in non-U.S. GAAP;

BV_{jt}^{US} is the fiscal year-end book value of shareholders' equity of firm j as reported in U.S. GAAP;

E_{jt}^{F} is the fiscal year earnings of firm j reported in non-U.S. GAAP;

E_{jt}^{US} is the fiscal year earnings of firm j reported in U.S. GAAP;

ΔE_{jt}^{F} is the change in fiscal year earnings (time $t-1$ to t) of firm j, reported in non-U.S. GAAP;

DE_{jt} $= E_{jt}^{US} - E_{jt}^{F}$;

ΔDE_{jt} is the change in DE_{jt} from time $t-1$ to t for firm j; and

DBV_{jt} $= BV_{jt}^{US} - BV_{jt}^{F}$.

utilizing *BV*. These observations are included in the returns tests. In each regression we delete any observation which yields an *R*-student ratio with an absolute value greater than three.[29]

The descriptive statistics in table 4 show a median (mean) annual stock return of 10 (15)% with an average return on domestic (non-U.S. *GAAP*) equity of around 15%. The mean and median aggregate earnings reconciliations are around –0.01 of domestic equity and price, indicating that, on average, U.S. *GAAP* earnings are lower. But the positive value at the third quartile indicates a large number of observations for which U.S. *GAAP* earnings are higher. The change in reconciliation items has some large differences as indicated by the median difference of –0.002 and the mean difference of 0.017 relative to beginning price.

The average adjustment for shareholders' equity is positive with a median of 0.01 and a mean of 0.25 indicating that, on average, U.S. *GAAP* shareholders' equity is higher. But the first quartile is –0.10 indicating a large number of observations for which U.S. *GAAP* results in lower shareholders' equity. The conflicting signs of the two adjustments are likely to be the result of a lack of articulation for many items, notably goodwill and asset revaluations.

The first test we perform is based on summary statistics of the ratios of price and book value of shareholders' equity (*PB*) as measured under U.S. *GAAP* and non-U.S. *GAAP*. The mean (median) values of *PB* based on non-U.S. *GAAP* and U.S. *GAAP* measures are 2.91 (1.74) and 2.38 (1.51) respectively. The variances (4.38 and 3.01) are clearly different given that we have the same observations in both cases. The mean of the differences is different from zero at the 0.01 level.

5.1 SHORT-WINDOW INFORMATION CONTENT ANALYSES

Table 5 reports the results of the tests of a market reaction to the aggregate reconciliation data with returns and market-adjusted returns measured over two short-windows. The shorter window is the five-day window around the earlier of the 20-F or annual report (with reconciliation) filing date, and the longer window extends from two days after the earliest earnings announcement to two days after the earlier of the 20-F or annual report (with reconciliation) filing date. Returns for the second window are divided by the number of days in the window to create a per-day return. The results do not reflect any market reaction, consistent with the results in McQueen [1993]. Given the discussion in section 4.1 this is not surprising and probably reflects an inability to clearly differentiate the news. We consider the components of the reconciliation as proxies for new information in section 6.

---

[29] The *R*-student ratio for observation *jt* is the standardized residual of this observation where the variance used in the standardization procedure excludes observation *jt*. See Belsey, Kuh, and Welsch [1980].

246   E. AMIR, T. S. HARRIS, AND E. K. VENUTI

TABLE 5

Regression Results for Associations between Short-Window Returns and Unexpected Earnings Information Based on Aggregate 20-F Reconciliations for the Full Sample:[1] 1982–91

$$R_{jt} = \omega_0 + \omega_{11}\frac{DE_{jt}}{P_{jt-\tau}^F} + \omega_{12}\frac{\Delta DE_{jt}}{P_{jt-\tau}^F} + \pi_{jt}$$

$$R_{jt} - R_{mt} = \rho_0 + \rho_{11}\frac{DE_{jt}}{P_{jt-\tau}^F} + \rho_{12}\frac{\Delta DE_{jt}}{P_{jt-\tau}^F} + \psi_{jt}$$

	ω_0/ρ_0	ω_{11}/ρ_{12}	ω_{12}/ρ_{12}	$\bar{R}^2$	N
Five-Day Return[2]	0.02	−0.04	0.04	0.00	278
	(7.3)***	(−0.8)	(0.8)		
Five-Day Market-Adjusted Return[2]	0.01	−0.01	0.07	0.01	278
	(5.1)***	(−0.3)	(1.5)		
Longer Event-Window Return[3]	0.01	0.05	−0.04	0.00	281
	(4.6)***	(1.2)	(−1.0)		
Longer Event-Window Market-Adjusted Return[3]	0.01	0.04	0.00	0.00	281
	(3.1)***	(1.1)	(0.1)		

[1]Sample firms are non-U.S. firms listed on a U.S. stock exchange or NASDAQ and filing Form 20-F.
[2]Five-Day Window: two trading days prior to the earlier of Form 20-F or annual report (with reconciliation) filing until two days after filing.
[3]Longer Window: two trading days after the earliest earnings announcement until 2 trading days after the earlier of Form 20-F or annual report (with reconciliation) filing.
t-statistics are in parentheses.
***Significant at the 1% level.
R_{jt} is the (domestic) return of firm j for the period $t-\tau$ to t standardized for the number of days in the longer-window case;
R_{mt} is a market return for the period $t-\tau$ to t based on the Morgan Stanley International Capital Index;
P_{jt}^F is the domestic price of firm j at time t (fiscal year-end plus six months);
E_{jt}^F is the fiscal year earnings of firm j reported in non-U.S. GAAP;
E_{jt}^{US} is the fiscal year earnings of firm j reported in U.S. GAAP;
$DE_{jt} = E_{jt}^{US} - E_{jt}^F$;
ΔDE_{jt} is the change in DE_{jt} from time $t-1$ to t for firm j; and
N is the number of observations.

5.2 ANNUAL RETURN ANALYSES

The results for the returns model in equation (4) are reported in table 6. We report the results for the full panel as well as for each of the years 1988–91 individually, and from 1982–87 as a combination because of the small number of observations in these years.

For the full sample the coefficients on earnings levels and changes variables are statistically significant at the 0.05 and 0.01 levels respectively. The coefficient on the level of reconciliation is statistically significant at the 0.01 level but the coefficient on the change in reconciliation is zero. The yearly regressions yield few significant coefficients except for 1989 when the coefficient on the reconciliation level is significant at the 0.01 level.[30] Overall, the return–earnings association

---

[30] The full-sample regression results may be affected by cross-correlations in the residuals. The lack of significant coefficients in the annual regressions increases the likelihood

TABLE 6

Regression Results for Annual Returns–Earnings Associations for
Aggregate 20-F Reconciliations for the Full Sample:[1] 1982–91

$$R_{jt} = \alpha_0 + \alpha_1 \frac{E_{jt}^F}{P_{jt-1}^F} + \alpha_2 \frac{\Delta E_{jt}^F}{P_{jt-1}^F} + \alpha_{31} \frac{DE_{jt}}{P_{jt-1}^F} + \alpha_{32} \frac{\Delta DE_{jt}}{P_{jt-1}^F} + \varepsilon_{jt}$$

	α_0	α_1	α_2	α_{31}	α_{32}	R^2	N
Full Sample	0.09	0.27	0.58	0.59	−0.00	0.12	349
	(4.5)***	(2.1)**	(3.6)***	(3.7)***	(−0.0)		
1991	0.05	1.15	−0.19	0.24	0.06	0.07	51
	(0.9)	(2.2)**	(−0.5)	(0.2)	(0.4)		
1990	−0.01	0.37	−0.05	−0.05	0.65	0.13	67
	(−0.1)	(0.6)	(−0.1)	(−0.1)	(0.8)		
1989	0.03	0.43	0.49	2.62	−0.72	0.21	66
	(0.6)	(0.9)	(2.6)**	(3.2)***	(−1.8)*		
1988	0.21	0.23	0.21	−0.01	0.85	0.12	60
	(5.5)***	(1.4)	(0.6)	(−0.0)	(1.2)		
Pre-1988	0.00	1.15	1.50	0.33	−2.59	0.22	102
	(0.0)	(1.4)	(1.6)	(0.4)	(−1.8)*		

[1]Sample firms are non-U.S. firms listed on a U.S. stock exchange or NASDAQ and filing Form 20-F.
t-statistics are in parentheses.
***Significant at the 1% level; **significant at the 5% level; * significant at the 10% level.
R_{jt} is the annual return of firm *j* for the period ending six months after the fiscal year-end;
P_{jt}^F is the domestic price of firm *j* at time *t* (fiscal year-end plus six months);
E_{jt}^F is the fiscal year earnings of firm *j* reported in non-U.S. *GAAP*;
E_{jt}^{US} is the fiscal year earnings of firm *j* reported in U.S. *GAAP*;
ΔE_{jt}^F is the change in fiscal year earnings (from *t* − 1 to *t*) of firm *j*, reported in U.S. *GAAP*;
DE_{jt} $= E_{jt}^{US} - E_{jt}^F$; and
ΔDE_{jt} is the change in DE_{jt} from time *t* − 1 to *t* for firm *j*.

results provide mixed evidence of the value-relevance of aggregate earnings reconciliations.[31]

5.3 MARKET-TO-BOOK ANALYSES

We report the results for the regression analysis using the aggregate reconciliations in table 7. Panel A reports results with the market-to-book ratio measures using the non-U.S. *GAAP* shareholders' equity. For the full sample, the adjusted R^2 is 0.47 and the coefficients on both *ROE* and shareholders' equity reconciliation are positive and significant at the 0.01 level. These results hold in each of the yearly regressions although the coefficient on shareholders' equity reconciliation is

---

that this correlation drives the results in the full (pooled) sample. However, the data limitations preclude any controls for this correlation.

[31] We ran the regression with U.S. and non-U.S. *GAAP* earnings measures (deflated by beginning price) together (not reported) to consider the relative versus incremental value-relevance of the two measures. We obtain a positive coefficient on the U.S. *GAAP* level of earnings (significant at the 0.01 level) and a positive coefficient for the non-U.S. *GAAP* change in earnings (significant at the 0.01 level).

248   E. AMIR, T. S. HARRIS, AND E. K. VENUTI

TABLE 7
Results for Market-to-Book Regressions for Aggregate 20-F
Reconciliations for the Full Sample:[1] 1981–91

Panel A: Non-U.S. *GAAP* Measure:

$$\frac{P_{jt}^{F}}{BV_{jt}^{F}} = \beta_0 + \beta_1 \frac{E_{jt}^{F}}{BV_{jt}^{F}} + \beta_{21}\frac{DBV_{jt}}{BV_{jt}^{F}} + \beta_{22}\frac{DE_{jt}}{BV_{jt}^{F}} + \eta_{jt}$$

	β_0	β_1	β_{21}	β_{22}	R^2	N
Full Sample	1.37	5.61	1.32	1.34	0.47	441
	(11.8)***	(10.3)***	(9.3)***	(1.2)		
1991	0.83	10.46	1.20	2.06	0.74	65
	(3.7)***	(7.8)***	(4.5)***	(1.3)		
1990	0.40	11.04	0.91	11.10	0.89	69
	(2.0)**	(9.2)***	(3.2)***	(3.3)***		
1989	0.81	7.87	1.17	8.77	0.37	61
	(1.9)*	(3.8)***	(2.3)**	(1.8)*		
1988	1.45	4.86	1.12	4.95	0.26	67
	(4.4)***	(3.6)***	(3.1)***	(1.9)*		
Pre-1988	1.49	6.38	0.68	−2.29	0.28	175
	(8.1)***	(6.7)***	(2.1)**	(−1.2)		

Panel B: U.S. *GAAP* Measure

$$\frac{P_{jt}^{F}}{BV_{jt}^{US}} = \theta_0 + \theta_1 \frac{E_{jt}^{F}}{BV_{jt}^{US}} + \theta_{21}\frac{DBV_{jt}}{BV_{jt}^{US}} + \theta_{22}\frac{DE_{jt}}{BV_{jt}^{US}} + v_{jt}$$

	θ_0	θ_1	θ_{21}	θ_{22}	R^2	N
Full Sample	1.44	4.12	0.06	−1.18	0.24	438
	(16.0)***	(9.4)***	(0.5)	(−1.3)		
1991	1.32	6.01	−0.19	1.20	0.34	65
	(6.8)***	(5.0)***	(−0.7)	(0.6)		
1990	0.57	9.73	0.35	9.82	0.70	69
	(2.9)***	(7.4)***	(1.6)	(3.4)***		
1989	0.75	7.31	1.07	4.68	0.16	61
	(2.0)*	(3.4)***	(2.2)**	(1.0)		
1988	1.50	3.42	0.65	1.93	0.09	67
	(5.8)***	(2.9)***	(1.5)	(0.8)		
Pre-1988	1.42	5.49	−0.16	−3.76	0.22	175
	(9.1)***	(6.7)***	(−0.8)	(−2.6)**		

[1]Sample firms are non-U.S. firms listed on a U.S. stock exchange or NASDAQ and filing Form 20-F.
t-statistics are in parentheses.
***Significant at the 1% level; ** significant at the 5% level; *significant at the 10% level.
P_{jt}^{F} is the domestic price of firm *j* at time *t* (fiscal year-end plus six months);
BV_{jt}^{F} is the book value of shareholders' equity of firm *j* at time *t* reported in domestic *GAAP*;
BV_{jt}^{US} is the book value of shareholders' equity of firm *j* at time *t* reported in U.S. *GAAP*;
E_{jt}^{F} is the earnings of firm *j* at time *t*, reported in domestic *GAAP*;
E_{jt}^{US} is the earnings of firm *j* at time *t*, reported in U.S. *GAAP*;
DE_{jt} $= E_{jt}^{US} - E_{jt}^{F}$ and
DBV_{jt} $= BV_{jt}^{US} - BV_{jt}^{F}$.

significant at the 0.05 level in 1989 and the pre-1988 period. The co-efficient on the earnings reconciliation is positive in the full sample and the yearly regressions from 1988–91, but it is significant (at the 0.01 level) only in 1990.

Results for the regressions using market-to-book based on U.S. *GAAP* shareholders' equity are reported in panel B. The adjusted R^2 is 0.24 for the full sample with the coefficients on both reconciliation measures not significantly different from zero. In the yearly regressions, the earnings reconciliation has a positive coefficient in 1990 (significant at the 0.01 level) and a negative coefficient in the pre-1988 period (significant at the 0.05 level). These results suggest that adjusting the shareholders' equity captures the material portion of the value-relevant aggregate reconciliation, as indicated by the results reported in panel A.

The results for the market-to-book tests provide evidence that the shareholders' equity reconciliations are value-relevant. Furthermore, the results suggest that the use of U.S. *GAAP* creates a market-to-book measure which captures all the information in the aggregate reconciliations, consistent with U.S. *GAAP* being perceived as more value-relevant.[32]

The apparently conflicting results for the various return analyses and the market-to-book tests may be due to two factors. First, as can be seen in table 4, the impact of the reconciliations on earnings is small relative to their effect on shareholders' equity. Second, as discussed in section 4, the reconciliations may be anticipated and therefore incorporated in the beginning-of-period price. Hence, the signal-to-noise ratio in the earnings reconciliation is too small to be captured by the aggregate reconciliation models. Yet, models which consider the price level itself, such as the market-to-book models, allow for value-relevant measurement differences to be reflected as such. This point is quite generic; that is, accounting measurements can be value-relevant if the measures affect price levels even if there is no effect on price changes. Relatedly, use of the aggregate reconciliations reduces the power of the tests by ignoring the details of the reconciliations themselves. We consider this issue next.

6. Analysis of Specific Differences in Accounting Practice

As explained, the 20-F reconciliation starts with earnings (shareholders' equity) under domestic non-U.S. *GAAP*, states specific material differences, and ends with earnings (shareholders' equity) under U.S. *GAAP*. Consideration of reconciliation components allows us to consider whether specific measurement differences are perceived by investors as

---

[32] When we use *ROE* based both on U.S. *GAAP* and non-U.S. *GAAP* earnings in the regression with market-to-book measured with non-U.S. *GAAP* we find the coefficient on U.S. *GAAP ROE* to be significantly different from zero (at the 0.01 level) if we include the shareholders' equity reconciliation, but not otherwise. However, when we consider the model using market-to-book based on U.S. *GAAP* shareholders' equity the U.S. *GAAP ROE* has no incremental explanatory power for any specification. These results are not separately reported.

value-relevant. We specifically identified four differences which apply to several companies and countries.[33] Each of these differences is described in more detail.

Under U.S. *GAAP* goodwill is calculated as the difference between the purchase price and the fair value of assets acquired, and amortized over a period up to 40 years. While practices differ in many countries some common differences are: goodwill is based on the book value of the assets; goodwill is written off against shareholders' equity immediately with no impact on the income statement; negative goodwill can be created without a write-down of the assets. While we also see limitations on the maximum amortization period in several countries, there need be no adjustment to comply with U.S. *GAAP* if a company's managers judge that the period is consistent with the expected economic life of the premium. The impact of the goodwill adjustment to U.S. *GAAP* usually increases shareholders' equity and reduces earnings.

U.S. *GAAP* uses historical cost (or lower of cost and market value) for most assets. In several countries assets are revalued either by government regulation (for example, occasionally in France and Italy) or at management's discretion (for example, Australia and the United Kingdom). At the time of revaluation assets and shareholders' equity are increased, usually with no immediate income effects. After revaluation the depreciation charge is based on the increased value while gains and losses on disposal of the assets may be based on either the new values or historical cost depending on the country and the company's choice. Thus, in general, under U.S. *GAAP* earnings will be higher and shareholders' equity will be lower.[34]

Accounting for pensions differs significantly around the world although private defined benefit plans are most common in the United States. Since many of the companies seeking a U.S. listing of their securities also have U.S. operations, we expect some of the difference to relate to accounting for the plans of these subsidiaries. However, for some non-U.S. plans companies may adopt conservative pension accounting practices, while others try to maintain off-balance sheet liabilities and account on a pay as you go basis. Given the potential mix of causes, it is not possible to predict the direction of the effect of the pension adjustment on earnings and shareholders' equity.

Throughout our sample period, U.S. *GAAP* required some form of deferred tax accounting. In some countries deferred taxes are not required while in others alternative treatments have been available, such as the liability method and the partial method (for example, in the

---

[33] Since the differences can be positive or negative if we compute the average absolute value of the specified differences relative to the sum of the absolute value of these and other differences, we cover about 70% of all recorded differences with the four differences categorized.

[34] Easton, Eddey, and Harris [1993] analyze asset revaluations in Australia. They find most of the asset revaluations relate to property so that the impact on depreciation expense is small.

United Kingdom). These items will generally lead to higher tax expense and lower shareholders' equity when U.S. *GAAP* is applied. However, the tax adjustment in the 20-F relates to the tax effect of other adjustments as well as differences in the accounting policy for taxation, so the net effect depends on other adjustments.

All other differences are accumulated in a final component. One item which occurs frequently is an adjustment for differences in the treatment of extraordinary items or prior-period adjustments. This was not classified separately because some of the adjustments are reclassifications; the specific items vary over time and across firms so that categorization into a separate component made no sense, and there was no balance sheet equivalent.

The components can be summarized as:

$$DE_{jt} = GE_{jt} + RVE_{jt} + PNE_{jt} + TXE_{jt} + OTHE_{jt} \qquad (9)$$

where:

GE_{jt} is the goodwill adjustment to earnings of firm j at time t;

RVE_{jt} is the asset revaluation adjustment to earnings of firm j at time t;

PNE_{jt} is the pension adjustment to earnings of firm j at time t;

TXE_{jt} is the tax adjustment to earnings of firm j at time t; and

$OTHE_{jt}$ is the net other adjustment to earnings of firm j at time t;

and:

$$DBV_{jt} = GBV_{jt} + RVBV_{jt} + PNBV_{jt} + TXBV_{jt} + OTHBV_{jt} \qquad (10)$$

where:

GBV_{jt} is the goodwill adjustment to shareholders' equity of firm j at time t;

$RVBV_{jt}$ is the asset revaluation adjustment to shareholders' equity of firm j at time t;

$PNBV_{jt}$ is the pension adjustment to shareholders' equity of firm j at time t;

$TXBV_{jt}$ is the tax adjustment to shareholders' equity of firm j at time t; and

$OTHBV_{jt}$ is the net other adjustment to shareholders' equity of firm j at time t.

All adjustments are included with the appropriate sign. For example, if goodwill expense is higher under U.S. *GAAP*, then the observation for GE_{jt} is negative.

Table 8 contains summary statistics for the reported (signed) and absolute values of the components after deflation by non-U.S. *GAAP* shareholders' equity. These statistics demonstrate that goodwill and revaluation adjustments have the largest relative effect and, consistent with table 4, the impact on shareholders' equity is larger than the impact on earnings. For example, the median adjustments for goodwill are around 0.4% of equity for earnings and nearly 6% of equity for the

252   E. AMIR, T. S. HARRIS, AND E. K. VENUTI

TABLE 8

Summary Statistics for Components of 20-F Reconciliations for the Full Sample of Firms:[1] *1981–91*
(All variables are deflated by BV_{jt}^F)

	Signed Values[2]					Absolute Values	
	Mean	SD	Median	Q1	Q3	Mean	Median
GBV_{jt}	0.404	1.02	0.055	0.000	0.422	0.408	0.059
$RVBV_{jt}$	−0.082	0.12	−0.034	−0.127	0.000	0.085	0.042
$PNBV_{jt}$	0.002	0.02	0.000	0.000	0.000	0.007	0.000
$TXBV_{jt}$	−0.114	0.22	−0.028	−0.146	0.000	0.117	0.029
$OTHBV_{jt}$	0.042	0.43	0.021	−0.003	0.074	0.183	0.052
GE_{jt}	−0.020	0.09	−0.004	−0.015	0.000	0.026	0.005
RVE_{jt}	0.010	0.08	0.000	0.000	0.005	0.016	0.000
PNE_{jt}	0.000	0.01	0.000	0.000	0.000	0.003	0.000
TXE_{jt}	−0.019	0.16	−0.000	−0.012	0.000	0.027	0.006
$OTHE_{jt}$	0.015	0.17	0.000	−0.007	0.009	0.046	0.008

[1] Sample firms are non-U.S. firms listed on a U.S. stock exchange or NASDAQ and filing Form 20-F.
[2] Positive values indicate that U.S. earnings (book value) increase as a result of the reconciling item; negative values indicate that U.S. earnings (book value) decrease as a result of the reconciling item.

BV_{jt}^F is the book value of shareholders' equity of firm j at time t reported in domestic GAAP;
GBV_{jt} is the goodwill adjustment to shareholders' equity of firm j at time t;
$RVBV_{jt}$ is the asset revaluation adjustment to shareholders' equity of firm j at time t;
$TXBV_{jt}$ is the tax adjustment to shareholders' equity of firm j at time t;
$PNBV_{jt}$ is the pension adjustment to shareholders' equity of firm j at time t;
$OTHBV_{jt}$ is the net adjustment to shareholders' equity of firm j at time t;
GE_{jt} is the goodwill adjustment to earnings of firm j at time t;
RVE_{jt} is the asset revaluation adjustment to earnings of firm j at time t;
TXE_{jt} is the tax adjustment to earnings of firm j at time t;
PNE_{jt} is the pension adjustment to earnings of firm j at time t; and
$OTHE_{jt}$ is the net other adjustment to earnings of firm j at time t.

shareholders' equity adjustment. This reflects an average amortization period of around 15 years. Similarly, the median earnings adjustment for asset revaluations is 0% of equity while the median adjustment to shareholders' equity is around 4% of equity.

Substituting (9) into the short-window returns model in (2) we obtain a specification with the components proxying for new information:[35]

$$R_{jt} - R_{mt} = \rho_0 + \rho_{11}\frac{GE_{jt}}{P_{jt-\tau}^F} + \rho_{12}\frac{RVE_{jt}}{P_{jt-\tau}^F} + \rho_{13}\frac{PNE_{jt}}{P_{jt-\tau}^F} + \rho_{14}\frac{TXE_{jt}}{P_{jt-\tau}^F} +$$

$$\rho_{15}\frac{OTHE_{jt}}{P_{jt-\tau}^F} + \rho_{16}\frac{\Delta GE_{jt}}{P_{jt-\tau}^F} + \rho_{17}\frac{\Delta RVE_{jt}}{P_{jt-\tau}^F} + \rho_{18}\frac{\Delta PNE_{jt}}{P_{jt-\tau}^F} +$$

$$\rho_{19}\frac{\Delta TXE_{jt}}{P_{jt-\tau}^F} + \rho_{20}\frac{\Delta OTHE_{jt}}{P_{jt-\tau}^F} + \psi_{jt}. \qquad (11)$$

---

[35] In the interest of parsimony we consider only the market-adjusted returns for the component analyses.

Nonzero coefficients indicate that the components are proxying for new information which the market prices. However, insignificant coefficients need not indicate a lack of value-relevance for the reasons outlined in section 4.

Similar to the short-window returns model (11), substituting (9) into the returns–earnings model in (4) we obtain a specification with the components:

$$R_{jt} = \phi_0 + \phi_1 \frac{E_{jt}^F}{P_{jt-1}^F} + \phi_2 \frac{\Delta E_{jt}^F}{P_{jt-1}^F} + \phi_3 \frac{GE_{jt}}{P_{jt-1}^F} + \phi_4 \frac{RVE_{jt}}{P_{jt-1}^F} +$$

$$\phi_5 \frac{PNE_{jt}}{P_{jt-1}^F} + \phi_6 \frac{TXE_{jt}}{P_{jt-1}^F} + \phi_7 \frac{OTHE_{jt}}{P_{jt-1}^F} + \phi_8 \frac{\Delta GE_{jt}}{P_{jt-1}^F} + \phi_9 \frac{\Delta RVE_{jt}}{P_{jt-1}^F} +$$

$$\phi_{10} \frac{\Delta PNE_{jt}}{P_{jt-1}^F} + \phi_{11} \frac{\Delta TXE_{jt}}{P_{jt-1}^F} + \phi_{12} \frac{OTHE_{jt}}{P_{jt-1}^F} + \upsilon_{jt}. \qquad (12)$$

Nonzero coefficients on the component variables indicate value-relevance. A positive sign on the coefficients of the levels components suggests that the U.S. *GAAP* are more value-relevant.

For the market-to-book analysis based on non-U.S. *GAAP* shareholders' equity we obtain the components model by substituting (9) and (10) into (6) and allowing the coefficients to vary:

$$\frac{P_{jt}^F}{BV_{jt}^F} = \gamma_0 + \gamma_1 \frac{E_{jt}^F}{BV_{jt}^F} + \gamma_2 \frac{GE_{jt}}{BV_{jt}^F} + \gamma_3 \frac{RVE_{jt}}{BV_{jt}^F} + \gamma_4 \frac{PNE_{jt}}{BV_{jt}^F} +$$

$$\gamma_5 \frac{TXE_{jt}}{BV_{jt}^F} + \gamma_6 \frac{OTHE_{jt}}{BV_{jt}^F} + \gamma_7 \frac{GBV_{jt}}{BV_{jt}^F} + \gamma_8 \frac{RVBV_{jt}}{BV_{jt}^F} + \gamma_9 \frac{PNBV_{jt}}{BV_{jt}^F} +$$

$$\gamma_{10} \frac{TXBV_{jt}}{BV_{jt}^F} + \gamma_{11} \frac{OTHBV_{jt}}{BV_{jt}^F} + v_{jt}. \qquad (13)$$

Again, if each type of adjustment to U.S. *GAAP* is value-relevant, then we expect all coefficients in (13) to be nonzero, with positive coefficients indicating greater value-relevance for the U.S. *GAAP* measurement practice.

As in the aggregate reconciliation model the variables in equation (13) capture both cross-sectional differences in measures of profitability and measurement choices in the accounting variables. So, for example, γ_8 may be positive, despite the inclusion of the revaluations in BV_{jt}^F, because of the value-relevance of the property revaluations themselves.

254   E. AMIR, T. S. HARRIS, AND E. K. VENUTI

However, by using BV_{jt}^{F} and BV_{jt}^{US} to calculate the market-to-book measure we can, at least partially, control for the extent to which the variable captures the accounting measurement difference as opposed to the value-relevance of the underlying measure. Hence, we also substitute (9) and (10) into (8) and obtain:

$$\frac{P_{jt}^{F}}{BV_{jt}^{US}} = \lambda_0 + \lambda_1 \frac{E_{jt}^{F}}{BV_{jt}^{US}} + \lambda_2 \frac{GE_{jt}}{BV_{jt}^{US}} + \lambda_3 \frac{RVE_{jt}}{BV_{jt}^{US}} + \lambda_4 \frac{PNE_{jt}}{BV_{jt}^{US}} +$$

$$\lambda_5 \frac{TXE_{jt}}{BV_{jt}^{US}} + \lambda_6 \frac{OTHE_{jt}}{BV_{jt}^{US}} + \lambda_7 \frac{GBV_{jt}}{BV_{jt}^{US}} + \lambda_8 \frac{RVBV_{jt}}{BV_{jt}^{US}} + \lambda_9 \frac{PNBV_{jt}}{BV_{jt}^{US}} +$$

$$\lambda_{10} \frac{TXBV_{jt}}{BV_{jt}^{US}} + \lambda_{11} \frac{OTHBV_{jt}}{BV_{jt}^{US}} + \xi_{jt}. \tag{14}$$

In this case, the expectations for the coefficients vary. We expect asset revaluations to be value-relevant (Easton, Eddey, and Harris [1993]), and since the U.S. *GAAP* shareholders' equity does not include the revaluation we expect λ_8 to be positive. Because the revaluation component of the earnings reconciliation includes a reversal of the additional depreciation expense we expect λ_3 to be negative if investors perceive that depreciation reflects a reduction in asset values.[36] Results consistent with the hypotheses would indicate a value-relevant element of non-U.S. *GAAP*. On the other hand, to the extent the reconciliation items reflect primarily accounting measurement issues which are "corrected" by using U.S. *GAAP* we expect all coefficients to be zero. Of course, it would be unrealistic to expect that each variable captures purely a measurement-error or value-relevant factor. However, comparing the results of tests based on (13) and (14) should permit inferences about each factor.[37]

The results of the short-window return model tests are found in table 9; the annual return window test results are shown in table 10; and results for the market-to-book models are reported in panels A and B of table 11. The regressions in these tables can be compared with the regressions based on the aggregate reconciliations reported in tables 5, 6, and 7 respectively.

For the short window analyses the results for the five-day return interval (panel A) for all available observations show that including the

---

[36] The expense reconciliation may be a mix of a depreciation adjustment and an adjustment for the gain or loss on disposal of property, which is treated differently for revalued assets in some countries.

[37] Comparisons of coefficients in equations (12) and (13) must be made cautiously since the dependent and independent variables have been adjusted.

components increases the adjusted R^2 from 0.01 to 0.03 (relative to the aggregate reconciliations). The only coefficient which is significant (at the 0.05 level) is on the change in the "other items" component. For the longer window (panel B) no coefficient is significant.[38]

For the annual returns (table 10) the adjusted R^2 are the same in the aggregate and component models. The coefficients on all the changes variables, except for pensions, are statistically significant at the 0.10 level or better. The only significant coefficient (at the 0.05 level) for a levels variable is for the "other items" variable.

For the market-to-book regressions we see in table 11 that the adjusted R^2 increases for both measures. As expected, the coefficients on the *ROE* measures are essentially unchanged. When the non-U.S. *GAAP* shareholders' equity is used (panel A) no earnings component coefficient is significantly different from zero at conventional levels. The coefficients for the shareholders' equity components are positive and significant at the 0.01 level, except for pensions which is significant at the 0.10 level.

For the market-to-book regression based on the U.S. *GAAP* measure of shareholders' equity (panel B), the significant coefficients for shareholders' equity adjustments include those for asset revaluations which is positive, "other" which is negative (both significant at the 0.05 level), and taxation (significant at the 0.10 level). The only significant coefficient for earnings reconciliations is for the asset revaluation adjustment which has a negative sign and is significant at the 0.10 level. The results suggest that asset revaluations are viewed as value-relevant by the market, and removing these measures in order to reconcile to U.S. *GAAP* reduces the value-relevance of the accounting data.[39] However, the difference between the results in panels A and B of table 11 suggests that other reconciliation items collectively act as an adjustment toward more value-relevant measures.

The positive coefficient on the shareholders' equity component of goodwill with market-to-book based on non-U.S. *GAAP* and the insignificant coefficient with market-to-book based on the U.S. *GAAP* deflator suggests that for our sample of firms the capitalization of goodwill is value-relevant. The coefficients on the tax component suggest that the tax reconciliation includes a value-relevant measurement change as well as an additional indicator of anticipated future profitability.

A potential problem with interpreting the results of the component specifications is that we may be capturing information about the underlying component itself rather than the reconciliation of the measurement difference. Since the actual component values are not reported

---

[38] We also included the change in non-U.S. *GAAP* earnings as a proxy for new information as a test of the assumption that this information had been impounded in the market, with no impact on the results reported in table 9.

[39] These results are consistent with those found in Easton, Eddey, and Harris [1993].

256   E. AMIR, T. S. HARRIS, AND E. K. VENUTI

TABLE 9
Regression Results for Associations between Short-Window Returns and
Unexpected Earnings Information Based on Components of 20-F Reconciliations:[1] 1982–91

$$R_{jt} - R_{mt} = \rho_0 + \rho_{11}\frac{GE_{jt}}{P^F_{jt-\tau}} + \rho_{12}\frac{RVE_{jt}}{P^F_{jt-\tau}} + \rho_{13}\frac{PNE_{jt}}{P^F_{jt-\tau}} + \rho_{14}\frac{TXE_{jt}}{P^F_{jt-\tau}} + \rho_{15}\frac{OTHE_{jt}}{P^F_{jt-\tau}} +$$

$$\rho_{16}\frac{\Delta GE_{jt}}{P^F_{jt-\tau}} + \rho_{17}\frac{\Delta RVE_{jt}}{P^F_{jt-\tau}} + \rho_{18}\frac{\Delta PNE_{jt}}{P^F_{jt-\tau}} + \rho_{19}\frac{\Delta TXE_{jt}}{P^F_{jt-\tau}} + \rho_{20}\frac{\Delta OTHE_{jt}}{P^F_{jt-\tau}} + \psi_{jt}$$

Panel A: Five-Day Return Interval[2]

	All Countries	United Kingdom and Australia	Other Countries
ρ_0	−0.00	−0.00	−0.01
	(−1.9)*	(−0.1)	(2.8)**
ρ_{11}	0.09	4.24	−0.13
	(0.2)	(1.4)	(−0.3)
ρ_{12}	0.05	0.93	0.12
	(0.3)	(1.0)	(0.9)
ρ_{13}	−0.02	3.34	−0.03
	(−0.2)	(0.9)	(−0.3)
ρ_{14}	0.05	−1.21	0.03
	(0.5)	(−0.8)	(0.3)
ρ_{15}	0.00	0.21	0.00
	(0.0)	(0.8)	(0.0)
ρ_{16}	0.17	−3.39	0.64
	(0.5)	(−1.4)	(2.0)**
ρ_{17}	0.04	−0.50	0.09
	(0.5)	(−1.4)	(1.1)
ρ_{18}	0.00	−3.93	0.05
	(0.0)	(−0.9)	(0.4)
ρ_{19}	−0.08	−0.99	0.04
	(−0.5)	(−1.0)	(0.3)
ρ_{20}	−0.17	0.04	0.05
	(−2.4)**	(0.2)	(0.6)
$\bar{R}^2$	0.01	0.00	0.00
N	275	159	114

Continued overleaf

separately under most non-U.S. *GAAP* systems we are unable to decompose the earnings measures into the relevant components to test for the incremental value-relevance of the reconciliation items.

7. Additional Specification Checks

Our tests assume that all coefficients are constant across countries. As shown in table 2, many of the sample firms are incorporated in the United Kingdom or Australia; both of these countries follow a similar Anglo-Saxon approach to accounting. To test whether the results vary across countries we rerun the tests on component reconciliations with

TABLE 9 —*continued*

Panel B: Longer Window Return Interval[3]

	All Countries	United Kingdom and Australia	Other Countries
ρ_0	0.00	0.00	0.00
	(0.7)	(0.6)	(1.0)
ρ_{11}	−0.19	−0.27	−0.37
	(−0.6)	(−0.1)	(−1.1)
ρ_{12}	0.04	−1.87	0.03
	(0.4)	(−2.0)**	(0.3)
ρ_{13}	0.10	3.45	0.04
	(1.2)	(1.0)	(0.5)
ρ_{14}	−0.01	-0.59	−0.07
	(−0.2)	(−0.4)	(−0.7)
ρ_{15}	−0.02	0.00	−0.05
	(−0.3)	(0.0)	(−1.0)
ρ_{16}	−0.12	0.55	−0.01
	(−0.4)	(0.3)	(−0.1)
ρ_{17}	0.01	0.59	−0.02
	(0.1)	(1.4)	(−0.3)
ρ_{18}	−0.07	-3.13	−0.13
	(−0.6)	(−0.8)	(−1.1)
ρ_{19}	−0.04	−0.01	−0.09
	(−0.3)	(−0.0)	(−0.7)
ρ_{20}	−0.02	−0.25	0.03
	(−0.4)	(−1.3)	(0.6)
$\bar{R}^2$	0.00	0.00	0.00
N	275	159	116

[1]Sample firms are non-U.S. firms listed on a U.S. stock exchange or NASDAQ and filing Form 20-F.
[2]Five-Day Window: two trading days prior to the earlier of Form 20-F or annual report (with reconciliation) filing until two days after filing.
[3]Longer Window: two trading days after the earliest earnings announcement until two trading days after the earlier of Form 20-F or annual report (with reconciliation) filing.
t-statistics in parentheses.
***Significant at the 1% level; **significant at the 5% level; *significant at the 10% level.

R_{jt}	is the (domestic) return of firm j for the period $t - \tau$ to t standardized for the number of days in the longer-window case;
R_{mt}	is a market return for the period $t - \tau$ to t based on the Morgan Stanley International Capital Index;
P^F_{jt}	is the domestic price of firm j at time t (fiscal year-end plus six months);
E^F_{jt}	is the earnings of firm j at time t, reported in domestic *GAAP*;
GE_{jt}	is the goodwill adjustment to earnings of firm j at time t;
RVE_{jt}	is the asset revaluation adjustment to earnings of firm j at time t;
TXE_{jt}	is the tax adjustment to earnings of firm j at time t;
PNE_{jt}	is the pension adjustment to earnings of firm j at time t;
$OTHE_{jt}$	is the net other adjustment to earnings of firm j at time t; and
Δ	reflects the change of the relevant variable from period $t - 1$ to t.

258   E. AMIR, T. S. HARRIS, AND E. K. VENUTI

TABLE 10
Regression Results for Returns–Earnings Associations for 20-F
Component Reconciliations:[1] 1982–91

$$R_{jt} = \phi_0 + \phi_1 \frac{E_{jt}^F}{P_{jt-1}^F} + \phi_2 \frac{\Delta E_{jt}^F}{P_{jt-1}^F} + \phi_3 \frac{GE_{jt}}{P_{jt-1}^F} + \phi_4 \frac{RVE_{jt}}{P_{jt-1}^F} + \phi_5 \frac{PNE_{jt}}{P_{jt-1}^F} + \phi_6 \frac{TXE_{jt}}{P_{jt-1}^F} +$$

$$\phi_7 \frac{OTHE_{jt}}{P_{jt-1}^F} + \phi_8 \frac{\Delta GE_{jt}}{P_{jt-1}^F} + \phi_9 \frac{\Delta RVE_{jt}}{P_{jt-1}^F} + \phi_{10} \frac{\Delta PNE_{jt}}{P_{jt-1}^F} +$$

$$\phi_{11} \frac{\Delta TXE_{jt}}{P_{jt-1}^F} + \phi_{12} \frac{\Delta OTHE_{jt}}{P_{jt-1}^F} + \upsilon_{jt}. \qquad (4)$$

	All Countries	United Kingdom and Australia	Other Countries
ϕ_0	0.08	0.18	−0.04
	(2.3)***	(5.6)***	(−0.8)
ϕ_1	0.39	−0.24	1.12
	(2.8)***	(−1.0)	(3.1)***
ϕ_2	0.41	1.43	0.04
	(2.3)***	(4.1)***	(0.2)
ϕ_3	0.08	2.31	−1.46
	(0.1)	(1.4)	(−0.4)
ϕ_4	0.43	1.68	0.20
	(0.9)	(1.0)	(0.3)
ϕ_5	−0.51	4.86	−0.42
	(−0.5)	(1.2)	(−0.3)
ϕ_6	−0.28	−2.61	0.94
	(−0.3)	(−1.0)	(0.8)
ϕ_7	0.65	0.43	2.30
	(2.3)**	(1.0)	(2.2)**
ϕ_8	1.07	−0.13	2.46
	(2.1)**	(−0.2)	(0.7)
ϕ_9	1.23	5.20	0.71
	(1.9)*	(3.5)***	(0.8)
ϕ_{10}	−0.37	−5.73	0.41
	(−1.0)	(−1.1)	(0.6)
ϕ_{11}	−0.63	3.67	−0.24
	(−1.9)*	(1.7)*	(−0.3)
ϕ_{12}	−0.14	−0.1	−0.69
	(−1.9)*	(−0.1)	(−0.8)
R^2	0.12	0.20	0.10
N	349	204	145

[1]Sample firms are non-U.S. firms listed on a U.S. stock exchange or NASDAQ and filing Form 20-F.
t-statistics are in parentheses.
***Significant at the 1% level; **significant at the 5% level; *significant at the 10% level.

R_{jt}	is the annual return of firm j for the period ending six months after the fiscal year-end;
P_{jt}^F	is the domestic price of firm j at time t (fiscal year-end plus six months);
E_{jt}^F	is the fiscal year earnings of firm j reported in non-U.S. *GAAP*;
GE_{jt}	is the goodwill adjustment to earnings of firm j at time t;
RVE_{jt}	is the asset revaluation adjustment to earnings of firm j at time t;
TXE_{jt}	is the tax adjustment to earnings of firm j at time t;
PNE_{jt}	is the pension adjustment to earnings of firm j at time t;
$OTHE_{jt}$	is the net other adjustment to earnings of firm j at time t; and
Δ	represents the change of the relevant variable from period $t-1$ to t.

the U.K. and Australian firms in one group and all other countries in a second group.[40] The results of these tests are reported in tables 9–11.[41]

Table 9 reports the results for the short-window regressions using market-adjusted returns; panel A reports tests using the five-day window; panel B reports tests using the longer window. For both windows the adjusted R^2 for the U.K. and Australia sample is zero and no coefficients are significant. For the other countries both return intervals yield essentially no results although the coefficient on change in (level of) goodwill is significant at the 0.05 level in the short (longer) window.

The results for the annual return model split into the two country groups shown in table 10 indicate a similar pattern. The adjusted R^2 is twice as high for the U.K. and Australia sample as for the other countries sample. The only significant coefficients are those on change in revaluation (at a 0.01 level) and change in tax (at a 0.10 level) for the U.K. and Australia sample and on the level of other items (at a 0.05 level) for the other countries group.

The component analyses of the market-to-book models for the country subsamples are reported in table 11. For the market-to-book measure based on non-U.S. *GAAP*, reported in panel A, the coefficients on shareholders' equity reconciliations of goodwill and asset revaluations are positive and significant at the 0.01 level for both country samples. Only the other countries group retains a significant coefficient on the asset revaluation component when the U.S. *GAAP* measure is used. This suggests that there is value-relevance in asset revaluations although it appears the revaluations are discounted in the U.K. and Australia group.[42]

Given the controversy over the immediate write-off of goodwill (Choi and Lee [1991]) the positive coefficient for goodwill with the non-U.S. *GAAP* measure but not the U.S. *GAAP* measure suggests that capitalizing goodwill is consistent with the way investors price this asset. For the U.S. *GAAP* measure there is a negative coefficient on the earnings goodwill component (significant at the 0.05 level) for the other countries group consistent with the goodwill amortization being too aggressive (that is, rapid) for this group.

The coefficients for the "other" category are significant at conventional levels for several specifications. Given the many items that make

---

[40] Repeating the analysis by country is not possible given the small number of observations for many countries.

[41] We do not report results for the aggregate reconciliations in the interest of parsimony. The results of the tests indicate some differences between the two country groups as may be gauged from the component results reported in tables 9–11. The results for the annual return models are also consistent with those in Pope and Rees [1993].

[42] This result appears to be inconsistent with the results in Easton, Eddey, and Harris [1993]. Since they have a more complete sample of Australian companies and exclude U.K. companies the results suggest that revaluations may be less value-relevant in the United Kingdom relative to Australia. This conjecture is consistent with the results in Barth and Clinch [1993].

TABLE 11

Results for Market-to-Book Regressions for 20-F Component Reconciliations:[1] 1981–91

Panel A: Non-U.S. GAAP Measure:

$$\frac{P_{ji}^F}{BV_{ji}^F} = \gamma_0 + \gamma_1 \frac{E_{ji}^F}{BV_{ji}^F} + \gamma_2 \frac{GE_{ji}}{BV_{ji}^F} + \gamma_3 \frac{RVE_{ji}}{BV_{ji}^F} + \gamma_4 \frac{PNE_{ji}}{BV_{ji}^F} + \gamma_5 \frac{TXE_{ji}}{BV_{ji}^F} + \gamma_6 \frac{OTHE_{ji}}{BV_{ji}^F} + \gamma_7 \frac{GBV_{ji}}{BV_{ji}^F} + \gamma_8 \frac{RVBV_{ji}}{BV_{ji}^F} + \gamma_9 \frac{PNBV_{ji}}{BV_{ji}^F} + \gamma_{10} \frac{TXBV_{ji}}{BV_{ji}^F} + \gamma_{11} \frac{OTHBV_{ji}}{BV_{ji}^F} + v_{ji}$$

	γ_0	γ_1	γ_2	γ_3	γ_4	γ_5	γ_6	γ_7	γ_8	γ_9	γ_{10}	γ_{11}	R^2	N
Full Sample	1.58	5.91	-4.13	-2.29	-6.38	0.06	1.06	0.97	3.69	9.32	1.46	0.82	0.50	440
	(11.0)***	(10.6)***	(-1.3)	(-1.2)	(-0.5)	(0.0)	(0.9)	(4.4)***	(4.7)***	(1.9)*	(2.7)***	(2.6)***		
United Kingdom and Australia	1.75	6.19	-1.84	8.51	-3.95	-0.70	2.31	0.84	3.90	2.96	1.49	-0.36	0.43	230
	(7.6)***	(6.8)***	(-0.5)	(1.7)*	(-0.5)	(-0.1)	(1.6)	(2.7)***	(3.9)***	(0.4)	(1.2)	(-0.7)		
All Other	1.09	7.58	-5.67	-0.23	7.09	1.90	3.11	1.45	5.07	4.92	2.94	1.93	0.52	206
	(6.8)***	(10.7)***	(-1.4)	(-0.1)	(0.4)	(1.0)	(1.6)	(5.0)***	(5.1)***	(0.9)	(5.2)***	(5.7)***		

Continued overleaf

TABLE 11 (cont.)

Panel B: U.S. *GAAP* Measure:

$$\frac{P_{jt}^F}{BV_{jt}^{US}} = \lambda_0 + \lambda_1 \frac{E_{jt}^F}{BV_{jt}^{US}} + \lambda_2 \frac{GE_{jt}}{BV_{jt}^{US}} + \lambda_3 \frac{RVE_{jt}}{BV_{jt}^{US}} + \lambda_4 \frac{PNE_{jt}}{BV_{jt}^{US}} + \lambda_5 \frac{TXE_{jt}}{BV_{jt}^{US}} + \lambda_6 \frac{OTHE_{jt}}{BV_{jt}^{US}} + \lambda_7 \frac{GBV_{jt}}{BV_{jt}^{US}} + \lambda_8 \frac{RVBV_{jt}}{BV_{jt}^{US}} + \lambda_9 \frac{PNBV_{jt}}{BV_{jt}^{US}} + \lambda_{10} \frac{TXBV_{jt}}{BV_{jt}^{US}} + \lambda_{11} \frac{OTHBV_{jt}}{BV_{jt}^{US}} + \xi_{jt}$$

	λ_0	λ_1	λ_2	λ_3	λ_4	λ_5	λ_6	λ_7	λ_8	λ_9	λ_{10}	λ_{11}	R^2	N
Full Sample	1.49	4.21	-0.79	-2.38	4.61	-0.05	0.72	0.33	0.61	5.47	0.59	-0.39	0.38	438
	(14.5)***	(9.8)***	(-0.3)	(-1.7)*	(0.5)	(-0.1)	(0.8)	(1.5)	(2.2)**	(1.4)	(1.9)*	(-2.3)**		
United Kingdom and	1.62	3.70	-2.11	0.34	0.35	-7.34	-0.21	0.41	0.61	4.63	0.46	-0.52	0.36	230
Australia	(10.0)***	(5.5)***	(-0.4)	(0.1)	(0.0)	(-1.8)*	(-0.1)	(1.1)	(1.6)	(0.9)	(0.8)	(-2.2)**		
All Other	1.28	5.26	-7.72	-0.63	2.61	1.15	1.95	-0.26	2.49	2.57	0.71	0.51	0.44	207
	(9.3)***	(8.3)***	(-2.0)**	(-0.3)	(0.1)	(0.7)	(1.1)	(-0.8)	(4.3)***	(0.4)	(1.7)*	(1.8)*		

1 Sample firms are non-U.S. firms listed on a U.S. stock exchange or NASDAQ and filing Form 20-F.
t-statistics in parentheses.
***significant at the 1% level; **significant at the 5% level; *significant at the 10% level.

P_{jt}^F　is the domestic price of firm *j* at time *t* (fiscal year-end plus six months);
BV_{jt}^F　is the book value of shareholders' equity of firm *j* at time *t* reported in domestic *GAAP*;
BV_{jt}^{US}　is the book value of shareholders' equity of firm *j* at time *t* reported in U.S. *GAAP*;
E_{jt}^F　is the earnings of firm *j* at time *t*, reported in domestic *GAAP*;
GE_{jt}　is the goodwill adjustment to earnings of firm *j* at time *t*;
RVE_{jt}　is the asset revaluation adjustment to earnings of firm *j* at time *t*;
TXE_{jt}　is the tax adjustment to earnings of firm *j* at time *t*;
PNE_{jt}　is the pension adjustment to earnings of firm *j* at time *t*;
$OTHE_{jt}$　is the net other adjustment to earnings of firm *j* at time *t*;
GBV_{jt}　is the goodwill adjustment to shareholders' equity of firm *j* at time *t*;
$RVBV_{jt}$　is the asset revaluation adjustment to shareholders' equity of firm *j* at time *t*;
$TXBV_{jt}$　is the tax adjustment to shareholders' equity of firm *j* at time *t*;
$PNBV_{jt}$　is the pension adjustment to shareholders' equity of firm *j* at time *t*; and
$OTHBV_{jt}$　is the net other adjustment to shareholders' equity of firm *j* at time *t*.

up this category we are unable to draw any useful inferences about this component.

Another possible confounding factor is the inclusion of 49 observations of financial institutions. Analysis of industrial firms alone yields results similar to those reported. As an additional check for the influence of multicollinearity we calculated condition indexes for the annual return and market-to-book regression models. Several of the component models have a maximum condition index between 5 and 15, suggesting mild collinearity. To test for the impact of collinearity we considered several alternative specifications. Constraining all component observations to have a maximum absolute value of 1 reduced the collinearity, with the maximum condition index for any model being around 7. As the results did not change qualitatively we do not report these results. From an economic perspective the tax component is the one most likely to be correlated with other adjustments as it is partially adjusting for the tax effect of each component reconciliation. Consequently, we reran all component regression models combining the tax and other components. Again the results were qualitatively unchanged. As a test of any influence from heteroscedasticity we recomputed all t-statistics using a White correction and found that no results differed qualitatively.

8. Concluding Comments

We use reconciliations to U.S. *GAAP* as provided on Form 20-F filings to evaluate the value-relevance of different accounting measurement systems. Our results suggest that the aggregate reconciliations of both shareholders' equity and earnings are value-relevant, consistent with U.S. *GAAP* measures being more value-relevant than the aggregate measures from the mix of non-U.S. *GAAP* systems.

In analyzing some of the systematic components which cause the differences between U.S. *GAAP* and non-U.S. *GAAP* earnings and shareholders' equity we find investors view both capitalized goodwill and asset revaluations as value-relevant. The taxation adjustments are also value-relevant, both as a result of indicating future dividends or profitability as well as capturing measurement differences.

These results should not be taken as bearing directly on the usefulness of the 20-F reconciliations as imposed by the SEC. Given that the variables which appear to be value-relevant are goodwill, asset revaluations, taxation, and a conglomeration of other items, it seems plausible that a careful investor may be able to reconstruct the value-relevant data from the reports presented in the home country. Further, removal of the asset revaluations appears to make the U.S. *GAAP* statements less relevant. Thus, while overall U.S. *GAAP* measures appear to be relatively more value-relevant our results do not indicate that the 20-F reconciliations themselves are required.

REFERENCES

ADLER, M., AND B. DUMAS. "International Portfolio Choice and Corporation Finance: A Synthesis." *Journal of Finance* (June 1983): 925–84.

AMIR, E. "The Market Valuation of Accounting Information: The Case of Post-Retirement Benefits Other Than Pensions." *The Accounting Review* (October 1993): 703–24.

BANK OF NEW YORK. *Global Offerings of Depositary Receipts: A Transaction Guide.* New York: BNY, 1992.

BARTH, M. E., AND G. CLINCH. "Market Perceptions of International Diversity in Accounting Standards." Working paper, Harvard Business School, June 1993.

BEAVER, W. H. "The Information Content of Annual Earnings Announcements." *Journal of Accounting Research* (Supplement 1968): 67–92.

BELSEY, D. A.; E. KUH; AND R. E. WELSCH. *Regression Diagnostics.* New York: Wiley, 1980. .

BERNARD, V. L.; R. C. MERTON; AND K. G. PALEPU. "Mark-to-Market Accounting for U.S. Banks and Thrifts: Lessons from the Danish Experience." Working paper, University of Michigan, August 1992.

CHOI, F. D. S., AND C. LEE. "Merger Premia and National Differences in Accounting for Goodwill." *Journal of International Financial Management and Accounting* (1991): 219–40.

EASTON, P. D.; P. EDDEY; AND T. S. HARRIS. "An Investigation of Revaluations of Long-Lived Tangible Fixed Assets." *Journal of Accounting Research* (Supplement 1993): 1–38.

EASTON, P. D., AND T. S. HARRIS. "Earnings as an Explanatory Variable for Returns." *Journal of Accounting Research* (Spring 1991): 19–36.

EASTON, P. D., AND M. E. ZMIJEWSKI. "SEC Form 10K/10Q Reports and Annual Reports to Shareholders: Reporting Lags and Squared Market Model Prediction Errors." *Journal of Accounting Research* (Spring 1993): 113–29.

EDWARDS, E. O., AND P. W. BELL. *The Theory of Measurement of Business Income.* Berkeley, Calif.: University of California Press, 1961.

FAIRFIELD, P. M., AND T. S. HARRIS. "An Investigation of Intrinsic Value and Risk as Explanations of the Returns to Price-to-Earnings and Price-to-Book Value Trading Strategies." Working paper, Columbia University, 1991.

FAMA, E. F., AND K. R. FRENCH. "The Cross-Section of Expected Stock Returns." *Journal of Finance* (1992): 427–65.

FELTHAM, G., AND J. A. OHLSON. "Valuation of Clean Surplus Accounting for Operating and Financial Activities." Working paper, Columbia University, March 1993.

FROST, C. A., AND G. POWNALL. "A Comparison of the Price Sensitivity of Accounting Disclosures in the U.S. and the U.K." Working paper, Washington University, October 1992.

FUERBRINGER, J. "S.E.C. Says No on German Stocks." *New York Times* (April 26, 1992).

HARRIS, T. S., AND E. YURKO. "Investor Preferences on Listing Issues and Accounting Practices: A Survey of Senior Money Managers of Major Non-US Institutions." Working paper, Columbia University, February 1993.

JARRELL, G. "SEC Crimps Big Board's Future." *Wall Street Journal* (June 19, 1992).

MCQUEEN, P. D. "The Information Content of Foreign and U.S. GAAP Earnings in SEC Form 20-F." Working paper, New York University, January 1993.

OHLSON, J. A. "Accounting Earnings, Book Value and Dividends: The Theory of the Clean Surplus Equation (Part 1)." Working paper, Columbia University, 1989.

————. "Earnings, Book Value and Dividends in Security Valuation." Working paper, Columbia University, 1991.

OU, J. A., AND S. H. PENMAN. "Financial Statement Analysis and the Evaluation of Market-to-Book Ratios." Working paper, University of California, Berkeley, August 1992.

POPE, P., AND W. REES. "International Differences in GAAP and the Pricing of Earnings." *Journal of International Financial Management and Accounting* (1993): 190–219.

ROSENBERG, B.; K. REID; AND R. LANDSTEIN. "Persuasive Evidence of Market Inefficiency." *Journal of Portfolio Management* (1985): 19–46.

264   E. AMIR, T. S. HARRIS, AND E. K. VENUTI

SICONOLFI, M., AND K. G. SALWEN. "Big Board, SEC Fight Over Foreign Stocks." *Wall Street Journal* (May 13, 1992): C1, C21.

WILSON, G. P. "The Relative Information Content of Accruals and Cash Flows: Combined Evidence at the Earnings Announcement and Annual Report Release Date." *Journal of Accounting Research* (Supplement 1986): 165–200.

Journal of Accounting Research
Vol. 31 Supplement 1993
Printed in U.S.A.

Discussion of
A Comparison of the Value-Relevance of U.S. versus non-U.S. GAAP Accounting Measures Using Form 20-F Reconciliations

PETER F. POPE*

1. Introduction

The SEC Form 20-F reconciliation requirements create opportunities to examine the abilities of different *GAAP* regimes to capture value-relevant information. In their paper, Amir, Harris, and Venuti (hereafter AHV) employ a multicountry analysis to examine the incremental information content of the reconciliations. The paper is a timely contribution to the literature in view of current debates concerning international disclosure regulation and accounting harmonization. AHV's results indicate that the aggregate reconciliations of both shareholders' equity and earnings and their components have information content, and these are interpreted as indicating that U.S. *GAAP* measures of earnings and book value are more value-relevant than the non-U.S. *GAAP* measures. This is a potentially important conclusion for accounting regulators and financial statement users.

The main issues raised by conference participants concerned the definition of value-relevance and the interpretation of the empirical tests. This discussion presents these and other issues in three parts: motivation; specification and interpretation of the value-relevance tests; and issues for future research.

*University of Lancaster. Thanks are due to Trevor Harris and John O'Hanlon for helpful comments on earlier drafts. Financial support from the Economic and Social Research Council (grant #R000233813) and the Research Board of the Institute of Chartered Accountants in England and Wales is gratefully acknowledged.

2. Motivation

Comparative research on the value-relevance of alternative *GAAP* measurements can be motivated from at least two perspectives. First, international and national accounting regulators may wish to select between measurement alternatives that have already been implemented in another *GAAP* regime, and evidence on the information content of such measurements will potentially be valuable in this context. Regulators may also wish to consider the introduction of supplementary disclosures. Perhaps the strongest motivation for AHV's research is the considerable policy interest in whether the Form 20-F disclosures are necessary. Debate on this issue has focused on the possible disclosure costs the SEC rules impose on foreign firms and the likelihood that, as a consequence of such costs, international securities business is being driven away from the United States toward markets with fewer disclosure requirements, such as SEAQ International in London. The results in AHV may contribute to this debate by providing evidence on the equity market's use of the reconciliations.

A second reason for interest in the value-relevance of *GAAP* alternatives lies in the concept of accounting quality (see, e.g., Lev [1989]). The fact that U.S.-listed foreign firms must report "competing" earnings and book value measures and associated reconciliation statements makes it possible to compare the abilities of different *GAAP* regimes to achieve accounting quality, defined in terms of the explanatory power of accounting numbers for stock prices. It may also be possible to identify the sources of quality differences by analyzing the value-relevance of specific accruals components across *GAAP* regimes.

3. Specification and Interpretation of Value-Relevance Tests

3.1 RELATIVE AND INCREMENTAL INFORMATION CONTENT

In testing the value-relevance of accounting numbers based on their statistical association with stock price (or return) it is important to distinguish between *relative* and *incremental* information content (Biddle and Seow [1993]). The relative information content of *GAAP* alternatives is indicated by the ranking of R^2 statistics obtained from separate regressions for each *GAAP* regime. In contrast, incremental information content is indicated by the additional explanatory power attributable to one measure after controlling for the information in the other, and this may be tested by examining the t statistics or partial F-statistic in a multiple regression including accounting measures from both *GAAP* alternatives. Two measures may both have incremental information content, but generally one cannot draw conclusions about relative information content from an incremental information test.

Depending on the motivation for the research and the questions we may wish to answer, different research designs will be appropriate.

Choices among measurement methods for the purposes of standard setting imply an interest in the relative information content of alternative measures. Similarly, the quality of different measures of the same underlying accounting construct (e.g., earnings, book value) will be reflected in tests of relative information content. In contrast, incremental information content tests will potentially be informative for regulation regarding supplementary disclosures. Throughout most of their paper AHV define value-relevance in terms of the increase in explanatory power for market-to-book ratios (or returns) attributable to the reconciliations. In other words, they adopt an incremental information content perspective. Conference participants noted that the study is similar in spirit to a test of incremental information content of footnote disclosures that enable the computation of alternative earnings measures in a domestic *GAAP* setting (e.g., the use of footnote disclosures to convert *LIFO* to *FIFO* earnings).

The distinction between relative and incremental information content is important in interpreting AHV's results. Although AHV concludes that their results are consistent with U.S. *GAAP* being *more value relevant* than the aggregate measures from the mix of non-U.S. *GAAP* systems, it should be recognized that this conclusion is based primarily on incremental information content tests. Although the incremental information content focus is most relevant to the policy debate concerning supplementary Form 20-F disclosures, AHV's tests do not provide rankings of the information content of the numbers generated by the foreign and U.S. *GAAP* regimes.[1]

AHV adopt three basic approaches to testing value relevance: short event-window tests, a long window returns association test, and tests based on market-to-book ratios. These approaches focus on the information content of different accounting variables and employ different control variables. This discussion considers each test in turn.

3.2 SHORT EVENT-WINDOW TEST

Conference participants suggested that if the Form 20-F disclosures are themselves informative, then a price response ought to be observed in the reconciliation announcement period. AHV's short window tests suggest that the earnings reconciliation does not contain incremental information beyond the information reflected in stock prices measured after foreign *GAAP* earnings announcements. The absence of an identifiable announcement effect could be due to difficulties in identifying information release dates and the unexpected news components of reconciliation announcements, as discussed by AHV. However, subject to this qualification, the results suggest that the value-relevance of the reconciliations indicated by AHV's other tests is most likely to be explained by information reaching the market through mechanisms

---

[1] Alford et al. [1993] report tests of relative information content.

other than the SEC filings. Examples of such mechanisms include foreign *GAAP* supplementary disclosures and voluntary disclosures. As AHV acknowledge, the main reconciliation components can probably be reconstructed from foreign *GAAP* disclosures. This possibility creates uncertainty about whether the paper should best be viewed as a test of the information content of the 20-F reconciliations, or as a commentary on the information content of disclosures that might be made irrespective of SEC disclosure rules. This ambiguity may be difficult to resolve, but one approach would be to attempt to refine the short window tests by more precise modeling of expectations relating to the reconciliations conditioned on prior disclosures, perhaps using methods similar to Wilson [1987]. Although this could be fairly complex, in view of international diversity in supplementary disclosure practices, the ability to attribute the value-relevance of the reconciliations to the SEC rules will be an important step in interpreting AHV's results for the SEC policy debate.[2]

3.3 ANNUAL RETURNS–EARNINGS ASSOCIATION TESTS

The second set of incremental information content tests reveals the ability of unexpected earnings from the foreign and U.S. *GAAP* regimes jointly to explain annual returns. AHV focus attention on whether U.S. *GAAP* earnings (or equivalently the earnings reconciliation) have incremental information content beyond foreign *GAAP* earnings. In equation (4) of the paper the hypothesis of no incremental information content is rejected if α_{31} or α_{32} is significantly different from zero. AHV report evidence in table 6 that the earnings reconciliation level is significant for the full sample. This indicates that U.S. *GAAP* earnings have incremental information content beyond foreign earnings, although quantifying this in terms of the incremental R^2 is not possible on the basis of the reported results.

Regression equation (4) contains the same information as a multiple regression of returns on foreign *GAAP* and U.S. *GAAP* earnings variables simultaneously. The implied coefficient on the foreign *GAAP* earnings level (change) is $\alpha_1 - \alpha_{31}$ ($\alpha_2 - \alpha_{32}$) and the coefficient on the U.S. *GAAP* earnings level (change) is a α_{31} (α_{32}). AHV do not discuss the incremental information content of foreign *GAAP* earnings variables beyond U.S. *GAAP* earnings, but the coefficient estimates reported in table 6 suggest that foreign earnings will be found to possess incremental information beyond U.S. *GAAP* earnings.[3]

Findings of incremental information content suggest a role for future research in explaining such results. Some evidence that differences in specific accruals procedures may be important is provided in

---

[2] An alternative approach would be to demonstrate that prior information disclosures captured by the reconciliations would not materialize in the absence of SEC regulation.

[3] Pope and Rees [1993] find such a result for U.K. firms.

the results of the components analysis in table 10. However, test misspecification could also provide an explanation. Easton, Eddey, and Harris [1993] suggest that under the characterization of valuation developed by Ohlson [1989; 1991] and under the assumption that U.S. *GAAP* approximate clean surplus accounting,[4] the appropriate specification for the returns regression includes the earnings changes and levels variables, as employed in AHV, plus a term reflecting deviations from clean surplus accounting under foreign *GAAP*. In common with previous research, where dirty surplus accounting could be relevant (e.g. Pope and Rees [1993]), AHV do not include such a term in their analysis. However, components of the earnings reconciliation variables (e.g., changes in goodwill and asset revaluation adjustments) may proxy for this omitted term, rather than reflecting information independent of the foreign *GAAP* regime. If so, U.S. *GAAP* measures may play no independent role in the valuation process. If the research focus is on the joint role of book value and earnings in valuation, then a more complex test of information content is suggested, involving a dirty surplus adjustment term as an additional regressor in equation (4). Unfortunately, the dirty surplus term may be difficult to estimate in practice.

3.4 MARKET-TO-BOOK RATIO TESTS

The market-to-book ratio (*MB*) is assumed by AHV to reflect differences between market and book values (unrecorded goodwill) arising from the application of conservative accounting principles and measurement error. Conservative accounting produces systematically biased book values that fail fully to reflect future growth opportunities. *GAAP*-specific measurement error may be present even if accounting is unbiased. However, Fama and French [1992] also show that *MB* and size jointly explain expected returns. They argue that if markets are rational, this implies that *MB* is an inverse measure of risk, perhaps associated with relative distress.[5] The existence of at least three sources of difference between market value and book value is important for the interpretation of the information content tests based on *MB*.

AHV initially test how "well aligned" book values are with market value by examining the first and second moments of *MB*. This may be interpreted as a simple test of the *relative* information content of alternative book value measures. The findings that *MB* under U.S. *GAAP* is closer to unity and has lower variance are interpreted by AHV as evidence that U.S. *GAAP* book value is a more value-relevant measure

---

[4] Easton, Eddey, and Harris [1993] suggest that although clean surplus account does not hold exactly in the United States, the dirty surplus component is unlikely to be material. However, to the extent that U.S. *GAAP* do deviate from clean surplus it will be necessary to incorporate the effects into the analysis.

[5] Fama and French [1992] analyze the book-to-market ratio rather than *MB*.

than its foreign *GAAP* counterpart. There are several reasons to be cautious about this interpretation of the distributional properties of *MB*. First, conference participants observed that *MB* reflects conservatism in accounting. In view of possible interdependence between the degree of conservatism, the existence of growth opportunities, and the complementary valuation roles of book value and earnings (see, e.g., Feltham and Ohlson [1992]), it seems important to control for such factors in comparisons of *MB* measures. Where conservatism may differ across *GAAP* regimes, the distributional properties of *MB* alone cannot be expected to be informative about the value-relevance of *GAAP* systems. In fact, this issue motivates the use of the market-to-book regression by AHV. A second limitation of *MB* as a measure of relative information content is due to its potential role as a risk measure. If *MB* measures risk, then the "correct" *MB* measure will be the one that best explains future returns. This need not be the *MB* measure having lower variance. A third reason for caution over drawing inferences from *MB* distribution is based on the recognition that, generally, the distributional properties of ratios are very complex. They rely critically on the functional form of the relation between numerator (market value) and denominator (book value) (see, e.g., Lev and Sunder [1979] and Whittington [1980]). Unless the relationship between market value and book value is proportional and deterministic, the distribution of *MB* will be skewed, the mean will fail to capture the average relation between market and book values, and the sample variance will be difficult to interpret. Table 4 suggests that both *MB* measures display skewness. Given such statistical considerations, the appropriate interpretation of distributional differences in *MB* across *GAAP* alternatives is unclear.[6]

In their market-to-book regression tests, AHV analyze the ability of reconciliation items to explain variation in the alternative *MB* measures. The regression results for equations (6) and (8) show that the book value reconciliation has incremental information content beyond earnings and foreign *GAAP* book value, but that only in 1989 does the book value reconciliation have incremental information content beyond earnings and U.S. *GAAP* book value. AHV interpret these results as indicating that the book value reconciliation corrects for measurement error in foreign *GAAP* book value.[7]

---

[6] The distributional properties of *MB* ratios may also lead to specification bias in the market-to-book regression models.

[7] The possibility cannot be ruled out that the book value reconciliation also plays a role as a proxy for the impact of foreign *GAAP* dirty surplus accounting on earnings and book value. This is one specific source of measurement error that is potentially identifiable from foreign *GAAP* disclosures alone.

The assumptions underlying the interpretation of equations (6) and (8) are important. In both regressions earnings have high explanatory power, and this is assumed to reflect the role of earnings as a proxy for growth opportunities. Earnings are implicitly assumed to be uncorrelated with any measurement error in U.S. *GAAP* book value. This is significant, because one possible alternative explanation for the results is that the earnings variables are correlated with measurement error in book values. Additionally, one or more of the regressors might reflect risk differences also reflected in the respective *MB* measures. It could be worthwhile for future research to attempt to resolve the ambiguity over the possible roles played by earnings and the book value reconciliation in equations (6) and (8), by introducing direct proxies for growth opportunities and risk.

In the conference discussion, the weak evidence of incremental information content obtained for the returns model was contrasted with the stronger results for the market-to-book regressions. AHV suggest that this may be due to the relatively small impact of the reconciliations on earnings compared to their impact on shareholders' equity, and to the low signal-to-noise ratio in the earnings reconciliation. It was also suggested that predictability in the book value reconciliations on the basis of previous reconciliations may create dependence in observations over time, and inefficiency and loss of degrees of freedom in the pooled regression estimates. The predictability of the book value reconciliations undercuts the ability of the market-to-book regressions to test the information content of the annual Form 20-F reconciliations. In the extreme, reconciliations published at the initial date of listing in the United States could be sufficient to explain cross-sectional variation in stock prices. Perhaps one way to establish the information content of *annual* reconciliations would be to show that contemporaneous values have incremental explanatory power beyond lagged values.

The results in table 11 are also consistent with foreign *GAAP* asset revaluations, deferred tax, and "other" book value components containing incremental information. One striking feature of the results based on the U.S. *GAAP MB* measure is the large increase in the R^2 statistic for the full sample, from 24% (in table 7) to 38%, resulting from the decomposition of the reconciliations. It appears that components of aggregate foreign book value (e.g., revaluation reserves) have incremental information content beyond U.S. *GAAP* book value, but that the aggregate book value reconciliation is too noisy to reveal this effect. Taken overall, the *MB* regression results are consistent with the book value reconciliation being value-relevant but with neither book value measure being valuation-sufficient.

A final issue relating to the *MB* regression and considered in the conference discussion is whether the market-to-book regression approach

272   PETER F. POPE

to testing incremental information content dominates direct estimation of an equation involving price as the dependent variable and alternative book value and earnings measures as regressors.[8] This approach would eliminate potential selection bias from the exclusion of negative book value observations and "outliers" caused by small book values. Another advantage is that the coefficients from a levels regression could be interpreted directly as valuation weights, consistent with Ohlson [1991]. Additionally, possible problems of spurious inference (Kuh and Meyer [1955] and Lev and Sunder [1979]) and bias due to measurement error in the denominator (Briggs [1962]) would also be avoided in a price regression.[9]

4. Further Issues for Future Research

Variations in *GAAP* result in both measurement and disclosure differences. Earnings and book value measurements differ across *GAAP* regimes and over time because of differences in conservatism, deviations from clean surplus accounting, and flexibility of accounting choice afforded to management. Disclosure differences will impact on the information environment within which accounting signals are evaluated by the market. If there is cross-sectional or time-series diversity in *GAAP*, tests based on the associations between stock prices (or returns) and accounting numbers will suffer from loss of power when *GAAP* are assumed to be homogeneous. Because of sample size considerations, AHV are only able to control for possible *GAAP* differences by partitioning their data into "United Kingdom/Australia" and "Other Countries" groups. However, there is some evidence in their results of regime-specific and time-specific effects. If subsequent research is to develop more powerful tests and perhaps attempt to model the conditions under which U.S. *GAAP* can be expected to have incremental information content, it will be necessary to consider how diversity in financial reporting environments could influence the relation between prices and accounting numbers. This issue will be discussed in the context of returns–earnings regressions.[10]

---

[8] Barth and Clinch [1993] use a price levels approach, although they do not include earnings variables to proxy for growth opportunities. Equivalently, price could be regressed on book value and earnings from one *GAAP* regime and the respective reconciliation adjustments.

[9] One reason for estimating a deflated regression is possible heteroscedasticity in a price levels regression. However, even if heteroscedasticity is known to be a problem, the procedures in White [1980] would provide a solution. In any case, even if the error variance in the price equation is proportional to book value, regressions (6) or (8) are not correct weighted least squares regression specifications because they should include one over book value as an additional regressor, to be consistent with a levels regression of price on a constant, earnings and book value.

[10] However, most of the points raised are relevant to price level or market-to-book-based regression models.

GAAP diversity will be expected to influence model coefficients and explanatory power for several reasons. First, differences in underlying accruals procedures may influence the time-series process of earnings, and hence the relevant weights for earnings levels and changes variables as complementary measures of unexpected earnings. Second, diversity across *GAAP* regimes in conservatism and growth opportunities will also imply regime-specific weights for earnings levels and changes variables under the Feltham and Ohlson [1992] characterization of valuation.[11] A third reason for *GAAP*-specific differences in the returns–earnings relation could be differences in the measurement error in unexpected earnings proxies across regimes. This situation may arise because of time-series changes in *GAAP*, because of accounting policy switches permitted by *GAAP*, or due to prices leading earnings. The returns–earnings regression specification involving earnings changes assumes time-series comparability of earnings, and changes in *GAAP* reduce comparability. Furthermore, when observations are pooled over time, stationarity in the earnings evolution process is assumed. Significant *GAAP* changes could affect this process. Although the problems caused by *GAAP* changes are not unique to international accounting research, they are particularly important in this context because of differences in the rates of innovation across *GAAP* regimes.

Measurement error in reported numbers perceived by the equity market also may depend on the degree of flexibility allowed to management under *GAAP* and the incentives for management to reduce or introduce measurement error. The degree of flexibility clearly varies across *GAAP* regimes. If a significant degree of accounting choice is available to management, the alignment of management and equity interests becomes an important consideration in determining whether flexibility in accounting choice will be used by management for signaling to the equity market or other user groups, or to manipulate numbers in their own self-interest. The expected motivations for accounting choices could influence the credibility and reliability of accounting numbers perceived by the equity market, and hence the statistical associations between stock price and accounting measures.

Additionally, flexibility in *GAAP* might itself reflect the endogeneity of *GAAP* depending on country-specific factors such as ownership and capital structure, linkages with the corporate tax system, and other historical influences. *GAAP* are most likely to reflect the information needs of equity market investors in countries where equity financing is dominant. Thus, the probability of finding incremental information content for U.S. *GAAP* reconciliations is likely to be higher for countries where domestic *GAAP* are oriented toward providing a base for corporate taxation or serving the needs of creditors. The subsample tests in AHV relating to the United Kingdom/Australia partition provide some preliminary

---

[11] Dirty surplus adjustment terms would also be affected.

274   PETER F. POPE

support for this conjecture. However, the interactions between *GAAP* differences, contracting arrangements, and the perceived credibility and value-relevance of foreign and U.S. *GAAP* accounting numbers are potentially very complex.

Another source of measurement error in the returns–earnings regression relates to the possibility that prices lead earnings (Beaver, Lambert, and Morse [1980]). The extent to which this occurs will be related to the frequency of voluntary or *GAAP*-mandated disclosures of value-relevant information that is subsequently reflected in future earnings. When stock prices lead earnings, an error-in-variables problem is effectively created with respect to unexpected earnings (Kothari [1992]). This is potentially very important for international research because the information environments for firms across *GAAP* regimes differ significantly as a result of differences in disclosure practices. The implication for future research is that more powerful tests of information content may be achieved by controlling for differences in disclosure practices.

Finally, a further issue raised by conference participants and related to voluntary disclosure is to consider why, if U.S. *GAAP* reconciliations have value-relevance, we do not frequently observe formal announcements of U.S. *GAAP* numbers or references to such numbers in the financial press. In attempting to answer this question, field research involving financial analysts might complement market association studies and shed some light on the possible roles of the reconciliation data in the valuation process and on differences in value-relevance across foreign *GAAP* regimes.

REFERENCES

ALFORD, A.; J. JONES; R. LEFTWICH; AND M. ZMIJEWSKI. "The Relative Informativeness of Accounting Disclosures in Different Countries." *Journal of Accounting Research* (Supplement 1993): 183–223.

BARTH, M. E., AND G. CLINCH. "International Accounting Differences and Their Relation to Share Prices: Evidence from U.K., Australian, and Canadian Firms." Working paper, Harvard University, May 1993.

BEAVER, W.; R. LAMBERT; AND D. MORSE. "The Information Content of Security Prices." *Journal of Accounting and Economics* (1980): 3–28.

BIDDLE, G. C., AND G. S. SEOW. "Relative versus Incremental Information Content." Working paper, University of Washington, July 1993.

BRIGGS, F. E. A. "The Influence of Errors on the Correlation of Ratios." *Econometrica* (January 1962): 162–77.

EASTON, P. D.; P. H. EDDEY, AND T. S. HARRIS. "An Investigation of Revaluations of Tangible Long-Lived Assets." *Journal of Accounting Research* (Supplement 1993): 1–38.

FAMA, E. F., AND K. R. FRENCH. "The Cross-Section of Expected Returns." *Journal of Finance* (June 1992): 427–65.

FELTHAM, G. A., AND J. A. OHLSON. "Valuation and Clean Surplus Accounting for Operating and Financial Activities." Working paper, University of British Columbia, 1992.

KOTHARI, S. P. "Price-Earnings Regressions in the Presence of Prices Leading Earnings." *Journal of Accounting and Economics* (1992): 173–202.

KUH, E., AND J. R. MEYER. "Correlation and Regression Estimates When Data Are Ratios." *Econometrica* (October 1955): 400–416.

LEV, B. "On the Usefulness of Earnings and Earnings Research: Lessons and Directions from Two Decades of Empirical Research." *Journal of Accounting Research* (Supplement 1989): 153–92.

LEV, B., AND S. SUNDER. "Methodological Issues in the Use of Financial Ratios." *Journal of Accounting and Economics* (December 1979): 187–210.

OHLSON, J. A. "Earnings, Book Value and Dividends: The Theory of the Clean Surplus Equation (Part 1)." Working paper, Columbia University, 1989.

———. "Earnings, Book Value and Dividends in Security Valuation." Working paper, Columbia University, 1991.

POPE, P. F., AND W. P. REES. "International Differences in GAAP and the Pricing of Earnings." *Journal of International Financial Management and Accounting* (1993): 190–219.

WHITE, H. "A Heteroskedasticity-Consistent Covariance Matrix Estimator and a Direct Test for Heteroskedasticity." *Econometrica* (May 1980): 817–38.

WHITTINGTON, G. "Some Basic Properties of Accounting Ratios." *Journal of Business Finance and Accounting* (1980): 219–32.

WILSON, G. P. "The Incremental Information Content of Accrual and Funds Components of Earnings after Controlling for Earnings." *The Accounting Review* (April 1987): 293–322.

[12]

Japan and the World Economy 2 (1990) 263–282
North-Holland

THE INTERNATIONAL PRICE–EARNINGS RATIO PHENOMENON

A Partial Explanation *

John S. BILDERSEE, John J. CHEH and Changwoo LEE

Leonard N. Stern School of Business, New York University, New York, NY 10003, USA

Received June 1989, final version received March 1990

The PE ratio is an important estimator of value in the US equity markets. However, there seem to be large differences between PE ratios in the US and Japan. It turns out that the differences can be reduced, on average, by adjustments to earnings due to differences in depreciation, leverage and ownership policies in the two countries. Further, it turns out that, different from the US market, net book value appears more stable than earnings as a measure of market values in Japan. This difference is reduced when policy differences are accounted for in the analysis. Further, perceived differences between the two markets seem to be narrowing.

Keywords: PE ratios, Japan, leverage, cross-holdings, volatility, interest expense, PE ratio adjustments, depreciation expense, international markets.

1. Introduction

The PE ratio is an important estimator of value in the US equity markets. However, this barometer, as we know it, has not been an effective investing tool in the Japanese markets. [1] The most troubling aspect of this issue is the high average PE ratio in the Japanese markets relative to those in other industrial nations such as the US, UK, West Germany and France. For example, the average ratio was 57.7 in Japan and 13.1 in the US at the end of May, 1988. [2]

Although this difference seems huge, it turns out that it can be reduced by adjustments to earnings due to differences in debt policy and depreciation

---

* This project has been partially supported by a research grant from the Center for Japan–US Business and Economic Studies of the Leonard N. Stern School of Business at New York University. We appreciate the help of our research assistant, Ajay Zutshi, and Hiroharu Tanaka of Nihon Keizai Shimbun America Inc. for helpful insights about Japanese Equity Markets. All mistakes remain our responsibility.
[1] The Japanese equity market is currently the largest in the world. As of December, 1988 the aggregative market value of securities in the Japanese stock markets was $3,500 billion while the United States market was valued at $2,638 billion and the markets in the United Kingdom, West Germany and France were $572 billion, $240 billion and $235 billion-respectively.
[2] The Japanese ratio came from the Report on Japan's Stock Price Level by the Japan Securities Research Institute.

policy between business in the two countries. Further, it turns out, different from the US market, that book value appears more stable than earnings as a measure of market values in Japan, but that this difference is reduced when these policy differences are accounted for in the analysis and that perceived differences between the two markets seem to be narrowing. After describing the background in section 2, section 3 provides a description of the data used in the analysis. Section 4 reports the results of our adjustments and tests of Japanese PE ratios. Section 5 summarizes the conclusions of the analysis.

2. Background

PE ratios play an important role in the US equity markets. The underlying rationale is that earnings per share is a good summary valuation measure and is a better summary measure for valuation than any other variables such as corporate book value. In fact, it appears that investors value firms based on their earnings power rather than on their asset ownership. This approach to valuation has been documented by Black (1980). He notes that the variability of earnings to price ratios is less than the variability of book value to price ratio suggesting that the greater consistency is symptomatic of its association with value. [3]

Despite the popularity of the ratio in the US, it has not received the same acceptance in Japan. Instead, some feel that, in Japan, asset ownership has a stronger association with market values than does earnings power. In particular, Tobin's Q ratio, has received increasing attention as an alternative to the PE ratio for use in equity valuation in Japan. This ratio of stock price per share to net asset value per share is supposed to indicate whether or not a firm is fully valued in the markets.

Wakasugi (1988a) and Viner (1988) imply that Japanese stocks may appear overvalued when investors focus on the earnings number, but that this may be due to high expectations for Japanese stocks. Further, Wakasugi (1988a) claims that the Q ratio is a better investing tool in the Japanese market than the PE ratio. He suggests that, in a transitional period, the PE ratio is a mismatched indicator of value because earnings reflects only past achievements. However, the Q ratio should not suffer this deficiency as its numerator and denominator both reflect potential future benefits.

Wakasugi (1988c) argues that stock prices may appreciate further because Q ratios for Japanese stocks remain below one. This appreciation may continue until prices more fully reflect the asset values used in the Q ratio. Taking the example of high land prices in Japan metropolitan areas, he argues that Japan equity investors can obtain the land more cheaply by buying firms

---

[3] He uses results from Stickell (1980). An extensive survey of PE ratios and anomalies can be found in Jacobs and Levy (1988).

in the stock markets and then selling off other assets until only the land remains. Even with some constraints on this activity he indicates that the land can generate high earnings so that asset based values can be different, and higher, than values based on historical earnings. In turn, this leads to high stock prices based on the asset values. As evidence, he points to stable Q ratios in the Japanese stock markets.

Differences in the use of the PE ratio in the US and Japan may be due to fundamentally different earnings and asset approaches to valuation in the two equity markets. In this case, market behaviors may be quite different and models usable in one economy may not be transferable to the other economy without substantial adjustment and recalibration.

However, differences in the use of the PE ratio in the US and Japan may be due to differences in business policies in the US and Japan. One difference is due to the selection of depreciation policy for financial reporting. Although many US firms use straight line depreciation for financial reporting purposes Japanese firms, according to Suzuki and Mashimo (1988) and Viner (1988), typically use accelerated depreciation for financial reporting reducing income. They do so because they must use the same depreciation reporting scheme for financial reporting as for tax reporting. In this case, a Japanese firm that is identical to an American firm will report lower income. If earnings are adjusted for accounting procedures, as suggested by Beaver and Dukes (1973), the PE ratio of the American firm should be lower than that for the Japanese firm. [4]

The other difference is that typical Japanese firms have capital structures different from the typical US capital structure. Japanese firms are far more highly levered than are typical American firms. However, this does not lead to an increased chance of default. Much of the borrowing is from a relatively small number of interested parties like banks so that the likelihood of a forced bankruptcy is small relative to that for an American firm with the same debt spread across a large number of disinterested parties. Moreover, there is a substantial amount of cross-holding among leading Japanese firms [Hodder and Tschoegl (1985) and Viner (1988)] increasing the likelihood of a private rescue in Japan relative to that in the US. [5] Cross-holding increases the shares outstanding so that a typical Japanese firm's leverage may be even greater than suggested in financial reports.

The different financial structure makes the Japanese earnings number different from the US number. Japanese firms have large interest expenses relative to US firms. Choi et al. (1983) reports that, during 1976–1978, 902

---

[4] Differences from those implied by Beaver and Dukes (1973) would be evidence of different valuation structures in the American and Japanese markets.
[5] Cross-holdings mean that firms hold portions of each other. In this case, if one firm has problems, it may be exported to other firms. Given this linkage, it is likely that other firms will support any firm in trouble.

American firms had an average times interest earned ratio equalling 6.5, four times higher than that for 976 Japanese firms which had a ratio of 1.6. They also report that the typical Japanese firm has an interest expense/income ratio three times that for the typical US firm and that the average debt to total assets ratio for the Japanese firms was 84% compared to 47% for the US firms.[6]

Both policies reduce the income number for a Japanese firm relative to that for a similar American firm. Adjustments for these differences cause PE ratios in Japan to become more like those in the US. This is consistent with past research in the area such as that of Beaver and Dukes (1973). They found that PE ratios of a portfolio of firms using accelerated depreciation were greater than the PE ratios of a portfolio of firms using straight-line depreciation after controlling for risk (beta) and growth. Moreover, when the earnings of the straight-line portfolio were converted according to the accelerated method, the PE differences in the two portfolios disappeared. Beaver and Morse (1978) found that differences in accounting methods among companies were the most likely explaining factor for PE ratio differences among US companies over long periods.

The cross-holding issue is different. Many Japanese firms hold shares in firms that, in turn, hold shares in them. The sale of shares to another company and reinvestment of the funds back in the other company leads to an increase in the number of shares outstanding.[7] However, the flow through overstates the net investment made by the companies. Further, assuming that the companies have no intention of trading securities in which they have invested, many shares are outstanding only in a technical sense.[8] Since increased shares outstanding is the major effect, the net result of cross-holdings is to reduce earnings per share and to increase the typical Japanese firm's PE ratio. The prime benefit of the stock issue and reinvestment is any resulting investment income which may actually increase the firm's earnings. The impact of cross-holding may be substantial as a survey of the ownership of listed firms in 1987 indicates that Japanese corporate and financial interests own 72.7% of stocks listed on Japan equity markets in terms of market value [Yasuda and Lin (1988)].

If the focus in Japan is on asset valuation rather than earning power as suggested by Wakasugi, then questions arise about the meaning, if any, we can

---

[6] This is equivalent to debt to book equity ratio of 5.25 in Japan and a ratio of 0.89 in the US.
[7] The cross-holding pattern can be complex. For example, company A may own a share in company B which, in turn, owns a share in company C which, in turn, owns a share in company A. Although cross-holding can occur when companies separately enter the secondary markets to acquire shares of other firms, this causes the firms to lose cash. The 'private' transfer does not require net cash flows to third parties.
[8] A counter argument would be that the linking of the firms allows the first firm to draw on the second firm's equity in a crisis so that effective equity available in a crisis may be substantially larger than that for an American firm with the same ratio.

draw from raw and adjusted PE ratios measured for Japanese firms? Do the PE ratios in Japan imply that Japanese securities are overvalued relative to other nation's securities and does any seeming overvaluation relative to the PE ratio preclude its use as a meaningful investment statistic? [9] Do adjustments in the ratios make them more useful for security analysis? [10]

3. Data and methodology

Accounting and stock price information for Japanese firms comes from the NEEDS data base provided by Nihon Keizai Shimbun Inc. Information for US firms is obtained from COMPUSTAT. The study covers the 1976–1987 period. The first year is 1976 because this is the year when most Japanese companies started reporting accounting information annually. Firms in the Japanese sample have March 31 fiscal yearends, a 12-month reporting period and no missing data. They also report positive ordinary income, positive net income before taxes, positive net income. Firms in the US sample have December 31 fiscal year ends, no missing data and report positive income before extraordinary items, positive net income before taxes, and positive net income.

Stock prices used in the PE ratios are closing fiscal year end prices for all firms. In addition, firms had to have positive earnings on various levels of income calculations. Since we compare several alternative PE ratios in this analysis, firms used here must have positive income before extraordinary items, income before taxes, and after taxes in any given year. Due to data availability the number of Japanese firms in the study increases from 303 in 1976 to 477 in 1985. The number of US firms increases from 750 in 1976 to 953 in 1987.

Adjustments for interest expense and depreciation expense involve adding back those expenses made different by systematically different Japanese and American policies. In effect, by removing the impacts of differing accounting and financial policies some of the calculated PE ratios focus on business operations and on operations excluding depreciation.

Precise information on corporate cross-holdings is not available. We approximate a cross-holdings ratio from NEEDS data. The impact of cross-holdings on the PE ratio is removed if the PE is adjusted by

$$PE_a = PE * (1 - CH),\qquad\qquad (1)$$

[9] The word 'overvalued' refers to the value of a security relative to what it would be if the security had a PE ratio typical of the US stock market.

[10] The nature of the usefulness might be different from that in the US markets. In any case, a more precise statement might be that the PE ratio's relation to market value in Japan would be structurally different from that in the US rather than necessarily being related to overvaluation.

where

PE = PE prior to adjustment for cross-holdings;

PE_a = PE after adjustment for cross-holdings; and

CH = estimated cross-holdings ratio.

If there are no cross-holdings, CH is 0 and the PE ratio is unchanged. As the proportion of cross-holdings increases, the adjustment causes a larger decrease in the adjusted PE ratio relative to the unadjusted PE ratio.

In addition to offering some insights into the distributions of a variety of PE ratios in the US and Japanese markets, we look at the volatility of selected price related ratios to gain some insight into differences, if any, between the PE and Q type ratios in each market.

We use the 'standardized hinge spread' or the ratio of the third quartile minus the first quartile relative to the median in order to focus on the relative volatility of the ratios used here. This statistic was used by Black (1980). Because we are dealing with a ratio of an accounting statistic to market price low volatility suggests a consistent relation between the two measures. Over time, if one of two distributions summarized in this nature is less volatile than the other, then the statistic making up that distribution is, on average, a more consistent measure of stock prices. [11]

4. Results of the tests

In this section we test the volatility of selected price related ratios in the US and Japanese markets. We also look at the impact of adjusting US and Japanese PE ratios so that they reflect only those aspects of firms which are not systematically different.

4.1. Volatility tests

These tests serve two purposes. First, they replicate and extend Black's analysis (1980). Second, insofar as book value asset based measures approximate, in concept, the asset based valuation arguments associated with the Q ratio, they give some sense of the relative consistency of earnings versus asset based valuation measures in the two markets.

Table 1 contains the standardized hinge spreads of the Earnings–Price (EP), Book Value of Assets–Price (BP), and Net Book Value of Equity–Price (NBP) ratios for each year of the sample period. [12] Based on this statistic, the EP and NBP ratios are less volatile on average than the BP ratio for US firms.

---

[11] No causality is implied here. This is an association test between alternative measures found useful or thought to be useful in a variety of equity markets. The hinge ratio does not measure the consistency of individual corporate PE ratios over time.

[12] The volatility of the EP measures are based on earnings statistics common to both markets. The EP ratio is based on net income before extraordinary items. The Japanese version of this measure is called ordinary income.

J.S. Bildersee et al. / International price–earnings ratio 269

Table 1
Volatilities [a] of EP, BP and NBP ratios.

Year	EP ratio		BP ratio		NBP ratio	
	Japan	US	Japan	US	Japan	US
76	1.0163	0.6135	0.8168	0.9369	0.3505	0.6449
77	0.7414	0.5386	1.0555	0.8925	0.4445	0.5913
78	0.7677	0.5800	1.0307	0.9681	0.3808	0.6170
79	0.7566	0.5968	1.1125	1.1580	0.4659	0.7180
80	0.8504	0.7748	0.9484	1.4029	0.5480	0.8866
81	0.7883	0.6633	1.0106	1.1610	0.5026	0.7419
82	0.7383	0.8204	1.0069	1.1758	0.4668	0.7284
83	0.9138	0.8577	1.0333	1.1962	0.5523	0.7000
84	0.8754	0.7163	1.1536	0.9896	0.6133	0.5939
85	0.7539	0.7917	1.1949	1.0127	0.6796	0.6191
86	0.8804	0.6846	0.9648	0.8545	0.6838	0.6409
87	0.8811	0.6788	0.8261	0.9018	0.7500	0.6913
Avg	0.8303	0.6930	1.0128	1.0542	0.5365	0.6811

[a] Volatility is measured as third quartile minus first quartile divided by median.
[b] The EP Ratio is based on net income before tax and extraordinary items. The Japanese version of this earnings number is called ordinary income.
[c] The BP ratio is based on the book value of total asset.
[d] The NBP ratio is based on the book value of equity.

The volatility of the EP ratio is always less than BP volatility and is less than NBP volatility in seven of 12 years including every year from 1976 through 1981. In those six years EP volatility averages 11% less than NBP volatility. This is consistent with the results reported by Black (1980). This pattern reverses from 1982 through 1987 when the volatility of the EP ratio is greater than that for the NBP ratio every year except 1987.

Contrary to the US case, the NBP ratio is the least volatile ratio for the Japanese firms. Moreover, unlike the US case, the NBP volatility is lower in every year for Japanese firms. [13] This is consistent with Wakasugi's argument (1988c) that an asset value approach is appropriate in Japanese equity markets.

There are some intriguing trends in the US and Japanese volatility measures. After peaking in 1983, the volatility of the US EP ratio falls through 1987. Likewise, US NBP volatility has fallen since 1980. Moreover, the US NBP ratio has been less volatile than the EP ratio during the second half of the sample period contrary to Black (1980). This may represent the beginning of a change in our valuation system. One is tempted to overlook the differences between book value and market value and speculate that the improved performance of this surrogate for the Q ratio represents an interna-

[13] A two-tailed difference of the means test indicates that the volatility statistic for the NBP ratio is significantly lower than that for the EP ratio at the 1% level.

Table 2
Comparison of PE ratios before adjustments. [a]

Year	Japanese firms			US firms		
	N	Mean	Median	N	Mean	Median
76	303	106.78	21.83	750	15.59	7.92
77	353	38.25	24.00	770	10.72	7.58
78	342	32.85	25.35	788	8.99	6.76
79	398	36.59	24.95	799	10.19	6.60
80	435	45.39	18.61	796	13.79	8.22
81	447	49.47	21.74	806	13.13	7.41
82	434	39.52	21.62	753	17.27	10.56
83	427	35.88	26.01	807	26.07	11.93
84	433	59.38	33.26	847	14.83	9.72
85	477	61.11	32.11	796	19.93	12.62
86	474	75.64	44.03	851	35.97	13.75
87	462	111.99	53.32	953	25.57	11.34

[a] PE ratios are based on earnings after tax.

tionalization of valuation methodologies for the US relative to Japan. Of course, this may be due to chance.

There is also some support for the internationalization of the financial markets in the Japanese results. The volatility of the Japanese NBP ratio increases throughout the sample period and is now at approximately the same level as US volatility. However, the volatility of the Japanese EP ratio, although higher in 1987 than during the late 1970s, appears to have stabilized. The gap between EP and NBP volatilities has diminished considerably suggesting that differences in the relative consistency of the two measures is narrowing. Apparently, there are forces in both markets causing any differences in valuation, after adjustments for accounting and financial policy differences, to decrease.

4.2. PE ratios in the US and Japanese markets

Table 2 shows PE ratios using after tax net income for both countries before any adjustments are made. Both the mean and the median PE ratios of Japanese firms are always greater than those of US firms. [14] Difference of the

---

[14] The PE ratios presented in table 2 and in later tables are equal weighted averages of PE ratios for individual firms without losses for the year in question. If a firm has low earnings for any reason, then it will have an abnormally high PE ratio. Market average ratios such as those used for Value Line are based on a market price divided by market earnings. Effectively, they are value weighted. They are usually lower than those presented here. However, in a given year, the value weighted ratio is one observation without a standard deviation for testing purposes and adjustments applied here are done on a firm by firm basis.

means tests indicate that the ratios are significantly higher than those of US firms at the 1% level. [15]

(A) PE ratios and earnings adjustments

Table 3, Panels A and B, reports various PE ratios using earnings numbers adjusted for taxes, depreciation, extraordinary items, interest expense and some appropriate combinations. Adjustments involve adding back those items to after tax earnings so that the resulting ratio is no longer affected by those activities that are systematically different in the two countries. This results in ratios that have been neutralized for the different policies, but which now reflect smaller portions of the firms' activities. Adjustments removing the impact of taxes (PE2) and removing the impacts of both taxes and extraordinary items to calculate ordinary income (PE0) reduce the gap between the two countries. But, substantial differences remain. Additional adjustments are made for depreciation expense (PE3), interest expense (PE4) and depreciation and interest expenses (PE5).

Panel C summarizes the percent differences between the comparative average ratios each year of the two countries. During the period the average PE ratio is 242% greater in Japan than in the US and the corresponding median ratio is 206% greater. Adjustments removing depreciation and or interest expense cause the difference in the average ratios to fall to within approximately 30% to 80% of each other. [16] This is consistent with the notion that the PE ratio difference between the two countries is due primarily to differences in leverage and depreciation policies. However, the average Japanese PE ratios at any point in time are significantly greater than US ratios irrespective of the associated adjustment.

The volatility of the adjusted EP ratios of both countries is in table 4. Panel A shows that for US firms, earnings–price ratios based on earnings after taxes (EP1) is less volatile than the NBP ratio from table 1. The other adjusted ratios, including those adjusted for interest expense, are more volatile than the NBP ratio.

Panel B offers two perspectives of the Japanese equity markets. First, the volatilities of the EP3, EP4, and EP5 ratios approximate those for the corresponding ratios in the US markets suggesting similarities in valuation of operations in both markets. Second, these similarities, while symptomatic of an internationalized market, are limited because none of the adjustments

---

[15] Due to the asymmetry of the distributions of PE ratios and the meaninglessness and exclusions of PE ratios for firms with losses the difference of the means tests are suspect. Due to this asymmetry we offer medians in addition to means for each distribution.

[16] Due to the question of the precise timing of fiscal years mentioned earlier, this test was repeated comparing US data with the Japanese data of the following March rather than the preceding March. The results are like those described in the text except that the differences between the medians of the ratios adjusted for interest expense were about 6% and the differences between the means were slightly less than those reported in table 3.

Table 3
Adjusted PE ratios. [a]

Year	N	PE1 Mean	PE1 Med	PE0 Mean	PE0 Med	PE2 Mean	PE2 Med	PE3 Mean	PE3 Med	PE4 Mean	PE4 Med	PE5 Mean	PE5 Med
Panel A: US firms													
76	750	15.6	7.9	6.2	4.8	6.2	4.8	4.1	3.4	4.7	3.7	3.5	2.8
77	770	10.7	7.6	6.0	4.4	6.0	4.4	3.7	3.1	4.3	3.4	3.2	2.6
78	788	9.0	6.8	5.6	4.1	5.6	4.1	3.5	2.9	4.1	3.1	2.9	2.4
79	799	10.2	6.6	6.2	4.2	6.2	4.2	4.1	3.0	4.3	3.2	3.4	2.5
80	796	13.8	8.2	10.0	5.1	10.0	5.1	5.9	3.5	6.8	3.8	4.8	2.8
81	806	13.1	7.4	12.5	4.7	12.6	4.7	5.1	3.3	5.6	3.4	4.2	2.6
82	753	17.3	10.6	16.8	6.3	16.8	6.3	6.4	4.3	7.6	4.8	5.2	3.4
83	807	-26.1	12.0	19.4	7.3	19.0	7.4	6.6	5.0	8.6	5.5	5.4	4.1
84	847	14.8	9.7	10.3	5.9	10.0	5.9	5.5	4.0	6.4	4.5	4.5	3.3
85	796	19.9	12.6	25.0	7.7	25.1	7.9	6.6	5.1	8.0	5.8	5.5	4.1
86	851	36.0	13.7	18.1	8.3	18.6	8.4	7.3	5.6	8.7	6.3	6.0	4.7
87	953	25.6	11.3	16.0	7.3	16.1	7.3	6.6	4.8	7.6	5.6	5.3	4.0
Panel B: Japanese firms (not adjusted for cross-holdings)													
76	303	106.8	21.8	43.8	12.3	18.0	11.8	7.4	6.5	5.4	4.7	4.0	3.4
77	353	38.2	24.0	18.9	11.1	24.6	11.9	7.0	6.5	5.5	4.9	4.1	3.6
78	342	32.9	25.3	18.5	12.1	16.4	12.6	7.8	7.1	6.6	6.1	4.8	4.4
79	398	36.6	24.9	18.5	11.4	19.3	11.8	8.6	7.1	7.6	6.6	5.5	4.7
80	435	45.4	18.6	19.0	9.1	16.7	9.5	7.3	5.7	5.9	5.2	4.4	3.7
81	447	49.5	21.7	19.0	10.5	16.8	11.1	7.4	6.6	5.7	5.2	4.3	3.8
82	434	39.5	21.6	21.4	9.6	13.1	9.8	6.6	5.7	5.5	5.3	4.0	3.7
83	427	35.9	26.0	22.8	12.1	17.4	11.8	8.4	6.9	7.1	6.1	5.0	4.3
84	433	59.4	33.3	33.0	15.4	26.4	15.7	10.7	8.5	9.8	7.7	6.8	5.3
85	477	62.1	32.1	24.7	13.7	23.3	14.4	10.4	8.4	9.9	8.0	7.0	5.7
86	474	75.6	44.0	38.9	21.0	31.8	20.8	14.6	11.7	14.3	11.8	9.6	8.1
87	462	112.0	53.3	38.3	22.9	51.8	24.4	17.2	13.1	18.0	15.1	11.8	9.7

Panel C: Percent differences (Japanese PE ratios / US PE ratios) [b]

76	585%	176%	606%	156%	190%	146%	80%	91%	15%	27%	14%	21%
77	257	216	215	152	310	170	89	110	28	44	28	38
78	266	272	230	195	193	207	123	145	61	97	66	83
79	165	277	198	171	211	181	110	137	77	106	62	88
80	229	127	90	78	67	86	24	63	−13	37	−8	32
81	278	193	52	123	33	136	45	100	2	53	2	46
82	128	104	27	52	−22	56	3	33	−28	10	−23	9
83	38	117	18	66	−8	159	27	38	−17	11	−7	5
84	301	243	220	161	164	166	95	113	53	71	51	61
85	212	155	−1	78	−7	82	58	65	24	38	27	39
86	110	221	115	153	71	148	100	109	64	87	60	72
87	338	372	139	214	222	234	161	173	137	170	123	143
Avg	242%	206%	159%	133%	119%	148%	76%	98%	34%	61%	33%	53%

[a] In computing the PE ratios here, the following denominators are used:

PE1 – net income after tax,

PE0 – ordinary income (income before tax and extraordinary items),

PE2 – net income before tax,

PE3 – ordinary income + depreciation expense,

PE4 – ordinary income + interest expense,

PE5 – ordinary income + depreciation expense + interest expense.

[b] One hundred percent has been subtracted from each statistic so that equal Japanese and US ratios have a difference of 0%. Numbers less than zero indicate that the US ratio is greater than the corresponding Japanese ratio.

Table 4
Volatility of adjusted EP ratios. [a]

Year	EP1	EP0	EP2	EP3	EP4	EP5
Panel A: US firms						
76	0.4857	0.6135	0.6111	0.6195	0.6159	0.6260
77	0.4767	0.5386	0.5350	0.5306	0.5217	0.5520
78	0.4989	0.5800	0.5684	0.5613	0.5869	0.6154
79	0.5973	0.5968	0.6040	0.6431	0.6746	0.7038
80	0.7666	0.7748	0.7574	0.7321	0.8916	0.9044
81	0.6556	0.6633	0.6627	0.6771	0.8086	0.7991
82	0.8823	0.8204	0.8294	0.8344	1.0922	0.9602
83	0.8129	0.8577	0.8638	0.8929	0.9829	1.0145
84	0.6935	0.7163	0.7140	0.7014	0.8626	0.8088
85	0.7577	0.7917	0.8073	0.7533	0.8964	0.8594
86	0.6339	0.6846	0.6890	0.6519	0.7455	0.7653
87	0.6460	0.6788	0.6836	0.6711	0.7175	0.7367
Avg	0.6589	0.6930	0.6938	0.6891	0.7830	0.7788
Panel B: Japanese firms						
76	0.6940	1.0163	0.8874	0.7133	0.7148	0.6588
77	0.5891	0.7414	0.7026	0.6510	0.7699	0.8312
78	0.6251	0.7677	0.7294	0.5722	0.7402	0.7728
79	0.7802	0.7566	0.8161	0.6540	0.7833	0.7755
80	0.8714	0.8504	0.8531	0.7386	0.7323	0.7249
81	0.7994	0.7883	0.8597	0.7597	0.7879	0.8222
82	0.7522	0.7383	0.7525	0.6070	0.6991	0.6342
83	0.8351	0.9138	0.8275	0.6917	0.7924	0.7547
84	0.8536	0.8754	0.8264	0.7407	0.9393	0.9745
85	0.8410	0.7539	0.8104	0.7204	0.8832	0.9188
86	0.9186	0.8804	0.9291	0.7843	0.8033	0.8059
87	0.8974	0.8811	0.9042	0.7636	0.8471	0.7593
Avg	0.7881	0.8303	0.8249	0.6997	0.7911	0.7861

[a] In computing the EP ratios for this table, the following earnings numbers are used:
EP1 – net income after tax,
EP0 – ordinary income (income before tax and extraordinary items) (as reported in table 1),
EP2 – net income before tax,
EP3 – ordinary income + depreciation expense,
EP4 – ordinary income + interest expense,
EP5 – ordinary income + depreciation expense + interest expense.

reduces volatility to the level of the NBP ratio. If Japanese equity investors rely as heavily on earnings numbers in measuring market values as they seem to on net asset values, then one or more of the adjusted earnings numbers would have shown greater stability than the NBP ratio. That is, after removing a major accounting choice and removing the impact of financial policies the ratios begin to look comparable but real economic differences may be the source of remaining differences.

Table 5
Average debt–book equity ratios. [a]

Year	Japanes firms				US firms			
	N	Current	Long term	Total	N	Current	Long term	Total
76	303	3.434	1.367	4.800	750	0.602	0.722	1.324
77	353	3.546	1.479	5.025	770	0.590	0.714	1.304
78	342	4.520	1.587	6.107	788	0.681	0.729	1.410
79	398	4.225	1.399	5.624	799	0.703	0.712	1.415
80	435	4.466	1.398	5.864	796	0.690	0.737	1.427
81	447	3.815	1.388	5.203	806	0.626	0.682	1.308
82	434	3.469	1.183	4.652	753	0.619	0.657	1.276
83	427	3.561	1.203	4.764	807	0.676	0.674	1.350
84	433	3.776	1.175	4.951	847	0.993	0.966	1.959
85	477	3.815	1.161	4.976	796	0.866	0.853	1.719
86	474	3.241	1.031	4.272	851	0.896	0.857	1.753
87	462	3.221	1.096	4.317	953	0.936	0.738	1.674
Avg		3.757	1.289	5.046		0.740	0.753	1.493

[a] From 1983 on, Japanese firms have included an item called 'Special Reserve' in owners' equity. To be consistent with this, the current and long-term debt–equity ratios reported above are based on current and long-term liabilities divided by owners' equity which includes the 'Special Reserve'. Our data analysis shows that the 'Special Reserves' are 3.4% to 8.6% of owners' equity from 1976 to 1982. If firms have missing data on 'Special Reserve', then the special reserves for those firms are set to 0.

(B) PE ratios and leverage ratios

Interest expense adjustments were made above to recognize and remove differential debt policies from the analysis. Table 5 summarizes the mean debt–book equity ratios of firms in both countries and outlines the accounting impact of those differences in respective debt policies. Consistent with results previously obtained by Choi et al. (1983) and Tschoegl (1985) the ratios for the US firms are always lower than those observed for Japanese firms. The average aggregate leverage ratio for Japanese firms is 5.046 for the sample period while the corresponding US ratio is 1.493.

The mean ratios for Japanese firms are 3.757 and 1.289 for current and long-term leverage, respectively. The corresponding ratios for US firms are 0.740 and 0.753. High current debt for Japanese firms reflects their tendency to borrow from banks. However, both current and long-term debt ratios have declined from peaks during the late 1970s. US firms have relatively low leverage ratios throughout the period. However, consistent with increasing American reliance on debt, the current leverage ratio has risen since the early 1980s while the long-term ratio peaked in the mid 1980s. Additionally, the ratios suggest an increasing reliance on short-term debt relative to long-term

Table 6
Spearman rank correlation coefficients (PE ratio and debt–equity ratio).

Year	PE1	PE0	PE2	PE3	PE4	PE5
Panel A: Japanese firms						
76	0.16879	0.13331	0.12906	−0.05681 [c]	−0.67539	−0.63593
77	0.19458	0.16110	0.15241	−0.14867	−0.71039	−0.68220
78	0.25194	0.18188	0.15462	−0.14197	−0.67453	−0.65467
79	0.19277	0.15761	0.16323	−0.05469 [c]	−0.56391	−0.53948
80	0.23441	0.23981	0.26764	0.06822 [c]	−0.47851	−0.46706
81	0.24453	0.24731	0.24418	0.01799 [c]	−0.61822	−0.60197
82	0.39595	0.31327	0.33490	0.05913 [c]	−0.53943	−0.52640
83	0.24268	0.23253	0.19723	−0.05947 [c]	−0.61708	−0.59005
84	0.15395	0.08287 [b]	0.10803	−0.16798	−0.64346	−0.62472
85	0.13255	0.09442	0.12678	−0.12214	−0.55761	−0.55106
86	0.24117	0.12836	0.18497	−0.01220 [c]	−0.44943	−0.41865
87	0.28171	0.11908	0.20177	0.07587 [c]	−0.35473	−0.27248
Panel B: US firms						
76	−0.32436	−0.21939	−0.21252	−0.35624	−0.52418	−0.54101
77	−0.22814	−0.12016	−0.11508	−0.26350	−0.45886	−0.48896
78	−0.25948	−0.15936	−0.15312	−0.30076	−0.49343	−0.51939
79	−0.19087	−0.09303	−0.08878	−0.25622	−0.43634	−0.47021
80	−0.28587	−0.22225	−0.22063	−0.35685	−0.52857	−0.54473
81	−0.31240	−0.22752	−0.22531	−0.34411	−0.54072	−0.54387
82	−0.39236	−0.34475	−0.33813	−0.47177	−0.63273	−0.65325
83	−0.33308	−0.31801	−0.31536	−0.46924	−0.60794	−0.64443
84	−0.28994	−0.29476	−0.28948	−0.42408	−0.59904	−0.62527
85	−0.28555	−0.31832	−0.30738	−0.44085	−0.60319	−0.61962
86	−0.18330	−0.22393	−0.22195	−0.35121	−0.51717	−0.53598
87	−0.22815	−0.23722	−0.23248	−0 40647	−0.53729	−0.57160

[a] The vast bulk of the rank correlations, including all but three in panel B, are significant at the 0.01% level. (Although the number of observations varies from year to year a correlation of approximately 0.10 (0.20) is necessary to achieve significance at the 1% (0.01%) level in panel A. For definitions of PE1–PE5, see table 3.
[b] *Not significant* at the 5% level.
[c] *Not significant* at the 10% level.

debt in the US markets. The decrease in aggregate Japanese leverage and the increase in aggregate US leverage plus the apparent reliance on short-term financing are again consistent with the notion of the internationalization of these equity markets relative to each other.

Table 6 has rank correlations between PE ratios and corporate leverage in the US and Japan. PE ratios after interest is added back (PE4 and PE5) are negatively ordered relative to corporate leverage in each economy. Moreover, the rank correlations are approximately −0.50 in each economy suggesting that, as a first approximation, each market's sensitivity to operating risks within the market appears similar. [17] The negative relationship persists for all PE ratios for US firms. This is equivalent to observing a positive ranking between a firm's capitalization rate or cost of capital and leverage like that found in numerous studies of US capital markets.

Japanese PE ratios based on after tax income and on ordinary income are positively ordered with corporate leverage. That is, unlike the US case where increased corporate debt in the US is associated with increased risk and reduced PE ratios, the primary empirical effect of increased corporate debt may be to magnify corporate PE ratios. Alternatively, price changes due to leverage do not reflect fully risks as they would be reflected in the US market. This is consistent with the possibility that high levels of leverage (as measured in the US) do not properly measure financial and default risks in Japan due, at least in part, to differences in perceptions of leverage based risk. These differences may reflect cultural and business differences as suggested in Choi, et al. (1983).

(C) PE ratios and cross-holdings

A possible explanation of differences in PE ratios and differences in perceptions of financial risk is the cross-holdings of securities in Japan. It has been widely reported that cross-holdings in Japan far exceed those in the US market.

Here, we consider alternative cross-holdings measures and then approximate the proportion of cross-holdings associated with the firm as the minimum value of investment by the company in other companies relative to net assets or investments by other companies in the company relative to the firm's shares outstanding. [18]

Table 7 provides distributions of cross-holdings of the Japanese firms. Panel A is based on measuring cross-holdings from the asset side. Cross-holdings are measured as the percent of investments in other firms relative to net asset values. Using this measure mean cross-holding of Japanese sample firms remains at about 30% throughout the sample period. Throughout the period over 10% of the cross-holdings are over 50% of equity. Based on this measure cross-holdings remain stable throughout the period.

Panel B looks at cross-holdings from the equity side. It is based on shares held by Japanese business interests as a percent of shares outstanding. Cross-holdings are measured as the shares held by all Japanese governments,

---

[17] Since this reflects an ordering based on corporate reports, it does not reflect on the linearities of any relationships nor even on the relative structures and driving forces generating the similar rankings.

[18] The ratio of cross-holdings used here has to be viewed as an estimate. For example, shares are issued by the firm at different prices. Also, if some cross-held shares are bought in the secondary market rather than from the company, then the market value of those shares will be reflected in the investment account used in the numerator of the ratio while the book value of the same shares will be reflected in the denominator.

Table 7
Distributions of cross-holdings for Japanese firms.

Year	N	5%	25%	50%	Mean	75%	90%	Maximum
Panel A: Cross-holdings through investment in other firms [a]								
76	285	5.42%	14.85%	27.07%	32.31%	41.03%	58.75%	305.34%
77	334	6.12	14.74	27.09	33.75	43.41	64.92	225.03
78	327	5.47	14.23	26.95	39.47	39.43	61.14	2309.17
79	384	5.65	14.08	25.18	35.96	41.66	60.68	944.86
80	421	6.22	14.54	27.21	36.03	44.11	65.85	670.49
81	437	5.49	13.84	23.86	34.29	39.31	63.64	638.42
82	422	5.27	12.83	22.54	30.77	36.92	57.05	468.58
83	414	5.30	12.38	21.68	32.40	37.17	60.48	439.02
84	425	5.45	10.97	21.68	32.29	38.15	62.54	210.09
85	473	4.41	11.04	20.95	31.13	38.31	61.42	325.66
86	472	4.56	10.84	20.17	29.22	35.69	57.05	201.96
87	459	4.66	10.91	19.41	30.11	37.15	61.76	231.35
Panel B: Cross-holdings reflected in shares held by other firms [b]								
76	285	33.26%	53.07%	64.38%	62.07%	71.93%	81.66%	95.36%
77	334	35.03	54.33	64.51	63.04	73.48	81.72	92.16
78	327	35.69	55.16	64.52	63.10	72.67	80.50	92.27
79	384	39.69	57.09	66.52	64.86	74.81	81.64	92.25
80	421	36.51	56.55	65.94	64.34	74.27	81.39	92.05
81	437	37.47	56.11	65.67	63.94	73.31	79.76	91.66
82	422	37.85	55.30	65.19	63.23	72.75	79.27	91.66
83	414	38.55	55.62	65.55	64.14	73.74	79.74	92.62
84	425	39.23	56.95	66.90	65.18	75.11	79.72	92.51
85	473	44.17	58.82	68.24	66.68	76.31	81.89	92.50
86	472	44.35	60.98	69.14	67.82	76.26	83.01	91.72
87	459	42.92	63.56	70.39	69.08	77.77	83.64	89.38
Panel C: Cross-holdings through net *investment in other firms* [c]								
76	285	5.42%	14.18%	26.86%	29.84%	40.36%	56.58%	95.36%
77	334	6.12	14.74	27.09	30.46	42.44	60.53	91.21
78	327	5.47	14.23	26.95	29.40	38.70	56.02	91.82
79	384	5.65	14.08	25.18	29.66	40.06	58.92	92.12
80	421	6.22	14.54	27.21	30.59	42.07	61.08	91.98
81	437	5.49	13.84	23.86	28.60	38.85	58.41	91.66
82	422	5.27	12.83	22.54	27.15	36.65	54.39	91.66
83	414	5.30	12.38	21.68	27.22	36.59	54.73	92.62
84	425	5.45	10.97	21.68	27.31	37.87	57.43	92.51
85	473	4.41	11.04	20.95	26.70	37.88	57.94	92.50
86	472	4.56	10.84	20.17	25.89	35.45	56.11	91.72
87	459	4.66	10.91	19.41	26.36	36.83	60.82	89.34

[a] These cross-holdings are computed as the long-term investment in other firms divided by book equity.
[b] These cross-holdings are computed as the number of shares held by other companies divided by the number of shares issued.
[c] These cross-holdings are computed as the minimum of long-term investment in other firms divided by book equity and the number of shares held by other companies divided by the number of shares issued.

financial institutions, investment trusts, securities companies and business corporations over total shares issued. These numbers tell a different story. The mean ratios are typically twice as large as those in Panel A. They indicate that cross-holdings have increased from 62% on average in 1976 to 69% in 1987. All fractiles in the table also show increases. These results are particularly intriguing as they run counter to the popular impression that the Japanese markets are becoming more internationalized. [19]

Neither one of these measures are perfect. Even the measure based on shares measures cross-holdings as the maximum possible cross ownership. However, it does not necessarily measure cross ownership where companies own portions of each other or of a small group of firms thereby being an effective barrier to activities such as hostile takeovers and mergers. [20]

Panel C contains the minimum value of investment by the company in other companies relative to net assets or investments by other companies in the company relative to the firm's shares outstanding. This approximates the amount of investments in other firms that are balanced by equivalent obligations to other firms estimating true cross ownership as opposed to the proportion of shares held by domestic firms. All cross-holding adjustments are based on the data used in Panel C.

Tables 8 and 9 contain the results of including firm by firm cross-holdings information in the analysis. Table 8 contains mean and median PE0 and PE1 ratios adjusted for approximate cross-holdings based on eq. (1). The adjustment for cross-holdings decreases PE ratios from 25% to 40% on average during the sample period. The other ratios behave the same way. [21]

Table 9 contains the percent differences between Japanese PE ratios after adjustments for cross-holdings and corresponding US PE ratios from table 3, Panel A. Removing the impact of cross-holdings reduces the differences in the ratios between the markets. The average difference in the mean PE1 ratio is 128%. However, after interest is added back the difference falls, on average, to 7%. After all adjustments this difference averages 1%. Further, US PE ratios were greater in 7 of the 12 years. The results are the same even if investment income is subtracted from earnings included as part of the adjustments.

It appears that, on average, adjustment for differences in the Japanese business environment from the US environment as represented by estimated

[19] We also looked at cross-holdings based on investment income relative to ordinary income. Accounting for investment income varies from firm to firm and investment to investment. Additionally, ordinary income fluctuates from period to period so this measure is more volatile than the other measure.

[20] For example, each of two firms may issue 30% of their shares to a third firm which, in turn, has no shares held by the first two corporations. Although there is, on average, 20% ownership of firms by other firms, there is no cross ownership.

[21] If investment income is subtracted from earnings and resulting extreme observations are removed, then the results are the same as those documented here. However, the actual adjustments are smaller.

Table 8

PE ratios [a] of Japanese firms adjusted for cross-holdings and results of matched pair mean difference *T*-Test.

Yr	N	PE1				PE0			
		Unadjusted		Adjusted for cross-holdings		Unadjusted		Adjusted for cross-holdings	
		Mean	Median	Mean	Median	Mean	Median	Mean	Median
76	285	111.67	21.83	62.24 [b]	15.12	33.60	12.27	20.59	8.16
77	334	32.86	23.85	22.90	16.22	17.97	11.09	11.77	8.08
78	327	32.87	25.08	22.41	16.88	18.76	12.11	13.02	8.41
79	384	36.14	24.98	24.26	17.65	18.15	11.37	12.49	8.09
80	421	46.19	18.61	29.91	12.75	18.63	9.05	12.56	6.06
81	437	49.65	21.74	35.23	15.10	18.73	10.46	11.98	7.51
82	422	39.64	21.30	26.50	15.00	21.39	9.51	14.83	6.82
83	414	35.79	26.08	24.86	18.15	22.85	12.10	16.43	8.88
84	425	59.07	33.26	40.01	23.39	33.05	15.41	25.00	10.97
85	473	61.35	31.99	41.61	22.56	24.58	13.66	17.36	10.35
86	472	75.68	44.03	53.07	31.53	38.92	20.99	27.11	15.06
87	459	111.66	53.20	72.03	39.84	38.11	22.86	26.55	17.85

[a] For definition of PE ratios, see table 3. The vast bulk of the difference of the means tests are significant at the 0.01% level.

[b] *Not significant* at the 10% level.

cross ownership, removes the remaining differences between PE ratios in the two markets. However, there seems to be consecutive periods when the adjusted Japanese ratio is greater than its American counterpart. Moreover, there are consecutive periods when this reverses. This pattern suggests that the relation between US and Japanese PEs varies with changes in relative economic conditions.

5. Conclusion

Differences in volatility of alternative ratios are consistent with previous conclusions that the US market is based primarily on earnings valuation while the Japanese market is based primarily on asset valuation. However, there are suggestions that differences between the markets are narrowing. Trends in the data, while not conclusive, point towards the relative internationalization or increasing similarity of the two markets.

Adjustment for systematic policy based differences explains some, but not all, of the differences in PE ratios between the US and Japanese markets. Since the adjustments are primarily for financial and depreciation policies, this suggests that investors in both countries value operating flows in parallel ways.

Financial obligations seem to be viewed differently. There is some evidence that the markets react differently to interest obligations. However, adjustments

J.S. Bildersee et al. / International price–earnings ratio 281

Table 9

Relative PE ratios after earnings and cross-holdings adjustments [percent differences (Japanese PE ratios/US PE ratios) adjusted for earnings and cross-holdings]. [a]

Year	PE1		PE0		PE2		PE3		PE4		PE5	
	Mean	Med	Mean	Med	Mean	Med	Mean	Med	Mean	Med	Mean	Med
76	299%	92%	232%	70%	99%	64%	26%	27%	-14%	-3%	-15%	-13%
77	114	113	96	84	106	85	32	41	-3	3	-4	2
78	149	148	133	105	104	106	60	74	23	50	28	36
79	138	167	101	93	103	99	47	71	32	49	20	35
80	117	55	25	19	12	26	-17	13	-38	-6	-35	-8
81	169	104	-4	60	-12	62	1	32	-25	-11	-24	2
82	53	42	-12	8	-48	11	-28	-3	-46	-23	-42	-19
83	-5	51	-15	22	-38	17	-7	0	-38	-19	-29	-22
84	170	141	143	86	88	84	42	52	19	24	18	23
85	109	79	-31	34	-37	31	15	22	-4	0	-2	0
86	47	130	50	81	18	77	48	53	27	40	24	31
87	181	253	66	145	115	142	83	103	80	104	67	84
Avg	128%	115%	65%	67%	43%	67%	25%	40%	7%	17%	1%	13%

[a] For definitions of PE ratios, see table 3.

based on a major difference in business environments eliminated most of the remaining differences between Japanese and US PE ratios. Of course, these are statements based on averages that may not be sensitive to changing relationships between these two markets and other markets nor to period to period changes in economic conditions. Studies evaluating associations between measures of operating performance, such as growth and business risk, and PE ratios and adjusting for differences in the distribution of assets across industrial, retailing and service industries in each country and studies of relative performance are appropriate extensions of this work.

References

Beaver, W.H. and R.E. Dukes, 1973, Tax allocation and depreciation methods: some empirical results, The Accounting Review, July, 549–559.

Beaver, W.H. and D. Morse, 1978, What determines price–earnings ratios?, Financial Analysts Journal, July/Aug., 65–76.

Black, F., 1980, The magic in earnings: Economic earnings versus accounting earnings, Financial Analysts Journal, Nov./Dec., 19–24.

Choi, F.D.S., H. Hino, S.K. Min, S.O. Nam, J. Ujiie and A.I. Stonehill, 1983, Analyzing foreign financial statements: The use and misuse of international ratio analysis, Journal of International Business Studies, Spring/Summer, 113–131.

Hodder, J.E. and A.E. Tschoegl, 1985, Some aspects of Japanese corporate finance, Journal of Financial and Quantitative Analysis, June, 173–191.

Jacobs, B.L and K.N. Levy, 1988, Disentangling equity return regularities: New insights and investment opportunities, Financial Analysts Journal, May/June, 18–43.

Japan Securities Research Institute, 1988, Report on Japan's stock price level, Oct.

Ozanian, M.K. and A. Ourusoff, 1989, The FW international 500, Financial World, March 7, 78–79.

Stickell, S.C., 1980, A comparative analysis of the relationships of price to earnings and price to book values, Master's thesis (MIT, Cambridge, MA).

Suzuki, O. and S. Mashimo, 1988, An international comparison of accounting systems and measuring standards for stock price levels, Report on Japan's stock price level, Oct., Ch. 3.

Viner, A., 1988, Inside Japanese financial markets (Dow Jones–Irwin, Homewood, IL).

Wakasugi, T., 1988a, General remarks, in: Report on Japan's stock price level Oct.

Wakasugi, T., 1988b, Reconsidering Japan's stock prices, Report on Japan's stock price level, Oct. Ch. 1.

Wakasugi, T., 1988c, Are stock prices too high in Japan?, Report on Japan's stock price level, Oct. Ch. 2.

Yasuda, O. and T. Lin, The boost effect of cross-shareholding on a P/E ratio, in: Report on Japan's stock price level, Oct.

Yoda, T., 1987, Tobin's Q, Japanese equities research memorandum (Daiwa Securities, Tokyo) March.

[13]

Japan and the World Economy 5 (1993) 51–72
North-Holland

Achieving comparability of US and Japanese financial statement data

Paul R. Brown

Stern School of Business New York University New York, NY 10012, USA

Virginia E. Soybel, Clyde P. Stickney

The Amos Tuck School of Business Administration Dartmouth College Hanover, NH 03755, USA

Received October 1991; accepted April 1992

Abstract: This paper develops a methodology for restating Japanese and U.S. financial statement data at the firm level to a comparable reporting basis. We apply the procedure to a sample of Japanese and U.S. firms for fiscal years 1985 through 1988. Previous studies which have investigated the disparity between U.S. and Japanese price-earnings ratios (PERs) have concluded that different accounting principles explain between one-half and virtually all of the difference between U.S. and Japanese PERs. In contrast, our results indicate that adjusting for different accounting principles explains very little of the difference in PERs.

Keywords: Price-earnings (PE) ratios; Japan, U.S. and Japanese financial reporting practices; Japanese accounting methods

1. Introduction

Several recent studies have investigated why Japanese price-earnings ratios (PERs) are so much higher than U.S. PERs (Aron, 1990; Bildersee et al., 1990; French and Poterba, 1991; Officer and Isgro, 1990). These studies have examined both differences in accounting principles, such as depreciation methods, and differences in business practices, such as the use of financial leverage or the extent of intercorporate cross-holdings, as possible reasons for the differences in PERs between the two countries.

This paper presents a methodology for restating U.S. and Japanese financial statement data to a comparable basis. Unlike earlier studies, most of the restatements we make are to U.S. financial statement data to achieve greater consistency with Japanese generally accepted accounting principles

Correspondence to: Paul R. Brown, Stern School of Business, New York University, New York, NY 10003, USA. Tel.: (212) 9980019.

(GAAP). Restating U.S. financial statements is usually easier than restating Japanese financial statements because of the extensive notes that accompany U.S. financial statements. We do make one adjustment, however, to the Japanese financial statement data. Thus, the resulting data reflect a blend of U.S. and Japanese accounting principles. Also unlike earlier studies, we make these adjustments at the level of the individual firm rather than at an aggregate level for all firms.

Given comparable financial statement data, the researcher can then focus attention on economic, strategic, institutional, and cultural reasons for differences in PERs or other financial ratios. We apply the restatement procedure to a sample of U.S. and Japanese firms in 13 industries for fiscal years 1985 through 1988. While other studies have found that accounting principles explain between one-half and virtually all of the difference between U.S. and Japanese PERs, our results show that the net effect of adjusting for different accounting principles explains only a small portion of the difference in PERs.

The next section of the paper identifies the principal differences between U.S. and Japanese GAAP. Section 3 reviews previous research that attempted to reconcile U.S. and Japanese PERs for alternative accounting principles. Section 4 describes our restatement methodology, while Section 5 presents the results of restating PERs and other financial ratios for a sample of firms to a comparable reporting basis. Section 6 sets out our conclusions.

2. Summary of alternative GAAP

Table 1 summarizes the most important differences between U.S. and Japanese GAAP. Japanese GAAP emanates from two sources. The Japanese Commercial Code sets forth the required accounting by firms in their annual reports to shareholders. This annual report typically follows a strict legal definition of the entity. Regulations of the Ministry of Finance stipulate the form and content of financial statements filed with this governmental agency. These financial statements tend to follow economic entity concepts more closely, with majority-owned subsidiaries consolidated and 20% to 50%-owned intercorporate investments accounted for using the equity method. The descriptions of Japanese GAAP in Table 1 apply to both Commercial Code and Ministry of Finance requirements unless otherwise noted.

Two recent changes in Japanese GAAP have significantly narrowed the distance between U.S. and Japanese financial reporting practices. The first of these changes was the elimination in 1982 of provisions of the Japanese Commercial Code that permitted firms to use reserves liberally to stabilize reported earnings (KPMG Peat Marwick, 1989, p. 36). Secondly, since 1983, Japanese companies have been required to use the equity method, consistent with U.S. GAAP, to account for intercorporate investments of 20% to 50% ownership in filings with the Ministry of Finance; similarly, consolidated

Table 1
Summary of generally accepted accounting principles in the U.S. and Japan

	United States	Japan
Marketable securities	Lower of cost or market	Acquisition cost (unless price declines considered permanent)
Inventories-valuation	Lower of cost or market	Acquisition cost (unless recovery of price declines is considered remote)
Cost flow assumption	FIFO, LIFO, average, specific identification	FIFO, LIFO, average, specific identification
Fixed assets–valuation	Acquisition cost less depreciation	Acquisition cost less depreciation
Depreciation	Straight line, declining balance, sum-of-the-years'-digits	Straight line, declining balance, sum-of-the-years'-digits
Research and development	Expensed when incurred	Expensed when incurred or capitalized and amortized
Leases	Operating and capital lease methods	Operating lease method
Deferred taxes	Deferred tax accounting required	Book/tax conformity generally required so deferred tax accounting not an issue
Investments in securities:		
0%–20%	Lower of cost or market	Acquisition cost (unless price declines considered permanent)
20%–50%	Equity method	Commercial Code Annual Report: Acquisition cost (unless price declines considered permanent) Filings with Ministry of Finance: Equity method
Greater than 50%	Consolidation	Commercial Code Annual Report: Acquisition cost (unless price declines considered permanent) Filings with Ministry of Finance: consolidation
Corporate acquisitions	Purchase and pooling of interests methods	Purchase method
Amortization of goodwill	Amortized over maximum of 40 years	Amortized over maximum of 5 years
Foreign currency translation	All current and monetary/nonmonetary methods	Monetary/nonmonetary and current/noncurrent methods
Appropriations of retained earnings	Not generally practiced	Annual bonuses paid to directors and Commercial Code auditors charged to retained earnings; pre-tax effects of special tax incentives recognized earlier for tax than for book purposes are charged to appropriated retained earnings (credit special reserve)

Continued overleaf

Table 1 (continued)

United States	Japan
	when they originate and are transferred out of appro-priated retained earnings (debit special reserve) when they reverse

Source: The Japanese Institute of Certified Public Accountants, *Corporate Disclosure in Japan* (July, 1987); KPMG Peat Marwick, *Comparison of Japanese and U.S. Reporting and Financial Practices* (1989).

financial statements with majority-owned subsidiaries have been required since 1977 (KPMG Peat Marwick, 1989, p. 13).

Several important differences in accounting principles remain. They include inventory cost-flow assumptions, depreciation methods, the treatment of directors' and statutory auditors' bonuses, and the treatment of deferred taxes and special tax reserves.

2.1. Inventory cost–flow assumptions

Although both U.S. and Japanese GAAP allow the same cost–flow assumptions in accounting for inventory, actual practices observed in each country differ considerably. Table 2 reveals that FIFO and LIFO dominate U.S. corporate reporting whereas average and specific identification methods (included in 'other' in Table 2) dominate Japanese reporting. The combina-

Table 2
Inventory cost flow assumptions in the United States and Japan

	United States			Japan		
	1987	1988	1989	1987	1988	1989
FIFO	37%	38%	39%	10%	11%	10%
LIFO	37	36	36	6	5	6
Average	21	21	20	48	47	48
Other	5	5	5	36	37	36

	Use of LIFO in the United States		
	1987	1988	1989
All inventories	5%	5%	7%
50% or more	56	55	52
Less than 50%	22	24	27
Not determinable	17	16	14

Sources: AICPA, *Accounting Trends and Techniques*, 1990, p. 105, for U.S. data and Arthur Andersen, *Companies' Accounting and Disclosure*, 1990, for Japanese data.

Table 3
Depreciation methods in the United States and Japan

	United States			Japan		
	1987	1988	1989	1987	1988	1989
Straight-line	81%	82%	82%	5%	3%	4%
Accelerated	18	17	17	70	70	69
Combination	– [a]	– [a]	– [a]	20	¯20	20
Other	1	1	1	5	7	7

[a] Firms using a combination of straight-line and accelerated depreciation methods in the U.S. appear in both of the preceding lines, whereas in the Japanese tabulation, such firms appear only on the 'combination' line. Thus, the data are not directly comparable.
Sources: AICPA, *Accounting Trends and Techniques*, 1990, p. 24, for U.S. data and Arthur Andersen, *Companies' Accounting and Disclosure*, 1990, for Japanese data.

tion of relatively low inflation rates in the U.S. and Japan during the last five years, rapid rates of inventory turnover in Japan, and increasingly rapid rates of inventory turnover in the U.S. suggest that differences in inventory cost–flow assumptions should be of little consequence. In fact, however, the magnitude of cost of goods sold relative to sales means that small changes in cost of goods sold can significantly affect net income. One cannot convert a FIFO or average cost firm to LIFO because LIFO layers cannot be built ex post. One can, however, convert U.S. firms from LIFO to FIFO using the required disclosures of the FIFO or replacement cost of beginning and year-end inventories, an adjustment which enables us to achieve greater comparability of U.S. and Japanese financial statement data.

2.2. Depreciation method

Table 3 sets out depreciation methods used for financial reporting in the U.S. and Japan. The dominant depreciation practices observed in each country are:

	United States	Japan
Financial reporting	Straight-line	Accelerated
Tax reporting	Accelerated	Accelerated

The overwhelming use of accelerated depreciation methods for financial reporting in Japan is explained by a tax requirement that a firm's depreciation method for tax purposes conform to its depreciation method for reporting purposes. To achieve comparability of U.S. and Japanese financial statement data, we must either convert U.S. firms to an accelerated basis or convert Japanese firms to a straight-line basis. As discussed in a later section, we restate U.S. financial statement data to an accelerated depreciation basis using information on the average life and growth rate in depreciable assets.

2.3. Bonuses to directors and statutory auditors

Japanese GAAP charges bonuses paid to directors and statutory auditors directly against retained earnings, whereas U.S. firms charge such compensation for services against net income. This item is not separately disclosed in the U.S. but is reported in Japan. Our adjustment charges the reported amount for Japanese firms against their earnings.

2.4. Deferred taxes and special tax reserves

In general, the amounts reported for financial and tax reporting are the same in Japan, so that the issue of deferred tax accounting does not arise. There is one type of timing difference in Japan, related to special tax incentives, for which deferred tax expense should be charged against net income to make Japanese data comparable to the U.S.

Japanese tax law provides tax incentives for certain activities, such as overseas equity investments and special first-year depreciation on investments in particular types of equipment. The pre-tax effects of these items do not flow through the income statement for financial reporting, consistent with reporting practices in the U.S. [1] However, the practice in the U.S. is to provide deferred taxes for these timing differences. To achieve comparability, income tax expense for Japanese firms should be increased and net income reduced by an amount equal to the tax rate times the timing difference.

The necessary information to make this adjustment is in appropriated retained earnings. Japanese tax law requires firms to reflect these special tax incentives 'on their books' (Japanese Institute of Certified Public Accountants, p. 31). Rather than flow these items through the income statement, Japanese firms transfer an amount from unappropriated retained earnings to appropriated retained earnings or special tax reserves equal to the pre-tax timing difference. When the timing difference reverses, usually when the asset is sold, the amount is reversed out of appropriated retained earnings. To achieve comparability with U.S. GAAP, the change in appropriated retained earnings relating to special tax incentives multiplied by the tax rate will yield the appropriate increase or decrease in income tax expense for Japanese firms.

2.5. Other GAAP differences

Other GAAP differences remain that we do not treat either because their effect is likely to be immaterial or there is insufficient information to make the required adjustments.

---

[1] One exception to this treatment occurs for the deferral of gains on sales of certain property where the proceeds are reinvested in similar property. In this case, the pre-tax gain does flow through the income statement in Japan, just as it does in the U.S.

(1) Research and development costs: Although not required by GAAP, dominant practice in Japan expenses these costs in the year incurred to obtain the tax benefits. Consequently, U.S. and Japanese firms treat research and development costs virtually the same.

(2) Leases: Japanese GAAP treats all leases as operating leases. Because Japanese companies provide no information on their leases, capitalization of all or part of their outstanding leases is not possible. U.S. companies do not uniformly disclose the amount of capitalized lease assets or liabilities or the amount of depreciation and interest expense relating to capitalized leases. Thus, any adjustment made to U.S. data to eliminate capitalized leases is likely to create more noise than is worthwhile. Failing to adjust for capitalized leases should affect only a few industries (some users of heavy equipment) in our sample and should have no material effect on earnings.

(3) Goodwill amortization: The difference in the amortization periods for goodwill (40 years in the U.S. and 5 years in Japan) should not be of major significance since Japanese companies historically have not undertaken substantial corporate acquisitions to the same extent as U.S. firms.

3. Literature review

Several studies have restated PERs for either (a) different accounting principles and/or (b) different business practices in attempts to explain the difference between U.S. and Japanese PERs. Aron (1990) uses information from *Morgan Stanley Capital International Perspective* (MSCIP) as the starting point for calculating Japanese EPS and PERs. His adjustments fall into three categories: correction of MSCIP data, adjustments for different accounting principles, and adjustment for cross-holdings. To correct the MSCIP data, Aron adjusts for different fiscal year-end dates and for intercorporate investments in subsidiaries that were reported as consolidated but were in fact accounted for using the cost method. His next series of adjustments are for changes in tax reserves, consolidation of subsidiaries comprising less than 10% of consolidated net income, sales or assets, and different depreciation methods. His last adjustment is for cross-holdings, as he argues that shares of Japanese companies held by institutional investors should be treated as if they were treasury stock and therefore deducted from shares outstanding to be consistent with U.S. practice.

The effects of Aron's adjustments on PERs for fiscal 1989 are summarized in Table 4. Aron's aim was to determine if, on average, differences between U.S. and Japanese PERs could be explained by his adjustments. Consequently, he used aggregate level factors for his adjustments rather than restating amounts at the individual-firm level. For example, he increased Japanese average EPS by an aggregate factor of 5.1% to reflect the difference in year end of the average U.S. firm versus the average Japanese firm.

Table 4

	United States	Japan
Average PER-reported	14.1	38.80
Correction of MSCIP Data		(4.20)
Subtotal		34.60
Adjustments for GAAP		
Tax reserves		(1.81)
Consolidation		(2.02)
Depreciation		(6.90)
Subtotal		23.87
Adjustment for cross-holdings:	–	(8.10)
Average PER-restated	14.1	15.77

Similarly, he increased Japanese average EPS by 5.61% for tax reserves. [2] While these aggregate level adjustments are informative in portraying a general picture of the difference in PERs, the analyst' s attention is likely to be directed at individual companies where averages such as those used by Aron may not be appropriate. The restatement methodology described in this paper is intended to be applied at an individual firm level.

Approximately 35% of the restatement in the Japanese average PER relates to Aron's cross-holdings adjustment. Aron's objective was to restate the PER so that (1) the numerator of the PER reflects only the portion of total market value of equity held by non-institutional investors (42.5% for fiscal 1989 in Aron's computations) and (2) the denominator of the PER reflects only the unconsolidated earnings of the parent company (to achieve consistency between the numerator and denominator).

French and Poterba (1990) also use aggregate data to adjust average U.S. and Japanese PERs for differences in accounting principles and other factors. They adjust Japanese average PERs for accounting practices related to consolidation, tax reserves, and depreciation. Their sample is drawn from 1975 to 1988; filings of consolidated financial statements were not required until 1977, and the equity method was not applied to 20%–50% intercorporate investments until 1983. Consequently, French and Poterba use parent-only, non-equity method financial statements to achieve consistency across all years in their sample.

---

[2] Aron *increased* Japanese EPS by (1–tax rate)(increase in appropriated retained earnings for tax reserves). The addback to net income for the *pre-tax* effect of these tax incentives rests on the assumption that Japanese companies initially flowed these tax incentives through their income statements, reducing net income. Our reading of Japanese reporting practices (KPMG Peat Marwick, 1989, pp. 11–12) is that, like U.S. companies, these timing differences do not affect Japanese reported earnings. Thus, Aron's adjustment appears to overstate Japanese EPS and understate their PER. Aron's reduction in Japanese earnings for the *tax effect* of these timing differences is consistent with the adjustment for tax incentives discussed in Section 2.4.

At the same time, they adjust for cross-holdings using a procedure similar to Aron's to obtain a numerator comparable to the denominator of the PER. They shrink the total market value of equity of firms by the portion attributable to institutional shareholders, and they shrink earnings for dividends paid to institutional shareholders. The aggregate level metrics that French and Poterba use to make these adjustments differ from those used by Aron, but their general approach is the same.

French and Poterba's adjustment for tax reserves relies on Aron's estimate that reserves averaged 4% of net income over the 1975–1988 period. Their adjustment increases net income by (1–tax rate of 52%)(4% of earnings). (See footnote 2 regarding the appropriateness of this adjustment.)

French and Poterba follow two approaches to converting Japanese firms from accelerated to straight-line depreciation. The first approach divides the reported depreciation in half on the premise that the depreciation rate for double declining balance depreciation is $2/n$ and the straight-line rate is $1/n$, where n is the total depreciable life. The adjustment to earnings is an increase of (1–tax rate)(0.5 × reported depreciation). Their second method is more complex as it considers growth rates in depreciable assets and the current stage in the assets' average depreciable life. They rely on economy-wide growth rates in business investment and the same average of depreciable assets for all companies in making their adjustments.

For 1988, French and Poterba's adjustments (employing the second method above for depreciation differences) have the following effects on PERs:

Average Japanese PER-reported	54.3
Adjustments	
Intercorporate investments and cross-holdings	(18.7)
Tax reserves	(0.7)
Depreciation Method 1	–
Depreciation Method 2	(2.2)
Average Japanese PER-restated	32.7

French and Poterba also adjust *U.S.* accounting data for intercorporate holdings to make them similar to Japanese data. They give no detail regarding their procedure but report that, because of a smaller level of intercorporate holding in the U.S. than in Japan, the change in U.S. PERs is insignificant (from 12.9 reported to 11.7 restated in 1988). Overall, French and Poterba's adjustments explain roughly one-half the difference between U.S. and Japanese PERs.

Officer and Isgro (1990) likewise make aggregate level adjustments and examine differences in accounting principles and other factors to reconcile

U.S. and Japanese PERs. They adjust for depreciation method differences by comparing straight-line and accelerated depreciation as a percentage of net income. Over their 1985–1989 sample period, reported depreciation expense was 93% of net income in the U.S. and 220% in Japan. Assuming that the U.S. percentage reflects straight-line depreciation and the Japanese percentage reflects accelerated depreciation, Officer and Isgro restate Japanese depreciation expense and earnings using these proportions. Their adjustment for intercorporate investments and cross-holdings is similar to Aron's and French and Poterba's, although they assume different cross-holding percentages and dividend payout rates. The results of their adjustments for the 1985–1989 period are summarized as follows:

Average Japanese PER-reported	37.6
Adjustments	
Depreciation	(15.0)
Cross-holdings	(9.1)
Average Japanese PER-restated	13.5

In a departure from prior studies, Bildersee (1990) apply their adjustments to individual firms rather than at an aggregate level to average PERs. Their restatement procedure addresses differences in both accounting principles and business practices.

Bildersee et al. begin by using net income before extraordinary gains and losses in an effort to measure more accurately permanent earnings. Capital markets research (Lev, 1989, pp. 169–170) in the U.S. suggests that market prices reflect only permanent earnings and do not incorporate such transitory components as extraordinary items. To eliminate differences in depreciation methods, Bildersee et al. add back depreciation expense to net income. Similarly, since U.S. and Japanese income tax rates differ (50%–55% in Japan versus 33%–36% in the U.S.), they add income tax expense back to net income. This adjustment also eliminates the effect of deferred tax accounting differences.

Prior studies (Holden and Tschoegl, 1985; Skully, 1981) have shown that Japanese firms carry significantly higher levels of financial leverage than U.S. firms. To eliminate the effects of differences in capital structure on PERs, Bildersee et al. add interest expense back to net income.

Bildersee et al.'s adjustment for cross-holdings is as follows:

$$PE_a = PE \times (1-CH),$$

where PE_a = PER adjusted for cross-holdings; PE = PER unadjusted for cross-holdings; CH = percentage of company's stock held intercompany.

Table 5

	United States	Japan
Median PER-reported	11.3	53.3
Adjustments		
Extraordinary items and		
income taxes	(4.0)	(30.4)
Depreciation	(2.5)	(9.8)
Interest	(0.8)	(3.4)
Subtotal	4.0	9.7
Cross-holdings (using		
measure (3) above)	–	(2.3)
Median PER-restated	4.0	7.4

They use three different measures of CH: (1) investments reported on the balance sheet divided by total assets, (2) percentage of total shares outstanding held by Japanese governments, financial institutions, investment trusts, securities companies, and other corporations, and (3) the lesser of (1) and (2).

The effects of all of these adjustments on median PERs in 1987 are shown in Table 5.Using mean rather than median PERs and aggregating data over the years 1976 to 1987, Bildersee et al. conclude that their adjustments eliminate all but 1% of the difference between Japanese and U.S. PERs.

Bildersee et al. have extended the literature on U.S. and Japanese PERs by examining data at the individual firm level. Their conclusion that attainment of similar market multiples on operating earnings (net income before extraordinary items, taxes, depreciation and interest), adjusted for cross-holdings 'suggests that investors in both countries value operating flows in parallel ways' (p. 280) seems flawed, however. The market prices used in the numerator of the PER reflect the effects of most of the items eliminated from the denominator. Differences in interest expense, for example, reveal substantive differences in firms' relative abilities to generate earnings available to common shareholders and should affect stock prices. It is, therefore, not clear what the restated ratios mean. To address this issue in our study, we have distinguished accounting principle differences whose effects on earnings are essentially cosmetic from business practice differences whose effects on both earnings and price may be substantive. We focus only on effects of differences in accounting principles in this paper.

4. Data and methodology

Our sample of Japanese firms is drawn from the NEEDS annual consolidated data base of Nihon Keizai Shimbun, Inc., for fiscal years 1985 through 1988. The sample of U.S. firms is drawn from the COMPUSTAT data base for the same period. The criteria used for inclusion of firms in the sample were as follows:

1. The accounting period ends in December, January, February, or March. Most U.S. firms use a December year-end and most Japanese firms use a March year-end.
2. The firm is in an industry that has a minimum of 10 firms in 1988. We wish to study differences across industries in the U.S and Japan, and some minimum number of participants is needed to make the average results meaningful.
3. Firms whose reported or restated PER exceeds three standard deviations from the mean were excluded to eliminate outliers. [3]
4. Some firms are excluded because of their inventory and/or depreciation methods, as discussed below.

Our final sample sizes grew from 595 in 1985 to 810 in 1988 for the U.S. and from 207 in 1985 to 352 in 1988 for Japan. Our adjustments, outlined below, are primarily (but not exclusively) to U.S. rather than Japanese financial data due to the greater availability of information. The resulting PERs are, therefore, not based on GAAP of a single country, but are based instead on a blend of Japanese and U.S. accounting principles. Table 8 sets out the effects on average PERs of adjusting for each of the differences in accounting principles discussed next.

4.1. Inventory cost flow assumptions

Japanese firms using a LIFO cost flow assumption have been eliminated from the sample because, unlike the U.S., these Japanese firms do not disclose their LIFO reserves. Note from Table 2 that only 6% of Japanese firms used LIFO in fiscal 1990. U.S. companies that account for inventory on a FIFO or weighted average basis are not restated, whereas those using LIFO have been adjusted to an 'as if' FIFO basis using -the reported LIFO reserve. The restatement of net income is as follows:

Change in reported net income for inventory adjustment $= (1-\text{statutory tax rate})(\text{LIFO reserve}_{t+1}-\text{LIFO reserve}_t)$

where t is the beginning of the fiscal year and $t + 1$ is the end of the fiscal year. The statutory tax rate used for U.S. firms is 46% for 1985 and 1986, 40% for 1987, and 34% for 1988. Because we examine briefly the effect of different accounting principles on the rate of return on assets and the rate of

---

[3] In addition, 5 outlying observations were eliminated from the Japanese sample due to their unusually high bonuses as a proportion of earnings. For the U.S. sample, 7 outlying observations were deleted due to unusually large differences between weighted average shares and shares outstanding at the end of the fiscal year.

return on common shareholders' equity, we restate balance sheet amounts as well. The restatement of total assets is as follows:

Change in reported assets for inventory adjustment = (1−tax rate)(LIFO reserve$_t$).

The adjustment to assets reflects (1) the increase in inventories by the amount of the LIFO reserve and (2) the reduction in cash (or other assets) for the additional taxes that would have been paid if the U.S. firm had used FIFO instead of LIFO. [4] The restatement of common shareholders' equity is:

Change in reported common shareholders' equity for inventory adjustment = (1−tax rate)(LIFO reserve$_t$).

The effect of these adjustments is to put all firms in both the U.S. and Japanese samples on FIFO, average, or specific identification cost flow assumptions. Although these three cost flow assumptions produce different income statement and balance sheet amounts, our adjustment for LIFO eliminates the major source of difference in the mix of cost flow assumptions for inventories.

4.2. Depreciation

Firms using either straight-line or a combination of accelerated and straight-line depreciation methods are excluded from the Japanese sample. The financial statement amounts for companies in both samples using accelerated depreciation remain unchanged. We convert U.S. firms using straight-line depreciation (the vast majority of U.S. firms) to double-declining balance depreciation. The relation between straight-line and double-declining balance depreciation amounts depends on (1) the average total life of fixed tangible assets (which we measure by dividing gross property, plant, and equipment by depreciation expense) and (2) the growth rate in capital expenditures (which we measure using the compound annual average rate of growth in depreciation expense over the preceding five years). Table 6 shows the percentage relation between double-declining balance depreciation expense and gross property, plant, and equipment (Panel A) and the percentage relation between double-declining balance accumulated depreciation and gross property, plant, and equipment (Panel B) for given average lives and growth rates as examples of the percentage relations. To make the conversions to accelerated depreciation for each firm in each year, we began by computing the compound annual growth rate in depreciation expense

---

[4] One can legitimately debate whether the deferred tax liability should increase rather than cash decrease for the tax effect of the adjustment. Our treatment reflects the conformity requirement in the U.S. that firms cannot use LIFO for tax purposes if they use FIFO for financial reporting. Also, assuming the use of FIFO for both tax and financial reporting puts U.S. firms on a comparable basis with Japanese firms.

Table 6
Factors for conversion from straight-line to double-declining balance depreciation given selected average lives and growth rates

Average life (years)	Growth rate					
	5%	6%	7%	8%	9%	10%
Panel A: Double-declining balance depreciation expense / gross property, plant and equipment						
5	0.22043	0.22162	0.22280	0.22398	0.22515	0.22632
6	0.17325	0.17454	0.17584	0.17712	0.17840	0.17967
7	0.15590	0.15701	0.15812	0.15923	0.16033	0.16143
8	0.13108	0.13228	0.13348	0.13468	0.13587	0.13706
9	0.12102	0.12210	0.12318	0.12425	0.12532	0.12638
10	0.10579	0.10695	0.10810	0.10925	0.11039	0.11153
11	0.09921	0.10027	0.10133	0.10238	0.10343	0.10447
12	0.08895	0.09008	0.09120	0.09231	0.09342	0.09453
13	0.08439	0.08534	0.08638	0.08743	0.08846	0.08949
14	0.07693	0.07803	0.07913	0.08023	0.08131	0.08239
15	0.07345	0.07449	0.07552	0.07655	0.07758	0.07859
Panel B: Double-declining balance accumulated depreciation / gross property, plant and equipment						
5	0.55484	0.55557	0.55626	0.55690	0.55749	0.55804
6	0.55078	0.55088	0.55092	0.55091	0.55084	0.55073
7	0.56036	0.55958	0.55874	0.55785	0.55689	0.55589
8	0.55343	0.55202	0.55054	0.54899	0.54739	0.54573
9	0.55957	0.55723	0.55481	0.55233	0.54980	0.54721
10	0.55209	0.54912	0.54608	0.54298	0.53981	0.53659
11	0.55606	0.55213	0.54814	0.54408	0.53998	0.53583
12	0.54866	0.54412	0.53952	0.53485	0.53014	0.52539
13	0.55114	0.54564	0.54008	0.53446	0.52882	0.52315
14	0.54400	0.53790	0.53174	0.52555	0.51932	0.51308
15	0.54541	0.53835	0.53124	0.52411	0.51697	0.50985

(straight-line) over the previous five years and the average total life of property, plant, and equipment. We then simulated the calculation of double-declining balance depreciation until the percentages (such as those in Panels A and B of Table 6) for that particular firm reached steady-state. This occurs after completing one retirement/replacement cycle for the average life under study.

The restatements to the income statement and balance sheet are as follows:

Change in reported net income for depreciation adjustment = (1–tax rate)(DDB depreciation expense–SL depreciation expense)

Change in reported assets for depreciation adjustment = DDB accumulated depreciation–SL accumulated depreciation

Change in reported common shareholders' equity for depreciation adjustment = (1–tax rate)(DDB accumulated depreciation–SL accumulated depreciation)

These adjustments assume that the tax effects result in a reduction in the deferred income tax liability rather than cash. The result of these adjustments is to put all companies in both samples on an accelerated depreciation basis for both tax and financial reporting.

4.3. Bonuses to directors and statutory auditors

Japanese GAAP charges directors' and statutory auditors' bonuses directly to retained earnings. To achieve comparability with U.S. GAAP, we subtract the reported amounts for these items from net income. Because these bonuses cannot be deducted for tax purposes (KPMG Peat Marwick, 1989, p. 18), the amount subtracted is the gross amount reported.

4.4. EPS calculation

Japanese GAAP does not require the complex computations of EPS followed in the U.S. for common stock equivalents and other potentially dilutive securities, nor do they require calculations of the weighted average number of shares. To achieve comparability and to eliminate transitory components of earnings, EPS calculations for both countries are equal to consolidated net income before extraordinary items available to common shareholders divided by the number of common shares outstanding at the end of the year.

4.5. Deferred taxes and tax reserves

As discussed earlier in Section 2.4, we should decrease EPS of Japanese companies for the tax effects of timing differences created by special tax incentives. The information needed to make this adjustment, the change in appropriated retained earnings for tax reserves, is not included on the NEEDS consolidated data base used in this study. The NEEDS unconsolidated data base reports the change in appropriated retained earnings but does not indicate whether the change relates to dividends, tax reserves, or other factors. Thus, short of gathering the necessary information directly from Japanese annual reports, we cannot make the needed adjustment for deferred taxes on tax reserves. We expect, however, that adjusting for this difference in GAAP would decrease average Japanese EPS and increase restated average Japanese PERs, thus broadening rather than diminishing the difference between U.S. and Japanese PERs.

4.6. Cross-holdings

Each of the studies discussed previously used unconsolidated earnings data and made adjustments for cross-holdings of shares between Japanese corporate entities. The need to adjust for cross-holdings arises because market prices in the numerator of the PER reflect the market value of both the parent entity and the value of its holdings in other companies, whereas earnings in the denominator of the PER include earnings of the parents plus dividends (not earnings) from intercorporate investments. Previous researchers adjust for this inconsistency between the numerator and denomina-

Table 7

	United States		Japan	
	Reported PER	Restated PER	Restated PER	Reported PER
1985	22.1	25.4	52.1	47.9
1986	22.8	26.8	56.9	54.1
1987	17.0	18.9	62.5	60.5
1988	17.2	20.4	60.8	58.8

tor by removing the portion of the market value and earnings, respectively, related to intercorporate investment. The result is a measure of a 'parent-company-only' PER.

In contrast, our study uses consolidated/equity method earnings so that no adjustment for cross-holdings is necessary. The numerator of the PER reflects the market value of the entire consolidated entity, which is consistent with consolidated earnings. Our result is a 'consolidated' PER.

The two approaches to dealing with intercorporate investments (cross-holdings) are reconcilable. Our approach starts with PERs that early researchers obtained after adjusting for cross-holdings and then aggregating PERs across firms.

5. Results

The net effects of adjusting at the firm level for differences in accounting practices on average Japanese and U.S. PERs are summarized in Table 7. These results show clearly that the net effect of adjusting for differences in GAAP is minimal. Unlike prior studies, our analysis suggests that differences in GAAP explain only a small portion of the difference between average U.S. and Japanese PERs. Table 8 summarizes the effects of each adjustment on average U.S. and Japanese PERs in each fiscal year, 1985–1988, and Table 9 summarizes the effects of each adjustment across years within each industry. [5] While converting U.S. firms from straight-line to double declining balance depreciation decreases EPS and increases the average U.S. PER as expected, its effect is usually counteracted (unless there are LIFO layer liquidations) by the conversion of cost of goods sold to a FIFO basis and by the change from weighted average shares and common stock equivalents to outstanding shares at fiscal year-end in calculating EPS. Furthermore, the effect of deducting bonuses from Japanese earnings increases the average Japanese PER and thus widens the difference between average U.S. and Japanese PERs.

[5] We also computed median PERs for each fiscal year and each industry; the differences in median PERs closely mirror differences in average (mean) PERs. We also performed a Spearman rank-order correlation of PERs for each year across industries and each industry across years; the rank order correlations were all above 90%.

Table 8

Effects of adjustments on annual average U.S. and Japanese price-earnings ratios, 1985–1988

	1985		1986		1987		1988	
	U.S.	Japan	U.S.	Japan	U.S.	Japan	U.S.	Japan
Average PER-reported	22.1	47.9	22.8	54.1	17.0	60.5	17.2	58.8
Adjustments for								
Depreciation	3.0	–	3.9	–	3.7	–	8.8	–
Inventory	0.3	–	0.5	–	(0.8)	–	(4.0)	–
Directors' bonuses	–	4.2	–	2.8	–	2.0	–	2.0
EPS calculation	0.0	–	(0.4)	–	(1.0)	–	(1.6)	–
Average PER-restated	25.4	52.1	26.8	56.9	18.9	62.5	20.4	60.8

Table 9
Effects of adjustments on industry average U.S. and Japanese price-earnings ratios, 1985–1988

	Automobiles		Chemicals		Clay, glass		Construction	
	U.S.	Japan	U.S.	Japan	U.S.	Japan	U.S.	Japan
Average PER-reported	13.7	49.5	14.2	45.5	12.0	64.5	19.6	60.4
Adjustments for								
Depreciation	4.1	–	3.0	–	3.9	–	1.3	–
Inventory	(0.6)	–	(0.3)	–	0.1	–	(0.1)	–
Directors' bonuses	–	3.6	–	1.4	–	4.2	–	2.9
EPS calculation	(1.8)	–	(1.7)	–	(1.1)	–	(0.4)	–
Average PER-restated	15.4	53.1	15.2	46.9	14.9	68.7	20.4	63.3

	Electrical		Food processing		Instruments		Machinery	
	U.S.	Japan	U.S.	Japan	U.S.	Japan	U.S.	Japan
Average PER-reported	21.7	58.0	17.0	54.4	23.7	67.2	20.6	71.7
Adjustments for								
Depreciation	4.6	–	3.4	–	9.0	–	2.7	–
Inventory	(0.3)	–	(0.2)	–	(1.2)	–	(0.2)	–
Directors' bonuses	–	2.9	–	1.4	–	2.4	–	6.4
EPS calculation	(0.2)	–	(0.2)	–	(1.6)	–	(0.3)	–
Average PER-restated	25.8	60.9	20.0	55.8	29.9	69.4	22.8	78.1

	Metals		Pharmaceuticals		Retailers		Textiles	
	U.S.	Japan	U.S.	Japan	U.S.	Japan	U.S.	Japan
Average PER-reported	14.9	45.9	27.6	74.7	19.9	57.4	13.2	50.5
Adjustments for								
Depreciation	3.3	–	5.8	–	4.5	–	2.0	–
Inventory	(0.7)	–	0.1	–	(1.7)	–	(0.0)	–
Directors' bonuses	–	1.4	–	1.1	–	1.0	–	1.9
EPS calculation	0.0	–	(0.8)	–	(0.3)	–	0.2	–
Average PER-restated	17.5	47.3	32.7	75.8	22.4	58.4	15.4	52.4

Average PER-reported	Wholesalers	
	U.S.	Japan
	19.3	35.4
Adjustments for		
Depreciation	3.9	–
Inventory	(1.1)	–
Directors' bonuses	–	0.9
EPS calculation	(0.1)	–
Average PER-restated	22.0	36.3

Table 10
Comparison of unadjusted and adjusted mean price-earnings ratios

	Using reported data			Using adjusted data		
	U.S.	Japan	Level of significance of difference	U.S.	Japan	Level of significance of difference
By year across industries						
1985	22.1	47.9	0.000	25.4	52.1	0.000
1986	22.8	54.1	0.000	26.8	56.9	0.000
1987	17.0	60.5	0.000	18.9	62.5	0.000
1988	17.2	58.8	0.000	20.4	60.8	0.000
By industry across years						
Auto	13.7	49.5	0.000	15.4	53.1	0.000
Chemical	14.2	45.5	0.000	15.2	46.9	0.000
Clay, glass	12.0	64.5	0.000	14.9	68.7	0.000
Construction	19.6	60.4	0.000	20.4	63.3	0.000
Electrical	21.7	58.0	0.000	25.8	60.9	0.000
Food processing	17.0	54.4	0.000	20.0	55.8	0.000
Instruments	23.7	67.2	0.000	29.9	69.4	0.000
Machinery	20.6	71.7	0.000	22.8	78.1	0.000
Metals	14.9	45.9	0.000	17.5	47.3	0.000
Pharmaceuticals	27.6	74.7	0.000	32.7	75.8	0.000
Retailers	19.9	57.4	0.000	22.4	58.4	0.000
Textiles	13.2	50.5	0.000	15.4	52.4	0.000
Wholesalers	19.3	35.4	0.000	22.0	36.3	0.000

Table 11
Comparison of unadjusted and adjusted rates of return

By year across industries / By industry across years	Return on assets						Return on common equity					
	Using reported data			Using adjusted data			Using reported data			Using adjusted data		
	U.S. (%)	Japan (%)	Level of significance of difference	U.S. (%)	Japan (%)	Level of significance of difference	U.S. (%)	Japan (%)	Level of significance of difference	U.S. (%)	Japan (%)	Level of significance of difference
1985	5.1	4.0	0.002	4.8	3.9	0.009	7.2	7.2	0.963	6.2	7.0	0.234
1986	4.8	3.2	0.000	4.6	3.1	0.000	6.9	6.0	0.207	6.3	5.8	0.476
1987	5.0	3.4	0.000	4.9	3.3	0.000	5.8	6.7	0.299	5.5	6.5	0.208
1988	5.7	3.7	0.000	5.5	3.6	0.000	7.1	7.6	0.574	6.7	7.4	0.452
Auto	7.6	3.1	0.000	7.5	3.0	0.000	12.0	6.4	0.000	11.3	6.1	0.000
Chemical	9.0	3.3	0.000	8.8	3.2	0.000	14.7	6.9	0.000	14.2	6.7	0.000
Clay, glass	5.6	3.7	0.048	5.2	3.6	0.096	8.8	6.4	0.206	7.8	6.3	0.401
Construction	3.9	2.8	0.387	4.1	2.8	0.280	6.2	7.4	0.670	5.4	7.2	0.524
Electrical	2.9	3.4	0.286	2.5	3.4	0.068	0.9	6.2	0.000	-0.3	6.0	0.000
Food processing	6.9	3.9	0.000	7.0	3.8	0.000	11.3	7.6	0.026	11.5	7.4	0.018
Instruments	3.5	2.9	0.338	3.2	2.7	0.373	3.6	4.6	0.387	3.1	4.5	0.225
Machinery	3.9	3.6	0.553	3.7	3.5	0.730	4.4	7.1	0.013	3.9	6.9	0.006
Metals	6.0	4.1	0.000	5.7	4.0	0.000	9.0	8.0	0.256	8.7	7.7	0.290
Pharmaceuticals	9.4	3.9	0.000	9.5	3.9	0.000	12.6	6.9	0.059	12.6	6.9	0.059
Retailers	7.5	3.9	0.000	7.3	3.9	0.000	11.5	7.7	0.000	11.2	7.6	0.000
Textiles	5.4	3.8	0.087	5.1	3.7	0.137	5.7	8.4	0.297	5.0	8.1	0.242
Wholesalers	4.6	3.5	0.008	4.5	3.4	0.010	5.9	7.1	0.198	5.6	6.9	0.167

Table 10 shows average reported and restated PERs for the U.S. and Japan by year (Panel A) and industry (Panel B) and summarizes the results of tests of the significance of the differences between reported PERs and the differences between restated PERs. The process of restating PERs has little effect on these results, as significance levels are unchanged in all but the instruments and wholesalers industries.

To examine the effect of different GAAP on other financial ratios, we conducted tests of significance of the difference between average reported and restated rates of return on assets and common equity. The results of these tests are shown in Table 11. Panel A provides the results of tests of rates of return averaged across industries within years, and Panel B provides results regarding rates of return averaged across years within industries. As seen in the tests of differences in average PERs, the effects of adjusting financial statement data on tests of differences in average rates of return are negligible. Differences that are statistically significant ($\alpha \leq 0.05$) using reported data remain significant using restated data. This consistency is not surprising given that each adjustment changes the numerator and denominator in the same direction; converting U.S. firms from LIFO to FIFO, for example, increases earnings in the numerator due to lower cost of goods sold and increases total assets in the denominator of rate of return on assets. Thus, the net effects of the adjustments on the ratios are insignificant.

6. Conclusions

Using large samples of publicly-traded U.S. and Japanese companies, we find that adjusting their financial statement data to the same accounting principles has only a minor effect on differences in average price-earnings ratios or rates of return. Unlike previous studies, we adjust the data at the individual firm level (rather than the aggregate level) by converting items to the same accounting basis (rather than eliminating items altogether). Also unlike prior work, we include an adjustment for different inventory cost-flow assumptions and use consolidated financial statement data.

Our purpose is to eliminate essentially cosmetic sources of differences in average ratios so that the remaining differences in average Japanese and U.S. PERs and rates of return may be attributed to substantive differences between the two countries. Our results indicate that differences in average U.S. and Japanese ratios are attributable primarily to substantive differences. Having eliminated differences in accounting practices as an explanation for differences in average ratios, we are undertaking the next step in this research which is to identify those substantive factors that can explain the differences we observe in average U.S. and Japanese PERs and rates of return.

Acknowledgements

The authors wish to express appreciation to Kathy Reinig and Ajay Zutshi for data collection and processing assistance and to the Center on Japanese Economy and Business at the Graduate School of Business, Columbia University, for permitting us to use the Nikkei-NEEDS data base.

References

Aron, P.H., 1990, Japanese P/E multiples in an era of uncertainty. Daiwa Securities America Report No. 38.

Bildersee, J.S., J.J. Cheh and C. Lee, 1990, The international price-earnings ratios phenomenon, Japan and the World Economy 2, 263–282.

French, K.R. and J.M. Poterba, 1991, Were Japanese stock prices too high?, Journal of Financial Economics 29, 337–363.

Hodder, J.E. and A.E. Tschoegl, 1985, Some aspects of Japanese corporate finance, Journal of Financial and Quantitative Analysis 2, 173–191.

Japanese Institute of Certified Public Accountants, 1987, Corporate disclosure in Japan.

KPMG Peat Marwick, 1989, Comparison of Japanese and U.S. Reporting and Financial Practices.

Lev, B., 1989, On the usefulness of earnings and earnings research: Lessons and directions from two decades of empirical research, Journal of Accounting Research, Supplement, 153–192.

McDonald, J., 1989, The *mochiai* effect: Japanese corporate cross-holdings, Journal of Portfolio Management, 90–94.

Nakatani, I., 1984, The economic role of financial corporate grouping, In: M. Aoki, ed., The economic analysis of the Japanese firm, (North-Holland, Amsterdam) 227–258.

Officer, R. and G. Isgro, 1990, The relative behaviour of price to earnings ratios in Australia, Japan, U.S. and U.K. and the implications, Working Paper, University of Melbourne.

Skully, M.T., 1981, Japanese corporate structure: Some factors in its development, The International Journal of Accounting, Spring, 67–98.

Tokyo Stock Exchange, 1990 Fact Book.

[14]

Journal of International Financial Management and Accounting 5:1 1994

A Comparison of Relations Between Security Market Prices, Returns and Accounting Measures in Japan and the United States

Charles Hall*, Yasushi Hamao** and Trevor S. Harris**

Abstract

We examine associations between accounting measures of earnings and stock returns in Japan over varying window lengths and compare them to those for the United States. Our results are consistent with the view that Japanese investors utilize less accounting information in their pricing of equities than do their U.S. counterparts. This was particularly evident in the 'boom' period of the mid to late 1980s when the fundamental values conveyed by accounting measures appear to have been largely ignored. The association increases with the inclusion of 1991, suggesting a return to more emphasis on fundamentals with the recent decline in stock prices.

I. Introduction

Extensive research and discussion has occurred over the last two decades relating to the relevance of accounting differences in the valuation of securities in international capital markets (Choi and Levich [1990]). Yet little empirical evidence exists which evaluates how the accounting measures in Japan are associated with stock prices or returns, especially over periods other than short-event windows of a few days, weeks or months.

The stock prices of companies listed on Japan's securities markets rose at a rapid pace in the 1980s and yielded price-earnings (henceforth P/E) and price-to-book value (henceforth P/B) ratios which many observers suggested were high by international standards (Aron [1987, 1989], French and Poterba [1991], Chan, Hamao and Lakonishok [1991] and Schieneman [1988]). The last few years have reflected an opposite trend. At the time of writing the Japanese stock market had lost about 50 percent

* Doctoral Candidate and **Associate Professors at Graduate School of Business, Columbia University. Address correspondence to authors at Graduate School of Business, Columbia University, Uris Hall, New York, NY 10027. We gratefully acknowledge funding from the Center on Japanese Economy and Business at Columbia University. Yasushi Hamao's research was supported in part by the Batterymarch Fellowship; Trevor Harris' research was sponsored in part by the Rudolph Schoenheimer Fellowship.

48   *Charles Hall, Yasushi Hamao and Trevor S. Harris*

of its market value since the 1989 high. The accounting measures of the Japanese firms listed on the stock market have not shown the same volatility. We see use of P/E relatives in discussions of cost of capital (for example, McCauley and Zimmer [1991] and Poterba [1991]) and broad international comparisons (for example, Bildersee, Cheh and Lee [1990], and Dontoh, Livnat and Todd [1991]). For such evaluations to be made usefully we should expect fundamental associations between the accounting and stock market measures to be equivalent across the countries, subject to accounting differences. That is, if equivalent basic associations do not exist then it is not clear what it means to make such international comparisons.

This paper evaluates such associations in Japan and compares them to a sample of firms in the United States using a methodology recently developed in Easton and Harris [1991b] and Easton, Harris and Ohlson [1992] and considered for Germany in Harris and Lang [1992].

Darrough and Harris [1991] and Sakakibara, Yamaji, Sakurai, Shiroshita and Fukuda [1988] provide evidence that Japanese reported accounting earnings and management forecasts do have information content around earnings announcement dates. Yet, it might be argued that despite the information content in earnings the relative returns-earnings associations are different across the U.S. and Japan because of both economic factors and accounting differences. For example, expected rates of return might affect the relative coefficients of earnings in returns-earnings association studies and be independent of any accounting differences. However, while such economic differences may affect the coefficient estimates in cross-sectional tests, they should not necessarily affect the degree of association as reflected in the R^2. On the other hand, the garbling of the accounting information may cause differences in both the coefficient estimates and the strength of the association. This would seem to be consistent with the results reported in Chan, Hamao and Lakonishok [1991]. The Easton, Harris and Ohlson [1992] methodology minimizes the influences of accounting measurement differences so the methods we use should control for much of the garbling effect. Also, Brown, Soybel and Stickney [1991] find that adjusting Japanese and U.S. financial statement data for differences in accounting principles has only a small impact on average P/Es or rates of return, and Harris and Lang [1992] find equivalent return-earnings associations in Germany and the U.S. These results suggest that we might reasonably expect equivalent associations in Japan without any accounting adjustments.

Security Market Prices, Returns and Accounting Measures 49

While we do not control for all accounting differences we do factor in a specific difference by considering both the parent-only and consolidated measures in Japan. Both popular perception in Japan and empirical evidence in Darrough and Harris [1991] suggest that the parent-only earnings appear to be the primary earnings information variable. Until 1991, consolidated data could be, and generally was, reported after the parent data had been presented. The parent data are considered in Aron [1987, 1989], Chan, Hamao and Lakonishok [1991] and French and Poterba [1991]. Yet the international trend is towards increased application of consolidation principles and there is a perception that consolidation differences are a major factor in explaining differences in Japanese P/E ratios (Aron [1989] and French and Poterba [1991]). We also consider the role of depreciation which is presumed to be relevant for explaining international differences in several of the cited studies.

The results suggest that Japanese stock prices were largely unrelated to fundamental values based on accounting measures for most of the 1980s and that, currently, we are seeing a correction towards these fundamentals. Thus, further studies which try to control for other differences in Japanese and U.S. accounting practice in order to explain apparent price differentials are questionable at best.

II. Development of Hypotheses

Recently, an advisory body to the Ministries of Finance and of International Trade and Industry:

'proposed the standardization of some national financial regulations around the world. They should include standardized methods of international securities settlements, release of information, (and) accounting standards . . . (The committee) said that standardization was needed to create smoother international financial transactions.'[1]

This proposal reflects the common sentiment that different accounting practices impact the international financial markets. Survey analysis (Choi and Levich [1990]) indicates that various participants in the capital markets are influenced by different practices and yet there are others who seem to be able to cope with the differences. The earlier quote suggests that some Japanese policy advisors believe that differences between Japanese and other countries' accounting practices impact the operation of international financial markets. Yet other have argued that stock prices and fundamental variables such as accounting earnings and book value of

50   *Charles Hall, Yasushi Hamao and Trevor S. Harris*

owners' equity are essentially unrelated in Japan. For example, Zielinski and Holloway [1991] state 'share prices have gradually lost touch with the earning power of the companies which they represent' (page 16) and Viner [1988] suggests that

'the Japanese stock market is only a market of stocks . . . Japanese investors will decide what they want and what they wish to discard on the basis of trends and fads which have no Western counterpart . . . If the Japanese market will give a kingdom for a horse then global valuation techniques and internationalization will have no bearing on that decision.' (page 124)

Furthermore, anecdotal evidence exists of 'ramping' of prices and deals between brokerage firms and important clients which create short term price movements which may be unrelated to the earning power of companies.

These two positions are somewhat contradictory. The first suggests that correcting for accounting differences will create a symmetry in the re-lations of stock prices and accounting fundamentals across countries. This is consistent with the argument made in Aron [1987, 1989]. The second position suggests that the basic associations are 'structurally' different. We have some evidence that correcting for accounting differences does not explain the relative Japanese and U.S. P/Es or costs of capital (for example, Brown, Soybel and Stickney [1991], and Poterba [1991]). Yet there appears to be little empirical evidence analyzing the relative as-sociations between accounting measures and stock prices or returns in Japan.[2] In general, the Japanese accounting system, as prescribed in the Commercial Code, is oriented more towards protection of creditors than to providing information for investors. In addition, there is a tax con-formity rule which requires legal entities to include expenses in the reported accounting income if they are to be included as expenses for tax purposes. Together these institutional characteristics suggest that Japanese firms' owners' equity and earnings will be biased downwards and be more conservative than the equivalent measures of their U.S. counterparts. The bias in the reported values will change the expected coefficient (multiple) in cross-sectional tests of the associations between the accounting and stock market measures but need not reduce the strength of the associations themselves. Harris and Ohlson [1987] have shown that U.S. investors rationally discriminate between the relative conservatism of successful efforts and full cost accounting for oil and gas producers. Also Harris and Lang [1992] have shown that associations between German accounting

Security Market Prices, Returns and Accounting Measures 51

and stock market measures are associated in a similar way to U.S. firms despite the potentially strong conservative bias in German accounting practice. In fact, the Japanese accounting system has its early roots (from the time of the Meiji restoration) in German practice. Thus, overall, even if the Japanese accounting system creates some measurement biases it need not reduce the power of associations with stock market measures if in fact Japanese investors consider accounting measures in their pricing decisions in a similar manner to U.S. investors. If Japanese investors largely ignore the accounting measures then it is harder to argue that effort should be spent on trying to adjust the accounting system to obtain measures which are closer to those provided in the U.S., so as to 'correct' for apparent differences in valuation.

The major accounting differences are summarized in other papers including Aron [1987, 1989], Brown, Soybel and Stickney [1991], French and Poterba [1991], Harris [1991] and Viner [1988]. Most studies suggest that the large differences relate to the issue of parent versus consolidated reporting and the choice of depreciation method.[3] The understatement of equity and earnings resulting from lack of consolidation varies substantially cross-sectionally, but on average, for our sample, the median ratio of consolidated to parent earnings (owners' equity) ranges from 1.08 (1.02) to 1.12 (1.03) for the years in which consolidation is required. Furthermore, we now have a reasonable period with which to use the consolidated data so that this should not be a concern.[4] The depreciation question is complicated by the fact that it has nothing to do with Japanese accounting per se. Of course one might argue that the tax conformity rules give Japanese companies an incentive to use accelerated depreciation rules but these rules are in conformity with U.S. generally accepted accounting practice (GAAP). Thus, we find U.S. firms using equivalent methods (e.g., General Motors and Ford) and the Japanese firms which use U.S. GAAP for their consolidated statements still use accelerated depreciation methods. The accelerated depreciation combined with a growth of investment in capital equipment can depress reported earnings in the short run but should have little impact over longer windows which cover the depreciation cycle. The methodology we employ will therefore largely control for any influence of 'excessive' depreciation.

In testing the associations between accounting and stock market measures we consider two basic approaches. The first simply looks at the basic association between price multiples relative to the fundamental accounting measures. In particular, we focus on the correlation between P/B and return on equity (henceforth ROE). This can be justified formally

52   *Charles Hall, Yasushi Hamao and Trevor S. Harris*

using the model outlined in Ohlson [1989, 1991]. The model shows price as a weighted average of earnings, book value of owner's equity and other information, formally:

$$P_{it} = k\theta x_{it} + (1-k)y_{it} - kd_{it} + v_{it} \tag{1}$$

where:

P_{it} is the share price of security i at time t,
x_{it} is accounting earnings for firm i at time t,
k is a weight indicating the degree of relevance of earnings,
θ.   is $R_F/(R_F-1)$ where R_F is the risk free rate,
y_{it} is the book value of owners' equity for firm i at time t,
d_{it} is dividends for firm i at time t, and
v_{it} is other information used to price firm i at time t, and is orthogonal to earnings and owners' equity.

Dividing through by y_{it} yields the P/B ratio on the left hand side and the ROE, dividend over owners' equity and (deflated) other information on the right hand side.[5] Thus, if earnings is considered to be weighted heavily in pricing companies we should expect a high correlation between P/B and ROE given the historically small dividends. Alternatively, if book value is weighted heavily in the pricing decision then we can expect a high negative correlation between P/E and ROE. If other information is being used primarily, that is accounting measures are being relatively under-utilized, then both correlations will be small.[6] Thus, our first test of the relative degree to which accounting measures are used in valuation in Japan is based on the simple correlations outlined above.

The second set of tests considers associations between security returns and measures of accounting earnings. Returns-earnings associations have been the focus of analyzing the value-relevance of accounting information for some time. But the focus has usually been in the form of assessing the information content of unexpected earnings. If one takes the first difference of the variables in equation (1) we have returns as a function of deflated earnings and changes in earnings. Therefore, at least for annual return intervals, we consider both earnings variables for explaining returns.[7]

The general model we use to test the returns-earnings associations is derived in Easton and Harris [1991b] and Easton, Harris and Ohlson [1992] and is represented as follows:

$$R_{iT} = \alpha_0 + \alpha_1 AE_{iT} + \alpha_2 \Delta AE_{iT} + \epsilon_{iT} \tag{2}$$

Security Market Prices, Returns and Accounting Measures   53

where:

R_{iT} is $(P_{iT}-P_{io} + FVS_{iT})/P_{io}$, with T being 1 in an annual window and varying up to $T = 20$ years,

FVS_{iT} is the cumulative dividends from time 1 to T and the earnings on the dividends (d_{it}) assuming a reinvestment at the risk free rate (R_F), that is:

$$FVS(d_{i1}, \ldots, d_{iT}) \equiv d_{i1}(R_F^{T-1}) + d_{i2}(R_F^{T-2}) + \ldots + d_{iT-1}(R_F) + d_{iT} \equiv FVS_{iT},$$

AE_{iT} is $\sum_{t=1}^{T} x_{it} + FVF_{iT}$, with x_{it} being accounting earnings from firm i at time t, and

$$FVF(d_{i1}, \ldots, d_{iT}) \equiv d_{i1}(R_F^{T-1} - 1) + d_{i2}(R_F^{T-2} - 1) + \ldots + d_{iT-1}(R_F - 1) \equiv FVF_{iT},$$

ΔAE_{iT} is $AE_{iT}-AE_{is}$, that is the change in aggregate earnings with respect to the relevant interval with s being equal to some time period prior to T and depending on the definition of change in earnings used,[8] and

ϵ_{it} is the residual error term.

If accounting data are considered to be valuation relevant, we should expect the earnings to be associated with returns. In short windows (up to a year) both the use of other information and potential leads and lags in accounting measurement or recognition of economic events can yield low association metrics. However, as demonstrated in Easton, Harris and Ohlson [1992], by extending the window length we minimize accounting measurement problems and, as Easton, Harris and Ohlson [1992] show, earnings explain more than half the returns over a ten year window in the U.S.[9] Hence, if the short window associations using Japanese data are lower than the U.S. this may be partly a result of accounting measurement issues. But, by extending the window length, any measurement problems should largely disappear so that any differences in Japanese and U.S. metrics of returns-earnings associations should converge. On the other hand, if differences remain it is more likely that Japanese investors are placing more weight on other information (relative to accounting measures) in their pricing of securities.

The analysis of the value-relevance of accounting measures is extended by comparing the returns-earnings associations for Japanese companies

54   *Charles Hall, Yasushi Hamao and Trevor S. Harris*

across the two reporting options—parent and consolidated. If the consolidated data are considered to be more value-relevant than the parent-only data then for the comparison using just Japanese companies we should expect the associations to be higher for the consolidated data. However, previous evidence in Darrough and Harris [1991] and anecdotal evidence suggests that investors focus on the parent report.[10] Hence, simple rule changes to provide superficial conformity of accounting rules will not necessarily create uniformity in the uses of the information.

III. Data and Sample Selection

Japan

The Japanese stock price data are taken from the database described in Hamao [1991], which covers monthly data from January 1970 to December 1992. Parent accounting and dividend data are provided by Daiwa Institute of Research. This is a monthly database which records the accounting information as it is released for all firms in Tokyo Stock Exchange Sections I and II from January 1970 to December 1991. The consolidated statement data are taken from the Nihon Keizai Shimbun Sha (Nikkei) NEEDS database. For each fiscal year we use the month in which the accounting data was released. The current and lagged prices are then utilized to calculate returns.

While a Japanese firm may choose any month as its accounting cycle end, several firms have changed the end month to March over the years. We drop observations when there is an irregular number of months in an accounting cycle because of the change. We also exclude financial institutions and twelve observations spread over the years with extreme values (e.g., an ROE of 264,000 percent). This leaves us with a minimum of 935 firms in 1971 and a maximum of 1,277 firms in 1986 in the parent sample.

Since full consolidated reporting became mandatory only after 1983, the consolidated data we have are useful only from 1984. The consolidated data sample consists of 364 firms for which current profit and price data are available for every year from 1984 to 1991. We repeated the tests with the full number of observations with consolidated data. As the results were qualitatively identical, we report only the restricted sample results.

Management forecasts of 363 firms' consolidated current profit are collected from the *Japan Company Handbook* published by Toyo Keizai Shimpo Sha. All data are converted to a per share basis adjusted for stock splits. The Gensaki (bond repo) rate, used as a short-term risk-free interest rate, is taken from Hamao and Ibbotson [1992].

Security Market Prices, Returns and Accounting Measures 55

United States

U.S. accounting data are collected from the 1991 Compustat Industrial database. This was the most recent data available so U.S. data are only available up to 1990 fiscal year-ends. Price and adjustment factor data are extracted from the Center for Research in Security Prices database for a date three months following the fiscal year end. T-Bill rates of return are taken from Ibbotson Associates [1992].

The U.S. sample of 262 firms is selected by matching Japanese firms in the consolidated sample on the basis of the 1990 market value of equity and four-digit SIC code. Japanese firms are assigned an SIC code based on their four-digit Securities Identification Code given by the Japan Securities Identification Code Conference. These codes yield 66 industry classifications. Japanese and U.S. market values of equity are put on a comparable basis by converting the Japanese values at the average 1990 exchange rate extracted from Datastream. U.S. firms are required to have return and earnings data in every year from 1983 to 1990, to ensure that we impose the same survival constraints that we use for the Japanese sample.

Data Summary

Some summary descriptive statistics for the samples are reported in Table 1. Panels A, B, and C describe the results for the Japanese parent, consolidated and U.S. data, respectively.

We report medians to eliminate the impact of a small number of extreme observations. The median returns for Japan are consistent with the market patterns. Notice that the rapid run-up in prices began in 1983 and continued through 1989. While 1989 marked the beginning of the slide in Japan's stock market prices, the 1990 returns still reflect a small average increase with 1991 showing the sharp decline of close to 23 percent for both parent and consolidated samples.

It is also interesting to observe that in 1971 through 1982 the median P/E was around 20 with much lower P/Es in 1971 and 1974. The latter was clearly affected by the high interest rates. From 1983 through 1991 the P/Es have remained at high levels with 1986 to 1991 having P/Es over 40. In contrast, for the U.S. sample, the median P/Es have ranged between 11 and 16. The P/B ratios reflect a similar pattern. For Japan, the P/B based on parent data was below 2.0 up 1978 as well as from 1981 to 1983. But from 1984 the P/B began moving away from this level based

56   Charles Hall, Yasushi Hamao and Trevor S. Harris

Table 1. *Summary Statistics*

Panel A

Japan – Parent

Yr	Median Return (%)	Median P/E	Median P/B	Median ROE (%)	Spearman Correlation			Int. Rate (%)	N
					P/E, ROE	P/B, ROE	Ret, ROE		
71	6.25	10.55	1.31	12.70	−0.20	0.53	0.17	6.61	935
72	41.18	17.38	1.85	10.05	−0.25	0.40	−0.06	4.83	967
73	7.00	15.61	1.79	11.14	−0.50	0.21	−0.06	7.40	985
74	0.47	13.55	1.70	11.83	−0.58	0.15	0.11	13.29	1009
75	−4.70	17.06	1.65	8.45	−0.23	0.14	0.20	11.21	1012
76	10.83	21.56	1.86	7.03	−0.16	0.18	0.27	7.20	1050
77	4.27	20.94	1.90	8.11	−0.27	0.21	0.19	5.94	1141
78	16.39	23.52	2.22	7.89	−0.17	0.14	0.04	4.94	1158
79	0.99	20.38	2.12	9.31	−0.39	0.10	−0.05	5.48	1166
80	−0.56	18.53	2.00	9.99	−0.50	0.19	0.09	10.74	1184
81	−3.98	19.53	1.86	8.87	−0.35	0.17	0.31	7.54	1194
82	−3.74	19.67	1.67	7.98	−0.31	0.00	−0.07	6.88	1203
83	16.11	25.45	1.94	6.95	−0.21	0.06	0.16	6.57	1213
84	14.46	29.19	2.25	6.83	−0.21	0.09	0.06	6.37	1230
85	17.95	32.04	2.56	7.01	−0.36	0.14	−0.07	6.55	1245
86	28.27	45.82	3.20	6.04	−0.29	0.03	0.13	5.19	1277
87	16.00	56.27	3.61	5.54	−0.26	0.16	0.14	3.93	1260
88	27.37	59.39	4.22	6.39	−0.38	0.18	−0.05	3.98	1197
89	12.32	59.24	4.29	6.95	−0.51	0.23	−0.01	4.68	1165
90	5.89	59.15	3.90	6.25	−0.48	0.32	0.17	7.00	1207
91	−22.76	45.61	2.99	6.36	−0.47	0.35	0.27	7.38	996

Panel B

Japan – Consolidated

Yr	Median Return (%)	Median P/E	Median P/B	Median ROE (%)	Spearman Correlation			N
					P/E, ROE	P/B, ROE	Ret, ROE	
84	15.71	27.90	2.26	7.24	−0.21	0.15	0.07	364
85	16.73	28.69	2.47	7.97	−0.39	0.22	−0.02	364
86	30.18	44.17	3.18	6.48	−0.30	0.03	0.15	364
87	14.20	50.00	3.46	5.48	−0.00	0.04	0.13	364
88	28.78	55.30	4.31	6.95	−0.28	0.22	−0.04	364
89	14.96	52.45	4.34	7.66	−0.42	0.34	0.02	364
90	0.36	53.78	3.86	6.77	−0.52	0.19	0.00	364
91	−22.82	41.27	2.82	6.61	−0.41	0.24	0.29	364

Security Market Prices, Returns and Accounting Measures 57

Table 1. *Summary Statistics (contd)*
Panel C
U.S. – Consolidated

					Spearman Correlation				
Yr	Median Return (%)	Median P/E	Median P/B	Median ROE (%)	P/E, ROE	P/B, ROE	Ret, ROE	Int. Rate (%)	N
84	6.77	10.76	1.34	12.80	0.03	0.53	0.43	9.85	262
85	18.53	12.36	1.49	10.97	0.18	0.46	0.43	7.72	262
86	25.01	15.79	1.83	9.87	0.21	0.52	0.45	6.16	262
87	−1.78	13.30	1.61	11.86	0.05	0.59	0.33	5.47	262
88	7.59	11.52	1.60	14.35	−0.15	0.57	0.10	6.35	262
89	11.52	11.08	1.58	13.34	0.14	0.54	0.38	5.46	262
90	−2.05	12.73	1.46	11.31	0.21	0.53	0.44	6.34	252

Notes to Table 1: The ROE is defined as earnings divided by book value of equity.

on both parent and consolidated samples. The peak was in 1989 with the median of 4.34 for the consolidated sample. In contrast, the median P/B in the U.S. never reached 2.0 with a peak of 1.83 in 1986. In principle, we might expect high P/Bs because of high profitability, but in fact, the trend was quite the opposite. The peak (median) ROEs in Japan occurred in the early 1970s when multiples were lowest. The median ROEs in Japan were below 8 percent from 1983 onwards while in the U.S., during the same periods, the median ROEs were around 11 percent. Some of this difference is related to accelerated depreciation methods and large capital investment in Japan, and to the interest differentials between Japan and the U.S. But even with these adjustments it would be hard to argue that Japanese firms were extraordinarily profitable. Next we consider the tests of associations between accounting and stock market measures.

IV. Results of Primary Tests

In most of the reported results we use the maximum number of observations available to ensure robust statistics. All tests were also run on the limited sample of 364 firms used in the long window analysis of consolidated data for Japanese firms. In all cases the qualitative conclusions are unchanged for all subsets.

58   *Charles Hall, Yasushi Hamao and Trevor S. Harris*

Price Ratio Tests

The first set of tests relate primarily to the correlations of P/B and ROE and secondarily to P/E and ROE. As discussed, if investors consider reported earnings to be value-relevant then we can expect that there is a high positive correlation between ROE and P/B. The annual correlations are reported in Table 1. We use rank correlations so that large or small observations do not have an undue weighting. The results are reported in panel A for the Japanese parent data, in panel B for the Japanese consolidated data and in panel C for the U.S. data. For the Japanese data, in all years except 1971 and 1972, we see that the correlation is below 0.40. For the parent reports the correlations are below 0.30 from 1973 to 1989. The correlations range from 0.03 in 1986 to 0.34 in 1989 for the consolidated data. In comparison the matched sample of U.S. firms has only two years in which the correlation is less than 0.50 and in both cases the correlation is greater than 0.45. These results are consistent with the view that on average Japanese investors pay less attention to earnings than do U.S. investors.

Similarly, the rank correlations of P/E and ROE are negative and quite high in contrast to the U.S. which varies around zero. This is consistent with a greater relative focus on accounting owners' equity than earnings in Japan as compared to the U.S. where earnings seem to be more important.

The comparison of parent and consolidated data for Japanese samples is inconclusive. This suggests that the consolidated data are not necessarily superior as we might naively expect from the push towards consolidation around the world.

Returns-Earnings Associations

First, we consider the tests based on annual return windows. These results are reported in Table 2, with panels A, B and C again reporting the Japanese parent, consolidated and then U.S. samples, respectively. We also report in the last column of panels A and B the adjusted R^2 from the regressions using parent data for the restricted sample of 364 Japanese firms. Beginning with the parent data full sample, we find an R^2 greater than 0.10 in only two years, and in 1982 this appears to be driven by outliers. Furthermore, in several years, particularly in the period from 1983 to 1989, the R^2 is below 0.05. We also find little consistency in the

Security Market Prices, Returns and Accounting Measures 59

Table 2. *One Year Window Regressions*
Panel A
Japan – Parent

Yr	α_0 (t-stat)	α_1 (t-stat)	α_2 (t-stat)	Adjusted R^2	Spearman Corr.	N	Adjusted R^2 for 364 firms
71	0.08	0.62	0.02	0.052	0.41	935	0.042
	(4.9)	(6.6)	(0.6)		0.49		
72	0.58	−0.01	0.52	0.042	0.35	969	0.074
	(25.8)	(−0.1)	(5.9)		0.33		
73	0.11	0.42	0.41	0.031	0.31	986	0.050
	(6.1)	(2.1)	(3.7)		0.33		
74	0.08	−0.60	1.61	0.160	0.34	1009	0.107
	(5.4)	(−3.5)	(10.4)		0.51		
75	0.01	0.36	0.10	0.021	0.37	1012	0.060
	(0.6)	(3.1)	(1.1)		0.27		
76	0.23	0.12	0.82	0.070	0.37	1051	0.239
	(15.7)	(0.8)	(6.6)		0.37		
77	0.09	0.28	0.06	0.034	0.39	1143	0.098
	(9.4)	(3.3)	(0.8)		0.35		
78	0.27	0.16	0.26	0.025	0.22	1157	0.047
	(19.7)	(1.2)	(3.4)		0.37		
79	0.10	−0.78	1.51	0.065	0.05	1166	0.016
	(8.3)	(−4.8)	(8.8)		0.25		
80	0.03	.0.39	0.15	0.011	0.19	1184	0.022
	(2.2)	(2.2)	(1.3)		0.29		
81	0.01	0.62	0.59	0.070	0.41	1194	0.067
	(1.1)	(3.8)	(4.6)		0.39		
82	0.01	−0.21	1.03	0.164	0.08	1203	0.000
	(0.8)	(−1.8)	(11.6)		0.22		
83	0.30	−0.23	0.98	0.059	0.13	1214	0.019
	(22.4)	(−1.6)	(8.2)		0.31		
84	0.24	0.04	0.68	0.019	0.09	1229	0.004
	(17.6)	(0.2)	(4.0)		0.29		
85	0.25	0.28	0.19	0.003	0.18	1246	0.011
	(15.3)	(1.0)	(1.3)		0.12		
86	0.43	−0.61	0.94	0.007	0.26	1277	0.023
	(20.7)	(−1.6)	(2.4)		0.31		
87	0.25	1.30	0.29	0.048	0.23	1260	0.009
	(14.2)	(4.6)	(1.6)		0.28		
88	0.37	0.50	1.02	0.016	0.16	1197	0.030
	(18.7)	(0.8)	(1.8)		0.22		
89	0.17	0.39	0.02	0.000	0.16	1165	0.004
	(12.1)	(0.7)	(0.0)		0.17		
90	−0.02	7.34	−1.4	0.062	0.34	1207	0.023
	(−0.9)	(8.3)	(−2.5)		0.28		
91	−0.27	3.95	−1.38	0.096	0.43	997	0.102
	(24.5)	(7.0)	(−2.6)		0.37		

Continued overleaf

60   *Charles Hall, Yasushi Hamao and Trevor S. Harris*

Table 2. *One Year Window Regressions (contd)*
Panel B
Japan – *Consolidated*

Yr	α_0 (t-stat)	α_1 (t-stat)	α_2 (t-stat)	Adjusted R^2	Spearman Corr.	N
85	0.23	0.06	0.70	0.015	0.14	364
	(8.4)	(0.1)	(2.2)		0.20	
86	0.45	0.31	1.14	0.020	0.23	364
	(11.7)	(0.4)	(1.5)		0.30	
87	0.20	0.36	1.20	0.025	0.16	364
	(10.6)	(0.7)	(2.8)		0.24	
88	0.37	0.47	1.54	0.009	0.16	364
	(9.7)	(0.3)	(2.1)		0.25	
89	0.17	−0.15	0.50	0.000	0.09	364
	(7.1)	(−0.1)	(0.5)		0.15	
90	0.04	2.39	−1.07	0.007	0.16	364
	(1.5)	(2.0)	(−0.8)		0.14	
91	(−0.29)	3.93	−0.20	0.140	0.44	364
	(−22.4)	(6.8)	(−0.3)		0.29	

Panel C
U.S. — *Consolidated*

Yr	α_0 (t-stat)	α_1 (t-stat)	α_2 (t-stat)	Adjusted R^2	Spearman Corr.	N
83	0.19	0.68	0.46	0.066	0.34	262
	(4.0)	(3.2)	(4.5)		0.28	
84	−0.08	1.41	−0.92	0.112	0.57	262
	(−2.3)	(5.9)	(−4.1)		0.19	
85	0.12	0.78	−0.68	0.123	0.46	262
	(3.9)	(4.5)	(−6.2)		0.17	
86	0.17	0.47	0.44	0.560	0.45	262
	(4.6)	(3.8)	(5.5)		0.19	
87	−0.14	1.07	0.37	0.223	0.38	262
	(−4.0)	(4.2)	(5.6)		0.36	
88	0.03	0.23	0.47	0.116	0.43	262
	(1.0)	(1.4)	(3.4)		0.36	
89	−0.05	1.47	−0.54	0.074	0.28	262
	(−1.3)	(4.7)	(−4.1)		0.29	
90	−0.06	0.21	−0.12	0.015	0.38	262
	(−2.1)	(2.4)	(−1.1)		0.27	

Notes to Table 2: The model is $R_{iT} = \alpha_0 + \alpha_1 AE_{iT} + \alpha_2 \Delta AE_{iT} + \epsilon_{iT}$. See text for notations used in the equation. The first row of Spearman correlation is between R and AE, the second row is between R and ΔAE.

Security Market Prices, Returns and Accounting Measures   61

relative importance of the earnings levels versus changes for explaining returns and the size of the coefficients vary from year to year more than one might expect from the interest rate changes reported in Table 1. In analyzing the data we found many extreme observations which had an impact on the parametric analysis so we also provide rank correlations for returns and each independent variable. One pattern that emerges, which is consistent with the regression results, is a generally poorer correlation in the 1980s beginning in 1982.

Moving to the consolidated data, we again find very low R^2 (below 0.03) and rank correlations except for 1991. Use of consolidated data did not affect the associations in any systematic way, in four of the seven years the R^2 are higher for the restricted sample using parent accounting data. Looking at the U.S. sample for a similar period we find much higher R^2 for every year and a higher rank correlation for the independent variables which are significant in the regression models.[11]

The annual window results are consistent with the interpretation that Japanese investors pay less attention to accounting earnings than U.S. investors, but this could plausibly be a reflection of measurement problems in the accounting process. By extending the window length we attempt to control for this explanation. The results, in the annual window also suggest that the period of the 1980s reflects an even greater disregard for fundamental accounting measures in the valuation of Japanese companies.

As explained in Section III of this paper, in analyzing the long window results we were constrained by the availability of data. Japanese companies have only been required to prepare full consolidated reports (that is, including equity accounting for their associate companies) since 1983, and 1984 was the first year with large numbers of companies presenting such data. For the parent data we use a similar interval as used for the consolidated data but also consider tests based on the full sample period available which yields 20 years as a maximum window. We also report results with 1990 and 1991 as the last date. These results should not be considered as independent but the contrast between the two end-periods is quite dramatic for all window lengths and indicates the strength of the adjustment back to fundamentals.

Table 3 reports the results for four and seven year windows for the Japanese parent, consolidated and U.S. data in panels A, B and C, respectively. Panel A also includes the results for 20 year windows ending in 1990 and 1991. To minimize any concerns about independence we use essentially non-overlapping years except for the windows ending 1990

62   *Charles Hall, Yasushi Hamao and Trevor S. Harris*

Table 3. *Long Window Regressions*
Panel A
Japan – Parent

Ending yr. – length of window	α_0 (t-stat)	α_1 (t-stat)	Adjusted R^2	Spearman Corr.	N	Adjusted R^2 for 364 firms
90 - 20	6.51 (13.7)	1.84 (13.0)	0.211	0.50	647	
91 - 20	3.35 (8.1)	1.84 (13.0)	0.372	0.56	507	
78 - 7	1.00 (14.0)	1.22 (15.6)	0.214	0.53	898	0.120
84 - 7	0.67 (7.8)	1.54 (9.9)	0.080	0.28	1111	0.139
90 - 7	2.27 (16.7)	3.03 (10.3)	0.102	0.38	923	0.058
91 - 7	1.36 (15.9)	1.88 (10.4)	0.136	0.49	688	0.167
75 - 4	0.43 (12.7)	0.88 (15.5)	0.207	0.52	924	0.036
79 - 4	0.61 (16.6)	0.79 (7.7)	0.054	0.34	1019	0.144
83 - 4	0.18 (5.4)	0.90 (7.1)	0.041	0.30	1159	0.058
87 - 4	1.49 (20.2)	1.60 (5.7)	0.026	0.28	1170	0.042
90 - 4	0.87 (19.2)	1.68 (6.4)	0.038	0.30	990	0.000
91 - 4	0.00 (0.0)	4.26 (14.7)	0.223	0.52	750	0.195

Panel B
Japan – Consolidated

Ending yr. – length of window	α_0 (t-stat)	α_1 (t-stat)	Adjusted R^2	Spearman Corr.	N
91 - 8	1.26 (8.9)	2.29 (8.7)	0.170	0.46	364
90 - 7	2.48 (13.9)	1.85 (4.7)	0.054	0.32	364
91 - 7	0.95 (7.7)	2.43 (8.1)	0.151	0.48	364
87 - 4	1.32 (12.4)	1.66 (3.8)	0.035	0.24	364
90 - 4	0.91 (11.1)	1.26 (2.1)	0.012	0.29	364
91 - 4	-0.04 (-0.8)	3.60 (9.0)	0.183	0.47	364

Security Market Prices, Returns and Accounting Measures 63

Table 3. *Long Window Regressions (contd)*
Panel C
U.S. – Consolidated

Ending yr. – length of window	α_0 (t-stat)	α_1 (t-stat)	Adjusted R^2	Spearman Corr.	N
90 - 7	−0.30 (−2.4)	2.04 (16.5)	0.510	0.80	262
87 - 4	0.07 (1.1)	1.91 (15.8)	0.489	0.76	262
90 - 4	−0.24 (−3.6)	1.64 (11.2)	0.323	0.55	262

Notes to Table 3: The model is $R_{iT} = \alpha_0 + \alpha_1 AE_{iT} + \epsilon_{iT}$. See text for notations used in the equation.

or 1991 for the reasons previously indicated. As large observations can have undue influence on the parametric results we also report the Spearman rank correlations for the return and aggregate earnings variables described in equation (2).

For the seven year windows, the Japanese parent data, we see the adjusted R^2 range from 0.21 with 1978 as the end-date to 0.08 with 1984 as the end-date.[12] While 1991 had nothing unusual about its earnings (see Table 1), the R^2 increased from 0.10 in 1990 to 0.14 in 1991. The relations among the rank correlations are even more striking. For the seven year window ending in 1978 the correlation was 0.53, the 1984 end-date correlation was the lowest at 0.28 and the correlation increased from 0.38 to 0.49 when changing the end-date from 1990 to 1991. Although not reported, the R^2 for seven year windows in the period between 1983 and 1989 were all less than 0.10. Note that even when we extend the window to 20 years the R^2 increases to only 0.21 when 1990 is the end-date and then jumps to 0.37 when we move the end-date to 1991. The pattern in the rank correlations shows a similar trend.

The four year window results in Panel A are generally lower than those for the seven year windows but they are very low with R^2 no greater than 0.06 in any four-year window other than the 1975 and 1991 end-years. While we only report the non-overlapping years no other four year window had an R^2 greater than 0.08. The rank correlations are also below 0.40 except for the first and last end-years.

In general, these long window results suggest that even when we extend the window up to 20 years there seems to be little association between

64   *Charles Hall, Yasushi Hamao and Trevor S. Harris*

aggregate earnings and stock returns. But it still might be perceived that the result is a function of the use of parent data and the general lack of usefulness of accounting data. To address this we first look at Panel B which contains the results for the consolidated data. Unfortunately, we only have the period beginning with 1984 which from the parent and annual window results appears to be a period with relatively low use of accounting data in Japan. The longest window of eight years yields an R^2 of 0.17 and a rank correlation of 0.46. The seven-year window ending in 1991 gives a similar result. But the seven year window ending in 1990 shows a much lower R^2 of 0.05 and the rank correlation drops from 0.48 to 0.32. The last column in Panel A of Table 3 presents the R^2 for the parent data for the subset of 364 firms being considered in Panel B and reflects similar patterns to those of the larger sample of parent data. The four year window results show an R^2 of 0.18 for end-date 1991 but 0.01 and 0.04 for 1990 and 1987 respectively with rank correlations below 0.30 for these two end-dates.

Two points can be made from the long-window results discussed to this point. Using consolidated data does not increase the associations between returns and reported earnings and lengthening the window has some effect but only a marginal one, unlike the pattern reported in Easton, Harris and Ohlson [1992] and corroborated in other studies. But perhaps these firms are unusual in some way. The results in Panel C report the results of the long-window tests for the matched sample of U.S. firms.

The results for the U.S. firms show that for the seven-year window ending in 1990 we have an R^2 of 0.51 and a rank correlation of 0.80. The four year windows show similar differences to the Japanese results. The differences in association are quite striking and it is hard to conceive that these could be a function of accounting differences or even interest rate differentials (see Table 1). Thus, once again, the results are consistent with the hypothesis that Japanese investors paid much less attention to the fundamental values reflected in accounting measures. The results also suggest that the price adjustments we have observed reflect a movement back towards the fundamentals but it would be hard to argue that this process is complete using only the 1991 data.

However, before drawing these conclusions too strongly we consider some additional factors which might be perceived to be omitted variables which would help to explain the results.

Security Market Prices, Returns and Accounting Measures 65

V. The Role of Earnings Forecasts and Depreciation

Management's Earnings Forecast

Darrough and Harris [1991] show that while investors do react to announcements of earnings, the reaction is affected by the management forecast of earnings issued simultaneously with historic earnings. We would expect rational investors who use earnings in their valuation of companies to incorporate the forecasted future earnings into the price. Consequently, we use the management forecast of consolidated earnings for 1992 (deflated by beginning price) as an additional variable in the regression model based on equation (2) with 1991 as the end-year, for the consolidated sample. These results are reported in Table 4.

For the seven and eight year windows we obtain an R^2 of 0.23 as compared to 0.15 and 0.17 (respectively) for the aggregate earnings alone. We see some increment in the four year window but only a small difference in the one year window. The results suggest that there is additional information in the earnings forecast but that it still leaves a significant amount of the stock returns unexplained especially as compared to the U.S. sample.

Depreciation

As discussed in Section II of this paper, many studies have argued that depreciation is a cause of differences between the U.S. and Japan which affects the relations of accounting and stock market data. While this is

Table 4. *Japan – Consolidated with Management Forecast*

Ending yr. – *length of* *window*	α_0 *(t-stat)*	α_1 *(t-stat)*	α_2 *(t-stat)*	*Adjusted* R^2	*Spearman* *Corr.* *between* *ret. and* *forecast*	*N*
91 - 8	1.16 (8.4)	1.74 (6.4)	2.30 (5.4)	0.229	0.56	364
91 - 7	0.83 (6.8)	1.55 (4.8)	3.41 (6.1)	0.227	0.55	364
91 - 1	−0.29 (−23.7)	3.33 (5.8)	0.46 (1.8)	0.146	0.43	364

Notes to Table 4: The model is $R_{iT} = \alpha_0 + \alpha_1 AE_{iT} + \alpha_2 FE_{iT} + \epsilon_{iT}$, where *FE* is forecast of earnings by management divided by the beginning stock price.

66   *Charles Hall, Yasushi Hamao and Trevor S. Harris*

spurious as an argument about alternative GAAP, it is conceivable that on average a more conservative depreciation policy may understate earnings in periods of rapid capital expansion as occurred in the 1980s in Japan. We also observe that Chan, Hamao and Lakonishok [1991] find that net income plus depreciation is more highly correlated with monthly returns than reported earnings.[13] In general, depreciation may be useful as an additional explanatory variable reflecting, or proxying for, the expected growth of a company. In relatively short windows depreciation may also reflect measurement errors in reported earnings. However, by extending the window we essentially control for such measurement problems. For U.S. companies, Ohlson and Penman [1992] have analyzed components of earnings within the long window framework. Over a ten year window, they found that depreciation has a negative coefficient approximating the (positive) earnings coefficient in magnitude. This suggests that once we control for measurement problems found in short windows, investors seem to price depreciation like any other expense. Consequently, to evaluate the value-relevance of depreciation in Japan we rerun the analysis for the parent sample using earnings plus depreciation and depreciation as separate variables.[14]

The results of these tests are reported in Table 5. Panels A and B report the results for the Japanese parent and U.S. samples respectively. The results for the Japanese parent show that depreciation seems to help explain more of the cross-sectional variation in returns. The R^2 for the one year regressions increase in each year and the depreciation variable has a significant coefficient in most of the years. But we see that in the U.S. sample while the impact on the R^2 is not as large, there is an increase in the one year windows and the coefficient on depreciation is generally positive. These results suggest that depreciation is probably proxying for some other value-relevant information variable or may be reflecting investors' perceptions of a measurement error. As we increase the window the increase in R^2 is maintained in the Japanese sample so, for example, we see the R^2 for the seven year windows ending 1978, 1984 and 1991 increasing from 0.21, 0.08 and 0.14 (in Table 3 panel A) to 0.37, 0.16 and 0.17 respectively. But the coefficients on the depreciation variables are now negative and quite similar in magnitude to the coefficient on aggregate earnings (especially if we adjust for earnings being an after-tax measure). These results are consistent with investors treating aggregate depreciation similarly to any other expense once we control for periodic measurement issues and also that depreciation may proxy for cross-sectional differences in anticipated growth via capital

Security Market Prices, Returns and Accounting Measures 67

expenditure. The results for the seven year window for the U.S. sample show a similar result in terms of the coefficients but the aggregate depreciation makes no incremental contribution to the R^2. Given the relatively heavy investment in capital equipment in Japan through much of the sample period it is perhaps not surprising that the depreciation expense proxies for some value-relevant information, however given the long window results it is hard to argue that this is purely a consequence of accounting measurement questions. Further analysis of this question is beyond the scope of this particular research.

VI. Summary and Conclusions

The debate on the consequences of differences in accounting practices and the effect of these differences on the valuation of securities has frequently considered adjustments to the accounting system with an assumption, at least implictly, that this would 'normalize' the comparative associations between accounting and stock market measures. Yet there has been little systematic evaluation of these associations, particularly where many of the measurement concerns are largely controlled for.

Table 5. *Regressions with Depreciation*
Panel A-1
Japan – Parent (Long Windows)

Ending yr. – length of window	α_0 (t-stat)	α_1 (t-stat)	α_2 (t-stat)	Adjusted R^2	Spearman Corr.	N
78 - 7	0.28 (3.1)	1.48 (15.6)	−1.08 (−8.9)	0.371	0.69 0.59	789
84 - 7	−0.13 (−1.1)	2.53 (12.4)	−2.04 (−8.2)	0.163	0.41 0.32	977
90 - 7	1.79 (9.6)	3.92 (9.5)	−3.51 (−7.0)	0.127	0.41 0.29	781
91 - 7	1.10 (10.4)	2.12 (10.6)	−1.82 (−6.9)	0.170	0.44 0.21	631
83 - 4	0.05 (1.1)	1.28 (8.6)	−1.15 (−6.4)	0.064	0.28 0.12	1069
87 - 4	1.34 (13.0)	1.80 (4.3)	−1.33 (−2.6)	0.024	0.32 0.23	1089
90 - 4	0.70 (12.6)	1.95 (7.3)	−1.12 (−3.0)	0.078	0.32 0.19	871
91 - 4	−0.15 (−3.4)	5.09 (16.7)	−4.85 (−12.9)	0.296	0.49 0.24	729

Continued overleaf

68   *Charles Hall, Yasushi Hamao and Trevor S. Harris*

Table 5. *Regressions with Depreciation (contd)*
Panel A-2
Japan – Parent (One Year Windows)

Yr	α_0 (t-stat)	α_1 (t-stat)	α_2 (t-stat)	α_3 (t-stat)	α_4 (t-stat)	Adjusted R^2	N
71	−0.03	1.12	−0.18	−1.05	0.61	0.092	925
	(−1.1)	(7.1)	(−1.3)	(−5.0)	(2.4)		
72	0.27	0.88	1.12	0.61	−0.48	0.260	945
	(8.3)	(4.5)	(6.0)	(3.0)	(−2.8)		
73	−0.11	1.09	0.26	0.44	−0.21	0.183	966
	(−4.6)	(5.0)	(1.7)	(1.9)	(−1.7)		
74	−1.10	0.30	1.25	0.85	−1.10	0.277	993
	(−5.2)	(1.7)	(8.1)	(4.2)	(−5.0)		
75	0.01	0.57	0.21	−0.55	1.06	0.066	966
	(0.5)	(3.2)	(1.3)	(−2.6)	(4.4)		
76	0.12	0.55	1.00	0.53	0.30	0.140	977
	(5.0)	(2.7)	(6.2)	(2.1)	(0.9)		
77	0.05	0.46	−0.02	−0.05	0.22	0.047	1073
	(3.5)	(4.0)	(−0.2)	(−0.3)	(0.6)		
78	0.17	0.65	0.70	0.36	−1.30	0.070	1089
	(7.9)	(3.1)	(5.0)	(1.3)	(−2.7)		
79	−0.04	−0.26	1.07	2.14	−4.30	0.141	1113
	(−2.3)	(−1.3)	(6.0)	(8.3)	(−5.4)		
80	0.04	0.22	0.27	−0.33	0.26	0.004	1146
	(2.0)	(0.9)	(1.5)	(−1.0)	(0.3)		
81	−0.02	0.95	0.28	−0.73	1.91	0.049	1153
	(−1.2)	(5.1)	(1.8)	(−3.1)	(2.6)		
82	−0.05	0.16	0.16	0.24	−0.80	0.020	1154
	(−3.9)	(1.2)	(1.8)	(1.4)	(−1.7)		
83	0.27	0.04	0.85	0.13	−0.53	0.019	1150
	(12.8)	(0.2)	(3.8)	(0.5)	(−0.7)		
84	0.20	0.10	0.48	0.51	−1.32	0.012	1164
	(9.6)	(0.3)	(1.9)	(1.4)	(−3.1)		
85	0.18	0.29	0.60	0.95	−1.00	0.030	1200
	(8.2)	(0.8)	(2.1)	(2.1)	(−2.5)		
86	0.47	−1.00	1.22	0.84	−2.10	0.005	1232
	(16.3)	(−2.1)	(2.6)	(1.4)	(−1.3)		
87	0.16	3.58	0.33	−2.36	−10.93	0.040	1198
	(5.9)	(4.8)	(1.7)	(−2.6)	(−4.0)		
88	0.17	3.03	0.36	0.85	0.00	0.086	1155
	(6.8)	(3.7)	(0.5)	(0.9)	(0.0)		
89	0.12	1.89	−0.44	−1.70	−2.98	0.010	1091
	(6.9)	(2.8)	(−2.1)	(−2.1)	(−1.4)		
90	0.02	5.75	1.18	−5.32	0.91	0.062	1113
	(1.1)	(5.4)	(1.1)	(−4.3)	(0.3)		
91	−0.27	4.14	−1.27	−4.35	1.77	0.096	994
	(−20.7)	(6.7)	(−2.0)	(−6.2)	(1.0)		

Security Market Prices, Returns and Accounting Measures 69

Table 5. *Regressions with Depreciation (contd)*
Panel B
U.S. – Consolidated

Ending yr. – length of window	α_0 (t-stat)	α_1 (t-stat)	α_2 (t-stat)	Adjusted R^2	Spearman Corr.	N
89 - 7	−0.39	1.94	−1.59	0.502	0.69	260
	(−1.9)	(12.9)	(−5.4)		0.26	
90 - 7	−0.23	2.11	−2.28	0.510	0.69	260
	(−1.6)	(15.0)	(−8.7)		0.31	
87 - 4	0.01	1.85	−1.6	0.492	0.68	260
	(0.1)	(14.3)	(−6.5)		0.20	
90 - 4	−0.43	1.57	−0.95	0.365	0.46	260
	(−5.4)	(11.0)	(−4.4)		0.09	

Notes to Table 5:
In Panel A-1 and B, the model is $R_{iT} = \alpha_0 + \alpha_1(AE_{iT} + D_{iT}) + \alpha_2 D_{iT} + \epsilon_{iT}$, where D_{iT} is cumulative depreciation per share divided by beginning stock price.
In Panel A-2, the model is $R_{iT} = \alpha_0 + \alpha_1(AE_{iT} + D_{iT}) + \alpha_2\Delta(AE_{iT} + D_{iT}) + \alpha_3 D_{iT} + \alpha_4\Delta D_{iT} + \epsilon_{iT}$. The first row of Spearman correlation in Panels A-1 and B is between R and $(AE + D)$, the second row is between R and D.
See text for notations used in the equations.

In this paper, we analyze the return-earnings associations over varying window lengths and compare the results for samples of Japanese and U.S. firms. Our results are consistent with the perception that Japanese investors utilize accounting information, particularly earnings, less in their pricing of companies than do U.S. investors. The corollary is that Japanese investors place a larger weight on 'other information' in their valuations. This conclusion was particularly evident in the 'boom' period of the mid-1980s when the fundamental values inherent in the accounting data appear to have been largely ignored. The increased associations we find with the inclusion of 1991 prices suggest that the current fall in prices is consistent with a return to more emphasis on fundamental values but that this process may not be complete.

We also find results consistent with the notion that depreciation is treated simply as an expense over long windows but it also appears to act as a proxy for anticipated growth from capital investment. Further research would be needed to test this hypothesis more directly.

A further implication of the research findings is that it is implausible that accounting differences can ever explain differences in the associations between accounting and stock market measure in Japan relative to other

70   *Charles Hall, Yasushi Hamao and Trevor S. Harris*

countries. The fact that the associations are so similar for consolidated and parent data itself indicates that using the lack of consolidation as an explanation for past differences is implausible. Rather, investors seeking to make investment decisions in Japan need to reconsider the underlying pricing and institutional practices. Using differences in accounting practice to justify the valuation differentials across countries is essentially using accounting as a scapegoat for more fundamental structural differences.

Notes

1. This was reported in *The Nikkei Weekly* of the week of June 13, 1992. The advisory body is a subcommittee of the Council on Foreign Exchange and Other Transactions.
2. In a study of the information content of Japanese earnings over short windows, Darrough and Harris [1991] show that there is a market reaction to the announcement of earnings and the management forecast of earnings with a more noticeable reaction occurring for the parent earnings. This suggests that investors do consider earnings as a measure of information about the firm. Also, Chan, Hamao and Lakonishok [1991] test associations between monthly returns and various fundamental variables, but their tests use 12 return measures for each accounting measure and use various combinations of variables over annual windows without considering the accounting or valuation characteristics of the variables.
3. The issue of cross-holdings is also sometimes considered (Aron [1987, 1989] and French and Poterba [1991]) but we view this as a moot point when evaluating returns-earnings associations as each share owns a portion of the net assets irrespective of who holds the share. To the extent the company owns in itself there would be a reduction in the net assets as well as the equity. This position is also taken in Brown, Soybel and Stickney [1991].
4. Of course, this presumes that, in fact, the consolidation rules reflect the notion of capturing the group structure. We would conjecture that in Japan a problem remains because of the nature of the stable shareholdings and the significant influence which exists in the keiretsu. This institutional characteristic would argue for equity accounting of these holdings even though the stakes are below the traditional twenty percent threshold. Thus, in Japan, we might reasonably expect an understatement of earnings and equity based on the as-if equity accounting measures that could be used. This does not presume a mark-to-market measure which would create a circularity in the associations.
5. A similar model derived more heuristically is found in Wilcox [1984]. Ohlson's model is found to have empirical validity in Easton and Harris [1991b] and Maydew [1992]. Dividend terms have been found to be empirically irrelevant in the studies on U.S. data. Given the relatively low dividend payouts in Japan, this insignificance should be even more true there. Consequently, we ignore dividends in the rest of the paper.
6. Fairfield and Harris [1991] and Penman [1991] have demonstrated a strong correlation between P/B and ROE for US firms.
7. Ohlson [1989] formally models this relation and Easton and Harris [1991a] derive and empirically test the relation between earnings levels, earnings changes and returns and show that on average the earnings level variable is relevant for explaining returns. Corroborating evidence can also be found in Easton and Harris [1991b], Easton, Harris and Ohlson [1992], Warfield and Wild [1992] for U.S. companies and Harris and Lang [1992] for German companies.

Security Market Prices, Returns and Accounting Measures 71

8. Easton, Harris and Ohlson [1992] and Ohlson and Penman [1991] and Lys, Ramesh and Thiagarajan [1992] use alternative definitions of change in earnings. Easton, Harris and Ohlson use the simple change based on an equivalent time period while the others view change in earnings based on the difference between earnings at the beginning and the end of the relevant window. In general, as one extends the window, the changes variable becomes less well-defined and has little relevance in explaining returns. Hence we do not incorporate the change variable into our long window analysis.

9. Other studies have corroborated these findings including, Lys, Ramesh and Thiagarajan [1992] and Warfield and Wild [1992].

10. A report in *The Nikkei Weekly* of January 11, 1992 states:

'Sony's stock has been performing poorly in recent months, and stock market observers are critical about the company's consolidated-based management style. . . . Even some Sony officials have begun voicing concern that the emphasis on the consolidation-based management might be wrong.

"That strategy might have resulted in our not paying enough attention to the parent company's profits," said one official.' (page 8)

11. Comparisons of R^2 must always be interpreted cautiously if the dependent variable changes in any way. The spirit of the comparisons is from the sense of accounting measures being fundamental measures of value or change in value and a standard worldwide valuation model. Thus, *ex ante*, each sample can be considered a random drawing from the same population.

12. Easton, Harris and Ohlson [1992] note that the choice of a start-date and end-date and the means of choosing the sample had little bearing on the correlations for the ten-year window correlations and R^2 for U.S. data.

13. Chan, Hamao and Lakonishok [1991] term this variable 'cash flow' as is often done in the finance literature, but this is clearly a misnomer given that depreciation is the only adjustment made to report earnings.

14. In principle we should adjust the depreciation addback to earnings for the tax rate. However, Chan, Hamao and Lakonishok [1991] and others have not done this and the data is not readily available to us. Thus the earnings plus depreciation variable is partially misspecified. In addition, we use the parent sample because the consolidated depreciation was only available to us for less than half the 364 firms. Given the lack of difference in consolidated and parent returns-earnings associations this should have little impact on the interpretation of our results.

References

Aron, Paul, "Japanese Price Earnings Multiples: Refined and Updated," Daiwa Securities America (May 1987).

Aron, Paul, "Japanese P/E Ratios and Accounting II: Rhetoric and Reality," Daiwa Securities America (August 1989).

Bildersee, John J., John J. Cheh, and Changwoo Lee, "The International Price-Earnings Ratio Phenomenon: A Partial Explanation," *Japan and the World Economy* (1990), 263–282.

Brown, Paul R., Virginia E. Soybel and Clyde P. Stickney, "Achieving Comparability of U.S. and Japanese Financial Statement Data," Working Paper, New York University (1991).

Chan, Louis, Yasushi Hamao and Josef Lakonishok, 1991, "Fundamentals and Stock Prices in Japan," *Journal of Finance* (December 1991), 739–1764.

72   *Charles Hall, Yasushi Hamao and Trevor S. Harris*

Choi, Frederick D. S., and Richard M. Levich, *The Capital Market Effects of International Accounting Diversity* (Homewood, IL: Dow Jones-Irwin, 1990).

Darrough, Masako N. and Trevor S. Harris, "Do Management Forecasts of Earnings Affect Stock Prices in Japan?" in William T. Ziemba, Warren Bailey and Yasushi Hamao eds. *Japanese Financial Market Research* (Amsterdam: North-Holland, 1991), 197–229.

Dontoh, Alex, Livnat, Joshua, and Rebecca Todd, "International Comparisons of Earnings Price Ratio, Estimation Risk and Growth," Working Paper, New York University (November 1991).

Easton, Peter D. and Trevor S. Harris, "Empirical Evidence on the Relevance of Earnings and Book Value of Owners' Equity in Security Valuation," Working Paper, Columbia University (1991a).

Easton, Peter D. and Trevor S. Harris, "Earnings as an Explanatory Variable for Returns," *Journal of Accounting Research* (1991b), 19–36.

Easton, Peter D., Trevor S. Harris and James A. Ohlson, "Accounting Earnings Can Explain Most of Security Returns: The Case of Long Return Intervals," *Journal of Accounting and Economics* (forthcoming, 1992).

Fairfield, Patricia M. and Trevor S. Harris, "An Investigation of Intrinsic Value and Risk as Explanations of the Returns to Price-to-Earnings and Price-to-Book Value Trading Strategies," Working Paper, Columbia University (1991).

French, Kenneth and James Poterba, "Were Japanese Stock Too High?" *Journal of Financial Economics* 29 (1991), 337–363.

Hamao, Yasushi, "A Standard Data Base for the Analysis of Japanese Security Markets," *Journal of Business* 64 (January 1991), 87–102.

Hamao, Yasushi and Roger G. Ibbotson, *SBI – Japan (with updates)* (Chicago: Ibbotson Associates, 1992).

Harris, Trevor S. and Mark Lang, "Relations Between Security Market Prices, Returns and Accounting Measures in Germany," Working Paper, Columbia University (September 1992).

Harris, Trevor S. and James A. Ohlson, "Accounting Disclosures and the Market's Valuation of Oil and Gas Properties," *The Accounting Review* (October 1987), 651–670.

Ibbotson Associates, *Stocks, Bills, Bonds and Inflation* (Chicago, 1992).

Lys, T., K. Ramesh and S. Thiagarajan, "The Role of Earnings Levels vs Earnings Changes in Explaining Stock Returns: Implications from the Time Series Properties of Earnings," Working Paper, Northwestern University (1992).

Maydew, Edmund L., "An Empirical Evaluation of Earnings and Book Values in Security Valuation," Working Paper, University of Iowa (1992).

McCauley, Robert N. and Stephen Zimmer, "The Cost of Capital for Securities Firms in the United States and Japan," Federal Reserve Bank of New York Quarterly Reviews (Fall 1991), 14–27.

Ohlson, James A., "Accounting Earnings, Book Value and Dividends: the Theory of the Clean Surplus Equation (Part I)," Working Paper, Columbia University (1989).

Ohlson, James A., "Earnings, Book Values, and Dividends in Security Valuation," Working Paper, Columbia University (1991).

Ohlson, James A. and Stephen H. Penman, "Disaggregated Accounting Data as Explanatory Variables for Returns," *Journal of Accounting, Auditing and Finance* (forthcoming, 1992).

Penman, Stephen H., "An Evaluation of Accounting Rate of Return," *Journal of Accounting, Auditing and Finance* (1991).

Security Market Prices, Returns and Accounting Measures   73

Poterba, James, ''Comparing the Cost of Capital in the United States and Japan: A Survey of Methods,'' *Federal Reserve Bank of New York Quarterly Reviews* (Winter 1991), 20–32.

Sakakibara, Shigeki, Hidetoshi Yamaji, Hisakatsu Sakurai, Kengo Shiroshita and Shimon Fukuda, *The Japanese Stock Market: Pricing Systems and Accounting Information* (New York: Praeger, 1988).

Schieneman Gary S., ''Japanese P/E Ratios: Are They Overstated By Conservative Accounting Practices?'' *International Accounting and Investment Review* (Prudential-Bache Securities, June 1988).

Tokyo Keizai Shimpo Sha, *Japan Company Handbook* (Tokyo, September 1992).

Viner, Aron, *Inside Japanese Financial Markets* (Homewood, IL: Dow Jones-Irwin, 1988).

Warfield, Terry D. and John Wild, ''Accounting Recognition and the Relevance of Earnings as an Explanatory Variable for Returns,'' *The Accounting Review* (forthcoming, 1992).

Wilcox, J.W., ''The P/B-ROE Valuation Model,'' *Financial Analysts Journal* (January-February 1984), 58–66.

Zielinski, Robert, and Nigel Holloway, *Unequal Equities: Power and Risk in Japan's Stock Market* (Tokyo: Kodansha International, 1991).

Part IV
Foreign Currency Translation
by US Multinationals

[15]

THE ACCOUNTING REVIEW
Vol. LIX, No. 3
July 1984

The Rationale Underlying the Functional Currency Choice

Lawrence Revsine

ABSTRACT: FASB Statement No. 52 on Foreign Currency Translation is designed to achieve compatibility between financial statement numbers and underlying economic effects of exchange rate changes. This result is accomplished through the selection of what the FASB terms the functional currency of the foreign subsidiary. Unfortunately, the rationale underlying the functional currency choice is complicated and not widely understood. To overcome the problem, this paper explains the objectives behind the functional currency choice by using three illustrative case settings.

FASB Statement Number 52 on Foreign Currency Translation was issued in December 1981. This Statement superseded the highly controversial Statement 8. Statement 8 was attacked because of the widespread belief that firms were compelled to report foreign currency gains and losses that bore little correspondence to the economic effects that they were actually experiencing. Under Statement 8, firms might report foreign exchange *gains* when their underlying real foreign exchange position was *deteriorating*, and vice versa. By contrast, Statement 52 is intended to achieve compatibility between firms' reported exchange gains and losses and these firms' underlying real economic changes.

Statement 52 tries to achieve compatibility between the accounting numbers and the underlying economic effects by allowing firms discretion in selecting a foreign subsidiary's *functional currency*. The FASB describes the subsidiary's functional currency as "the currency of the primary economic environment in which the entity operates..." To illustrate, if a U.S. parent has a Dutch subsidiary that conducts business in both Holland and France, the functional cur-

rency might be the parent's currency (the dollar), or the subsidiary's currency (the guilder), or even the French franc. Individual circumstances must be used to determine which currency should be selected as the functional currency.

Understanding the factors that govern the functional currency choice is crucial for achieving the primary objective of Statement 52—i.e., compatibility between financial numbers and underlying economics. Unfortunately, the underlying goals and objectives for selecting among the possible functional currencies of a subsidiary are complicated. The concepts underlying the procedures are often particularly difficult for students to grasp. To overcome the problem, this paper explains the rationale behind the functional currency choice by using three illustrative case settings.

The author gratefully acknowledges the helpful comments of Arthur R. Wyatt of Arthur Andersen & Co. and Professor Robert P. Magee of Northwestern University.

Lawrence Revsine is Eric L. Kohler Professor of Accounting and Information Systems, Northwestern University.

Manuscript Received July 1983.
Accepted October 1983.

The Accounting Review, July 1984

Case I presents a series of foreign currency transactions and shows their financial statement effects. Case II is identical to Case I in an economic sense except that the foreign transactions are undertaken through a subsidiary that acts as a conduit for transforming foreign currency flows into dollars. The example demonstrates that applying the FASB's functional currency guidelines in Case II leads to financial statements identical to those derived in Case I. This equivalence is not accidental; instead, the FASB guidelines are designed to generate consolidated results for a conduit subsidiary that are identical to the statement results that arise when the foreign transactions are undertaken directly by the parent. Finally, Case III introduces a modification of the Case II assumptions that alters the underlying economics. The example shows how the FASB guidelines lead to the selection of a different functional currency in Case III and why the chosen functional currency captures the altered economic circumstances.

Thus, the objective of this paper is to clarify the rationale underlying the functional currency choice. A thorough understanding of the rationale should enable students (who will soon become managers, auditors, and external statement users) to apply and interpret Statement 52 in an informed manner and thereby achieve the compatibility benefits sought by the FASB.

FOREIGN CURRENCY TRANSACTIONS: CASE I

The need to select a functional currency exists only when the financial statements of a foreign subsidiary are consolidated with those of the parent or when the equity method is used. While the functional currency choice arises only as a prelude to combining intercorporate interests, it is easier to under-

stand the rationale behind the Statement 52 rules if we first consider a simple nonconsolidation setting which will be called Case I.

Assume in Case I that the Wildcat Corporation, a U.S. company, desires to sell its product in Britain. On January 1, 19x5, when the exchange rate was 1£ = 1.50$, Wildcat purchased a warehouse building in London to facilitate product distribution. The building cost £200,000, which is equivalent to $300,000 at the date of purchase. It also deposited £5,000 (equivalent to $7,500) in a London bank. On July 1, 19x5, it makes credit sales totalling £100,000 when the exchange rate is still 1£ = 1.50$. Wildcat produced these goods in the U.S. at a total cost of $110,000. The receivables are collected on August 1, 19x5, when the exchange rate is 1£ = 1.40$. The proceeds are converted into dollars and remitted to Wildcat's U.S. headquarters. (For simplicity, we ignore all other costs which might be incurred.) Further assume that the exchange rate was 1£ = 1.39$ at December 31, 19x5.

In Case I, there is no foreign subsidiary. The facts simply describe a series of foreign currency transactions encompassing purchase of a foreign nonmonetary asset (a building), a monetary asset (the £ deposit), and the credit sale.

The accounting for these transactions is straightforward and noncontroversial under the assumed conditions. The transactions that would be recorded on Wildcat's books are described below.

Purchase of a Foreign Nonmonetary Asset (*London Building*)

At the time of purchase, the dollar equivalent cost of the building would be recorded. The entry would be:

DR   Building $300,000
    CR   Cash $300,000
(To record purchase of building for £200,000 when the exchange rate was 1£ = 1.50$.)

No adjustment to the gross book value is needed at the end of 19x5, despite the fact that the exchange rate is then $1£ = 1.39\$$. This is a direct consequence of historical cost accounting; original transaction amounts (in this case, the dollar equivalent cost) are entered and not subsequently adjusted. (For simplicity, we ignore depreciation.)

Purchase of a Monetary Asset (Sterling Deposit)

When the pound sterling account is opened, the following entry is made:

```
DR   Cash ($ equivalent of £
        deposit)              $7,500
   CR      Cash                        $7,500
(To record deposit of £5,000 when the exchange rate
was 1£ = 1.50$.)
```

Again for simplicity, we assume that the account balance was maintained intact throughout the year. Since the year-end exchange rate has fallen to $1£ = 1.39\$$, the dollar equivalent of the sterling deposit is only $6,950; thus, a loss has arisen as a consequence of the foreign currency transaction. In accordance with existing U.S. accounting practice, monetary assets are shown at net expected realizable value and therefore the loss to date must be recognized in the accounts of Wildcat. The entry is:

```
DR   Foreign exchange loss   $550
   CR      Cash                        $550
(To reflect the decline in the dollar equivalent of the
foreign currency deposit balance; $7,500 – $6,950.)
```

Foreign Currency Sales Transaction

Wildcat Corporation's British sales were denominated in pounds sterling; these are clearly foreign currency transactions. Exchange rate changes between the time of the original transaction and the time of eventual conversion into dollars result in foreign exchange gains or losses. The accounting entries are:

```
DR   Accounts receivable   $150,000
   CR      Sales revenue                $150,000
```

```
DR   Cost of goods sold     $110,000
   CR      Inventory                     $110,000
(To record sterling denominated sales of £100,000 at
their dollar equivalent in terms of the then prevailing
exchange rate of 1£ = 1.50$ and to record associated
cost of goods sold.)
```

Upon collection, the foreign currency receivables are immediately converted to dollars at the exchange rate of $1£ = 1.40\$$. The entry on Wildcat's books would be:

```
DR   Cash                    $140,000
DR   Foreign exchange loss   $ 10,000
   CR      Accounts receivable          $150,000
(To record collection of £100,000 receivables and
conversion to dollars at a rate of 1£ = 1.40$.)
```

To help the reader visualize the overall effect of this accounting treatment, a partial balance sheet and income statement for Wildcat Corporation are presented in Figure 1. These statements include only the foreign assets and results of the foreign operations that are included in the example.

It will be useful to summarize the accounting treatment incorporated in the example. First, foreign currency transactions, whether completed (i.e., the dollar proceeds from sales) or uncompleted (i.e., the sterling deposit), have an immediate or potentially immediate impact on future dollar cash flows. Because of this dollar flow impact, foreign currency gains or losses are recorded as they occur and are included in income. Second, nonmonetary asset acquisitions follow the historical cost convention; therefore, the original dollar cash equivalent of the nonmonetary asset cost is carried forward in the accounts, despite subsequent exchange rate changes.

With this background, we are now able to turn to the central issue —an explanation of the rationale underlying the choice of functional currency.

THE DOLLAR AS THE FUNCTIONAL CURRENCY: CASE II

The theory underlying the selection of a functional currency will be illustrated

The Accounting Review, July 1984

FIGURE 1

WILDCAT CORPORATION PARTIAL BALANCE SHEET
(AS OF DECEMBER 31, 19x5) AND INCOME STATEMENT
(FOR THE YEAR ENDED DECEMBER 31, 19x5)

Balance Sheet

Cash
Dollar deposits $140,000
Sterling deposit—
dollar equivalent   6,950

		Retained earnings
Building	300,000	($150,000 – 110,000
		– 10,000 – 550)
		$29,450

Income Statement

Sales revenues	$150,000
Cost of goods sold	(110,000)
Foreign exchange loss	
(10,000 + 550)	(10,550)
Net Income	$ 29,450

using a slightly altered version of the
Wildcat Corporation example, called
Case II. All assumptions in Case I are
retained except that we now further assume that Wildcat forms a wholly owned
British subsidiary, Proper Kitty, Ltd.,
which handles British sales. As before,
however, all goods are shipped from the
U.S., and British sales receipts are converted into dollars and remitted back to
the U.S.

When Proper Kitty, Ltd. is formed,
Wildcat Corporation would make the
following entry:

DR   Investment in subsidiary $307,500
      CR   Cash $307,500
(To record formation of subsidiary which purchases a
building for £200,000 and deposits £5,000 in a London
bank. The exchange rate at the time of formation is
1£ = 1.50$.)

Immediately after formation, Proper
Kitty, Ltd.'s balance sheet would appear
as follows:

Proper Kitty Ltd.
Balance Sheet as of January 1, 19x5

Cash	£ 5,000		
Building	200,000	Equity	£205,000
	£205,000		£205,000

Notice that Proper Kitty's equity
(£205,000) when translated at the exchange rate of 1£ = 1.50$ is precisely
equal to the $307,500 investment in sub-
sidiary account on Wildcat's books.

When Wildcat ships goods to Proper
Kitty, we assume that the following entry
is made on Wildcat's books:

DR   Receivable due from
         subsidiary $150,000
DR   Cost of goods sold   110,000
      CR   Inventory $110,000
      CR   Sales revenue   150,000
(To reflect shipment of goods to subsidiary, accounted
for at eventual sales value.)

Assuming that Wildcat bills Proper Kitty
Ltd. in sterling, when the dollar proceeds
from the £100,000 sales are remitted to
Wildcat on August 1, 19x5, the following
entry would be made on Wildcat's books:

DR   Cash $140,000
DR   Foreign exchange loss   10,000
      CR   Receivable due from
                 subsidiary $150,000
(To reflect receipt of proceeds from £100,000 sales
when the exchange rate was 1£ = 1.40$.)

After remitting the cash back to Wildcat,
Proper Kitty's balance sheet will be identical to that shown above for January 1,
19x5. Since no further entries take place
during 19x5, these balances also reflect
balance sheet carrying amounts at December 31, 19x5. The income statement
would show:

Property Kitty, Ltd.
Income Statement for the Year Ended
December 31, 19x5

Sales revenues	£100,000
Cost of goods sold	100,000
Net Profit	0

Obviously, forming a subsidiary has
complicated Wildcat's accounting entries
considerably. Intercompany accounts
must now be kept and consolidation adjustments and eliminations must be
made. However, the reader should verify
that the underlying transactions and

basic economic effects in Case II are absolutely identical to those in Case I. Whereas Wildcat itself undertook the transactions in the earlier example, here these same transactions are performed through a subsidiary. But the organizational form does not alter the ultimate economic effects. *The two cases are completely equivalent in an economic sense.*

If the two cases are equivalent, logic suggests that the consolidated numbers that result from a subsidiary's foreign transactions should be identical to those that would have resulted if the parent had undertaken the transactions directly. This is precisely what the FASB's functional currency guidelines accomplish. Let's see how.

Prior to consolidation, Statement 52 requires a company to identify the functional currency of its foreign subsidiaries. In Case II, the question is whether Proper Kitty's functional currency is the pound or the dollar. It is important to understand two characteristics of this choice:

1) The functional currency will not *always* be the currency in which the subsidiary's statements are expressed; and
2) The functional currency choice is intended to trigger a set of accounting mechanisms which result in reported foreign exchange numbers that correspond to the underlying economics.

The FASB presents guidelines for choosing the functional currency. These guidelines are reproduced in Table 1.

The FASB guidelines help determine whether the subsidiary is a free-standing unit or simply an intermediary that exists only as a conduit for transforming foreign currency transactions into dollar cash flows. When the subsidiary is simply a conduit, the consolidation approach treats the foreign currency statements of the subsidiary as artifacts which must be remeasured into dollars.

In Case II, FASB indicators A(2), D(2), and F(2) identify Proper Kitty as simply a conduit for foreign transaction cash flows back into dollars. In other words, the subsidiary is artificial; it is as if Wildcat had engaged in the foreign transactions directly. In such situations, the functional currency is the dollar, not the pound. The reporting goal is to end up with financial statements equivalent to those that would have resulted had Wildcat entered into the foreign transactions directly (i.e., as in Case I), rather than through Proper Kitty. This result is accomplished by using the temporal method [FASB, 1975, Appendix D] to remeasure pounds into dollars and by treating any remeasurement gains or losses as an element of Wildcat's income.

In the temporal method, monetary assets are translated at the current rate of exchange, nonmonetary assets at the historical rate of exchange, and income statement items at the rate that was in effect at the time of the transaction.[1] After using these rates to remeasure Proper Kitty's accounts, the result yields a dollar measure for each account that would have resulted had the original transactions been recorded initially in dollars. This is illustrated in Figure 2, where the temporal method is applied to Proper Kitty Limited and the resulting dollar measures are consolidated with Wildcat Corporation.

Notice that the consolidated dollar numbers in the right-hand column of Figure 2 are identical to the numbers shown in Figure 1 where Wildcat undertook the foreign transactions directly, rather than through a subsidiary. This

---

[1] An exception exists for nonmonetary asset expirations. These expenses on the income statement are usually translated at the historic rate that existed at the time of original asset acquisition. Since our example does not encompass such items, we ignore this issue.

510   The Accounting Review, July 1984

TABLE 1
STATEMENT 52 GUIDELINES FOR FUNCTIONAL
CURRENCY CHOICE*

A. Cash Flow Indicators
  (1) Foreign Currency—Cash flows related to the foreign entity's individual assets and liabilities are primarily in the foreign currency and do not directly affect the parent company's cash flows.
  (2) Parent's Currency—Cash flows related to the foreign entity's individual assets and liabilities directly affect the parent's cash flows on a current basis and are readily available for remittance to the parent company.

B. Sales Price Indicators
  (1) Foreign Currency—Sales prices for the foreign entity's products are not primarily responsive on a short-term basis to changes in exchange rates but are determined more by local competition or local government regulation.
  (2) Parent's Currency—Sales prices for the foreign entity's products are primarily responsive on a short-term basis to changes in exchange rates; for example, sales prices are determined more by worldwide competition or by international prices.

C. Sales Market Indicators
  (1) Foreign Currency—There is an active local sales market for the foreign entity's products, although there also might be significant amounts of exports.
  (2) Parent's Currency—The sales market is mostly in the parent's country or sales contracts are denominated in the parent's currency.

D. Expense Indicators
  (1) Foreign Currency—Labor, materials, and other costs for the foreign entity's products or services are primarily local costs, even though there also might be imports from other countries.
  (2) Parent's Currency—Labor, materials, and other costs for the foreign entity's products or services, on a continuing basis, are primarily costs for components obtained from the country in which

the parent company is located.

E. Financing Indicators
  (1) Foreign Currency—Financing is primarily denominated in foreign currency, and funds generated by the foreign entity's operations are sufficient to service existing and normally expected debt obligations.
  (2) Parent's Currency—Financing is primarily from the parent or other dollar-denominated obligations, or funds generated by the foreign entity's operations are not sufficient to service existing and normally expected debt obligations without the infusion of additional funds from the parent company. Infusion of additional funds from the parent company for expansion is not a factor, provided funds generated by the foreign entity's expanded operations are expected to be sufficient to service that additional financing.

F. Intercompany Transactions and Arrangements Indicators
  (1) Foreign Currency—There is a low volume of intercompany transactions and there is not an extensive interrelationship between the operations of the foreign entity and the parent company. However, the foreign entity's operations may rely on the parent's or affiliates' competitive advantages, such as patents and trademarks.
  (2) Parent's Currency—There is a high volume of intercompany transactions and there is an extensive interrelationship between the operations of the foreign entity and the parent company. Additionally, the parent's currency generally would be the functional currency if the foreign entity is a device or shell corporation for holding investments, obligations, intangible assets, etc., that could readily be carried on the parent's or an affiliate's books.

---

* Note: Table 1 is taken directly from FASB [1981], pp. 26–27.

equivalence is no accident. Since the economics of the two cases are identical, the FASB has selected an accounting method for the foreign subsidiary which leads to the same dollar result that would have existed had the transactions been undertaken directly by Wildcat.

To summarize, when the Statement 52 guidelines identify the parent's currency as the functional currency:

1) The subsidiary is treated for accounting purposes as a mere conduit.

2) One implication is that foreign transactions are deemed to have an immediate (or potentially immediate) impact on dollar cash flows of the parent. For this reason, all foreign exchange gains and losses are taken through income.

3) Since the subsidiary is an artifact, all balance sheet numbers are reflected at amounts that would have existed had the subsidiary's account initially been recorded in the functional currency. The temporal

FIGURE 2
PARTIAL CONSOLIDATED FINANCIAL STATEMENTS
(Includes Only Foreign Assets and Results of Foreign Operations)
CASE II

Account Title	Property Kitty, Ltd. £'s	Exchange Rate (Temporal Method)	Remeasured In $'s	Wildcat Corporation	Consolidation Eliminations (DR) CR	Consolidated $'s
Dollar deposit				$140,000		$140,000
Sterling deposit	£ 5,000	1.39	$ 6,950			6,950
Investment in subsidiary				$307,500	(1) 307,500	
Building	200,000	1.50	300,000			300,000
	£205,000		$306,950	$447,500		$446,950
Original Equity	205,000	1.50	307,500		(1) (307,500)	
Retained Earnings			(550) ←	40,000 ← (10,000)		29,450 ←
	£205,000		$306,950	$ 30,000		$ 29,450
Sales	£100,000	1.50	$150,000	$150,000	(2) (150,000)	$150,000
Cost of Goods Sold	100,000	1.50	150,000	110,000	(2) 150,000	110,000
				40,000 ←		
Foreign Exchange Loss			(550) ←	(10,000)		(10,550)*
Net Income				$ 30,000		$ 29,450 ←

* Note: This total is comprised of:

Foreign exchange loss on sale proceeds	$10,000
Foreign exchange loss on sterling deposit	550
	$10,550

method is designed to achieve this result.

THE FOREIGN CURRENCY AS THE FUNCTIONAL CURRENCY: CASE III

We have seen that when the foreign subsidiary is merely a conduit for dollar cash flows, the functional currency is the dollar. By contrast, when the foreign subsidiary's operations "are relatively self-contained and integrated within a particular country or economic environment" [FASB, 1981, para. 80], then the functional currency is the currency of that foreign country.

To illustrate the rationale behind this rule, we introduce a Case III variation on the Wildcat Corporation setting. Consistent with Case II, we assume in Case III that Wildcat Corporation forms a U.K. subsidiary, Proper Kitty, Ltd., by investing $307,500 when the exchange rate was 1£ = 1.50$. Again, as in Case II, the investment proceeds are used to buy a building for £200,000 and to open a £5,000 account in a London bank. Sales totalling £100,000 are again made on July 1, 19x5, and collected on August 1. In contrast to the previous cases, however, we now assume that these goods were not shipped from the U.S.; instead, they were acquired by Proper Kitty from an unaffiliated U.K. supplier at a cost of £73,333 (which is equivalent to $110,000 at the then prevailing exchange rate). The sales proceeds are used to pay the supplier and the remaining cash (£26,667) is retained in the London account to finance Proper Kitty's future operations, expansion, and growth.

Notice that the economics of this case are quite different from the previous ones. In Case III, Proper Kitty does not engage in transactions merely to influence near-term dollar cash flows. Thus, the effect of an exchange rate change on future dollar cash flows is unclear.

In its Conceptual Framework, the FASB [1978] argues that the goal of financial reporting is to provide a forecast base for assessing "the amounts, timing, and uncertainty of prospective net cash inflows." Applying this logic to the circumstances of Case III (where the cash-flow impact of exchange rate changes is unclear), these exchange rate changes are not included in income under FAS 52. Specifically, in Cases I and II the decline in the pound from $1.50 to $1.40 between the time of sale and the time of collection resulted in an unequivocal $10,000 foreign exchange loss, which is deducted from income. No such loss is included in the Case III income number since Proper Kitty is an on-going, self-contained entity that will redeploy the sales proceeds in the U.K. In other words, it is not at all clear that a loss has occurred in Case III. Under such circumstances, the functional currency is designated as the foreign currency, and the decline in the dollar equivalent of the sales proceeds is taken directly to a special owners' equity account, rather than deducted from income. Similar treatment is accorded to the change in the dollar equivalent of the £5000 deposit in the London bank.

Furthermore, when the foreign entity is a self-contained unit, as in Case III, the FASB contends that the balance sheet translation process "should retain the financial results and relationships that were created in the economic environment of the foreign operations" [FASB, 1981, para. 74]. In other words, after translation, the foreign subsidiary's financial statement items should bear the same proportionate relationship to one another in dollars as they did in the foreign currency. This can be accomplished only if all items are translated using the same exchange rate. For this purpose, the FASB mandates the use of the current rate as of the balance sheet date. Using the current rate method on the income statement, all items are translated at the rate of exchange as of the transaction date.

Considering Proper Kitty's functional currency to be the pound and using the current rate method leads to the consolidated result shown in Figure 3. Notice carefully that the consolidated result in Figure 3 is quite different from the Case I result that was derived in Figure 1. This difference reflects the fact that Case III and Case I are not identical. In Case III, it is not at all clear that the impact of the exchange rate changes on the initial cash balance and subsequent cash collections will necessarily affect future *dollar* flows. Since Proper Kitty is a self-contained entity, these pound balances will be redeployed within the U.K., and the eventual dollar impact of these reinvestment activities may not materialize for years. For this reason, the FASB concludes that the effect of these rate changes should be excluded from the income computation.[2]

---

[2] The FASB's decision to exclude from income uncompleted foreign transactions with uncertain dollar flow effects is arguable. Although consistent with the dominant treatment of uncompleted transactions in existing practice, the FASB approach ignores the fact

Revsine

FIGURE 3

PARTIAL CONSOLIDATED FINANCIAL STATEMENTS
(Includes Only Foreign Assets and Results of Foreign Operations)
CASE III

Account Title	Property Kitty, Ltd. £'s	Exchange Rate	Translated In $'s	Wildcat Corporation	Consolidation Eliminations (DR) CR	Consolidated $'s
Cash	£ 31,667	1.39	$ 44,017			$ 44,017
Investment in subsidiary				307,500	(1) 307,500	
Building	200,000	1.39	278,000			278,000
	£231,667		$322,017			$322,017
Original equity	205,000	1.50	307,500		(1) (307,500)	
Retained earnings	26,667	1.50	40,000			40,000
Cumulative translation adjustment			To balance (25,483)*			(25,483)
	£231,667		$322,017			$ 14,517
Sales	£100,000	1.50	$150,000			$150,000
Cost of goods sold	73,333	1.50	110,000			110,000
	£ 26,667		$ 40,000			$ 40,000

* Note:
    The cumulative translation adjustment in this simplified example is determined by multiplying the decline in the value of the £(1.50 – 1.39) by the net asset balance of £231,667 just prior to the decline.

Also notice that the dollar equivalent carrying balance for the nonmonetary asset differs from Case I. In Case I, the building was translated at the historic rate of exchange, in accordance with historical cost accounting principles. But in Case III, Proper Kitty is a self-contained entity. The FASB contends that in such circumstances, financial statements are more informative if they maintain proportionate relationships that exist in the functional currency. Thus, the building is also translated at the current rate of exchange and most ratio relationships for Proper Kitty's dollar statements are equal to those contained in the pound statements (i.e., compare ratios based on column 3 data versus column 1 data in Figure 3).

To summarize, when a foreign entity is a self-contained unit:

1) The functional currency is the currency of the foreign economic environment.

2) The impact of rate changes on future dollar flows is uncertain. Thus, translation gains and losses are not run through income; instead, they are accumulated in a separately designated owners' equity account.

3) Subsidiary balance sheets should preserve the proportionate relationships that existed in the functional currency. Therefore, all assets

that existing rates in foreign exchange markets may be a least biased indicator of dollar flows that will ultimately be realized. In this view, changes in exchange rates signal changes in expected future flows. Since the FASB views income as a potential cash flow predictor, such exchange rate changes might (consistent with FASB [1978]) be includable in income.

and liabilities are translated at the current rate of exchange. Any gain or loss on translation is put into a special owners' equity account rather than through income.

WILL STATEMENT 52 LEAD TO COMPATIBILITY?

The previous analysis demonstrates how the functional currency choice required by Statement 52 is crucial for achieving compatibility between accounting signals and underlying economic consequences. But since choice injects potential for error, it is legitimate to question whether Statement 52 will lead to its intended result.

To some accountants, the latitude inherent in the functional currency choice may be troublesome, since the existence of latitude raises the specter of statement manipulation. However, statement manipulation via the functional currency choice does not appear to be a major threat since firms have a built-in motive to make the "correct" choice. For example, firms would be ill-advised to select the dollar as the functional currency in order to gain some near-term income enhancement (i.e., from foreign exchange gains that are included in income under the temporal method). The reason is that this short-run benefit may backfire if and when the foreign exchange effect reverses in subsequent years. That is, today's income enhancement may lead to to-morrow's income decrement. Thus, the likelihood of statement manipulation arising from the functional currency choice appears slight.

A much more real danger is that firms, their auditors, and outside analysts may not understand the subtle philosophy that underlies the functional currency choice. As a consequence, innocent but incorrect choices and assessments may be made, and compatibility may not be achieved. Unfortunately, the FASB's guidelines for the functional currency choice, reproduced in Table 1, may increase the likelihood of this possibility. That is, unless the theory underlying the selection mechanism is understood, some firms may be tempted to merely count-up the indicators in each direction; the choice would simply depend on which currency (the dollar or the foreign currency) garners more indicators. This simplistic application of Statement 52 is unsatisfactory since, for example, five indicators may point to the foreign currency as the functional currency and only one may point to the dollar. Despite this, the one criterion which points to the dollar may clearly dominate. Unless those making the selection clearly understand the theory underlying the choice, an incorrect selection is very likely using a straightforward tally of the indicators in each direction. It is to forestall precisely this possibility that this paper was written.

REFERENCES

Financial Accounting Standards Board, *Statement of Financial Accounting Standards No. 8*, "Accounting for the Translation of Foreign Currency Transactions and Foreign Currency Financial Statements" (October 1975).
——, *Statement of Financial Accounting Concepts No. 1*, "Objectives of Financial Reporting by Business Enterprises" (November 1978).
——, *Statement of Financial Accounting Standards No. 52*, "Foreign Currency Translation" (December 1981).

[16]

PAUL A. GRIFFIN

Management's Preferences for
FASB Statement No. 52:
Predictive Ability Results

Research attempting to explain or predict preferences with respect to accounting rules is a relatively new branch of accounting research. Factors
affecting a manager's welfare (e.g., political costs) are identified and then
evaluated empirically to ascertain whether such factors are helpful in predicting a manager's decision to respond to proposed changes in the Financial
Accounting Standards Board's (FASB's) rules on foreign currency translation. FASB Statement No. 52, issued December 1981, replaced FASB Statement No. 8 and required U.S. multinational corporations to switch from
the 'temporal' to the 'current rate' method of translating foreign currency
financial statements into U.S. dollars. The models use current economic data
as well as information about managers' responses to earlier changes in the
rules for translating foreign currency statements. While the models adequately describe management's behaviour, and hence are consistent with
earlier research, their predictive ability is only a modest improvement over
naive prediction rules.

Key words: Accounting policies; Foreign exchange translations (ALL).

I. INTRODUCTION

This study evaluates the predictive ability of a model formulated by Griffin (1982).
That model attempted to explain and describe managers' preferences for the accounting choices inherent in Financial Accounting Standards Board's (FASB) Statement
No. 8, *Accounting for the Translation of Foreign Currency Financial Statements*. Using non-overlapping and randomly-chosen holdout samples, the model is evaluated
in terms of its ability to predict managers' preferences regarding subsequent foreign
currency accounting proposals, specifically, those that culminated ultimately in the
December 1981 issuance of FASB Statement No. 52, *Foreign Currency Translation*.

The study also responds to recent criticisms of the developing literature on management preferences and accounting choices.[1] Ball and Foster (1982), for instance, note

---

[1] A sampling of the literature includes Hagerman and Zmijewski (1979), Collins, Rozeff, and Dhaliwal
(1981), Bowen, Lacey, and Noreen (1981), Zmijewski and Hagerman (1981), and Griffin (1982). Im-
petus for such research can be traced to Watts and Zimmerman (1978) who argued that enterprise
managers are likely to select or prefer an accounting standard over others only when that selection or
preference augments their pecuniary and non-pecuniary wealth (expected future consumption). For a
general criticism of the Watts-Zimmerman arguments, see Christenson (1983).

PAUL GRIFFIN is an Associate Professor of Accounting, Graduate School of Administration, University
of California at Davis, California.

that the various earlier studies' approaches are still predominantly at a single-period, single-issue level and display little or no interest in the validation of their results. For example, the earlier studies fail to control for overfitting by using holdout samples and, as a result, remain essentially incomplete in a practical sense. The present study employs current accounting and economic data in addition to information about how managers responded to the May 1978 invitation to comment on FASB standards. Hence, it uses data pertaining to more than one accounting proposal.

In the context of the proposals that preceded Statement 52, the model appears to describe managers' preferences with reasonable adequacy, is consistent with earlier research, and provides modestly-improved predictions compared to those generated by a naive prediction rule. Managers, policy makers, and others, therefore, may find this statistical device of limited assistance in predicting the responses of those who participate in setting accounting standards.

II. ACCOUNTING CHOICES AND MANAGEMENT'S PREFERENCES

The conceptual underpinnings of this research relate to the issue of what motivates managers (and others) to submit letters of comment to an accounting rule-making body such as the FASB. While no cogent theory of accounting choice exists, numerous overlapping and often competing motivational perspectives have been articulated, among which are the following. Managers prefer accounting standards that (1) present a fair statement of financial condition and performance to all users — present and potential, (2) maximize the wealth of the present shareholders, (3) maximize the market value of the firm's assets, (4) satisfy regulations, (5) maximize the utility of managers' pecuniary and non-pecuniary wealth, and (6) present numbers in conformity with generally accepted accounting principles, applied consistently over time. In a sense, these perspectives connote paradigms, each which suggests a somewhat different underlying story to explain preferences for and ultimately choices of accounting alternatives.

This paper embraces the fifth view — that corporate managers act in a self-interested manner preferring accounting proposals that enhance rather than diminish the utility of their wealth. Wealth increases, according to Watts and Zimmerman (1978) among others, are captured as either direct cash payments tied to accounting rules or indirect cash payments secured as returns on securities held, which themselves are conditioned by accounting rules. Managers' wealth, for example, may be affected by an accounting proposal that potentially affects incentive compensation payments, modifies tax calculations (income, sales, excise, etc.), provides costly information for investors, creditors, competitors, and other users of financial statements, alters investment and financing opportunities (e.g., restrictions in debt covenants), or changes the perceptions of interested outside parties such as regulators, elected officials, labour, and public interest groups.

Apparently, foreign currency accounting rules have affected managers' wealth in one or more of the preceding ways. It is well documented, for instance, that foreign exchange risk management practices changed measurably after the introduction of Statement 8 in 1976 (see, for example, Evans, Folks, and Jilling, 1978). Manage-

ABACUS

ment, apparently, consumed real resources attempting to hedge the firm's accounting exposure to minimize fluctuations in earnings due to currency swings. Risk averse managers, whose compensation is based on reported net income surely prefer such smoother earnings streams. The magnitude of the potential impact of proposed foreign currency accounting rules on earnings, then, may prompt managers to respond thereto.

Other variables that might provide clues about the effects of accounting alternatives on management wealth include firm size, performance, and leverage. Firm size captures numerous aspects of a firm's attitudes and subsequent behaviour. Larger firms, in all probability, are more sensitive to the political consequences of the regulatory process, have greater access to experts, and thus can participate in the regulatory process at a lower cost (per unit of output). Moreover, in the context of foreign currency accounting rules, larger firms would seem more likely to be invested internationally, actively managing their economic and accounting exposure to minimize foreign exchange risk. Hence, larger firms are more likely to be participants rather than bystanders in the standard setting process.[2]

Performance indicators such as accounting rates of return and market rates of return may also provide clues about wealth effects in that less-than-expected results may impose significant costs on managers (e.g., as a reduction in value of their human capital in the labour market). The belief that such costs may be reduced by participating in the standard setting process will, of course, precipitate such participation.

Finally, a leverage factor is proposed as a proxy for management's concern about the firm's future costs of financing. While accounting leverage may not directly influence the market's discount rate, such variables are often significant in debt covenants, specifically, in deciding whether such covenants are violated. However, since a firm's debt to equity ratio per se does not necessarily measure closeness to violation, it is not obvious what directional hypothesis might be stated regarding this factor. Earlier research, nonetheless, has argued that firms with higher leverage are more likely to be concerned with potentially binding constraints in lending agreements than other firms. Such highly-levered firms may seek accounting changes in order to loosen those constraints (see, for example, Collins, Rozeff, and Dhaliwal, 1981).

In short, this research uses foreign currency adjustment and three more-encompassing financial variables (size, return, and leverage) as possible determinants of management's interest in foreign currency accounting rules. Of course, in examining responses to the proposals that gave rise to Statement 52, knowledge of whether management provided comments on earlier similar proposals should convey important information. Management's response regarding Statement 8 is utilized as an additional explanatory variable.

III. RESEARCH METHODOLOGY

The research approach parallels Griffin's 1982 analysis of responses to the FASB's May 1978 call for comments, principally on Statement 8. Firms were classified as

---

[2] For a detailed examination of the relationship between political costs and firm size, see Zimmerman (in press).

FASB STATEMENT NO. 52

respondents or non-respondents — respondents being those firms that submitted comments regarding the proposal that resulted in Statement 52.

Samples and Data

The 'population' comprised the 174 firms that submitted comments to the FASB regarding Statement 52 and the 479 multinational firms employed by Dukes (1978) in his study of the security price effects of Statement 8. Four hundred and fifty-two firms were then selected as those listed on the Annual Industrials COMPUSTAT file having one or more requisite data items available for years 1976. Of the 452 firms surviving the COMPUSTAT screen, 156 were Statement 52 respondents while 296 were not. Respondent firms were identified by checking the public files of the Financial Accounting Standards Board. The maximum number of firms from one industry classification was 22 (petroleum refining). (A list of the 452 firms is available from the author by request.)

Variable Definition

Except for variable 1, the variables defined below are identical to those used earlier. Variables 2-9 were utilized as predictor variables in analysing Statement 52 responses.

1. FAS 52   = 1 if firm responded to August 1980 exposure draft that preceded Statement 52.
      = 0 if firm did not.
2. FAS 8   = 1 if firm criticized Statement 8 in response to May 1978 invitation.
      = 0 if firm did not.
3. $DTEQ_t$ = long term debt (t)/common equity (t); $t = 1976-9$.
4. $VMKT_t$ = [common shares outstanding (t) X price (t)]/1000; $t = 1976-9$.
5. $SAAS_t$ = sales (t)/total assets (t); $t = 1976-9$.
6. $RMKT_t$ = [price (t) + dividends (t) − price (t − 1)]/price (t − 1) adjusted for stock splits and dividends; $t = 1976-9$.
7. $REEQ_t$ = earnings available for common (t)/common equity (t); $t = 1976-9$.
8. $FCAJ_t$ = [foreign currency adjustment (t) − foreign currency adjustment (t − 1)]/net income before taxes (t); $t = 1976-9$.
9. $BETA_t$ = beta coefficient from one-factor market model based on three years of monthly return CRSP data (to 31 December 1978).

Since outliers can have an influence on discriminant function parameter estimates, each of variables 3-9 was rank-ordered so that the tails of the distribution could be carefully screened. Nine firms with $-1.07 > BETA > 3.0$ were designated as having missing values on that variable and 3 firms with negative common equity were designated as having missing values on variables DTEQ and REEQ. For purposes of analysing financial ratios, the deletion of outliers provides more normal distributional characteristics (see Frecka and Hopwood, 1983, among others). Also, in a further attempt to achieve approximate normality variables 3 through 8, after adjusting for outliers, were transformed using the square root and cube root functions (see, for example, Kendall and Stewart, 1977). Distributions of individual variables were shifted to the right to make values positive, if required by the transformation. The transformations, however, did not consider higher order moments.

ABACUS

TABLE 1

FAS 52 RESPONDENTS VS. OTHER MULTINATIONALS:
SELECTED FINANCIAL CHARACTERISTICS

Variable*	Year	N	FAS 52 Respondent Mean	Other Multinationals Mean	Significance $[F(1,N-2)]$†
	1976	96	0.43	0.56	0.347
Debt/Equity	1977	101	0.37	0.75	0.246
	1978	116	0.42	0.56	0.210
	1979	115	0.36	0.55	0.101
	1976	96	2,936.86	629.59	0.0002
Market Value ($M)	1977	101	3,433.03	762.49	0.0001
	1978	116	2,231.34	624.86	0.0001
	1979	115	2,549.80	749.27	0.0001
	1976	96	1.17	1.45	0.082
Sales to Assets	1977	101	0.48	0.88	0.073
	1978	116	1.19	1.41	0.041
	1979	115	1.24	1.46	0.062
	1976	96	0.27	0.43	0.059
Market Return	1977	101	0.16	0.33	0.003
	1978	116	0.10	0.09	0.939
	1979	115	0.34	0.35	0.900
	1976	96	0.03	0.16	0.377
Foreign Currency	1977	101	0.05	0.21	0.348
Adjustment	1978	116	0.03	0.04	0.512
	1979	115	0.03	0.09	0.300
	1976	96	0.46	0.20	0.008
FAS 8 Respondent	1977	101	0.49	0.38	0.005
	1978	116	0.41	0.18	0.007
	1979	115	0.38	0.19	0.022

* For definitions, see Section III.
† Test is equivalent to a two-tailed test of the relationship between FAS 52 response/no response and the explanatory variables (see Kmenta, 1971, p. 238).

IV. RESULTS

Tables 1 and 2 present the primary results. Univariate F statistics in Table 1 test for a significant relationship between the dependent variable (variable 1) and each separate independent or explanatory variable. Discriminant analysis results are presented in Table 2.[3] For each year and each model, firms eligible for analysis (i.e., no missing discriminating variables) were randomly split into two approximately equal groups — one for computing the discriminant function coefficients, the other for estimating

[3] Since the primary emphasis is on classification and prediction, multivariate discriminant analysis was selected as the dominant statistical procedure. Maximum likelihood techniques such as logit analysis, of course, have advantages regarding coefficient estimation and hypothesis testing. However, as Griffin (1982) reveals, classification error rates are essentially similar using either multivariate discriminant or multivariate logit analysis.

FASB STATEMENT NO. 52

MULTIVARIATE DISCRIMINANT ANALYSIS: SUMMARY OF MODELS CLASSIFYING FAS 52 RESPONDENTS AND OTHER MULTINATIONALS

Panel	1976				1977				1978				1979			
	1	2	3	4	1	2	3	4	1	2	3	4	1	2	3	4
A. *Standardized Discriminant Coefficients*																
Relative Risk (BETA)	−0.29	−0.31	−0.38	−0.37	−0.27	−0.26	−0.31	−0.32	−0.23	−0.22	−0.30	−0.30	−0.19	−0.20	−0.26	−0.24
Debt/Equity (DTEQ)	−0.29	−0.29	−0.16	−0.15	−0.22	−0.21	−0.14	−0.14	−0.45	−0.42	−0.28	−0.33	−0.44	−0.39	−0.30	−0.35
Market Value (VMKT)	0.48	0.50	0.66	0.66	0.52	0.52	0.61	0.61	0.44	0.44	0.61	0.61	0.43	0.46	0.57	0.54
Sales/Assets (SAAS)	−0.35	−0.38	−0.42	−0.41	−0.39	−0.39	−0.42	−0.42	−0.45	−0.44	−0.48	−0.50	−0.49	−0.29	−0.32	−0.52
Market Return (RMKT)	−0.16	−0.14	−0.17	−0.18	−0.42	−0.42	−0.45	−0.45	−0.08	−0.07	−0.09	−0.10	−0.14	−0.11	−0.12	−0.15
Earnings/Common Equity (REEQ)	0.10	0.13	0.06	0.04	0.00	0.00	−0.04	−0.04	0.23	0.21	0.19	0.23	0.43	0.33	0.33	0.42
Exchange Gain or Loss (FCAJ)	−0.18	N.A.	N.A.	−0.12	0.03	N.A.	N.A.	0.03	0.10	N.A.	N.A.	0.14	0.35	N.A.	N.A.	0.36
FAS 8 Respondent (FASB)	0.44	0.41	N.A.	N.A.	0.25	0.25	N.A.	N.A.	0.40	0.41	N.A.	N.A.	0.28	0.29	N.A.	N.A.
Number of Observations																
B. *Classification and Prediction Analysis*																
Test Sample: Percent Correct	73.96	72.64	71.96	73.20	74.26	75.24	72.64	74.51	68.10	70.48	72.64	70.09	73.04	73.91	73.68	70.69
Number of Observations	96	212	214	97	101	210	212	102	116	210	212	117	115	207	209	116
Holdout Sample: Percent Correct	58.42	69.74	65.94	55.45	65.55	71.49	65.94	63.87	62.71	71.49	65.50	60.17	58.10	68.02	65.02	56.19
Naive Model:* Percent Correct	55.45	64.47	64.19	55.45	57.98	64.47	64.19	57.98	57.63	64.47	64.19	57.63	55.24	64.86	64.57	55.23
Number of Observations	101	228	229	101	119	210	229	119	118	228	229	118	105	222	223	105
Percentage Increase: Holdout/Naive −1.00	5.36	8.17	2.72	0.00	13.06	10.89	2.73	10.16	8.81	10.89	2.04	4.41	5.18	4.87	0.70	1.74
C. *Classification and Prediction Analysis: Cube Root Transformation*																
Test Sample: Percent Correct	81.71	80.11	78.57	80.72	91.49	83.67	84.85	85.42	68.42	70.23	71.21	66.23	75.28	76.00	75.00	74.44
Number of Observations	82	181	182	83	47	98	99	48	76	131	132	77	89	175	176	90
Holdout Sample: Percent Correct	64.89	68.93	68.60	69.15	71.15	77.67	68.27	65.38	60.76	65.97	66.44	62.03	62.24	67.01	66.50	63.27
Naive Model:* Percent Correct	59.97	65.53	65.22	59.57	75.00	75.72	75.00	75.00	63.29	63.89	63.01	63.29	57.14	63.96	63.96	58.33
Number of Observations	94	206	207	94	52	103	104	52	79	132	146	79	98	197	197	96
Percentage Increase: Holdout/Naive −1.00	8.93	5.19	5.18	16.08	−5.13	3.56	−8.97	−12.83	−4.00	3.26	5.44	−1.99	8.93	17.27	3.97	8.47

* Predicts all firms are 'other multinationals', i.e., non-respondents.

a classification error rate. Such classification error rates are unbiased since none of the observations used in establishing those rates is used in estimating the discriminant function's parameters.

Univariate Analysis

Table 1 shows that relative to other multinationals, FAS 52 respondents appear to be larger (Market Value), less profitable (Sales to Assets, Market Return), and have responded earlier in conjunction with Statement 8 (FAS 8 respondent). Such relationships are statistically significant and consistent with the conceptual underpinnings discussed earlier.[4]

However, contrary to the earlier findings (i.e., Griffin, 1982) pertaining to FAS 8, FAS 52 respondents seemingly exhibit lower leverage and smaller impact of foreign exchange gains and losses on earnings, though the univariate relationships for such variables are not statistically significant.

Correlation matrixes of both the transformed and untransformed independent variables were computed for each year 1976-9. The correlations were low in both cases. For example, the matrixes of the untransformed variables yielded only two instances of correlations in excess of ± 0.40 (out of 36x4 individual computations).

Tests of Predictive Ability

Table 2 presents the key findings of this study. For each of four years, twelve discriminant functions were estimated (4 models x 3 transformations (none, square root, cube root)). Discriminant function coefficients for the untransformed data are reported in Panel A. These confirm the univariate findings in Table 1, showing VMKT and FAS 8 as increasing the likelihood of FAS 52 response, and BETA, DTEQ, and SAAS as decreasing that likelihood. The statistical significance of those parameters, however, was not evaluated in part because in none of the 48 analyses were the group covariance matrixes statistically equal.[5] Further, there was no assurance that the independent variables were multivariate normally distributed, despite the different transformations. Discriminant function coefficients reported in this study are, of course, biased — bias being inversely proportional to sample size.

Rather than focusing on individual parameters, classification and prediction analysis, whose justification does not hinge directly on various statistical requirements, was emphasized as the primary test of model adequacy. Panels B and C present the results for untransformed and cube-root transformed data, respectively. The model parameters estimated on the test sample were used to predict whether firms in the holdout sample responded to Statement 52. Success rates are stated as percentage of firms correctly classified. Panels B and C compare those success rates with the percent correct from a naive rule — predict all firms as 'other multinationals', i.e., non-FAS 52 respondents. The relative improvements in predictive ability for model 2 with untransformed variables are 8.17, 10.89, 10.89, and 4.87 for 1976-9 (Panel B);

---

[4] Note that the finding regarding market return (greater for non-respondents) is also consistent with the size effect, as documented in Banz (1981), among others.

[5] A jackknife estimator, however, has been proposed (for recent cases, see Crask and Perreault, 1977, and Fenwick, 1979) to attend to this issue.

for model 2 with the cube-root transformation are 5.19, 3.56, 3.26, and 17.27 for 1976-9 (Panel C) and for model 2 with the square root transformation are 11.68, 0.01, 1.18, and 1.82 for 1976-9 (not reported in Table 2). Also, model 2 predictions appear to be statistically more accurate than the naive predictions in that repeated application of the random-splitting procedure showed the holdout samples percent correct to be greater than the naive model (without exception for the untransformed data).

The discriminant model (specifically, model 2) thus exhibits a modest incremental ability to predict those firms likely to submit comments regarding Statement 52. Confidence in the model's modest success was underscored by two design features: first, the variables selected were based on a prior analysis of Statement 8 responses and, second, the parameters were estimated on independent and randomly-generated test samples.

V. RELEVANCE OF RESULTS

Absent the loss functions of policy makers and others who might be interested in identifying likely respondents to an accounting proposal and assessing preferences toward such proposal, one can only conjecture about likely uses of statistical models of the kind examined in this research. Nonetheless, if it is acknowledged that respondents' views on accounting issues matter to policy makers — and it seems inconceivable that they do not, given the self-regulatory nature of the accounting standard setting process — then techniques which might readily recognize those likely to submit comments (and the nature thereof) could aid, and ultimately make more efficient, the standard setters' research process. Non-respondents' views might also be inferred from statistical techniques of this kind. Indeed, knowledge of the likely comments of those who do not participate in standard setting could be potentially useful for policy, especially if the statements of those who do respond are predisposed to a particular viewpoint. It should be noted that when applied to an independent sample of firms that commented on the Statement 52 proposal, one version of the model (Model 2) using untransformed data correctly classified approximately two-thirds of the holdout sample, an average improvement of 8.71 percent over a naive benchmark for years 1976-9.

However, the analysis described in this paper can only be viewed as an initial step in developing a useful predictive tool for policy makers and others. The model is preliminary in that it is contextually specific (focusing on foreign currency accounting rules only), does not exhaust all possible variables that might depict how management's wealth is affected by accounting policy, and is economically and statistically incomplete in defining the constructs and providing error-free measurements of those constructs. Future studies, hopefully, will address these and other limitations of the general methodology. Certainly, there is no shortage of accounting regulations to analyse. Such analyses should eventually be moulded into a more cogent explanation of why managers select accounting rules.

A B A C U S

REFERENCES

Ball, Ray and George Foster, 'Corporate Financial Reporting: A Methodological Review of Empirical Research', Supplement to *Journal of Accounting Research,* Vol. 20, 1982.

Banz, Rolf W., 'The Relationship Between Return and Market Value of Common Stocks', *Journal of Financial Economics,* March 1981, pp. 3-18.

Bowen, Robert M., John M. Lacey, and Eric W. Noreen, 'Determinants of the Corporate Decision to Capitalize Interest', *Journal of Accounting and Economics,* August 1981, pp. 151-67.

Christenson, Charles, 'The Methodology of Positive Accounting', *The Accounting Review,* January 1983, pp. 1-22.

Collins, Daniel W., Michael S. Rozeff, and Dan S. Dhaliwal, 'The Economic Determinants of the Market Reaction to Proposed Mandatory Accounting Changes in the Oil and Gas Industry: A Cross-Sectional Analysis', *Journal of Accounting and Economics,* August 1981, pp. 37-72.

Crask, Melvin R., and William D. Perreault, Jr., 'Validation of Discriminant Analysis in Marketing Research', *Journal of Marketing Research,* February 1977, pp. 60-8.

Dukes, Roland E., *An Empirical Investigation of the Effects of Financial Accounting Standards Board Statement No. 8 on Security Return Behavior* (Stamford, Conn.: FASB, December 1978).

Evans, Thomas G., William R. Folks, and Michael Jilling, *The Impact of Statement of Financial Standards No. 8 on the Foreign Exchange Risk Management Practices of American Multinationals: An Economic Impact Study* (Stamford, Conn.: FASB, November 1978).

Fenwick, Ian, 'Techniques in Market Measurement: The Jackknife', *Journal of Marketing Research,* August 1979, pp. 410-14.

Frecka, Thomas J., and William S. Hopwood, 'The Effects of Outliers on the Cross Sectional Distributional Properties of Financial Ratios', *The Accounting Review,* January 1983, pp. 115-28.

Griffin, Paul A., 'Foreign Exchange Gains and Losses: Impact on Reported Earnings', *Abacus,* June 1982, pp. 50-69.

Hagerman, Robert L., and Mark E. Zmijewski, 'Some Economic Determinants of Accounting Policy Choice', *Journal of Accounting and Economics,* August 1979, pp. 141-61.

Kendall, M., and A. Stewart, *The Advanced Theory of Statistics: Volume I,* Macmillan Publishing Co., New York 1977.

Kmenta, Jan, *Elements of Econometrics,* The Macmillan Company, New York 1971.

Watts, Ross L., and Jerold L. Zimmerman, 'Towards a Positive Theory of the Determination of Accounting Standards', *The Accounting Review,* January 1978, pp. 112-34.

Zimmerman, Jerold L., 'Taxes, and Firm Size', *Journal of Accounting and Economics,* in press.

Zmijewski, Mark E., and Robert L. Hagerman, 'An Income Strategy Approach to the Positive Theory of Accounting Standard Setting Choice', *Journal of Accounting and Economics,* August 1981, pp. 129-49.

[17]

Journal of Accounting and Economics 8 (1986) 143–158. North-Holland

CHARACTERISTICS OF FIRMS ELECTING EARLY ADOPTION OF SFAS 52*

Frances L. AYRES

The University of Oklahoma, Norman, OK 73019

Received July 1985, final version received January 1986

In 1981 the FASB issued a new standard for accounting for foreign currency translation, SFAS 52. The standard provided a gradual transition period, allowing firms to select from several possible adoption dates. This study extends the research on the positive theory of accounting choice to examine the factors associated with a management's choice of adoption date. The comparison reveals that early adopters were smaller, typically decreased in pre-change earnings the year before adoption, had less stock owned by directors and officers, and were more constrained on dividend payouts and interest coverage ratios than later adopters.

1. Introduction

Accounting for foreign currency translation by multinational companies has been an area of controversy for some time. According to Statement of Financial Accounting Standards No. 8 (SFAS 8), issued in 1975, translation gains and losses were included in the determination of net income. Thus, financial reporting under SFAS 8 often resulted in large fluctuations in income when inventories and fixed assets held in foreign countries were translated from foreign currencies to the US dollar.

In response to criticisms of SFAS 8, the Financial Accounting Standards Board (FASB) agreed to reconsider the method of accounting for foreign currency translation, and in December of 1981 issued SFAS 52. One major difference between SFAS 8 and SFAS 52 is that gains and losses occurring from foreign currency translation no longer flow through income. SFAS 52 requires that these gains and losses be reported directly to owners' equity bypassing the income statement.

A number of recent studies have investigated the relation between various firm-specific variables and accounting choice [see, for example, Hagerman and Zmijewski (1979), Zmijewski and Hagerman (1981), Bowen, Noreen and Lacey

*The research assistance of Soon-Yong Kwon on this project is gratefully acknowledged. I would also like to thank Julie Collins, William R. Kinney, Shane Moriarity, Judy Rayburn, Jerry Salamon, Jerold Zimmerman, and the reviewer Eric Noreen for their helpful comments.

(1981), Dhaliwal (1980) and Daley and Vigeland (1983)]. Models have been developed which seek to explain managements' selection of different accounting alternatives for cases where voluntary choice exists.

The purpose of this study is to extend this line of research to the area of accounting for foreign currency translation. The study provides evidence that the positive theory of accounting applies to the selection by firms of the adoption date of mandatory accounting policies during the phase-in-period.

Although SFAS 52 was a mandatory accounting change, firms had a choice of adoption dates. SFAS 52 was required to be adopted for fiscal years beginning on or after December 15, 1982, but an earlier adoption date was encouraged. Since SFAS 52 was enacted in December of 1981, this meant that for calendar year firms there were three possible adoption years (1981, 1982 and 1983). This study tests for the existence of systematic differences among the firms which chose different adoption dates for SFAS 52. Specifically, I consider the relation between adoption date and (a) earnings before adoption of SFAS 52, (b) the percentage of stock held by management, (c) firm size, (d) interest coverage and (e) dividend payout restrictions.

2. SFAS 52 and earnings

Under SFAS 8 certain balance sheet accounts (primarily inventory and property) and related income statement accounts of foreign subsidiaries were translated at historical exchange rates. All translation adjustments were made directly to income. Under the requirements of SFAS 52, balance sheet accounts are now translated from the functional currency into U.S. dollars at the current rate of exchange at year end.[1] Income statement accounts are translated at average exchange rates for the year. The resulting translation adjustments are made to a separate component of owners' equity.

The earnings impact from adopting SFAS 52 is influenced by a foreign subsidiary's mix of monetary and non-monetary assets as well as the acquisition dates of inventory and depreciable assets. When the dollar strengthens relative to foreign currencies, as it did during most of 1981 and 1982, the cost of sales and depreciation charges will translate into fewer dollars under SFAS 52 than under SFAS 8. Sales however are translated at an average rate for the year under both standards. Further, under SFAS 8, subsidiaries in a net monetary liability (asset) position also incur translation gains (losses) on the balance sheet which flow through income. In contrast, under SFAS 52 these gains and losses move directly to owners' equity. The financial press indicated a general belief that the net effect of these factors was to yield higher income under SFAS 52 than under SFAS 8 for most companies in 1981 [Bettner

---

[1]A subsidiary's functional currency is the currency of the country in which it conducts its primary operations and expends cash.

(1981a, b), Mathur and Loy (1981)].[2]

The earnings effect of the choice to adopt SFAS 52 was disclosed for firms adopting the standard in 1981. That is, the standard required that firms adopting it for a fiscal year ending before March 31, 1982 must disclose the effect on income from adopting the new standard. For firms which elected to adopt early, the earnings effect was, in general, positive. Of the 103 firms in this study that adopted SFAS 52 in 1981, only one reported decreased earnings as a result of the adoption. The effect of adoption of SFAS 52 in 1982 and after is less clear. This is because (1) SFAS 52 did not require that the effect on earnings from adoption after March 31, 1982 be disclosed, and (2) a company which adopted SFAS 52 later than 1981 may have terminated some or all of its currency hedges of SFAS 8 exposure rendering determination of the effect on earnings of adoption of the standard virtually impossible (FASB Accounting Standards, p. 1662).[3]

3. Research hypothesis

Recall that firms with calendar fiscal years had three possible adoption dates available. The study design in this paper is based on the premise that initially (in December 1981) managers were faced with a dichotomous choice – adopt SFAS 52 or continue to use SFAS 8. Then, in 1982 managers again made a choice of whether to adopt the new standard or defer adoption until 1983. Because 1981 was the only year for which the income effect was disclosed, the hypotheses developed here relate to the decision of whether to adopt the new standard in 1981. The hypotheses tested in this study are based on the assumption that adoption of SFAS 52 in 1981 would have increased earnings reported for the non-adopting firms as well.

3.1. Relation between control of the firm and adoption date

Dhaliwal et al. (1982) found that management-controlled (MC) firms are more likely than owner-controlled (OC) firms to adopt accounting methods which increase reported earnings. There are a number of possible reasons for this. Hindley (1970) and Williamson (1967) argue that managers of MC firms

[2] From a group of thirty-nine countries, for which exchange rates were available in the *Wall Street Journal* for the three years ending on December 31, 1980, 1981 and 1982, there were only four cases where foreign currencies gained against the dollar, and all of the gains were insignificant. The average percentage change in US dollar equivalents for the thirty-nine countries was −15.8% for 1981 and −16.7% for 1982.

[3] I examined the disclosures related to the adoption of SFAS 52 for a subsample of sixty-one of the sample firms adopting SFAS 52 after 1981. Only seven firms provided information on the earnings effect of adoption. Of these seven, five reported earnings increases, and two reported earnings decreases. Most firms either did not disclose the effect, or indicated that it was immaterial. This reporting was consistent with the requirements of SFAS 52.

influence information released regarding firm performance in order to present the results about firm operations in the most favorable light. The positive theory of accounting method choice leads us to a similar conclusion. Because the proportion of earnings-based management compensation is larger for MC firms than for OC firms, managers of MC firms are more likely than those of OC firms to choose accounting methods leading to higher reported income.

A company may be thought of as owner-controlled if one party (or block) holds a sufficient level of stock to exercise active control over corporate policies. Companies which are more widely held tend to be controlled by managers.[4] I used the percentage of stock owned by directors and officers as a group as a measure of the extent of control held by owners. Firms with a lower percentage of stock held by directors and officers are generally more widely held and may be thought of as manager-controlled, while as the percentage of stock held by directors and officers increases the company becomes more owner-controlled (and managed). The first hypothesis, stated in alternative form, is:

> H1: Firms electing to adopt SFAS 52 in 1981 have a lower percentage of stock owned by directors and officers than later adopters.

3.2. Political costs hypothesis

Watts and Zimmerman (1978) argue that managements' preference for an accounting method depends on the income effect of the method and the size of the firm. They argue that, because of political exposure, large firms tend to adopt income reducing accounting methods. Evidence supporting this hypothesis was found by Watts and Zimmerman (1978), Hagerman and Zmijewski (1979), and Zmijewski and Hagerman (1981), and to a lesser extent by Bowen, Noreen and Lacey (1981). Since early adoption of SFAS 52 would ordinarily increase income, this suggests that firm size is likely to be inversely related to the probability of early adoption. The second hypothesis tested is:

> H2: Firms adopting SFAS 52 in 1981 are smaller than later adopters.

MC firms tend to be larger than OC firms, hence a negative correlation between the percentage of stock owned by management and the size of the firm is expected, and was found by Dhaliwal et al. (1982). This correlation between size and control tends to reduce the power of the tests of H1 and H2. This problem is partially mitigated by the use of multivariate testing procedures.

---

[4] The terms OC and MC are used here to provide consistency with Dhaliwal et al. (1982). Monson and Downs (1965) use the terms owner-managed and managerial firms to distinguish between those firms that are closely held and managed by owners and diffusely held firms run by professional managers.

3.3. Earnings and accounting choice

Management bonuses or salary adjustments are often a function of some earnings-based measure of performance. A number of researchers have tested whether or not earnings-based compensation schemes affect managements' choice of accounting policy. The results have been mixed. There are several problems with using the existence of a bonus plan as a determinant of accounting choice. First, most companies have some sort of bonus plan. Over 90% of the companies used in this study had a bonus plan. Second, in many cases discretionary bonuses are not based on a formula or prespecified plan. For example, FMC indicates in their March 1981 proxy statement that 'awards are based on individual performance and company success'. Thus, the variable 'existence of a bonus plan' does not tell us whether or not management has an incentive to increase earnings.

Most bonus plans are based, directly or indirectly, on some measure of profitability. A survey conducted by Martin E. Segal and Company of 980 large industrial companies examined the relation between the percentage change in firms' bonuses and the percentage change in their return on investment. They found that a modest (0–5%) increase in profitability is associated with a large (35.5%) increase in bonuses, while profitability increases in excess of 10% led to only slight incremental increases in bonuses (*Execucomp 1983*). This finding suggests that management has an incentive to increase earnings, but not by a large amount. This is consistent with Healy's (1984) paper which showed that when earnings exceeded or fell below the bounds on bonus plans, accruals tended to be negative, while if earnings were between upper and lower bounds, accruals were, on average, positive. Management may thus be characterized as striving to attain a target level of earnings growth which is some increasing function of prior years' earnings.[5] Thus, managers of firms with earnings below an upper-ceiling target level may be motivated to adopt income increasing accounting policies in order to improve earnings.

The third hypothesis tested in this study is:

H3:   Firms electing to adopt SFAS 52 in 1981 have a smaller percentage growth in pre-adoption earnings than later adopters.

3.4. Financial constraints

Debt agreements often contain restrictive covenants designed to limit wealth transfers between debt and equity holders [see Jensen and Meckling (1976) and Smith and Warner (1979) for a discussion of these issues]. Common limitations

---

[5] This characterization is consistent with that employed in previous studies which used the existence or non-existence of a bonus plan as a dichotomous variable. It is based on the more general premise that managements' future wealth is linked to reported earnings. Because of this linkage, management has an incentive to attempt to achieve some target level of earnings growth.

include limits on the long-term debt to total assets ratio and limits on the interest coverage ratio. Dividend payments are also restricted to the pool of unrestricted retained earnings. The change from SFAS 8 to SFAS 52 can alter a firm's closeness to debt constraints and its dividend paying ability through the accounting impact of the change on the financial statement variables used to measure these constraints. The force of the impact of the accounting change depends on the form of the debt covenant. Some debt agreements contain provisions which insulate the firm and its creditors from the impact of accounting changes.

The direction of the impact from the adoption of SFAS 52 on the ratio of long-term debt to total assets is ambiguous. Although the earnings effect was generally positive, the effect of adoption on net assets depends on the relation between historical and current exchange rates and a company's mix between monetary and non-monetary assets. Because of this ambiguity, no relation between early adoption and long-term debt/total assets is hypothesized.

The interest coverage ratio is directly affected by SFAS 52 adoption. Because SFAS 52 increased earnings in most cases, the interest coverage ratio would be increased by SFAS 52 adoption. Bowen et al. (1981) and Daley and Vigeland (1983) hypothesize that because firms with lower interest coverage ratios are likely to be closer to default on debt covenants, these firms are more likely to select an income increasing accounting choice than firms with higher levels of interest coverage. The results from both of the aforementioned studies weakly support this hypothesis. Even if companies are not in violation of existing covenants, low levels of interest coverage may make obtaining additional debt financing more difficult and/or affect a firm's bond ratings. Thus low interest coverage may be of concern to management, regardless of the specific form of existing debt covenants.

A limitation of these prior studies is that they did not control for the level of long-term debt. Interest coverage restrictions relate to the minimum level required. Beyond this level we would not expect managers to be motivated to take action to increase interest coverage. While specific details of coverage restrictions are not readily available, Sherwood (1976, p. 35) notes that Standard and Poor's generally requires a coverage ratio of seven or eight times for a bond to receive an AAA rating and a ratio of over two for a BBB rating. A firm with a small proportion of debt financing may achieve a high coverage ratio with much lower income than a higher debt firm. Hence, ceteris paribus, the higher a firm's degree of leverage, the greater the probability that the firm will approach interest coverage restrictions. To the extent that firms with relatively little long-term debt are not impacted by interest coverage restrictions, the power of tests of this variable in explaining managerial choice is reduced. This may explain, in part, the marginal significance of this variable in prior studies. In order to control for this, I divided the sample into two groups based on the median level of long-term debt to total assets (*LEV*). Firms with a *LEV* value of less than 16% were classified as low-debt, while firms with *LEV* of 16% or greater were classified as high-debt.[6] The fourth hypothesis (restricted to high-debt firms) is:

> H4:   High-debt firms electing to adopt SFAS 52 in 1981 had lower interest coverage ratios than later adopters.

In addition to examining this hypothesis, the dichotomy between high- and low-debt firms allows me to examine whether the interest coverage ratio is a significant variable for low-debt firms (which are less likely to be in close proximity to interest coverage restrictions).

Dividend payments are restricted to the pool of available or unrestricted retained earnings. Adoption of SFAS 52 would increase unrestricted retained earnings to the extent that earnings are increased and hence would relax the dividend pay-out constraints. Hence the fifth hypothesis is:

> H5:   Firms electing to adopt SFAS 52 in 1981 had higher ratios of dividends to unrestricted retained earnings than later adopters.

4. Sample, design and methodology

The initial sample of firms was obtained from the firms listed in the 1981–1983 volumes of *Accounting Trends and Techniques* (AT&T) that reported the adoption of SFAS 52 in one of these years. Additional selection criteria required (1) a December 31 fiscal year end, (2) financial data available on the Compustat Annual Industrial Tape from 1979–1982, and (3) proxy statements and annual reports available on the National Databank Microfich file for the year of adoption.[7] These selection criteria resulted in a sample of 103 firms adopting in 1981, 91 firms adopting in 1982, and 38 firms adopting in 1983. Table 1 provides a summary of the firms included in the initial sample and the reasons for deletion of firms not meeting the additional selection criteria. A breakdown by two-digit industry codes of the firms in the sample is

---

[6] The sample median for *LEV* was 16.2 and the mean was 16.5. There exists no generally accepted value as to what constitutes a 'significant' level; hence the choice of the median level is somewhat arbitrary. The results reported in this study do not differ materially for any cut-off between high- and low-debt firms in the range of 15–18%, which is approximately equal to a 95% confidence interval for the sample mean. Four firms had no debt. Two of these were early adopters, and two were later adopters. No material difference in the results were found when these firms were excluded.

[7] The requirement for a calendar year end was used to assure that the sample could be dichotomized on the variable of adoption year *and* that the income effect of the early adoptions would be disclosed. Firms which elected to adopt during 1982, but did not have a calendar year end were in fact adopting SFAS 52 as early as possible. Those with fiscal years ending after March 31, 1982 were not, however, required to disclose the effect of the change.

150   *F. Ayres, Characteristics of early adopters of SFAS 52*

Table 1

Firms included in the sample.

	1981	1982	1983
Firms reporting change to SFAS 52 in AT&T[a]	141	167	64
Deleted due to non-12/31 fiscal year	(6)	(67)	(19)
Inadequate Compustat data	(32)	(9)	(7)
Proxy not available	(1)		
Firms included in sample	103	91	38

[a]*Accounting Trends and Techniques.*

given in table 2. The breakdown indicates a fairly even distribution across industries and adoption years. Noticeable exceptions were fabricated metal, food and kindred products, and petroleum refining. The first of these groups adopted SFAS 52 primarily in 1981, while the latter two tended to be later adopters. The effects of industry clustering are considered in the subsequent analysis.

Using data collected from Compustat and proxy statements the following variables were computed for each firm for 1981:

$CEPS$ $= ([EPS_{1981} - CPS - EPS_{1980}]/|EPS_{1980}|) \times 100$, where $EPS_T =$ primary earnings per share excluding extraordinary items and discontinued operations for year T, and $CPS =$ the per share effect of adoption of SFAS 52 for 1981 adopters; for later adopters $CPS = 0$ in 1981;

$COVINT = $ (income before extraordinary items and discontinued operations − income effect of adoption of SFAS 52)/interest expense;

LEV $= $ (long-term debt/total assets) $\times 100$;

$DIVURE = $ ([preferred dividends + common dividends]/unrestricted retained earnings) $\times 100$;

$SIZE$ $= $ total assets (in millions);

DO $= $ percentage of stock held by directors and officers as a group.

The variable $COVINT$ was very large in three cases due to a small denominator. To correct for this, I coded this variable as fifty if it was greater than fifty. Other than the coded observations, the next largest observation was 28.5. In two cases $DIVURE$ was very large. These two observations were coded as 100. The change in earnings per share variable ($CEPS$) was also very large for a number of companies. Twenty-three companies had earnings changes in excess of 100%. For these companies $CEPS$ was coded as either +100 (for positive changes) or −100 for negative changes. The sensitivity of the results to these conventions is discussed later.

Table 2

Industry membership of sample firms.

SIC	Industry	SFAS 52 adoption years			
		1981	1982	1983	1982 + 1983
10	Metal Mining	0	1	1	2
12	Bituminous Coal & Lignite Mining	0	1	0	1
13	Crude Petroleum & Natural Gas	0	2	0	2
14	Non-metallic Minerals Mining & Quarrying	1	0	0	0
16	Construction other than Building	0	2	0	2
20	Food & Kindred	2	6	1	7
21	Tobacco	1	2	0	2
22	Textile	1	1	0	1
23	Apparel & Other Finished Products of Fabrics	2	1	0	1
24	Lumber & Wood	0	0	2	2
26	Paper	9	5	0	5
27	Printing & Publishing	1	4	0	4
28	Chemicals	20	15	9	24
29	Petroleum Refining	1	8	7	15
30	Rubber	4	0	1	1
32	Stone, Clay, Glass, Concrete	6	5	1	6
33	Primary Metal	3	5	3	8
34	Fabricated Metal	11	1	0	1
35	Machinery	11	12	5	17
36	Electrical Equipment & Supplies	10	4	4	8
37	Transportation Equipment	8	5	3	8
38	Professional, Scientific Instruments	5	4	1	5
40	Railroad Transportation	1	0	0	0
42	Motor Freight Transportation	0	1	0	1
48	Communication	1	0	0	0
49	Electric, Gas, Sanitary Service	0	2	0	2
50	Wholesale Trade: Durable goods	1	0	0	0
51	Wholesale Trade: Non-durable goods	0	1	0	1
54	Food Stores	0	2	0	2
58	Eating & Drinking Places	1	1	0	1
73	Misc. Business Service	2	0	0	0
89	Misc. Service	1	0	0	0
		$\overline{103}$	$\overline{91}$	$\overline{38}$	$\overline{129}$

Table 3

Descriptive statistics and univariate tests of the relation between explanatory variables and adoption year of SFAS 52 (all variables are measured in 1981).

| Variables[a] | Hypotheses | Year of adoption | | | | Mann–Whitney U one-tailed significance |
| | | (1) 1981 | | (2) 1982 and 1983 | | |
		Mean (s.d.)	Maximum Minimum	Mean (s.d.)	Maximum Minimum	
CEPS	(1) < (2)	−10.00 (39.80)	100.00 −100.00	11.32 (39.95)	100.00 −100.00	0.0000
CPS		0.38 (.37)	1.65 −0.03	—	—	—
COVINT (LEV < 16%)	(1) ≤ (2)	7.40 (10.28)	50.00 −1.47	8.23 (8.63)	50.00 0.33	0.0325
COVINT (LEV ≥ 16%)	(1) < (2)	1.44 (1.27)	6.61 −0.98	2.27 (2.10)	15.67 −0.37	0.0007
LEV	(1) = (2)	16.52 (9.84)	41.77 0	16.48 (9.29)	52.28 0	0.4641
DIVURE	(1) > (2)	21.81 (38.33)	344.07 0	12.36 (9.50)	52.45 0	0.0014
SIZE	(1) < (2)	1,982 (2,172)	15,052 45	5,248 (8,791)	62,931 44	0.0000
DO	(1) < (2)	6.53 (9.73)	44.7 0.17	8.51 (13.13)	67.28 0.10	0.2480

[a]$CEPS = ([EPS_{1981} - CPS - EPS_{1980}]/|EPS_{1980}|) \times 100$, where $EPS_T =$ primary earnings per share excluding extraordinary items and discontinued operations for year T, and $CPS =$ the per share effect of adoption of SFAS 52 for 1981 adopters; for later adopters $CPS = 0$ in 1981;

$COVINT =$ (income before extraordinary items and discontinued operations − income effect of adoption of SFAS 52)/interest expense;

$LEV =$ long-term debt/total assets × 100;

$DIVURE =$ (preferred dividends + common dividends)/retained earnings × 100;

$SIZE =$ total assets (in millions);

$DO =$ percentage of stock held by directors and officers as a group.

5. Results of analysis

5.1. Descriptive statistics and univariate tests

Table 3 presents descriptive statistics for the variables of interest. In every case, the mean differences are in the hypothesized direction. A Mann–Whitney U-test was conducted to provide a univariate test of the hypotheses. The variables *CEPS*, *SIZE* and *DIVURE* are all significant at $\alpha < 0.01$ based on a one-tailed test. *CONVINT* was significant at $\alpha < 0.01$ for high ($\geq 16\%$) leverage firms and at $\alpha < 0.05$ for low ($< 16\%$) leverage firms. *DO* did not differ significantly between early and late adopters.

As predicted by H3, the 1981 adopters reported a decrease in earnings (before the effect of SFAS 52 adoption) of 10.0%, while 1982 and 1983 adopters reported an increase in earnings of 11.3% in 1981. The *CEPS* for the 1981 adopters was significantly less than that of later adopters at $\alpha < 0.0001$. The average *CPS* was 0.38, which is 11.4% of the average pre-change earnings per share for the change firms. These results are consistent with the hypothesis that firms reporting earnings decreases are more likely to select an income-increasing accounting policy. The results are also consistent with Healy's (1985) findings regarding the relationship between accruals and bonuses.

SIZE was highly significant ($\alpha < 0.0001$) with early adopters being smaller on average than later adopters. *DIVURE* was significant at $\alpha = 0.0014$, indicating that early adopters had more binding constraints on dividend payout than later adopters. *LEV* did not differ significantly between early and late adopters. This variable has been found to be a significant factor in other accounting choice studies when the accounting choice made a difference in leverage. If significant differences between groups were found on this variable, it would serve as an indicator that other factors might be driving the results, or that *LEV* should be considered as a covariate. Since I used *LEV* as a factor to split the sample in the interest coverage variable, it is important that this variable not differ between the two groups.

Several points are worth noting with respect to interest coverage. The mean value of the *COVINT* was much higher for firms with low leverage than for firms with high leverage. The mean levels of *COVINT* for low-leverage firms were 7.40 and 8.23 for early and late adopters, respectively. For high-leverage firms the mean levels of *COVINT* were 1.44 for early adopters and 2.27 for late adopters. Furthermore, the level of significance of the *COVINT* variable was much higher for the high-leverage firms than for low-leverage firms ($\alpha = 0.0007$ compared to $\alpha = 0.0325$). These findings are consistent with the argument that coverage restrictions are likely to be of less importance to firms with low levels of debt in their capital structure than to high debt firms.

Table 4 presents the correlation matrix among the variables. The strongest correlation was -0.540 between interest coverage and leverage. Several other variables exhibited statistically significant correlations at $\alpha < 0.05$. As expected, *DO* and *SIZE* were negatively correlated. *DIVURE* was positively correlated with *LEV*. *COVINT* was positively correlated with *CEPS* at $\alpha < 0.05$. I also calculated the coefficient of multiple correlation R^2, between each variable and all of the other variables using a procedure suggested by Johnston (1972) and applied by Daley and Vigeland (1983). This provides an estimate of the degree to which each independent variable is related to all other variables as a group. The largest multiple correlation was for *COVINT* ($R^2 = 0.312$). The degree of intercorrelation among the variables suggests that a multivariate approach is an appropriate means to consider the simultaneous effect of the variables on the adoption decision.

154   *F. Ayres, Characteristics of early adopters of SFAS 52*

Table 4

Correlation among explanatory variables.

Variables[a]	Pairwise correlation coefficients					
	CEPS	*COVINT*	*DIVURE*	*SIZE*	*DO*	*LEV*
CEPS	1.000	—	—	—	—	—
COVINT	0.140[b]	1.000	—	—	—	—
DIVURE	−0.067	−0.124	1.000	—	—	—
SIZE	0.039	−0.037	−0.113	1.000	—	—
DO	0.073	0.099	0.025	−0.173[c]	1.000	—
LEV	−0.069	−0.540[c]	0.204[c]	−0.060	−0.023	1.000
Multiple $R^{2\ d}$	0.028	0.312	0.055	0.050	0.043	0.047

[a] Variables are as defined in table 3.
[b] Significant at the 0.05 level.
[c] Significant at the 0.01 level.
[d] R_i^2 coefficient of multiple determination between variable i and all other independent variables.

5.2. Multivariate analysis

A logistic model was employed to test the overall significance of the variables in the model. The logistic model is based on the assumption that the dependent variable is an estimate of the probability that an observation belongs in one of two groups. It assumes that the probability function has a logistic distribution. Both the logistic model and the similar probit model have been used in several accounting choice studies [see for example Elliot et al. (1984), Bowen, Noreen and Lacy (1981) and Hagerman and Zmijewski (1979)].

In order to allow for a different effect of interest coverage on high- versus low-leverage firms, a dummy variable, *COVDUM*, was created. This variable was set equal to one when *LEV* was less than 16, and zero otherwise. In order to allow for a different slope coefficient between high- and low-leverage firms, I multiplied *COVDUM* by *COVINT*. For high-leverage firms the effect of interest coverage is captured in the *COVINT* variable. The effect of interest coverage on low-leverage firms is the sum of the coefficients for *COVINT* and *COVDUM* × *COVINT*. If there is no difference in the impact of interest coverage on the adoption decision between high- and low-leverage firms then the coefficient for *COVDUM* × *COVINT* is expected to be insignificant. If interest coverage is less important for low-leverage firms than for high-leverage firms, then the coefficient of *COVDUM* × *COVINT* will be positive.[8]

---

[8] I also ran the model with *COVDUM* included to allow for a different intercept between high- and low-leverage firms. This variable was insignificant and was dropped from the final model.

Table 5

Logistic model of SFAS 52 adoption year decision; 1981 versus later (1982 and 1983) adopters; total sample.

	Const.	CEPS	COVINT	COVDUM × COVINT	DIVURE	SIZE/100	DO
				Variables[a]			
Expected sign	?	−	−	+ or 0	+	−	−
Coefficient	0.308	−1.24	−0.219	0.213	0.030	−0.019	−0.028
t-value	0.91	−2.92	−1.63	1.66	2.57	−3.24	−1.99
Significance (one-tailed)	(0.182)	(0.002)	(0.051)	(0.048)	(0.005)	(0.001)	(0.023)

Percentage correctly classified: 69.0%
Value of chi-squared statistic for model: 52.14, d.f. = 6
Probability under H_0 < 0.0001
Dependent variable = 1 if adoption date of SFAS 52 is 1981, $N = 103$
                 = 0 if adoption date of SFAS 52 is 1982 or 1983, $N = 129$

[a]See table 3 for variable definitions. Further, $COVDUM$ = dummy variable coded one if LEV < 16, and zero otherwise; and $COVDUM \times COVINT$ = interaction term which measures the difference in the impact of interest coverage between low-leverage firms and high-leverage firms.

Table 5 presents the results of the logistic model using the complete sample of firms for the initial 'adopt versus defer' decision.[9] As was true in the univariate test, all of the coefficients have the predicted sign. The overall model was significant at α < 0.0001. All of the coefficients on individual variables were significant at $\alpha = 0.05$ or less providing support for H1–H5.[10] The significance of the $COVDUM \times COVINT$ variable indicates that for low-leverage firms interest coverage does not appear to be a significant factor in the decision to adopt SFAS 52.[11]

[9]The logistic model was run with LEV included and as expected it was insignificant. The results were not materially altered by the inclusion of this variable. I also ran the model with $SALES$ as an alternative measure of size and found no material difference in the results.

[10]I also ran the model separately on the 1981 versus 1982 adopters, and 1981 versus 1983 adopters. The 1981 versus 1982 results were virtually identical to the complete sample. The results of the 1981 versus 1983 subgroup resulted in coefficients in the predicted direction, however the only significant variable was $SIZE$. Since the 1983 sample consisted of only thirty-seven firms, this result may be a function, in part, of the small sample size.
In order to determine the sensitivity of the model to the coding of outlier observations in the $COVINT$, $DIVURE$ and CPS variables, I ran the model with the coded observations deleted. This reduced the sample size to 205 observations. The results remained similar to those in table 5. All coefficients were significant in the predicted direction at $\alpha = 0.05$ or less except for DO. The coefficient for DO was significant at $\alpha = 0.09$.

[11]The sum of the coefficients for $COVINT$ and $COVDUM \times COVINT$ is −0.006 for low-leverage firms, which is insignificant ($t = 0.045$).

5.3. Industry as an omitted variable

To control for industry, an additional test was run in which the firms in the 1981 sample were matched with firms from the 1982 and 1983 samples on the basis of at least two-digit SIC codes.[12] This resulted in a sample of seventy-seven matched pairs of firms. Using a method employed by Bowen, Noreen and Lacy (1981) the logistic model was run using the differences in the independent variables for the matched pairs in the analysis. This procedure controls for the effect of different industry intercepts. These results are presented in table 6. The overall model was significant at $\alpha < 0.0001$ and all of the coefficients except those related to interest coverage were significant at $\alpha < 0.05$. *COVINT* and *COVDUM × COVINT*, although in the predicted direction, were not significant. This could be due to some industry effect attributable to this variable, or to the reduced power of the test due to the reduction in sample size.[13]

6. Conclusions

This study investigated whether the choice of adoption date is related to firm control, proximity to debt and dividend constraints, size and reported earnings. It was found that firms choosing to adopt SFAS 52 at the earliest possible adoption date (1) had a lower percentage of stock owned by directors and officers, (2) had smaller percentage earnings increases from the previous year, (3) were smaller, and (4) were closer to debt and dividend constraints than later adopters.

The results are consistent with previous research which suggests that systematic differences exist between firms that choose alternative accounting policies. Hence, the results provide further support in the developing framework of a positive theory of accounting choice. This study also used a variable that has not been previously employed to measure managements' incentive to increase earnings, the percentage *change* in reported earnings per share in the adoption year of the accounting policy change (*CEPS*). This variable was found to be highly significant and is consistent with a management strategy aimed at achieving some target earnings goals.

[12] I used four-digit SIC codes whenever possible. For firms that could not be matched on four-digit codes, three- and two-digit SIC codes were used. If a firm could not be matched on at least two digits it was dropped from the sample.

[13] While the Bowan et al. method controls for industry effects on the intercept, it reduces the sample size considerably. By using differences in matched pairs rather than the individual values as the independent variables, the seventy-seven matched pairs constitute a sample size of seventy-seven. However, if the actual values are used, the total sample size is doubled. Implementation of their method requires that the matched pairs be randomly assigned to two groups. For the first group, the differences in the independent variables are calculated as $(X_f - X_{f'})$, where firm f is the 1981 adopter and f' is the matched later adopter. The dependent variable for this group is coded one. In the second group the differences are calculated as $(X_{f'} - X_f)$ and the dependent variable is coded zero.

Table 6

Logistic model of SFAS 52 adoption year decision; industry-matched sample; 1981 versus later (1982 and 1983) adopters.

				Variables[a]			
	Const.	*CEPS*	*COVINT*	*COVDUM* $\times$ *COVINT*	*DIVURE*	*SIZE*/100	*DO*
Expected sign	?	–	–	+ or 0	+	–	–
Coefficient	–0.258	–0.720	–0.245	0.288	0.045	–0.016	–0.051
t-value	–0.83	–3.16	–1.15	1.10	2.58	–1.77	–2.05
Significance (one-tailed)	(0.203)	(0.001)	(0.124)	(0.135)	(0.005)	(0.038)	(0.020)

Percentage correctly classified: 77.9%
Value of chi-squared statistic for model: 38.05, d.f. = 6
Probability under H_0 < 0.0001
Dependent variable = 1 if independent variable j is calculated as $(X_{fj} - X_{f'j})$ where firm f is the 1981 adopter and f' represents the matched late adopter, $n = 38$
= 0 if independent variable j is calculated as $(X_{f'j} - X_{fj})$, where f' represents the late adopter, and firm f is the matched 1981 adopters, $n = 39$

[a]See tables 3 and 5 for definitions of variables. Independent variables are the differences between the values of the named variables for the 1981 adopter and the later adopter in a matched pair.

The results are consistent with an ordering effect taking place with respect to the adoption of SFAS 52. By allowing the change over a period of several years, the FASB permits systematic earnings manipulation. The FASB has formally instituted a policy of enacting new standards with a gradual transition period. An alternative approach to implementation of new standards would be to pass accounting changes with a delayed adoption date which is the same for all firms.

References

Bettner, Jill, 1981a, Major accounting rule change adopted covering foreign currency translation, Wall Street Journal, Dec. 8, 8.

Bettner, Jill, 1981b, Companies press for new accounting method that could improve 1981 per-share earnings, Wall Street Journal, Nov. 9, 56.

Bowen, R.E. Noreen and J. Lacey, 1981, Determinants of the corporate decision to capitalize interest, Journal of Accounting and Economics 3, 151–179.

Daley, L.A. and R.L. Vigeland, 1983, The effects of debt covenants and political costs on the choice of accounting methods: The case of accounting for R&D costs, Journal of Accounting and Economics 5, 195–211.

Dhaliwal, D., 1980, The effects of the firm's capital structure on the choice of accounting methods, Accounting Review, Jan., 78–84.

Dhaliwal, D., Gerald L. Salamon and E. Dan Smith, 1982, The effect of owner versus management control on the choice of accounting methods, Journal of Accounting and Economics 4, 41–53.

Elliot, J., G. Richardson, T. Dyckman and R. Dukes, 1984, The impact of SFAS No. 2 on firm expenditures on research and development: Replications and extensions, Journal of Accounting Research, Spring, 85–102.

Execucomp, 1983 ed. (Martin E. Segal Company).

Financial Accounting Standards Board, 1984, Accounting standards: Original pronouncements, 1984–85 ed. (McGraw-Hill, New York).

Hagerman, R. and M. Zmijewski, 1979, Some economic determinants of accounting policy choice, Journal of Accounting and Economics 1, 142–161.

Healy, Paul M., 1985, The effect of bonus schemes on accounting decisions, Journal of Accounting and Economics 7, 85–107.

Hindley, B., 1970, Separation of ownership and control of the modern corporation, Journal of Law and Economics, April, 185–222.

Jensen, M. and W.H. Meckling, 1976, Theory of the firm: managerial behavior, agency costs and ownership structure, Journal of Financial Economics 3, 305–360.

Johnston, J., 1972, Econometric methods, 2nd ed. (McGraw-Hill, New York).

Mathur, Ike and David Loy, 1981, Foreign currency translation: Survey of corporate treasurers, Management Accounting (NAA) 63, 33–38.

Monson, Joseph R. and Anthony Downs, 1965, A theory of large managerial firms, Journal of Political Economy 53, 221–236.

Sherwood, Hugh C., 1976, How corporate and municipal debt is rated (Wiley, New York).

Smith C. and J. Warner, 1979, Financial contracting: An analysis of bond covenants, Journal of Financial Economics 7, 117–162.

Watts, R. and J. Zimmerman, 1978, Towards a positive theory of the determination of accounting standards, Accounting Review, Jan., 112-134.

Williamson, O.E., 1967, A dynamic stochastic theory of managerial behavior, in: A. Phillips and O. Williamson, eds., Prices: Issues of theory, practice and public policy (University of Pennsylvania Press, Philadelphia, PA).

Zmijewski, Mark and Robert L. Hagerman, 1981, An income strategy approach to the positive theory of accounting standard setting/choice, Journal of Accounting and Economics 3, 129-150.

[18]

Further Evidence on the Impact of SFAS 52 on Analysts' Earnings Forecasts

Frances L. Ayres
University of Oklahoma

Jacci L. Rodgers
Oklahoma City University

Abstract

This study examines the impact of Statement of Financial Accounting Standards Number 52 (SFAS 52) on analysts' earnings forecasts. Value-Line forecasts of multinational firms' earnings were examined for the years 1979–1984. Forecast errors did not exhibit a significant linear trend. However, the results show a decline in signed forecast errors from the pre-SFAS 52 to the post-SFAS 52 period reflecting a change from an overstatement bias to relatively unbiased forecasts.

Overall, the results suggest that (1) overstatement errors were greater in the pre-SFAS 52 period than in the post SFAS 52 period, and (2) overstatement errors in the year that SFAS 52 was adopted were greater than surrounding years. In addition, a strong negative relation was found between 1981 signed forecast errors and both revisions in forecasts and the income effect of the accounting change.

This study examines the impact of the introduction of a mandatory change in accounting for foreign currency translation, SFAS 52, on analysts' forecasts of multinational firms' earnings [FASB (1981)]. The findings of prior studies with regard to the impact of foreign currency accounting standard changes on forecast accuracy have been mixed [see Brown (1983), Elliott and Philbrick (1990), and Griffin and Castanias (1987)].

Griffin and Castanias, using absolute forecast errors, report that the change in reporting from SFAS No. 8 [FASB (1975)] to SFAS 52 was associated with a gradual increase in forecast accuracy following the initial adoption of SFAS 52. Brown found no change in forecast accuracy following the enactment of SFAS No. 8 which he hypothesized would impair forecast accuracy. Elliott and Philbrick examined SFAS 52 in conjunction with several other changes (both mandatory and discretionary). They reported that (1) absolute forecast errors were higher during

---

Frances Ayres would like to acknowledge the financial support of the University of Oklahoma College of Business Samuel Roberts Noble Foundation and the KPMG Peat Marwick Foundation. The authors would also like to acknowledge the helpful comments of two anonymous referees.

the change year than nonchange year for firms with no prior disclosure of the change, and (2) a negative relation was found between signed forecast revisions and the income effect of the change. Their findings on the relation between signed forecast errors and the income effect of the accounting change were mixed, and support a weak, but overall positive relation for mandatory accounting changes. Elliott and Philbrick concluded that the results are consistent with the hypothesis that accounting changes are made with an income smoothing motivation.

Elliott and Philbrick examined both signed and unsigned forecast errors. However, the adoption of SFAS 52 was one of a large number of accounting changes examined in their study, comprising about 23 percent of their total sample. While examining the impact of a broad spectrum of accounting changes on forecast accuracy is useful in assessing the average impact of accounting changes on forecasts it does not test whether a particular standard (i.e., SFAS 52) impacted forecast accuracy. Differences across accounting method changes may help to explain the mixed results they report in their examination of the relation between signed forecast errors and the income effect of accounting changes.

The impact of SFAS 52 on signed forecast errors is of particular interest in its own right. Complete analysis of the impact of accounting standards on forecast behavior requires an assessment of the effect on forecast bias, as well as the effect on absolute forecast errors. A major criticism of SFAS 8 was that the impact of foreign currency fluctuations on earnings made earnings and financial statement relationships difficult to interpret (SFAS 52. π 153). If analysts are unable to anticipate the impact of foreign currency gains and losses on earnings we would expect that analysts' forecasts would be upwardly biased when companies incur foreign currency translation losses as was generally the case in the late 1970s and early 1980s. During this period the dollar rose relative to foreign currency leading to translation losses for multinational companies. Virtually all sample companies reported a significant negative balance in stockholders' equity upon adoption of SFAS 52, reflecting cumulative translation losses.

SFAS 52 was not enacted until December of 1981. This meant that for 1981 adopters the possibility of adoption could not be assessed until fairly late in the year, if at all. Griffin and Castanias interviewed analysts to determine when and if they revised their 1981 forecasts in response to the enactment of SFAS 52. They found that about half the analysts interviewed revised forecasts in response to SFAS 52 enactment and half did not. However of those who did revise, most reported that they did so either in the next forecast following SFAS 52 enactment or when a

122 *Frances L. Ayres and Jacci L. Rodgers*

company first disclosed under SFAS 52. This suggests that analysts' forecasts made during 1981 were based on SFAS 8 earnings expectations. The income effect of SFAS 52 adoption tended to be positive.

Our results suggest that while analysts tended to revise earnings forecasts downward during the year, initial forecast errors were negative consistent with an overstatement bias on the part of analysts. The overstatement bias was negatively correlated to the percentage change in earnings as a result of SFAS 52 enactment. In general, firms that adopted SFAS 52 early had a decline in pre-change earnings which analysts failed to anticipate.

This research extends prior studies in two respects. First, we examine signed forecast errors over a six year period surrounding the enactment of SFAS 52. Griffin and Castanias utilized a similar time frame for their examination of absolute forecast errors. The use of signed forecast errors allows us to examine the direction of and change in the bias in analysts' forecasts surrounding SFAS 52 adoption. Knowledge of whether particular accounting practices are associated with bias in forecasts is important for several reasons. First, the FASB Concepts Statement #2 *Qualitative Characteristics of Accounting Information* (1980) states that financial accounting disclosures should be neutral and not lead to biased judgments by those who rely upon them (FASB Concepts Statement No. 2 paragraphs 98–110). If a particular accounting method leads to biased forecasts, then this suggests that the goals of the Conceptual Framework are not being met. Second, systematically biased forecasts may be associated with market inefficiencies. Abarbanell and Bernard (1992) found that analysts underreact to recent earnings changes and that this underreaction is related to the post-earnings-announcement drift phenomena. If the degree of bias differs across accounting methods this suggests that there may be differences in the speed of the market reaction to earnings as a function of the method of accounting used. Third, the costs to investors who rely on analysts are likely to differ for under-estimates and over-estimates of earnings. The use of absolute forecast errors implies a symmetric loss function.

A second contribution of this study is that we used Value-Line rather than aggregate analysts' forecasts which were employed in prior studies. The Institutional Brokers Estimate System (I/B/E/S) was used by both Griffin and Castanias and Elliott and Philbrick. I/B/E/S reports mean and median forecasts at different points in time as well as information on the number of analysts reporting. Hence it can provide insight on an aggregate level into change in accuracy as well as forecast revision behavior. It does not, however, allow assessment of whether or not particular analysts (or analyst firms) revise specific forecasts or reduce forecast errors in response to a particular accounting change. Value-Line provides four forecasts per year of annual earnings for firms which it follows making it possible to examine the changes in specific forecasts. I/B/E/S data, by using medians, is smoothed and thus does not allow one to focus on directional changes in specific forecasts. The I/B/E/S data provides monthly values of median forecasts and forecast revisions but does not indicate if or when particular analysts revise forecasts. By using one analyst group data (Value Line), we can observe true directional changes in forecasts which show us how this set of analysts accounted for uncertainty and responsed to changes in expected earnings during the year.

The remainder of this paper is divided as follows. First, the research hypotheses are described. Next, the sample and research design are discussed. Third, the results are presented. The final section presents the conclusions.

Hypotheses

SFAS 52 possesses several characteristics which cause it to serve as a particularly rich source of information regarding analysts' forecasts. First, the income effect of adoption for companies disclosing an effect was generally large and positive. This is because the dollar gained relative to most foreign currencies during the adoption period of SFAS 52 (1981–1983). As a result, companies that experienced translation losses which would have flowed through income under SFAS 8 were able to move the losses directly to owners' equity under SFAS 52. The mean increase in earnings for the companies in this study was 12.5 percent.[1] Second, SFAS 52 was enacted late in 1981 (December 7) which meant that specific predictions of which companies would elect immediate adoption and the income effects of the change were unlikely prior to the year end. A review of the *Wall Street Journal Index* for 1980–1982 indicated that while the proposed new standard was known as early as late 1980 when the exposure draft was issued, most of the press information regarding the effects of SFAS 52 was published in December 1981 immediately after its enactment.

During the transitional period (1981–1982) the impact of SFAS 52 on forecast accuracy depended upon a number of factors. These include; (1) the extent to which analysts were able to predict whether management would elect to adopt SFAS 52 in 1981 (the year of its enactment), (2) the

124   *Frances L. Ayres and Jacci L. Rodgers*

extent to which information about the probable passage of SFAS 52 had already been incorporated into previous forecasts and (3) the ability of analysts to determine the income impact of the new standard. The uncertainty about earnings related to these factors suggests that forecast errors of multinational firms would be higher in 1981 and 1982 (the transitional years) than in surrounding periods.[2] The longer term effect on forecast accuracy depends on the extent to which the prior standard (SFAS 8) impaired forecast accuracy by including in income the impact of translation gains and losses. The null hypotheses is:

H0: The accounting change from SFAS 8 to SFAS 52 was not associated with a change in the accuracy of analysts' forecasts.

Rejection of the null suggests that the accounting change from SFAS 8 to SFAS 52 changed analysts' forecast accuracy. The specific timing and nature of the change depends on the behavior of analysts during the transitional period and after SFAS 52 adoption. The following alternative hypotheses, conditional on rejection of the null, address specific expectations about analysts' behavior during the transitional years and following SFAS 52 adoption. Because of the uncertainty created by the possibility of an accounting change of this magnitude, we expected that the transitional years (1981 and 1982) would have higher forecast errors. Griffin and Castanias report results for absolute forecast errors which are consistent with this.[3] However, the expected direction and magnitude of the signed forecast errors during the transitional period is uncertain. If uncertainty about SFAS 52 effects led to more uncertainty, but no directional bias in forecasts, then the mean signed forecast errors would be expected to be insignificantly different from zero. On the other hand if uncertainty about the impact of SFAS 52 on earnings led to systematic under-(over-)forecasts of earnings then signed forecast errors will be negative (positive). The first hypothesis is:

H1: Signed Value-Line Analysts' forecast errors of multinational firms' earnings were greater in magnitude in 1981 and 1982 than in surrounding years.

A related question is whether the forecast error difference between transitional and surrounding years is due to general uncertainty regarding multinational firms' earnings throughout the transitional period, or is primarily caused by uncertainty about the level of earnings in the adoption year. If the former applies then we would expect to observe greater than normal forecast errors throughout the transition period regardless of the year that a particular firm adopted SFAS 52. The latter case implies higher forecast errors in the adoption year only. That is, we would expect that 1981 adopters would have the highest forecast errors in 1981 and 1982 adopters would have the largest errors in 1982. The second hypothesis is:

H2: Signed Value-Line Analysts' forecast errors of multinational firms' earnings were greater in magnitude in the year of adoption than in surrounding years.

One factor motivating the issuance of SFAS 52 was a concern that earnings were excessively volatile under SFAS 8 because of the inclusion of translation gains and losses in net income [Seidler, 1982]. To the extent that inclusion of these gains and losses in earnings made income more difficult to predict, we would expect that removal of this effect would lead to improved earnings forecasts. If SFAS 52 did lead to a reduction in forecast errors then we would expect, ceteris paribus, that forecast errors in the SFAS 52 period (1983 and 1984) would be lower than those in the SFAS 8 period (1979 and 1980). The transitional period is excluded because of the potential for increased forecast errors due to the uncertainty of time of adoption. The third hypothesis:

H3: Signed Value-Line Analysts' forecast errors of multinational firms earnings were smaller in magnitude in 1983 and 1984 than in 1979 and 1980.

The fourth and fifth hypotheses relate to the relation between analysts' forecast errors and the income effect of the change. As Elliott and Philbrick (1990) note, a positive association between the income effect of the change and forecast errors would be consistent with analysts failing to anticipate the change. This is consistent with the findings of Biddle and Ricks (1988), Hughes and Ricks (1986) and Ricks and Hughes (1985). A negative relation between the income effect of the change and the forecast error suggests that either (1) analysts overestimated the income effect of the change or that (2) management used the accounting change to increase income and that the extent of manipulation relates to the degree of overoptimism of analysts.

The results of Elliott and Philbrick on this issue were mixed. The strongest positive correlation (0.30) was reported for a single mandatory

126   *Frances L. Ayres and Jacci L. Rodgers*

change with prior disclosure and more than five analysts following. For the remaining mandatory changes (less than five analysts with prior disclosure, less than five analysts without prior disclosure and more than five analysts with prior disclosure) the correlations were:- 0.07, 0.05 and 0.09 respectively.

Approximately half of Elliott and Philbrick's sample of mandatory accounting changes were SFAS 52 adopters. The remaining changes included lease accounting, interest capitalization, vacation accruals and other miscellaneous changes. The mixed results obtained suggest that the relation between forecast errors and the income effect of the change was not constant across mandatory changes suggesting that more detailed examination of particular types of accounting changes may be fruitful. The fourth hypothesis is:

H4: There is a cross-sectional association between signed forecast errors and the signed income effect of SFAS 52 adoption.

Forecast revisions would be expected to be positively related to the income effect of the change if analysts revised their forecasts in anticipation of SFAS 52 adoption. No association between forecast revisions and the signed effect of the change would be expected if analysts did not adjust forecasts to capture the effect of the change. A negative relation between forecast revisions and the income effect of the change suggests that management uses the change to adjust for unexpected earnings decreases (because the income effect of the change is positive). Alternatively if analysts fail to anticipate the change and revise earnings estimates downward through the year in response to concern with the negative impact of foreign currency fluctuations, the behavior of analysts rather than management may be the causal factor in an observed negative relation. The fifth hypothesis is:

H5: There is a cross-sectional association between signed revisions of analysts' forecasts and the signed income effect of SFAS 52.

Sample and research design

The sample firms were selected from *Accounting Trends and Techniques* group of firms. Firms disclosing a change to SFAS 52 in either 1981 or 1982 were included. Additional selection criteria were availability of earnings information on Compustat and a calendar year end. A sample of domestic control firms matched on the basis of SIC industry codes was obtained from a group of firms used in Salatka (1989). The final sample consisted of eighty-three firms: twenty-nine 1981 adopters, thirty 1982 adopters and twenty-four domestic control firms.[4] Because the industry matching was not exact, the sample of firms is treated as three random samples rather than as a paired control sample. Table 1 presents the industry distribution of the sample firms by two-digit SIC code.

For each company in the sample, Value-Line earnings forecasts were obtained for the period 1979–1984. Value-Line publishes four annual forecasts per year for the companies that it follows. A total of 24 quarterly forecasts of annual earnings was obtained for each firm. The first three Value-Line quarterly forecasts for 1981 were issued prior to the issuance of SFAS 52. The fourth quarter forecast was issued prior to the annual earnings announcement and in most cases subsequent to the passage of the standard.

Following Baldwin (1984), multivariate analysis of variance (MANOVA) was used to test whether there was a significant difference between sample and control firms' forecast errors for different years and quarters in the test period. Specific contrasts were then tested to explain the nature of the effects.

Table 1. *Industry Membership of Sample Firms*

Number of Firms			
Two-digit SIC code	1981 adopters	1982 adopters	Control firms
20	2	2	1
21	1	1	1
22	1	1	1
26	4	4	5
27	1	1	3
28	5	5	1
29	1	1	1
30	1	—	1
32	2	2	1
33	1	1	2
34	—	1	2
35	6	6	1
36	3	4	3
37	1	1	1
	29	30	24

128   *Frances L. Ayres and Jacci L. Rodgers*

The following error metric was computed for each sample firm for the years 1979–1984:

$$FE_{ijk} = (EPS_{ik} - FEPS_{ijk})/|EPS_{ik}| \qquad (1)$$

where,

FE_{ijk} = signed annual forecast error for year i in quarter j for firm k

EPS_{ik} = Value-Line actual earnings per share for year i for firm k and

$FEPS_{ijk}$ = Value-Line forecast of annual earnings per share for year i in quarter j for firm k.

The absolute value of earnings per share was used as the deflator for two reasons. First, using realized earnings per share results in error measures which are readily interpretable as the percentage forecast error by analysts. Second, since we looked at four forecasts per year, realized earnings per share provides a consistent deflator over quarters.

Error metric (1) was transformed in order to test H1–H3 as follows: First, the control firms were used to remove economy wide effects unrelated to SFAS 52 from both early and late adopters by subtracting from each forecast error the average signed forecast error for the control group for year i in quarter j.[5] This transformation resulted in the following variable:

$$UFE_{ijk} = FE_{ijk} - AVGFE_{ij} \qquad (1')$$

$AVGFE_{ij}$ = mean signed forecast error for year i and quarter j for the control group

The transformed error metric (1′) was then transformed to create three variables designed to test H1–H3. These variables were as follows, (firm and quarter subscripts are eliminated for expositional convenience except where needed for clarity).

Variable used to test H1:

$$TRANS = (UFE_{81} + UFE_{82})/2$$
$$- (UFE_{79} + UFE_{80} + UFE_{83} + UFE_{84})/4 \qquad (2)$$

Equation 2 was used to test whether the transition years had higher average forecast errors than the average of the surrounding years.

Variable used to test H2:

$$ADOP = (UFE_{81}) - (UFE_{79} + UFE_{80} + UFE_{83} + UFE_{84})/4, \qquad (3)$$
for 1981 adopting firms and
$$ADOP = (UFE_{82}) - (UFE_{79} + UFE_{80} + UFE_{83} + UFE_{84})/4,$$
for 1982 adopting firms

Equation 3 was designed to test specifically for adoption year effects. The tests of adoption year effects and transitional effects are related in that the transformed variables both contain either 1981 or 1982 adjusted forecast errors. However we would expect that if the transition effect dominated, stronger results would obtain for the Equation 2 contrasts, while if adoption year effect dominated, stronger results would obtain for Equation 3. Significant results for both would suggest both a transition and an adoption year effect.

Variable used to test H3:

$$CHG = (UFE_{83} + UFE_{84}) - (UFE_{79} + UFE_{80}) \qquad (4)$$

Equation 4 provides a test of whether the forecast error changed significantly from the pre- to the post-SFAS 52 period.

H4 and H5 were tested using cross-sectional regression models. The dependent variables were unexpected forecast error (1') for H4 and forecast revisions for H5. The dependent variables were regressed against the pre-SFAS 52 adoption earnings change and the income effect of SFAS 52 adoption (SFAS52). Pre-adoption earnings change (ECHG) was used as a control variable. To the extent that analysts use prior years' earnings to forecast future years, a positive relation between earnings changes and forecast errors is expected. This relation would be expected to be strongest early in the year (quarter 1 forecasts) and to decline through the year as additional evidence became available regarding earnings realizations. This would result in a positive relation between earnings changes and forecast revisions as well. Both independent variables were weighted by the absolute value of 1981 actual earnings to ensure consistency with the dependent variable. The models are shown below.

130   *Frances L. Ayres and Jacci L. Rodgers*

To test H4 the following model was used:

$$UFE_{81jk} = a_j + b1_j \; ECHGk + b2_j \; SFAS \; 52_k + e_{jk}, \tag{5}$$
$$j = 1,4 \; quarters, \; k = 1,29 \; firms$$

$$ECHG = ((EPS_{81k} - SFAS52) - EPS_{80k}) / |EPS_{81k}|$$

$$SFAS52 = primary \; earnings \; per \; share \; effect \; of \; SFAS \; 52$$
$$adoption / |EPS_{81k}|$$

To test H5 the model was:

$$REV_{81mk} = a_j + b_{1j} \; ECHG_k + b2_j \; SFAS52_k + e_{mk}, \tag{6}$$
$$m = 1,3 \; revisions$$

$$REV_{81mk} = (FEPS_{81jk} - FEPS_{81j-1,k}) / |EPS_{81k}|$$

Results

Table 2 Panels A and A' present means and standard errors for the adjusted forecast errors (1') and the transformed variables (2–4). The results indicate an overstatement bias from 1979–1982 followed by relatively unbiased adjusted forecast errors in 1983 and 1984. Panel A' also shows that the overstatement was generally greater in the adoption year. The change in forecast error was positive (CHG in Panel A') and ranged from seven percent in the fourth quarter to nearly twenty percent in the second quarter forecasts. Interpretation of this must be made in light of the finding that the pre-SFAS 52 forecast errors were negative reflecting overestimates of earnings. Hence, the positive sign of the change in forecast error suggests a movement from overstatements to unbiased forecasts.[6]

Multivariate Tests for Hypothesized Effects

Table 3 presents the results of the overall MANOVA for tests of time and time × quarter interactions. These tests reveal whether there are significant differences in forecast errors for any combination of time and quarters. Our expectation was that the results of the hypothesis test would tend to be strongest in the first quarter and decline as the year progressed and more information about earnings became available. The results in Table 3 are based on the adjusted transformed variables (Equation 1'). The results reveal no overall effect for time although fourth quarters forecast

Table 2. *Panel A Means and standard errors for signed adjusted forecast errors*[1]

Variable	Quarter Q1	Q2	Q3	Q4
1979				
Mean	−0.0504	−0.2079	−0.2222	−0.0777
std.error	(0.0834)	(0.0644)	(0.0688)	(0.0631)
1980				
Mean	−0.1904	−0.1212	−0.1346	−0.0591
std. error	(0.0761)	(0.0636)	(0.0782)	(0.0594)
1981				
Mean	−0.0982	0.0279	−0.1091	−0.0450
std. error	(0.0544)	(0.0750)	(0.0658)	(0.0441)
1982				
Mean	−0.2142	−0.3625	−0.2387	−0.1108
std. error	(0.1040)	(0.0962)	(0.0835)	(0.0657)
1983				
Mean	0.0331	0.0441	0.0155	0.0102
std. error	(0.0892)	(0.1047)	(0.0880)	(0.0697)
1984				
Mean	0.0224	0.0238	0.0025	0.0016
std. error	(0.1020)	(0.1024)	(0.0915)	(0.0881)

Panel A′ Means for transformed variables

Variable|Hypothesis		Quarter Q1	Q2	Q3	Q4
TRANS	H1				
Mean		−0.1099	−0.0909	−0.0891	−0.0458
std. error		(0.0775)	(0.0834)	(0.0744)	(0.0416)
ADOP	H2				
Mean		−0.2011	−0.2120	−0.1569	−0.0267
std. error		(0.1058)	(0.1098)	(0.1164)	(0.0702)
CHG	H3				
Mean		0.1482	0.1986	0.1877	0.0727
std. error		(0.0920)	(0.0985)	(0.0902)	(0.0696)

[1] UFE_{ij} = $FE_{ij} - AVGFE_{ij}$.
where FE_{ij} = $(EPS_{ij} - FEPS_{ij})/|EPS_{ij}|$
EPS_{ij} = Value Line reported earnings per share for year i in quarter j
$FEPS_{ij}$ = Value Line forecasted earnings per share for year i in quarter j
$AVGFE_{ij}$ = mean absolute forecast error for year i and quarter j for the control group
$TRANS_{ij}$ = $(UFE_{81} + UFE_{82})/2 - (UFE_{79} + UFE_{80} + UFE_{83} + UFE_{84})/4$
$ADOP_{ij}$ = $(UFE_{81}) - (UFE_{79} + UFE_{80} + UAFE_{83} + UFE_{84})/4$ for 1981 adopting firms and
$ADOP_{ij}$ = $(UFE_{82}) - (UFE_{79} + UFE_{80} + UFE_{83} + UFE_{84})/4$ for 1982 adopting firms.
CHG_{ij} = $(UFE_{83} + UFE_{84}) - (UFE_{79} + UFE_{80})$

132   *Frances L. Ayres and Jacci L. Rodgers*

Table 3. *Multivariate Repeated Measure Analysis of Variance for Signed Forecast Errors 1979–1984 (All years and quarters combined)*

	Quarter	Time	Time*Quarter
Wilke's Lambda	0.8909	0.8950	0.4271
F	2.29	1.27	3.93
Prob > F	0.0866	0.2922	0.0002

errors were smaller than first quarter as expected. However, a highly significant time × quarter interaction was found suggesting that significant differences exist across time for some quarters. Because of this our hypothesis test results are analyzed by quarter.

The results of the hypothesis tests are presented in Table 4. Transition year effects (TRANS) were significantly different from surrounding years in the first quarter ($p = 0.08$) supporting H1. For the remaining quarters the transition year errors tended to be more negative (overstated) but not significantly so. The p-values for quarters 2–4 ranged from 0.12–0.14. Table 2 shows that for the first quarter mean overstatement errors were about 11 percent greater than for surrounding years.

The adoption year tests (H2) were significant in quarters 1–3, but not in the fourth quarter. Average overstatement errors for quarters 1–3 ranged from 16–20 percent. For the fourth quarter the adoption year mean signed forecast errors were only 2.7 percent.

The forecast error change was significant for quarters 1–3 and in the predicted direction in the fourth quarter. The change in forecast error in quarter 1–3 ranged from 15–20 percent and was in a positive direction indicating a movement from overstatement bias in the pre-SFAS 52 period to unbiased forecasts after the enactment of SFAS 52.

Table 4. *Tests for Hypothesized Effects*

Quarter	Transition p-value H1 TRANS	Adoption year p-value H2 ADOP	Forecast Error Change p-value H3 CHG
1	0.0809	0.0311	0.0563
2	0.1401	0.0292	0.0243
3	0.1180	0.0826	0.0209
4	0.1379	0.3524	0.1502

Examination of Adoption Year Effects

H4 and H5 were tested using only the 1981 adopters because 1981 was the only year for which the income effect of the change was available. SFAS 52 did not require disclosure of the effect of SFAS 52 adoption on earnings for calendar year end companies adopting after 1981. Recall that the dependent variables were the unexpected forecast error $(1')$ for each quarter (1–4) for H4 and forecast revisions for H5. The independent variables were the earnings change (pre-SFAS 52 adoption) (ECHG) and the income effect of SFAS 52 adoption (SFAS 52).

Table 5 indicates a consistent positive relation between the pre-adoption earnings change (ECHG) and the forecast errors. However, a significant *negative* relation was found between the earnings effect of SFAS 52 adoption and the signed forecast errors. The SFAS 52 effects were positive for all firms in this sample and range from 1.7 to 71.4 percent of earnings. Recall that negative (positive) forecast errors imply overestimates (underestimates) of earnings. Thus the negative relation between the impact of SFAS 52 on earnings and forecast errors suggest that the greater the level of analysts' overestimation (underestimation) of earnings, the larger (smaller) the change in earnings due to SFAS 52 adoption.

The independent variables in the regressions are also related. Companies adopting SFAS 52 in 1981 tended to have a decrease in earnings prior to adoption.[7] The correlation between the change in earnings prior to SFAS 52 adoption and the income effect of SFAS 52 adoption was -0.66 indicating the existence of multicollinearity. In the case where there are two independent variables which are negatively correlated, the estimation errors in the coefficients will tend to be positive which could cause the estimated coefficient to be positive for one variable when both are in the model.[8] To control for this the effects of both variables were examined separately as well as jointly.

Table 5 shows that the relation between forecast errors and the change in earnings is positive and significant in all four quarters when the income effect of SFAS 52 is not included. The income effect of SFAS 52 is negative and significant in all quarters when examined alone. When included with the earnings change the SFAS 52 effect is not significant in the first two quarters. However, in the last two quarters, the SFAS 52 effect dominates the effect due to the change in earnings. An examination of the adjusted R^2 reveals an interesting trend. In the first two quarters (forecasts issued by April and July respectively) the adjusted R^2 using only the earnings change is equivalent to that with the SFAS 52 effect

134   *Frances L. Ayres and Jacci L. Rodgers*

Table 5. *Relation Between Forecast Errors, Earnings Change and Change in Earnings due to SFAS 52 Adoption (1981 Adopters only)*

Model: UFE_{kj} = $a_j + b1_j\ \text{ECHG} + b2_j\ \text{SFAS52}$ = j = 1–4 quarters, k = 1.29 firms

      UFE   = unexpected forecast error for firm k for quarter j

      ECHG = change in primary earnings per share for firm k prior to SFAS 52 adoption[1]

      SFAS52 = earnings per share effect of SFAS 52 adoption for firm $k / |\text{EPS}_{81k}|$

Quarter 1	Intercept	b1	b2	Adjusted R^2
Coefficient	0.062	0.973	0.206	0.770
t-value	(0.690)	(7.440)	(0.352)	
pr $|t| > 0$	0.500	0.000	0.728	
Coefficient	0.092	–	−2.680	0.290
t-value	(0.580)		(−3.480)	
pr $|t| > 0$	0.565		0.002	
Coefficient	0.077	0.942	–	0.780
t-value	(1.000)	(9.790)		
pr $|t| > 0$	0.350	0.002		

Quarter 2	Intercept	b1	b2	Adjusted R^2
Coefficient	0.196	0.767	−0.456	0.780
t-value	(2.570)	(6.940)	−(0.920)	
pr $|t| > 0$	0.016	0.000	0.3665	
Coefficient	0.220	–	−2.740	0.400
t-value	(1.710)		(−4.390)	
pr $|t| > 0$	0.097		0.000	
Coefficient	0.162	0.836	–	0.780
t-value	(2.430)	(10.120)		
pr $|t| > 0$	0.022	0.000		

[1] $\text{ECHG} = \dfrac{(\text{EPS}_{81k} - \text{SFAS52}) - \text{EPS}_{80k}}{|\text{EPS}_{81k}|}$

Table 5. (continued)

Quarter 3	Intercept	b1	b2	Adjusted R^2
Coefficient	0.197	0.301	−2.190	0.750
t-value	(2.710)	(2.860)	(−4.650)	
pr $|t|>0$	0.012	0.001	0.000	
Coefficient	0.206	–	−3.090	0.690
t-value	(2.510)		(−7.750)	
pr $|t|>0$	0.018		0.000	
Coefficient	0.032	0.627	–	0.550
t-value	(0.380)	(5.930)		
pr $|t|>0$	0.707	0.000		

Quarter 4	Intercept	b1	b2	Adjusted R^2
Coefficient	0.109	0.950	−0.869	0.370
t-value	(1.910)	(1.150)	(−2.330)	
pr $|t|>0$	0.067	0.262	0.029	
Coefficient	0.112	–	−1.150	0.370
t-value	(1.950)		(−4.100)	
pr $|t|>0$	0.061		0.000	
Coefficient	0.044	0.224	–	0.270
t-value	(0.830)	(3.240)		
pr $|t|>0$	0.417	0.002		

included. In the third quarter (forecast issued between July and October) the adjusted R^2 is greatest with both variables in the model although the SFAS 52 effect appears to contribute somewhat more explanatory power. By the fourth quarter forecast (issued between October and January) the SFAS 52 effect clearly dominates the change in earnings. This is what we would expect if analysts revised earnings forecasts in response to quarterly earnings without taking into account the potential adoption of SFAS 52.

The negative relation between forecast errors and the income effect due to SFAS 52 adoption appears anomalous at first pass. It indicates that the greater the change in earnings induced by SFAS 52 the more analysts' forecasts tend to exceed actual earnings. Elliott and Philbrick reported a weak positive relation between the income effect of adoption and signed forecast errors. However, their results were for a broad spectrum of accounting changes and differed in direction and significance levels across

136   *Frances L. Ayres and Jacci L. Rodgers*

Table 6. *Relation Between Forecast Revisions, Earnings Change and Change in Earnings due to SFAS 52 Adoption (1981 Adopters only)*

Model: $\text{REV}_{mk} = a_j + b1_j \text{ ECHG}_k + b2_j \text{ SFAS52}_k$, k = 1.29

REV = revision of EPS forecast for firm k at time m, $m = 1$–3

ECHG = change in primary earnings per share prior to SFAS 52 adoption for firm k[1]

SFAS52 = earnings per share effect of SFAS 52 adoption for firm k

Rev1	Intercept	b1	b2	Adjusted R^2
Coefficient	0.110	0.291	−1.450	0.640
t-value	(1.510)	(2.750)	(−3.060)	
pr $|t|>0$	0.143	0.010	0.005	
Coefficient	0.119	–	−2.310	0.550
t-value	(1.460)		(−5.820)	
pr $|t|>0$	0.565		0.000	
Coefficient	0.002	0.506	–	0.520
t-value	(0.020)	(5.550)		
pr $|t|>0$	0.350	0.002		

Rev2	Intercept	b1	b2	Adjusted R^2
Coefficient	−0.170	0.492	0.917	0.380
t-value	(−2.040)	(4.070)	(1.690)	
pr $|t|>0$	0.051	0.000	0.1025	
Coefficient	−0.155	–	−0.544	0.000
t-value	(−1.470)		(−1.060)	
pr $|t|>0$	0.097		0.000	
Coefficient	−0.101	0.356	–	0.330
t-value	(−1.350)	(3.807)		
pr $|t|>0$	0.022	0.000		

[1] $\text{ECHG} = \dfrac{(\text{EPS}_{81k} - \text{SFAS52}) - \text{EPS}_{80k}}{|\text{EPS}_{81k}|}$

Table 6. *(continued)*

Rev3	Intercept	b1	b2	Adjusted R^2
Coefficient	0.099	0.227	−2.280	0.850
t-value	(1.950)	(3.090)	(−6.920)	
pr $|t| > 0$	0.061	0.004	0.000	
Coefficient	0.106	–	−2.950	0.790
t-value	(1.820)		(−10.390)	
pr $|t| > 0$	0.080		0.000	
Coefficient	−0.071	0.565	–	0.570
t-value	(−0.970)	(6.123)		
pr $|t| > 0$	0.342	0.001		

groupings. This suggests that the relation may differ across accounting changes. Elliott and Philbrick argue that a negative relation between forecast errors and the income effect of accounting changes is consistent with analysts overestimating the impact of the accounting change.

Table 6 shows the relation between forecast *revisions*, earnings changes and SFAS 52 adoption. The relation between earnings changes and revisions remained positive which is consistent with forecasts gradually moving in the direction of realized earnings. The relation between revisions and SFAS 52 adoption was negative when included without the earnings change in the model. When the earnings change was included in the model the coefficient was significant and negative only for the first and third revisions (REV1 and REV3). The negative relation between forecast *revisions* and the income effect of SFAS 52 is consistent with the findings of Elliott and Philbrick (1990).

Additional Analyses

In an attempt to provide additional insight into the relation between analysts' forecasts and earnings changes during the SFAS 52 transition, we also examined an additional variable, the percentage of foreign assets. One possible explanation for the strong negative relation between forecast errors and the impact of SFAS 52 adoptions is that analysts' forecasts under SFAS 8 are related to the importance of foreign operations. This would suggest that we would expect to observe a positive relation between the percentage of assets in foreign countries and the magnitude of pre-change earnings in 1981. Since pre-adoption earnings changes tended to

138   *Frances L. Ayres and Jacci L. Rodgers*

be negative, this suggests a negative relation between the percentage of foreign operations and signed forecast errors. Using 1981 disclosures from sample firms' notes to the financial statements the percentage of foreign assets (PERFOR) was computed for both early and late adopters. Consistent with results reported by Brown (1985) no difference between early and late adopters on this variable was found. We examined the relation between PERFOR and SFAS52, ECHG and UFE two different ways. First, the Pearson correlation between PERFOR and the above variables was computed. The results were insignificant. Next, the variable PERFOR was included as an additional independent variable in equations (5) and (6). The results were insignificant and did not change the sign, magnitude or significance of the remaining independent variables. Thus we were unable to conclude that the importance of foreign assets to total operations helped to explain either the size of the earnings impact or the size and magnitude of forecasts errors surrounding SFAS 52 adoption.

We also examined the relation between earnings change and forecast errors for late adopters of SFAS 52 and the control firms. This was done in order to determine if the relation between ECHG and UFE (REV) was similar for these firms to that for early adopters. The results are qualitatively similar to those in Tables 5 and 6. That is, the coefficient on ECHG is initially near one and positive and declines throughout the year in both magnitude and significance.

Discussion

The results from Tables 5 and 6 pose some interesting questions regarding the behavior of analysts and managers during the transition from SFAS 8 to SFAS 52. The negative relation between forecast errors and the income effect of SFAS 52 adoption indicates that the greater the increase in earnings associated with the accounting change the more analysts over-forecast pre-change earnings. One possible explanation for this is earnings management behavior. That is, management concern with overly optimistic forecasts could lead managers to try to meet the forecast by early adoption of an income increasing accounting change. Lev (1992) suggests that pressure to meet analysts forecasts often drives managers to manipulate earnings.

A second possible explanation is that the degree of overoptimism by analysts is greater for firms with the largest translation losses. That is, analysts failure to take account of foreign currency earnings in their forecast, coupled with a general tendency towards overoptimism could lead to the observed negative relation between forecast errors and SFAS 52 adoption.

In the aggregate it is difficult to assess expost what occurred behaviorally on the part of managers and analysts during the SFAS 52 transition. Anecdotal evidence for one company is available in the case of Revlon. Revlon was one of the sample companies which adopted SFAS 52 in 1981. During 1981 Revlon indicated several times during the year (following quarterly earnings announcements) that foreign currency was an important determinant of earnings. For example, on 27 July 'Heard on the Street,' stated that:

> Last week's report of relatively flat earnings for the first half on sales up 18% surprised nobody. Revlon blames the impact of foreign currency translations for the weak profit picture (*Wall Street Journal*, p. 37).

In late October of 1981 Revlon called a press conference indicating that 1981 earnings would be \$3.50–3.60 per share rather than the \$4.60 that most analysts had forecast. Revlon management attributed this to foreign currency swings which were greater than anticipated. When SFAS 52 was passed on 7 December 1981 no new earnings projections were issued by management. Actual earnings (announced in February 1982) were \$4.10. The earnings announcement on 24 February 1982 indicated that the higher than expected earnings were due to a late change in the rules for accounting for foreign currency. The reported impact of SFAS 52 on earnings per share was a \$.40 per share increase. The behavior of the Value-Line analysts during 1981 seems to indicate that they did not anticipate that Revlon would adopt SFAS 52. The first three annual forecasts issued by Value-Line for Revlon ranged from \$5.15 to \$5.35. Then in January 1982 Value-Line reduced its earnings forecast dramatically downward to \$3.70, presumably in response to the announcement of management in October. The behavior of Revlon parallels that of the statistical results reported in Tables 5 and 6 in the first three quarters. That is, the early forecasts were overly optimistic. The fourth quarter results differ in that they indicate that Value-Line forecasted in the fourth quarter Revlon's actual prechange annual earnings. Hence for Revlon the relation between the fourth quarter forecast error and the income effect of SFAS 52 adoption was positive. The difference between Revlon and the remainder of the sample in the fourth quarter is likely due to the press conference called by Revlon management in October.[9] This suggests that Value-Line did not predict

140   *Frances L. Ayres and Jacci L. Rodgers*

early adoption of SFAS 52 despite the fact that Revlon's heavily publicized woes regarding translation losses suggest that adoption of SFAS 52 *could* have a beneficial impact on earnings.

Conclusions

This research examined Value-Line analysts' forecasts during the periods surrounding the enactment and adoption of SFAS 52 by multinational firms. Forecast errors decreased by 14 percent for first quarter forecasts from pre to post SFAS 52. In addition, higher forecast errors were found in the year of SFAS 52 adoption. In general, overstatement errors were greater during the year of SFAS 52 adoption and were strongly correlated with the income effect of SFAS 52 adoption. A negative relation was found between signed forecast errors and the income effect of SFAS 52 adoption. After adoption of SFAS 52 multinational firms forecasts were relatively unbiased.

Notes

1. For the sample of firms used in this study there were no earnings decreases associated with SFAS 52 adoption. This is generally consistent with other studies examining the income effect of SFAS No. 52 adoption [see Ayres (1986) and Elliott and Philbrick (1990)]. The group of firms reporting the income effect of adoption consists primarily of 1981 (early) adopters. This is because SFAS No. 52 only required disclosure of the income effect for firms adopting in 1981.

2. In this study we define 1981 and 1982 to be the transitional years, although adoption of the standard was allowed as late as 1983. However, most firms adopted the standard by the end of the 1982 fiscal year. *Accounting Trends and Techniques* reported that only 16% of their December 31 fiscal year end firms adopted SFAS 52 in 1983. The firms in our sample all adopted the standard in either 1981 or 1982.

3. Analyses were also run using absolute forecast errors. These results are generally consistent with the findings reported and are available from the authors.

4. The major constraint in the sample was the selection of control firms. To avoid concentration in any particular industry, we required that sample firms be matched on at least the one-digit SIC code. This resulted in a sample of firms from the 2000 and 3000 SIC code group.

5. To control for outliers, in excess of two in absolute value were coded as +2 or −2 for signed forecast errors.

6. Recall that these are *adjusted* forecast errors from which the effect of economy wide factors has been subtracted. Thus, the raw forecasts may still contain bias. What these results suggest is that the bias related to foreign currency reporting is essentially zero by 1984.

7. This was also documented in Ayres (1986). Also Ricks (1982) reports that LIFO adoptions tend to occur during years when income is rising.

8. Bernard and Ruland (1987) note a similar problem in their analysis of the information of historical cost versus current cost earnings. However, in their case the independent variables were positively correlated leading to spurious negative coefficients.

9. Only one other sample company had a fourth quarter forecast error equal to the change in earnings caused by SFAS 52 adoption. All companies had non-zero forecast errors.

References

Abarbanell, J. A. and V. L. Bernard. 1992. Tests of analysts' overreaction/underreaction to earnings information as an explanation for anomalous stock price behavior. *Journal of Finance* (July): 1181–1268.

Ayres, F. L. 1986. Characteristics of firms electing early adoption of SFAS 52. *Journal of Accounting and Economics* (June): 143–158.

Baldwin, B. A. 1984. Segment earnings disclosure and the ability of security analysts to forecast earnings per share. *The Accounting Review* (July): 376–389.

Bernard, V. L. and R. G. Ruland. 1987. The incremental information content of historical cost and current cost income numbers: time-series analyses for 1962–1980. *The Accounting Review* (October): 707–722.

Biddle, G. C., and W. E. Ricks. 1988. Analyst forecast errors and stock price behavior near the earnings announcement dates of LIFO adopters. *Journal of Accounting Research* (Autumn): 169–194.

Brown, B. 1985. The relationship between firm attributes and early adoption of the foreign currency accounting standard, SFAS 52: An empirical investigation. *International Journal of Accounting* (Fall): 1–19.

Brown, L. D. 1983. Accounting changes and the accuracy of analysts' earnings forecasts. *Journal of Accounting Research* (Autumn): 432–443.

Elliott, J. A. and D. R. Philbrick. 1990. Accounting changes and earnings predictability. *The Accounting Review* (January): 157–174.

Financial Accounting Standards Board (FASB). 1975. *Accounting for the Translation of Foreign Currency Transactions and Foreign Currency Financial Statements*, Statement of Financial Accounting Standards No. 8, Stamford, Conn. (October).

———. 1980. *Qualitative Characteristics of Accounting Information*, Statement of Financial Accounting Concepts No. 2 (May).

———. 1981. *Foreign Currency Translation*, Statement of Financial Accounting Standards No. 52, Stamford, Conn. (December).

Griffin, P. A. and R. P. Castanias. 1987. *Accounting for the Translation of Foreign Currencies: The Effects of Statement 52 on Equity Analysts*. Research Report, Financial Accounting Standards Board, Stamford, Connecticut.

Hughes, J. S. and W. E. Ricks. 1986. Market reactions to mandated interest capitalization. *Contemporary Accounting Research*. (Spring). 222–241.

Lev, B. 1992. The curse of great expectations. *The Wall Street Journal* (November 30), p. A12.

Ricks, W. E. 1982. The market's response to the 1974 LIFO adoptions. *Journal of Accounting Research* (Autumn): 367–387.

Ricks, W. E. and J. S. Hughes. 1985. Market reactions to non-discretionary accounting change: The case of long-term investments. *The Accounting Review* (January): 33–52.

Salatka, W. K. 1989. The impact of SFAS No. 8 on equity prices: An events study and cross-sectional analysis. *Journal of Accounting and Economics* (February): 35–70.

Seidler, L. 1982. Changes in FASB no. 8 suggested by study showing harmful impacts of translation accounting. *Bear Stearns Accounting Issues*, Bear Stearns and Company Investment Research (January 18), pp. 30–33.

The Wall Street Journal. 1981. Heard on the Street (July 27), p. 37.

Received October 1991
Accepted October 1993

[19]

Noisy Accounting Earnings Signals and Earnings Response Coefficients: The Case of Foreign Currency Accounting*

DANIEL W. COLLINS   *University of Iowa*

WILLIAM K. SALATKA   *Wilfrid Laurier University*

Abstract. This paper extends the growing literature on factors affecting cross-sectional and intertemporal variation in earnings response coefficients. It tests the empirical implications of recent theoretical work by Choi and Salamon (1989) and Holthausen and Verrecchia (1988), who model the degree of price adjustment associated with earnings announcements as a function of the amount of noise or garbling in the accounting earnings signal relative to valuation-relevant cash flows or dividends. The particular earnings measurements considered relate to U.S. multinational companies and to the differences in income determination under *Statement of Financial Accounting Standards (SFAS) No. 8* and *SFAS No. 52*. The study finds a modestly smaller relative price adjustment for a given amount of unexpected earnings for multinational firms than for nonmultinationals during the *SFAS No. 8* period. This finding is consistent with multinationals producing "noisier" earnings signals during this time period. However, several indirect measures suggest that there was greater prior probability uncertainty associated with the future cash flows or dividends of the nonmultinational sample. Accordingly, this cannot be ruled out as a competing explanation for the observed differences in the market's response to earnings signals during the *SFAS No. 8* period. Following the implementation of *SFAS No. 52*, the earnings response coefficient increased substantively for firms whose accounting for translation gains or losses was most affected by this standard. These results suggest that the earnings measurements produced under *SFAS No. 52* were perceived by market participants to be of higher quality (less noisy) than those produced under *SFAS No. 8*. The framework and analysis in this paper hold promise for investigating the relative informativeness of earnings signals produced under alternative income determination rules.

Résumé. Les auteurs apportent leur contribution personnelle aux publications de plus

* The authors acknowledge the financial support provided by the Fuqua School of Business at Duke University, the College of Business at the University of Iowa, and the Eller Center for Entrepreneurial Studies at the University of Arizona. The authors thank Sati Bandyopadhyay, Sung Choi, Bruce Johnson, S.P. Kothari, Johannes Ledolter, Tom Linsmeier, Khalid Nainar, Gordon Richardson, Terry Warfield, and CAR Conference discussants Jennifer Kao and Paul Griffin for their helpful comments. They also acknowledge comments from accounting workshop participants at the following universities: Arizona, Connecticut, Harvard, Iowa, Kansas, McMaster, New York, Ohio State, Purdue, Rice, St. Louis, San Diego State, and Vanderbilt.

120   D.W. Collins   W.K. Salatka

en plus nombreuses portant sur les facteurs qui touchent la variation transversale et temporelle des coefficients de réaction aux bénéfices. Ils vérifient les conséquences empiriques des travaux théoriques récents de Choi et Salamon (1989) et de Holthausen et Verrecchia (1988), qui modélisent le degré d'ajustement du cours des valeurs associé aux annonces de bénéfices comme étant fonction de la quantité de parasites ou de l'importance du brouillage dans le signal que constituent des bénéfices comptables par rapport aux flux monétaires ou aux dividendes pertinents à l'évaluation. Les mesures particulières des bénéfices auxquelles s'intéressent les auteurs sont celles de multinationales des États-Unis et font état de la variation des bénéfices, selon qu'ils sont évalués conformément au SFAS n° 8 ou au SFAS n° 52. Pour un montant donné de bénéfices inattendus, les auteurs constatent un ajustement relatif du cours des valeurs légèrement plus faible dans le cas des multinationales que dans celui des entreprises d'envergure plus modeste, au cours de la période d'application du SFAS n° 8. Cette constatation est conforme à l'hypothèse voulant que les multinationales aient produit des indicateurs de bénéfices plus « brouillés » au cours de cette période. Toutefois, plusieurs mesures indirectes donnent à penser qu'il existait une incertitude plus grande quant à la probabilité a priori des flux monétaires ou des dividendes futurs dans l'échantillon des entreprises d'envergure plus modeste. Les auteurs ne peuvent donc écarter cette hypothèse à titre d'explication concurrente des différences observées dans la réaction du marché aux indicateurs de bénéfices, au cours de la période d'application du SFAS n° 8. À la suite de l'instauration du SFAS n° 52, le coefficient de réaction aux bénéfices a sensiblement augmenté dans le cas des entreprises dont la méthode comptable relative à la conversion des gains et des pertes était davantage touchée par cette norme. Ces résultats laissent croire que les mesures des bénéfices conformes au SFAS n° 52 ont été perçues par les intéressés comme étant de plus grande qualité (c'est-à-dire moins brouillées) que les mesures conformes au SFAS n° 8. Le cadre de référence et l'analyse contenus dans cet article sont prometteurs pour l'analyse de la qualité relative de l'information livrée par les indicateurs de bénéfices conformes à d'autres règles d'évaluation des bénéfices.

Background

The effect of accounting earnings signals on investors' appraisal of the future cash flows and dividend-paying ability of publicly traded companies has long been of interest to accountants and members of the investment community. *Ceteris paribus*, changes in security prices around earnings announcement dates provide evidence that accounting earnings signals convey useful information to investors regarding the amount, timing, and/or uncertainty of future cash flows of an enterprise. Numerous studies have documented the information content of earnings numbers. For example, Foster (1977) and Hagerman, Zmijewski, and Shah (1984) demonstrate that the sign and magnitude of unexpected quarterly earnings are related to abnormal security returns measured around earnings announcements.

Recently, a number of studies have documented that earnings response coefficients (ERCs), which map unexpected earnings into security returns, are not constant; instead, these coefficients exhibit considerable intertemporal and cross-sectional variation.[1] (i.e., Kormandi and Lipe 1987, Collins and Kothari 1989, and Easton and Zmijewski 1989). For the most part, the work to date has focused on fundamental characteristics or properties of firms' earnings-generating process, such as the persistence, growth, and riskiness of earnings.[2]

This paper provides further evidence about factors that contribute to differences in the return/earnings relation across firms and over time. Unlike the previous work in this area, however, the present analysis focuses on how differences in the perceived quality of earnings signals manifest themselves in differential ERCs. The study allows for the possibility that across firms and over time, earnings measurements may not be equally informative with respect to assessing future cash flows and dividend-paying ability of an enterprise. Instead, it is hypothesized that reported earnings numbers will be tainted with different levels of noise or garbling, depending upon the particular set of accounting measurement rules used to describe the underlying economic events. Following the theoretical work of Choi and Salamon (1989) and Holthausen and Verrecchia (1988), it is hypothesized that differences in the perceived noise imbedded in reported earnings figures are inversely related to the magnitude of ERCs.

The particular accounting controversy considered in this paper relates to foreign currency accounting for U.S. multinational companies and the methods for measuring and reporting translation gains (losses) under *Statement of Financial Accounting Standards (SFAS) No. 8* and under *SFAS No. 52*. Following its issuance, *SFAS No. 8* was severely criticized for introducing artificial variability (i.e., noise) into reported earnings and for producing reported results that were frequently inconsistent with economic reality.[3] Interestingly, the Financial Accounting Standards Board (FASB) itself apparently concurred with this assessment, noting in *SFAS No. 52* (Appendix C, par. 63) that "*SFAS No. 8* has produced results that the Board and many constituents believe *do not reflect the underlying economic reality of many foreign operations and thereby produces results that are not relevant.*"

The rules for measuring and reporting translation gains (losses) were substantially modified under *SFAS No. 52*. Many believed that these changes significantly improved the quality of the reported earnings figures of multinational companies (Griffin and Castanias 1987). However, Beaver and Wolfson (1982) argue that this conclusion may be unwarranted, particularly when the translation gain/loss is excluded from income.

This study tests assertions about the relative quality of earnings signals under *SFAS No. 8* and *SFAS No. 52* by comparing the amount of price response to earnings surprises for a set of multinational and a set of domestic corporations during the *SFAS No. 8* and *52* periods. Consistent with alleged deficiencies of income determination under *SFAS No. 8*, the study finds weak evidence that the relative price adjustment for a given amount of unexpected earnings was smaller for multinational firms than for nonmultinationals during the *SFAS No. 8* period. This result is consistent with multinational firms producing lower-quality earnings signals during the *SFAS No. 8* period than did their nonmultinational counterparts. However, several indirect measures suggest that there was greater prior probability uncertainty associated with the future cash flows or dividends of the nonmultinational sample during this time frame. Accordingly, this cannot be ruled out as a competing explanation for the observed differences in the markets' response to earnings signals during the *SFAS No. 8* period.

Following the implementation of *SFAS No. 52*, the ERCs increased substantively for firms whose accounting for translation gains or losses was most affected by this standard (i.e., multinationals using the local currency as the functional currency). In the *SFAS No. 52* period, unlike the *SFAS No. 8* period, this study finds no significant difference in the market response to earnings surprises for these firms relative to that observed for the nonmultinational control firms. This result suggests that the market perceives the earnings of these two sets of firms to be of comparable quality.

We do not find this to be the case, however, for the multinational firms that use the U.S. dollar in total or in part as the functional currency. These firms essentially follow the translation procedures set forth in *SFAS No. 8* and continue to report translation gains/losses on the income statement under *SFAS No. 52*. For these firms, there was no evidence of ERCs increasing from the *SFAS No. 8* to the *SFAS No. 52* period. Moreover, we find that the degree of price response to earnings surprises for these firms remains well below that observed for either the multinational-local currency firms or the nonmultinational control firms in the sample. This result suggests that the market perceives the earnings of firms to be of lower quality if they use the U.S. dollar as the functional currency and carry translation gains/losses to the income statement.

The remainder of the paper is organized as follows. The second section outlines the theoretical relation between relative price changes and accounting signals using the general Bayesian framework proposed by Choi and Salamon (1989) and Holthausen and Verrecchia (1988). These studies highlight how differences in the perceived level of noise in earnings measurements manifests itself in differential ERCs. The third section briefly reviews the major differences in the income determination process of multinational companies under *SFAS No. 8* and *SFAS No. 52* and the alleged deficiencies and/or distortions associated with the former method. These allegations lead to the prediction that the earnings reported under *SFAS No. 8* will have a smaller impact on investor expectations with respect to future cash flows than will *SFAS No. 52* earnings and, therefore, will exhibit a lower ERC. The fourth section outlines the sample and methodology used to test this hypothesis. Section five contains the results of the analysis and an investigation of potential confounding influences on the findings. The sixth section presents a summary and suggestions for future research.

Theoretical framework

Studies that investigate the information content of earnings signals have generally used variants of the following linear model relating abnormal security returns ($U\tilde{R}$) measured around earnings announcement dates to some measure of unexpected earnings ($U\tilde{E}$), which is typically scaled by price two days before to the earnings announcement (P_{it-2})

$$U\tilde{R}_i = a + b\frac{UE_{it}}{P_{it-2}} + \tilde{e}_{it} \tag{1}$$

Typically, the model is estimated with data pooled across firms and over time under the maintained hypothesis that the ERC (b) is intertemporally and cross-sectionally constant.

Choi and Salamon (1989) (C&S) and Holthausen and Verrecchia (1988) (H&V) relax the assumption that the ERC in (1) is constant and model firm-specific determinants of price reactions to information releases.[4] In both studies, the price of a particular firm j is modeled as a linear function of future (random) cash flows or liquidating dividends ($\tilde{X}_j$), which are normally distributed with mean μ_j and variance σ_j^2.[5] To formalize the role of accounting signals in changing beliefs about the underlying cash flows or liquidation dividends, C&S and H&V introduce an information system (η_j) that stochastically relates an outcome $\tilde{X}_j = X_j$ to a signal $\tilde{Y}_j = \eta_j (X_j)$. Therefore, the informativeness of a signal $\tilde{Y}_j$ vis-à-vis the valuation-relevant future cash flows or liquidating dividends depends on the characteristics of the information system (and, thus, its signals) as *perceived* by investors. To express the idea that the accounting information system and its earnings signals are "noisy," the following relation between the earnings signal and the future underlying cash flows or liquidating dividend is assumed:

$$\tilde{Y}_j = \tilde{X}_j + \tilde{\epsilon}_j \tag{2}$$

where ϵ_j represents the noise or garbling in the earnings measurement process with variance $\phi^2(\epsilon_j) = \phi_j^2$. The reciprocal of the variance, $1/\phi_j^2$, can be thought of as an indicator of the quality or informativeness of the accounting earnings information signal vis-à-vis the underlying cash flows or liquidating dividends.

Given this simplified setting together with rational Bayesian investors, C&S and H&V derive the amount of price change (ΔP_j) at the time of an information (earnings) release as a function of (1) the prior probability uncertainty with respect to the firm's valuation-relevant cash flows or liquidating dividend (σ_j^2), (2) the variance of the noise term of the information release (ϕ_j^2), and (3) the deviation of the signal realization from its expected value ($Y_j - \mu_j$).[6] More formally

$$\Delta P_j = \frac{\sigma_j^2}{\sigma_j^2 + \phi_j^2} (Y_j - \mu_j) \tag{3}$$

Scaling both sides of (3) by price immediately prior to the information release yields an expression analogous to (1) but with the earnings response coefficient (ERC) reparameterized as a function of σ_j^2 and ϕ_j^2. In particular, (3) demonstrates that for a given amount of unexpected earnings (i.e., earnings surprise), the amount of price change associated with the signal is posi-

124   D.W. Collins   W.K. Salatka

tively related to the prior probability uncertainty associated with the future cash flows or liquidating dividends and negatively related to the perceived noise in the information signal. That is,

$$\frac{\partial ERC}{\partial \sigma_j^2} > 0 \qquad\qquad\qquad (4a)$$

$$\frac{\partial ERC}{\partial \phi_j^2} < 0 \qquad\qquad\qquad (4b)$$

The second comparative static result is of primary interest in the present study. Specifically, (4b) implies that the lower the perceived quality of the earnings signal (i.e., the *higher* ϕ_j^2), the *smaller* the impact of a given amount of unexpected earnings on a firm's own price change.

The institutional setting in which the empirical implications of this latter result are tested focuses on the debate surrounding the measurement of earnings for multinational companies. The next section of the paper reviews the major alleged deficiencies of *SFAS No. 8* for measuring the earnings performance of multinational companies.

SFAS No. 8 and garbled earnings
SFAS No. 8, "Accounting for the Translation of Foreign Currency Transactions and Foreign Currency Financial Statements," is arguably one of the most controversial standards issued by the FASB to date. This standard proposed the so-called temporal method to translate the results of operations and financial position of foreign subsidiaries. Under this method, sales are converted at the exchange rates prevailing when the transactions occur while the cost of goods sold is converted at the historical exchange rates when the inventory units are purchased.[7] Many who opposed *SFAS No. 8* claimed that this conversion process resulted in operating margin distortions when the exchange rates fluctuated because sales and cost of goods sold would be translated at different rates. For example, consider a situation in which all purchases and sales are in the local (foreign) currency, and the foreign operating unit follows a pricing policy of maintaining a constant profit margin. Despite the constant profit margins in the foreign currency, the translated operating margins would narrow when the foreign currency weakens relative to the dollar and would widen when it strengthens. In this situation, the translated operating margins would not reflect the economic circumstances (i.e., constant profit margins) of the foreign operating unit.

Another concern centered on the required recognition of exchange adjustment gains and losses in quarterly earnings for monetary items and incomplete transactions. Under *SFAS No. 8*, cash, receivables, and both short- and long-term debt were translated at the exchange rates prevailing at the balance sheet date. Thus, any change in exchange rates from one balance sheet date to another resulted in a recorded (but unrealized) gain or loss despite the fact that there was no immediate cash flow effect. Many argued that this requirement introduced artificial variability into quarterly income figures that was inconsistent with economic reality.[8] For example, if a foreign currency strengthened relative to the dollar, translation of foreign debt would result in an unrealized loss being recorded under *SFAS No. 8*. If, in fact, the dollar recovered by the time the debt was settled, no economic gain or loss would have been realized. Yet the reported earnings figures would have included translation gains and losses over time that would be offsetting and largely transitory in nature.

Typical of the concerns about the artificial volatility introduced in the earnings figures under *SFAS No. 8* are the following statements by senior corporate executives.

Quarterly earnings reports have been bouncing around unpredictably ever since *SFAS No. 8* took effect for most companies Jan. 1 [1976]. It will be years before anybody can work with a comparative financial statement with any degree of certainty again. [Herbert Knortz, vice-president, International Telephone and Telegraph, *The Wall Street Journal*, December 8, 1976]

The shortcomings in the rule [*SFAS No. 8*] itself are magnified by the wide swings in currency values. The fluctuations, and the unsound formula for recognizing them, produce wide swings in the profit-and-loss statement which don't necessary reflect economic realities. [William Strong, senior vice-president, Firestone Tire and Rubber Company, *The Wall Street Journal*, December 8, 1976]

A divergence between economic reality and reported accounting results under *SFAS No. 8* also arose when foreign debt was issued to finance the acquisition of property, plant, and equipment used in foreign operations. The debt would be translated at current rates while the fixed assets would be translated at historical rates. If the U.S. dollar subsequently weakened against the foreign currency, the temporal method under *SFAS No. 8* would result in a translation loss being included in accounting income. However, if the purchasing power parity (PPP) theory holds (Balassa 1964), the value of the real property would be expected to rise to offset the experienced changes in exchange rates.[9] Thus, from an economic perspective, one could argue that the foreign entity experienced no loss.

The preceding discussion suggests that the reported accounting earnings of U.S. multinational companies may have provided garbled or noisy signals of the true underlying economic performance of these firms and that the noise was due to the vagaries of the foreign exchange market and various inconsistencies in the translation process under *SFAS No. 8*. If the market indeed *perceived* the reported accounting earnings of multinationals to be tainted or misleading as a result of the translation process, then the model outlined in the second section would predict *less* change in security prices for a given amount of unexpected earnings for those firms than for firms that had little or no foreign operations or sales. An alternative interpretation of the points raised above by critics of *SFAS No. 8* is that although the translation gains/losses carried to income under *SFAS No. 8* may not be totally irrelevant to assessing future cash flows or liquidating dividends, their relation with price changes may nevertheless be weaker because such gains and losses tend to be more transitory in nature as compared to most other components of earnings.[10] Evidence presented by Lipe (1986) suggests that shocks to earnings that are less permanent in nature are associated with lower ERCs. Thus, the predictions made above remain intact. That is, the ERCs of multinational companies are expected to be *smaller* than those for nonmultinationals during the time that *SFAS No. 8* was in effect, either because the translation process called for in this standard was viewed as adding noise or largely transitory (but, nevertheless, price-relevant) components to earnings. Tests of this prediction are carried out in the fifth section.

Did SFAS No. 52 improve the quality of earnings?
The issuance of *SFAS No. 52* in December 1981 brought about major changes in the translation of foreign currency financial statements. These changes, it is alleged, reduced or eliminated many of the distortions in reported income that resulted from *SFAS No. 8*. *SFAS No. 52* sought to restore the compatibility between the financial accounting numbers and underlying economic reality by allowing firms to select a foreign subsidiary's *functional currency*. The functional currency is described as "the currency of the primary economic environment in which the entity operates" (*SFAS No. 52*, par. 5). For foreign entities that operate relatively independently of their U.S. parents, the functional currency is the local (foreign) currency, and *SFAS No. 52* calls for all account balances (except for retained earnings) to be translated at the current rate. Moreover, any resultant translation gain or loss bypasses the income statement and is carried directly to stockholder's equity. If the foreign subsidiary is merely a conduit of the U.S. parent for transforming foreign currency flows to dollars, then the dollar is the functional currency, and the translation process and recognition of exchange gains or losses are virtually identical to that specified by *SFAS No. 8*. Thus, unrealized exchange adjustment gains or losses that may be largely transitory are still imbedded in the reported earnings numbers of these firms, as are the effects of translating sales and costs of goods sold at different rates.

Supporters of *SFAS No. 52* see two advantages to translating all accounts at current exchange rates. The first is that it recognizes the fact that real assets provide an effective hedge for liabilities when exchange rates change because of different inflation rates. Second, it helps preserve important operating margins and accounting relationships that better reflect economic reality. By eliminating the immediate recognition of unrealized translation gains and losses from the income statement, *SFAS No. 52* reduces the volatility of earnings caused by temporary fluctuations in exchange rates. Many argue that *SFAS No. 52* thereby removes a major transitory component from earnings, one that had obscured the true operating performance of multinationals.

In a survey of equity analysts conducted for the FASB, Griffin and Castanias

(1987) reported that 62.5 percent of the analysts interviewed believed that the quality of earnings increased under *SFAS No. 52* from *SFAS No. 8*. The survey results suggested that analysts were "more comfortable" with the financial statement information under *SFAS No. 52* because currency adjustments were eliminated from the income statement and because the local currency perspective maintained critical financial statement relationships that had been distorted by the translation procedures in *SFAS No. 8*.

Griffin and Castanias summarized their interview results as follows (1987, 74):

The interviews also confirmed the supposition that Statement 52 reduces the uncertainty inherent in both reported and projected earnings. Such uncertainty reduction, among other factors, led some analysts to assert that the *quality of financial information has increased*. However, the respondents were unclear about whether Statement 52 per se prompted changes in companies stock values....If a weak connection exists between stock values and Statement 52, the comments suggest that it would most likely be due to a *shift in capitalization rates because of changes in earnings quality*. [Emphasis added.]

If, as the survey results suggest, investors perceived the earnings signals under *SFAS No. 52* to be of higher quality than those reported under *SFAS No. 8*, then the model outlined in the second section predicts that the ERCs of multinational companies will *increase* under *SFAS No. 52* relative to what they were while *SFAS No. 8* was in effect. An increase in the ERC would be consistent with a "shift in capitalization rates because of changes in earnings quality," as suggested by Griffin and Castanias.

An alternative prediction regarding the informativeness of earnings signals under *SFAS No. 52* versus *SFAS No. 8* is derived from a more formal analysis of the properties of major foreign currency translation methods conducted by Beaver and Wolfson (1982). Under the assumptions that (1) markets are perfect and complete (therefore, current market values are readily available for all assets and liabilities) and (2) exchange rate changes are driven solely by differential rates of inflation between the two countries, Beaver and Wolfson analyze the extent to which various combinations of accounting measurement techniques/translation methods possess the properties of *economic interpretability* and *symmetry*. *Economic interpretability* is defined as (1) the reported book values on the balance sheet being equal to the present value of the future cash flows of the assets, liabilities, and net worth of the firm and (2) the reported return on investment (net income divided by beginning-of-the-year assets) equaling the nominal rate of return on investment, denominated in terms of the domestic currency. *Symmetry* occurs when two economically equivalent investments (i.e., real rate of return for foreign investment equals the real rate of return for domestic investment) produce the same financial statement numbers when the investments are translated into a common currency.

Beaver and Wolfson examine the properties of economic interpretability and symmetry for three accounting measurement technique/translation method combinations: (1) historical cost accounting with foreign financial statements

128   D.W. Collins   W.K. Salatka

translated at historical exchange rates (H/H), (2) comprehensive market value accounting with translation at current rates of exchange (C/C), and (3) historical cost accounting with translation at the current exchange rate (H/C). Their basic findings with respect to these three combinations are as follows: (1) the C/C method possesses both economic interpretability and symmetry, (2) the H/H method possesses symmetry but not economic interpretability, and (3) the H/C method possesses neither property except in trivial cases.

In practice, the temporal method of translation adopted by *SFAS No. 8* is a hybrid of all three combinations noted above: current assets valued at market and current liabilities are translated at current exchange rates (C/C), fixed assets and inventory valued at historical cost are translated at historical rates (H/H), and long-term monetary assets and liabilities valued at historical cost are translated at current rates (H/C). Thus, the resultant numbers produced on the financial statements, including translated income, do *not* possess the desired properties of economic interpretability or symmetry. Loosely speaking, under *SFAS No. 8*, translated income produces a garbled signal of the real return on assets. This is particularly true for firms with relatively large amounts of foreign fixed assets and long-term debt for which the H/H and H/C combinations apply.

The current method of translation adopted under *SFAS No. 52* (when the functional currency is the local currency) results in all accounts being translated at current exchange rates at each balance sheet date. As such, it is a combination of the C/C and H/C methods, and the problems associated with the latter combination remain. Moreover, the translation gain or loss is *excluded* from income. Given the stylized conditions underlying their model, Beaver and Wolfson show that *inclusion* of the translation gain or loss in income is necessary for a given method to achieve either economic interpretability or symmetry. Interestingly, they conclude that a major empirical implication of their model is that an imperfect correlation will exist between investors' market returns (price changes plus dividends) and reported accounting rates of return on equity under *SFAS No. 52* because of the exclusion of the translation gain or loss from net income.[11] Thus, contrary to the assertions made in the popular press and in the Griffin and Castanias (1987) survey results, the analysis presented by Beaver and Wolfson suggests that earnings numbers produced under *SFAS No. 52* may be no more informative than those produced under *SFAS No. 8*. If so, we would expect to observe no increase in the ERCs of the multinational sample from the *SFAS No. 8* to the *SFAS No. 52* period, and we would expect the ERCs of the nonmultinational firms to exceed those of the multinational firms for both periods.

Sample and research design

Treatment and control firms

To test the implications of the model and the competing arguments regarding the relative informativeness of earnings signals produced under *SFAS No. 8* and *SFAS No. 52* outlined in the previous sections, an initial sample of 30 multinational treatment firms was selected. The firms available from the Value Line tape were sorted according to the average (over 1977 to 1981) variance of foreign currency adjustments divided by total assets. The 30 firms selected had the highest variance of foreign currency adjustments and met the following criteria:

1 At least 12 percent of average total sales consisted of foreign sales during the years 1977 through 1981.
2 Quarterly earnings per share forecasts from the Value Line Investment Survey were available from 1976 through 1987.
3 Security return data were available from a 1988 version of the Daily CRSP tape for the years 1976 through 1987.

The selection screens based on variance of foreign currency adjustments and foreign sales were used to identify firms whose financial statements were most affected by *SFAS No. 8*. The second and third selection criteria were used to ensure that sufficient earnings and return data were available to obtain reasonably efficient estimates of ERCs during both the *SFAS No. 8* and *SFAS No. 52* time periods.

To test for cross-sectional differences in ERCs due to differential noise in earnings signals, control firms were matched with the treatment firms by industry (SIC code) and firm size (total sales). In three cases, it was not possible to locate a control firm (followed by Value Line) that approximated the size of the treatment firm in the corresponding industry. Accordingly, the final sample consists of 54 firms (27 multinationals and 27 nonmultinationals).

Ideally, the control firms would have no foreign operations or transactions, so that their reported earnings would be totally free of any effects from *SFAS No. 8*. Unfortunately, the matching criteria and the data availability requirements in equations (2) and (3) prevented the formation of such a control sample. Therefore, firms with foreign sales of up to 11 percent of average total sales over the period 1977 through 1981 were included. Although these firms have some foreign currency translation adjustments imbedded in their earnings figures, these adjustments tend to be relatively small, as reported in Table 2. Obviously, this concession works against finding any differences in the ERCs between the treatment and control firms. Table 1 presents an industry profile of the firms in the treatment and control samples. Given the constraint that the control firms have no more than 11 percent of foreign sales to average total annual sales, 16 matches were found at a four-digit SIC level, none at a three-digit level, and 11 at a two-digit level.

Table 2 displays statistics for the distribution of total sales, the proportion of foreign sales, the absolute value of foreign currency adjustment as a percentage of net income, and the variance of foreign currency adjustments. The summary statistics for total sales suggest that treatment firms are slightly larger in average size, but these differences are not statistically significant. The summary statistics for the remaining three variables in Table 2 reveal substantive differences between the treatment and control samples on these dimensions, differences that are desirable given the thrust of this paper. Note that

130   D.W. Collins   W.K. Salatka

TABLE 1
Distribution of pairwise industry matches between treatment and control firms

Two-digit industry code	Number of two-digit matched pairs	Number of three-digit matched pairs	Number of four-digit matched pairs	Total number of matched pairs
20	0	0	2	2
26	0	0	1	1
28	5	0	1	6
29	0	0	1	1
30	1	0	2	3
32	1	0	1	2
34	1	0	0	1
35	1	0	4	5
36	1	0	3	4
37	0	0	1	1
38	1	0	0	1
Totals	11	0	16	27

the average (median) absolute value of foreign currency adjustment as a percentage of net income before extraordinary items is 9 percent (4 percent) for the treatment sample and 2 percent (0 percent) for the control sample. Thus, the translation gains/losses represent a nontrivial component of reported earnings for the multinational sample.

Matching criteria and controls for differences in information environment and prior probability uncertainty
Matching by industry and firm size is an attempt to control for differences in the information environment that are likely to influence the magnitude of the ERCs related to earnings announcements. Work by Atiase (1985), Grant (1980), and Holthausen and Verrecchia (1988) suggests that the variance of price adjustment associated with an accounting signal (announcement) is inversely related to the availability of prior information signals and the extent to which these earlier signals are correlated with the valuation-relevant cash flows ($\tilde{X}_j$) and the firm's accounting earnings signal ($\tilde{Y}_j$). Firms in similar industries and of similar size are expected to exist in roughly equivalent information environments. By analyzing firms from similar industries over the same time frame, differences between the two samples in economywide and industrywide sources of information are minimized. As in Atiase (1985) and Grant (1980), firm size measured by sales is used to proxy for the availability of firm-specific nonaccounting information.

A second reason for matching treatment and control firms by industry is to try to minimize differences in prior probability uncertainty with respect to the underlying valuation-relevant cash flows. Firms in the same industry are

TABLE 2
Summary statistics on total sales, foreign sales and variance of foreign currency
adjustment 1977–1981

Variable/group membership	Mean	Std dev.	Percentile			t-value
			90	50	10	
Firm size (sales)*						
Treatment	761.29	565.63	1510.01	653.90	143.02	0.36
Control	720.59	602.80	1562.26	521.56	99.91	
Proportion of foreign sales†						
Treatment	0.32	0.14	0.54	0.31	0.13	8.91
Control	0.07	0.07	0.11	0.08	0.03	
Absolute value of foreign currency adjustment ÷ N.I.‡						
Treatment	0.09	0.16	0.20	0.04	0.00	5.18
Control	0.02	0.04	0.05	0.00	0.00	
Variance of foreign currency adjustments§						
Treatment	0.42	0.61	1.28	0.15	0.02	227.51
Control	0.04	0.06	0.16	0.01	0.00	

*Sales (in millions of dollars) denotes average annual sales over 1977 through 1981 obtained from a 1981 version of the Value Line tape.
†Proportion of total sales is the average of annual foreign sales divided by total annual sales calculated over the period 1977 through 1981.
‡N.I. = Net income before extraordinary items and discontinued operations. This ratio is based on annual figures. Amounts greater than 100 percent are set equal to 100 percent.
§The variance of foreign currency adjustments is the variance of annual foreign currency adjustments divided by total assets (where the function has been multiplied by 10,000) calculated over the period 1977 through 1981. The annual foreign currency adjustments, which are obtained from a 1981 version of the Value Line tape, include both translation as well as transaction adjustments to reported earnings.

assumed to face similar factor and product markets and, therefore, the level of uncertainty associated with the outcome of their production/investment decisions is roughly similar. Recall from the model outlined in the second section that ERCs are an increasing function of investors' uncertainty with respect to the unobservable future cash flows prior to receiving an earnings signal. Thus, systematic differences in this variable across the two samples could either attenuate or magnify ERC differences, thereby limiting the ability to draw inferences about the quality or informativeness of earnings signals under *SFAS No. 8* and *SFAS No. 52*. By industry matching of treatment and control firms, we attempt to hold the σ_j^2 determinant of ERCs in the C&S (1989) and H&V (1988) model roughly constant across these two samples. Indirect evidence on the success in achieving this goal is provided in the fifth section.

Proxies for unexpected earnings
Value Line analysts' forecast errors are treated as an exogenous predetermined variable in the empirical model (presented below) used to test for differ-

132   D.W. Collins   W.K. Salatka

ential ERCs. The tests that follow focus on the relation between analysts' earnings forecast errors and security returns measured around quarterly earnings announcement dates. Evidence presented by Brown, Foster, and Noreen (1985) and Brown, Griffin, Hagerman, and Zmijewski (1987) suggests that analysts' forecast errors, especially errors for short horizons determined relative to quarterly earnings announcement dates, are related to security returns. Moreover, by focusing on return performance measured over relatively short windows around quarterly earnings announcement dates, one can more readily attribute differences in how the price responds to a given amount of unexpected earnings (i.e., ERCs) to differences in the informativeness or quality of the earnings signal, per se. Accordingly, differences in the information environment that contribute to differences in the surprise in the earnings signal are effectively captured by the magnitude of the analysts' earnings forecast error.

Empirical model for cross sectional differences in earnings response coefficients

To test whether the market perceived the earnings signals of multinationals produced under *SFAS No. 8* to be of lower quality (i.e., possessed greater amounts of noise) than the earnings signals of nonmultinationals and whether *SFAS No. 52* reduced some of that noise, the following pooled cross-sectional regression model is estimated:

$$PE_{iq} = \frac{b_o}{PE_{it-2}} + b_1 \times \frac{UE_{iq}}{P_{it-2}} + b_2 \left[T \times \frac{UE_{iq}}{P_{it-2}} \right] + b_3 \left[GRPL_i \times \frac{UE_{iq}}{P_{it-2}} \right]$$

$$+ b_4 \left[GRPC_i \times \frac{UE_{iq}}{P_{it-2}} \right] + b_5 \left[T \times GRPL_i \times \frac{UE_{iq}}{P_{it-2}} \right]$$

$$+ b_6 \left[T \times GRPC_i \times \frac{UE_{iq}}{P_{it-2}} \right] + \epsilon_{iq} \tag{5}$$

where

PE_{iq} = The prediction error from a market model cumulated over the day before and the day of firm *i*'s quarterly earnings announcement for quarter *q*. The market model parameters are estimated over a 200-day trading period running from day $t = -100$ *to* $t = 100$, in which day $t = 0$ is the day of the firm's quarterly earnings announcement.

P_{it-2} = The price of firm *i*'s stock two days prior to the quarterly earnings announcement at $t = 0$, obtained from a 1988 version of the CRSP Stock Price Master tape.

UE_{iq} = Unexpected earnings of firm *i* for quarter *q*, calculated as the difference between reported earnings for quarter *q* and the most recent earnings forecast for quarter *q*, both of which were obtained from the Value Line Investment Survey.[12]

T = 1 if quarterly earnings announcement is in *SFAS No. 8* time frame, and

0 if quarterly earnings announcement is in *SFAS No. 52* time frame.

$GRPL_i$ = 1 if multinational firm that uses local (foreign) currency as functional currency under *SFAS No. 52*, 0 otherwise.

$GRPC_i$ = 1 if multinational firm that uses both U.S. dollars and local currency as functional currency under *SFAS No. 52*, 0 otherwise.

e_{iq} = A random disturbance distributed $N(0, \sigma_e^2)$.

Equation (5) is estimated with quarterly data over the combined *SFAS No. 8* and *SFAS No. 52* time periods. The *SFAS No. 8* time period is defined to begin with the first quarter of 1976 and end in the fourth quarter of 1980. The *SFAS No. 52* period begins with the fourth quarter of 1983 and ends with the fourth quarter of 1987.[13] The combination of both periods for all sample firms (both treatment and control firms) results in 1,998 possible quarterly earnings announcements. Missing earnings forecasts, quarterly announcement dates, and/or return data result in an initial sample of 1,823 firm/quarters for estimation of equation (5). Based on an analysis of influential data points using the diagnostic checks in Belsley, Kuh, and Welsch (1980), 11 firm/quarters (0.6 percent of the sample) were identified as outliers that significantly influenced the point estimates of ERCs across the various samples and time periods.[14] These observations were subsequently deleted, producing a final sample of 1,812 firm/quarters for estimating the parameters reported below.

Specification of relevant contrasts and tests
Equation (5) is essentially an analysis of covariance estimated as a constrained regression. To maximize the power of the tests, (5) was estimated by pooling data across firms and over time and simultaneously testing for both cross-sectional and temporal differences in ERCs. In most cases, we are *not* interested in testing the significance of individual coefficients but are interested in testing differences in *combinations of coefficients* that constitute the average ERC for a particular firm type/time period. These differences are referred to as contrasts.

The regression coefficients that constitute the ERC for a particular type of firm in the *SFAS No. 8* and *52* periods are summarized in Table 3. Note that the regression coefficients constituting an ERC depend upon the values of the indicator variables for a particular firm type/time period.

To illustrate how the model is used to test the contrasts of interest, consider the "firm contrasts" in Table 3, where the ERCs of multinational firms and control firms in the *SFAS No. 8* period were compared. Note that there are three indicator variables: one (T) to distinguish between the *SFAS No. 8* and *52* periods and two others (*GRPL* and *GRPC*) to distinguish between three possible group memberships. In the *SFAS No. 8* period, T = 1. Therefore, for

134   D.W. Collins   W.K. Salatka

TABLE 3
Summary of earnings response coefficients by type of firm and time period

$$\text{Model: } PE = b_0 \left[\frac{1}{P_{t-2}} \right] + b_1 \left[\frac{UE}{P_{t-2}} \right] + b_2 \left[T \times \frac{UE}{P_{t-2}} \right] + b_3 \left[GRPL \times \frac{UE}{P_{t-2}} \right]$$

$$+ b_4 \left[GRPC \times \frac{UE}{P_{t-2}} \right] + b_5 \left[T \times GRPL \times \frac{UE}{P_{t-2}} \right]$$

$$+ b_6 \left[T \times GRPC \times \frac{UE}{P_{t-2}} \right] + e$$

Type of firm	SFAS No. 8 period	SFAS No. 52 period
	◄——Time period contrasts ——►	
Control firms	$b_1 + b_2$	b_1
Multinational firms functional currency = Local currency	$b_1 + b_2 + b_3 + b_5$	$b_1 + b_3$
Firm contrasts	Restriction* $b_3 + b_5 = b_4 + b_6$	Firm contrasts
Multinational firms functional currency = U.S. \$ + Local	$b_1 + b_2 + b_4 + b_6$	$b_1 + b_4$

*The restriction applies because the *GRPC* or *GRPL* designations for the nature of functional currency was first introduced in *SFAS No. 52*. Therefore, this distinction has no meaning in the *SFAS No. 8* time frame.

PE = Two-day (day -1 and 0) prediction error from market model around quarterly earnings announcement
P_{t-2} = Price two days before quarterly earnings announcement
UE = Actual EPS_q – VL forecasted EPS_q
T = 1 if in *SFAS No. 8* time frame
    0 if in *SFAS No. 52* time frame
$GRPL$ = 1 if multinational firm with functional currency equal local currency under *SFAS No. 52*
    0 otherwise
$GRPC$ = 1 if multinational firm with both U.S. dollars and local currency as functional currency under *SFAS No. 52*
    0 otherwise

the control firms, the ERC is estimated by $b_1 + b_2$. For these firms, the *GRPL* and *GRPC* indicator variables are 0; therefore, b_3 through b_6 do not apply. For the multinational treatment firms, the estimated ERC is either $b_1 + b_2 + b_3 + b_5$ or $b_1 + b_2 + b_4 + b_6$. However, because the distinction between functional currencies (local currency or a combination of U.S. dollar and local currency) has meaning only in the *SFAS No. 52* period, $b_3 + b_5$ was restricted to equal $b_4 + b_6$ in the *SFAS No. 8* period.[15] Hence, the relevant contrast between the ERCs of treatment and control firms is represented by $b_3 + b_5$ (or $b_4 + b_6$). The null hypothesis is that $b_3 + b_5$ (or $b_4 + b_6$) is equal to or greater than 0; the alternative is that the sum of these two coefficients is negative. The remainder of the contrasts is discussed in the empirical results section.

The relevant contrasts are tested using a standard F-test described in Kmenta (1986, 479):

$$F(r, n-k) = \frac{(SSE_R - SSE_U)/r}{SSE_U (n-k)} \tag{6}$$

where n is the number of observations, r is the number of restrictions, and k is the number of unrestricted coefficients. For each of the contrasts, the number of observations is 1,812, with one restriction and seven unrestricted coefficients (six in *SFAS No. 8* period). The error sum of squares from the restricted model (SSE_R) is compared with the error sum of squares from the unrestricted model (SSE_U) to form the relevant test statistic in (6).

Empirical results

Table 4 presents means, standard deviations, and selected decile values for analysts' earnings forecast errors (*FEs*) and two-day abnormal returns (*PEs*) for the treatment and control samples for each of the two test periods. The *FEs* are divided by price two days before the quarterly earnings announcement to adjust for scale differences and to provide a measure that allows for meaningful aggregation across firms. To provide a more appropriate basis for assessing forecast accuracy, the median absolute value of *FE* scaled by price is also reported in the last column of Table 4.

For the signed analysts' *FEs*, there is no difference in either the mean or median values between the multinational and nonmultinational samples. This result holds for both the *SFAS No. 8* and *SFAS No. 52* periods. However, differences in forecast accuracy were found across the two samples of firms in both test periods. In the *SFAS No. 8* (52) period, the median absolute FE/P_{t-2} is .0031 (.0016) for the multinational sample and .0050 (.0028) for the nonmultinational sample. According to a Wilcoxon medians test (two tailed), both of these differences are significant at an α level of .0001. Thus, despite the presence of significantly larger translation gains/losses in the earnings of

136   D.W. Collins   W.K. Salatka

TABLE 4
Summary statistics for analysts' forecast errors and abnormal returns for *SFAS No. 8* versus *SFAS No. 52* periods and for treatment versus control firms

	Mean	Std. dev.	Deciles					Median abs. value
			1	3	5	7	9	
A. Analysts' forecast errors*—*SFAS No. 8* period								
Multinational treatment firms	−0.0043	0.0488	−0.0131	−0.0015	0.0005	0.0027	0.0090	0.0031
Nonmultinational control firms	−0.0023	0.0273	−0.0163	−0.0030	−0.0007	0.0040	0.0127	0.0050
p-value for difference†	(.4119)				(.4673)			(.0001)
B. Analysts' earnings forecast errors—*SFAS No. 52* period								
Multinational treatment firms	−0.0048	0.0485	−0.0082	−0.0014	0.0000	0.0008	0.0040	0.0016
Nonmultinational control firms	−0.0021	0.0136	−0.0095	−0.0025	−0.0002	0.0016	0.0053	0.0028
p-value for difference	(.3048)				(.9552)			(.0001)
C. PE (−1,0)‡—*SFAS No. 8* period								
Multinational treatment firms	−0.0014	0.0337	−0.0351	−0.0134	−0.0016	0.0116	0.0321	n/a
Nonmultinational control firms	0.0002	0.0378	−0.0416	−0.0148	0.0000	0.0127	0.0411	n/a
p-value for difference	(.5700)				(.4420)			
D. PE (−1,0)—*SFAS No. 52* period								
Multinational treatment firms	−0.0011	0.0344	−0.0378	−0.0126	−0.0004	0.0106	0.0353	n/a
Nonmultinational control firms	−0.0012	0.0422	−0.0392	−0.0126	0.0014	0.0141	0.0434	n/a
p-value for difference	(.9711)				(.4801)			

*Earnings forecast errors are calculated as (actual expected) and are scaled by stock price two days before the earnings announcement.
†p-values are reported probabilities for two-tailed tests for significant difference in means or medians of indicated variables.
‡PE (−1,0) are the two-day cumulative abnormal returns or prediction errors from the market model measured over the day before and the day of the quarterly earnings announcement.

the multinational sample (see Table 2), analysts were apparently able to predict more accurately the earnings of these firms than those of the nonmultinationals, although the differences in median absolute value of *FE/P* (.12 percent to .19 percent of price) are not all that large. Note that in the *SFAS No. 52* period, the median absolute FE/P_{t-2} is roughly half as large as it is in the *SFAS No. 8* period. This result is consistent with the finding reported in Griffin and Castanias (1987, Tables 5.4 and 5.5) that the average analyst forecast error for the *SFAS No. 52*–affected companies decreased after the adoption of *SFAS No. 52*. However, because the control sample of nonmultinationals also exhibits a smaller FE/P_{t-2} in the *SFAS No. 52* period, we are reluctant to attribute this improvement in forecast accuracy to the elimination of translation gains/losses from the income statement for at least some of the multinational firms.

Turning to the summary statistics for the two-day abnormal returns $[PE(-1,0)]$ reported in panels C and D of Table 4, we find no significant differences between means, medians, or dispersion characteristics of the two samples. Again, this result holds for both the *SFAS No. 8* and *SFAS No. 52* periods.

Table 5 presents the individual coefficient estimates and related *t*-values from estimating (5) across the 1,812 firm/quarters that constitute the sample. Two sets of estimates are provided: one set for the unrestricted version of (5) and a second set wherein the coefficients were restricted on the two types of

TABLE 5
Pooled cross-sectional regression results

Model: See Table 3.

Parameter	Unrestricted version		Restricted version*	
	Coef. est.	*t*-value	Coef. est.	*t*-value
b_0	0.024	2.09	0.024	2.09
b_1	1.044	7.22	1.044	7.22
b_2	−0.282	−1.60	−0.282	−1.60
b_3	0.429	0.71	0.430	0.71
b_4	−0.497	−2.80	−0.496	−2.80
b_5	−0.635	−1.02	−0.597	−0.96
b_6	0.429	1.58	0.329	1.47
Adjusted R^2	.089		0.086	
F-value	25.131 ($p < .001$)		29.257 ($p < .0001$)	
Number of quarterly earnings announcements	1,812		1,812	

*Restricting $b_3 + b_5 = b_4 + b_6$ in *SFAS No. 8* period. *F*-value for restriction = .429 ($p = .513$).

138   D.W. Collins   W.K. Salatka

multinational firms (those using the local currency as the functional currency and those using a combination of the U.S. dollar and the local currency) to be equal in the *SFAS No. 8* period. Restricting $(b_1 + b_2 + b_3 + b_5) = (b_1 + b_2 + b_4 + b_6)$ effectively amounts to estimating a single ERC across the entire sample of multinational firms in the *SFAS No. 8* period. During this time period, the notion of a functional currency for reporting foreign operations had not yet been established, and the translation procedures and reporting of associated gains and losses was the same for all multinational firms. Consequently, the distinction between a "local currency" firm or a "U.S. dollar functional currency" firm is artificial and of little practical consequence for this time frame. Accordingly, the restricted version of (5) was used to estimate a single coefficient for the total sample of multinational firms for purposes of carrying out the between-group comparisons in the *SFAS No. 8* period.[16] For the *SFAS No. 52* between-group comparisons and the comparisons over time, the distinctions between multinationals on the basis of their functional currencies become important. Therefore, the estimates from the unrestricted version of the model were used for these tests.

The individual coefficient estimates reported in Table 5 are combined as indicated in Table 3 to form ERC estimates and related firm and time period contrasts that are of primary interest in this study. Therefore, we do not comment on the sign and significance of individual coefficients at this point.[17] When appropriate, individual coefficients will be discussed as they relate to particular contrasts or differences in ERCs. Note, however, that the *F*-value for the overall regression is 25.131 (unrestricted version), which is highly significant ($p < .0001$). Yet the rather low explanatory power of our model (adjusted R^2 of 8.9 percent for the unrestricted version) suggests there are a variety of factors, aside from accounting method differences, that contribute to cross-sectional and intertemporal differences in the return/earnings relation.[18]

Table 6 summarizes the value of the indicator variables and the combination of coefficients that compose the estimated ERC for a particular group of firms in a particular time period. Also presented in this table are the predicted sign of each contrast, according to the garbling hypothesis and the Beaver-Wolfson hypothesis, the estimated value, the associated *F*-statistic, and the significance level for each contrast. Because the reported results favor the garbling hypothesis over the Beaver-Wolfson hypothesis, the following discussion is framed in terms of the garbling hypothesis. The various contrasts summarized in Table 6 are also presented graphically in Figures 1 and 2, where the ERCs of each group contributing to a particular contrast are plotted. Each of these contrasts is next considered in turn.

Firm contrasts

The sign of the contrast between the ERCs of multinational treatment firms and control firms in the *SFAS No. 8* period ($b_3 + b_5$ or $b_4 + b_6$) is predicted to be negative. That is, the slope of the return/earnings relation is expected to be lower for the multinational firms if the market perceives their earnings numbers to be of lower quality due to the *SFAS No. 8* translation procedures. The results reported in Table 6 and Figure 1 panel A are weakly consistent with this prediction. The estimated ERC of multinational treatment firms is approximately 22 percent smaller than that of the nonmultinational control firms (.595 versus .762). The value of the contrast (−0.167) yields an *F*-value of 1.45, which is significant at $p = .114$.[19]

Turning to the *SFAS No. 52* period, three contrasts are of interest. Firms that use local currencies as the functional currency under *SFAS No. 52* do not include translation gains or losses in income, and all accounts are converted at current exchange rates. However, firms with foreign operations that are an extension of their domestic operations or that operate in highly inflationary economies are required to determine translation gains and losses following the same procedures used under *SFAS No. 8*.[20] In addition, these gains and losses must be included in the determination of periodic income. Thus, firms using a combination of local currency and U.S. dollars as functional currencies are predicted to have noisier earnings signals in the *SFAS No. 52* period than (1) the control firms or (2) the multinational firms using exclusively local currencies as the functional currency.[21] Because firms using the local currency as the functional currency convert all accounts at the current exchange rates and exclude translation gains/losses from income, their reported earnings numbers under *SFAS No. 52* are expected to be relatively free of any garbling that might result from the translation techniques and recognition of unrealized translation gains and losses under *SFAS No. 8*. Therefore, it was expected that no significant differences would be found between the ERCs of the multinational-local currency sample and the control sample in the *SFAS No. 52* period.

The results reported in Table 6 and Figure 1 are uniformly consistent with all of these predictions. The second contrast in Table 6 (depicted graphically in panel B of Figure 1) compares the ERC of multinational firms using a combination of U.S. dollars and local currency as the functional currency with the ERC of control firms. The estimated ERCs are 0.547 and 1.044, respectively. The difference of −0.497 yields an *F*-statistic of 7.86, which is significant at the .003 level.

The third contrast in Table 6 and in panel C of Figure 1 compares the ERCs of the two multinational treatment groups in the *SFAS No. 52* period. As predicted, the multinational firms using both U.S. dollars and local currency exhibit a much smaller ERC than do the multinational firms using only local currency as the functional currency (0.547 versus 1.473). The difference of −0.926 produces an *F*-value of 2.39, which is significantly different from 0 at $p = .061$.

The final firm contrast compares the ERCs of multinational-local currency firms and control firms in the *SFAS No. 52* period (panel D of Figure 1). Although the multinational-local currency firms have a somewhat larger ERC than the control firms (1.473 versus 1.044), the difference of 0.429 yields an *F*-

140   D.W. Collins   W.K. Salatka

TABLE 6
Response coefficients and contrasts among response coefficients resulting from the regression model

Model: See Table 3

Contrasts	Values of indicator in regression model			Response coefficients resulting from the regression model*	Contrasts (differences) between the coefficients	Predicted sign of contrast		Estimated value of contrast	F-statistic (significance)‡
	T	GRPL	GRPC			Garbling	B&W†		
Firm contrasts									
All multinational firms in SFAS No 8. period	1	1 or 0	1 or 0	$b_1 + b_2 + b_3 + b_5$ or $b_1 + b_2 + b_4 + b_6 = 0.595$ (Restrict $b_3 + b_5 = b_4 + b_6$)	$b_3 + b_5$ or $b_4 + b_6$	(−)	(−)	−0.167 (.114)	1.45
versus									
Control firms in SFAS No 8 period	1	0	0	$b_1 + b_2 = 0.762$					
Multinational comb. Sample in SFAS No. 52 period	0	0	1	$b_1 + b_4 = 0.547$	b_4	(−)	(−)	−0.497	7.86 < (.003)
versus									
Control firms in SFAS No. 52 period	0	0	0	$b_1 = 1.044$					
Multinational comb. Sample in SFAS No. 52 period	0	0	1	$b_1 = 0.547$	$b_4 - b_3$	(−)	(no difference)	−0.926	2.39 (.061)
versus									
Multinational local Sample in SFAS No. 52 period	0	1	0	$b_1 + b_3 = 1.473$					

Continued overleaf

TABLE 6 (cont.)

			Contrast		Predicted contrast	Predicted sign	Estimate	t-statistic (p-value)
Multinational local sample in SFAS No. 52 period	0	1	0	$b_1 + b_3$	= 1.473				
versus									
Control firms in SFAS No. 52 period	0	0	0	b_1	= 1.044				
				b_3		(no difference)	(−)	−0.429	0.50 (.480)
Time period contrasts									
Multinational comb. Sample in SFAS No. 52 period	0	0	1	$b_1 + b_{43}$	= 0.547				
versus									
SFAS No 8 period	1	0	1	$b_1 + b_2 + b_4 + b_6$	= 0.694	$-(b_2 + b_6)$	(+ or no)	(no change) −0.147	0.51 (.476)
Multinational local Sample in SFAS No. 52 period	0	1	0	$b_1 + b_3$	= 1.473				
versus									
SFAS No 8 period	1	1	0	$b_1 + b_2 + b_3 + b$	= 0.556	$-(b_2 + b_5)$	(+)	(no change) 0.917	2.34 (.063)
Control firms in SFAS No. 52 period	0	0	0	b_1	= 1.044				
versus									
SFAS No 8 period	1	0	0	$b_1 - b_2$	= 0.762	$-b_2$	(no prediction)	(no prediction) 0.281	2.56 (.110)

*Estimates for the *SFAS No. 8* contrast are from the restricted version of (5). Estimates for all other contrasts are based on the unrestricted version of (5).

†Predicted sign of contrast based on the modeling in Beaver and Wolfson (1982).

‡Based on 1 and 1,811 degrees of freedom. Significance levels are for individual contrasts and for one-tailed tests where the predicted contrast is directional. The p-values are based on the relation between $F(1,N)$ and $t(N)$. In those cases where the predicted contrast is nondirectional, the reported p-values are for two-tailed tests.

Significance levels for jointly determined contrasts can be determined via the Bonferroni method (see Neter and Wasserman 1973, 146–148).

§Comb. sample = firms whose functional currency is a combination of local currency and U.S. dollars.

¶Local sample = firms whose functional currency is the local ((foreign) currency only.

142   D.W. Collins   W.K. Salatka

Figure 1 Comparison of earnings response coefficients across firms

Panel A *SFAS No. 8 period*

Panel B *SFAS No. 8 period*

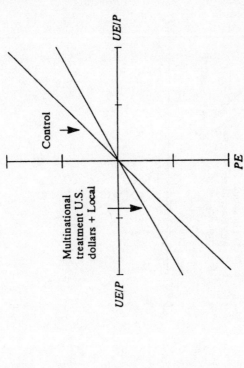

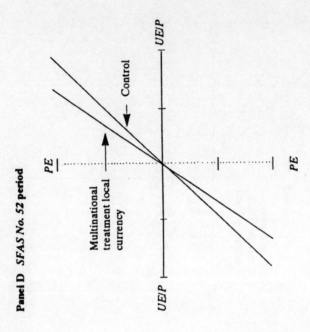

Panel C *SFAS No. 52 period*

Multinational treatment U.S. dollars + Local

Multinational treatment local currency

Panel D *SFAS No. 52 period*

Multinational treatment local currency

Control

144   D.W. Collins   W.K. Salatka

Figure 2 Comparison of earnings response coefficients across firms

Panel A Multinational firms'   **Panel B Multinational firms' functional**   **Panel C Control firms**
functional currency = U.S. dollars + Local   **currency = U.S. dollars + Local**

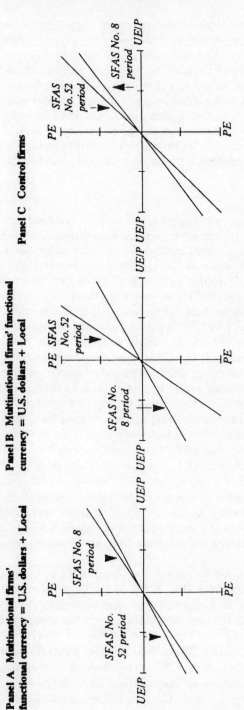

value of only 0.50, which is not significant. These results suggest that the earnings signals produced by multinational-local currency firms after *SFAS No. 52* were of similar quality to those of the nonmultinational control firms.

In summary, the firm contrast results are uniformly consistent with the hypothesized effect of noise or garbling in reported earnings numbers on ERCs. Specifically, for multinational firms whose reported earnings numbers contain unrealized translation gains and losses determined under the temporal method of *SFAS No. 8*, the price response to a given amount of unexpected earnings is consistently smaller than for firms whose reported earnings figures exclude these effects. This result holds true in both the *SFAS No. 8* and *SFAS No. 52* periods.

Time period contrasts

The results of the time period contrasts are reported in the last three sections of Table 6 and in Figure 2. The change from the temporal method of translation under *SFAS No. 8* to the current method of translation under *SFAS No. 52* is expected to reduce or eliminate the operating margin distortions that were alleged to exist under the former method. In addition, the elimination of translation gains/losses from income is predicted to enhance the informativeness (i.e., reduce the noise) of the earnings signals of multinational firms from the *SFAS No. 8* period to the *SFAS No. 52* period. However, the multinational firms that use a combination of both U.S. dollars and local currency as functional currency continue to convert at least some account balances at historical exchange rates and continue to report at least some translation gains/losses as part of income. Therefore, we expect to find little or no evidence of an increase in ERCs for these firms from the *SFAS No. 8* period to the *SFAS No. 52* period as compared to the multinational companies using local currency only as the functional currency. With respect to the control firms, no prediction was made about changes in ERCs from one time frame to another. However, this contrast was examined to see whether there are confounding time-related influences on ERCs that are not specified in the model (e.g., differences in growth opportunities or changes in the level of interest rates used to capitalize earnings innovations at different points in time). Any observed changes over time in the ERCs of control firms can be viewed as a way to isolate or control for the influences of these unspecified time-related factors on ERCs.

The first time period contrast in Table 6 is depicted in Figure 2, panel A. This contrast compares the average ERC in the *SFAS No. 8* period and the *SFAS No. 52* period for the multinational firms using a combination of U.S. dollars and local currency as the functional currency. For this group of firms, the estimated ERC exhibits a slight decrease from 0.694 to 0.547 from the *SFAS No. 8* to *SFAS No. 52* period. The decrease of 0.147 yields an *F*-statistic of 0.51, which is insignificant (*p*-value = .476). Thus, there is no evidence of a change in the markets' response to earning surprises for those firms that continued to translate at least some account balances as they did under *SFAS No.*

146   D.W. Collins   W.K. Salatka

8 and to report unrealized translation gains/losses on the income statement.

For the multinational-local currency firms (panel B, Figure 2), there is a significant increase in ERCs from the *SFAS No. 8* to *SFAS No. 52* periods (0.556 to 1.473). The estimated change is 0.917, which is significant at the .063 level. Subject to the qualification noted below, these results are consistent with the conclusions reached by Griffin and Castanias (1987) that investors perceive the earnings signals under *SFAS No. 52* to be of higher quality than those reported under *SFAS No. 8*—particularly for the multinational-local currency firms whose reporting was most affected by the shift from *SFAS No. 8* to *SFAS No. 52*.

There is one important caveat to this interpretation of the results, however. The final time period contrast in Table 6 (panel C, Figure 2) reveals that the control firms also experienced a modest increase in their ERC from the *SFAS No. 8* to *SFAS No. 52* period (from 0.762 to 1.044, an increase of 0.281). This increase is significantly different from 0 at $p=.110$. Although several firms in this sample had small amounts of foreign operations, it is difficult to attribute the increase in their ERCs to changes in foreign currency accounting. Rather, it would appear that differences in macroeconomic conditions or changes in firm-specific factors (addressed later) contributed to at least some of the differences in ERCs between the *SFAS No. 8* and *SFAS No. 52* periods.

The preceding result suggests that other factors, aside from changes in earnings quality, may have contributed to the changes in ERC estimates over time. For the moment, these "other factors" are unspecified and their influence on ERCs is assumed to be the same across all three groups. Under this assumption, the change in ERCs of the control group (and to some extent, the multinational-combination sample) captures the effects of these unspecified factors and provides a measure of the change in the market's responsiveness to earnings surprises in the *absence of accounting method changes* with respect to translation gains/losses. Consequently, the relevant comparison or contrast is the magnitude of the time period contrast of each group vis-à-vis the others.

Reading from Table 6, the time period contrast of the control firms is given by $-b_2$, the time period contrast of the multinational-combination firms is $-(b + b_6)$, and the time period contrast of the multinational-local currency firms is $-(b_2 + b_5)$. Therefore, the relevant comparisons between each multinational group and the control group are represented by $-b_6$ and $-b_5$, respectively. The comparison of ERC change for the multinational-local currency group vis-à-vis the multinational-combination group is $b_6 - b_5$. All of these contrasts are predicted to be positive if the changes in reporting under *SFAS No. 52* improved earnings quality as perceived by investors.

The t-tests on $-b_6$ and $-b_5$ reported in Table 5 (unrestricted version) are equivalent to F-tests on these contrasts. These results show that $-b_6$ is negative ($-.429$) and marginally significant ($t = -1.58$), indicating that there was *less* an increase in the ERCs of multinational firms using a combination of U.S. dollars and local currency as a functional currency than there was for the control firms over the same time period.

The results for the multinational-local currency firms compared to the control firms and the contrasts between the two multinational groups suggest quite a different interpretation, however. From Table 5 we see that $-b_5 = 0.635$ is positive as expected, but the reported t-value is significant only at $p = .155$. A somewhat stronger result obtains for the comparison between the multinational-local and multinational-combination currency groups ($b_6 - b_5 = 1.064$), which is positive as predicted and significant ($F = 2.81$, $p > 0.046$). Thus, for those firms that experienced the greatest change in reporting for foreign currency gains and losses because of changing from *SFAS No. 8* to *SFAS No. 52* (multinational-local currency firms), there is some (albeit weak) evidence that this group's *quality of earnings increased* compared to the control firms and compared to multinationals not experiencing as large a change in foreign currency reporting (the multinational-combination group).

A closer look at confounding factors

The model outlined in the second section parameterizes ERCs as an increasing function of investors' uncertainty with respect to unobservable future cash flows or liquidating dividends, and a decreasing function of the perceived noise or garbling in the earnings signal. To draw inferences about the latter, it is important that prior probability uncertainty (σ_j^2) be similar across the relevant samples. As noted in the fourth section, matching treatment and control firms by industry was an attempt to hold the σ_j^2 roughly constant across the two samples. Here indirect evidence on the success in achieving this goal is presented.

Table 7 presents between-group and over-time median comparisons for three alternative proxies for the unobservable prior probability uncertainty with respect to valuation-relevant future cash flows or dividends: (1) the coefficient of variation on ex post operating cash flows, (2) the standard deviation of market model residuals, and (3) the Value Line Earnings Predictability Index.[22] Intuitively, prior probability uncertainty (σ_j^2) is expected to be positively related to the first two measures and negatively related to the last measure.

The evidence presented in Table 7 suggests that industry matching is only partially successful in controlling for differences in prior probability uncertainty.[23] For the *SFAS No. 8* period, the evidence is very consistent across all three measures and suggests that there was greater uncertainty associated with the cash flows and earnings of the nonmultinational control sample than for the multinational treatment sample. All of the differences in medians are significant at $p = .04$ or below. Given the comparative statics in (4a), these differences should contribute to *higher* ERCs for the nonmultinational sample relative to the multinational sample. Note that this is the same prediction that we make based on perceived differences in the quality (informativeness) of earnings for nonmultinationals versus multinationals. Thus, the effects of differential earnings quality on observed differences in ERCs during the *SFAS No. 8* period is potentially confounded by differences in prior probability uncertainty.

148　　D.W. Collins　　W.K. Salatka

TABLE 7

Between-group and over-time comparisons of alternative proxies for prior probability uncertainty for *SFAS No. 8* and *SFAS No. 52* periods

Group comparisons	Coef. of variation on operating cash flows			Market model residuals			VL earnings predictability index		
	SFAS No. 8 period median	*SFAS No. 52* period median	p-value*	*SFAS No. 8* period median	*SFAS No. 52* period median	p-value*	*SFAS No. 8* period median	*SFAS No. 52* period median	p-value*
Nonmultinationals versus	.354	.451	(.307)	.019	.017	(.207)	45.0	47.0	(.234)
All multinationals	.301	.324	(.322)	.015	.016	(.296)	75.0	55.0	(.140)
p-value†	(.041)	(.339)		(.015)	(.015)		(.031)	(.418)	
Nonmultinationals versus	.354	.451	—‡	.019	.017	—	45.0	47.0	—
Multinational local	.316	.238	(.625)	.015	.016	(.666)	76.9	72.0	(.410)
p-value†	(.077)	(.290)		(.050)	(.562)		(.017)	(.140)	
Nonmultinationals versus	.354	.451	—	.019	.017	—	45.0	47.0	—
Multinationals comb.	.271	.413	(.074)	.016	.016	(.443)	60.0	53.0	(.320)
p-value†	(.340)	(.750)		(.026)	(.026)		(.112)	(.891)	
Multinational local versus	.316	.238	—	.015	.016	—	76.9	72.0	—
Multinational comb.	.271	.413	—	.016	.016	—	60.0	53.0	—
p-value†	(.243)	(.243)		(.554)	(.869)		(.353)	(.091)	

*Significance level for Wilcoxon matched-pairs signed-ranks test, two tailed (see Siegel 1956, Ch. 5).

†Significance level for two-sample medians test, two tailed (see Siegel 1956, Ch. 6).

‡Dash indicates that results for same comparison are reported above in the same column.

Turning to the comparisons for the *SFAS No. 52* period, the differences in median values between the nonmultinational and multinational samples are generally smaller across all three measures, and for most comparisons the differences are not statistically significant. Thus, for the *SFAS No. 52* period, matching by industry to control for differences in prior probability uncertainty appears to have worked reasonably well. This enhances our ability to draw inferences about differences in earnings quality from estimated differences in ERCs during this time frame.

A major unexpected result in this section is the marginally significant increase in the ERCs of the control sample over time. Evidence in Table 7 suggests that this increase cannot be explained readily by significant shifts over time in prior probability uncertainty with respect to future cash flows. The following briefly examines alternative explanations for the ERC increases, both for the control firms and the multinational treatment firms.

Previous work by Kormendi and Lipe (1987), Collins and Kothari (1989), and Easton and Zmijewski (1989) suggest four factors that may influence ERCs: earnings persistence, beta risk, growth opportunities, and risk-free interest rates. The first factor, earnings persistence, is defined as the extent to which a current earnings shock causes investors to revise future earnings expectations. All three of these studies found a positive relation between persistence measures and ERCs. Accordingly, if earnings persistence is found to be systematically higher in the *SFAS No. 52* period than in the *SFAS No. 8* period, this factor could contribute to the observed increases in ERCs. The present study estimates persistence in the manner suggested by Easton and Zmijewski (1989), running the following time-series regression for each firm in each of the test periods.

$$\frac{REV_{iq}(q + 1)}{P_{it-2}} = a_i + b_i \frac{FE_{iq}}{P_{it-2}} + e_{iq} \tag{7}$$

where

$REV_{iq}(q + 1)$ = The revision in the one-quarter-ahead Value Line earnings forecast of firm *i* for quarter $q + 1$ following the earnings announcement in quarter q

FE_{iq} = The Value Line earnings forecast error for quarter q measured as (actual-expected), where the expected number is the most recent Value Line forecast prior to the earnings release for quarter q

P_{it-2} = The price per share two days before the earnings announcement for quarter q.

b_i = Estimate of persistence for firm $_i$

The second factor, market beta, is expected to be negatively related to ERCs (Collins and Kothari 1989, Easton and Zmijewski 1989). Therefore, a

150   D.W. Collins   W.K. Salatka

decrease in beta from the *SFAS No. 8* to *SFAS No. 52* period would be consistent with an increase in ERCs. Betas were estimated by applying the standard market model to 200 days of return data centered on each quarterly earnings announcement and then computing the average for each firm across all quarters within each of the two sample periods.

The third factor is growth opportunities, expected to be positively related to ERCs. Following Collins and Kothari (1989), we use the average ratio of market to book value of equity computed over each of the two test periods. Significant increases in this ratio from the *SFAS No. 8* to *SFAS No. 52* period would be consistent with an increase in ERCs.

The fourth and final factor is risk-free interest rate. Collins and Kothari (1989) find a negative relation between risk-free rates and ERC estimates. The present analysis uses the median yield on 20-year government bonds issued within each of the two test periods. A decrease in risk-free rates from the *SFAS No. 8* to *SFAS No. 52* period would be consistent with an increase in ERCs.

Table 8 presents the median value of each variable for each of the sample groups and for each test period. Also presented are the associated *p*-values for testing for differences in the reported median values.[24] For the nonmultinational control sample, the median persistence measure is slightly lower in the *SFAS No. 52* period than in the *SFAS No. 8* period, while for the two multinational samples persistence increases slightly. None of these differences is significantly different from 0, however.

For market beta, the nonmultinational control sample exhibits a significant decrease from the *SFAS No. 8* to the *SFAS No. 52* period of −.098 (roughly 10 percent of the *SFAS No. 8* beta level). There are no significant beta changes for either of the multinational groups. As noted, a decrease in beta over time is consistent with the increase in ERCs observed for the control sample.

The growth proxy is significantly larger in the *SFAS No. 52* period than in the *SFAS No. 8* period for each of the sample groups. Thus, the possibility cannot be ruled out that at least part of the observed increase in ERCs for the control sample and for the multinational-local sample is due to enhanced growth prospects in the *SFAS No. 52* period.

Finally, the median yield on 20-year government bonds issued during the *SFAS No. 52* period is 9.58 percent and in the *SFAS No. 8* period 8.87 percent. Given a negative relation between risk-free interest rates and ERCs, this works against the finding of an increase in ERCs over time.

Overall, Table 8 provides mixed evidence on the potentially confounding influences of firm-specific and economywide factors on ERC estimates over time. The most striking result is for the control group that exhibits a significant decrease in beta and a significant increase in growth from the *SFAS No. 8* to *SFAS No. 52* period. Both effects would tend to increase ERCs for the control group over time, which is consistent with the last contrast reported in Table 6. On the other hand, the decrease in persistence and the increase in risk free rates, although not significant, would tend to decrease ERCs over time.

For the two multinational groups, the growth variable is the only factor that exhibits a significant increase from the *SFAS No. 8* to *SFAS No. 52* period. This difference is consistent with the observed change in ERCs for the multinational-local sample but is inconsistent with the ERC change for the multinational-combination sample. Unlike the control sample, there is no evidence of a significant change in beta risk over time for either of the multinational treatment groups.

In sum, the evidence in Table 8 suggests plausible explanations for the marginally significant increase in the ERCs of the control sample from the *SFAS No. 8* to *SFAS No. 52* period.[25] Two of the four factors (beta risk and growth) exhibit significant changes consistent with an increase in ERCs over time. For the two multinational groups, the growth variable is the only factor to exhibit a significant change that is consistent with ERC increases. Thus, this is a potential confounding variable when evaluating the time period contrasts of the two multinational samples in Table 6. Because this is the only factor that exhibits a significant change across all three groups, comparing the time period contrast of the multinational-local currency sample to the time period contrasts of the multinational-combination and control samples (as in the previous section) provides a control for the effects of this factor when testing for the influence of accounting method changes on earnings quality and ERCs over time.

For completeness, Table 8 also presents tests of median differences between the various subgroups within the *SFAS No. 8* and *SFAS No. 52* periods for each of the variables noted above. Only 1 of the 24 comparisons is significant at $p = .10$ or below; the growth measure for the multinational-local sample (1.869) is significantly higher (p-value $= .078$) than that for the nonmultinational sample (1.336) in the *SFAS No. 52* period. In general, there is no evidence that any of the firm (between-group) contrasts is severely compromised due to systematic differences in these other determinants of ERCs.

Summary and conclusions

Following the adoption of *SFAS No. 8*, managers of multinationals and financial analysts expressed concern that the translation method that called for the inclusion of translation gains/losses in the determination of quarterly income added significant noise or garbling to the reported earnings figures. The changes in translation methods and the removal of certain exchange adjustment gains/losses from the income statement called for in *SFAS No. 52* were claimed to have made the earnings numbers of multinational companies significantly more informative.

This study examines the relative price adjustment for a given dollar amount of unexpected earnings determined under *SFAS No. 8* and *SFAS No. 52* for a set of multinational firms and a set of nonmultinational firms. We test the

152   D.W. Collins   W.K. Salatka

TABLE 8
Test of differences in selected determinants of ERCs for *SFAS No. 52* versus *SFAS. No. 8* period and between groups within each period

Group comparisons	Persistence*			Beta			Growth†			Risk-free rate‡		
	SFAS No. 8 period median	SFAS No. 52 period median	p-value‖	SFAS No. 8 period median	SFAS No. 52 period median	p-value	SFAS No. 8 period median	SFAS No. 52 period median	p-value	SFAS No. 8 period median	SFAS No. 52 period median	Difference
Nonmultinationals versus	0.382	0.306	(.782)	0.961	0.863	(.022)	0.979	1.336	(.028)	8.87%	9.58%	0.71%
All multinationals	0.319	0.329	(.789)	0.875	0.900	(.540)	0.999	1.504	(.006)	—	—	—
p-value‖	(.787)	(.783)		(.419)	(.787)		(.787)	(.498)		—	—	—
Nonmultinationals versus	0.382	0.306	—**	0.961	0.863	—	0.979	1.336	—	—	—	—
Multinational-local	0.329	0.364	(.475)	0.867	0.911	(.968)	1.384	1.869	(.068)	—	—	—
p-value	(.562)	(.921)		(.916)	(.562)		(.916)	(.078)		—	—	—
Nonmultinationals versus	0.382	0.306	—	0.961	0.863	—	0.979	1.336	—	—	—	—
Multinational-comb.	0.263	0.291	(.798)	0.875	0.813	(.514)	0.930	1.392	(.033)	—	—	—
p-value	(.750)	(.750)		(.340)	(.750)		(.750)	(.750)		—	—	—
Multinational-local versus	0.329	0.364	—	0.867	0.911	—	1.384	1.869	—	—	—	—
Multinational-comb.	0.263	0.291	—	0.875	0.813	—	0.930	1.392	—	—	—	—
p-value	(.865)	(.873)		(.866)	(.866)		(.353)	(.243)		—	—	—

*Persistence = Slope from following time-series model.

Continued overleaf

TABLE 8 (cont.)

$$\frac{REV_q}{P_{t-2}} = a + b\,\frac{FE_q}{P_{t-2}} + e_q$$

$$\dagger\text{Growth} = \frac{1}{T}\sum_{t=1}^{T}\frac{P_t}{BV_t}$$

P_t = Price per share in year t

BV_t = Book value of equity per share in year t

T = Number of years in *SFAS No. 8* (1976-1980) or *SFAS No. 52* (1983 to 1987) period.

‡Median yield on 20-year government bonds issued during the indicated period.

§Significance for Wilcoxon matched-pairs signed-ranks test

¶Significance for two-sample medians test, two tailed.

**Dash indicates that results for same comparison are reported above in the same column.

154   D.W. Collins W.K. Salatka

empirical implications of the theoretical work of Choi and Salamon (1989) and Holthausen and Verrecchia (1988), who model the price adjustment associated with earnings announcements as a function of the amount of perceived noise or garbling in reported earnings signals.

The results of the present study indicate that ERCs (the price adjustment for a given dollar of unexpected earnings) for multinational companies were marginally lower than those for nonmultinational companies during the time that *SFAS No. 8* was in effect. This finding is consistent with greater noise or garbling in the earnings signals of the multinational firms relative to the non-multinational firms and/or to greater uncertainty surrounding the future cash flows or dividends of the latter set of firms. Following the adoption of *SFAS No. 52*, the ERCs of those firms whose reporting of foreign operations was most affected by this standard (i.e., the multinational-local currency firms) increased significantly and were slightly higher than those of the control firms (but not significantly so). This result is consistent with an increase in the earnings quality of the multinational-local currency firms relative to the control firms from the *SFAS No. 8* to *SFAS No. 52* period.

A similar increase in the market's response to earnings surprises was not observed, however, for the multinational-combination sample. These firms use the U.S. dollar (in whole or in part) as the functional currency and continued to report translation gains/losses on the income statement as called for under *SFAS No. 8*. The ERCs of this group of firms did not increase from the *SFAS No. 8* to the *SFAS No. 52* period (in fact, they decreased slightly), and they remained significantly below those of the control firms and of the multinational-local currency firms in the *SFAS No. 52* period. Thus, there is little evidence that the quality of earnings improved for those firms whose reporting for foreign operations was least affected by *SFAS No. 52*.

This paper represents an initial attempt to investigate the effects of differential earnings quality on the return/earnings relation as called for in Lev (1989). There are many situations that could affect the quality of reported earnings, such as those in which accruals are adjusted by managers in connection with maximizing remuneration under compensation agreements, those in which changes in accounting methods occur, or those in which accounting standards increase the variability of reported earnings. The framework and methods presented in this paper hold promise for investigating these and many other issues affecting the informativeness of earnings signals produced under alternative income determination rules.

Endnotes
1   This result is documented for both "association" studies, in which unexpected earnings are related to security returns measured over quarterly and annual periods, and for "events" studies, in which security returns are measured over a narrow window (two to five days) around earnings announcements.

2   Miller and Rock (1985) characterize earnings persistence as the extent to which a
    current shock or innovation in earnings affects expectations of future earnings.
3   For a review of the various criticisms of earnings measurements reported under
    SFAS No. 8, see Aggrawal (1978) and Nobes (1980).
4   We acknowledge that there are other theoretical specifications of ERCs in the liter-
    ature that, perhaps, could have been used as a backdrop for the present study. We
    opted for the simpler specification in H&V and C&S over the more complex specifi-
    cations in Kormendi and Lipe (1987), Collins and Kothari (1989), and Easton and
    Zmijewski (1989) because the former highlight the qualities of a firm's reporting
    system in determining the degree of market response to earnings signals produced
    by that system. As such, the H&V and C&S framework ties naturally into the "qual-
    ity of earnings" concerns raised by Lev (1989) and frequently cited in the debate
    over *SFAS No. 8*. In contrast, the theoretical determinants of ERCs presented in
    Kormendi and Lipe (1987), Collins and Kothari (1989), and Easton and Zmijewski
    (1989) tend to downplay the role of the information system and focus, instead, on
    the economic characteristics of the firm or macroeconomic conditions (e.g., risk,
    growth opportunities, and interest rates). Nevertheless, we recognize that the influ-
    ence of these factors may confound the tests for differences in ERCs over time and
    across firms. Section five takes a closer look at these and other potential confound-
    ing factors.
    H&V (1988) actually derive predictions about the relative magnitudes of price
    change variances around earnings announcements rather than predictions about
    earnings response coefficients per se. However, the implication of noise or garbling
    in earnings signals is the same for ERCs and variance of price changes around earn-
    ings announcements.
5   C&S (1989) assume that investors are risk averse and have a negative exponential
    utility function for consumption/wealth, while H&V (1988) assume that investors
    possess risk-neutral utility functions. Both utility functions exhibit constant
    absolute risk aversion. This implies that prices of risky assets are independent of
    investors' initial wealth and are linearly related to investors' (homogenous) expec-
    tations with respect to "true" economic earnings or cash flows at any point in time.
    The C&S model implies that the expected earnings that are capitalized must be
    risk adjusted while the H&V pricing equation contains no risk adjustment.
6   The model developed by C&S focuses on the valuation effects of a *single* public
    information signal such as an earnings announcement. H&V, on the other hand,
    derive their model of the relation between the variance of price changes and earn-
    ings signals in a setting with a sequence of two public signals and two risky assets.
    This setting allows them to investigate how cross-sectional and intertemporal cor-
    relations between information releases affect the degree of price response to new
    information. The relations and comparative static developed below relate to the
    first information release in the single asset case of the H&V framework (1988,
    82–87), which parallels the derivation in C&S (1989).
7   One exception to this rule occurs when inventories are valued at the lower of cost or
    market and market is below cost. In this case, the inventory valued at current mar-
    ket prices would be converted at current exchange rates.
8   Economic exposure is the extent a firm's present value of future cash flows is
    affected by exchange rate fluctuations. The discussions in Madura (1989) and
    Shapiro (1986) suggest that accounting exposure lacks real cash flow implications
    and, therefore, accounting translation gains/losses may be largely irrelevant for
    stock valuation purposes.
9   Purchasing power parity (PPP) theory links currency exchange rates to the relative
    inflation rates between two countries. Considerable research has been conducted to
    evaluate whether changes in currency exchange rates are consistent with the PPP
    theory (see papers by Gailliot 1970, Frenkel 1978, Cornell and Dietrich 1978,

156   D.W. Collins   W.K. Salatka

Officer 1980, Roll 1979, and Rush and Husted 1985). In general, these studies tend to reach conflicting conclusions. On the one hand, while there appears to be substantial deviations from PPP in the short run, the bulk of the evidence suggests that PPP holds in the long run (three- to five-year horizons). However, most empirical tests have been unable to reject the hypothesis that the real exchange rate follows a random walk process. If this is true, then shocks to the real exchange rate are permanent and will never reverse, implying that there is no tendency for PPP to hold in the long run. Thus, evidence purporting to show that real exchange rates follow a random walk process (and, hence, all shocks to this series are permanent) is *inconsistent* with PPP theory holding in the long run.

Recent studies by Abuaf and Jorion (1990) and Whitt (1992) reconcile the conflicting findings noted above. These studies demonstrate that the failure to reject the random walk hypothesis in earlier studies can be attributed to the low power of the statistical tests employed. Using alternative and more powerful testing procedures, Abuaf and Jorion and Whitt find that real exchange rates do not follow a random walk process (hence, shocks are not permanent). Rather, they find that exchange rates have a sizable autoregressive component implying that shocks die out over time, making the return to equilibrium a multiyear process, which is consistent with evidence that PPP tends to hold in the long run.

10 The evidence in Abuaf and Jorian (1990) and Whitt (1992) suggests that shocks to exchange rates are not permanent but die out over a period of years. If this is true, then the future cash flow implications of the translation gains/losses reflected in income under *SFAS No. 8* are problematic. The ultimate pricing effect of current period exchange rate movements depends on when (and how far) in the future the foreign source monetary assets/liabilities will be repatriated or settled, and the likelihood that exchange rate changes occurring in the current period will be offset or reversed prior to settlement and/or repatriation.

   Consider, for example, foreign source debt with maturities 10 to 20 years in the future, which the U.S. parent intends to pay off with foreign source income. If the dollar weakens relative to the foreign currency, the firm would report a translation loss under *SFAS No. 8*. However, given that shocks in exchange rates tend to die out over time, it is problematic whether the firm would actually suffer a corresponding decline in future cash flows. Thus, it is questionable whether stock price movements would mirror the accounting exchange loss reported under *SFAS No. 8* in this case.

11 Beaver and Wolfson (1982) caution that the success of their predictions regarding the correlations between market returns and accounting returns under the II/II, II/C, and C/C methods depends on the realism of their assumptions about perfect and complete markets and about exchange rate changes being driven solely by differential rates of inflation among the respective countries. Shifts in hedging behavior and changes in the mix of foreign-denominated debt that accompanied the adoption of *SFAS No. 8* suggest that certain market imperfections and/or incompleteness were present. Thus, the extent to which we can rely on the predictions derived from the Beaver and Wolfson analysis when carried to the empirical domain may be limited.

12 Note that because of the staggered cycle on which Value Line releases each of its 13 editions, some of the earnings forecasts are actually released after the close of the fiscal quarter but before the quarterly results are announced. Systematic differences in the forecast horizons between treatment and control firms could introduce differential measurement error into our unexpected earnings measure, which could confound the interpretation of our results. However, a comparison of the forecast horizons (not presented here) indicates that the treatment and control groups have similar forecast horizon characteristics.

13 Data for 1981 and 1982 are omitted because this was a transition period during

which some firms adopted *SFAS No. 52* early and others adopted it later. Furthermore, results reported in Griffin and Castanias (1987) indicate that, although *SFAS No. 52* seemed to improve analysts' ability to forecast earnings of multinationals by eliminating the translation adjustment from income, the improvement was not immediate. This finding suggests there was some sort of "learning effect" period during which time analysts and other statement users gradually became aware of the full impact of *SFAS No. 52* and then began to use this information to improve their ability to forecast the performance of multinationals.

14 Two of the outliers were caused by unusually large price changes and the remaining nine were caused by unusually large earnings forecast errors. Virtually all of the large forecast errors were due to special one-time charges to earnings related to plant closings or corporate restructuring disclosed to the market at the time of the earnings announcement. Evidence in Elliott and Shaw (1988) and Freeman and Tse (1991) suggests that the market heavily discounts the significance of large forecast errors, particularly those caused by one-time special charges or credits to earnings. Accordingly, such observations tend to attenuate the estimated slope of the return/earnings relation (i.e., the ERC) toward zero.

15 This restriction was subsequently relaxed when we compared the changes in ERCs from the *SFAS No. 8* to the *SFAS No. 52* period for our two groups of multinational treatment firms.

16 Note from Table 5 that the F-value for testing the restriction is 0.429, which is insignificant (p-value of .513). This indicates that the ERC estimates for the two sets of multinational firms are not significantly different from one another during the *SFAS No. 8* period.

17 White's (1980) test for heteroscedasticity was conducted for both the restricted and unrestricted versions of (5) and was insignificant. Heteroscedasticity-consistent covariance estimates yielded significance levels for coefficient estimates that are similar to the values reported in Table 5.

18 Other possible factors affecting the return/earnings relation include risk, growth, and persistence of earnings innovations and interest rate differences over time. See Kormendi and Lipe (1987), Easton and Zmijewski (1989), and Collins and Kothari (1989). These influences are examined further in the fifth section.

19 Because the F-test is nondirectional and the predicted contrasts are directional for all but two of our comparisons, we use the relation between $F(1,N)$ and $t(N)$ to convert the significance levels on the reported F-statistics, which are two tailed to the significance level on an equivalent one-sided t-test with N degrees of freedom.

20 Highly inflationary economics are defined in paragraph 11 of *SFAS No. 52* to be those that have experienced cumulative inflation of 100 percent or more over the most recent three-year period.

21 In the sample of 27 multinational treatment firms, 12 firms used local currency, 12 firms used a combination of U.S. dollars and local currency, and 3 firms used U.S. dollars only as the functional currency. For purposes of testing, the latter two groups are combined.

22 Value Line includes in its quarterly survey of each company an index (scored from 0 to 100) to indicate the relative ease (high values) or difficulty (low values) in predicting earnings for that firm. Among other things, this index takes into account past volatility in the earnings series and changing economic circumstances that might make the firm's earnings more difficult to predict in the future.

23 The focus is on the median results because of the relatively small sample sizes and distortions in averages caused by outliers in such settings.

24 The p-values reported in the columns of Table 8 are for the Wilcoxon matched-pairs signed-ranks test of differences over time. The row p-values are for two-sample medians test between the indicated groups.

25 In lieu of the series of univariate tests conducted here and in Table 7, we considered

158   D.W. Collins   W.K. Salatka

expanding (5) to conduct a simultaneous multivariate analysis of all the potential confounding variables in Tables 7 and 8. We rejected this approach as being impractical and excessively complex in that it would necessitate adding 42 terms to the 6 terms already in (5) (i.e., 7 additional variables $\times$ 2 time periods $\times$ 3 groups = 42). Moreover, such an approach would tend to introduce considerable estimation error into the analysis. Virtually all of the variables in Tables 7 and 8 (except the interest rate variable) are estimated from individual firm time-series data. In many cases, the number of time-series data points underlying these estimates is relatively small, resulting in large standard errors. Comparing group or time-period averages as we do in Tables 7 and 8 helps to minimize the sampling (estimation) error problems that would arise from using firm-level estimates in a multivariate regression (analysis of covariance).

References

Abuaf, N., and P. Jorion. Purchasing Power Parity in the Long Run. *Journal of Finance* (March 1990), 157–174.

Aggrawal, R. FASB No. 8 and Reported Results of Multinational Operations: Hazard for Managers and Investors. *Journal of Accounting, Auditing and Finance* (Spring 1978), 197–216.

Atiase, R. Predisclosure Information, Firm Capitalization and Security Price Behavior around Earnings Announcements. *Journal of Accounting Research* (Spring 1985), 21–36.

Balassa, B. The Purchasing-Power Parity Doctrine: A Reappraisal. *The Journal of Political Economy* (December 1964), 584–596.

Beaver, W., and M. Wolfson. Foreign Currency Translation and Changing Prices in Perfect and Complete Markets. *Journal of Accounting Research* (Autumn 1982, Part II), 528–550.

Belsley, D., E. Kuh, and R. Welsch. *Regression Diagnostics: Identifying Influential Data and Sources of Collinearity.* Wiley, 1980.

Brown, L., P. Griffin, R. Hagerman, and M. Zmijewski. An Evaluation of Alternative Proxies for the Security Market's Expectation of Corporate Earnings. *Journal of Accounting and Economics* (July 1987), 159–194.

Brown, P., G. Foster, and E. Noreen. *Security Analyst Multi-Year Earnings Forecasts and the Capital Market*, Accounting Research Study. American Accounting Association, 1985.

Choi, S., and G. Salamon. External Reporting and Capital Asset Prices. Working paper, Vanderbilt University, 1989.

Collins, D., and S.P. Kothari. An Analysis of Intertemporal and Cross-Sectional Determinants of Earnings Response Coefficients. *Journal of Accounting and Economics* (July 1989), 143–181.

Cornell, W.B., and J.K. Dietrich. The Efficiency of the Market for Foreign Exchange under Floating Exchange Rates. *The Review of Economics and Statistics* 10 (1978), 111–120.

Easton, P., and M. Zmijewski. Cross-Sectional Variation in the Stock Market Response to Accounting Earnings Announcements. *Journal of Accounting and Economics* (July 1989), 117–141.

Elliott, J., and W. Shaw. Write-offs as Accounting Procedures to Manage Perceptions. *Journal of Accounting Research* (Supplement 1988), 91–119.

Financial Accounting Standards Board. Statement of Financial Accounting Standards No. 8, "Accounting for the Translation of Foreign Currency Transactions and Foreign Currency Financial Statements." October 1975.

————. Statement of Financial Accounting Standards No. 52, "Foreign Currency Translation." December 1981.

Foster, G. Quarterly Accounting Data: Time-Series Properties and Predictive-Ability Results. *The Accounting Review* (January 1977), 1–21.

Frenkel, J. Purchasing Power Parity: Doctrinal Perspective and Evidence from the 1920's. *Journal of International Economics* 8 (1978), 169–191.

Freeman, R., and S. Tse. A Nonlinear Model of Security Price Responses to Unexpected Earnings. Working paper, University of Texas at Austin, 1991.

Gailliot, H. Purchasing Power Parity as an Explanation of Long-Term Changes in Exchange Rates. *Journal of Money, Credit, and Banking* 2 (1970), 348–357.

Grant, E. Market Implications of Differential Amounts of Interim Information. *Journal of Accounting Research* (Spring 1980), 255–268.

Griffin, P., and R. Castanias II. Accounting for the Translation of Foreign Currencies: The Effects of *SFAS No. 52* on Equity Analysts. Research Report. Financial Accounting Standards Board, 1987.

Hagerman, R., M. Zmijewski, and P. Shah. The Association between the Magnitude of Quarterly Earnings Forecast Errors and Risk-Adjusted Stock Returns. *Journal of Accounting Research* (Autumn 1984), 526–540.

Holthausen, R., and R. Verrecchia. The Effect of Sequential Information Releases on the Variance of Price Changes in an Intertemporal Multi-Asset Market. *Journal of Accounting Research* (Spring 1988), 82–106.

Kmenta, J. *Elements of Econometrics*. 2nd ed. Macmillan, 1986.

Kormendi, R., and R. Lipe. Earnings Innovations, Earnings Persistence and Stock Returns. *Journal of Business* (July 1987), 323–346.

Lev, B. On the Usefulness of Earnings and Earnings Research: Lessons and Directions from Two Decades of Empirical Research. *Journal of Accounting Research* (Supplement 1989), 153–192.

Lipe, R. The Information Contained in the Components of Earnings. *Journal of Accounting Research* (Supplement 1986), 37–64.

Madura, J. *International Financial Management*. West Publishing, 1989.

Miller, M., and K. Rock. Dividend Policy under Asymmetric Information. *Journal of Finance* (September 1985), 1031–1052.

Neter, J., and W. Wasserman. *Applied Linear Statistical Model*. Richard D. Irwin, 1974.

Nobes, C. A Review of the Translation Debate. *Accounting and Business Research* (Autumn 1980).

Officer, L. Effective Exchange Rates and Price Ratios over the Long Run: A Test of the Purchasing-Power-Parity Theory. *Canadian Journal of Economics* (May 1980), 206–230.

Roll, R. Violations of Purchasing Power Parity and Their Implications for Efficient International Commodity Markets. In *International Finance and Trade*, vol. 1, ed. M. Sarnat and G. Szego. Ballinger, 1979.

Rush, M., and S. Husted. Purchasing Power Parity in the Long Run. *Canadian Journal of Economics* (February 1985), 137–145.

Shapiro, A. *Multinational Financial Management*. Allyn and Bacon, 1986.

Siegel, S. *Nonparametric Statistics for the Behavioral Sciences*. McGraw-Hill, 1956.

White, H. A Heteroscedasticity-Consistent Covariance Matrix Estimator and a Direct Test for Heteroscedasticity. *Econometrica* 48 (1980), 817–838.

Whitt, J. The Long-Run Behavior of the Real Exchange Rate: A Reconsideration. *Journal of Money, Credit and Banking* (February 1992), 72–82.

Discussion of "Noisy Accounting Earnings Signals and Earnings Response Coefficients: The Case of Foreign Currency Accounting"*

JENNIFER L. KAO   *University of Waterloo*

Collins and Salatka (1993) follow a task similar to that of Pincus (1991) and Wasley (1990) in examining how voluntary and mandatory accounting method choice may affect the quality of earnings. The policy under investigation in this paper is foreign currency accounting. The authors argue that, *ceteris paribus,* earnings produced under *SFAS No. 52* are less noisy (garbled) and hence are of higher quality than those produced under *SFAS No. 8*. Relating this claim to theoretical predictions from Holthausen and Verrecchia (1988) (HV) leads to the following hypothesis: earnings response coefficients (ERCs) for multinational companies using local currency as functional currency (MNC-local) would increase following the implementation of *SFAS No. 52*. The results in the paper moderately support this so-called garbling hypothesis.

My remarks focus on two areas: (1) theoretical support for the study and (2) confounding effects and experimental design. These will be discussed in turn.

Theoretical support for the study
Nature of translation gains or losses
A major assumption maintained in the paper is that *SFAS No. 52* substantially improved the quality of reported earnings figures because artificial volatility caused by the inclusion of mostly transitory translation gains or losses in income was eliminated. This assumption is supported by practitioner quotes, survey results, and several studies of exchange rate determination and time-series behavior of exchange movements. In particular, the authors observe that if shocks to exchange rates are not permanent and die out over time, then

* The discussant acknowledges the financial support provided by the Centre for Accounting Research and Education at the University of Waterloo. The comments of Sati Bandyopadhyay, Jack Hughes, Gordon Richardson, and especially Bill Scott are gratefully acknowledged.

Contemporary Accounting Research Vol. 10 No. 1 (Fall 1993) pp 161–166 ©CAAA

162   J.L. Kao

"the future cash flow implications of the translation gains/losses reflected in income under *SFAS No. 8* are problematic."

However, evidence documented in these studies is far from conclusive and does not appear to have completely resolved the issue of whether or not the real exchange rates follow a random walk process. To the extent that fluctuations in exchange rates are closely approximated by a random walk (i.e., shocks are permanent), one might argue that profit variation under *SFAS No. 8* reflects the underlying real exchange movements and hence is price relevant rather than a mere garbling of price-relevant information.

Of course, as the authors pointed out in their response to my comments at the Conference, the exchange rate movements and translation gains or losses may not exhibit similar time-series behavior. But, if that is the case, it might call into question the economic support that the authors draw in the paper.

Effect of nonearnings information

Assume that accounting exposure to currency fluctuations is indeed mostly transitory. It may be preempted or undone, however, by alternative sources of information available to the investors both prior to and contemporaneous with the release of earnings announcements.

For instance, a recent study by Ou and Penman (1989) shows that the accounting reports contain a wide range of nonearnings information that can be used to filter out transitory components of current earnings and help better predict future earnings. Ramakrishnan and Thomas (1991) also demonstrate the potential of incorporating other information to estimate not just the transitory, but also the permanent and price-irrelevant components of reported earnings. Such nonearnings information may affect the relationship between returns and earnings. In particular, a large ERC is, according to Lipe (1990), consistent with inaccurate alternative information in forecasting future earnings. Shores (1990) also finds a negative association between the information content of earnings announcements and the level of interim information.

If the market is efficient, then, holding aside the contractual or political arguments,[1] stock prices at the time of earnings announcements could remain invariant to the choice of foreign currency accounting measurement rules. That is, the ERCs for the MNC-local may not increase significantly following the *SFAS No. 52* pronouncement, as conjectured.

Summary

The point here is that, without a deeper understanding of how the accounting and economic exposure to currency fluctuation given alternative information maps into market prices, it is not intuitive why unrealized exchange gains or losses are mostly transitory, or the earnings response coefficients under *SFAS No. 52* are necessarily higher. In fact, as discussed above, economic arguments can be made to support either the opposite prediction or the null hypothesis. Thus, rather than imposing an ordering over the relative informativeness of

Discussion of "Noisy Accounting Earnings Signals"   163

SFAS No. 8 versus *SFAS No. 52*, it might be more appropriate to conduct a nondirectional test of the null hypothesis.

Confounding effects and experimental design

Changes in macroeconomic trends

Under the assumption that *SFAS No. 52*'s reported earnings are less noisy than those of *SFAS No. 8*, ERCs for MNC-local are shown to increase significantly from the period 1976–1980 to 1983–1987. Although this time contrast is consistent with the inverse relationship between ERCs and the perceived noise in information implied by the HV model, it can just as easily be explained by the changes in macroeconomic trends over the 12 years under investigation.

For instance, if domestic and/or foreign governments had opted in favor of policies that encouraged setting up foreign operations through MNCs in the second sample period, then ERCs could exhibit the change reported even without the alleged accounting policy effect.

Alternatively, the strong market response might have reflected the proliferation of hedging instruments that sprang up following a long period of instability in currency value in the late 1970s. This wide array of sophisticated techniques would allow MNCs to manage more effectively their economic and accounting exposure to exchange risk in the second sample period, compared to the first.

In the paper, the authors use matched-pair design to deal indirectly with these and other time-dependent confounding factors. The idea behind such a control group technique is that both control and treatment firms are homogeneous except for the method of accounting for translation adjustments. This *ceteris paribus* assumption is nonetheless quite tenuous because the control firms, by design, had very little foreign operations and should therefore have remained relatively unaffected by the changes in government policies or risk management techniques. It follows that tests on the time contrast of MNC-local, using the time contrast of control firms as a benchmark, may not rule out macroeconomic factors as competing explanations for the reported shift in ERCs.

Differences in operating environments

Besides the macroeconomic factors discussed above, the *ceteris paribus* assumption can also be challenged on the grounds that the environments in which firms operate might have been different.

For instance, according to Table 8, the control firms and MNC-local registered differential growth rates in not just the *SFAS No. 52* period but also the period from *SFAS No. 8* to *SFAS No. 52*. Moreover, Table 7 reports that, irrespective of the measures used, control firms faced significantly greater prior uncertainty than the treatment firms in the *SFAS No. 8* period. This suggests that the degree of diversification may be different for these two groups of firms. The more certain priors along with the "purportedly" lower quality of earnings signal for the treatment firms, compared to the control firms, should, according to the ERC literature, contribute to considerably smaller ERCs for the treatment firms during the period when *SFAS No. 8* was in effect. However, the firm contrasts between control and treatment firms reported in Table 6 provide only weak support at 11.4 percent significance level. One explanation could be that these firms might have been different in other aspects of operation that mitigate the disparity in both the degree of diversification and quality of earnings.[2]

By comparison, the homogeneity assumption may be relatively easier to accept when the comparison is between MNC-local and MNC-combined. Nonetheless, my confidence in the reported firm contrasts would be increased if the authors could demonstrate the equality of ERCs for MNCs in the *SFAS No. 8* period rather than merely constrain them to be equal.

An implication from the preceding discussion is that matching firms along size and industry dimensions might not have achieved the homogeneity necessary for one to make conclusive statements about either the firm contrasts between MNCs and control firms, the firm contrasts between the two subgroups of MNCs, or the time contrasts for the MNCs.

Selection of MNC-combined

For testing purposes, MNC-combined includes three firms that used U.S. dollars only and nine firms that used a combination of U.S. dollars and local currency as their functional currencies. This definition may pose a problem if the majority of foreign operations carried out by these nine multiple functional currency MNCs were consolidated using local currencies. In this case, MNC-combined is for all intents and purposes MNC-local. Thus, without a detailed analysis, it is difficult to determine whether both MNC-combined and MNC-local should indeed exhibit dissimilar ERC trends and have statistically distinguishable ERCs in the post–*SFAS No. 52* period, as claimed by the authors.

In light of the potential complications described above, it may not be straightforward to sign the time and firm contrasts involving MNC-combined. This in turn could weaken the support these results offer to the main conclusion that only the MNC-local experienced higher ERCs following the implementation of *SFAS No. 52*.

Self-selection bias

Under *SFAS No. 52*, many MNCs can still use the temporal method to translate balance sheet items and include translation adjustments in net income if their reporting currency is used as the functional currency. To identify the functional currency, management is required to take into account a set of indicators provided by the Financial Accounting Standards Board (FASB). However, the application of such guidelines criteria does involve judgement and could sometimes entail ambiguities.

In a recent study, Bartov and Bodnar (1992) suggest that cross-sectional variation in the choice of functional currency is common and can be explained by predictions from positive accounting theory. Specifically, local currency is

Discussion of "Noisy Accounting Earnings Signals"   165

favored by firms to reduce the likelihood of abnormally large positive (negative) currency shock to earnings when their political exposure (the interest coverage) is high (low). Conversely, the U.S. dollar is likely to be chosen by firms with high debt-equity ratios to avoid violating their debt-equity ratio constraint caused by a large translation shock to the owners' equity.

These results imply that the choice of functional currency under *SFAS No. 52* might have been discretionary, reflecting the fundamental differences among MNCs along several dimensions perceived to have economic consequences in the positive accounting literature. Such self-selection bias could have complicated the interpretation of firm contrast between these two groups of MNCs in the *SFAS No. 52* period, as well as the time contrasts of these firms relative to the control group.

Summary
The authors present results in support of the hypothesis that ERCs increased for the MNC-local over the two sample periods. What is not so evident is whether the observed trends are attributable to foreign currency accounting alone. Growth is offered as an alternative explanation in the paper, but that is clearly not the only one. Part of the difficulty lies in the dilemma posed by the use of matched-pair experimental design. On the one hand, it seems necessary to use the control group technique to isolate the effect of accounting standard changes on ERCs. Yet, on the other hand, one might argue that tests that fail to address many potentially important (granted difficult to control for) confounding variables may present an even greater challenge for proper inferences to be drawn.

Based on the discussion in this and the preceding sections, it appears that, in addition to the extent of noise contained in the earnings signals, the ability of market to process the signals produced by different accounting measurement rules, the nature of underlying operating and reporting environments facing firms, and/or the characteristics of firm-specific variables may have also contributed to the observed shifts in ERCs. In the absence of a comprehensive theory on the accounting method choice, it might be more appropriate to view the paper as a descriptive study that documents the differential change in ERCs following a mandated accounting policy change for three groups of firms under investigation.

Endnotes
1 The consequence of relaxing this assumption is considered in the next section.
2 Alternatively, it might also suggest that the quality of earnings might not have been lower for the treatment firms, as the authors hypothesize.

References
Bartov, E., and G. Bodnar. Determinants of the Choice between Foreign Currency and Dollar as Functional Currency by Multinational Firms. University of Rochester, 1992.

166   J.L. Kao

Collins D.W. and W.K. Salatka. Noisy Accounting Earnings Signals and Earnings Response Coefficients: The Case of Foreign Currency Accounting. *Contemporary Accounting Research* (Fall 1993), 119–159.

Holthausen, R. and R. Verrecchia. The Effect of Sequential Information Releases on the Variance of Price Changes in an Intertemporal Multi-Asset Market. *Journal of Accounting Research* (Spring 1988), 82–106.

Lipe, R. The Relation between Stock Returns and Accounting Earnings Given Alternative Information. *The Accounting Review* (January 1990), 49–71.

Ou, J.A., and S.H. Penman. Accounting Measurement, Price-Earnings Ratio, and the Information Content of Security Prices. *Journal of Accounting Research* (Supplement 1989), 111–144.

Pincus, M. Accounting Methods and Differential Stock Market Response to the Announcement of Earnings. Washington University, 1991.

Ramakrishnan, R.T.S. and J.K. Thomas. Valuation of Permanent, Transitory and Price-Irrelevant Components of Reported Earnings. Columbia University, 1991.

Shores, D. The Association between Interim Information and Security Returns Surrounding Earnings Announcements. *Journal of Accounting Research* (Spring 1990), 164–181.

Wasley, C. Mandatory Accounting Changes and Earnings Response Coefficients: SFAS No. 2 and Accounting for Research and Development Costs. Washington University, 1990.

Discussion of "Noisy Accounting Earnings Signals and Earnings Response Coefficients: The Case of Foreign Currency Accounting"

PAUL A. GRIFFIN   *University of California, Davis*

This paper by Collins and Salatka (hereafter C&S) investigates whether the relation between stock returns and accounting earnings differs for firms substantially affected by the Financial Accounting Standards Board (FASB) *Statement of Financial Accounting Standards (SFAS)No. 8*, and whether the relation changed as those firms implemented FASB *SFAS No. 52* following its issuance in 1981. The approach taken uses a firm's earnings response coefficient (ERC) to examine the effects of the accounting rule change, where the ERC is defined as the responsiveness of a firm's (abnormal) stock return to unexpected (quarterly) earnings.

Just as the earlier abnormal performance index studies (e.g., Ball and Brown 1968) and cross-sectional valuation methodologies (e.g., Litzenberger and Rao 1971) were applied to evaluate issues of accounting policy, the C&S approach is a natural and logical application of the use of the ERC. However, the innovative nature of the paper also raises many thorny issues in both the theoretical and empirical domains. Some are specific to the approach taken by the authors, some apply to ERC research in general, and yet others pertain broadly to the application of the quasi-experimental research approach based on samples of pre-post and experimental-control companies.

I present my views as follows. The next section comments on the theoretical specification of the earnings-return relation. Following this is a discussion on the choice of the accounting issue investigated. Then I examine the research design and focus on several issues of econometrics, including the potential implications of measurement error. The final section summarizes my remarks.

Specification of the earnings-return relation

To specify an ERC, C&S adopt a model of returns that links unexpected earnings (UE_{it}) to abnormal returns (UR_{it}), modeled linearly as $UR_{it} = a + bUE_{it} + e_{it}$. A firm's stock price just before an information release is based on a one-period capital asset pricing model (Choi and Salamon 1989, Holthausen and

Contemporary Accounting Research Vol. 10 No. 1 (Fall 1993) pp 167–178 ©CAAA

168   P.A. Griffin

Verrecchia 1988) that assumes a probability distribution over the uncertain but measurement-error-free earnings or cash flow variable $f(X_{it})$. C&S then compare this stock price with a revised stock price immediately following an information release Y_{it}. The revision is based on the posterior density function $f(X_{it}|Y_{it})$, where $Y_{it} = X_{it} + \epsilon_{it}$ and the likelihood function $f(Y_{it}|X_{it})$ reflects uncertainty or error in the mapping from the firm's underlying cash flow to an information release about that cash flow. A single information release about cash flow—namely, reported earnings—is assumed. The result is a theoretical ERC whose maximum is 1 and whose partial derivatives with respect to $var(X_{it})$ and $var(\epsilon_{it})$ are positive and negative, respectively. *Ceteris paribus*, assuming $var(\epsilon_{it} |SFAS\ No.\ 8\ earnings) > var(\epsilon_{it} |non-SFAS\ No.\ 8\ earnings)$, C&S predict that ERC|non-*SFAS No. 8* earnings > ERC|*SFAS No. 8* earnings. Similarly, for $var(e_{it} |SFAS\ No.\ 8\ earnings) > var(\epsilon_{it} |SFAS\ No.\ 52\ earnings)$, C&S predict ERC|*SFAS No. 52* earnings > ERC|*SFAS No. 8* earnings.[1]

How well does this relation capture those factors that affect the ERC? To be sure, except in the one-period setting as modeled by C&S, no one would suggest that the ERC is bounded from above at 1. Several studies have reported empirical ERCs of more than 1 in both reverse and nonreverse regression contexts (e.g., Beaver, Lambert, and Ryan 1987). Others have further suggested that the number of upper bounds on the theoretical magnitude of the ERC is without limit due, for instance, to the dependency of the ERC on an assumed pricing relation (e.g., Easton and Zmijewski 1989) and the properties of the earnings process (e.g., Lang 1991).

By comparing C&S's specification of the ERC to others found in the literature, I find that several additional factors are not included at the specification stage, which in the context of this (or any other) study of a change in accounting policy may be relevant.[2] These include the impact of temporal changes in the risk free-rate, R_f ($\delta ERC / \delta R_f < 0$), changes in the market risk premium, $\lambda = R_m - R_f < 0$ ($\delta ERC / \delta \lambda < 0$), and cross-sectional differences or temporal changes in other value-relevant parameters which might naturally occur in alternative valuation settings (e.g., the earnings capitalization rate, ρ ($\delta ERC/\delta \rho < 0$) (e.g., Miller and Modigliani 1961), the ratio of market value to book value, μ ($\delta ERC/\delta \mu < 0$) (e.g., Ohlson 1991), and growth opportunities in excess of normal return, $\pi - \rho(\delta ERC / \delta \pi - \rho > 0$).[3]

For instance, if one of the hypothesized effects of a change from *SFAS No. 8* to *SFAS No. 52* is a decrease in the underlying earnings capitalization rate (or similar variable such as the CAPM expected rate of return), then it follows naturally that such variable should be considered in the theoretical analysis. To exclude such at the conceptual level discounts the importance of such variable. I spotlight the earnings capitalization rate (or its reciprocal, as a capitalization multiple) because the Griffin and Castanias (1987) survey of the equity analysts suggests—as do C&S—that it is here that the market effects if any of the switch to *SFAS No. 52* might be revealed. Thus, in my view, an appropriate structure for ERC specification would include an underlying earnings capitalization rate (or similar variable, depending on the asset pricing model) and

Discussion of "Noisy Accounting Earnings Signals"   169

recognition that such rate, or change in rate, functionally depends on the accounting standard or change in standard.

Another variable to consider explicitly at the theoretical level would be the degree of persistence of earnings (e.g., Beaver, Lambert, and Morse 1980, Miller and Rock 1985, Kormendi and Lipe 1987). One straightforward approach would consider earnings changes as generated by a first-order, moving average (ARIMA 0,1,1) process parameterized by θ, where the lower and closer to 0 the θ parameter, the more persistent the series. Presumably, for a non–U. S. functional currency firm, *SFAS No. 52* reported earnings should have a higher persistency coefficient θ than *SFAS No. 8* earnings because earnings changes for the former series are more likely to be more permanent than transitory.

Such an earnings process and rudimentary asset pricing model may be stated as follows.[4]

$x_t = x_{t-1} + a_t - \theta a_{t-1};$	Underlying earnings or cash flow
$X_t = x_t + \epsilon_t;$	Error in measuring x_t
$P_t = E(x_t).[1 \div \rho_t + \gamma(\rho)_t];$ and	Asset pricing
$\Delta P_t = \alpha_t + ERC.\Delta X_t + v_t$	ERC regression

where ϵ_t, a_t, v_t and $\gamma(\rho)_t$ are random variables with 0 mean and constant variance. I therefore specify an underlying earnings or cash flow–generating process, $x_t = x_{t-1} + a_t - \theta a_{t-1}$, a measurement error model for reported earnings, $X_t = x_t + \epsilon_t$, and a simple asset pricing equation, $P_t = E(x_t).[1 \div \rho_t + \gamma(\rho)_t]$, where E is the expectation operator.

It is reasonably straightforward to show that $\Delta ERC/\Delta \theta < 0$, $\Delta ERC/\Delta \sigma(\epsilon) < 0$ $\Delta ERC / \Delta \rho < 0$, and $\Delta ERC/\Delta \sigma(\gamma) < 0$. The change to *SFAS No. 52* could therefore be hypothesized to increase ERC for at least four basic reasons. First, under the new standard, the expectation would be that earnings is more persistent under the new standard and thus $\Delta \theta < 0$. Second, reported earnings under *SFAS No. 52* should contain less error, that is, $\Delta \sigma(\epsilon) < 0$. Third, investors could decrease their capitalization rates in response to the new standard, namely, $\Delta \rho < 0$, and, fourth, investors may be less uncertain about those earnings capitalization rates, hence $\Delta \sigma(\gamma) < 0$. However, if any one of the above-mentioned variables potentially changes for reasons other than the change to *SFAS No. 52* (which empirically may have been the case as note 3 suggests), then the choice of an appropriate experimental design also becomes paramount, regardless of the model specification.

Another aspect of the theoretical domain that may give rise to testable predictions relates to the length of the holding period for returns and earnings. C&S concentrate on two-day event windows around the quarterly earnings announcements. But what if the effects are captured over longer intervals?[5] For example, the market may view the accounting choice simply as an accrual accounting issue. In this situation, the cash flows are unchanged and should

170   P.A. Griffin

eventually be revealed by the reporting process, though not necessarily in full, at each earnings announcement or other information release. As such, the hypothesis would be that the longer the holding period, the less likely that the accounting choice affects the ERC. On the other hand, an alternative hypothesis might be that if differences or changes in the ERC persist over the longer holding periods, then the standard most likely has real rather than purely cosmetic effects (ruling out other factors, of course). In terms of the previous model, however, this would suggest that ϵ_{it} (the error in reported earnings) is not entirely independent of a_{it} (the error in underlying earnings or cash flows) and the theoretical structure above would need to be respecified to incorporate such nonindependence.

Choice of accounting issue

The appropriate choice of accounting rule is an important consideration in the application of the ERC methodology. The accounting issue and its effects should a priori be sufficiently clear so that the experimental design is not swamped by the effects of type I and type II error. In other words, if the market in fact responded to *SFAS No. 52*, then the ERC results should indicate that and vice versa. Two considerations come to mind.

The first concerns the strength of the rationale for the hypotheses. Though empirical results based on affected companies (e.g., Nance and Roemmich 1983; Hosseini and Aggarwal 1983) indicate that *SFAS No. 52* earnings did in fact produce the smallest variability of reported earnings relative to other translation techniques, the link to stock market variables of a shift to *SFAS No. 52* is less clear cut. The Griffin and Castanias survey, for example, while spotlighting market capitalization rates as a potential explanatory variable, suggests that the market effects were quite subtle and, from the viewpoints of the survey respondents, were jointly affected by management decisions such as balance sheet hedging to avoid earnings fluctuations (Evans and Doupnik 1986). Economic factors in other markets, including the foreign exchange market, were also mentioned as conditioning the market's interpretation of the firm's accounting choice. The survey further reminds us that the analyst community was less than fully convinced that *SFAS No. 52* caused substantive market effects. Though some analysts were quite sure that the market applied a higher capitalization multiple to *SFAS No. 52* earnings, others were less certain and argued that any such effects would be unlikely to be captured by short-term movements in stock prices. Given these kinds of potentially confounding factors, the ability of the ERC approach to detect changes in market behavior induced by the accounting standard may be limited. Dealing formally and empirically with such potentially confounding factors presents a major research challenge and opportunity.

A second consideration relates to the Beaver and Wolfson (1982; 1984) analysis of foreign currency accounting, which further spotlights the complexity of testing for a market response to changes in foreign currency accounting. They argue that investors in perfect and complete markets would anticipate all translation gains and losses, fully reflecting these amounts in market rates of return. To exclude the gains and losses from earnings increases earnings variability and by implication decreases the ERC. However, the impact of changes in exchange rates on earnings must consider expected and unexpected rate changes, and it may well be the latter that dominated during the transition in accounting rule. For example, with respect to this period, the evidence indicates an erosion of the forecasting abilities of professional exchange forecasters since 1978 (Levich 1983) and a sharp deterioration in forecasting ability in 1982 (Jaycobs 1984). Thus, C&S's view (C&S, note 1) that "the extent to which we can rely on the predictions derived from the Beaver and Wolfson analysis...may be limited..." has merit. Interesting questions, nonetheless, manifest themselves in this issue. For instance, how do imperfections in the foreign exchange market and the forecasting abilities of exchange rate forecasters affect the estimation of the ERC?

Overall, these issues suggest that the market impact of the change in foreign currency accounting was probably quite small and cross-sectionally heterogeneous. So a key issue is whether the ERC approach has sufficient diagnostic ability to trace these foreign currency effects given the other possible influences.

Research design
C&S use an analysis of covariance approach, examining differences between multinational and nonmultinational firms across a *SFAS No. 8* period (1976-1Q to 1980-4Q) and *SFAS No. 52* period (1983-4Q to 1987-4Q). Multinational firms are split into U.S. dollar and non–U.S. dollar functional currency firms. Dummy variables or groups of dummy variables test for cross-sectional and intertemporal differences among the multinational and control groups. Systematic influences on ERC from other than foreign currency effects are held constant by use of a size- and industry-matched control group.

Rather than include the nonaccounting variables directly in the analysis of covariance model, the authors examine the similarity of the groups based on proxies for factors potentially affecting the ERC (e.g., prior period uncertainty, earnings persistence, beta risk, growth opportunity, and risk-free interest rate). Their univariate profile analyses of the other factors partially explain the ERCs cross-sectionally and temporally, and often in a direction consistent with the hypothesized effects of the foreign currency standards. This raises an issue of interpretation. For example, the sample data suggest that prior period uncertainty is greater for the nonmultinational sample in both periods (consistent with a higher ERC for the nonmultinationals) and increases for the multinationals from the *SFAS No. 8* to the *SFAS No. 52* period (consistent with an increase in the ERC). Thus, the predicted and observed directional effects on the ERC of differences and changes in $\sigma(a_t)$ are the same as those for the foreign currency standard. Similarly, the growth factor—as proxied by the market-to-book value of equity—increases from the *SFAS No. 8* to the *SFAS No. 52* period for both groups. Although we do not know how much foreign cur-

172   P.A. Griffin

rency accounting has to do with this, reasons other than foreign currency accounting may play a role given that the median increase across the two groups remains mostly unchanged (e.g., $1.336 \div 0.979 = 1.364$ and $1.869 \div 1.384 = 1.350$ for nonmultinationals and multinationals-local: C&S, Table 8).

One reason for an increase in the market-to-book ratio is inflation, whose average annual rate decreased from 9.264 percent during 1976 to 1980 to 3.412 percent during 1983 to 1987 (Ibbotson Associates 1991). These data are shown in Figure 1 (and note 3). Because reported accounting values are mostly unaffected, a decline in the rate of inflation is salutary for the market-to-book ratio. Nominal risk-free interest rates also decreased during this period. Thus, the authors' ex post analysis of nonforeign currency factors that potentially explain the ERC offers an alternative explanation of the basic results. Whether those same conclusions would hold if such factors were jointly analyzed in the empirical analysis is unclear because the present approach does not take into account the associations among such factors and across the foreign currency variables themselves.

Other variables to consider are the characteristics of the accounting change, such as the impact of *SFAS No. 52* on prior period earnings and the magnitude of (or changes in) the cumulative foreign currency adjustment account. To the extent that these characteristics are uncorrelated with the more general economic factors, they can provide a useful means to highlight the accounting effects, if any. Hence, an alternative approach would be to analyze intertemporally (and cross-sectionally) a sample of affected companies (e.g., non– U.S. dollar functional currency firms), where the predicted effects on ERC are derived in part from the characteristics of the accounting change.

Also, I would examine the impact of the change on ERCs during period of transition,[6] where the ERC is estimated cross-sectionally each quarter relative to the first quarter that a company disclosed results under the new standard (or using pooled data for the transition period). This approach has the advantage that it recognizes the learning period associated with the interpretation of results under the new accounting standard, which is a period when it may be having the most influence on market behavior.[7]

Econometric issues
As with other papers in this area, the econometric issues are substantial and particularly complex with regard to measurement error, for it is differential error across firms and over time that is one basis for the hypothesized differences or changes in the ERC. Measurement error must be addressed, of course, but the use of techniques to reduce the bias in regression coefficients (e.g., by grouping or instrumental variables) may well obscure or eliminate the effects that the experiment seeks to identify. Moreover, not all change in measurement error may be attributable to the accounting choice being studied, and so the researcher faces a difficult task.

Though none is entirely satisfactory, two possible suggestions for future research come to mind. First, the abnormal return results could be rerun over

Discussion of "Noisy Accounting Earnings Signals" 173

Figure 1 Basic series: 1976–1987

Panel A: Return on government securities

Annualized rate of return

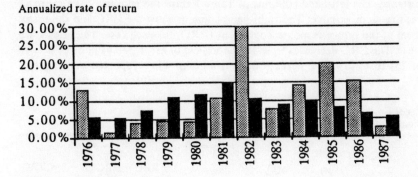

■ U.S. Treasury bills
▓ U.S.U.S. intermediate term bonds

Panel B: Common stock index and inflation

Common stock index (1975 = 100)   Annualized rate of return

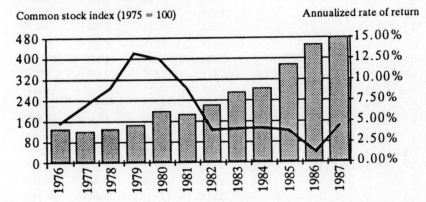

Data from Ibbotson Associates, Inc. *Stocks, Bonds, Bills, and Inflation: 1991.* Total
return series used for Treasury bills, intermediate term government bonds, and common stock. Inflation based on U. S. consumer price index.

a nonannouncement period. Specifically, I would regress two-day abnormal
returns for several nonoverlapping intervals around each announcement date
(e.g., −10 to −9, −8 to −7, and so on) on unexpected earnings. Such results
might help calibrate the reported results based on abnormal returns over days
−1 and 0 so that the influences of the general variables relative to the
accounting effects are better understood.

A second possibility would use simulation to focus on the effects of measurement error. I show some preliminary results in Table 1, where the model

174   P.A. Griffin

structure is adapted from Beaver et al. (1980) and Beaver et al. (1987). The random variables ϵ_t, a_t, and $\gamma(\rho)_t$ are regenerated within each simulation and assume a uniform distribution for each variable with zero mean and constant variance. The left-hand columns of Table 1 show the choices of the range of each random variable. The right-hand columns show the ERC and the reciprocal of the return response coefficient (RRC) for each case. The effects are clear. The ERC decreases from its theoretical or error free value ($1 \div \rho = 10$ or 15) to as low as 2 percent of that amount when reported earnings are

TABLE 1
Simulated earnings response and return response coefficients

				$1 \div \rho = 10$		$1 \div \rho = 15$	
θ	ϵ_t	a_t	$\gamma(\rho)_t$	ERC	1 = RRC	ERC	1 = RRC
0	0	1	0	10.000	10.000	15.000	15.000
0.2	0	1	0	7.679	7.985	11.546	12.007
0.4	0	1	0	5.122	5.919	7.748	8.983
0	0.5	1	0	6.573	9.942	9.910	15.110
0.2	0.5	1	0	5.174	8.066	7.731	11.945
0.4	0.5	1	0	3.682	6.018	5.428	9.048
0	1	1	0	3.496	9.571	5.007	14.783
0.2	1	1	0	2.595	7.796	3.959	12.010
0.4	1	1	0	1.879	5.841	2.844	9.047
0	2	1	0	1.115	9.927	1.663	15.193
0.2	2	1	0	0.877	8.473	1.307	12.411
0.4	2	1	0	0.697	5.590	1.054	8.438
0	4	1	0	0.308	10.198	0.432	18.290
0.2	4	1	0	0.233	9.085	0.377	12.816
0.4	4	1	0	0.194	5.817	0.293	8.779
0	1	1	1	3.040	14.509	4.958	16.709
0.2	1	1	1	2.514	12.207	3.468	14.544
0.4	1	1	1	1.688	12.569	2.772	14.764
0	4	1	1	0.351	13.000	0.497	17.368
0.2	4	1	1	0.237	15.184	0.365	17.448
0.4	4	1	1	0.208	11.383	0.293	15.218

Underlying earnings model: $x_t = x_{t-1} + a_t - \theta a_{t-1}$; Measurement error model: $X_t = x_t + \epsilon_t$; Pricing equation: $P_t = E(x_t).[1 \div \rho_t + \gamma(\rho)_t]$; ERC regression: $\Delta P_t = \alpha_t + \text{ERC}.\Delta X_t + u_t$; RRC regression: ΔX_t 5 α_t + RRC.$\Delta P_t + w_t$; where ϵ_t, a_t, and $\gamma(\rho)_t$ are random variables with 0 mean and constant variance.

Starting values for each simulation: Underlying measurement error-free earnings, $x_0 = 5$; market capitalization, $1 \div \rho = 10$ or 15; number of trials per simulation/regression, n = 500; number of simulated regressions per row value mean = 10.

Random variables regenerated with each simulation and assumed distributed uniformly with 0 mean and constant variance. The numbers for ϵ_t, a_t, and $\gamma(\rho)_t$ shown in the table represent the range for each random variable.

assumed to contain error uniformly distributed over the range $4 = -2$ to 2 (e.g., reported earnings at $t = 0$ would thus be uniformly distributed over the range $5-2 = 3$ to $5 + 2 = 7$). Table 1 also shows the effect of increasing the coefficient θ in a regression context, which is to reduce further the ERC. For instance, with earnings error distributed over range $4 = -2$ to 2, the ERC whose theoretical value is 10 drops from 0.308 to 0.194. This model, however, does not provide sufficient realism as a benchmark for the C&S results. But to the extent that others may, then differences between simulated and empirical results may offer fresh insights into the relative effects of specification error versus measurement error in defining an appropriate structure for estimating the ERC.

Summary

This study represents an initial application of the ERC to the evaluation of an accounting policy. The approach offers promise, but the way is fraught with many challenges to research design, especially in the context of the change in foreign currency accounting given that the effects are not clearly manifested in market behavior. C&S have done much to alleviate many of the methodological concerns. But others abound, given the constraints of their experiment, none the least of which is to control explicitly for other systematic influences on the ERC. Further, some aspects may be partially obscuring the very effects that they seek to identify. In closing, we should recall that Charles Darwin sat on his theory of evolution for almost 20 years, reworking the results and gathering additional evidence, before it was published, always afraid that he would be branded a traitor, a heretic, and worse. C&S should fear not, and I am sure that future research will give this work its due recognition.

Endnotes

1 The authors base the signs of the hypotheses mostly on empirical and survey evidence. I comment further on this in a later section on the choice of accounting issue.
2 Many of these factors, however, are considered in the C&S paper in their section on confounding factors.
3 The annualized measures presented in Appendix 1 suggest that value-relevant factors such as those mentioned were probably not temporal constants for the period under consideration. Source: *Stocks, Bonds, Bills, and Inflation: 1991 Yearbook* (Ibbotson Associates, Inc., 1991), 37. See also Figure 1.
4 This model is similar, though not identical, to that outlined in Beaver et al. (1980) and Beaver et al. (1987). In a later section, I simulate the model to examine the likely effects of measurement error on the relation between earnings changes and price changes.
5 Evidence on the behavior of financial analysts does not rule out this possibility, in that at the moment of an earnings announcement, analysts seldom have the time to analyze complex accounting issues to the fullest extent possible. They normally respond quickly to the earnings announcement and then follow up later over a number of days. Their follow up normally includes a detailed study of the financial statements as well as requests for further information and clarifications from management.

176   P.A. Griffin

Appendix 1

Return/% change	1976	1977	1978	1979	1980	1981	1982	1983	1984	1985	1986	1987
Treasury bills	5.08	5.12	7.18	10.38	11.24	14.71	10.54	8.80	9.85	7.72	6.16	5.47
Int. govt. bonds	12.87	1.41	3.49	4.09	3.91	9.45	29.10	7.41	14.02	20.33	15.14	2.90
S&P 500 stocks	23.84	-7.18	6.56	18.44	32.42	-4.91	21.41	22.51	6.27	32.16	18.47	5.23
Inflation	4.81	6.77	9.03	13.31	12.40	8.94	3.87	3.80	3.95	3.77	1.13	4.41

Discussion of "Noisy Accounting Earnings Signals"   177

6 The period of transition covers the period of adjustment of analysts and other users to information under a new accounting rule. This period may be defined by the standard itself or empirically based on the "abnormality" of analyst or market behavior.
7 For an analysis of the impact on earnings response coefficients of *SFAS No. 87* on pension accounting during the transition period, and a discussion of the advantages of aligning the data in event rather than calendar time, see Cerf (1991).

References
Ball, R., and P. Brown. An Empirical Evaluation of Accounting Income Numbers. *Journal of Accounting Research* (Autumn 1968), 159–178.
Beaver, W., R. Lambert, and D. Morse. The Information Content of Security Prices. *Journal of Accounting and Economics* (March 1980), 3–28.
Beaver, W., R. Lambert, and S. Ryan. The Information Content of Security Prices: A Second Look. *Journal of Accounting and Economics* (July 1987), 139–157.
Beaver, W., and M. Wolfson. Foreign Currency Translation and Changing Prices in Perfect and Complete Markets. *Journal of Accounting Research* (Autumn 1982, Pt.II), 528–550.
———. Foreign Currency Translation Gains and Losses: What Effect Do They Have and What Do They Mean?" *Financial Analysts Journal* (March/April 1984), 28–36.
Cerf, D. A Study of the Intertemporal Variation in Earnings Response Coefficients: The Case of the Mandated Change in Accounting Rules to SFAS #87 on Pensions. Doctoral dissertation, University of California, Davis, 1991.
Choi, S., and G. Salamon. External Reporting and Capital Asset Prices. Working paper, Vanderbilt University, 1989.
Collins, D., and W. Salatka. Noisy Accounting Earnings Signals and Earnings Response Coefficients: The Case of Foreign Currency Accounting. *Contemporary Accounting Research* (Fall 1993), 119–159.
Easton, P., and M. Zmijewski. Cross-Sectional Variation in the Stock Market Response to Accounting Earnings Announcements. *Journal of Accounting and Economics* (July 1989), 117–141.
Evans, T., and T. Doupnik. FASB Research Report, *Foreign Exchange Risk Management Under Statement 52*. FASB, 1986.
Griffin, P., and R. Castanias, II. FASB Research Report, *Accounting for the Translation of Foreign Currencies: The Effects of Statement 52 on Equity Analysts*. FASB, 1987.
Holthausen, R., and R. Verrecchia. The Effect of Sequential Information Releases on the Variance of Price Changes in an Intertemporal Multi-Asset Market. *Journal of Accounting Research* (Spring 1988), 82–106.
Hosseini, A., and R. Aggarwal. Evaluating Foreign Affiliates: The Impact of Alternative Foreign Currency Translation Methods. *The International Journal of Accounting Education and Research* (Fall 1983), 65–87.
Ibbotson Associates, Inc. *Stocks, Bonds, Bills, and Inflation: 1991 Yearbook*. Ibbotson Associates, Inc., 1991.
Jaycobs, R. Getting It Right at the Right Time. *Euromoney* (August 1984), 148–154.
Kormendi, R., and R. Lipe. Earnings Innovations, Earnings Persistence, and Stock Returns. *Journal of Business* (July 1987), 323–346.
Lang, M. Time-Varying Stock Price Response to Earnings Induced by Uncertainty About the Time-Series Process of Earnings. *Journal of Accounting Research* (Autumn 1991), 229–257.
Levich, R. Currency Forecasters Lose Their Way. *Euromoney* (August 1983), 140–147.
Litzenberger, R., and C. Rao. Estimates of the Marginal Rate of Time Preference and Average Risk Aversion of Investors in Electric Utility Shares: 1960–66. *The Bell Journal of Economics and Management Science* (Spring 1971), 265–277.

178   P.A. Griffin

Miller, M., and K. Rock. Dividend Policy under Asymmetric Information. *Journal of Finance* (September 1985), 1031–1052.

Miller, M., and M. Modigliani. Dividend Policy, Growth, and the Valuation of Shares. *Journal of Business* (October 1961), 411–433.

Nance, J., and R. Roemmich. Financial Statement Impact of Foreign Currency Translation Alternatives. *The International Journal of Accounting Education and Research* (Fall 1983), 89–113.

Ohlson, J. A. The Theory of Value and Earnings, and an Introduction to the Ball–Brown Analysis. *Contemporary Accounting Research* (Fall 1991), 1–19.

Part V
Geographic Segment Reporting by US Multinationals

[20]

Journal of Accounting Research
Vol. 28 No. 2 Autumn 1990
Printed in U.S.A.

Research Reports

The Predictive Ability of Geographic Segment Disclosures

RAMJI BALAKRISHNAN,* TREVOR S. HARRIS,† AND
PRADYOT K. SEN††

1. Introduction

This research is aimed at evaluating whether geographically segmented (*GEOG*) data provide incremental information about the earnings process. Previous research on segment data has focused on the relevance of line-of-business (*LOB*) segment reports.[1] But, to our knowledge, no similar research has been done on the *GEOG* disclosures which have been required since the introduction of *Statement of Financial Accounting Standard (SFAS) No. 14*.

The issue of providing segment disclosures has renewed significance because the SEC has been considering the extension of segment disclosures (both *LOB* and *GEOG*) to all interim financial statements (Ernst and Whinney [1985] and Craven and Feller [1984]).[2] In addition, segment

* University of Iowa; † Columbia University; †† University of California, Berkeley. We are grateful to Dan Collins, Jim Ohlson, and the reviewer for comments made on this paper. This research was partially supported by the Faculty Research Fund, Graduate School of Business, Columbia University.

[1] Kinney [1971] and Collins [1976] found that forecasts based on *LOB* data were more accurate than forecasts based on consolidated (*CONS*) data. *LOB* data have also been shown to be relevant to the pricing of securities (e.g., Kinney [1972] and Ajinkya [1980]) and related assessments of risk (Kinney [1972] and Collins and Simonds [1979]). Finally, Baldwin [1984] found that *LOB* data were useful for analysts' forecasts.

[2] In 1988 the SEC indefinitely postponed a decision on segment disclosures in interim reporting.

disclosure requirements have been a major barrier to listings on U.S. stock exchanges by some foreign firms.[3]

GEOG data are usually disclosed only in annual reports, so it is difficult to control for potential confounding variables in price or return association studies. Consequently, we evaluate the specific contribution of sales and income *GEOG* data by estimating their predictive ability, in the spirit of Kinney [1971] and Collins [1976].[4] Reported *GEOG* data (in U.S. dollars) are based on the local currency data translated at some exchange rate. Consequently, when using the *GEOG* data to forecast their *CONS* equivalents, we employ country- (or region-) specific expected exchange rate changes together with any expected growth rates. The predictive ability of these *GEOG*-based forecasts is then compared with the predictive ability of *CONS* forecasts (based on *CONS* data only).

Two sets of *GEOG* predictions are used in the predictive accuracy tests. To control for errors in predicting exchange rates and regional growth, the first set of predictions assumes perfect foresight (*PF*) and uses the realized values of the macroeconomic variables. The results of these tests indicate that, relative to *CONS* data, *GEOG* data can enhance the prediction of income and, to a lesser extent, sales. The second set of tests relaxes the *PF* assumption and uses various forecasts of the exchange rate and growth variables; in most cases this additional forecast error clearly dilutes *GEOG*'s predictive ability.

Our sample period spans the introduction of *Statement of Financial Accounting Standard No. 52 (SFAS 52)* which applies to foreign currency translation. One argument for the introduction of *SFAS 52* was that it reduced the variability of reported *CONS* income. If so, *CONS* forecasts will be more accurate in the post-*SFAS 52* period. When we repeated the analysis using only post-*SFAS 52* data, we found that *SFAS 52* marginally improves the relative predictive ability of the consolidated data.

Section 2 of the paper develops the hypothesis and models to be tested. Section 3 describes the data and test statistics. The results of the full sample tests are reported and discussed in section 4. Tests examining the robustness of the results are discussed in section 5.

---

[3] For example, Japanese companies avoided listing on U.S. exchanges from 1982 to October 1987. Papers made available to one of the authors by Mr. Stephen A. Grant of Sullivan and Cromwell reveal that a primary reason for this avoidance was concern about *GEOG* disclosures. Once these concerns were allayed, the Keidanren reduced its objections and in turn the Japanese Ministry of Finance initiated segment disclosure requirements as of April 1, 1987. The first new Japanese listing in the United States was by Tokio Marine and Fire Insurance Company in October 1987.

[4] Freeman, Ohlson, and Penman [1982] suggest that return on equity (*ROE*) more accurately predicts next period's earnings than do simple random walk models. Since *GEOG* data on assets are disclosed, we evaluated the predictive accuracy of *GEOG* data for forecasts of return on assets as a proxy for *ROE*. The results were essentially the same as those for earnings and sales and can be obtained from the authors.

2. *Hypothesis and Models to Be Tested*

Freeman, Ohlson, and Penman [1982, p. 640] argue that "forecasts of future (expected) earnings are based on an information set which is potentially much larger than that of current and past earnings." We are primarily interested in evaluating whether *GEOG* data can be considered as a relevant part of this larger information set.

While segment data are trivially finer than consolidated data (one can always aggregate the segment income to get consolidated income), the fineness criterion is not sufficient to justify the relevance of *GEOG* data. If the *GEOG* data are reported with error, with the errors offsetting in the aggregate, it can be shown that forecasts using these data need not be as good as forecasts using consolidated data.[5] The reason is that forecasts which use the expanded segment data potentially compound the error in the additional information during the translation process.

Various parties have suggested that the *GEOG* data contain too much error to be informative. Bavishi and Wyman [1980, p. 163] suggest that the way companies classify and report the geographic segments implies that "present disclosures are almost useless." Also, anecdotal evidence suggests that companies may choose to garble their *GEOG* disclosures. For example, managers distort the disclosures to prevent "dumping" or tax disputes resulting from international transfer-pricing questions.[6] This is illustrated, anecdotally, in a September 1985 letter from Stephen A. Grant of Sullivan and Cromwell, to Japan's Keidanren (Chamber of Commerce) which encourages them to recommend the adoption of segment reporting.[7] Mr. Grant states on the second page of his letter: "Industry segment reporting does not require disclosing profits by individual products, and U.S. companies have shown the way in combining different operations into broad segments which do not disclose sensitive information. Geographic segment reporting does not require showing profits in different areas that can be compared when products are manufactured in Japan and sold abroad." Given the likelihood that *GEOG* data are measured with error, it is an empirical matter whether any such errors render the *GEOG* data irrelevant for forecasting earnings.

To evaluate *GEOG* data's relevance to the information set of future (expected) income, we test the following hypothesis:

H_N: The forecast errors of income (sales) are the same when either the

---

[5] A formal proof of this statement is available from the authors.

[6] Analogously, Dye [1986] provides a model which shows conditions under which both proprietary and nonproprietary information may rationally not be disclosed. Thus, the noisy disclosures may be rational.

[7] The letter summarizes memoranda provided by the SEC, the FASB, the NYSE, the Big Eight accounting firms, the Financial Analysts Federation, the major investment banks, and law firms. The set of papers made available by Mr. Grant were part of an effort to get Japan to provide segment disclosures.

308   R. BALAKRISHNAN, T. S. HARRIS, AND P. K. SEN

CONS or the *GEOG* data disclosed in annual financial statements are used to make the predictions.

The alternative hypothesis is that there is a difference in the predictive ability of the *CONS* and *GEOG* data sets for sales and income.

2.1 MODEL SPECIFICATION

2.1.1 Random Walk Models. Although evidence exists that forecasts of income using time series of quarterly income (Hopwood, McKeown, and Newbold [1982]) or security analysts' forecasts (Fried and Givoly [1982]) outperform annual time-series models, we cannot use those forecasts without biasing against *GEOG* by the use of updated information. For example, analysts' forecasts which are made at any time should include relevant *GEOG* information. Even year-ahead forecasts made prior to the publication of an annual report (at $t - 1$) have the prior years' *GEOG* segments (i.e., in the reports at $t - 2, t - 3, \cdots$) to use in their forecasts. Thus we choose to use historical data in the forecast models.

The consensus of much prior research is that when annual data are used to predict income, the random walk model performs as well as more complex time-series prediction models (e.g., Bao et al. [1983] and Hopwood, McKeown, and Newbold [1982]). Thus one model we use for the prediction of consolidated data is:[8]

$$E(X_{it}^c) = X_{it-1}^c \tag{C1}$$

where superscript c represents consolidated data, $E(X_{it})$ is the expected value (in U.S. dollars) at time $t - 1$ of income or sales for company i at time t, and X_{it-1} is the actual value (in U.S. dollars) of income or sales for company i at time $t - 1$.

We assume that the random walk model is equally relevant for local currency (LC) forecasts of income for countries without high inflation. This is equivalent to assuming zero expected growth within the LC. A *GEOG* forecast of segment U.S. dollar income is obtained by adjusting the prior period's reported income by the expected rate of change in the exchange rate. The right-hand side of equation ($G1$) is equivalent to multiplying the local currency value of income or sales by the expected U.S. dollar/local currency exchange rate. Formally, we have:

$$E(X_{it}^r) = X_{it-1}^r [1 + E(\Delta FX_t^r)] \tag{G1}$$

where superscript r represents the region or country for which the

---

[8] An alternative to the RW model is the RW model with a drift term, i.e.:

$$E(X_{it}^c) = \theta_i^c + X_{it-1}^c \tag{C1'}$$

where θ_i is the drift term for company i.

We considered model ($C1'$) in our empirical tests. However, for our sample, it unambiguously underperformed the pure RW model ($C1$). Hence, we have excluded it from the rest of the paper in the interest of parsimony.

segment information is given. $E(\Delta FX_t^r)$ is the expected rate of change of the exchange rate (in U.S. dollars per LC unit) for region r from time $t - 1$ to t. The exchange rate to be used is the average rate for the period, since this is the rate used to translate the income statement. And all other variables are as previously defined.

The random walk assumption for LC income is likely to be violated for hyperinflationary countries (three-year inflation of 100% or more). For these countries, we assume a random walk model of real income and adjust the previous year's value by the (expected) inflation rate and rate of change in exchange rate.[9] For these countries ($G1$) becomes:

$$E(X_{it}^r)' = X_{it-1}^r[1 + E(INF_t^r)] \, [1 + E(\Delta FX_t^r)] \qquad (G1')$$

where $E(INF_t^r)$ is the expected rate of change in the price level in region r for period $t - 1$ to t. To obtain the forecast of X_{it} using $GEOG$ data we aggregate across regions, i.e.:

$$E(X_{it}^R) = \sum_{r=1}^{n} E(X_{it}^r) + \sum_{r=n+1}^{N} E(X_{it}^r)' \qquad (\overline{G1})$$

where R represents a value based on aggregated $GEOG$ data, N is the number of regions for a company, and n is the number of regions not experiencing hyperinflation.

The first test of the null hypothesis compares the forecast errors using ($C1$) and ($\overline{G1}$) for income and sales.

2.1.2. Growth-Adjusted Models. The random walk model is supplemented by a model used in both Kinney [1971] and Collins [1976], which adjusts the prior period's value by a growth factor. The choice of a growth factor is limited by the detail of the disclosure and data availability. Since no LOB data are provided by region, we use a broad regional growth factor.

The variable chosen as a proxy for growth is nominal gross national product ($NGNP$). For the $CONS$ model we use $NGNP$ of the holding company's country, i.e., the United States in this study. We adjust for consolidated growth using $\Delta NGNP_t^{US}$ rather than some "world" measure of $\Delta NGNP_t$ for several reasons. First, the objective of the study is to test the predictive ability of $GEOG$ data relative to a benchmark which ignores the international characteristics of the firm. Second, in most cases, the U.S. segment accounted for at least half of total operations. Third, the form of international diversification varied widely by firm. Thus, the second $CONS$ model is:

$$E(X_{it}^c) = X_{it-1}^c[1 + E(\Delta NGNP_t^{US})]. \qquad (C2)$$

In the case of the $GEOG$ data we apply a region-specific (expected)

---

[9] We are grateful to the reviewer for this suggestion.

310   R. BALAKRISHNAN, T. S. HARRIS, AND P. K. SEN

NGNP growth factor as well as the (expected) rate of change in the exchange rate to each region's data, i.e.:

$$E(X_{it}^R) = X_{it-1}^r[1 + E(\Delta NGNP_t^r)] \, [1 + E(\Delta FX_t^r)]. \qquad (G2)$$

To obtain a forecast of consolidated X_{it} using the *GEOG* data we sum ($G2$) across regions as in model ($\overline{G1}$). The resulting forecast is denoted ($\overline{G2}$). Since *GNP* is a measure of activity, we believe that the *NGNP* growth model is likely to be particularly appropriate for sales estimates.[10]

To summarize, we use two models, random walk and *NGNP*-based growth, for predicting consolidated income and sales using either *CONS* or *GEOG* data. The initial hypothesis tests reported in section 4 use forecasts based on the same model applied to the *CONS* and *GEOG* data, i.e., ($\overline{G1}$–C1) and ($\overline{G2}$–C2). Other combinations are discussed in section 5.

3. Data, Sample Selection, and Test Statistics

Data on *GEOG* sales and income were extracted from relevant annual reports and 10-Ks. Reasonableness checks were performed to ensure that measurement errors from the extraction process were minimized.

3.1 CRITERIA USED IN SELECTION OF SAMPLE COMPANIES

Since this research was conducted over a number of years, the data were collected in two stages. In the first stage 324 companies were identified for 1979 to 1983 from the *Value Line* data base, which contains data on foreign sales and assets. Although *SFAS 14* became effective for companies with fiscal year-ends subsequent to December 15, 1976, segment data through 1978 fiscal year-ends contained many classification adjustments consistent with a learning process. Thus, we decided to eliminate the learning years and begin our sample with 1979. 1983 was the last year of available data when the first stage of the project was completed.

GEOG data should be most useful for companies with a "significant" proportion of their operations in foreign countries. Our criterion for significance, although arbitrary, is that a company had a ratio of foreign assets to total assets or a ratio of foreign sales to total sales of at least 25% in one year, and not less than 10% in all years of the initial test period (1979 to 1983).

Two hundred and twelve companies were excluded from the initial sample if (*i*) the company did not have a fiscal year-end between October 31 and March 31, since the forecasts for macroeconomic variables were

---

[10] Most of the existing evidence on the time-series properties of accounting data relates to income. However, Abdel-khalik and El-Sheshai [1983, p. 361] found that at least for quarterly series the sales and income series were of the same form. Also, Collins [1976] utilized the same estimates for both variables in his study.

PREDICTIVE ABILITY OF SEGMENT DISCLOSURES   311

for the following calendar year; (*ii*) the company had no more than two segments unless the non-U.S. segment was a specific country—for example, a company disclosing the two segments as U.S. and other was excluded but a company disclosing the segments as U.S. and West Germany was retained; (*iii*) the segments were given as regions and there was no information in the 10-K or annual report to indicate the countries in which the company operates; (*iv*) the company reclassified its segments or restated its financial statements because of a restructuring or a change in a significant accounting policy (other than foreign currency translation); (*v*) companies were not incorporated in the United States or were financial institutions, advertising agencies, or independent oil and gas companies, since these firms were not expected to conform to the specified prediction models.

We were left with 112 companies for the first stage. The collection and analysis process took several years so we extended the number of years (to include 1984 and 1985) for this sample. Imposing the above criteria for the additional years reduced the final sample to 89 firms. Table 1 summarizes the sample selection process.

3.2 CLASSIFICATION OF COUNTRIES WITHIN EACH SEGMENT

Companies invariably report *GEOG* data by region rather than by country. To establish the countries included in each region, we used three basic sources of information: (*i*) direct reference to the countries in the notes to the financial statements or in management's discussion of the results; (*ii*) reference to properties owned or operated by the company, usually disclosed in the 10-K; and (*iii*) the list of significant subsidiaries, frequently disclosed in the annual report.

A weighting scheme based on relative dollar *NGNP*s was applied to the countries within a region to ensure that, unless explicitly stated to

TABLE 1

Summary of the Filter Process Used in Extracting the Sample of Firms with Significant Geographic Segment Data, 1979–85

Companies from *Value Line* Meeting Criterion of Significant Geographic Operations in 1979 Through 1983	324
Companies with Fiscal Year-Ends Not Between October and March	(30)
Companies with Poor Geographic Disclosure (i.e., Two General Regions or No Information on Countries in a Region)	(64)
Companies with Changes in Year-End, Restatement of Data, or Significant Restructuring of the Company	(74)
Companies for Which Annual Reports or 10-Ks Not Available	(37)
Companies Registered Outside the United States	(12)
Companies in Financial Services or Advertising Industries	(15)
Independent Oil and Gas Companies	(3)
Final Sample Size	**89**

312   R. BALAKRISHNAN, T. S. HARRIS, AND P. K. SEN

the contrary, there was not a disproportionate weighting for the small countries. For example, if a region consisted of France and Spain, the proportion of income (sales) attributed to each country was based on their relative (dollar equivalent) *NGNP*s. We also observed in the extraction process that where there was more specific detail given (e.g., the number of outlets for McDonald's) the weighting would have been reasonably approximated by use of the *NGNP* weights. We are aware that our assignments of countries to regions, and the relative weights we use, are a potential source of measurement error, yet we believe we have extracted the maximum amount of information from the public disclosures of the *GEOG* data which we are testing.

3.3 COUNTRY GROWTH RATE AND EXCHANGE RATE DATA

In order to estimate models (C2) and (G1–G2) we needed one-year-ahead forecasts of *NGNP*s and/or exchange rates. For each of the two models being considered, we use both perfect foresight measures as well as forecasts of the macroeconomic variables. The forecast methods are described in detail in Appendix A.

3.4 FORECAST ERROR MEASURES

To compare predictive ability we first compute the relative absolute error (*AE*) of the predicted value of X_{it}:

$$AE_{imt}^{j} = \left| \frac{E(X_{it}^{j} \mid model\ m) - X_{it}}{X_{it}} \right| \qquad (M1)$$

where j is R or c, and m represents a random walk or growth model. Then we calculate the mean absolute error (*MAE*) for each combination of j and m:[11]

$$MAE_{im}^{j} = \frac{1}{T} \sum_{t=1}^{T} (AE_{imt}^{j}). \qquad (M2)$$

Having computed *MAE* for each model, we estimate the difference in the *MAE*s for the relevant *GEOG* and *CONS* model, i.e.:

$$D_{im} = MAE_{im}^{c} - MAE_{im}^{R}. \qquad (M3)$$

3.5 TEST STATISTICS

We computed both parametric and nonparametric test statistics. To reduce the influences of outliers we truncated each D_{im} at + or −1 (i.e. 100%), which is consistent with the *LOB* studies. Previous studies (e.g.,

---

[11] *MAE* is commonly used in accounting research. Studies using *MAE* include Collins [1976], Collins, Hopwood, and McKeown [1984], and Hopwood, Newbold, and Silhan [1982].

PREDICTIVE ABILITY OF SEGMENT DISCLOSURES   313

Collins [1976]) concentrated on parametric tests by computing average *MAE*s. Despite truncation, the parametric tests may be sensitive to violations of the normality assumption, so we conduct nonparametric tests as well. The two nonparametric statistics used are the Wilcoxon Signed Rank Test (Lehman [1975]) and the Fisher Sign Test (Hollander and Wolfe [1973]). The sign test ignores magnitudes and reflects only the direction of predictive ability.

4. Results

4.1 RESULTS OF TESTS USING "PERFECT FORESIGHT" MEASURES

The results of the perfect foresight tests on sales and income for the random walk (panel A) and growth (panel B) models are reported in table 2.

The results for income show statistically significant increases in predictive accuracy from use of the *GEOG* data. The growth model yields a mean differences of 4.5% and a median difference of 0.8%, with all test statistics significant at the 1% level. The random walk model indicates smaller differences of 3.6% for the mean (significant at the 1% level) and 0.1% for the median. The contrast between the mean and median differences as well as the differences at the quartiles suggests that there are some relatively large positive differences (i.e., *GEOG* superiority).

The results for sales are not as consistent. For the random walk model the *GEOG* forecast is worse than the *CONS* forecast, with mean and median differences of −0.4%. These differences are small but statistically significant at a level of less than 1%. On the other hand, the growth model favors *GEOG* data, yielding mean and median differences of 0.7%, also significant at the 1% level. The difference at the third quartile of 1.8% and at the first quartile of only −0.1% reflects the fact that the *GEOG* data help to improve the sales forecast by over 1% for 36 firms but adversely affect the forecast for just 10 firms by an equivalent amount.

For both income and sales the Wilcoxon and Fisher test statistics indicate that *GEOG* data provide more accurate predictions when the growth model is used, compared with use of the random walk model. This is consistent with our expectation that a potential advantage of segment data is its ability to differentiate the trends in the different segments. The success of *GEOG* forecasts with the growth model also indicates that $\Delta NGNP$ is a reasonable proxy for growth in activity and that nonaccounting information is useful in the prediction of future income and sales.

4.2 RESULTS OF TESTS USING FORECASTS OF EXCHANGE RATES AND NGNP

The results reported in table 3, which use forecasts of changes in both FX_t and $NGNP_t$ to generate the relevant prediction, generally indicate

TABLE 2

Summary Statistics from Tests of Differences in Mean Absolute Forecast Errors[1] for the Full Sample (1979–85) Assuming Perfect Foresight for Exchange Rate Changes and NGNP Growth Rates (89 Companies)

| | Mean Difference | t Value | Difference | | | Sign of Wilcoxon Test Statistic | Fisher Test Statistic |
			1st Quartile	Median	3d Quartile		
Panel A: Random Walk Models ($\overline{G1}$, C1)							
Sales	−0.004	−2.52*	−0.011	−0.004	0.005	−**	−4.07**
Income	0.036	2.77**	−0.009	0.001	0.024	+	0.42
Panel B: Growth Models ($\overline{G2}$, C2)							
Sales	0.007	4.39**	−0.001	0.007	0.018	+**	5.19**
Income	0.045	2.92**	−0.003	0.008	0.024	+**	5.47**

[1] The forecast errors are based on mean absolute error (CONS) − mean absolute error (GEOG). Thus a positive (negative) sign indicates a superior *GEOG* (*CONS*) forecast.

($\overline{G1}$, C1) represents random walk models (adjusted for hyperinflation) for forecasts using *GEOG* and *CONS* data.

($\overline{G2}$, C2) represents *NGNP* growth-adjusted models for forecasts using *GEOG* and *CONS* data.

* $p < 0.05$.

** $p < 0.01$.

PREDICTIVE ABILITY OF SEGMENT DISCLOSURES   315

TABLE 3

Summary Statistics of Tests of Differences in Mean Absolute Forecast Errors[1] for the Full Sample (1979–85) Using Forecasts for Foreign Exchange Rate Changes and NGNP Growth Rates (89 Companies)

| Forecast Model for Exchange Rate[2] | Mean Difference | t Value | Difference | | | Sign of Wilcoxon Test Statistic | Fisher Test Statistic |
			1st Quartile	Median	3d Quartile		
Panel A: Random Walk Models ($\overline{G1}$, C1)							
Sales ....FO	0.003	2.80**	−0.002	0.004	0.009	+**	5.19**
RW	0.001	1.41	−0.003	0.003	0.008	+**	3.51**
Income ....FO	−0.005	−0.89	−0.008	0.001	0.005	−	0.98
RW	0.003	0.89	−0.001	0.001	0.003	+*	4.91**
Panel B: Growth Models ($\overline{G2}$, C2)							
Sales ....FO	−0.002	−2.43*	−0.009	−0.003	0.008	−*	−2.38*
RW	−0.001	−0.74	−0.006	0.001	0.005	+	0.14
Income ....FO	−0.004	−0.75	−0.008	−0.001	0.004	−	−1.26
RW	0.005	1.82	−0.001	0.002	0.004	+*	3.79**

[1] The forecast errors are based on mean absolute error (*CONS*) − mean absolute error (*GEOG*). Thus a positive (negative) sign indicates a superior *GEOG* (*CONS*) forecast.

[2] *FO* represents the forward rate forecast and *RW* represents the random walk forecast of foreign exchange rates.
($\overline{G1}$, C1) represents random walk models (adjusted for hyperinflation) for forecasts using *GEOG* and *CONS* data. ($\overline{G2}$, C2) represents *NGNP* growth-adjusted models for forecasts using *GEOG* and *CONS* data.

* $p < 0.05$.
** $p < 0.01$.

that the errors introduced by forecasting the macroeconomic variables reduce the predictive power of *GEOG* data.

When the random walk model is used, the sales forecasts based on *GEOG* data are significantly better, at a 1% level, than the forecasts based on *CONS* data for both exchange rate forecast models. However, both mean and median differences are below 0.5%. This improvement in the sales forecasts is surprising. Since we are generally dealing with local subsidiaries of multinational corporations, we conjecture that their sales policies (e.g., prices) may be based on predicted exchange rates, and these cannot be adjusted quickly for unexpected exchange rate changes. Thus the sales forecasts using exchange rate predictions do quite well.

On the other hand, firms are better able to influence cost and other income factors (such as interest) or even hedge exposures as exchange rates vary from their expected values. So it is less surprising that the income forecasts provide a slightly different picture. When a random walk (*RW*) exchange rate prediction model is used, the income forecasts based on *GEOG* data are superior to the forecasts based on *CONS* data, but the differences are smaller than those in the perfect foresight case (panel A of table 2). The mean difference is 0.3%, in contrast to 3.6% (in the *PF* case), and is not significant. Also, the third quartile difference is 0.3% in the *RW* case versus 2.4% in the *PF* case. Both the Wilcoxon and Fisher sign tests are significant at levels of 5% and 1%, respectively. Interestingly, using the forward rate (*FO*) model to predict exchange rates further reduces the forecast accuracy from using *GEOG* data. While the median difference is still positive, the Fisher test statistic is no longer significant at a 5% level. Also, the mean and Wilcoxon test statistics are both negative, suggesting some relatively large forecast errors from the use of *GEOG* data.

The results reported in table 2 reflect a marked improvement in *GEOG* forecasts when growth models ($\overline{G2}$, *C2*) are used in conjunction with *PF* forecasts. In contrast, the results for the growth models using forecasts of growth and exchange rates, reported in panel B of table 3, show a deterioration in the predictive accuracy of the *GEOG* forecasts compared with the random walk models ($\overline{G1}$, *C1*). The *CONS* forecasts of sales are significantly more accurate than *GEOG* forecasts at the 5% level, when the growth models and *FO* are used, with a mean difference of −0.2% and a median difference of −0.3%. In the case of income the use of a growth model has little impact on the forecast accuracy of *GEOG* data. When *RW* forecasts are used for exchange rates the *GEOG* forecasts are still more accurate than *CONS* forecasts, with mean and median differences of 0.5% and 0.2%, respectively. Both nonparametric statistics are positive and significant at the 5% level for the Wilcoxon test and the 1% level for the Fisher test. In sum, the deterioration in the accuracy of *GEOG* forecasts with growth suggests that the consensus forecasts of growth we use are relatively inaccurate, at least when combined with exchange rate changes. The results in table 3 also suggest that *RW*

PREDICTIVE ABILITY OF SEGMENT DISCLOSURES   317

forecasts of exchange rates are relatively more accurate than the *FO* forecasts, as might be expected from past research (see Appendix A).

Considering the results based on the *RW* exchange rate forecasts, *GEOG* data provide more accurate forecasts of income using either the random walk or growth model, and more accurate forecasts of sales using the random walk model. However, the magnitude of the differences suggests that the inaccuracy in forecasting macroeconomic variables over a long period, such as a year, restricts the potential usefulness of the *GEOG* data. The relative accuracy of the *PF* results in table 2 suggests that income forecasts should be revised as macroeconomic factors change. Furthermore, segment disclosures in interim reports should be useful for updating the income forecasts to reflect more closely the results that can be achieved with perfect foresight. In the case of sales forecasts, interim segment reporting appears to be redundant.

5. *Extensions of the Hypothesis Tests*

The results reported in section 4 indicate that these segment data enhance the predictive accuracy of annual income and sales, for our sample. However, recall that the sample selection process eliminated many of the companies with poor *GEOG* disclosures. Given the results for the full sample, the hypothesis test is extended to consider the robustness of the results.[12]

Ideally, the predictive ability of *GEOG* and *LOB* data could also be compared. However, in our sample only 13 companies had sufficiently systematic *LOB* data to facilitate a direct comparison. Given the crudeness of statistics used in predictive ability tests, the sample was considered too small to provide a robust test of the relative predictive ability of *GEOG* compared to *LOB* data.[13]

5.1 COMPARISON OF GEOG GROWTH AND CONS RANDOM WALK FORECAST MODELS

Some readers may also believe it is useful to compare forecasts based on *CONS* and *GEOG* data using (*i*) forecasts of growth but not exchange

---

[12] The sample was partitioned to include only the companies with three or more regions outside the United States. The results for the remaining subsample of 31 companies are quite similar to the full-sample results. This suggests that the relevance of *GEOG* disclosures is robust and does not depend on the number of regions reported.

[13] The predictive accuracy of the growth models for *LOB* and *GEOG* income for these 13 companies was tested. The *LOB* forecasts used data and models equivalent to those used in Collins [1976]. The *LOB* forecasts were more accurate than *CONS* forecasts with a mean difference of 0.003 and a median difference of 0.002. For the *GEOG* forecasts with *PF* the mean difference was 0.095 and the median difference was 0.012. When the forecasts were used for growth and exchange rates (*RW*) the mean difference was 0.099 and the median difference was 0.044. The Wilcoxon and Fisher test statistics were both significant at the 1% level. These results suggest that some combination of *LOB* and *GEOG* disclosure would probably improve predictive accuracy of income forecasts.

318   R. BALAKRISHNAN, T. S. HARRIS, AND P. K. SEN

rates or (*ii*) growth models for *GEOG* data and random walk models for *CONS* data (i.e., ($\overline{G2}$–C1). These comparisons can be easily made but are not reported in detail because, while they are appropriate in a *LOB* study, they make less sense in the case of forecasts using *GEOG* data.

GEOG disclosures provide local currency values translated (or converted) into U.S. dollars. Ignoring the exchange rates thus excludes the essential difference in *GEOG* data. In addition, a *nominal* (*LC*) growth rate of 10% can easily be offset by a decline in the exchange rate. Incorporating both effects will lead to a lower dollar growth rate, which is all that is economically relevant in a comparison to the *CONS* dollar value.

The reason for not fully reporting the comparison between forecasts using a growth model and *GEOG* data versus the random walk model and *CONS* data ($\overline{G2}$, C1), or vice versa ($\overline{G1}$, C2), is much simpler. First, we do not compare forecasts ($\overline{G1}$) and (C2) because, as discussed in section 2, (C1) is generally a better prediction model than (C2) for consolidated U.S. income. In the case of the comparison of forecasts ($\overline{G2}$) and (C1), when a growth model is applied to *GEOG* data the growth in *NGNP* is applied to all segments. In our sample, the U.S. segment is generally at least half of total sales and income. It is difficult to conceive of a forecaster applying a growth rate to U.S. values when using segment data but not when using *CONS* data. Nevertheless, in the interest of completeness, we report some results (in table 4) that can be used to compare the two *GEOG* forecast models with the widely utilized *CONS* random walk model. However, we believe that any comparison of the ($\overline{G2}$, C1) forecasts should be made cautiously.

The results for sales forecasts reveal that when we assume *PF* the forecasts using *GEOG* data are more accurate than the simple *CONS* random walk forecast. A comparison of the mean and median differences of 1.1% to the equivalent values in table 2 suggests (*i*) that a growth model using *NGNP* is better than a random walk model for sales forecasts, and (*ii*) that forecasts using *GEOG* data and *PF* provide more accurate predictions of group sales. When forecasts of growth and exchange rates are used the conclusion is a little different. Comparing the results reported in tables 3 and 4 we see that random walk sales forecasts using *GEOG* data are the most accurate. Given the predictive accuracy of *GEOG* data for random walk forecasts of sales with forecasted exchange rates (panel A of table 3), the mean difference of −0.2% and the median difference of −0.6%, reported in table 4, suggest that use of the consensus forecasts of *NGNP* reduces the predictive accuracy of the forecasts for both *CONS* and *GEOG* data.

The results in table 4 for forecasts of income show that random walk forecasts using *CONS* data are more accurate than growth forecasts using *GEOG* data for both *PF* and forecasted growth and exchange rates. Comparison of these income forecasts to those in tables 2 and 3 suggests that the random walk forecasts are more accurate than forecasts using a

TABLE 4

Summary Statistics of Tests of Differences in Mean Absolute Forecast Errors[1] for the Full Sample (1979–85) Using the Growth Model for Forecasts Using GEOG Data and the Random Walk Model for Forecasts Using CONS Data (G2, C1) (89 Companies)

	Mean Difference	t Value	Difference			Sign of Wilcoxon Test Statistic	Fisher Test Statistic
			1st Quartile	Median	3d Quartile		
Sales:							
—With Perfect Foresight Growth and Exchange Rates	0.011	3.70**	−0.008	0.011	0.033	+**	3.23**
—With Random Walk Exchange Rate and Growth Forecasts	−0.002	−0.58	−0.026	−0.006	−0.022	−	−1.82
Income:							
—With Perfect Foresight Growth and Exchange Rates	−0.035	−2.45*	−0.036	−0.007	0.012	−*	−1.54
—With Random Walk Exchange Rate and Growth Forecasts	−0.086	−4.21**	−0.078	−0.034	0.005	−**	−5.4**

[1] The forecast errors are based on mean absolute error $(CONS)$ − mean absolute error $(GEOG)$. Thus a positive (negative) sign indicates a superior $GEOG$ $(CONS)$ forecast.

* $p < 0.05$.
** $p < 0.01$.

320   R. BALAKRISHNAN, T. S. HARRIS, AND P. K. SEN

NGNP growth rate. Thus, based on the conclusions in section 4.1, when we assume *PF* or a *RW* exchange rate forecast the *GEOG* data, at least weakly, help to increase the accuracy of predictions of random walk model forecasts of income.

5.2 HYPOTHESIS TESTS FOR POST-SFAS 52

A stated motivation for *SFAS 52*, introduced in 1981, was a reduction in the volatility of reported income. The introduction of *SFAS 52* should therefore reduce the benefits from *GEOG* disclosures. The sample is partitioned into pre- and post-*SFAS 52* subsamples based on the year of adoption, extracted from each company's annual report.

Table 5 reports the results of the tests for the post-*SFAS 52* subsample.[14] In all cases *GEOG* forecasts are still more accurate than *CONS* forecasts. When perfect foresight of exchange rates and *NGNP* is assumed the results are consistent with a hypothesis that *SFAS 52* reduces the volatility of *CONS* income as the values and significance levels of all reported statistics decline. When the *RW* forecasts of exchange rate are used, with income forecasts based on a random walk model, the post-*SFAS 52* results indicate slightly higher differences in the mean (0.7% vs. 0.3%) and the first and third quartiles, but are similar to the full-sample results shown in panel A of table 3. When the growth model with the forecast growth rate is used the post-*SFAS 52* mean difference is higher, the median difference is the same, and the Wilcoxon and Fisher test statistics are more significant compared with the full-sample results shown in panel B of table 3. These results thus suggest that the *GEOG* data still (weakly) enhance the accuracy of income forecasts subsequent to the introduction of *SFAS 52*.

6. Conclusion

This paper provides evidence that geographic segment data enhance predictive ability for annual income and sales. The usefulness of these data is reduced because detailed geographic segments are frequently not reported and because of inaccuracy in annual forecasts of country-specific growth and exchange rates. Providing segment data in interim reports and updating forecasts as macroeconomic factors change should enhance the predictive usefulness of geographic segment disclosures.

APPENDIX A

This appendix describes the derivation of the forecasts of nominal gross national product (*NGNP*) and exchange rates.

---

[14] The tests for the post-*SFAS 52* subsamples are relevant only for income since sales should be unaffected by *SFAS 52*.

PREDICTIVE ABILITY OF SEGMENT DISCLOSURES   321

TABLE 5

Summary Statistics of Tests of Differences in Mean Absolute Forecast Errors[1] of Income for the Subsample of Observations Subsequent to the Adoption of SFAS 52 (89 Companies)

Model and Macroeconomic Variable Forecast Used	Mean Difference	t Value	Difference			Sign of Wilcoxon Test Statistic	Fisher Test Statistic
			1st Quartile	Median	3d Quartile		
Random Walk ($\overline{G1}$, C1) with Perfect Foresight Exchange Rates	0.019	1.82	−0.013	−0.001	0.020	+	−0.42
Growth ($\overline{G2}$, C1) with Perfect Foresight Growth and Exchange Rates	0.021	1.87	−0.007	0.002	0.012	+*	1.87
Random Walk ($\overline{G1}$, C1) with Random Walk Exchange Rate Forecasts	0.007	1.03	−0.003	0.001	0.008	+*	2.95*
Growth ($\overline{G2}$, C2) with Random Walk Exchange Rate and Growth Forecasts	0.008	1.30	−0.001	0.002	0.006	+**	4.07**

[1] The forecast errors are based on mean absolute error (CONS) − mean absolute error (GEOG). Thus a positive (negative) sign indicates a superior GEOG (CONS) forecast.

($\overline{G1}$, C1) represents random walk models (adjusted for hyperinflation) for forecasts using GEOG and CONS data.

($\overline{G2}$, C2) represents NGNP growth-adjusted models for forecasts using GEOG and CONS data.

* $p < 0.05$.

** $p < 0.01$.

322   R. BALAKRISHNAN, T. S. HARRIS, AND P. K. SEN

1. NGNP Forecasts

In general, countries either provide data on Gross National Product (*GNP*) or on Gross Domestic Product (*GDP*) but not both. Of the countries used in this study, all but four[15] use *GDP* rather than *GNP*. For ease of exposition both measures are referred to as *GNP* in this paper.

We used an average of published forecasts to proxy a "consensus" forecast of the expected rate of change in *NGNP*. The sources of these forecasts were "The Quarterly Economic Review" for the relevant country prepared by The Economic Intelligence Unit of *The Economist*, various publications of Business International Corporation,[16] and "The OECD Economic Outlook." For the major countries all three sources were available, and only one forecast was available in only two cases of small countries.

The forecasting services provide real *GNP* (*RGNP*) growth rate data. To obtain *NGNP* rates we adjust the *RGNP* rates by relevant inflation factors. The expected rate of change in a region's *NGNP* is given by:

$$E(\Delta NGNP_t^r) = \{1 + E(\Delta RGNP_t^r)\} \{1 + E(INF_t^r)\} - 1$$

where $E(\Delta NGNP_t^r)$ is the expected rate of change in nominal *GNP* in region r for period $t - 1$ to t, $E(\Delta RGNP_t^r)$ is the expected rate of change in real *GNP* in region r for period $t - 1$ to t, and $E(INF_t^r)$ is the expected rate of change in the price level in region r for period $t - 1$ to t.

As with *RGNP*, the expected rate of inflation is a consensus estimate of the three forecast services.

Clearly, the forecast of $E(\Delta NGNP_t^r)$ introduces measurement error. As expected, the largest forecast errors occur in high-inflation countries. For the major industrial countries the forecast errors are generally less than 5% except for 1982 when a period of unexpectedly rapid growth began for many of these countries.

2. Exchange Rate Forecasts

Consensus forecasts could not be used for exchange rates as such forecasts were provided only by Business International and only for some currencies. Consequently, the model used for exchange rate forecasting was based on the type of exchange arrangement in operation in each year[17] (e.g., independent floating, managed floating via a cooperative

---

[15] These countries are Canada, Japan, the United States, and West Germany. The difference between the two measures is generally not material for time-series analyses.

[16] Specifically, "Business Europe," "Business Asia," "Business Latin America," and "Business International."

[17] The information on exchange arrangements was obtained from *International Financial Statistics* (*IFS*) published by the International Monetary Fund.

PREDICTIVE ABILITY OF SEGMENT DISCLOSURES 323

arrangement,[18] other forms of managed floating,[19] and pegging to a major currency).

For floating and certain managed floating currencies, two forecasts were made. First, the current consensus is that a random walk model performs as well as any other model in forecasting exchange rates (Meese and Rogoff [1983] and Callan, Kwan, and Yip [1985]), so we use a random walk (*RW*) model for the major currencies. Second, we have a measure of the market's expectation of future spot exchange rate changes through the discount or premium on forward exchange rates.[20] Hence we use the forward rate discount or premium to develop an expected rate of change in the spot rate for those (major) currencies with active forward exchange markets.[21] The relevant data were extracted from the *International Financial Statistics Tapes.*

The other (minor) currencies either had a managed float or pegged their currencies to a major currency. For the former we tried to emulate the nature of the floating arrangement in preparing our forecast. The best example of this is the case of highly inflationary economies where the exchange rates periodically adjust by the change in the local price level relative to the change in the U.S. price level (e.g., Brazil and Argentina). The forecast of the change in exchange rate used is thus a direct function of the expected relative inflation rates.[22] Finally, we base the forecast of a pegged exchange rate on the expected rate of change of the currency to which it is pegged.

To summarize, for major floating currencies we have two measures of expected exchange rates, one based on a random walk model and one based on the forward market premium or discount. For other managed floating currencies which had high inflation we use a purchasing power parity (*PPP*) approach. For remaining countries with pegged currencies, we use the fixed historic rate. Our exchange rate forecasts are imprecise, but the forecasts used are the best available according to the extant literature.

The forecasts of *NGNP*s and exchange rates can be obtained from the authors.

---

[18] The most prevalent example of this arrangement is the European Monetary System (*EMS*) which includes the major European currencies except for the British pound.

[19] In the most common example of managed floating, countries make periodic adjustments to their currencies based on relative economic indicators such as price levels. Brazil and Argentina are examples of countries which used such an arrangement.

[20] The evidence on the efficiency of forward exchange markets is mixed. For example, Frankel [1980] finds the market to be efficient but Cumby and Obstfeld [1981] do not.

[21] The countries are Austria, Belgium, Canada, Denmark, France, Italy, Japan, the Netherlands, Switzerland, the United Kingdom, and West Germany.

[22] This conforms to a purchasing power parity (*PPP*) theory which has been shown to hold for hyperinflationary economies (Frenkel [1978]).

324   R. BALAKRISHNAN, T. S. HARRIS, AND P. K. SEN

REFERENCES

ABDEL-KHALIK, A. R., AND K. M. EL-SHESHAI. "Sales Revenues Time Series Properties and Predictions." *Journal of Forecasting* 2 (1983): 351–62.

AJINKYA, B. B. "An Empirical Evaluation of Line-of-Business Reporting." *Journal of Accounting Research* (Autumn 1980): 343–61.

BALDWIN, B. A. "Segment Earnings Disclosure and the Ability of Security Analysts to Forecast Earnings Per Share." *The Accounting Review* (July 1984): 376–89.

BAO, D.-H., M. T. LEWIS, W. T. LIN, AND J. G. MANEGOLD. "Applications of Time-Series Analysis in Accounting: A Review." *Journal of Forecasting* 2 (1983): 405–23.

BAVISHI, V. B., AND H. E. WYMAN. "Foreign Operations Disclosures by U.S.-Based Multinational Corporations: Are They Adequate?" *International Journal of Accounting Education and Research* (Fall 1980): 153–68.

CALLAN, J. L., C. C. Y. KWAN, AND P. C. Y. YIP. "Foreign-Exchange Rate Dynamics: An Empirical Study Using Maximum Entropy Spectral Analysis." *Journal of Business Economics and Statistics* (April 1985): 149–55.

COLLINS, D. W. "Predicting Earnings with Sub-Entity Data: Some Further Evidence." *Journal of Accounting Research* (Spring 1976): 163–77.

COLLINS, D. W., AND R. R. SIMONDS. "SEC Line-of-Business Disclosure and Market Risk Adjustments." *Journal of Accounting Research* (Autumn 1979): 352–83.

COLLINS, D. W., W. S. HOPWOOD, AND J. C. McKEOWN. "The Predictability of Interim Earnings over Alternative Quarters." *Journal of Accounting Research* (Autumn 1984): 467–79.

CRAVEN, D. W., AND M. FELLER. "SEC Moves to Increase Interim Segment Disclosure." *CPA Journal* (October 1984): 93, 95.

CUMBY, R. E., AND M. OBSTFELD. "A Note on Exchange Rate Expectations and Nominal Interest Differentials: A Test of the Fisher Hypothesis." *Journal of Finance* (June 1981): 697–703.

DYE, R. A. "Proprietary and Nonproprietary Disclosures." *Journal of Business* (April 1986): 331–66.

ERNST & WHINNEY. *Financial Reporting Developments: April 1985.* Cleveland, 1985.

FINANCIAL ACCOUNTING STANDARDS BOARD. *Statement of Financial Accounting Standards No. 14: Financial Reporting for Segments of a Business Enterprise.* Stamford, Conn.: FASB, 1978.

———. *Statement of Financial Accounting Standards No. 52: Foreign Currency Translation.* Stamford, Conn.: FASB, 1981.

FRANKEL, J. "Tests of Rational Expectations in the Forward Exchange Market." *Southern Economic Journal* (April 1980): 1083–1101.

FRENKEL, J. A. "Purchasing Power Parity: Doctrinal Perspective and Evidence from the 1920s." *Journal of International Economics* (May 1978): 169–91.

FREEMAN, R. N., J. A. OHLSON, AND S. H. PENMAN. "Book Rate-of-Return and Prediction of Earnings Changes: An Empirical Investigation." *Journal of Accounting Research* (Autumn 1982, pt. II): 639–52.

FRIED, D., AND D. GIVOLY. "Financial Analysts' Forecasts of Earnings: A Better Surrogate for Market Expectations." *Journal of Accounting and Economics* (October 1982): 85–107.

HOLLANDER, M., AND D. A. WOLFE. *Nonparametric Statistical Methods.* New York: Wiley, 1973.

HOPWOOD, W. S., J. C. McKEOWN, AND P. NEWBOLD. "The Additional Information Content of Quarterly Earnings Reports: Intertemporal Disaggregation." *Journal of Accounting Research* (Autumn 1982, pt. I): 343–49.

HOPWOOD, W. S., P. NEWBOLD, AND P. A. SILHAN. "The Potential for Gains in Predictive Ability Through Disaggregation: Segmented Annual Earnings." *Journal of Accounting Research* (Autumn 1982, pt. II): 724–32.

KINNEY, W. R., JR. "Predicting Earnings: Entity vs. Sub-Entity Data." *Journal of Account-

ing Research (Spring 1971): 127–36.

————. "Covariability of Segment-Earnings and Multisegment Company Returns." *The Accounting Review* (April 1972): 339–45.

LEHMAN, E. L. *Nonparametric Statistical Methods Based on Ranks.* Oakland, Calif.: Holden-Day, 1975.

MEESE, R. A., AND K. ROGOFF. "Empirical Exchange Rate Models of the Seventies: Do They Fit Out of Sample?" *Journal of International Economics* (February 1983): 3–24.

21

Int J Acctg (1990) 25:252–267
© 1990 The University of Illinois

**The International
Journal of
Accounting**

Geographic Area Disclosures and the Assessment of Foreign Investment Risk for Disclosure in Accounting Statement Notes

Timothy S. Doupnik and Robert J. Rolfe

Associate Professors of Accounting, University of South Carolina, Columbia, SC 29208, USA

Key words: CFAs; Experiment; Geographic segments; SFAS 14; Investment

Abstract: An experiment was conducted to investigate the relevance of data on less aggregated geographic areas. Chartered Financial Analysts (CFAs), assigned to six different treatment groups, were presented with financial statement data, (including geographic area disclosures) and asked to assess the riskiness of investing in the hypothetical multinational corporation (MNC) depicted. Relevance was measured as the difference in risk assessment between groups receiving different levels of aggregated geographic area data. The results indicate that the level of aggregation can significantly affect financial statement users' risk assessments.

Publicly held US multinational corporations (MNCs) are required by the Financial Accounting Standards Board's (FASB) Statement of Financial Accounting Standards (SFAS) No. 14[1] to include in the notes to financial statements information on their foreign operations. SFAS 14 requires firms to report certain items of information by geographic area. Management has the responsibility of deciding how individual countries should be grouped together to form reportable geographic areas. Although some guidance is provided by SFAS 14, so much discretion is left to management in determining reportable geographic areas that the degree of aggregation selected by many firms may not provide adequate information for financial statement users to assess the riskiness of a company's foreign operations. Claiming that the FASB requirements are inadequate, several researchers have called for more stringent requirements so that the presentation is made on a less aggregate basis.[2]

This study used an experimental framework to examine whether the level of aggregation of geographic area data is relevant in making investment decisions. The subjects, Certified Financial Analysts (CFAs), were asked to indicate the level of risk associated with an investment in common stock of a hypothetical multinational corporation. An across-persons design was employed wherein different groups

Accepted for publication: September 26, 1990

evaluated the risk of different hypothetical MNCs. As the level of aggregation was different for each group, relevance was measured by changes in the risk assessments of the firms between the groups. The results show that the level of aggregation of geographic area does influence the risk assessment of financial statement users.

Development of the Research Problem

SFAS 14 requires firms to present data on foreign operations by significant geographic areas if (1) revenues generated from total foreign operations are 10% or more of consolidated revenues or (2) identifiable assets of total foreign operations are 10% or more of consolidated total assets. A geographic area is defined as significant if its revenues or identifiable assets are 10% or more of the related consolidated amounts.

Reportable geographic areas can be either individual countries or groups of countries. Determination of geographic area is left to management's discretion. Factors to be considered include proximity, economic affinity, similarities in business environment, and the interrelationship of the firm's operations in the various countries.[3] For each significant geographic area, firms must report revenue, operating profit, and identifiable assets.[4]

Emmanuel and Gray[5] suggest that under SFAS 14, a firm wishing to provide minimum disclosure could argue that its "Japanese, Korean and Philippine operations which separately meet the 10% revenue rule are in fact one geographic area, that is Asia". In their view, adequate disclosure of information by geographic area depends upon management's good intentions.

Studies by Arnold, Holder, and Mann[6] and Bavishi and Wyman[7] indicate that management has been reluctant to provide information on relatively disaggregated geographic area. Arnold, Holder, and Mann examined 10-K reports of 131 of the *Fortune* 500 firms with regard to geographic area disclosure. They found that only 17.6% of all disclosures were by country, 34.8% were at a continent or subcontinent level, and 12.8% were global in nature. "Other" was the geographic area used in 25.2% of all disclosures. Although each firm technically complied with the letter of SFAS No. 14, they may have violated its intent. The authors believe that the factors listed by the FASB for selecting appropriate geographic areas imply greater disaggregation than a single global category or continent. "Such data is important due to political (for example, expropriation) and economic (for example, currency exchange and translation) implications".[8] They recommend separate disclosure of each country in which 10% of total revenues is generated.

Bavishi and Wyman examined geographic area disclosures of 296 of the *Fortune* 500. Seventy-three percent of their sample firms used only one or two geographic areas (other than the United States). Of 17 firms in the pharmaceutical industry, 12 different classification schemes were used, including:

USA – Americas and Far East – Europe and Mideast and Africa

and

USA – Europe and Africa – Canada and Latin America – Other

Table 1. Number of significant geographic areas reported

Number of areas	Number of companies	Percentage ($n = 120$)	Cumulative percentage
1	30	25	25
2	50	41	66
3	26	22	88
4	13	11	99
5	1	1	100

The lack of cohesiveness in these areas led them to ask, "Where is the 'proximite, economic affinity, similarities in business environment' apparent in a classification, such as 'Europe/Mideast/Africa'?" They concluded that "the difficulty of assessing foreign risk of one company or comparing foreign risk between companies is apparent from the variety and vagueness of titles".[9]

These two studies used data gathered from annual reports for the year 1978. It is possible that in the intervening period of time companies have voluntarily decreased the level of aggregation in their geographic area disclosure and that over time the geographic areas defined by companies have become more cohesive. To examine this the annual reports of a sample of 120 companies reporting geographic area information in 1986 were examined to determine the number of areas reported (other than the USA) and the level of aggregation used for reporting purposes. Table 1 shows that 25% of sampled companies reported only one geographic area other than the USA generally labeled "Foreign". Another 41% reported only two areas, typically "Europe" and "Other", or "Eastern Hemisphere" and "Other Western Hemisphere". Only 12% reported more than three areas. General Motors, for example, reported on four areas: Canada, Europe, Latin America, and Other.

General Motors provides a good example of the different levels of aggregation used by companies for their geographic areas – country (Canada), continent (Europe), super continent (Latin America), and global (Other). Table 2 shows the frequency with which companies used these different levels of aggregation.

It can be seen that 73% of the companies sampled used a global category (Foreign or Other) to describe one of the geographic areas in which they had operations. This category represented 32.8% of all the geographic areas reported on.

Countries were aggregated at the hemisphere level (Eastern or Other Western) or the super continent level (e.g., Europe/Middle East/Africa, Latin America and Canada) by 32% of companies sampled. Of the 120 companies examined, only five did not use a global or super continent level of aggregation.

Table 2. Level of aggregation of significant geographic areas

Level of Aggregation	Number of companies	Percentage of companies
Global (Foreign, Other)	88	73%
Hemisphere, Super Continent	38	32%
Continent	69	58%
Country	31[a]	26%

[a] 26/31, Canada.

Countries were aggregated at a continent level (e.g., Europe, Africa, and South America) by 58% of companies. Only 26% of companies reported on individual countries, and of those, Canada was the individual country reported 84% of the time.

For the most part companies distinguish between the eastern and western hemispheres in defining geographic areas. Countries in the western hemisphere are generally reported in aggregate as "Other Western Hemisphere" or "Canada and Latin America", or decomposed into two areas "Canada" and "Latin America". More variety exists in the way the countries of the eastern hemisphere are reported. Some companies aggregate at the "Eastern Hemisphere" level, whereas others decompose this region into two or more areas. The ways in which the eastern hemisphere is decomposed include:

Two areas
    Europe Asia/Africa/Australia
    Europe Far East
    Europe/Africa Pacific
    Europe/Middle East/Africa Far East
Three areas
    Europe Pacific Africa
    Europe Africa/Middle East Asia/Pacific
Four areas
    Europe Asia Africa Oceania

Still other companies aggregate countries across hemispheres to create geographic areas, such as:

    Americas/Far East
    Americas/Pacific
    Latin America/Asia Pacific/Canada
    Pacific/Canada

Three conclusions can be drawn from an examination of companies' geographic area disclosure. First, virtually all companies aggregate some countries at a super continent or higher level, and other than Canada, companies do not report on an individual country basis. Second, the vast majority of companies aggregate countries into three or fewer geographic areas for reporting purposes. Third, there is no standardisation in the manner in which US companies decompose the world for geographic area reporting purposes. Thus, the potential limitations in geographic area disclosure identified by previous researchers continue.

The highly aggregated geographic areas used by firms to divide the world hide differences in investment risk that exist between countries within those areas. The perceived risk of investing in the Philippines is likely to be far different from that for Australia, yet both are encompassed in a single geographic area such as Far East/Pacific. Even within a fairly homogenous continent, such as Europe, there is likely to be a difference in perceived risk between a country, such as the Netherlands and Yugoslavia.

Implicit in the conclusions drawn by previous researchers is the assumption that providing data on less aggregated geographic areas could increase the relevance of information to financial analysts and other financial statement users. This assumption is the basis for the research question addressed in this study:

Are data on less aggregated geographic areas more relevant than data on more highly aggregated geographic areas in assessing the riskiness of investing in a firm with foreign operations?

Before recommending a policy decision that firms should provide information on less aggregated areas, research is necessary to determine whether that data would be used. Two issues are considered jointly by this research question: (1) whether geographic area data are important in the investment decision process and (2) whether users can differentiate between relatively low risk and high risk areas in the world.

Theoretical Framework

A theoretical basis for the disclosure of geographic area information is found in the "fineness theorem" of information economics.[10] Mohr argues that the fineness theorem has direct applicability to segmental reporting, "since the provision of segmental data in conjunction with consolidated data represents an information system which is "finer" than the disclosure of consolidated data alone".[11] Although this argument was offered for segmental reporting by industry, the same argument can be made for geographic segment reporting. Mohr continues:

Furthermore, by viewing the incremental disclosure of segmental sales, earnings, or other data as successively "finer subpartitions" of the information set, a number of "fineness" comparisons are possible. And, in accord with the theoretical result, each of these comparisons would imply that the "finer" information system is at least as valuable to the decision maker as the reporting of consolidated data alone (or of a less detailed set of segmental data) [emphasis added].

Thus, disaggregation of geographic areas as currently reported by companies in the US would lead to a finer information set which would be at least as valuable to financial statement users as the less detailed set of information.
In portfolio theory, it is suggested that decision makers utilize the available information set to acquire a portfolio of investments with a utility maximizing risk/ return relationship.[13] In this context, the disclosure of geographic area data on a less aggregated basis results in a finer information set which could lead to a revision in the decision maker's assessment of risk and/or return.

Prior Research

The relevance of geographic area disclosure has only recently become a topic of empirical research. Prodhan[14] examined the association between geographic segment disclosure and systematic risk of stock returns for a group of companies listed on the London Stock Exchange. Using an interrupted time series analysis he found that geographic disclosures and systematic risk were related. These results imply that geographic segment disclosures have information content to market participants in UK.

Balakrishnan, Harris, and Sen[15] examined the relevance of geographic segment disclosures per SFAS 14 in predicting sales and earnings of US companies. Using both random walk and growth adjusted models, they found that geographic area disclosures can enhance the information set used to predict annual earnings. It should be noted, however, that theirs was not a true test of SFAS 14 disclosures. Rather than using the actual geographic areas reported, they used information provided in 10-Ks on significant properties and references in the annual report to specific countries to disaggregate the geographic areas actually reported to a country basis. The percent of total operations allocated to individual countries within a reported region was arbitrarily based upon the relative GNPs of countries referred to located in that region.

Doupnik and Rolfe[16] [DR] conducted a laboratory experiment to examine whether different levels of aggregation of geographical area affect subjects' assessment of the risk of investing in a US MNC. They asked student subjects to evaluate 27 cases which represented all combinations of three variables having three treatment levels. The treatment variables were three different geographic areas and the treatments involved disaggregating to a country level of disclosure. They found that for the most part disaggregating geographic areas from a continent level to a country level significantly affected subjects' risk assessments.

There are several limitations in the DR study. The internal validity of their experiment is subject to question due to the demand effect of a within person, repeated measures design. The subjects may have perceived the manipulation of treatment variables and provided the responses they felt the experimenters were looking for. The external validity is questionable due to the use of student subjects, who may or may not react as actual financial analysts, and due to the use of individual countries as significant geographic areas in building hypothetical MNCs in the case scenarios. As noted above, very few companies use single countries as reportable areas.

This study seeks to improve upon the methodology employed by DR by (1) using CFAs as subjects, (2) employing an across-persons experimental design, and (3) building cases using geographic areas at a level of aggregation commonly used by US MNCs to divide the world.

Methodology

An across-persons experimental approach was used to determine the impact level of aggregation of geographic area data has on financial analysts' assessments of investment risk. CFAs were randomly assigned to one of six different groups. Each group received a different experimental instrument depicting a hypothetical MNC with common background information. The only difference between each group was in the level of aggregation of the geographic areas reported on in the notes to the financial statements.

Background Information

Subjects were given summary financial information on a hypothetical firm with no foreign operations (Domestic Corporation) whose stock was traded on the New York Stock Exchange. Summary financial statement data for the years 1982–1986 were provided. These data were constructed by taking average amounts for the *Fortune* 500 firms that had complete data on the COMPUSTAT tape. The subjects were told than an investment in the common stock of this firm was of moderate risk; on a scale of 1 (low) to 9 (high), the risk was assigned a rating of 5. This information was common to each of the cases for the six groups.

Experimental Task

Subjects were then provided information on a second hypothetical firm (Multinational Corporation) which was similar in all ways to Domestic Corporation other than the location of its operations. Fifty percent of Multinational's revenues, operating profit, and identifiable assets were located outside of the United States. The manner in which this 50% was reported varied from group to group. The subjects were asked to indicate the level of risk they associated with an investment in Multinational Corporation on the same nine point scale used for Domestic Corporation. They were told that risk was the possibility that the actual return from an investment would deviate from expected return, which could be caused by many factors, including the economy in general, competition, technological development, and government interference. A sample case is presented in Fig. 1.

Case #6

	Percentage of Total Located in Each Area		
	Revenues	Operating Profit	Identifiable Assets
United States	50%	50%	50%
Other Western Hemisphere	20%	20%	20%
Europe	20%	20%	20%
Middle East/ Africa	5%	5%	5%
Far East/ Pacific	5%	5%	5%
Total	100%	100%	100%

PLEASE INDICATE ON SCALE OF 1 (low) TO 9 (high):

(a) the level of risk you associate with an investment in the common stock of
    Multinational Corporation and
(b) the degree of confidence you place in your risk assessment made in (a).

Level of risk
    low risk 1 2 3 4 5 6 7 8 9 high risk
Degree of confidence
    low confidence 1 2 3 4 5 6 7 8 9 high confidence

Fig. 1. Sample Case

Since risk evaluation is an integral part of the investment decision process, differences in risk assessment among the groups served as an operational measure of the relevance of the level of aggregation of geographic area data. Six cases were developed to determine the impact the level of aggregation of geographic area data has on risk assessment.

Subjects were also asked to indicate the degree of confidence they placed in their risk assessment on a scale of 1 (low confidence) to 9 (high confidence). Information is defined as relevant if it has the capacity to change a decision or if it reduces the uncertainty surrounding a decision already made.[17] Differences in the degree of confidence among the groups were used as a second measure of the relevance of less aggregated geographic area data. Thus, the two dependent variables were risk assessment and decision confidence.

Cases

As can be seen in Fig. 2, the level of aggregation varied from three areas being reported in Case 1 to five areas in Cases 5 and 6. In each case 50% of revenues, operating profit, and identifiable assets were located in the United States. Of the remaining 50%, 20% was always located in the Western Hemisphere (other than in the United States) and 30% was always in the Eastern Hemisphere. Case 1 presents this information in the most aggregated fashion possible; simply stating that 20% of

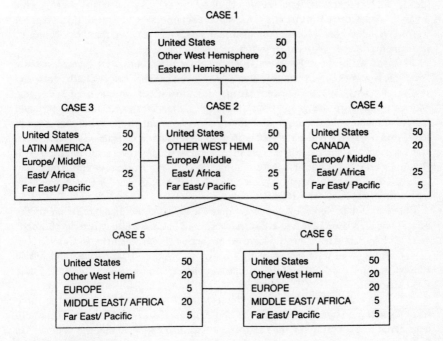

Fig. 2. Case treatments

operations were in "Other Western Hemisphere" and 30% were in the Eastern Hemisphere. Case 2 disaggregated the 30% of operations located in the Eastern Hemisphere into two components: 25% in "Europe/Middle East Africa" and 5% in "Far East/Pacific". These groupings were chosen because they are commonly used by US MNCs in their geographic area disclosures. Note that under SFAS 14, a US MNC with 25% of operations in Europe/Middle East/Africa and 5% in Far East/ Pacific could choose to report on two separate geographic areas or could opt to combine those two areas into one for financial reporting purposes. This is true because SFAS 14 establishes 10% of total operations as the threshold for a separate geographic area. Thus, a single MNC could have defined its significant geographic areas either as in Case 1 or as in Case 2.

Although Case 2 provides geographic area data at a less aggregated level than Case 1, it is unclear whether any additional information is provided. Whether subjects would react differently to Case 2 than to Case 1 would depend upon their assumption of the percentage of Eastern Hemisphere operations located in "Europe/Middle East/ Africa" and the percentage assumed to be in the Far East and Pacific region, and the relative risks perceived to be associated with operations in these two regions of the world.

The grouping "Other Western Hemisphere" contains very heterogeneous countries in terms of investment risk. Investment in Latin America is generally considered riskier than investment in Canada, yet it is very common for both to be grouped into the category "Other Western Hemisphere". To determine whether specifically identifying investment in Other Western Hemisphere as being located in the geographic areas "Canada" or "Latin America" had an impact on risk assessment, Cases 3 and 4 were developed. These cases are identical to Case 2 except for the location of investment in Other Western Hemisphere.

In Case 3 all of the Other Western Hemisphere operations were located in Latin America. It was expected that this would be viewed as more risky than the company in Case 4 where all Other Western Hemisphere operations were located in Canada. Moreover, because the geographic grouping "Other Western Hemisphere" could include Canada, subjects might base their risk assessment on the belief that some of the Other Western Hemisphere operations were located in Canada. Consequently it was expected that the risk assessment for Case 2 would be lower than that for Case 3 (Latin America). Yet because the grouping "Other Western Hemisphere" could also include Latin America, it was expected that the risk assessment for Case 2 would be higher than that for Case 4 (Canada).

Cases 5 and 6 were developed to investigate whether disaggregation of the geographic area "Europe/Middle East/Africa" used in Case 2 into two areas "Europe" and "Middle East/Africa" would have an impact on risk assessment. In Case 5, 20% of operations were reported as being located in "Middle East/Africa" and 5% in Europe, and in Case 6, 20% of operations were located in Europe and 5% in "Middle East/Africa".

It was expected that the company depicted in Case 5 would be viewed as more risky than the company in Case 6 as the Middle East and Africa are generally considered to be more risky than Europe. It was also expected that the company in Case 5 would be perceived as more risky than the company in Case 2. When given information that 25% of operations was located in "Europe/Middle East/Africa", it was anticipated that subjects could assume that more than 5% of operations was located in Europe. Thus, when 20% of operations was reported in "Middle East/Africa" with only 5% in Europe subjects might consider this case to be more risky. No *a priori* expectations could be developed for a comparison of Cases 2 and 6. Whether Case 2 could be considered more or less risky than Case 6 would depend upon whether subjects assumed that of the 25% located in "Europe/Middle East/Africa", more than 5% or less than 5% of operations were located in "Middle East/Africa".

Hypotheses

The above discussion leads to the following hypotheses related to risk assessment tested in this study:

Null Hypotheses	Alternative Hypothesis
Ho1: $R(1) = R(2)$	Ha1: $R(1) \neq R(2)$
Ho2: $R(3) = R(4)$	Ha2: $R(3) > R(4)$
Ho3: $R(2) = R(3)$	Ha3: $R(2) < R(3)$
Ho4: $R(2) = R(4)$	Ha4: $R(2) > R(4)$
Ho5: $R(5) = R(6)$	Ha5: $R(5) > R(6)$
Ho6: $R(2) = R(5)$	Ha6: $R(2) < R(5)$
Ho7: $R(2) = R(6)$	Ha7: $R(2) \neq R(6)$

where R = subject's mean risk assessment
    1–6 = Cases 1–6

A second set of hypotheses was developed for the decision confidence variable. If less aggregated geographic area data provide relevant information for assessing risk, then the subjects' confidence with regard to their risk assessments should increase as data become increasingly less aggregated. Specifically, confidence should be lowest for that case which provides information at the most aggregated level (Case 1) and confidence should be greatest for those cases which provide information at the least aggregated level (Cases 5 and 6). The null hypothesis tested with regard to decision confidence was:

Ho8: There is no difference in the degree of confidence across cases.

The alternative was:

Ha8: The degree of confidence where five areas are reported (Cases 5 and 6) is greater than where four areas are reported (Cases 2, 3, and 4) which in turn is greater than where three areas are reported (Case 1).

Symbolically:

Ho8: $C(1) = C(2, 3, 4) = C(5, 6)$
Ha8: $C(5, 6) > C(2, 3, 4) > C(1)$
where C = subjects' mean confidence level
1–6 = Cases 1–6

Table 3. Profile of respondents

Age	20–29	30–39	40–49	50–59	Over 60
%	4.8%	27.4%	31.5%	29.0%	7.3%
Education	No Degree	Bachelor's	Master's	Law	Doctorate
%	0.0%	23.4%	72.6%	2.4%	1.6%
Experience	0–5	6–10	11–15	16–20	Over 20
%	4.0%	17.7%	18.5%	22.6%	37.1%
Type of firm	Investment	Insurance	Bank	Mfg	Other
%	66.1%	12.9%	17.7%	0.8%	2.4%
Percent of time spent on MNCs	0–10	11–20	21–40	40–60	Over 60
%	21.0%	25.8%	26.6%	18.5%	8.1%

Subjects

A random sample of 500 members of the Institute of Chartered Financial Analysts was selected for contact by mail. CFAs represent an important group of financial statement users as they routinely assist investors in the evaluation of potential investments. Subjects were randomly assigned to each of the six treatments. Twenty-eight mailed instruments were undeliverable, reducing the contact pool to 472 CFAs. One hundred twenty-four usable responses were received, yielding a response rate of 26.3%.

To develop a profile of the respondents in this study subjects were asked to provide certain demographic information after completing the research task. A summary of this information is presented in Table 3. That table shows that the majority of respondents (a) were highly educated (77% had a master's degree or higher), (b) had at least 10 years of experience as a financial analyst (60% had 16 years or more), (c) were employed by investment firms (66%), and (d) spent at least 20% of their time dealing with MNCs (53%).

Subjects were also asked to indicate the importance attached to "financial statements" and "notes to financial statements" in making investment decisions on a scale of 1 (not important) to 9 (very important). The responses to these questions are

Table 4. Perceived importance of financial statements and notes to financial statements in making investment decisions

Financial statements

	not important								very important
	1	2	3	4	5	6	7	8	9
%	0.0%	0.0%	3.2%	3.2%	1.6%	4.0%	17.7%	26.6%	43.5%

Notes to financial statements

	not important								very important
	1	2	3	4	5	6	7	8	9
%	0.0%	1.6%	3.2%	0.8%	3.2%	3.2%	15.3%	23.4%	49.2%

Table 5. Summary statistics on risk assessments by case

Case	N	Mean risk assessment	Standard deviation
1	18	6.33	0.84
2	26	5.73	1.37
3	21	6.76	1.18
4	22	4.64	1.22
5	19	6.84	0.83
6	18	5.00	0.91

shown in Table 4. The vast majority of respondents considered both financial statements and the notes thereto to be important in making investment decisions. Over 85% rated both sources of information at 7 or higher.

This demographic information indicates that the majority of respondents in this study were highly experienced users of financial statements accustomed to dealing with MNCs in making investment decisions. Thus, the experimental task was appropriate for this group of subjects.

Analysis and Results

Analysis of variance was used to test for an overall difference in the mean risk assessments across Cases 1–6. The hypothesis of no difference was rejected at the .0001 level. The specific research hypotheses discussed above were then tested by making pairwise comparisons between cases. The experimentwise error rate for multiple comparisons was controlled using a procedure suggested by Tukey.[18]

Summary statistics on risk assessments by case are presented in Table 5. Not surprisingly, that table shows that Case 5 (20% of operations in Middle East/Africa) was perceived as the most risky by CFAs, followed by Case 3 (20% of operations in Latin America). The case in which 20% of operations were located in Canada was rated least risky (Case 4), followed by Case 6 (20% of operations in Europe). The cases providing the least amount of detail (Cases 1 and 2) fell in the middle in terms of mean risk assessment. It is interesting to note that except for Case 4 (20% in Canada) the CFAs, on average, perceived each of the MNCs depicted to be more

Table 6. Tests of hypotheses

Hypothesis	Case Comparison	Difference between means	Significance
1	1–2	0.60	ns
2	3–4	2.13	**
3	2–3	−1.03	*
4	2–4	1.09	**
5	5–6	1.84	**
6	2–5	−1.11	*
7	2–6	0.73	ns

* significant at 0.05 level; ** significant at 0.01 level; ns, not significant at 0.05 level

risky than the Domestic Company. (Recall that the subjects were instructed to assume that Domestic Company had a risk rating of 5 on a nine-point scale).

Results of the risk hypothesis testing are reported in Table 6. That table shows that for each of the directional hypotheses (Ha2–Ha6) the sign of the difference between means was as expected and that each of these alternative hypotheses was supported at the 0.05 level or better. Neither Ho1 nor Ho7, for which no directional alternatives were developed, could be rejected at the 0.05 level. As expected the strongest results were obtained for the comparison of Cases 3 and 4 (Latin America vs. Canada) and the comparison of Cases 5 and 6 (Middle East/Africa vs. Europe).

The inability to reject Ho1 and Ho7 indicates that disaggregation of reported geographic areas, in and of itself, does not necessarily mean that relevant information has been provided. Examining the comparison between Cases 1 and 2 more closely, the inability to reject Ho1 could be explained in three ways. The first is that subjects may view the areas "Europe/Middle East/Africa" and "Far East/Pacific" as being equally risky for foreign direct investment. The second explanation is that those subjects responding to Case 1 may have implicitly assumed that if 30% of operations are in the eastern hemisphere, then about 25% would be in Europe/Middle East/ Africa and 5% in Far East/Pacific. A third possible explanation is that the less aggregated areas "Europe/Middle East/Africa" and "Far East/Pacific" are themselves highly aggregated areas which provided no additional information for assessing investment risk. Perhaps the subjects implicitly combined these two areas and made their risk assessment thinking in terms of 30% of operations located in the eastern hemisphere.

These results imply that aggregation of geographic areas reduces information content only if the areas being aggregated are perceived to have different risk profiles. The results also imply that disaggregation of geographic areas provides relevant information only if areas of different risk are shown separately.

Degree of Confidence

Summary statistics on degree of confidence by case are presented in Table 7. Although in general mean confidence increased as the number of reported areas increased, the null hypothesis of no difference in degree of confidence across cases could not be rejected ($P = 0.7529$). Therefore, subsequent pairwise comparisons to test the confidence hypotheses were not made.

The small differences in confidence across cases could be explained in at least two ways. One possibility is that although geographic areas were less aggregated in the higher number cases, countries were still aggregated at the continent level or higher (except for Case 4 - Canada) and subjects still felt a great deal of uncertainty in their risk assessments. For example, knowing in Case 6 that 20% of Eastern Hemisphere operations were in Europe caused subjects to rate that hypothetical MNC as less risky than the subjects rated the hypothetical MNC in Case 1. However, not knowing in which European countries operations were located caused respondents to Case 6 not to be significantly more confident in their risk assessment than the respondents to Case 1. Although it is possible that further disaggregation of geographic areas to a country level would have caused significant differences in confidence to

Table 7. Summary statistics on confidence by case

Case	N	Mean confidence	Standard deviation
Three areas reported			
Case 1	18	4.55	1.72
Four areas reported			
Case 2	26	4.88	1.56
Case 3	21	4.57	1.72
Case 4	22	5.13	1.28
Five areas reported			
Case 5	19	5.00	1.67
Case 6	18	5.11	1.49

arise, we felt that it was important to use areas reported by companies at the levels of aggregation actually used.

Another possible explanation for the small differences in confidence between cases relates to the realism of the experimental task. The subjects were asked to make risk assessments using only a subset of the actual information that they would normally use in their investment analysis. Perhaps the relatively low confidence placed in risk assessments across all cases and the small differences across cases was a result of the subjects being forced to make decisions without being allowed to make a more complete data search that might have increased their confidence.

Summary and Conclusion

The results of this study indicate that the level of aggregation of geographic areas can be relevant to financial analysts in assessing the risk of investing in a company with foreign operations. This study has shown that decomposing a hemisphere level of aggregation (Other Western Hemisphere) into two components can significantly affect risk assessments, and that decomposing a super continent (Europe/Middle East/Africa) into two components can significantly affect risk assessments at least when a surprise is involved. These results are consistent with those of prior research.

The policy implication from the results of this study is that perhaps firms should be required to provide disclosure on less aggregated geographic areas. This suggestion raises the need to develop criteria for when and how to disaggregate. The two relevant dimensions are: (1) materiality and (2) differential investment risk. The first dimension relates to whether disaggregation of geographic information makes a difference in investors' decisions. Because limited activities in high risk areas should not have much impact on overall investment risk, those operations probably need not be disaggregated in the financial statements. In contrast, relatively large investments in high risk areas do make a difference in risk assessment. For example, in this study, subjects perceived the situation where 20% of operations were in the Middle East/Africa region as the most risky scenario. Further research needs to be conducted to determine at what level investment becomes material enough to affect investment decisions.

Disaggregation by itself does not automatically provide useful information. In this study, the disaggregation of the Eastern hemisphere category into "Europe/ Middle East/Africa" and "Far East/Pacific" did not significantly affect the subjects' perception of risk. Possibly this was because of the amount of variability that exists in each of the categories. The group "Europe/Middle East/Africa" contains very low risk countries such as Switzerland and the Netherlands and also high risk countries such as Lebanon and Libya. As these are precisely the type of groupings that are used by many US MNCs, the FASB should consider mandating further disclosure.

A possible way to avoid this problem is by further disaggregating geographic areas into groups that better reflect differences in investment risk. One obvious was to disaggregate the grouping "Europe/Middle East/Africa" would be to divide it into two groups: "Europe" and "Middle East/Africa". On the other hand, simply grouping operations by continents can also mask risk differences. For example, although Latin America is generally perceived as a risky location for foreign direct investment, some countries such as Costa Rica and Ecuador are significantly less risky than others such as Peru and El Salvador. If a US MNC is investing in the lower risk countries within a geographic area, it would be advantageous to disclose that fact. Disclosure could result in financial statement user perceiving the firm as less risky, perhaps resulting in higher stock prices and a lower cost of capital. Further research is needed to determine how these differences in country risk should be reflected in geographic area disclosures.

Footnotes

1. Financial Accounting Standards Board, "Financial Reporting for Segments of a Business Enterprise." *Statement of Financial Accounting Standards No. 14*. Stamford, CT: FASB, 1976.
2. See, for example, J. Arnold, W. Holder, and M. Mann, "International Reporting Aspects of Segment Disclosure." *The International Journal of Accounting*, Fall 1980, 125–135 and V. Bavishi and H. Wyman, "Foreign Operations Disclosure by US Based Multinational Corporations: Are They Adequate?"; *The International Journal of Accounting*, Fall 1980, 153–168.
3. op. cit., paragraph 34.
4. International Accounting Standards 14 also recommends that firms report sales or other operating revenues, segment result, and segment assets employed by geographic area. However, unlike SFAS 14, IAS 14 does not provide guidance as to how geographic segments should be determined or what constitutes a "significant" segment. International Accounting Standards Committee, "Reporting Financial Information by Segment." *International Accounting Standard 14*. London: IASC, 1981.
5. C. Emmanuel and S. Gray, "Corporate Diversification and Segmental Disclosure Requirements in the USA." *Journal of Business Finance and Accounting*, Winter 1977, 407–418.
6. J. Arnold, W. Holder, and M. Mann, "International Reporting Aspects of Segment Disclosure." *The International Journal of Accounting*, Fall 1980, 125–135.
7. V. Bavishi and H. Wyman, "Foreign Operations Disclosure by US-Based Multinational Corporations: Are They Adequate?" *The International Journal of Accounting*, Fall 1980, 153–168.
8. Arnold, Holder, and Mann, p.135.
9. Bavishi and Wyman, p.159.
10. See, for example, J. Marschak and R. Radner, *Economic Theory of Teams*. New Haven, CT: Yale University Press, 1971.
11. R. Mohr, "The Segmental Reporting Issue: A Review of Empirical Research." *Journal of Accounting Literature*, 1983, 41.
12. ibid.

Geographic Area Disclosures and Investment Risk   267

13. See, for example, H. Markowitz, "Portfolio Selection." *Journal of Finance*, March 1952, 77–91.
14. B. Prodhan, "Geographical Segment Disclosure and Multinational Risk Profied." *Journal of Business Finance and Accounting*, Spring 1986, 15–37.
15. R. Balakrishnan, T. Harris, and P. Sen, "The Predictive Ability of Geographical Segment Disclosures." Unpublished working paper presented at the 1988 annual meeting of the American Accounting Association, July 1988.
16. T. Doupnik, and R. Rolfe, "The Relevance of Level of Aggregation of Geographic Area Data in the Assessment of Foreign Investment Risk." *Advances in Accounting*, 1989, 51–65.
17. Financial Accounting Standard Board, "Qualitative Characteristics of Accounting Information." *Statement of Financial Accounting Concepts No. 2*, Stamford CT: FASB, 1980.
18. See, SAS Institute Inc, *SAS User's Guide: Statistics*. Cary, NC: SAS, 1985, 473.

Correspondence and offprint requests to: Professor Timothy S. Doupnik, School of Accounting, College of Business Administration, The William Close Building, University of South Carolina, Columbia, SC 29208, USA.

22

Journal of Business Finance & Accounting, 16(4) Autumn 1989, 0306 686X $2.50

SYSTEMATIC RISK AND THE DISCRETIONARY DISCLOSURE OF GEOGRAPHICAL SEGMENTS: AN EMPIRICAL INVESTIGATION OF US MULTINATIONALS

BIMAL K. PRODHAN AND MALCOLM C. HARRIS*

INTRODUCTION

Product market diversification within the country as well as transnational and conglomerate mergers of recent years across the world have resulted in increasingly less meaningful financial reports to the users giving rise to the need for unbundling or segment reporting.[1] Segment reporting recommendations in the recent past include the UK Companies Act 1985, the International Accounting Standard No. 14, the Statement of Financial Accounting Standard No. 14 in the USA, and pronouncements by the UN, the OECD and others[2] requiring line of business (LOB) as well as geographical disclosure. More recently the Accounting Standards Committee in the United Kingdom has produced an exposure draft on the subject of segment reporting (ASC 1988).

While the LOB disclosure impact has been investigated by many,[3] this has not been the case with geographical segment disclosure.[4] This research investigates the impact of geographical segments disclosure on the systematic risk of a group of US Multinationals quoted on the New York Stock Exchange during the period 1968—1984.

The paper is organised as follows: the first section explores the theory of disclosure, while the second section discusses the issues and develops hypotheses; method and data are described in the third section, and results are analysed in the fourth section; possible confounding variables are investigated in the fifth section, which is followed by conclusions in the final section.

THEORY

Discretionary Disclosure and the Diffusion Process

Discretionary disclosure decisions by firms are products of managerial actions in response to demands from user groups (Chambers, 1951; and Watts and Zimmerman, 1986).

* The authors are respectively from, the Department of Accounting and Finance, the University of Strathclyde; and the Department of Finance, St. John's University, New York. (Paper received June 1987, revised September 1987)

Firms have an incentive to disclose good news so as to distinguish themselves from the 'Lemons' in the market place who have no good news to disclose (Akerlof, 1970). But discretionary signalling of good news to the market takes place only when marginal analysis so demands; i.e. when the benefits from disclosure exceed the costs of disclosure — costs of information gathering and dissemination for instance (Verrecchia, 1983). Although this marginal analysis establishes how much to disclose it does not explain the mechanism of disclosure. The mechanism of disclosure is explained by the incentive signalling theory (Ross, 1979) or the 'lemons' process in reverse (Beales, Craswell and Salop, 1981), which works as follows:

Initially firms with good news disclose, following which firms with not so bad news have an incentive to disclose in order to distinguish themselves from those with really bad news. Even those with no news to disclose in such situations will have an incentive to disclose their state to avoid being lumped in with those with really bad news. Thus, the competitive disclosure process facilitates the diffusion of 'discretionary' disclosure in which discretion ultimately disappears.

Investor Perception

While managerial decision results in disclosure, the underlying causal variable which motivates managerial decision is the expectation of an improved perception of the fortunes of the firm in the minds of the users (investors).

Choi (1973) has argued that

'increased firm disclosure tends to improve the subjective probability distributions of a security's expected return streams in the mind of an individual investor by reducing the uncertainty associated with that return stream. For firms which generally outperform the industry average, it is also argued that improved disclosure will tend to increase the relative weighting which an investor will place on favourable firm statistics relative to other information vectors which he utilizes in making judgements with respect to the firm.' (p. 289)

This improved subjective probability distribution can be due to

(a) the contents of the disclosure, such as fineness of the data;
(b) the 'Hawthorne Effect'[5] i.e., 'the imputed motivation for the act of voluntary disclosure as distinguished from its content' (Patell, 1976, p. 248); or
(c) both.

As is the case in all joint tests of hypotheses it is difficult to disentangle the contents of the disclosure from its imputed motivation, and it is safe to assume that the competing hypotheses are not mutually exclusive.

The existence of Hawthorne effect in security prices does not negate market efficiency. Management disclosure of segment information does not necessarily amount to cosmetics to fool the market, but that investors perceive that management are conscientious in discharging their responsibility to the market. Such disclosure of finer information even if it does not contain any surprise reassures the market, resulting in less speculation about the future prospects of the company.

Disclosure and Systematic Risk

Apart from reducing the speculative element in investor perception, disclosure may also alter managerial behaviour in the real sector. So far as the contents of segment disclosures may affect investor perception of the firm's prospects, management will be more cautious in undertaking or expanding activities in sectors from which the cashflow and return prospects are uncertain. This argument is well supported in the literature (Collins and Simonds, 1979). Theoretical linkages between managerial actions in the real sectors and firm risk measures have also been provided by Dhaliwal et al. (1983), Subrahmanyam and Thomadakis (1980), Rubinstein (1973) and Hamada (1972) via operating risk and financing risk.

In brief, disaggregation results in finer information leading to a better understanding of the past and improved forecast for the future. For the disclosing group as a whole this results in lower stock price volatility, hence lower variance of stock prices. Although it is conceivable that for individual firms, the ratio of systematic risk to total risk may go up as well as down, there is no reason to believe that for a group of companies this will not remain unchanged. If systematic risk as a proportion of total risk is held constant, then any reduction in total risk will result in a reduction of systematic risk for the disclosing group of companies.

Geographical Segment Disclosure and Systematic Risk

Segment disclosure recommendations by The Accounting Standards Committee in the UK, The Financial Accounting Standards Board in the US, and others, have suggested a line of business (LOB) disclosure as well as geographical segments disclosure. Disclosure benefit studies of an empirical kind in the literature (Collins and Simonds, 1979; and Emmanuel and Pick, 1980) have however, been only of the LOB disclosure as documented in Mohr (1983). An early study by Kinney (1972) even suggested that geographical segments did not contain any significant information while LOB disclosure did so, as follows:

> 'The geographical data firms cannot be considered as multi-segment firms in the same sense as those reporting on a product line or divisional basis. Firms reporting on a geographic basis are likely to be in the same industries both the foreign and domestic markets and thus have a smaller incidence of covariance ratio less than one due to worldwide industry effects.' (p. 342)

The contention of this paper is that geographical segments disclosure has information content in the same manner as LOB disclosure. It is also suggested that some of the negative results in empirical studies of LOB disclosure (Horwitz and Kolodny, 1977; and Dhaliwal et al., 1983) could have been due to their exclusion of geographical segments from their investigation and concentrating exclusively on LOB disclosure as determinants of changes in systematic risk.

Segmentation on a geographical basis is not just an alternative to LOB disclosure but is distinctly and significantly different. The power of multi-nationals to control and coordinate resources internationally has given rise to demands for extensions in public accountability and control. Geographical disclosure is one of the mechanisms in achieving public accountability and control of multinationals because multinational firms' market related risk, which is a combination of operating risk and financing risk, is a function not only of the lines of businesses but also of the environment in which such businesses are conducted. For a firm which is internationally diversified such environment includes country risk: political risk as well as economic risk.

Shareholder benefit from corporate international diversification is well documented in the finance literature. Fatemi (1984) for instance states:

'To the extent that economic activity in foreign countries is less than perfectly cor-related with domestic economic activity (due to various legal, informational, and economic barriers which segment national financial markets), foreign operations should provide the stockholders of MNCs risk-return opportunities superior to those available to the stockholders of purely domestic firms' (pp. 1325–1326).

Similar arguments have been presented by Grubel (1968), Agmon and Lessard (1977), Cohn and Pringle (1973), Lessard (1974), Rugman (1978), Calvet (1981), and Adler and Dumas (1983).[6]

While the LOB disclosure benefits are influenced by both national and inter-national factors, geographical disclosure benefits are located entirely in inter-national settings. To distinguish the international settings from the purely domestic settings an economic concept of nationhood is useful. According to the theory of international trade, nations are zones within which physical factors of production are confined, while Ricardian theory identifies countries by their consumption preferences and technologies.

The concept of nationhood results in the segmentation of the real goods market which is a contributory cause for the segmentation of capital markets (Adler and Dumas, 1983). Independently however, capital market segmentation along national lines may also be due to investor inhibitions or official restrictions. Factors contributing to investor inhibitions include lack of information, fear of expropriation, and discriminatory taxation. Official restrictions include access to local capital markets via ceilings on foreign equity participation and freedom to repatriate dividends and capital. To the extent that such segmentation of capital market may exist in practice, multinational corporations may be able to reap benefits for their shareholders in the form of lower risk and

SYSTEMATIC RISK AND GEOGRAPHICAL SEGMENT DISCLOSURES   471

higher returns. Since the risk-return opportunities can vary in different countries, and the international corporations may also vary in their abilities to organize the firms' resources to take advantage of them, it is suggested that disclosure of geographical segment sales and profits data may alter the firm's systematic risk profile.

Benefits from corporate international diversification by multinational firms may not always be apparent unless the geographical spread is disclosed to the investors. In the context of geographical disclosure, if there is no way for investors to learn about the firms' geographical spread of business across countries then all firms could be perceived as being of equal risk. Similarly, if there is no way for firms in less volatile geographical segments to distinguish themselves from firms in more volatile geographical segments, then firms in more volatile segments will find it in their interests to hide their less favourable geographical spreads. Firms with geographical spreads in less risky regions will therefore have an incentive to disclose the status of their geographical portfolio in order to distinguish themselves from below average competitors.

ISSUES AND HYPOTHESES

Given the differential incentives to disclose segment information, SFAS 14 in the US required the disclosure of sales and trading profits by geographical segments. This was required for the fiscal year beginning after 15 December 1976, for US companies with foreign sales of ten per cent or more of total sales, as well as disclosure of lines of businesses. However, LOB disclosure was already required of US companies from 1970 onwards in their annual reports filed with the Securities and Exchange Commission (SEC) on form 10K.[7] The major new segmental disclosure required from 1977 onwards was thus of geographical segments.

Because information gathering and dissemination is not costless, preparers of financial statements, standard setters, and regulators would be interested in knowing whether such segment information is useful to users and whether there are benefits to reporting firms. Kochanek (1974) argued that improved segments disclosure should reduce uncertainty in forecasting earnings thus reducing stock price variability. Yet unless this reduction in stock price variability reduces systematic risk, modern capital market theory predicts that such disclosure will not reduce the firm's cost of capital — a major benefit of risk reduction. Choi (1973) found evidence that disclosure reduces cost of capital. Collins and Simonds (1979) showed that LOB disclosure reduced the systematic risk of US Multisegment firms, while Prodhan (1986a) showed similar effects for geographical segment disclosures for UK multinationals.

Kochanek (1974, p. 246) specifically set a criterion for determining the impact of segmental disclosure:

472   PRODHAN AND HARRIS

'Applied to the problem of segmental disclosure, to the extent that investors utilizing annual corporate reports containing subentity data generate a predicted security
market reaction significantly different from investors utilizing reports prepared on
an entity basis, such reaction may be viewed as evidence that segmental financial
disclosure does possess information content.'

To test this information content of geographical segment disclosure two groups
of firms matched by size, listing, financial year end, foreign sales and line of
business disclosure, but differing in geographical segment disclosure practice
were compared around an intervention date when SFAS 14 became operative.

The overall hypothesis being tested is that if geographical segment disclosure
contains information then firms newly disclosing geographical segment data
will show a reduction in systematic risk relative to firms consistently disclosing
such geographical segment data.

To be more precise, there were four hypotheses. These were as follows:

1. If segmental geographical disclosure reduces the disclosing group's
   systematic risk, then the treatment group average betas should be lower
   in the post-disclosure period when compared with the pre-disclosure
   period.

$$\text{i.e., } \bar{B}_{T(post)} < \bar{B}_{T(pre)}$$

2. Since in the post disclosure period both the treatment and control group
   companies follow the same practice so far as geographical segments are
   concerned, in the post disclosure period there should be no significant
   difference between the treatment and control group average betas.

$$\text{i.e., } \bar{B}_{T(post)} = \bar{B}_{C(post)}$$

3. If incentives to discretionary disclosure lie in the possession of good news,
   and by inference those who do not disclose voluntarily have something
   to hide, or no good news to disclose, then a priori control group betas
   in the pre-disclosure time segment are likely to be smaller than the non-
   disclosing treatment group pre-disclosure betas.

$$\text{i.e. } \bar{B}_{C(pre)} < \bar{B}_{T(pre)}$$

4. Since the control group has not changed its disclosure practices, in the
   absence of extraneous environmental factors, post-disclosure control group
   betas should not be different from the pre-disclosure betas.

$$\text{i.e., } \bar{B}_{C(pre)} = \bar{B}_{C(post)}$$

METHOD AND DATA

To identify a sample of large multinational companies, firms included in the
Standard and Poor's 500 Composite Stock Price Index in 1983 were examined.

SYSTEMATIC RISK AND GEOGRAPHICAL SEGMENT DISCLOSURES   **473**

These are well traded, widely followed firms that are likely to have significant international operations. Of these 64 per cent had December 31 fiscal year ends. Only firms with December fiscal year ends were chosen to enhance comparability.

To determine the international exposure of the firms in the sample, their annual reports, 10K filings with the SEC, proxy statements and prospectuses were examined. The sample was limited to firms which obtained at least ten per cent of revenues from foreign sources in each year 1968–1983. This materiality criterion was influenced by the benchmark chosen by the SEC, FASB and the UN who have used this minimum cut off for line of business disclosure as well as geographical disclosure. Only firms which had consistently disclosed line of business data in each year from 1968–1983 were included. Firms' disclosures were further examined as to their segmental geographical disclosure practices which was a new requirement under SFAS14 for the financial year beginning after 15 December 1976. Companies consistently disclosing geographical segment data from 1969 through 1983 were included in the control group while companies which disclosed such information starting in 1977 were categorized as the Treatment Group.

Benefits from geographical segment disclosure were tested in the security markets context rather than in the context of user behaviour, predictive ability or consensus studies on the grounds that in an efficient market all such benefits are likely to be impounded in security prices.

To examine the impact of disclosure on stock prices, monthly prices data for the companies on the Compustat PDE file was examined to calculate the monthly holding period yields from October 1968 through August 1984. These procedures resulted in 82 companies, 42 in the control group and 40 in the treatment group. No further matching by industry, leverage or any other criterion was undertaken since a much smaller sample size would not be very meaningful for testing purposes.

Appendix A documents the sample selection process. Appendix B lists companies in the treatment and control groups, and firm characteristics are listed in Appendix C.

Monthly, rather than weekly or daily stock prices data were chosen on the grounds that monthly prices are more likely to approximate to normal distribution (Fama, 1976; and Diacogiannis, 1986), avoiding thin trading problems (Dimson, 1979) and problems of nonsynchronous measurement (Scholes and Williams, 1977); allow for comovements between national stock indices (Ripley, 1973) and not impair parameter stability significantly (Collins et al., 1986).

Monthly security prices were regressed against a proxy for the market to identify systematic risk. Systematic risk is typically estimated from the market model — a linear regression of returns on the market index (Sharpe, 1963):

$$r_{jt} = \alpha_j + B_j R_{mt} + e_{jt}$$

where r_{jt} is the return on the jth stock for period t

R_m is the return on the market index, and

α_j and B_j are intercept and slope parameters respectively.

Standard and Poor's Composite stock index was used as the proxy for the market. Standard and Poor's Composite 500 stock index is a market-value-weighted average of 500 stocks and is a representative measure of the US market used by most institutional investors (Sharpe, 1985, p. 636). Although it can be argued that an international index would be more appropriate in measuring the stock price movements of international companies, a representative US index was chosen on the following grounds:

(a) There are two choices in world index at present: (i) The Financial Times Actuaries World Index and (ii) the Capital International Perspective's world index.[8] The Financial Times world index was launched on 17 March, 1987, and its database does not go back beyond the year 1986 at present. Since the period of investigation in this research is 1968–1983, clearly the Financial Times world index was inappropriate.

(b) The Capital International Perspective's (CIP) world index was the other choice, which has been used by researchers in international finance (Fatemi, 1984). The CIP index is not available for periods before 1970, thus this too was not appropriate for the time series being analysed in this research.

(c) Further, the CIP index excludes foreign domiciled companies' to avoid double counting. Thus US domiciled companies quoted on the New York Stock Exchange which are also quoted on the London or Tokyo Stock Exchange would be excluded from the CIP index.

(d) So far as the composition of the CIP index is concerned, the US market dominates the CIP world capitalization. As at 31 March, 1977, for instance, of the total world capitalizaton of $783 billion included in the index, United States stocks accounted for $458 billion, or 58.5 per cent of the index (CIP, 1977).

(e) The CIP index is also somewhat limited in its scope as it excludes South Africa, New Zealand, Malaysia, Mexico, and Ireland which are included in the Financial Times world index for instance.

(f) Moreover, to the extent that there are comovements in the world's equity markets (Ripley, 1973; and Panton et al., 1976), the US Market which is the largest component in any world index is likely to reflect the world market sufficiently. Fatemi (1984, p. 1332) found that regardless of the choice of proxy for the market portfolio, NYSE index or the CIP index, multinational companies' betas have been considerably lower and less volatile than uni-national companies' betas.

ANALYSES AND RESULTS

The hypotheses require an analysis of betas over time to assess changes in the model. Since structure has meaning only in a temporal framework, changes

SYSTEMATIC RISK AND GEOGRAPHICAL SEGMENT DISCLOSURES   475

in the firms' relative risks over time must be allowed for. Brown et al. (1975) have suggested the analysis of moving betas when such issues arise. In the accounting and finance literature, to allow for changes in firms' relative risk over time, moving betas have been used by Gonedes (1978) and Collins and Simonds (1979). Gonedes used a fifty-nine month moving regression on a database spanning twenty years, while Collins and Simonds have used a forty month moving regression over eight years' monthly prices.

Firm Level Analyses

At the firm level, following procedures similar to those of Collins and Simonds, a thirty-one month moving betas were calculated for the price series. Since the point of interest in current research is changes in beta levels rather than absolute levels of betas, a thirty one month moving regression was considered appropriate as this generates a long enough time series to be meaningful for testing purposes.

The application of thirty-one month moving regression to the entire time period of 191 months, October 1968 through August 1984, resulted in 160 moving betas. Centering on a disclosure month of December 1977, twelve months after December 1978 when SFAS 14 became operative, the moving betas were subdivided into pre- and post-disclosure segments of 80 moving betas each. This was designated as series A.

In series A the moving regression slope parameter of 31 items are attributed to the 31st month. This results in pre-disclosure betas overflowing into post-disclosure time segment. To avoid this overflow problem, a contamination free series B was designed where the pre-disclosure period was the 42 months of July 1974 to December 1977 while the post-disclosure period was the 42 months of November 1980 through April 1984.

Finally, there was an anticipation problem. Although SFAS 14 was mandatory for the financial year beginning on or after 15 December, 1976, earlier implementation was encouraged by the SEC. To avoid this anticipation problem a further series C was designed where the pre-disclosure period was July 1973 through December 1976, while the post disclosure period was November 1980 through April 1984, the same as in series B. Series C is designed to avoid both the contamination problem due to the overflow of moving betas from pre- into post-disclosure segment, as well as the possibility of early disclosure in response to the encouragement given by the SEC.

The three series can now be summarised as follows:

Series	Pre-disclosure	Post-disclosure	No. of months
A	5/71 — 12/77	1/78 — 8/84	80
B	7/74 — 12/77	11/80 — 4/84	42
C	7/73 — 12/76	11/80 — 4/84	42

Figure 1 shows the pre and post-disclosure betas for the treatment and control groups, while Figure 2 shows the differences in the betas between the treatment and the control groups for series C.

476   PRODHAN AND HARRIS

Figure 1

Average Moving Betas: Treatment and Control Groups

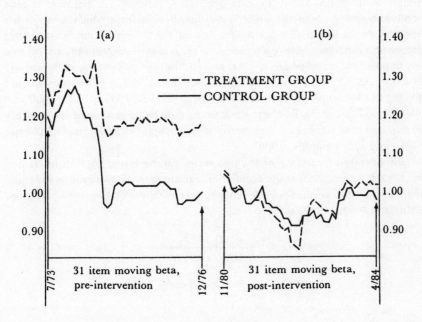

Figure 2

31 Item Moving Beta: Treatment-Control Group Averages (Differences)

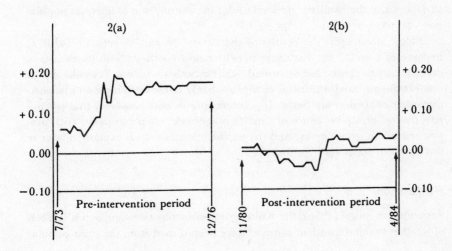

SYSTEMATIC RISK AND GEOGRAPHICAL SEGMENT DISCLOSURES   **477**

Parametric Test

In order to perform a statistical test of any hypothesis, it is necessary to make certain assumptions about the data generating process. For parametric tests some knowledge about the underlying distribution from which samples are selected are required. To justify the use of the t distribution in problems involving a difference between means, one must make two assumptions: (a) that the populations sampled are normal and (b) that the population variances are homogenous. Of the two, normal distribution assumption is of less consequence so long as the sample size is reasonably large (Hayes, 1963, p. 321–322; and Blalock, 1972, p. 223). Further, stock prices data being examined are monthly prices, and monthly stock prices distribution are approximately normal (Fama, 1976; and Diacogiannis, 1986).

Homogenity of variance of the two series can be tested by F ratio. If it is not tenable to assume that the population variances in the two groups are equal then a separate-variance t-test is appropriate with Welch degrees of freedom (Afifi and Azen, 1979, p. 77).

$$t = \frac{\bar{X}_1 - \bar{X}_2}{(S_1^2/N_1 + S_2^2/N_2)^{1/2}}$$

$$df = \left[\frac{C^2}{N_1 - 1} + \frac{(1 - C)^2}{N_2 - 1}\right] - 1$$

where

$$C = \left[\frac{S_1^2/N_1}{S_1^2/N_1 + S_2^2/N_2}\right]$$

N_1, N_2 being sample sizes, $\bar{X}_1$, $\bar{X}_2$ sample means, and S_1^2, S_2^2 sample variances.

However, when samples with an equal number of observations are considered, the t statistic derived under the assumption of equal population variances and the *t*-statistic derived under the assumption of unequal population variances are equal. (Hayes, 1963, p. 322).

Table 1 documents the results of the *t* tests. As can be seen in Table 1, hypotheses 1 and 2, on disclosure benefits and hypothesis 3 on incentives to discretionary disclosure are supported, while hypothesis 4 is not. It would appear that extraneous environmental factors are likely to have been present in post-disclosure control group betas. It is interesting to note however, that (i) pre-post control group betas are of smaller magnitude when compared with pre-post treatment group betas; and (ii) portfolio level analysis explained later in this research supports hypothesis 4.

Non-parametric Test

According to Siegel (1956), the Kolmogorov-Smirnov two sample test is a test of whether two independent samples have been drawn from the same popula-

PRODHAN AND HARRIS

Table 1

Differences Between Average Betas: 'T' Test

Series	A		B		C	
N =	Pre 80	Post 80	Pre 42	Post 42	Pre 42	Post 42
Means						
x_1 (Treatment)	1.195	1.061	1.206	0.973	1.220	0.973
x_2 (Control)	1.065	1.026	1.028	0.969	1.079	0.969
Variances						
S_1^2 (Treatment)	0.0047	0.0113	0.0024	0.0025	0.0036	0.0025
S_2^2 (Control)	0.0074	0.0049	0.0026	0.0013	0.0112	0.0013
t Statistics *(Treatment-Control)*						
Pre	10.51		16.18		13.00	
Post	1.48		0.42		0.42	
(Pre-Post)						
Treatment	9.42		21.30		20.25	
Control	3.13		6.59		6.30	
Table Values at:						
1%	3.46		3.55		3.55	
1%	2.60		2.70		2.70	
2%	2.33		2.40		2.40	
5%	1.99		2.00		2.00	

tion. The two-tailed test is sensitive to any kind of difference in the distributions from which the samples have been drawn: differences in central tendency, dispersion, skewness or kurtosis. If the two samples have in fact been drawn from the same population distribution then the cumulative distributions of both samples may be expected to be fairly close to each other in as much as they both should show only random deviations from the population distribution. A large enough deviation between the two sample cumulative distribution is evidence for rejecting H_0.

Assuming that the underlying distribution of the moving betas were unknown, the distribution free Kolmogorov-Smirnov two sample test was used for testing differences between the treatment and control group betas. These were conducted on the contamination-free series B as shown in Table 2. The '*D*' statistics for the treatment minus control group difference was 0.9523 pre-disclosure and 0.1905 post-disclosure. Since 0.2968 is the critical value at the five per cent level of significance, the pre-disclosure difference was seen as significant while post-disclosure was not. This supports hypotheses 2 and 3, of benefits of geographical segment disclosure and incentives to discretionary disclosure.

Table 2

Kolgomorov-Smirnov Two Sample Test
Series B: (Cumulative Frequency Percentages)

Average Beta Values	Pre-intervention (7/74−12/77)			Post intervention (11/80−4/84)		
	Treatment $F_o(X)$	Control $S_N(X)$	Difference	Treatment $Fo(X)$	Control $S_N(X)$	Difference
0.85−0.86				4.76	—	4.76
0.87−0.88				7.14	—	7.14
0.89−0.90				9.52	—	9.52
0.91−0.92				14.28	11.90	2.38
0.93−0.94				26.19	33.33	7.14
0.95−0.96	—	2.38	2.38	40.47	42.85	2.38
0.97−0.98	—	21.43	21.43	59.52	61.90	2.38
0.99−1.00	—	33.33	33.33	61.90	80.95	19.05*
1.01−1.02	—	61.90	61.90	88.10	95.23	7.13
1.03−1.04	—	73.80	73.80	95.23	97.62	2.39
1.05−1.06	—	80.90	80.90	100.00	100.00	0.00
1.07−1.08	—	80.90	80.90			
1.09−1.10	—	80.90	80.90			
1.11−1.12	—	95.23	95.23*			
1.13−1.14	—	95.23	95.23			
1.15−1.16	14.20	95.23	81.03			
1.17−1.18	47.60	100.00	52.40			
1.19−1.20	71.40	100.00	28.60			
1.21−1.22	73.80	100.00	26.20			
1.23−1.24	76.20	100.00	23.80			
1.25−1.26	80.90	100.00	19.10			
1.27−1.28	88.10	100.00	11.90			
1.29−1.30	97.60	100.00	2.40			
1.31−1.32	97.60	100.00	2.40			
1.33−1.34	97.60	100.00	2.40			
1.35−1.36	100.00	100.00	0.00			

Critical value of $D = \text{Max } F_o(X) - S_n(X)$ at the 5 per cent significance level is given by

$$1.36 \, ((n_1 + n_2)/n_1 n_2)^{1/2}$$

where n_1 and n_2 are number of companies in the treatment and control groups respectively. For the present samples

$$D = 1.36 \, ((40 + 42)/(40)(42))^{1/2} = 0.300$$

Preintervention $D = 0.9523$ which is highly significant; postintervention $D = 0.1905$ which is not significant at the 5 per cent level.

Portfolio Level Analysis

The treatment and control group firms were combined into two separate, equally weighted portfolios. To determine whether the treatment group experienced a reduction in systematic risk due to new disclosures, the market model was estimated for each portfolio over the 160 months in series A. Since we are interested in any differences in the coefficients before and after disclosure, the market model was tested for structural change. This required regressing portfolio returns against the market index over the entire 160 month period, restricting the coefficient on the market index to be the same both pre- and post-disclosure, and re-estimating the model for each of the eighty months, pre and post disclosure. Table 3 reports the unrestricted regression results for both groups pre- and post-disclosure. The dependent variable is portfolio return; the independent variable is the return on the S & P 500. Post-disclosure, the control group betas show a small decline, from 1.0492 to 1.0315 while the treatment group beta drops from 1.2013 to 1.0416.

To test whether the post disclosure declines of the two groups were significant, an analysis of covariance (or Chow test) was employed to test for structural change in the slope parameter. Since the results might be sensitive to the choice of disclosure date, the analysis was repeated for the reporting date; reporting date being defined as three months after the fiscal year end. Which ever date is chosen, we cannot reject the hypothesis that the pre and post disclosure betas are the same for the control group, but not for the treatment group. Treatment group betas, pre and post, were different at the one per cent significance level. Chow test results supporting hypotheses 1 and 4 are shown in Table 4.

Table 3

Equally Weighted Portfolios: Market Model Regressions

Pre- and Post-Disclosure Based on the Fiscal Year End Date:

Period	Group	Beta	Standard Error	$\bar{R}^2$	Number of Months
Pre-Disclosure	Control	1.0492	0.0372	0.9105	80
Post-Disclosure	Control	1.0315	0.0359	0.9137	80
Pre-Disclosure	Treatment	1.2013	0.0412	0.9158	80
Post-Disclosure	Treatment	1.0416	0.0470	0.8628	80

Pre- and Post-Disclosure Based on the Reporting Date:

Pre-Disclosure	Control	1.0512	0.0361	0.9128	83
Post-Disclosure	Control	1.0296	0.0372	0.9107	77
Pre-Disclosure	Treatment	1.1975	0.0402	0.9164	83
Post-Disclosure	Treatment	1.0422	0.0487	0.8590	77

Table 4

Equally Weighted Portfolios: Tests for Structural Change (Chow Test)

	Sums of Squares	N	Sums of Squares	N
Control:	Reporting Date		Fiscal Year End	
Same Coeff.	338.07	160	338.07	160
Same Slope	337.44	160	337.61	160
Pre:	184.07	80	183.37	80
Post:	153.00	80	153.99	80
Sum:	337.07		337.36	

Ho Slopes are the Same $F(1,156)$:

$F =$	0.17	F	
		$=$	0.12

	Sums of Squares	N	Sums of Squares	N
Treatment:	Reporting Date		Fiscal Year End	
Same Coeff.	510.09	160	510.09	160
Same Slope	509.48	160	509.93	160
Pre:	228.06	80	224.89	80
Post:	262.16	80	264.49	80
Sum:	490.22		489.38	

Ho Slopes are the Same $F(1,156)$:

$F =$	6.13	F	
		$=$	6.55

Critical values:

at 5%	3.19
at 1%	6.81

CONFOUNDING VARIABLES

Results of tests documented in this research have supported the hypothesis that post-disclosure treatment group betas are likely to be smaller than pre-disclosure treatment group betas. To be able to conclude that this change in average betas was due to changes in segmental geographical disclosure practice, it will be helpful to show that confounding variables were unlikely to have been responsible for this change in betas. One such confounding variable was SFAS No 8, Accounting for the Translation of Foreign Currency Transactions and Foreign Currency Financial Statements, issued by the Financial Accounting Standards Board in October 1975, effective for fiscal years beginning on or after 1 January, 1976.

482   PRODHAN AND HARRIS

However, SFAS 8 did not affect companies which

(i) had US $ as functional currency; or

(ii) had already complied with the SFAS 8 voluntarily before 1976; or

(iii) whose unrealised exchange gains or losses were of minimal impact due to tax effect.

Further, the impact of SFAS 8, if any, was usually reversed in the next fiscal year as follows:

Exchange gains in operating income in the current period results in the following sequence of events:

(a) Higher inventory value at the close of the current year, which results in

(b) Higher inventory value at the beginning of next year, resulting in

(c) Higher cost of production, leading to

(d) Lower profits, thus eliminating any gain in the previous year.

Dukes (1978) investigated the impact of SFAS 8 on the common stock security returns of multinational firms, and concluded that the issuance and implementation of SFAS 8 did not have any significant detectable effects when compared to (i) domestic firms of equal risk; (ii) multinationals already complying with SFAS 8 at the time of issuance in October 1975, and (iii) the market portfolio. Makin (1978) supports similar conclusions to that of Dukes.[9]

Finally, even if SFAS 8 had any impact, it should have affected both the treatment and control groups in the same manner.

CONCLUSION

Disclosure reduces uncertainty, and can result in lower cost of capital to the disclosing group of firms, when compared with the non-disclosing group. Previous disclosure studies have been mainly in the area of line of business, to the exclusion of geographical segments. This study has examined the information content of segmental geographical disclosures for multinationals in the US and found that geographical segmental disclosure, similar to line of business disclosure, does appear to have information content which affects market risk assessments.

NOTES

1 The total merger activity in the USA for instance, in recent years has set new records, rising from $12 billion in 1971 to $100 billion in 1984 (Boesky, 1986, p. 22).

2 See Prodhan (1986b) *Multinational Accounting*, Croom-Helm, London, p. 48 for a summary.

3 Collins and Simonds (1979), Emmanuel and Pick (1980) and Mohr (1983).

4 Prodhan (1986a) is an exception.

5 Hawthorne effect refers to the effect of employee attitudes towards production in the Hawthorne works of the Western Electric Company in Chicago, the supply organization for the telephone companies in the Bell System, during 1927–1932. The experiments were attempts at investigating the effects on production of such factors as temperature, humidity, lighting,

SYSTEMATIC RISK AND GEOGRAPHICAL SEGMENT DISCLOSURES   **483**

rest pauses and the length of the work day. Results showed that the factors under investigation could not explain many of the improvements in productivity obtained. It was established that improved productivity was recorded simply because the employees believed that management cared. (Roethlisberger and Dickson, 1939).

6 Jorion (1985) has suggested that international portfolio diversification results primarily in the form of risk reduction. With estimation risk being present gains in returns are usually overstated in a CAPM framework.

7 SEC (1970).

8 Capital International world index (1 January, 1970 = 100) is an arithmetic weighted average of market prices of 1112 companies listed in eighteen stock exchanges across the world, and is expressed in US dollars. The countries included are from three regions: (i) North American continent: US and Canada; (ii) Europe: UK, Germany, France, Italy, Belgium, Netherlands, Austria, Spain, Switzerland, Denmark, Norway and Sweden and (iii) the East: Japan, Hong Kong, Singapore and Australia.

9 Ziebart and Kim (1987) have found limited impact of SFAS 8 on multinational stock prices, but on a very short time series.

REFERENCES

Accounting Standards Committee (1988), *Proposed Statement of Standard Accounting Practice — ED 45: Segment Reporting*, ASC (London, 1988).

Adler, M. and B. Dumas (1983) 'International Portfolio Choice and Corporate Finance: A Synthesis', *Journal of Finance* (June 1983), pp. 925–984.

Afifi, A.A. and S.P. Azen (1979), *Statistical Analysis: A Computer Oriented Approach*, London (Academic Press, 1979).

Agmon, T. and D.R. Lessard (1977), 'Investor Recognition of Corporate International Diversification', *Journal of Finance* (September 1977), pp. 1049–1055.

Akerlof, G.A. (1970), 'The Market for "Lemons": Quality Uncertainty and the Market Mechanism,' *Quarterly Journal of Economics* (1970), pp. 488–500.

Beales, H., R. Craswell and S.C. Salop (1981), 'The Efficient Regulation of Consumer Information', *Journal of Law and Economics* (December 1981), pp. 491–544.

Blalock, H.M. (1972) *Social Statistics*, London (McGraw Hill, 1972).

Boesky, I.F. (1986) *Merger Mania*, London (Bodley Head, 1986).

Brown, R.L., J. Durbin and J.M. Evans (1975), 'Techniques for Testing the Constancy of Regression Relationship Over Time', *Journal of the Royal Statistical Society*, Series (B), (1975), pp. 149–192.

Calvet, A.L. (1981), 'A Synthesis of Foreign Direct Investment Theories and Theories of the Multinational Firm', *The Journal of Business Studies* (Spring/Summer 1981) pp. 43–59.

Capital International (1977), *Perspectives* (Geneva 1977).

Chambers, R. (1951), 'Disclosure is a Matter of Managerial policy, not Accounting', *The Journal of Accountancy* (August 1951), p. 223.

Choi, F.D.S. (1973), 'Financial Disclosure in Relation to a Firm's Capital Costs', *Accounting and Business Research*, (Autumn 1973), pp. 282–292.

Cohn, R.A. and J.J. Pringle (1973), 'Imperfections in International Financial Markets: Implications for Risk Premia and the Cost of Capital to Firms', *Journal of Finance*, (March 1973), pp. 59–66.

Collins, D.W., J. Ledolter and J. Rayburn (1986), Some Further Evidence on the Stochastic Properties of Systematic Risk, University of Iowa Working Paper (February 1986).

Collins, D.W. and R.R. Simonds (1979), 'SEC Line of Business Disclosures and Market Risk Adjustments', *Journal of Accounting Research* (Autumn 1979), pp. 352–383.

Companies Act, HMSO, London (1985).

Dhaliwal, D.S., F.M. Mboya and R.M. Barefield (1983), 'Utilization of SFAS No 14 Disclosures in Assessing Operating Risk', *Journal of Accounting and Public Policy* (Summer 1983), pp. 83–98.

Diacogiannis, G. P. (1986), 'Some Empirical Evidence on the Intertemporal Stationarity of Security Return Distributions', *Accounting and Business Research*, (Winter 1986), pp. 43–48.

Dimson, E. (1979), 'Risk Measurement when Shares are Subject to Infrequent Trading', *Journal of Financial Economics*, Vol. 7 (1979), pp. 197–226.

484   PRODHAN AND HARRIS

Dukes, R.E. (1978), *An Empirical Investigation of the Effects of Statement of Financial Accounting Standards No. 8 on Security Return Behaviour*, (Financial Accounting Standards Board, December 1978).

Emmanuel, C. and R. Pick (1980), 'The Predictive Ability of UK Segment Reports', *Journal of Business Finance and Accounting* (Summer 1980), pp. 201–218.

Fama, E.F. (1976) *Foundations of Finance* (Basic Books, 1976).

Fatemi, A.M. (1984), 'Shareholder Benefits from Corporate International Diversification', *Journal of Finance* (December 1984), pp. 1325–1344.

Financial Accounting Standards Board (1975), Accounting for the Translation of Foreign Currency Transactions and Foreign Currency Financial Statements, *Statement of Financial Accounting Standard No 8* (FASB, 1975, Stamford, Connecticut).

_____ (1976) Financial Reporting for Segments of a Business Enterprise, *Statement of Financial Accounting Standards, No. 14*, (FASB, 1976, Stamford, Connecticut).

Financial Times, London, (March 17, 1987).

Gonedes, N.J. (1978), 'Corporate Signaling, External Accounting, and Capital Market Equilibrium: Evidence on Dividends, Income and Extraordinary Items', *Journal of Accounting Research* (Spring 1978), pp. 26–79.

Grubel, H.G. (1968) 'Internationally Diversified Portfolios: Welfare Gains and Capital Flows', *American Economic Review* (December 1968), pp. 1299–1314.

Hamada, R.S. (1972), 'The Effect of the Firm's Capital Structure on the Systematic Risk of Common Stock', *Journal of Finance* (May 1972), pp. 435–458.

Hayes, W.L. (1963), *Statistics*, London (Holt Rinehardt and Winston, 1963).

Horwitz, B. and R. Kolodny (1977), 'Line of Business Reporting and Security Prices: An Analysis of SEC Disclosure', *Bell Journal of Economics* (Spring 1977), pp. 234–249.

International Accounting Standards Committee (1981), Reporting Financial Information by Segment, *IAS 14*, London (IASC, 1981).

Jorion, P. (1985) 'International Portfolio Diversification with Estimation Risk', *Journal of Business* (July 1985), pp. 259–278.

Kinney, W. (1972), 'Covariability of Segment Earnings and Multisegment Company Returns', *The Accounting Review*, (April 1972), pp. 339–345.

Kochanek, R.F. (1974), 'Segmental Financial Disclosure by Diversified Firms and Security Prices', *The Accounting Review* (April 1974), pp. 245–258.

Lessard, D.R. (1974), 'World, National and Industry Factors in Equity Returns', *Journal of Finance* (May 1974), pp. 379–398.

Makin, J.H. (1978), 'Measuring the Impact of Floating and FASB Statement No. 8 on Costs of Capital for Multinationals', pp. 41–69 in *Economic Consequences of Financial Accounting Standards, Selected Papers* (FASB, July 1978).

Mohr, R.M. (1983), 'The Segmental Reporting Issue: A Review of Empirical Research', *Journal of Accounting Literature* (1983), pp. 39–72.

Organisation for Economic Cooperation and Development (1979), *International Investment and Multinational Enterprises*, Paris (OECD, 1979).

Panton, D.B., V.P. Lessig and O.M. Joy (1976), 'Comovement of International Equity Markets: A Taxonomic Approach', *Journal of Financial and Quantitative Analysis* (September 1976), pp. 415–432.

Patell, J.M. (1976), 'Corporate Forecasts of Earnings per Share and Stock Price Behavior: Empirical Tests', *Journal of Accounting Research* (Autumn 1976), pp. 246–276.

Prodhan, B. (1986a), 'Geographical Segment Disclosure and Multinational Risk Profile', *Journal of Business Finance and Accounting* (Spring 1986), pp. 15–37.

_____ (1986b), *Multinational Accounting: Segment Disclosure and Risk*, London (Croom-Helm, 1986).

Ripley, D.M. (1973), 'Systematic Elements in the Linkage of National Stock Market Indices', *Review of Economics and Statistics* (August 1973), pp. 356–361.

Roethlisberger, F.J. and W.J. Dickson (1939), *Management and the Worker*, Cambridge, Mass. (Harvard University Press, 1939).

Ross, S.A. (1979), 'Disclosure Regulation in Financial Markets: Implications of Modern Finance Theory and Signalling Theory', pp. 177–193, in *Issues in Financial Regulation*, F.R. Edwards (Ed) (McGraw-Hill, 1979).

Rubinstein, M.E. (1973), 'A Mean-Variance Synthesis of Corporate Financial Theory', *Journal of Finance* (March 1973), pp. 167–181.

SYSTEMATIC RISK AND GEOGRAPHICAL SEGMENT DISCLOSURES   **485**

Rugman, A.M. (1978), International Diversification and the Multinational Enterprise (Lexington Books, 1978).

Scholes, M. and J. Williams (1977), Estimating Betas from Non-synchronous Data', *Journal of Financial Economics*, Vol. 5(1977), pp. 309–327.

Securities and Exchange Commission (1970), *Securities Act, Release No 34-9000*, Washington DC (SEC October 1970).

Sharpe, W.F. (1963), 'A Simplified Model for Portfolio Analysis', *Management Science* (January 1963), pp. 277–293.

———— (1985), *Investments*, N.J. (Prentice-Hall, 1985).

Siegel, S. (1956), *Nonparametric Statistics for the Behavioural Sciences* (McGraw-Hill, 1956).

Subrahmanyam, M.G., and S.B. Thomadakis (1980), 'Systematic Risk and the Theory of the Firm', *Quarterly Journal of Economics* (May 1980), pp. 437–451.

United Nations Economic and Social Council (1977), *International Standards of Accounting and Reporting for Transnational Corporations* (New York, 1977).

Verrecchia, R.E. (1983), 'Discretionary Disclosure', *Journal of Accounting and Economics*, Vol. 5 (1983), pp. 179–194.

Watts, R.L. and J.L. Zimmerman (1986), Positive Accounting Theory (Prentice-Hall, 1986).

Ziebart, D.A. and D.H. Kim (1987), 'An Examination of the Market Reactions Associated with SFAS No. 8 and SFAS No. 52', *The Accounting Review* (April 1987), pp. 343–357.

APPENDIX A

Sample Identification

S & P 500 for 1983

(500)

Financial year end
December 31

(323)

At least 10% of total sales
$ obtained outside the USA
in each of the years 1968–1983

(183)

Continuous disclosure of LOB data 1968–1983, and continuous disclosure of geographical segments sales and trading profits data in annual reports in each year 1968–1983

(45)

Continuous disclosure of LOB data 1968–1983, but change in geographical segment sales and trading profits data disclosure practice from non-disclosure to full disclosure starting December 1977, followed by continuous disclosure in annual reports in each year 1977–1983.

(48)

Continuous monthly stock prices listing for 191 months (October 1968–August 1984) available in Compustat files

(42)

(40)

CONTROL GROUP   TREATMENT GROUP

486   PRODHAN AND HARRIS

APPENDIX B (i)

Control and Treatment Group Companies

Control Group (N = 42)

Ticker Symbol	Company Name	Standard & Poor's Industry: No.	Name
ABT	Abbott Laboratories	2834	Pharmaceutical Preparations
ALD	Allied Corp.	2800	Chemicals & Allied Prods.
AMF	AMF Inc.	3940	Toys & Amusement Sport Goods
AMX	AMAX Inc.	1000	Metal Mining
AST	American Standard Inc.	3740	Railroad Equipment
BGH	Burroughs Corp.	3680	Electronic Computing Equip.
BMS	Bemis Co.	2649	Convert Paper-Paperbd PD Nec.
CCC	Continental Group	3410	Metal Cans & Shipping Cont.
CHA	Champion International Corp.	2600	Paper & Allied Products
CPC	CPC International Inc.	2000	Food & Kindred Products
CZ	Celanese Corp.	2820	Plastic Matr. & Synthetic Resin
DD	Du Pont (E.I.) De Nemours	2800	Chemicals & Allied Prods.
DOW	DOW Chemical	2800	Chemicals & Allied Prods.
EAF	Emery Air Freight Corp.	4700	Transportation Services
F	Ford Motor Co.	3711	Motor Vehicles & Car Bodies
GM	General Motors Corp.	3711	Motor Vehicles & Car Bodies
GRA	Grace (W.R.) & Co.	2800	Chemicals & Allied Prods.
HON	Honeywell Inc.	3680	Electronic Computing Equip.
JNJ	Johnson & Johnson	2649	Convert Paper-Paperbd Pd Nec
MLL	Macmillan Inc.	2731	Books: Publishing & Printing
MRK	Merck & Co.	2830	Drugs
MTC	Monsanto Co.	2800	Chemicals & Allied Prods.
NB	Nabisco Brands Inc.	2000	Food & Kindred Products
PD	Phelps Dodge Corp.	1021	Copper Orcs
RD	Royal Dutch Pete-NY Gldr 10	2911	Petroleum Refining
REV	Revlon Inc.	2844	Perfumes Cosmetics Toil Prep.
SA	Safeway Stores Inc.	5411	Retail-Grocery Stores
SKB	Smithkline Beckman Corp.	2834	Pharmaceutical Preparations
SMF	Singer Co.	3630	Household Appliances
SN	Standard Oil Co (Indiana)	2911	Petroleum Refining
SOC	Superior Oil Co.	1311	Crude Petroleum & Natural Gs
SRL	Searle (G.D.) & Co.	2834	Pharmaceutical Preparations
TRW	TRW Inc.	3662	Radio-TV Transmttng Equip.-AP
TX	Texaco Inc.	2911	Petroleum Refining
UK	Union Carbide Corp.	2800	Chemicals & Allied Prods.
UN	Unilever NV	2000	Food & Kindred Products
USG	US Gypsum Co.	3270	Concrete Gypsum & Plaster
WWY	Wrigley (WM) Jr Co.	2065	Candy & Other Confectionery
XON	Exxon Corp.	2911	Petroleum Refining
XRX	Xerox Corp.	3861	Photographic Equip. & Suppl.
Z	Woolworth (F.W.) Co.	5331	Retail-Variety Stores
ZE	Zenith Electronics Corp.	3651	Radio-TV Recieving Sets

SYSTEMATIC RISK AND GEOGRAPHICAL SEGMENT DISCLOSURES   **487**

APPENDIX B (ii)

Treatment Group (N = 40)

Ticker Symbol	Company Name	Standard & Poor's Industry: No.	Name
AA	Aluminium Co. of America	3330	Prim Smelt-Refin Nonfer Mtl.
ACK	Armstrong World Inds. Inc.	3079	Misc Plastic Products
AHP	American Home Products Corp.	2830	Drugs
AMP	AMP Inc.	3679	Electronic Components NEC
AXP	American Express	6199	Finance-Services
BA	Boeing Co.	3721	Aircraft
BAX	Baxter Travenol Laboratories	3841	Surg. & Med. Instruments & App.
BC	Brunswick Corp.	3510	Engines & Turbines
BNL	Beneficial Corp.	6140	Personal Credit Institutions
C	Chrysler Corp.	3711	Motor Vehicles & Car Bodies
CAT	Caterpillar Tractor Co.	3531	Construction Machinery & Equip.
CBM	Chesebrough-Pond's Inc.	2844	Perfumes Cosmetics Toil. Prep.
CCK	Crown Cork & Seal Co. Inc.	3410	Metal Cans & Shipping Cont.
CDA	Control Data Corp.	3680	Electronic Computing Equip.
CGG	Chicago Pneumatic Tool Co.	3540	Metalworking Machinery & Equip.
CHM	Champion Spark Plug	3699	Electrical Machy. & Equip. NEC
CMK	Carnation Co.	2000	Food & Kindred Products
CSP	Combustion Engineering Inc.	3533	Oil Field Machinery & Equip.
ETN	Eaton Corp.	3820	Measuring & Controlling Inst.
FNB	First Chicago Corp.	6025	Natl. Banks-Fed Reserve Sys.
GSX	General Signal Corp.	3825	Elec. Meas. & Test Instr.
HPC	Hercules Inc.	2800	Chemicals & Allied Prods.
IBM	Intl. Business Machines Corp.	3680	Electronic Computing Equip.
IFF	Intl. Flavors & Fragrances	2844	Perfumes Cosmetics Toil Prep.
INI	Internorth Inc.	4923	Natural Gas Transmis-Distr.
K	Kellogg Co.	2000	Food & Kindred Products
LLY	Lilly (ELI) & Co.	2834	Pharmaceutical Preparations
LOF	Libbey-Owens-Ford Co.	3210	Flat Glass
N	Inco Ltd.	1000	Metal Mining
NAC	National Can Corp.	3410	Metal Cans & Shipping Cont.
NCR	NCR Corp.	3680	Electronic Computing Equip.
OXY	Occidental Petroleum Corp.	1311	Crude Petroleum & Natural Gs
PBI	Pitney-Bowes Inc.	3570	Office Computing & Acctg. Mch.
PFE	Pfizer Inc.	2834	Pharmaceutical Preparations
ROH	Rohm & Haas Co.	2800	Chemicals & Allied Prods.
SGP	Schering-Plough	2830	Drugs
SWK	Stanley Works	3429	Hardware-NEC
TGT	Tenneco Inc.	4922	Natural Gas Transmission
TXN	Texas Instruments Inc.	3674	Semiconductors & Rel. Devices
WHR	Whirlpool Corp	3630	Household Appliances

488   PRODHAN AND HARRIS

APPENDIX C (i)

Sample Group Characteristics 1983

	Control Group	*Treatment Group*
No. of Companies		
(N)	42	40
Average Sales $m	12,447	4,818
Average Export $m	5,215	1,420
Export as % of Sales	42	29
Assets, $m	9,081	6,124
Assets/Sales	0.73	1.27

Control group companies were larger in size both in terms of total assets, as well as sales; they were more dependent on foreign sales. Treatment group companies were, however, more capital intensive, requiring $1.27 of capital to generate each dollar of sales.

APPENDIX C (ii)

Line of Business Analysis of Control and Treatment Group Companies

	Industry Category	*Number of Companies*	
No.	*Description*	*Control Group*	*Treatment Group*
	I Engineering related		
10	Metals, Mining	2	1
13	Crude Petroleum/Gas	1	1
30	Plastic Products	0	1
32	Glass, Concrete	1	1
33	Smelting	0	1
34	Metal Cans	1	3
35	Engines, Turbines	0	5
37	Railroad, Aircraft	3	2
38	Surgical Appliances	1	3
49	Gas transmission	0	2
		9(21.4%)	20(50.0%)
	II Service Sector		
20	Food	4	2
26	Paper converters	3	0
27	Publishing	1	0
39	Toys	1	0
47	Transportation	1	0
53	Retail stores	1	0
54	Grocery	1	0
60	Banking	0	1
61	Finance	0	2
		12(28.6%)	5(12.5%)

SYSTEMATIC RISK AND GEOGRAPHICAL SEGMENT DISCLOSURES   489

	Industry Category	*Number of Companies*	
No.	*Description*	*Control Group*	*Treatment Group*
	III Growth Sector		
28	Drugs, Perfumes	12	8
29	Petroleum refining	4	0
36	Electronics	5	7
		21(50.0%)	15(37.5%)
	Total	42(100%)	40(100%)

APPENDIX C (iii)

Sample Characteristics: Pre- and Post Intervention

	Treatment Group (N = 40)		*Control Group (N = 42)*	
	Pre 1971–77	*Post 1978–84*	*Pre 1971–77*	*Post 1978–84*
*Market Value of Firms**				
Mean	2630	3819	3639	5206
S.D.	5921	7871	4987	6722
Coeff. of Variation	2.25	2.06	1.37	1.29
*Sales**				
Mean	1936	3984	5279	11178
S.D.	2693	5182	8781	18636
Coeff. of Variation	1.39	1.30	1.66	1.67
*Total Assets**				
Mean	2307	4745	4024	7842
S.D.	3527	7367	6243	11902
Coeff. of Variation	1.53	1.55	1.55	1.52
Debt/Equity				
Mean	0.5644	0.6387	0.4803	0.3936
S.D.	0.5731	0.8680	0.2538	0.2026
Coeff. of Variation	1.02	1.36	0.53	0.51
Beta				
Mean	1.2013	1.0416	1.0400	1.0315
S.D.	0.2712	0.2844	0.2670	0.3010
Coeff. of Variation	0.23	0.27	0.26	0.29

* Million dollars.
MV of Firm = M.V. of Equity + Book Value of Debt
Debt/Equity = Book value of all interest bearing debt/M.V. of Equity
Beta = A single regression slope for each of pre and post series for the control and the treatment group companies averaged across companies. These are not moving betas, which have been used earlier.

PRODHAN AND HARRIS

APPENDIX C (iv)

Cross Correlations Between Beta and Other Characteristics of Firms

	Treatment Group (N = 40)		Control Group (N = 42)	
	Pre 1971–77	Post 1978–84	Pre 1971–77	Post 1978–84
M.V. of firm	0.22431 (0.1641)	−0.08638 (0.5961)	−0.32327 (0.0368)	−0.13875 (0.3809)
Sales	0.15266 (0.3470)	0.18047 (0.2651)	−0.36733 (0.0167)	−0.19782 (0.2092)
Total Assets	0.01580 (0.9229)	0.17650 (0.2759)	−0.34865 (0.0236)	−0.13894 (0.3802)
Debt/Equity	0.19396 (0.2304)	0.24717 (0.1241)	0.46098 (0.0021)	0.32628 (0.0350)
Beta	1.0000 (0.0000)	1.0000 (0.0000)	1.0000 (0.0000)	1.0000 (0.0000)

Figures in parenthesis represent significance levels.

APPENDIX C (v)

Pre: 1971–77 (average)
Post: 1978–84 (average)

Firm Level Characteristics: Control Group

Control Group Stock Symbols	Sales $m		Assets $m		M.V. of Firm $m		Debt/Equity	
	Pre	Post	Pre	Post	Pre	Post	Pre	Post
ABT	805	2173	819	2165	1287	4093	0.5480	0.4867
ALD	2085	5953	2083	5206	1572	2701	0.5679	0.5425
AMF	999	1264	758	930	767	626	0.8931	0.4886
AMX	1084	2512	2060	4612	1756	3734	0.5795	0.7171
AST	1565	2332	1115	1484	532	1086	0.7940	0.5242
BGH	1484	3296	2052	3804	3904	3112	0.4755	0.3726
BMS	531	682	300	379	162	196	0.5371	0.5040
CCC	2875	4738	1967	3770	1294	1999	0.4931	0.5309
CHA	2378	3831	1890	3288	1338	2225	0.8551	0.5769
CPC	2257	3914	1304	2269	1160	2009	0.4762	0.3477
CZ	1786	3197	1831	2649	1150	1532	0.7668	0.6741
DD	6488	21388	5711	16529	7477	11809	0.2436	0.4244
DOW	4177	10035	5110	11143	7590	9294	0.9356	0.8747
EAF	220	558	65	208	353	347	0.0000	0.8020
F	24850	40525	14043	23138	7350	7974	0.2993	0.4789

SYSTEMATIC RISK AND GEOGRAPHICAL SEGMENT DISCLOSURES   491

Control Group Stock Symbols	Sales $m		Assets $m		M.V. of Firm $m		Debt/Equity	
	Pre	Post	Pre	Post	Pre	Post	Pre	Post
GM	37702	64094	21435	37246	19382	20323	0.1147	0.2184
GRA	3109	5758	2304	4389	1560	3302	0.8183	0.7051
HON	2465	4879	2413	3923	1958	2738	0.6469	0.3404
JNJ	1953	4947	1387	3515	5530	6858	0.0614	0.1048
MLL	450	482	453	412	197	277	0.3635	0.4072
MRK	1301	2723	1300	3151	5399	6488	0.1793	0.2366
MTC	3278	6226	3091	5824	2842	4099	0.4396	0.4469
NB	1586	4278	893	2501	1013	2054	0.6517	0.4848
PD	877	1184	1440	2020	1166	1292	0.4867	0.6286
RD	15698	41985	16038	37607	8525	18351	0.4478	0.5336
REV	687	2078	661	1963	1187	1859	0.5592	0.4905
SA	8255	15695	1540	3505	1321	2260	0.3403	1.1176
SKB	538	2004	510	1933	1074	4719	0.3796	0.2049
SMF	2272	2615	1720	1477	1159	729	1.1174	1.0605
SN	8224	24227	8817	20740	8306	17676	0.3198	0.3509
SOC	308	1534	789	3736	1074	4709	0.2817	0.5295
SRL	545	959	679	1158	1190	1839	0.8015	0.644
TRW	2381	4874	1587	2896	1146	2333	0.5746	0.3609
TX	18538	43806	15446	25246	10277	12185	0.2956	0.2786
UD	4944	9212	5158	9610	4281	5670	0.5396	0.5031
UN	7046	12811	3761	6751	2052	3478	0.3930	0.6142
USG	827	1471	734	1107	478	789	0.2330	0.2188
WWY	287	547	201	312	258	309	0.0686	0.0509
XON	36346	89404	29416	55963	24169	33983	0.2984	0.2507
XRX	3497	7789	3688	7353	7823	5621	0.5670	0.3575
Z	4169	6318	1976	2800	1211	1511	0.5203	0.6188
ZE	882	1186	474	649	595	483	0.2115	0.4787

APPENDIX C (vi)

Pre: 1971–77;
Post: 1978–84.

Firm Level Characteristics: Treatment Group

Treatment Group Stock Symbols	Sales $m		Assets $m		M.V. of Firm $m		Debt/Equity	
	Pre	Post	Pre	Post	Pre	Post	Pre	Post
AA	2389	4812	3168	5329	2327	3640	0.6944	0.4737
ACK	838	1335	697	902	837	622	0.2961	0.2428
AHP	2038	3972	1264	2472	5316	5590	0.0237	0.0130
AMP	430	1161	381	959	1171	2229	0.2426	0.1664
AXP	2290	8554	8178	24814	3293	8055	0.6088	1.4858

Treatment Group Stock Symbols	Sales $m		Assets $m		M.V. of Firm $m		Debt/Equity	
	Pre	Post	Pre	Post	Pre	Post	Pre	Post
BA	3447	8829	2024	6070	961	3621	0.4009	0.0978
BAX	490	1431	627	1557	1500	2724	0.7810	0.4579
BC	764	1159	690	914	547	577	0.5837	0.4835
BNL	452	1261	2545	5843	2271	4556	2.4092	4.0820
C	12049	11492	6335	6593	2474	3063	0.5389	2.3174
CAT	3985	7413	2931	6331	4594	6380	0.4709	0.5293
CBM	559	1393	406	949	910	1269	0.3619	0.3870
CCK	723	1358	502	832	428	489	0.2280	0.0959
CDA	1042	3139	1743	4212	1062	2999	0.6550	1.0788
CGG	242	422	226	342	181	195	0.1206	0.6431
CHM	441	778	373	603	533	443	0.1392	0.2001
CMK	1762	3123	899	1588	1420	1501	0.3422	0.2555
CSP	1505	3118	1035	2398	688	1216	0.3474	0.2318
ETN	1578	2937	1215	2277	940	1549	0.5773	0.6724
FNB	1170	3389	16681	31452	3340	5544	2.9206	3.6723
GSX	495	1466	339	1120	386	1197	0.2133	0.1737
HPC	1304	2432	1181	1904	1450	1514	0.4806	0.4272
IBM	12907	28961	14131	28562	38197	50444	0.0748	0.1100
IFF	208	431	214	411	1075	874	0.1477	0.0567
INI	1034	3378	1790	3572	1413	2491	1.1609	0.8340
K	1050	2126	577	1203	1479	1852	0.1434	0.1310
LLY	1103	2564	1244	2718	4247	4504	0.1732	0.1348
LOF	715	1161	547	839	404	475	0.1791	0.3510
N	1462	1984	2850	3913	2873	2622	0.5450	0.7358
NAC	694	1394	394	734	207	376	0.7723	0.5739
NCR	1974	3271	2024	3200	1426	2518	0.9670	0.2852
OXY	4463	13386	3269	8736	1950	4431	1.0270	0.7565
PBI	440	1245	394	1107	314	771	0.6319	0.4280
PFE	1494	3099	1719	3414	2896	4950	0.5309	0.5856
ROH	880	1693	905	1289	1013	1118	0.5714	0.4031
SGP	695	1615	692	1981	2785	2241	0.0541	0.3425
SWK	470	920	346	617	305	627	0.4179	0.6444
TGT	4932	13014	6182	14633	4768	9615	1.1871	1.0959
TXN	1377	3827	904	2249	2042	2747	0.2066	0.2058
WHR	1564	2327	751	1151	1085	1129	0.3488	0.0952

Name Index